Mountain Republic

PHILIPPA HARRISON had a long and distinguished career in publishing: managing director and publisher of Macmillan and then chief executive and publisher of Little, Brown UK, she became the first female president of the Publishers Association. Born in Cartmel Priory Vicarage, she now lives with her husband in the same vicarage that Canon Rawnsley lived in when he co-founded the National Trust.

'…prompt / And watchful more than ordinary men'.
From 'Michael' by William Wordsworth

Mountain Republic

A Lake District Parish:
Eighteen Men, The Lake Poets
and the National Trust

Philippa Harrison

An Apollo Book

First published in the UK in 2021 by Head of Zeus Ltd
This paperback edition first published in 2022 by Head of Zeus Ltd,
part of Bloomsbury Publishing Plc

9 7 5 3 1 2 4 6 8

A catalogue record for this book is available from the British Library.

ISBN (PB): 9781838931834
ISBN (E): 9781838931841

Typeset by Ed Pickford
Maps by Jeff Edwards

Printed and bound in Great Britain
by CPI Group (UK) Ltd, Croydon CR0 4YY

Head of Zeus Ltd
5–8 Hardwick Street
London EC1R 4RG
WWW.HEADOFZEUS.COM

*To the memory of my mother, Alexina, and my dear friend Gill,
both of whom loved the Lake District.
And for Anthony, who brought me back here.*

Contents

PART THREE

Living in Interesting Times, 1829–74

Afterglow

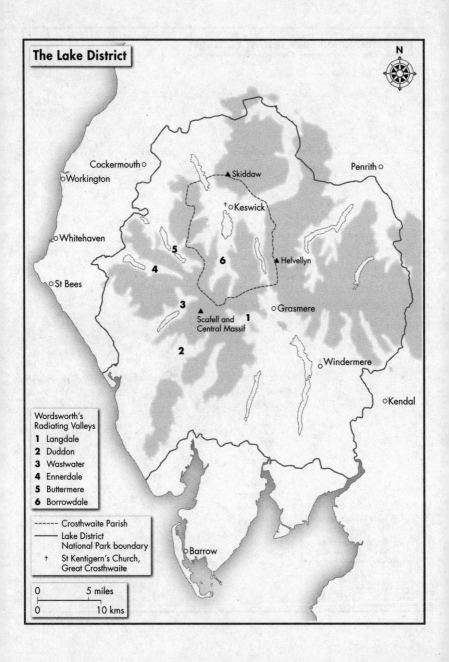

The Lake District

N

Cockermouth ○
○ Workington
○ Whitehaven
○ St Bees

▲ Skiddaw
† Keswick
Penrith ○

5
4
▲ Helvellyn

6

3
▲ Scafell and
Central Massif
○ Grasmere
1

2
○ Windermere

○ Kendal

○ Barrow

Wordsworth's
Radiating Valleys
1 Langdale
2 Duddon
3 Wastwater
4 Ennerdale
5 Buttermere
6 Borrowdale

------- Crosthwaite Parish
——— Lake District
National Park boundary
† St Kentigern's Church,
Great Crosthwaite

0   5 miles
0   10 kms

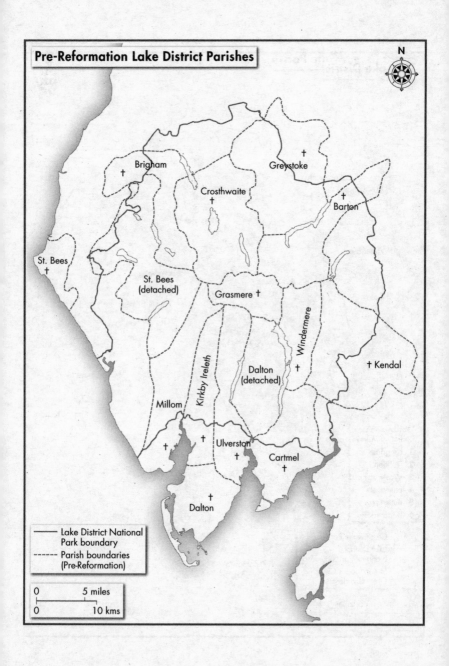

Pre-Reformation Lake District Parishes

N

† Brigham

† Greystoke

Crosthwaite
†

Barton
†

St. Bees
†

St. Bees
(detached)

Grasmere †

Windermere

Kirkby Ireleth

Dalton
(detached)
†

† Kendal

Millom

†

Ulverston
†

Cartmel
†

†
Dalton

Lake District National
Park boundary

Parish boundaries
(Pre-Reformation)

0   5 miles
0   10 kms

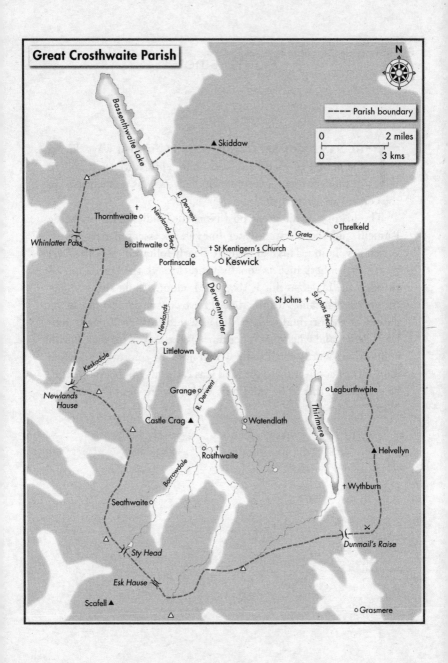

Great Crosthwaite Parish

N

- - - - Parish boundary

0   2 miles
0   3 kms

Bassenthwaite Lake

▲ Skiddaw

R. Derwent

† Thornthwaite

Newlands Beck

○ Threlkeld

R. Greta

Whinlatter Pass

Braithwaite ○

† St Kentigern's Church

Portinscale ○

○ Keswick

Derwentwater

St Johns †

St Johns Beck

Newlands

Keskadale

† ○ Littletown

○ Legburthwaite

Newlands Hause

Grange ○

R. Derwent

Thirlmere

Castle Crag ▲

○ Watendlath

▲ Helvellyn

Borrowdale

○ † Rosthwaite

† Wythburn

Seathwaite ○

× Dunmail's Raise

Sty Head

Esk Hause

Scafell ▲

○ Grasmere

Author's note

THE NAME 'CUMBRIA' can be used in different ways during the period covered here, and I have chosen to use it only in its modern sense, except when the word was publicly used in the context of Strathclyde.

The history of the great post-Norman landholdings of the de Rumelli and the Derwentwater lines is an essential part of the Parish's evolution. This can be more clearly followed, in both cases, by treating inheritance as equally valid through the female line as through the male, so this is the path I adopt. While always using the correct surnames for the time, I have continued also to use the names of the original owners of Derwentwater, de Rumelli and, later, Percy land when that inheritance is the reason for their Parish connection. Wordsworth sadly would not have approved as, while longevity of connection to the land was certainly important to him, he considered this to be valid only if there were ties of '*name* and blood'.

Introduction

U NTIL THE NINETEENTH century, most of today's Cumbria
was virtually cut off from the rest of England for reasons
geography makes clear. Its central mountain range of
Scafell throws up a huge volcanic mass, which has to be circum-
navigated, forcing transport to its edges. This is the core of the
Lake District, some 30 miles wide, and it excites passion in all
those who love it.* Like the millions who live here or visit, I lift
my eyes unto the hills and encounter constancy and majesty, a
grandeur that lifts me away from the mundane.

Yet it took me much of a lifetime fully to realise that this awe-
inspiring, contained world is also the scene of an exceptional social
history. Essentially shaped by an unusual form of tenancy and
by the landscape, this is usually elided into a broader history of
Cumbria, where it can get lost. So, ten years ago, I embarked upon
a project to unravel the history of an iconic area within it and then,
as it were, to restitch its tapestry, as I had come to believe that the
detail would bring alive the story of the indigenous people of the
whole district: the people who became for Wordsworth the paradigm of a life well lived. Here, their story is set in its rightful place
for the first time since the poet introduced them: within the heart
of the Lake District, the poet's 'visionary mountain republic'.[1]

The locus of the story is the 90 square miles of Great
Crosthwaite's Old Parish,† its place in the district well captured by

---

* For Canon Rawnsley it was 20 miles by 20 miles wide, presumably exclud-
ing what some call the Lake Margins, like Windermere and Grasmere.
† According to the Cumberland Post Office Directory 1873 and Bulmer's *History,
Topography and Directory* it was 58,330 acres, i.e. 91.14 square miles. In his 1994
book *Keswick: The Story of a Lake District Town*, the venerable George Bott, the
local Keswick expert, claimed 'at least 150 square miles' (p.125), but I think this
is an illustration of the awe often produced by the Parish's size and variety. Also, a
demonstration of how difficult it is to judge the extent of variable shapes.

Wordsworth himself, when he wrote one of the first comprehensive descriptions of the whole area.[2] Imagining a bird's-eye view from a point between the tops of Great Gable and Scafell in the central mountain range, and starting from the southeast and the Langdale Valley, he described an incomplete circle of valleys running from it 'like spokes from the nave of a wheel'. Crosthwaite Parish encompassed the eighth and northernmost valley, Borrowdale.*

By far the largest parish within the heart of the Lake District, Crosthwaite's old boundary travelled the tops of a magic circle of Lake District mountains: Skiddaw, Helvellyn and Great Gable. And it includes the area where every fell-walker feels they have come home – at the high crossroads of the central mountains, where the wall shelter near Esk Hause provides a natural meeting place for all en route east, west, north or south. Home also to two lakes, Derwentwater and Thirlmere[3], and their accompanying valleys, as well as part of Bassenthwaite Lake, Great Crosthwaite and Keswick are found at the northern end of Derwentwater, for Wordsworth 'distinguished from all other Lakes by being surrounded with sublimity'.[4]

Attractively asymmetrical, Derwentwater is bordered on its eastern and western sides by mountains and high fells, which can be reflected, along with the sky, in the lake's often glass-like water: vivid light green or burnished copper-brown, depending on the seasons and the bracken. At the southern end of the lake, Castle Crag, a small, steep, pine-covered Italianate hill, believed to have been the site of an Iron Age fort,[5] hides Borrowdale from the rest of the valley. Behind Crosthwaite and Keswick is Skiddaw, Coleridge's 'God made manifest', formed of the most ancient rock in the Lake District; a massive guard against the north wind and an emphatic scenic full-stop. When the bright golden light of evening spotlights its top from late summer, the heather adds another colour to the range, a brooding saturated purple combusting with the gold. And in painting after painting, the brightly whitewashed Crosthwaite church is seen, standing alone at its foot, an essential part of the artist's composition.

* Alfred Wainwright's 'loveliest square mile in the district'.

According to tradition, the church's dramatic placement on a slightly raised site was ordained during a missionary visit from Glasgow's and Strathclyde's St Kentigern around 553. Crosthwaite (and much of old Cumberland) had been part of the British kingdom of Strathclyde for most of the period between the departure of the Romans in the early fifth century and 1092, by which time Strathclyde had become part of Scotland. Thus, our Parish was not covered by the Domesday Book commissioned by William the Conqueror, and when his successor, William II, claimed 'the land around Carlisle' in 1092, it was, surprisingly, allowed to stay under its Scottish lord. In the twelfth century, Alice de Rumelli, Baroness of all Allerdale – a vast territory stretching from the south of Cumbria to the north, and east from the sea to the Helvellyn range – built her only Cumbrian church here. By far the largest church of its time in the Lake District, it was soon to become the first parish church within 'the heart of the fells'.[6]

Alice's church is still called St Kentigern's today, while Keswick, half a mile away from the church and first mentioned in the context of an 1190s Rumelli seigneurial gift, became the Lake District's first market town at the end of the thirteenth century. But the remarkable social history of the Parish only really emerged at the end of the fourteenth century[7] when the last de Rumelli bequeathed her ancient land to the Percys from Northumberland,[*] for, from then on, all the Parish business was to be administered, right up to the second half of the nineteenth century, by tenants who became known as 'customary'. These tenants had an exceptional advantage and, from the early seventeenth century onwards, a virtually unique one. Despite their many burdens of feudal obligation, for most of their time their land passed on to their heirs, only reverting to 'the lord' if they did not have a direct heir, had not paid their dues or had carried out a criminal act. This gave them a sense of future possibility and a quite different level of connection to their land than people elsewhere in Britain. In time they had been able also to sell or lease their holdings.

---

* This was Maud de Lucy.

Eighteen customary tenants were chosen annually at St Kentigern's for the particular form of governance in the Parish, the 'rule of select vestry'. In place before 1400, from the beginning the vestry oversaw a school and was entirely responsible for the appointment and regulation of the schoolmasters and administering the money and land that had been given to endow it. By Elizabethan times, vestry governance was publicly recognised for the first time in legal statutes, and the Eighteen Men began to *officially* oversee taxation, maintenance of the poor, education and infrastructure. From then on the whole of rural England was governed by 'the parish' until Victorian times, when parishes progressively lost their powers as the state began to intervene. A process which has seldom been traced right through in a single parish.

The Eighteen Men were strongly connected to the juries of the manor courts, always came from the same class, and often included members of the same families. Their history covers the period when William Wordsworth would describe the Lake District as a 'pure commonwealth'. And the unique freedom enjoyed by the upland customary tenants was underlined in the seventeenth century, when local political life in the rest of the country was being transformed by the much debated rise of the gentry. Largely owing to the arcane effects of old forest laws, Crosthwaite Parish did not follow suit[8].

From 1571 (when the Elizabethan religious settlement was finalised) to 1834 (when the state started to move responsibility for provision for the Parish poor to Cockermouth), the hill farmers 'were practically their own masters. They were forced to be careful, but they had no-one to cringe to'.[9] These were the glory days of the hill-farming community and the customary tenant and they gave both the Parish and the Lake District their particular character.

Wordsworth was to become their poet and used the inclusive word 'estatesman' to cover everyone, wealthy yeoman and poor subsistence farmer alike, who worked his own land and could pass both it and its stock on to his children. He believed that the statesmen's lives – lived entirely in response to the natural world and the needs of family, community and flock – best represented human nature, and wrought parables for mankind from their stories. The publication of Thomas Gray's journal of his visit to the Lake District in 1769 had

introduced, probably for the first time, the two words that are used
to identify the region today* and by Wordsworth's time picturesque
tourism had already become established. By the 1790s the Lakes had
become the principal English destination, with Crosthwaite Parish
– Derwentwater, Borrowdale, Keswick – its focal centre, until the
railways brought tourists to the south Lakes in 1847.

Once Wordsworth had immortalised the recently conceived
'English Lakes', intertwining its landscape with the romantic
imagination for ever – and indeed largely creating that imagination – the area became clearly recognised as a *peopled* landscape,
and the course was set more widely for the transformation of what
had been the largest isolated area of England into one of its most
visited. Samuel Taylor Coleridge and Robert Southey both lived
in Great Crosthwaite Parish;† Wordsworth first gained his right
to vote by owning a patch of land within it; and all three poets
tramped to see each other 'ower t'raise' to Grasmere (see the story
of Dunmail Raise in chapter 1), often meeting in Thirlmere Valley.
At the heart of the Lake Poets' landscape, along with Grasmere
and Rydal – key locations in the great change of the Lake District
– as I have already implied, Crosthwaite Parish can also be read as
a paradigm for Wordsworth's 'perfect Republic of Shepherds and
Agriculturalists'.[10] Thus, establishing the true history of its people
– their land, their work and the changes wrought by time – can, I
believe, both give the reader enough detail to judge the validity of
Wordsworth's claim and illuminate the whole history of the Lake
District in a way that a broader brush does not quite achieve.

*

Part One of *Mountain Republic* tells the story of the Parish from
the age of St Kentigern to that of the early Georgians. The first
element of this 1,200-year span covers the period (from the sixth
to the late eleventh centuries) when the Parish was largely cut off

* *Thomas Gray's Journal of his Visit to the Lake District in October 1769*, in
which he described the Keswick/Crosthwaite Valley as 'the Vale of Elysium'.
† Southey's forty years in Crosthwaite Parish probably make him its most
distinguished long-term inhabitant.

from what would become the rest of England; the second embraces an era (from the mid-1100s to 1745) during which the parishioners of Great Crosthwaite shared the experience of the whole of the North of England (considered to be a different country by those on both sides of the River Trent). This was a time when war with Scotland and raiding – writing out the long Parish history as part of Strathclyde – denied the border fifty years of consecutive peace.

Both Alice de Rumelli and her daughter passed much Parish land to the two great Cistercian abbeys of Furness and Fountains, considerably improving the efficiency of its sheep farming. Some three and a half centuries later, fourteen years into the reign of Henry VIII, Sir John Radcliffe, a member of the influential Derwentwater family, started a second great rebuilding of St Kentigern's. The exterior, broadly as you find it today, was unornamented, and buttressed and battlemented like the medieval pele towers of Cumberland; built to protect both people and livestock from Scottish or border raiders. Forty-seven yards long, it sits low on its land, like the Lakeland stone farmhouses of the seventeenth century, yet is conspicuous from the tops of the fells all around. The view from the church's short 56-foot square tower, added at the end of the Tudor rebuilding, is as lovely and as dramatic as that from any church in England. Entirely without ostentation, Crosthwaite's church nevertheless breathes confidence in its permanence and the centrality of its position.

However, within only a few years of St Kentigern's recreation, the North's difference from the rest of England was magnified by the Reformation (almost uniformly unpopular here), with extremely brutal consequences. The violent punishment of two revolts in thirty-three years bled it into submission. Wounds seemed to have been healed by the unification of the Scottish and English crowns under James VI and I but were opened again by the Civil War. Then, after the Restoration of 1660, stone houses were built for permanence in the Parish for the first time. Soon mortgages and money, and eventually turnpikes, would pave the way for 'the discovery of the Lakes'.

Part Two (starting in 1769, the last year of Wordsworth's unadulterated 'pure commonwealth' and the year Gray wrote his

Journal) traces the last flowering of the old values built up through the Parish's long history and the new flowering of the Romantic movement. William Gilpin, the progenitor of 'picturesque' paintings, had the 'visionary idea' of landscaping the whole of the Derwentwater shore, encouraging gentry from outside the area to buy land in the Keswick/Crosthwaite valley for the first time. Southey became the historian of the Parish,* Wordsworth the historian of its people, and, bizarrely to the modern eye, the two men turned Crosthwaite Parish and the core Lake District into a *casus belli* in a vituperative public battle about the future of Britain after the end of the Napoleonic wars.

Different prescriptions for the best method of alleviating poverty and reactions to the burgeoning Industrial Revolution were at the heart of the battle. Land use became an essential issue, both poets believing that life lived on the land was better for the poor. Wordsworth explicitly built his argument on the history of 'a class of men who are now almost confined to the north of England',[11] his fight, above all, to save a hard-working egalitarian way of life. This was only possible, he added – crucially – 'if these men are placed above poverty'.[12] And both he and Southey fought for state aid for small landowners as well as the landless.

Part Three charts the fall of old Crosthwaite Parish, as Whig championing of industrialisation, profit and change held sway. Most of the values that Wordsworth and the Parish had stood for were rooted out as the state and new seigneurs began to take control of the area so long overseen by the Eighteen Men. The Marshall family, flax millionaires, bought the old Derwentwater manor in the 1830s, and in 1836 felt they had a seigneurial obligation to build the church of St John's in Keswick and ensure that it had a Parish attached. So, from 1856, the old Crosthwaite Parish ceased to exist, despite St Kentigern's third renovation eleven years earlier by George Gilbert Scott, making it 'the Lake cathedral'[13] and a suitable home for Southey's effigy. Then, in 1874, the Parish grammar school was seized by the state, which at first provided a considerably poorer

---

* The Parish is at the centre of Southey's *Colloquies*, which sum up his adult conclusions 'as a moral and political writer'.

education for the parishioners' children. Control of all the endowments given to and husbanded by the Eighteen Men for almost five hundred years was swept away to London.

At a stroke, the whole value system of the old Parish was undone, the state legislating away the eighteen trustees of the grammar school and the select vestry at the same time. What of the Parish customary tenants? Historical orthodoxy has it that various economic pressures after the end of the Napoleonic wars caused 'the demise of the statesmen' in the Lake District. But a closer look at the Parish provides an alternative view.

*

Everything had not been lost, for when Canon Rawnsley took over St Kentigern's in 1883 some core Parish values were redeemed. A whirlwind of a man, the canon identified instantly with his parish and fell in love with its history, writing and preaching dramatic accounts of the lives of St Kentigern and the other Parish saint, St Herbert. Immensely responsive to the beauty of the Lake District landscape and strongly connected with his pastoral parishioners, he formed the Lake District Defence Society in the year he joined the Parish and soon took on his wealthy parishioners in order to keep footpaths open for the people. Once he decided to take the passions informed by the Parish, the Lake District and his hero, Wordsworth, on to the national stage, he prompted the inauguration of the National Trust.

Much of the Derwentwater shore, lost to the people in the landscaping of the late eighteenth century, was freed for them,* including boating rights on the lake. The fields in which the magnificent Castlerigg stone circle stood were bought originally by Rawnsley himself, to avoid their damage or exploitation. In doing so, Rawnsley saved not just the stone circle but as great a three-hundred-and-sixty-degree prospect of the Lake District as one can find. His campaign to protect the soul of the district was so significant that the Trust rightly asks today, 'Has anyone done more for

* With three purchases totalling 220 acres on the west side of the lake.

the Lake District in the last 200 years?'[14]

Crosthwaite and St Kentigern's, having lost their vast Parish earlier in the century, had nurtured and energised its saviour. Living as I do in his old vicarage, I have been inspired by Rawnsley's prodigious work ethic to keep researching in order to bring the history of the 'statesman' class alive and to honour their innumerable centuries of unremitting toil and shepherding; work and lives that have created and maintained a landscape from which millions have drawn inspiration, and which Wordsworth heralded as a divine symbiosis of beauty and use. These qualities lie at the heart of the 2017 award of World Heritage status to the Lake District for 'the outstanding universal value of a cultural landscape which deserves protection for the benefit of all humanity'.[15]

Old Crosthwaite Parish lies at the heart of that landscape, and it was on the shores of Derwentwater that HRH The Prince of Wales unveiled a magnificent slate memorial, made from a Honister clog, inscribed with words that I hope this book illuminates: 'The Lake District is an evolving masterpiece shaped and modified by people, nature, farming and industry for thousands of years. In turn, this spectacular landscape has inspired artists and writers of the Picturesque and Romantic movements and has generated ideas about the relationship between humans and landscape that have global influence.'

The masterpiece of the 90 square miles of the old Crosthwaite Parish could never have been achieved without the hundreds of years of guardianship and guidance from the Eighteen Men, without Wordsworth and Southey, without Rawnsley's saving of land and landscape for the people, and without its shepherds, from the Vikings until today. This is their story.

Part One

The Making of Crosthwaite Parish, 553–1769

A Secret Place

A fine engraving of Crosthwaite Church, commissioned from William Westall by Robert Southey, its most famous parishioner, for his *Colloquies*.

I

From St Kentigern and Strathclyde
to the Normans

IT WAS DURING the Celtic mists of the sixth century that St
Kentigern planted his cross at a place the Anglo-Saxons later
named 'Crosfeld'; 'feld' changed to 'thwaite' after the arrival
of the Vikings, meaning, in what was a thickly wooded area, a
clearing in the forest. An oak forest. For the Old Celtic word for
oak, 'derva', is enshrined in the words Derwent and Derwentwater.
So, Crosthwaite's name, a cross in a clearing in the oak forest,
described its very origins.

The saint is the first of the two characters without whom there
would be no story of the Parish to tell; the second making her
entrance six hundred years later. But Robert Southey would have
to reintroduce his name to a place that had long forgotten him,
an action Canon Rawnsley cemented when he adorned the church
with the symbols of St Kentigern's life, to keep his story forever
alive there. Kentigern had been the religious heart of Strathclyde,
an old Roman buffer state that in his time stretched down to the
shore of Morecambe Bay, in the south of Cumbria. Celtic-speaking
Britons peopled western Britain and left many signs that suggest
a unified Celtic culture, each area, for instance, using the same
methods of counting sheep, in multiples of five: one 'yan', five
'pimp', and ten 'dick'. This was as true of Cornwall and Brittany
as the Lake District. In Crosthwaite Parish, the Borrowdale count
of 'yan, tyan, tethera, methera, pimp'* was still bewildering the
uninitiated at sheep auctions as late as the early twentieth century.

---

* This method of local Brythonic counting was used across much of the old
county of Cumberland.

The people of the north of Strathclyde had elected St Kentigern bishop, his many converts named the 'Clasgu' (dear family) – the origins of the name Glasgow, in whose cathedral the saint is buried. To this day the figure of the saint, and the symbols associated with his legend, make up the crest of the city. Threatened by royal paganism, Kentigern had taken up his wooden shepherd's crook and begun to walk towards Wales, to better teach the simplicity of life. According to his biography,[*] commissioned by the Bishop of Glasgow in 1180, as Kentigern entered the mountains of Cumbria, he stayed in a 'thickly planted place to confirm and strengthen the men that dwelt there ... The saint erected a cross ... whence it took its name in English of Crosfeld ... in which very locality a Basilica recently erected is dedicated to the name of the blessed Kentigern.'[1]

Almost all the churches named after Kentigern have an association with a well (common meeting places) where the saint is thought to have baptised and preached. The Crosthwaite Holy Well[†] lay at the foot of Holy or High Hill, close to the church. The Howrah meadows, lying within a great bend in the River Greta before it glides into the How Wray (holy corner) of the River Derwent, were probably the route for early baptisms. Seven other churches in northwestern Cumberland dedicated to Kentigern seem likely to reflect the course of the saint's journey, and these are the only other churches in England with dedications to him. But Crosthwaite church, which claims a founding date of 553, is the only building in England whose association with St Kentigern is a matter of record. The consequences were to be large.

---

[*] By Jocelyn of Furness c.1185. His sources included an Irish manuscript, a vernacular Scottic life and a copy of part of St Asaph's biography, the original of which had been lost; however, some of his material, such as Kentigern's visit to Rome, was imagined for clerical political reasons. A body of thought considers that there is no real evidence that Kentigern ever travelled to Crosthwaite and Cumberland, and suggest that the naming of Crosthwaite Church (and the other Cumberland associations with his journey) were created by the Bishop of Glasgow's successful efforts to raise St Kentigern's profile during a re-build of his cathedral. I hope my later suggestion about the reasoning behind the building of Crosthwaite's twelfth-century church will be added to the scales of judgement weighing the question.
[†] The well was finally obliterated in the mid-nineteenth century.

By the time of St Kentigern's legendary journey, most of England was under the sway of the pagan Anglo-Saxons, Germanic tribesmen who had come to Britain in the aftermath of the Roman withdrawal. So the Christian core of Britain lay in the Celtic west until Augustine reconverted the southeast of England to Roman Christianity from 597. By the latter half of the seventh century, the two forms of Christianity were vying for supremacy in the northeast, the religious clash finally settled by the Synod of Whitby in 664 in favour of the Roman version. While the power of Celtic Christianity swiftly declined in most of England, in Strathclyde, and in much of what is now Scotland, it was to last for more than another 400 years.

Soon Anglo-Saxon settlers migrated, usually peacefully, from Northumbria to the hospitable land of the Cumberland plains and coast and, in time, along the Derwent to the larger valleys: Keswick and Thirlmere are the two principal Anglo-Saxon names in the Parish. But throughout the Lake District it appears that the effects on the Celts, keeping to their higher, clearer ground, was small; virtually no names with Anglo-Saxon origins are to be found over 250 feet.

We catch a tantalising glimpse of life in the Parish in this period via one of the earliest surviving works of British literature, a poignant celebration of country living written probably in the seventh century, before *Beowulf* – and over a millennium before Wordsworth. The poem is a lullaby sung to a child, Dinogad, about his father, who used to go hunting with his dogs along the River Derwent – but apparently does so no more. The waterfall to which it refers has been identified as Lodore Falls, the subject of one of Southey's best-loved poems:[2]

> *Dinogad's smock is pied, pied*
> *Made it out of marten hide*
> *Whit, whit, whistle along,*
> *Eight slaves with you sing the song.*
>
> *When your dad went to hunt,*
> *Spear on his shoulder, cudgel in hand,*
> *He called his quick dogs, 'Giff, you wretch,*
> *Gaff, catch her, catch her, fetch, fetch!'*

From a coracle he'd spear
Fish as a lion strikes a deer.
When your dad went to the crag
He brought down roebuck, boar and stag,
Speckled grouse from the mountain tall,
Fish from Derwent waterfall.

Whatever your dad found with his spear,
Boar or wild cat, fox or deer,
Unless it flew, would never get clear. *

Nearly seventy years after the Synod of Whitby, the great Anglo-Saxon historian Bede tells the story of the other early saint associated with Crosthwaite church, the anchorite St Herbert. It would be good to imagine St Herbert glimpsing Dinogad's father skimming past his island in his coracle, for Bede tells us 'Herebert … lived a solitary life on an island in that great lake which is the source of the river Derwent, and used to visit Cuthbert† every year and listen to his lessons of eternal salvation'.[3] In return, monks from Lindisfarne went each year on a pilgrimage to Derwentwater to be blessed by St Herbert. The last meeting of the two saints was in Carlisle in 687. There, having 'inspired each other with intoxicating draughts of the life of Heaven', the bishop told Herbert: 'we shall never see each other again with bodily eyesight, for I am certain that the time is at hand for my release…'[4]

Hearing this, the anchorite fell at his feet with tears and sighs … and beseeched God that, 'as we have served Him together on earth, so may we depart together'. The bishop prostrated himself in prayer, and, at once, his spirit reassured that he had obtained his request from the Lord, said, 'Rise up, my brother, and do not

---

* This verse was introduced to me by Tom de Wesselow. It was preserved as a later interpolation into 'Y Gododdin', a famous series of prose poems thought to have been composed by the Welsh bard Aneirin sometime in the mid to late sixth century. Dinogad, attended by his eight singing slaves, was evidently a child of importance, and his father may have been a local clan chief subject to the king of Strathclyde.
† The Bishop of Lindisfarne in Northumberland, who also oversaw Carlisle.

weep, but be full of joy. For the Lord in His mercy has granted our request.' The truth of this promise and prophecy was confirmed by the outcome of events ... their souls left their bodies on one and the same day, the twentieth of March, and were soon united in the beatific vision and borne by the ministering angels to the heavenly kingdom.'[5]

St Cuthbert, always associated with miracles, became even more famous in death than he was in life.[*] Eleven years after his interment, the monks, 'opening the sepulchre ... found the body intact and whole, as if it were alive'.[6] Mummification being then unknown, this was seen as miraculous. St Herbert's Island became famous too – so much so that, over 800 years later, Henry VIII's antiquarian places the 'lyttle poore market town cawlled Keswicke ... a mile fro St Hereberts isle that Bede speketh of'. Wordsworth was to write of 'this sainted spot' and J. M. W. Turner and many others painted it.

Shortly before the saints' deaths, the Anglo-Saxons had moved into southwest Scotland, cutting Cumberland off from Strathclyde for about 200 years and leaving the Parish in a sort of no man's land, loosely under Anglo-Saxon Northumbrian rule. The Cymric age and any sort of unified Celtic culture was finally over as links became more tenuous and Wales was isolated. But the land of Crosthwaite's Parish remained at the heart of Cumbria's experience of the great age of Celtic saints; and their religion, far less centralised and with a liberating emphasis on human perfectibility rather than original sin, was practised there into the next millennium.

The Vikings and a fell battle

In 793, the first Viking attack on Lindisfarne reverberated through the Christian world: 'Never before has such terror appeared in Britain as we have now suffered from a pagan race ... the church

* Cuthbert had become a hermit on the island of Inner Farne. On his death, a monk lit two torches on the headland as a signal to Lindisfarne, where the community sang 'Lord thou hast cast us out and scattered us abroad' – a requiem for the two men's spirits.

of St Cuthbert splattered with the blood of the priests of God ... a place more venerable than all in Britain is given as prey to pagan people.'[7] Two years later the Norwegian Vikings pillaged the monasteries on Ireland's west coast, in time proceeding to settle parts of the country, while the raids on Britain's east coast continued.

In 865, a Danish 'Heathen Army' arrived off East Anglia, inaugurating a century of Viking settlement and warfare with the Anglo-Saxons. By the mid-870s, the northeast of England had fallen to the Danes, who, in the words of the *Anglo-Saxon Chronicle*, began 'to plough and support themselves'. Meanwhile, the fulcrum of the Norwegian Vikings' maritime trading had become the Isle of Man, roughly equidistant from the Cumberland and Irish coasts. It was the disenchanted second- or third-generation Norse Irish from both Ireland and Man who began to settle Cumberland from around 925.[8]

Viking settlement of Cumbria continued throughout the tenth and eleventh centuries, a generally peaceful process, in strong contrast with the ravages wreaked in other parts of Britain. And, since the Vikings' interests were always fundamentally pastoral, unlike those of the Anglo-Saxons, they gradually moved up into the fells, usually as self-sufficient sheep farmers, eventually settling the whole of the Lake District – probably for the first time in its history. By far the most powerful progenitors of the mountain hill farmers, the Vikings bequeathed remnants of their legal heritage[*] and the resilience necessary for a hard, independent way of life.

Norse names replaced Celtic in the central fells – and old Norse gave birth to the Cumberland dialect. With its grating, clattering sounds and elongated vowels, the original dialect was well-nigh unintelligible to southerners. And it is still strongly alive today in Crosthwaite Parish. As recently as 1990, well over a hundred dialect variations of the verb 'to beat' could still be heard, the vast majority of them quite unknown outside the area.[9]

Words such as 'tarn', 'dale', 'beck', 'ghyll' and 'scree' have long marked their territory as clearly as the scent marks of any hunting animal and established a different landscape from the

---

* Such as 'cornage'.

South; there is no mistaking a 'fell' for a 'hill'. Signs of this first colonisation of the land, enclosed areas cleared from woodland in the form of 'thwaites' and mountain pasture created for grazing ('sheilings' or 'saetrs'), can still be seen in the Parish.

For the entire period between the departure of the Romans and the coming of the Normans, the Parish lands and the wider Lake District were remote from any unifying central force and had remained free of violent invasion. The relationship between its peoples thus evolved naturally.[*] The mix of local cultures, with its strong Viking overlay, formed a seedbed for the growth of the particular customs, habits and language that defined the Cumberland character. Neighbours, once with different languages and cultures, having to depend upon each other in the harsh conditions of farming self-sufficiency on poor land – and free from almost any oversight 'from above' – inevitably created a mixture of community and independence, of self-assertiveness and honour (values that may have been equally encouraged by the freedom of their Celtic Christianity).

Other essential characteristics flow from this. A tough, never-ending working life needs 'a good crack' (a lively gossip), wild breakouts for 'a good do' and both humour and stoicism to get by, all underscored by a natural conservatism, relying on inherited experience of what will and won't work on the land. At the same time, hill farmers are tough, doughty fighters who can keep a battle going for generations in rock-solid defence of their land, their families or their people.

Around 920, Crosthwaite was again back in Strathclyde,[10] which had been badly weakened fifty years earlier when the Viking Irish had conquered its capital, Dumbarton, and was on the way to becoming an under-kingdom of the Gaelic-speaking Scotti. Nevertheless, Strathclyde cautiously expanded its southern boundary to the River Derwent, placing Crosthwaite right on the border. The modern nation of Scotland was becoming ever

---

[*] Melvyn Bragg put it well in his book *Land of the Lakes*: 'The history of the Lake District from the Bronze Age is largely the story of a natural fortress continuously evading conquest because it contained little the invaders wished to hold or loot' (p. 31).

clearer[11] as the smaller kingdoms had either been incorporated earlier or were in the process of being subdivided between rival rulers.* However, the ancient Scottish system of tanistry, which fundamentally favoured the strongest candidate from among the chief's kin rather than the eldest son, and was historically responsible for the nasty, brutish and short life expectancy of their kings,† led to constant change. And from the time that the Parish was back within the country's borders, the title of King of Strathclyde became commonly given to a younger son of the King of Scotland, who had become the Prince of Cumbria upon his birth.[12] Soon the names of Strathclyde and Cumbria themselves became virtually synonymous; though Cumbria, oddly, appeared to be the more frequently used of the two.

Close to the middle of the tenth century, a great battle took place on the southern edge of the Parish, at Dunmail Raise, the high point in the pass connecting the Vale of Grasmere with the Thirlmere valley. Dunmail, for Strathclyde and Cumbria, was defeated by Edmund, the Saxon king of England, aided by Malcolm I, king of 'Scotland'. After the English king confirmed Malcolm as king of the Scots and overlord of Strathclyde, the Scot agreed to defend northern England against the Vikings. A great cairn, still standing today on the central reservation of the Grasmere–Thirlmere road, traditionally – but entirely inaccurately – marks the warrior's burial place (Dunmail in fact survived the battle). Wordsworth, bringing alive an episode in Parish history and far from averse to tales of Cumbrian prowess, writes of:[13]

* Since Kenneth I MacAlpin became king of the Picts, finally uniting the old Gaelic kingdoms in 834/5. Although his daughter married the king of Strathclyde and there was a short period of joint kingship, battles between Strathclyde and the king of the Scots then continued intermittently until Malcolm II, prince of Cumbria and king of Strathclyde, became king of Scotland. From c.1016 he became king of Lothian too and was thus the first effective ruler of the whole of Scotland. See Weir, *Britains Royal Families*, pp.178–79.
† They were murdered by their successors, killed in regicidal battles again and again, strangled at birth, and deposed or abdicated as the crown passed backwards and forwards from one branch of a family to another. Ibid, passim, pp. 164–247.

> *... that pile of stones*
> *Heaped over brave King Dunmail's bones;*
> *He who once had supreme command,*
> *Last king of rocky Cumberland;*
> *His bones, and those of all his Power*
> *Slain here in a disastrous hour!*

The story features strongly in Lake District histories and brochures, but 'king of rocky Cumberland', the title often given to Dunmail, he was not.[14] The brochures are simply repeating a legend that expresses a passionate desire for Cumberland to be an ancient nation. Historical facts all too often lack the necessary romance: in reality, the next Saxon king ravaged all of Cumberland after Malcolm's son refused him payment to see off the Danes, claiming his duty was to fight not fund. In the Parish, some of its Vikings are believed to have survived only by retiring into a fort at Castle Rock in St John's in the Vale.[15]

Joseph Wilkinson's *Dunmail Raise*, the large pile of stones on the right revered as Dunmail's grave. Wordsworth wrote the first version of his *Guide to the Lakes* as a text to accompany Wilkinson's *Views*.

Far better to have stories. Dunmail's two sons are said to have been blinded in the battle – and may have been – but Dunmail's magic crown joins its brethren in the annals of mythology. Its magic was so strong that anyone who wore it would become ruler of Strathclyde/Cumbria and his warriors threw it deep into Grizedale Tarn in the high Helvellyn fells at the edge of the Parish, in accordance with their leader's last words: 'My crown – bear it away; never let the Saxons flout it, until I come to lead you.' Every year they are said to return to the tarn, somehow recover the crown, and troop off to the cairn on the Raise.

There they strike it with their spears and hear a voice, deep within the stones, saying, 'Not yet, not yet; wait awhile my warriors.'[16]

Allerdale and the Normans

Soon after the battle, the future of the Parish could be smelt in the air with the emergence of the title 'Lord of Allerdale', an area that was soon to become the bedrock of the Norman administration of the Parish (and much of Cumberland). The title was created for Maldred, Regent of the Kingdom of Strathclyde, by his elder brother, King Duncan I* – the historical basis for Shakespeare's King Duncan. The Regent was to die in battle in 1045 avenging his brother's murder by Macbeth. Many battles later, in 1057, Maldred's nephew Malcolm III seized the Scottish throne, and began to anglicise the old Celtic institutions of Strathclyde and to Romanise its religion, changing the holy day from Saturday to Sunday. This process of religious and secular reformation would continue under Malcolm's son, David I (whose sister was married to King Henry I of England), and the Scottish government became Normanised.

Unlike southern Cumbria, which was under Norman rule following the Conquest, 'the land of Carlisle' remained part of Strathclyde and Scotland. The Parish was untouched by William I's infamous 'Harrying of the North', during which lands in the

---

* Duncan I had inherited a fully united Scotland from his grandfather, Malcolm II, in 1034.

northeast were laid waste; homes, crops, livestock and food burned to ashes, and many thousands said to have perished of hunger.* It wasn't until 1092 that the Conqueror's son, William II, 'marched north to Carlisle with a large army, and re-established the fortress, and built a castle'.[17] However, he was to find that reclaiming the Strathclyde lands from the Solway to the Derwent was a far from simple process, and northern suspicion would prompt him to transplant a colony of people from the south of England up to Carlisle.[18]

Thirty years later William the Conqueror's fourth son, Henry I, came north and created Cumberland baronies, answerable directly to the crown, several of which appear to have shadowed pre-Conquest estates. The Parish spanned two of the new baronies – Copeland, soon to be called Allerdale above Derwent, and Allerdale below Derwent.† The first of these baronies, which extended south from the River Derwent to the River Duddon, was confirmed to the Norman William le Meschin, who had married a fellow countrywoman, Ciceley de Rumelli, Lady of Skipton, from Yorkshire. Surprisingly, however, Maldred's eldest grandson, Waltheof, was allowed to keep the lands associated with his inherited Scottish title of Lord of Allerdale – 'Lord' changing to 'First Baron'. Of royal Scottish, British and Saxon descent, Waltheof was son, brother, brother-in-law and uncle to four Scottish kings. With English royal blood in his veins too,‡ he greatly excited the Victorians, who hallooed that 'no more noble and ancient strain of blood flows in the veins of any in our land'.[19]

Crucially for the future Crosthwaite Parish, Waltheof continued the de facto Norman acceptance of indigenous landowners by confirming the traditional overlordship§ of Castlerigg and Derwentwater. This

---

* In 1072 William the Conqueror forcibly 'persuaded' Malcolm to offer him homage for his English territories.
† Finally, Henry, either pleasantly or emphatically, confirmed the English barony of Greystoke upon Lord Forne FitzLyulph, siring an illegitimate son with his daughter. FitzLyulph gave his name to Ullswater, originally Lyulph's Water, Lyulph deriving from the Scandinavian for wolf (Lefebure, *Cumbrian Discovery*, p. 179).
‡ Internet genealogists today add that their old line also bred the Wessyngtons (Washingtons), who eventually linked Cumberland with America's first president.
§ 'Tallentir and Castlerig with the forest between Greta and [the unidentifiable] Caltre' given to 'Odard, Son of Lioff'. *Distributio Cumberlandiae*.

estate covered a considerable area of Parish land, running north–south from Threlkeld,[20] just outside the northeastern border of the Parish, spilling over into the Thirlmere valley then up to Dunmail Raise and west to Derwentwater. But the family held other territories outside the Parish, too, primarily Tallentire, 5 miles or so from the Cumberland coast. Their descendants, settled at Castlerigg, soon became known as de Derwentwater, adapting their name to their territory.[21] An ancient family, the Derwentwaters would remain the only major landed family living for any length of time in the Crosthwaite Parish.

Waltheof's demesne was soon extended by his baronial neighbour, who made over to him 'the honour of Cockermouth',* the town subsequently becoming his headquarters. Cockermouth was to remain the centre of the area's administration – as headquarters of the ward of Allerdale below Derwent – until the mid-nineteenth century. His nephew founded the house of Curwen, a family whose story marches with Crosthwaite through history, and Waltheof was to bequeath Bassenthwaite to his illegitimate son, Gospatrick.

In 1133, there was to be more change, as Henry, unamused to discover that the Bishop of Glasgow was running Carlisle, created the bishopric of Carlisle to oversee the areas his brother had recently reclaimed from Strathclyde.† The new diocese included Allerdale below Derwent and some of Westmorland but excluded Copeland; Dunmail Raise marked its southern boundary.

The names of the two Cumberland baronies carry down the ages a lasting echo of Crosthwaite's Strathclyde history. Allerdale above Derwent and Allerdale below Derwent subsequently became two wards of the old county of Cumberland, while Allerdale survives to this day as a district council of the modern county of Cumbria. And yet the lands of Allerdale above Derwent‡ lay *south* of the river and Allerdale below Derwent extended *north* and *east* of it,[22] the original baronies unequivocally described, as they continued to be for ever, from the Scottish rather than

---

* Reserving for his clerk 'the fourth part of Crosthwaite ... for keeping his Goshawkes'. William Camden quoted in Lefebure, *Cumbrian Discovery*, p. 87.
† The last bishopric to be created before the Reformation.
‡ In today's Cumbria now reverting to the name of Copeland.

English perspective. Presumably, this was the way their peoples – and the Normans – saw their history, natural allegiance and forebears.

Another new and emphatic distinction between the land surrounding the Parish and the rest of England emerged in the late eleventh century. The Domesday Book of 1086, in which the Parish does not feature, ascribes just 5 per cent of English landownership to its pre-Norman population. Yet the heart of Cumberland, including Allerdale below Derwent – around 20 per cent of the county – initially lay under the overlordship of barons without a drop of Norman blood in their veins: from Ullswater, Dacre, Greystoke, Crosthwaite and Bassenthwaite in the east and centre, to Cockermouth and on to Dean and, in terms of underlordship, Workington in the west.

Very few of the places that appear in this book, except for Carlisle and Egremont, were originally granted to Normans, despite Norman rule. This distinction between Cumberland and the rest of England would soon diminish in importance, as Saxons and Vikings began to intermarry with Normans. Nonetheless, it was one of a number of factors – not least the effects of the area's geographical isolation – that came together to ensure that the Parish maintained a sense of rugged independence, including its long history as part of Strathclyde and the continued absence of memories of mutual slaughter, given a broadly peaceful Norman settlement.

Alice de Rumelli and the Parish church*

The death of Henry I in 1135 ushered in a period of civil war between his daughter Matilda and his nephew Stephen, who seized the throne of England on his uncle's demise. Matilda's claims

---

* The early period covered in this chapter has many variable spellings and dates, depending upon the source. I have used Weir's *Britain's Royal Families: The Complete Genealogy* for Maldred and Waltheof, but I have changed her spelling of de Romelli to accord with Farrer and Clay, *Early Yorkshire Charters*, whose dates I have used for the de Rumelli stories.

were supported by her uncle David I of Scotland, one of the most powerful of Scotland's medieval kings,* who invaded northern England within days of Stephen's usurpation. Once he had rebuilt the fortress of Carlisle, the town began to replace Roxburgh as his favoured residence, and his bloody, largely successful, fighting for the rest of his reign introduced the border to its new future.

One of the Scottish king's most ferocious fighters was William FitzDuncan, a nephew of both Waltheof *and* David I, who had inherited Allerdale below Derwent from one uncle and been given the very considerable Scottish title of Earl of Moray by the other.[23] His marriage to Alice de Rumelli, heiress of Allerdale above Derwent, probably ordained by King David to cement his hold on northwest England, introduces the second character essential to the emergence of Great Crosthwaite Parish. Like Waltheof, William was without a drop of Norman blood, while Alice was thoroughly Norman, and their joint Cumbrian territory was vast, marching down to the south of Cumbria on the west coast and spanning the whole of Cumberland west of its border on the Helvellyn range. Together with Alice's lands in Yorkshire and William's in Scotland, this was a very grand alliance indeed. And an ingenious one, likely to prove unproblematic whichever nation had control over their Cumbrian territories.

Having been dispatched by King David to lead his western army, William FitzDuncan, almost as a honeymoon, ravaged his way down the Cumberland coast. The monks of Calder Abbey had fled in terror at his approach and in the spring of 1138, he moved east into Yorkshire, where Alice's mother's lands at Skipton were to be on the front line of a brutal campaign. The violence there became legendary:[24] 'They first slew children and kindred in the sight of their relations, lords in the sight of their serfs and the opposite, and husbands in the sight of their wives'.[25]

By the time King David died in Carlisle in 1153, Alice and

---

* The last to inherit the title of Prince of Cumbria, the kingship of Strathclyde having apparently disappeared just before the end of the eleventh century. He attracted many Anglo-Norman families to settle in Scotland, including the Bruces and the Stewards, later to use the French version of their name, Stuart. See Weir, *Britain's Royal Families*, pp. 209, 214, 246.

William had had five children: two boys, the eldest of whom
had died young, and three girls, all of them soon to be second
cousins to the Scottish and English kings, Malcolm IV and Henry
II. There had been much Gaelic and Viking harrumphing about
the succession of Malcolm IV, David's eleven-year-old grandson;
the eldest son of the eldest son, he gained the first unequivocal
inheritance in Scotland through the Norman principle of primo-
geniture.* Scurrilous rhymes circulated and the *Orkneyinga Saga*
reported of William FitzDuncan and his son that 'he was a good
man, and that his son was William the Noble, whom all the Scots
wished to take for their king'.[26] But William FitzDuncan died, as
did King Stephen of England – just a year after David I.[27] Tragedy
and legend take over.

Some ten years later, William the Noble, 'the Boy of Egremont'
(a title referred to as early as 1223 in a legal document),[28] also died
while staying in his mother's lands in Yorkshire. Leaping across the
Strid, a deep chasm in the River Wharfe, his leashed greyhound
hung back, distrusting the leap, and 'the boy' drowned. According
to legend, when his mother was told, she replied 'Endless sorrow'
to the question 'What is good for a bootless bene?' (i.e., 'whence
can comfort spring / When Prayer is of no avail?[29]'). A tradition
grew up, expressed in song and story, that Alice founded Bolton
Priory in memory of her son and to pray for his soul. Wordsworth
would tell the tale of the legendary founding of the Priory in his
poem 'The Force of Prayer'. And as with so much Cumberland
legend, truth and fiction co-exist. Alice and William did indeed
move their priory from the village of Embsay to Bolton in 1155,[30]
but the names of both mother and son appear on the charter, so,
demonstrably, Alice did not found Bolton Priory out of grief at the
death of her son.

However, like all legends, the tale of the Boy of Egremont
transmits an emotional truth down the ages. For, in plain truth,

* William FitzDuncan's father, who had spent much of his childhood in the
English court, had reigned briefly as Duncan II in 1094, when he had tried
to exercise the principle by deposing his uncle, Donald III. However, later the
same year, he died defending his position and his uncle resumed the throne.
Weir, *Britain's Royal Families*, pp. 188–189.

the Boy of Egremont's untimely death unravelled the fortunes of Alice's marriage, her estate to be divided into three between her daughters. For the passionate, early-twentieth-century historian of the Lake District, W. G. Collingwood,* to be at Egremont was to learn 'of the boy who would have been King of Scotland'.[31] It must have felt like a tragedy for Cumberland that such a great estate, centred upon Egremont, with such royal possibility and so many ancient links, should suddenly evaporate. As with the legends attached to Dunmail, the story is a lament for lost grandeur and it needed a suitably tragic emphasis; enter Bolton Priory, which quickly became a famous and much loved place and was situated in the valley where 'the boy' had drowned.

Might there have been some kernel of fact behind the legend? By the 1150s, chapel building had begun to flourish in Cumbria as the paying of tithes was becoming formalised, and landlords were able to endow them.[32] Alice did build a church, which she may well have raised in memory of her son,† the Norman church of St Kentigern's in Great Crosthwaite, described in Jocelyn of Furness's biography of St Kentigern (c.1181) as the 'Basilica, recently erected'.[33] A monk and scholar from the greatest monastery in Cumbria, founded not long before he wrote, Jocelyn's 'basilica' was a church of more than usual size: certainly, the Lake District then had no other church approaching it. It had an internal span of over 37 feet (a width that would probably have required wooden pillars on each side to support the roof),[34] a chancel arch and no tower.[35]

There is no certain date of construction. But there are some clues. Eeles, who did a great deal of work on the fabric of the church, considers it to be transitional rather than pure Norman, a period commonly considered to begin c.1160, and a lead coin

---

* The link between John Ruskin and Arthur Ransome.
† The Boy of Egremont was certainly alive in 1154 (the year of Stephen's death) and it has generally been believed that he died sometime before 1160. However, some detailed material in the *Early Yorkshire Charters* suggests that he died around 1163. See Farrer and Clay, *Early Yorkshire Charters*, Vol 7, pp. 13–14, 71.

from Stephen's reign* was found in the church, minted at a time when there were regular changes of coinage.[36] The only expert who has offered a date suggested 1160; I would consider the early 1160s to be the most likely period. But, whatever the exact date, it is extremely unlikely that the building of St Kentigern's could have been finished before 1157, when the still teenage Malcolm IV finally gave back to England the lands taken by the Scots during the years of civil war.

To its newly English parishioners, living in a sparsely populated valley full of 'wild beasts and birds of prey',[37] who had hitherto been used to a small thatched church, this unimaginably large building, in stone, must have seemed almost miraculous. Standing alone atop a small rise in the ground, visible from the hills around from miles away, the church must have inspired feelings of awe. This was a place of sanctuary, and an expression of De Rumelli power; a church destined to play a central role in the local community over the next 700 years. Whether it still retained the traditional Celtic religious services, far as it was from the modernising centre of Strathclyde, we will never know for certain. But it is thought to be more than another hundred years before churches in the remote mountainous regions of the northwest were cajoled into forsaking their old ways; and it seems likely that Celtic Christianity initiated the worship in the new basilica, built in honour of the great Celtic saint.

The mystery is why Alice chose to build the only religious building either she or William built in Cumbria just west of Great Crosthwaite. For the Normans, belief in the truth of religion was as strong as their love of conquest. Building monasteries or priories therefore made practical sense; the monks' devotions – mass and seven hours of daily prayer – aided not only the administration of their rule but their progression heavenwards. During the twelfth century, five monasteries were built either within Allerdale or holding land in Crosthwaite Parish. Alice may have built her church both as a Norman acknowledgment that her family had not created a religious insurance policy in Cumberland and, perhaps, to atone

* Discovered under the floor of the nave in the nineteenth century.

for the savagery of her first husband's battles for Scotland. But the couple's Cumbrian lands included many more obvious places to build, in particular William's headquarters at Cockermouth and her own at Egremont, and there will have been many other rustic churches in the couple's vast territories that she could have chosen to replace.*

A practical attraction of Crosthwaite may have been that it was a relatively safe place to build: difficult to access, surrounded by mountains and irrelevant to direct lines of attack. When churches were later built near the border on Solway Firth, their towers, built for defence, dwarfed their naves. Alice built a church with a nave of infinitely greater size and *no* tower. But this is hardly a sufficient explanation of its placement.

William Fitz Duncan had no Norman blood in him, and I think this is the key. The old Crosthwaite church was dedicated to St Kentigern, the Scottish patron saint of Glasgow Cathedral and Strathclyde. The placement of Alice's surprisingly grand church – a startlingly large one for its time and position – was surely chosen to honour her husband and her 'Boy's' lineage; built to assuage her grief over the tragic death of her son, and the stark diminishment of their family's power. And perhaps Alice built a Parish church for the people, rather than the more conventional priory or monastery, as the sort of act of true generosity that sometimes comes after suffering.

So, it would have made both practical and emotional sense for her to build her only Cumbrian religious building in Crosthwaite, leaving a permanent reminder of the Scottish heritage of her family on land that was newly English again. And her legacy was remarkable. St Kentigern's Parish would contain more than a third of the pre-eighteenth-century chapelries in the whole of the Carlisle diocese,† as well as a chantry chapel. Described by all as the 'mother

---

* Egremont may have had a chapel, as one was built or rebuilt there around 1220 – see Collingwood, *The Lake Counties*, p. 89 – and its parish church at St Bees was 3 miles away. Cockermouth's parish church at Brigham was several miles away and the stone church of St Bega's, Bassenthwaite's parish church, was some 4 miles (less by water) from Crosthwaite.
† Five out of fourteen.

church' of the Northern Lakes, St Kentigern's is also considered the original parish church of the Lake District.[38]

Southey was the first person to bring Alice de Rumelli back to mind as the builder of the Norman Parish church.[39] And when Wordsworth visited Bolton Abbey in 1807, and burrowed into its history,[40] her story touched him to his core. Ever since his brother's death, two years earlier, the poet had been trying to come to terms with his grief and achieve an acceptance of his loss. He worked this through by returning once again to Alice's story about 'the boy' in his long poem *The White Doe of Rylstone*, which centred on a later tragic event:[41]

> From which affliction – when the grace
> Of God had in her heart found place –
> A pious structure, fair to see,
> Rose up, this stately Priory!
> To the grief of her soul, that doth come and go,
> In the beautiful form of this innocent Doe:
> Which, though seemingly doomed in its breast to sustain
> A softened remembrance of sorrow and pain,
> Is spotless, and holy, and gentle, and bright;
> And glides o'er the earth like an angel of light.

In the poem's exploration of hidden strength, Wordsworth brought the peace of acceptance to Alice. He believed *The White Doe of Rylstone* to be 'in conception' the highest he ever produced, and when he finally published the poem, in 1815, he ensured that it appeared in an expensive quarto edition 'to show the world his opinion of it'. He also added some prefatory stanzas reflecting the new agony of the loss of two of his own young children, from which he never entirely recovered.

Both Lake Poets loved St Kentigern's. What might Wordsworth have felt had he known that Alice's salvation from her 'bootless bene' could never have been the building of Bolton Priory, and that the construction of her one and only religious building in Cumbria, St Kentigern's, close to the death of her son, appears to be the grandly magnified fact behind the centuries of feeling prompted by the legend he was so moved by.

2

Parish, Manor Governance and War,
1183–1370

WHEN THE BOY of Egremont's inheritance was split between his three sisters after Alice's death in 1187, her daughter – another Alice – became the new Lady of Allerdale. She too had a considerable impact upon the Parish. Between 1192 and 1195, after the death of her first husband, Gilbert Pipard (a man of real substance and achievement, who was even granted the king's rights for the great Forest of Inglewood), Alice II granted Fountains Abbey, in Yorkshire, the greatest Cistercian abbey in Britain, the right to choose the rector of St Kentigern's.[1] This will have been both a homage to her mother, who had promised gifts to the abbey, and, again, a part of the Normans' religious insurance policy. On becoming a widow for a second time, before the end of 1209, Alice paid the king 250 marks, ten palfreys and ten fillies to have the liberty of her own lands and a reasonable dower (income) from the lands of her two husbands, so that she would not be compelled to marry again.[2]

Pragmatically, she then sold most of Borrowdale, along with its hunting rights,[3] to Furness Abbey for £156 13s. 4d. in 1209/10[4] and at the same time awarded the manor of Thornthwaite, south of Bassenthwaite, to Patrick of Workington (an early member of the influential Curwen family) as a cousinly gesture. Describing herself as Alice de Rumilly, daughter of William, son of Duncan, she followed this with a flurry of gifts to Fountains in 1212,[5] given 'for the health of her soul and the souls of all her ancestors and successors and of her late husbands'. These gifts included the Derwentwater island of Hest-holm (Norse for 'Stallion Island', its name would be changed by Fountains to Vicar's Island), along with free transit of the lake for their boats. Also included was the land of Watendlath in the high fells east of Derwentwater and the Langstrath valley to the south, in Borrowdale – one of the principal routes to the central mountains; a gift that turned Stonethwaite into common land for both Fountains and Furness. She also gave Fountains the land around the church, the whole 'vill'* of Crosthwaite, along with its mill on the land of 'Kesewic' (this being the first recorded mention of Keswick).[6]

The Parish of Crosthwaite must have emerged soon after the new church was built as the rector was receiving tithes[7] well before Alice II's complicated negotiations with Furness and Fountains, although the vicarage is first found on record in 1283.[†] Roughly ten miles by nine, it encompassed a large but underpopulated area of some 90 square miles, stretching southeast from Threlkeld Bridge, and south along the tops to Helvellyn, before descending to Dunmail Raise. From there the boundary went west across the mountains, through Esk Hause and over the top of Great End to Sty Head. Climbing the tops of Great Gable and Brandreth, it continued across the Honister, Newlands and Whinlatter passes, onto Bassenthwaite Lake, which it crossed just before Beck Wythop, landing east of Mirehouse and just before Little Crosthwaite. It then rises to the top of Skiddaw before descending to follow the Glenderaterra river into the Greta and thence to Threlkeld Bridge.[8]

These boundaries were largely natural, defined by features in the landscape, at times coinciding with the boundary between Cumberland and Westmorland, counties which had emerged in the

---

* A 'vill' then meant a defined area of land strong enough to take a manor to court, and this one presumably included Great Crosthwaite, in so far as it was not already owned by the Derwentwaters, and (as the deeds make apparent) at least some of Little Crosthwaite.

† In most of England parish boundaries had been fixed long before, among the most durable legacies from Anglo-Saxon England but with the frequent transference of land from English to Scottish hands, the Northwest of England was unlikely to have had parish boundaries in mind, particularly in the wild semi-populated Lake District.

mid-twelfth century. The only exception lay in the northeast near Threlkeld, the Viking valley settlement on the border of Greystoke parish. It seems the Baron of Greystoke, whose appointment just predated the two Allerdale baronies, must have got his parish established first.

As the only parish church in the heart of the fells,[9] St Kentigern's would have drawn people to its vicinity.* A small area in Newlands Valley, the next valley west from Crosthwaite, was settled close to the time the church was built:[10] the early origins of the village of Braithwaite. Over a hundred years later, in 1296, Keswick,† half a mile east of the church, became the Lake District's only market town and long remained so. While the whole of Derwentwater was allocated to the township, it only held a small extent of land, bounded by the Derwent and Greta rivers and the manor of Castlerigg.[11]

The whole district was at the time more extensively forested than anywhere else in Britain,[12] the Parish cover so thick that 'the red squirrel is said to have gone from Keswick to Wythburn [at the southern end of Thirlmere] without touching the ground'.[13] But, owing to the Normans' passion for the hunt (almost an extension of warfare), the ancient right of the parishioners to forage the forest had been withdrawn when the upland territory of the two Allerdale barons was designated as private forest, subjecting vast areas (including treeless land) to forest law. Initially, only pigs were allowed to share the forest with the game, grubbing away at acorns to fatten up in the autumn,‡ the barons recompensed by a fee called pannage.§ Even though the forest law was soon curtailed,¶ feelings of alienation and anger echoed down the centuries in Cumberland ballads, the poacher emerging as even more of a hero than the later vaunted fighters against the Scots.

---

* Until the nineteenth century, most Lake District valleys had chapels of ease and were outlying parts of the large parishes they served.

† The town of Keswick is generally considered to have been deliberately planned by the Derwentwaters, rather than to have grown organically.

‡ Notably at Sty Head in Borrowdale and at Swinside in Portinscale.

§ In the Derwentfells as late as 1282, annual pannage was paid for over 250 pigs that had travelled to join their local brethren. Winchester, *Landscape and Society*, p. 101.

¶ To cover just Inglewood Forest.

Derwentwater and Bassenthwaite Lake from the Ashness Bridge, on the track up to Watendlath; the first general view of the heart of the Parish.

The only visible building is the whitewashed Crosthwaite church in the far distance.

The barons had complete control over their upland territory, which was designed to supplement their arable lands in the lowlands outside the Parish. These lands were often on the west coast, usually farmed by tenants in conventional feudal relationships. Although the unique upland/lowland organisation of the Lake District would later have unintended consequences, the barons' legal entitlements were to be further extended in 1235, when a new legal concept of 'manorial waste' was created,[14] over which they were again able to assert their rights. Thus, the vast no man's land of Lake District upland waste, largely unimprovable fellside, was claimed for the first time. But, presumably in an acknowledgment of pre-Norman conventions of land use, both Viking and Celtic, it was accepted that tenants could continue to exercise their common rights, principally grazing and turbary (peat cutting).

By the mid-thirteenth century, after Alice II's death in 1214,[15] the Parish had become split again between the baronies of Above Allerdale and Below Allerdale. The descendants of Alice's sister Cecily – mostly using the title of the Count of Aumale or de Fortibus – inherited Copeland and the Derwentfells, and Amabel's descendants inherited Allerdale below Derwent and were called de Lucy. They still owned Parish land directly (although much fighting over both territory and inheritance ensued over the next 150 years), as did the Derwentwaters, but it was the two Cistercian monasteries, Fountains and Furness, who now oversaw almost all the land in the Keswick/Crosthwaite valley.* The Cistercians placed their monasteries in secluded and solitary places and their rule stressed the importance of manual work: 'our food is scanty, our garments rough, our drink is from the stream, our sleep is often upon the book ... Self-will has no scope, there is no moment for idleness or dissipation ... Everywhere peace, everywhere serenity and a marvellous freedom from the tumult of the world.'[16] The 'white monks' spun their habits from their own white, undyed wool and became the first people to develop sheep-keeping into a trade in England.

---

* Fountains Abbey also started to graze their sheep in the Thirlmere Valley in the thirteenth century, where it is thought that Armboth may have been their 'grange'. Darrell, *Wythburn Church and the Valley of Thirlmere,* p. 10.

Alice I's fulling mill in Cockermouth,* known to be in existence by the mid-1150s, indicates that sheep had already begun to be profitable for the few who paid for their loosely woven cloth to be soaked in fresh water and fuller's earth and then stamped by human feet in tubs of stale urine. This process, known as 'walking', helped to remove the natural oils and to shrink and felt the cloth. (Feet would later be replaced by water-powered hammers.)[17] The Cistercians became ever more professional in their approach, introducing sheep farms – the herd-wyck – and the concept of wool and sheep as merchandise. They obtained export licences, and by 1315 had become the only group in England to divide their wool into three levels of quality.[18] Furness Abbey established their central Parish farm in Grange, at the southern end of Derwentwater, overseeing both their tenants and the management of the wool trade, complete with boats to transport the wool down the lake. Monk Hall in Great Crosthwaite (now the site of Keswick hospital) became the Fountains headquarters, and probably their storage barn.† All this provided work for the parishioners, whose numbers increased significantly throughout the thirteenth century.

The effective pastoral farming of the Cistercians is likely to have been instrumental in helping Thomas de Derwentwater persuade Edward I to grant a royal charter for a market in Keswick in 1276. By that time, the upland barons and their stewards were ignoring their status as lords of the chase and beginning to actively generate income from their upland; the possibilities for the parishioners expanded accordingly. Grazing and stock-rearing had been allowed in parts of the forests and by 1278 the Derwentfells had eight tanneries, making use of the ubiquitous oak bark to tan animal skins.[19] Then, a second wave of colonisation of the land created new communities of pastoral frontiersmen.

From the mid-thirteenth century, farmers and peasants, some organised by the monks and the barons' stewards, began to clear stony ground, drain the bog and create 'closes' (enclosed plots of

---

* The first fulling mill recorded in Cumberland.
† Among many others, the Penrith surveyor James Clarke confidently states in 1787 that 'the monks had a steward here and here the tenants paid their rates'. Clarke, *Survey*, p. 100.

land) and 'assarts' (land cleared from woodland for cultivation). The stones from the cleared ground were sometimes used for boundary walls in small irregular fields, but earth or turf banks topped with 'dry' hedges of stakes interwoven with brushwood were the norm,[20] as boundaries could still change. The pattern of this old landscape is still visible in several small areas in the Parish today.* Newlands earned its name from the introduction of a system of dykes and drainage channels to reclaim the low-lying impassable marshland, including a large shallow tarn. The small village core at Braithwaite expanded, and new settlements sprang up elsewhere, including the west side of Derwentwater, a scatter of farmsteads with newly enclosed fields rising up the lower slopes of the fellside. Between 1266 and 1310 rents rose steadily, despite the decidedly small size of the initial tenant farms.[21]

Tenants were free to achieve this transformation, as they were to farm, partly because of the absence of their baronial overlords and partly because of a particular northern tenancy system. In the north of England the obligation to be forever available to fight had been part of the original Norman grants of land, the duty defined early in the thirteenth century as to 'go at the king's precept in the army to Scotland; viz, in going, in the vanguard; and, in returning, in the rearguard'.[22] Uniquely, this service would soon become extended to the tenants at will, due to the uneasy relations with Scotland. There had been a risk of renewed war in 1215, when Alexander II of Scotland, exploiting the chaos of the war in England between King John and his barons, invaded the North to press his ancestral claims and the canons of Carlisle Cathedral happily elected a Scottish bishop. But things calmed down after John's death the following year. Then in 1249, prompted by the pope, Henry III of England and Alexander III of Scotland established the Laws of the Marches to 'regularise' behaviour on the border.

Three Marches were created in each country and in both

---

* For instance, Legburthwaite, at the northeast end of Thirlmere, probably wood originally cleared in medieval times, is still surrounded by a small area of ancient enclosures, as is Wythburn at the southeast end of the lake. See Historic Landscape Characterisation on the Cumbria County Council website for more.

England and Scotland each of the marches were responsible for the security of the region, and for the administration of the march laws. Despite the Scots' razing large parts of Carlisle Castle just six years after Henry and Alexander's treaty, Alexander's marriage to Henry's daughter Margaret kept things relatively quiet until the Scottish king's death in 1286. Over time, the Dacres, whose original lands lay some 8 miles from the Parish's eastern boundary, frequently became wardens of the western march. Since Dacre is the Celtic name for a trickling stream, and no specific grant of land has been found, the family are likely, along with their friends the Derwentwaters, to have been indigenous rather than Norman.

It is thought to have been the English wardens of the marches who enforced border tenant service over the tenants at will, creating a feudal obligation to the crown, albeit via the lord of the manor.[23] Reflecting the original form of knight's service, which exchanged military service for land, the exchange for the tenant was 'border service' for either assured or hereditary tenancy. There remains considerable debate about which it was, due to lack of clear evidence,[24] but once hereditary rights to farmed land were acknowledged in law, they were inviolable, unless the tenant was found guilty of a criminal act or died without a legally defined heir, in which case the tenement reverted to the lord of the manor.*

Since the sixteenth century, this Cumberland and Westmorland tenancy has usually been referred to as 'customary tenancy', a practice I follow here. In Elizabethan court cases, which offer the first recorded examples of the resolution of territorial disputes between tenant and landlord, the exchange would be described as 'tenant right' – unequivocally hereditary. But it is simply as 'tenants at the will of the lord' that we first officially meet customary tenants in the Parish, in a 1303 inquisition into the lands of Sir Thomas de Derwentwater (who had been knighted after getting Keswick its market charter)† sometime after his death.

---

* At times it was possible that there was a break clause.
† As had his father and grandfather before him.

We learn that the Derwentwater lands were held of the king in exchange for a cornage* rent of 10s., homage and serving for the king at his court in Cockermouth 'from three weeks to three weeks'. Sir Thomas's obligations to the court were shared by his nine 'free tenants' or freeholders, all outside the Parish, who provided the jury and court officials for the head (or 'leet') court, which was held twice a year, around Easter and Michaelmas. Upon Alice II's death without issue in 1214,[25] an equivalent court, overseeing Parish lands west and southwest of the River Derwent,† had been created in Braithwaite to deal with the division of her Rumelli lands between the representatives of her two sisters.

These courts dealt with both criminal and seigneurial matters. The seigneurial side dealt with the breaking of by-laws or infringements of the lord's right, which included licences to fish, hunt and cut timber, and the requirement of tenants to grind corn at the lord's mill. Fines were levied when a tenant 'broke the lord's soil', that is, encroached on his land. The criminal side dealt with breaches of the king's peace, whether 'affrays' (fighting), 'hubbleshows' (causing an uproar or hubbub), 'blouds' or 'bloodwites' (incidents involving the shedding of blood), 'petty micherie' (pilfering) or eavesdropping – no one was allowed to 'lye or harken at any man's doors or windows'.[26] The money raised from these fines flowed into the lord's estate and, given the freeholder status of the jurors, the court probably displayed little sympathy for the tenants.[27]

Sir Thomas's freeholders owned holdings of approximately 280 acres of land each. They had various obligations in addition to the maintenance of their land, all of them, along with cornage, apparently reflecting the antiquity of their landownership. Some freeholders had to feed Derwentwater's foresters for ten days each year. Two individuals who owned a hamlet between them had to pay Derwentwater's cornage fee. The Abbot of Calder, who was obliged to pay half a pound of pepper on Christmas Day, was

---

* An ancient North English tenure of land, which obliged the tenant to give notice of an invasion of the Scots by blowing a horn.

† Newlands, Borrowdale, Thornthwaite and Coledale (Portinscale) and the then seldom-mentioned Rumelli territory in the northwest of the Parish, running along the foot of Skiddaw.

typical of the west coast, where the majority of vills were cor-
nage-paying freeholds.

Sir Thomas also had 'thirty tenants who hold in burgage in a
place called Kesewik'.[28] Burgage plots, only created in town boroughs chartered by the king, were, in the Parish, directly leased
from the Derwentwaters.* However, the holder was subject to a
form of cornage and so qualified as a free tenant, able to sell or let
his plot or the remains of his lease and unburdened by most of the
feudal obligations of the countryside.[29] The plots were about 40
feet wide, with the height and line of the buildings controlled, and
in Keswick the burgesses usually held some of the Derwentwater
975 acres of demesne land[30] (mainly south and east of the town)
to farm as well. Their houses or huts, timber framed with rough
wood, would all have been thatched, usually with bracken, nearly
down to the ground, covering thick 'toppin' peat turves; thinner
ones, 'riggin sods', formed the roof ridge.[31] The walls, which were
mostly circular, would have been made of rough field stone or
wattle and daub.

However, it was the 'divers tenants at the will of the lord' who
held the considerable majority of Derwentwater land. Each acre
was assessed for annual rent and, although the tenant's feudal services are not mentioned in the inquisition of 1303, every tenant
will probably have paid some token (often called a God's Penny) to
mark the change of the lord or the tenant. The need to mark the
change of the lord was, along with hereditary rights, a particular
distinction of this form of tenancy.[32] All paid 'heriots' and gave
'boon days'. The heriot was a tax due on estates after the death
of the holder, and was often the best animal or, if the holding was
too poor to have one, a quantity of grain or wool. Boon days were
days when tenants gave their labour for free. There were generally
six such days, occurring at specified times of the farming year, but
in some manors the number of boon days was as high as sixteen.
However, the new colonisers in the forest communities in the Parish
hills seem to have been free of these feudal obligations, simply
paying rent and 'giving evidence to the foresters when necessary'.[33]

---

* In other contexts, burgage plots were, on occasion, freehold.

Finally, the Derwentwater Inquisition recorded twelve land-less cottagers, paying noticeably more rent per annum, 12d., than the tenants at will. Outside the Derwentwater estate but still in the Parish, there were eleven cottagers in the Newlands valley c.1270, and twenty-seven at Braithwaite in 1305.* The cottag-ers, usually including the women, lived off a variety of work for hire as the farming year progressed (including 'dongscaleing', i.e., muck-spreading).[34] The copper mines in Newlands, which were worked intermittently from the early 1200s,[†] offered another source of employment.[35] The estate accounts suggest that, in both Derwentwater and Bassenthwaite Lake, the local community had the right to fish freely; so, it seems that in the thirteenth century fishing could help provide a living for the landless.[36]

At the bottom of the Cumberland social scale were the bondsmen implied by the name of nearby Threlkeld (in Norse, 'the spring of the thralls or serfs'), which presumably referred to bondsmen brought in by the Vikings who settled there.[37] A Derwentwater bondsman had been recorded at Tallentire a few years earlier[38] but, since there is no reference to one in the inqui-sition, they were presumably entirely absent from the Parish, at least by the beginning of the fourteenth century. Indeed, all the evidence suggests that in the Lake District generally this group made up a very small part of the population.[39] Yet, in the rest of England, more than half the population were serfs, or chattels, who could be bought, sold and married by their masters as late as 1350.

The distinction between a 'tenant at will' and a 'bondsman' is one of many examples of the history of the Crosthwaite Parish lands creating a different, and preferable, environment for its people.[‡]

*

* However, the numbers declined steeply after the drop in population in the fourteenth century made more land available: by 1547 Braithwaite had only three, Newlands none.
† Lead too was mined in the Derwentfells, between 1266 and 1290.
‡ The distinction between a 'tenant at will' and a 'bondsman' argues, for me, for the early establishment of customary tenancy.

The growth of the population of the Parish by the end of the thirteenth century was underlined by its seven recorded mills;* and there may have been others, albeit unrecorded, as tithes from mills made up a good part of the income of the vicar of St Kentigern's from as early as 1251. Nevertheless, the evolving pastoral frontiersmen, the progenitors of the Parish's hill farmers, had tough lives. The ravages of wolves and eagles undermined the efficiencies introduced by the monks, so that sheep farming was, at this time, a much smaller affair in the Parish than it would later become.

The essential bulwark that tenants had to create and maintain was the head dyke, a stone wall that, often using large boulders, separated their few acres of fertile farmland in the lower valley from the open fell they used for coarse grazing.[40] In Borrowdale, it was called the 'fellgarth'. Behind the head dyke, the valley land *had* to be kept stockproof while the oats ripened to feed the family, the hay meadow grew, and good-quality grazing remained to feed what livestock could be kept through the winter. All of this activity, including following rules for grazing on the manorial waste, must have involved not just mutual cooperation but some form of communal organisation. The details of the latter, however, can only be traced in the Parish some hundred years later.

Once the head dykes were in place, the open and close seasons dictated the essential rhythm of the farmer's year. Stock was removed from the fertile land in the valley in spring, usually at Ellenmas or St Helen's Day,[†] to allow the crops and hay to grow during the close season behind the head dyke. And as ewes and rams were not easily separated on the hills, the 'clowting' of rams was universal: a piece of cloth strategically placed as a hopeful

---

* William de Derwentwater had had a mill dam built on his land of 'Kesewic' some forty years before it became a market town, and there was a mill at Millbeck, a mile or so north of Crosthwaite, first recorded in 1260 and mostly used for grinding oats. Forty years later, a mill at Brundholme, near the River Greta just north of Keswick, was recorded and the one at Crosthwaite given to Fountains by Alice II remained, as did the one she had granted at Braithwaite. There was also a water mill and a fulling mill at Wythburn.

† The Feast of the Invention of the Holy Cross celebrated on 3 May was especially significant in parts of the country that relied on the farming of livestock.

contraceptive device.[41] The return of the sheep to the lower land in the autumn* heralded the open season† behind the head dyke and the tupping (mating) time for the sheep. In the Lake District, this season was held back until November, some two months later than the south of England, so that by the time the lambs were driven out to the fells in springtime, the bracken was sprouting along with the first flush of plant growth.[42]

The Vikings had long used high summer pastures for grazing, migrating with their stock to their 'sheilings', temporary summer huts. As the population had expanded, the use of sheilings spread throughout the Parish – a process that continued until around 1350. The sheilings were closely associated with cattle, rent for grazing duly paid to the 'forest' landlords. In the Newlands valley the herders would frequently take their cows backwards and forwards for milking from as much as a mile away every day, the average size of a herd being ten.‡ A dairy enclosure at the head of the valley,[43] 4 miles away from the tenant farm near Portinscale,[44] underlines the value and rarity of good pasture – sufficiently important to offset the considerable extra work for the milkmaids.[45] Sometime before 1302, Fountains had created a professional vaccary or cattle ranch by enclosing their land around Stonethwaite. (This caused a long dispute with Furness, finally settled in Fountains' favour in 1304.)[46]

Cattle were sent to market in the late autumn; before the agricultural revolution, farmers usually lacked enough fodder to overwinter. Those animals that were kept were slaughtered and cured, by drying or pickling – a vital source of food to sustain the family and supplement the oats that were the core of their subsistence diet. Fishing, alongside cow-herding and shepherding, was another element of the parishioners' self-sufficiency. Fountains Abbey co-owned the rights to the River Derwent and opened a

---

* Usually on All Saints Day (1 November) or Martinmas (11 November).
† This phrase was often literal, with all the enclosures within the head dyke opened to allow the livestock of the whole community free access.
‡ As time went on, specialism began to appear, reflected in the early-four-teenth-century surnames – the specialist herder for calves (Calvert) and lambs (Lambert) for instance.

fishery at Portinscale. In 1230, a Nicholas de Linford,* one of the many men with whom Alice II had done business in Parish land, gave the monks the right to dam the river at their mill.[47] He also gave them the right to open a fishery in Derwentwater, where, with a pleasant biblical resonance, the monks used nets anchored on the shore, which they fed out into the water by boat, hauling in their catch by hand. Cumberland and the Derwent were by now already famous for their salmon and would remain so for another 500 years.

The commonest method of catching both salmon and sea trout in the river was the 'fishgarth', a wooden structure spanning the river with a net or wicker box at its centre, known as a 'coffin' or 'coop'. These were popular and effective devices – but they were illegal, since ancient custom (which was beginning to have legal force) demanded a clear midstream passage wide enough for 'a sow and her five pigs'.[48] In 1278, in order to preserve salmon stocks, a close season was introduced, enforced by twelve conservators[49] who were to cover all of Cumberland; fishing was proving another profitable business. The surname 'Fisher' soon became the most frequently used in the Parish.

The church and the 'terrible fourteenth century'

The basic transaction of the ancient ecclesiastic parish was that the priest was responsible for the 'cure of souls', the spiritual needs of the parishioners, who recompensed him through their tithes. But it took more than a century to sort out the effects of Alice II's gifts of land and church to the two monasteries on the Crosthwaite priests' tithes. The first rector was a relation of Alice II's second husband,[50] and the second was Adam de Crosthwaite,† who gave up the Borrowdale tithes to Furness in 1210, soon after Alice had sold its land to the abbey. But he strongly opposed the

* A place in Craven, connected to Fountains. Part of the Rumelli land in the West Riding of Yorkshire.
† To whom Alice had granted a quarter of the land of Crosthwaite, which would save the pannage fee for the pigs of his tenants.

previous rector's gift of his church to Fountains – which Alice
had supported – since this turned him into a mere vicar, a word
derived from the Latin *vicarius*, meaning substitute. Adam's
apparently sensible objection was that, because the gift had been
made long after the rector retired, it had no legality. However,
the judgment went against him, on the condition that Fountains
made an annual payment of 100s. to any vicar they appointed and
that Adam would keep the right to appoint his successor during
his lifetime.[51]

The terms of the deal were confirmed only after Adam's death
in 1251: the new vicar was to have the lands that had formerly
belonged to the rector, along with the vast majority of tithes, while
Fountains was to enjoy 'the small tithes, also tithes of sheaves, vegetables in the fields and ferms of lands held from the church and 10
marks per annum'.[52] The abbey relinquished its direct control of
the choice of vicar by giving the privilege to the Bishop of Carlisle,*
thus saving themselves their annual £5 fee.[53] Finally, almost a

Thomas Allom's *Derwentwater and the Village of Grange*.
The second general view of the heart of the Parish.

---

* It remains in the Bishop of Carlisle's hands to this day.

hundred years later, it was agreed that the abbey was to pay half the cost of repairing the church roof.* In exchange, and for the cancellation of *his* old obligations for roofing the chancel, the vicar wisely gave up any claim to the rector's land, keeping 'an acre to the south of his messuage, tithes of sheaves and garden produce and of wages of abbey servants in the parish'.[54]

New deaneries were created at the end of the thirteenth century, the two connected to the Parish mirroring the old Allerdale baronies. Allerdale Above Derwent joined the Richmond Deanery in the diocese of Chester, yet their land in the west of the Parish joined St Kentigern's, Keswick, Castlerigg, St John's in the Vale and Wythburn in the Allerdale deanery of the diocese of Carlisle. Legally, and for land disputes, Thornthwaite, Portinscale, Newlands and Borrowdale fell within Allerdale Above Derwent but, within the church administration, Crosthwaite Parish proved strong enough to, again, create its own exception. Its own vill was apparently reserved for Fountains Abbey.

Around this time,[55] when Edward I levied a tax on all the northern churches,† we get our first real sense of the relative wealth of the Parish, and the effectiveness of the parishioners' land clearing and farming. St Kentigern's was valued at £30 13s. 4d., its living at £20, about two-thirds up the scale of all the Cumbrian parishes and the fourth highest in Allerdale. A rector's salary was expected to be divided into thirds, one for his upkeep, one for church upkeep, and one for the poor. Vicars appear not to have had these defined obligations – if so, Crosthwaite's vicar would have been very comfortably off. In contrast, unbeneficed curates – those without their own livings – earned much the same as a peasant with 20 acres of plough land.[56]

The valuation of St Kentigern's may perhaps have been diminished by Alice's gifts to the two monasteries, but by the end of the thirteenth century there is real evidence that the vicar was doing

---

* The disappearance of this obligation after the Reformation would be a cause of constant trouble.

† Edward had been temporarily granted the use of the pope's tithes to help defray costs of a possible crusade. This computation remained the basis of church taxes until the reign of Henry VIII.

his job, both pulling his Parish together as a community and persuading people to attend church on Sunday. Official news and notices were proclaimed, usually by the parish clerk, outside the church – the best way of circulating intelligence in such a widely dispersed Parish; thus, such urgent matters as the loss of livestock or the finding of strays were quickly relayed around the locality. In 1300, the Lady of Allerdale was summoned to prove by what right she held a market outside Crosthwaite church. She denied that she held a market there: it was rather, she explained, 'that the men of the neighbourhood met at church on festival days, and there sold flesh and fish' from which, despite being lady of the manor, she took no toll.[57]

These markets clearly continued, for in 1306 Cockermouth was sufficiently incensed to send a petition to Parliament complaining that 'there was a great concourse of people every Sunday at Crosthwaite church, where corn, flour ... and other merchandise were bought and sold'.[58] They traded so successfully that the people of Cockermouth who 'farmed the tolls of the king'*, running their legitimate market, were quite unable to pay their rent. This was clearly unacceptable to Parliament, and Crosthwaite was forbidden to continue to hold markets.[59] However, the church market, a half-mile away from the only market town in the Lake District, at Keswick (which raised no complaint), was an emphatic mark of the vibrancy of Crosthwaite church as the cohesive centre of its Parish.

*

The fourteenth century had begun badly for the Parish, as the small tenant farmers, already seriously weakened by bad harvests,[60] were hit by a plague that affected sheep and cattle.[61] The gradually colonised high valleys and uplands were particularly vulnerable, since many pastoral farms had been created on marginal land, much of which would not be used again until the national food

* By then the Honour of Cockermouth had fallen to the king.

shortages caused by the Napoleonic wars. These agrarian disasters, exacerbated by real climate deterioration, mark a turning point: the steady population growth and expansion of farming that had taken place since the arrival of the Normans was replaced by a pattern of rising poverty and abandonment of land that would continue until the mid-fifteenth century.[62]

Initially, the greatest curse was war. By 1292 the Scottish royal house of Dunkeld was exhausted, leaving no direct heir, either male or female. Largely owing to two centuries of Anglo-Scottish marital diplomacy, the Scottish magnates invited King Edward I of England to adjudicate between the thirteen contenders for their throne. He chose the nobleman John Balliol, a man whom he proceeded to treat as a puppet. When the disgruntled Scots concluded a treaty with France (the 'auld alliance'), Edward I invaded Scotland (subjecting the town of Berwick to a brutal sacking), and by the end of 1296 had imprisoned Balliol and declared himself the ruler of Scotland. The Scots promptly rebelled, led by the Scottish knight William Wallace. Edward chose not to call up his northern foot soldiers because of their lack of experience and summoned the disciplined men from the Welsh borders to battle, on whom Wallace inflicted a famous defeat at Stirling Bridge in 1297, going on to burn the land for thirty leagues around Carlisle.

When Edward I did call for two thousand infantry from Cumberland in 1301, only 940 men turned up, almost all of whom left within a few days, worried that raiders might attack their homes (even though the fighting was taking place on Scottish soil). However, by the end of Edward's reign (1307), 'hobelars', light unarmoured lancers on fast-moving fell ponies, who avoided the battle but harried the opposing army, were playing a prominent military role and would prove 'the most useful soldiers of any English army'[63] until the arrival of horse archers with Edward III. The same ponies, 'hobblers' and weapons were used by the newly formed Border reivers. Unknown before Edward I's wars, they raided violently for cattle and goods and, originally patriotic, clan loyalty soon became more significant than country.

In 1314, eight years after he had assumed the Scottish crown, Robert Bruce defeated the English under Edward II at Bannockburn and campaigned as ferociously in northwest England as Edward I had done in Scotland. Cumberland began to provide many more soldiers, supplying around a thousand of the 6,000 foot raised and half of the 900-odd hobelars.[64] But still more force was needed, and in 1322, for the first time in history, the foot was drawn from every county in England. Four years earlier, in 1318, such was the damage done by Bruce's marauding troops that it caused a general re-evaluation of taxation for the northern clergy. A considerable majority of parish churches in the Carlisle and Copeland deaneries (many of them on the coast) had absolutely no value attributed to them at all. Even the Crosthwaite vicar found that the taxation value of his living dropped from the £20 of less than thirty years before to just £4.[65]

Derwentwater lands were dispersed; their land at Tallentire, close to the west coast, was deemed in 1317 as 'worth per annum, clear, 100s. and not more on account of the war; but in time of peace, it used to be worth £10'. The family had recently purchased some land in the Greystoke barony, including Threlkeld, for which they owed service to the Greystokes, whose parish was far more exposed to the fighting. The Dacre family nearby were fighters extraordinaire. Later, Allerdale (which of course included the Parish) was named in a legal enquiry of 1341[66] as one of the areas where the principal cause of impoverishment was the absence of men fighting in the Scottish wars. So, in all, it would be wrong to assume that St Kentigern's parishioners were never called to battle. Nevertheless, since Crosthwaite did not lie on an easily negotiated route south and was sufficiently sparsely populated to be largely ignored as a source of booty, the Parish itself was never directly attacked. A raid of 1322 at Embleton, two-thirds of the way to Cockermouth, in which the lord of the manor was killed and twelve of the twenty-six peasant holdings burnt and destroyed, was its closest sacking.[67]

Although Cumberland was so impoverished, in the Parish there was enough money available for a major church restoration around 1340. A chapel, with a north wall lying *outside* today's, was added at the northeast end of St Kentigern's, incorporating a tall three-light east window. However, in 1348/9, the first of the three fourteenth-century bouts of plague struck the Carlisle diocese. Over in the Kendal parish, the numbers of dead were so great and the numbers of fit men so small that the journey for burial at the mother church had become impracticable; and Grasmere and Windermere joined Crosthwaite as the next two Lake District parish churches. At last, in 1357, the Treaty of Berwick brought relative peace to the border for twenty-three years but just four or five years later the plague returned to the diocese. There were so few clergy left that the bishop petitioned the pope for a faculty to dispense forty twenty-year-olds,[68] '12 persons of illegitimate birth and 6 others, being sons of priests or illegitimate sons of married men, so that they may be ordained'.[69]

The combined episodes of plague are estimated to have killed up to 40 per cent of the Cumberland population. However, it is probable that the outbreaks were less severe in Crosthwaite Parish and in other areas deep within the Lake District; mountainous areas apparently proved more immune to the effects of the plague than agricultural ones.[70] Soon after the war restarted in 1380, *all* the Cumberland and Northumberland benefices were entirely exempted from tax, being described as 'so devastated by hostile incursions of Scots and the depredations of Englishmen passing through them towards Scotland that they are not capable of paying'.[71] This exemption lasted from 1385 until 1420. The ravages of the Scottish wars and the human and animal plagues had changed everything; monks begged and houses were abandoned.

The lasting reminders today of this embattled century in Cumberland are the stone pele towers that stand sentinel across the county. Like castle keeps, they were oblong or square, with walls 5 to 10 feet thick, entered by a narrow staircase from the basement. Offering temporary refuge from raiding parties, with space for livestock in the basement, pele towers were, above all, fireproof. Today, occasionally, they stand alone, more often as part of a building or with later buildings around them. A farmhouse in the north of the Parish probably began as a pele tower, but the nearest unequivocal examples are found at Dacre and Greystoke, both far too close to Penrith and the route south to leave themselves defenceless. The border churches, similarly fortified, are grim reminders of the scope of the fourteenth-century wars. And they left a lasting legacy: on both sides of the border, the old links of blood and custom were forgotten; Strathclyde was effectively buried.

There was an England and a Scotland; enmity between them became the new passion.

The Last of the Rumellis, the Eighteen Men and Belief, 1371–1534

I N 1374, SOME 700 years after his death, St Herbert came alive
again to the Crosthwaite Parish. Bishop Appleby of Carlisle
had 'come upon' Bede's history, and wrote to Sir Thomas de
Eskhead, the Vicar of Crosthwaite, telling him the story of the two
deaths, a 'holy fact which we believe … is unknown to many, if not
all'. And 'because it does not seem good that we should not know
the doings of the Lord that he thought worthy to be revealed to the
glory of His holy saints',[1] Bishop Appleby commanded Eskhead
to go to St Herbert's Island and celebrate the special mass of St
Cuthbert, offering an indulgence of forty days to all parishioners
who made the trip. For some reason, the bishop believed St Herbert
and St Cuthbert had died on 13 April and so it was on that day in
1374 that Eskhead duly took his congregation to the island, where
he soon built a chapel upon the remains of Herbert's hermitage
– paid for, it is said, by the bishop.[2] Pilgrimage to the island soon
provided some good extra business for the parishioners too,* and
the chapel bell would ring to summon the people of Crosthwaite
Parish to services in the island chapel. 'For two hundred years, all
but three'[3] – until well after the Reformation.

Eskhead's appointment (he was vicar from 1368 to 1390) was

---

* Some late-fourteenth/early-fifteenth-century stone moulds for Christian
ornaments were found near Nichol End, on Derwentwater's west shore, the
closest harbour from which to reach the island. And there is general acceptance
of Canon Rawnsley's hypothesis that they indicate local trade with pilgrims
going to the island.

later described by Canon Rawnsley 'as the best way of restoring peace to a then distracted parish, the fruits of whose benefice had been almost exhausted by contention among rival claimants'[4] (namely previous vicars and Fountains Abbey). Word of the dispute had even reached Rome, and Thomas, who had trained as a priest in the eternal city, had been called to the Parish to help adjudicate.[5] However, this brought the case to the attention of the king and his lawyers, and henceforth the Bishop of Carlisle was prohibited from admitting any new vicar until the king's right to choose him had been considered by the courts. Upon Eskhead's death, no other vicars are recorded at Crosthwaite until after the Reformation.

One of the great treasures of the church, the octagonal font, one of the only two highly-decorated pre-Reformation fonts in what used to be called 'the four northern counties'[6] was created in his memory. Its north side displays the arms of England and France. Also present are miniature shields of the Derwentwater, Curwen and Lucy families, and – perhaps – the arms of the Bassenthwaites (the detail of the carvings on the font has been difficult to read for a long time). These armorial devices are interleaved by flowers and leaves and a green man. Four lions stand just below the font, with four indecipherable animals at its foot, and around the bowl's chamfered edge one can read the words, in Latin, 'Pray for the soul of Sir Thomas of Eskhead, formerly vicar of this parish'.* The font was given to the church before 1400 by Maud Lucy, who had become the sole Rumelli heiress upon the death of her brother around 1368.†

---

* The words were apparently interspersed with the description of the shields. Eeles, the church historian, considers this to be a unique medieval configuration, although it too is impossible to decipher now.

† For generations, Maud's Lucy arms on the font have caused perplexity as it was known that the condition of her marriage was that the Percy arms should be forever quartered with the arms of the Lucys. This was thought to imply a date for the font before the marriage settlement of 1384, despite Sir Thomas de Eskhead, for whom we are bidden to pray, living at least until 1390. However, in fact (see Bouche's note *Prelates and People*, p. 118.) Maud's provision came into effect after her death, when Henry's son, 'Hotspur', carried out the agreement by quartering his arms with hers in acknowledgment of his extra inheritance. So, the font can now be clearly dated to between 1390 and 1398.

Over time, litigation, childlessness or the lack of a male heir had brought almost all of Alice and William's old Cumbrian lands (split three ways upon Alice's death) back together again. This history had long lent an element of Grecian tragedy to individual de Rumelli fortunes, but with Maud's marriage to Henry Percy, the first Earl of Northumberland, in 1384, those shadows grew darker.

She had first married the Earl of Angus – a good Scottish match after such things had stopped being fashionable. Her union with the Earl of Northumberland, the greatest landowner of the Northeast, made them substantially the most powerful family of the north. Maud bore no children with Percy, but she had produced a daughter, Elizabeth, by the Earl of Angus. Before Maud's second marriage to Percy, Elizabeth had herself been given to Henry Percy in marriage. The chronicler of the Percy family, having suggested – wisely and devoutly, if surprisingly – that upon her death, 'Elizabeth departed a Vergin to God's mercy',[7] then continues his story:

> Then afterwards Margret, the Lord Nevills daughter his
> Second wife married hee
> By whom hee had three sones whose names be ...
> Margarte dyed and after her fourtuned the case
> Hee married Maude Countess of Anguest his therd wife
> Which mother was to Elizabth his first wife
> And by the said Maud forthwithall
> The Lord Lucy Lands by her guift came to him all.

And then the scribe got to his real point, that Percy now had double insurance to the title of his new lands, from both Elizabeth and Maud, 'of which noe lawe may his heires defeate'. The strength of the dynastic alliance seems to have been the only consideration, and indeed, on Maud's death, the Rumellis' extensive lands in Cumberland, including their land in the Parish, passed to the Percys. However, this was a clear choice on Maud's part. She *could* have left these territories to distant blood relations. But she chose to consider the de Rumelli line extinct, like the

A pastoral view of the Vale of St John's.

House of Dunkeld in Scotland, and transferred the majority of the Boy of Egremont's lands – all that she had – to her husband and his sons by Margaret Neville, daughter of another powerful northern family.

Alice II had given Crosthwaite valley to the monks 'for the health of her soul and the souls of all her ancestors and successors'. Perhaps, Maud – her great-great-grand-daughter – thought that if she produced no heirs the honour of her family would be heightened by the power and fertility of the Percys. But they would make tough landlords in the Parish. The Northumberland family were notorious for relying on violence to achieve their ends. When the fifth Earl of Northumberland died in 1527, he was the first head of his family to die quietly in bed for 150 years.

Whatever Maud's reasoning, the Parish had finally lost the human link to its Scottish origins. This was not just the last time the legacy of the Boy of Egremont can be seen with any clarity in the Parish, but the last time a direct descendant of the builder of the church had care over it; and so the last time Crosthwaite was of primary importance to its overlord.

Governance and the school

After Maud's death in 1398, the coherence of the Parish continued to unravel. The Braithwaite court stopped overseeing Borrowdale (which admittedly paid its tithes to Furness), but now included Buttermere, which lay outside the Parish, within its ambit. However, the courts had evolved. Gradually, manor or baron courts, held 'for lord and neighbourhood', with a primary function of protecting the customs of the manor and resolving disputes involving 40 shillings or less, had been introduced to back up the leet courts. The Braithwaite and Keswick manor courts met every three to four weeks, and their existence, over time, was to change the balance of power in the Parish. For, unlike the leet, or head court, the twelve-man jury was entirely made up of customary tenants.

Numerous orders and by-laws came into being during this period, whether personal – relating, say, to the settling of the unpaid debts of neighbours – or manorial, for instance prohibiting fishing in the close season or the keeping of '20 foreign sheep in the Common'.[8] The tenants' first and essential duty remained maintaining stock-proof barriers around the head dyke but soon the new courts would attempt to ensure that houses didn't fall into disrepair too. At the same time, the by-law forbidding the illegal split of tenements, 'taverning', extended to include prosecution for keeping under-tenants or lodgers, indicated the jurors' legal attitude to the poor. However, the manor courts, knowing their place, duly passed their by-laws up to the head court for confirmation or amendment; and if they found people guilty of misconduct, those recommendations were sent on to the head court too.[9]

Both controlling and controlled by the community, the courts relied on the promotion of 'good neighbourhood' and 'ancient custom' as the underlying principles for settling disputes. The strength of the pull of 'ancient custom' was particularly prominent after Maud's death as the beginning of a resurgence of population levels inevitably affected the balance between society and its resources. By then, the church organisation of the Parish had also become deeply intermingled with both the aims and outcomes of manorial oversight. All the parishioners who attended church constituted its 'vestry', and 'vestry governance' became, over time, responsible for choosing parish officers. But in the Parish there was a 'select vestry', chosen from the customary tenants, who represented all the major areas of the Parish and originally met in the vestry of the church, giving a double meaning to the emerging term.

Their meetings helped ensure the courts' decision-making was informed by ancient practice, and frequently acquainted them with the precise circumstances surrounding particular misdemeanours. Select vestry governance, pacifying and preventative as much as accusatory, and rare in much of England, makes absolute sense when you consider the unusual size of the Parish, its small population, and the distance of so much of the commons from the nearest legal authority. Called the 'Eighteen Men'[10,11] in the Parish, the select vestry was appointed annually at St Kentigern's; they were sworn in at a service at the church[*] and chose their own successors, although it wasn't until the time of Elizabeth I that their obligations were spelt out.

Select vestries were common only in London, Bristol and the North, where their origins were probably connected to land tenure, primarily the use of the commons. In Cumbria they were usually found in two types of parish: large rural parishes, like Crosthwaite, which needed a knowledgeable centralising focus; and, later, those parishes that took over from abbeys dissolved after the Reformation, which badly needed to hold on to some of the abbey's administrative structure. Under a third of Cumbrian parishes had select vestries, most of them of sixteen men, with a particular weighting of twenty-fours in Lancashire North of the Sands.[†] Only Grasmere and Crosthwaite sported eighteen men.

---

[*] Using an oath that may, or may not, have changed when it was amended by court decree in 1571 (see page 100).
[†] The Webbs (see page 474) concluded that vestry governance may have existed in some parishes ever since legal memory began, and today it is considered that the majority of select vestries were formed around the late sixteenth century. Tate, *The Parish Chest*, p. 19.

Whether or not its members numbered eighteen at the outset, the
select vestry was alive in Crosthwaite Parish by the end of the
fourteenth century, which was unusually early, and their rule was
to become the defining distinction of the Parish.

Since the Parish vestry, like the jurors of the Parish manor
courts whom they advised, was made up entirely of customary tenants, the class both held remarkable power and enjoyed
extraordinary freedom for the time. However, in due course,
both juries and the select vestry became restricted in practice
to the more substantial tenants, from whom the officers of the
court were also drawn. So, all was not quite as democratic as the
class correlation of the juries and the Eighteen Men might imply
and, in time, legislation inevitably shored up the bias against
the landless, lest they became a burden on the community. In
this, the rule of Eighteen Men was broadly mirrored by some
other Cumbrian parishes, where 'substantial yeomen, resident in
a specific locality for perhaps several generations, could form an
effective ruling elite through the parish vestry of the Anglican
church, active and influential both in local politics and the
church itself'.[12]

In the country as a whole, the scarcity of labour after the Black
Death had led to a rapid decline in the number of serfs and the
widespread growth of 'copyhold' tenancies. This new type of
tenancy had several variations and often many of the same obligations and advantages of customary tenants, including inheritance
for some, but its name referred to its legal difference. The copy-
holder technically 'surrendered' his copy of the manorial court
roll registering his tenancy (the only document that recorded
his copyhold agreement) every time the tenancy changed, while
the customary tenant held his own deed, underlining his right
to bequeath the land.[13] However, as late as 1625 the King's Bench,
in the most important ruling in the history of customary tenancy,
described their tenancies as held 'at the will of the lord' when
legally confirming their hereditary rights.[14]

*

The outstanding pre-Reformation achievement of Crosthwaite's Eighteen Men was their stewardship of the Rumellis' final legacy, the Parish school, which for the Parish would prove to be a pearl without price. The North has always rated education, the first school in Cumberland starting as early as 1188 in Carlisle.[15] However, it had fallen away before the end of the fourteenth century and was only replaced, with a small grammar school, in the 1540s.* Penrith and Cockermouth both had chantry schoolmasters by 1395, the Cockermouth chantry started by Henry Percy, Maud's husband. But since chantries would be proscribed by Edward VI, these schools didn't last either, although Penrith soon acquired a replacement when Queen Elizabeth I, using the crown's chantry income, founded a grammar school in 1564, with the majestic endowment of £6 a year.[16] The school at St Bees started in 1583. A sprinkling of other schools would appear before the end of the eighteenth century, but the vast majority of Cumberland schools began life only in the nineteenth.

Crosthwaite's school is the only one in Cumberland† known to have had an uninterrupted existence from pre-Reformation times to the late nineteenth century. This unique achievement was made possible by a large endowment, its exact date unknown, and the efforts of the Eighteen Men. The school could not have existed without the latter, as they were the only body allowed to spend charitable donations on matters other than church maintenance. By carefully nurturing the endowment (which in time attracted more charity from the parishioners), maintaining the school, appointing the schoolmaster and overseeing his work during the pre-Reformation period without official Parish vicars, the Eighteen Men established their absolute authority over Crosthwaite School. Their success was such that when the courts first came to look at the school, in 1571 – even though the court case was to change old Parish practices – it was ruled unquestioningly that the vicar had no authority to interfere with the school

---

* Part of Henry VIII's establishment of the cathedral.
† At least, the only one that can be traced. I have found no other recorded example where the vicar, and soon the whole church hierarchy, were legally banned from interference.

in any way. And their absolute control over the Parish school appears to be unique.

Nestling on the edge of St Kentigern's 'acre', the school was surrounded on three sides by thick oak forest of a density hard to imagine today, the tall oaks covering 'all the shores and islands of this beautiful lake'.[17] They flowed down the incline from the school to carpet the shores of Derwentwater for the next 300 years: '...the wood was so even at the top, each tree being about eighteen yards high and very thick, that it looked like a field; and so interwoven that boys could have gone from tree to tree like squirrels.' But it was on a yew tree by the school, one of the 'finest and oldest yew trees in the country' (Robert Southey's description), that an actual memory of the schoolchildren's arboreal attractions was captured in the late eighteenth century by Sir George Beaumont:* 'all the boys, some forty in number, perched at one time upon its boughs'.[18] Like starlings.

The first extant documentary reference to the school's endowment appeared in the 1571 court case, when the commissioners judging it were worried about whether there was enough money to pay for a first-class teacher. In 1636, it was spelt out on oath that 'there has been a Grammar School within the Parish at Crosthwaite … time whereof the memory of Man knoweth not the contrary'.[19] In neither case was there any speculation about the original endowment that had allowed the school to come into existence. Had the money come from the Derwentwaters or the monks *they* would have remembered and, probably, been remembered. Maud's family had been by far the richest ever connected with the Parish, and Maud had an exceptionally talented and highly educated vicar in Sir Thomas de Eskhead to undertake the task of launching a school. But by the second half of the sixteenth century, she was quite forgotten.

When a sense of history, rather than just remembering, became more common in the Parish, local nineteenth- and twentieth-century historians and lawyers would consider Sir Thomas to be the

---

* Artist, friend and patron of the Lake Poets and one of the founders of the National Gallery.

school's 'onlie begetter'; this was partly because of his eminence but largely because of the lack of any other registered vicars between his death and the Reformation. Indeed, the prospectus for today's extremely successful Keswick School states that 'Its origins date back over 650 years to the mid fourteenth century when it was thought to have been founded by the vicar of Crosthwaite church, Sir Thomas de Eskhead.' Well, yes (although I would have thought the date may be two or so decades early) but, again, no one has thought about the endowment that allowed him to do this.* And the benefactress can *only* have been Maud.

Just as her forebears had chosen to build St Kentigern's in Crosthwaite to affirm their presence when so much had been lost, might not Maud, when she finally relinquished the old Rumelli power and oversight, also have sowed a seed that could grow from generation unto generation? If her husband was founding a chantry in Cockermouth, would Maud not have wished to leave her own mark on Crosthwaite? The last gift of the Lucys to their ancient lands and church. And just as Alice built a church for the people, rather than a more conventional priory or monastery, with their built-in years of prayer for their founder, is it not plausible that Maud too would have preferred to leave a memorial with no obvious personal advantages that could potentially obscure the successful functioning of her school?

The early endowment that brought Crosthwaite school into being, apart from a local tax raised after 1571, is the only money known to have been gifted to the school before 1687. Indeed, the endowment would help keep it afloat until well into the second half of the nineteenth century, when the government took over the school's governance and the funding. While we may not be able to *prove* that Maud was the original benefactress, it is certain that the people of this cut-off, sparsely populated Parish, in the midst of the fells, founded the school and managed it right through to the late nineteenth century. It was a triumph for its people and for its vestry governance.

---

* It has never been suggested that Sir Thomas could have endowed the school himself.

Fifteenth-century life on the land

The fourteenth and fifteenth centuries are likely to have seen the leasing of some Derwentwater demesne land,[20] and the mid-fifteenth century was an encouraging time for the hill farmer. Land was easily available after the traumatic fourteenth century and the farmers introduced an important new way of extending their land. All over the Parish, customary tenants began to enclose common land adjacent to their holdings within the head dyke, creating 'intakes' – the name still used today – often to the very edge of improvable land. This process continued for some 200 years, as the consequent extra manure from stock grazing within an enclosed area of land soon provided far better results than the rest of the manorial waste land.* The irregular shapes of the intakes, usually enclosed by stone walls, and offering a sharp contrast with the ruler-straight enclosures of the nineteenth century, are another ancient feature of the Parish that survives to the present day.

The move from medieval hunting forest to a landscape of hill farmers was virtually complete. Around Wythburn, still referred to as the Forest of Wythburn as late as 1675, 'dale male' (valley money) and 'forest silver' may still have been paid as a fee for six months' summer pasturing, in a process called 'agistment': where the landlord had defined a certain area of land as available for pasture, frequently for lowland flocks from some distance away.[21] However, in the colonised land within the Parish the old distinction between 'forest' and 'manorial waste' was finally on the way out, as it was across the Lake District and the traditional pasture 'without number' of manorial waste became the norm. However, fears of overstocking prompted the introduction in the mid-century of a new law of 'levancy and couchancy' in the Lake District and the North Pennines, which ruled that the tenants could only graze the number of animals in the summer that they could keep through the winter. All was becoming more ordered.

The demise of the wolf meant sheep were becoming much more

---

* In Braithwaite things went further, when nine tenants enclosed Braithwaite How and held it as a shared pasture. Winchester, *Landscape and Society*, p. 52.

important for the tenant farmer. Specialist herders developed into general herdsmen (usually young men and women) who tended the stock of the whole community.[22] Romantic paintings leap to mind. One of the shepherd's tasks was to preserve the unmarked boundaries of the village's grazing rights by turning away straying stock, a task that was carried out with care and calm: the sheep were 'luffyngly and easfully rechased and dryven agayn'.[23] Increased demand at the beginning of the fifteenth century led to the building of more fulling mills. However, after mid-century, southeastern Cumbria became the dominant local centre of the woollen industry. By the sixteenth century it would be supplying the whole of England with its coarse Kendal green cloth, which even gets a Shakespearean mention: in *Henry IV, Part 1*, Falstaff, with typical bravado, claims to the future Henry V that he had been attacked by 'three misbegotten knaves in Kendal green' although 'it was so dark, Hal, that thou couldst not see thy hand'.

The fell areas of the Parish were noticeably more extensive than we are used to today. But even then some animals were excluded, or restricted, from the fells; scabbed horses, for instance, had to be kept on the owner's private ground until a jury of four deemed them cured.[24] Pigs, of which only one or two were now kept by each farm – for family consumption – were nose-ringed to stop them grubbing up the soil. In places they were 'yoked or bowed', i.e. fitted with a triangular wooden collar with projecting ends to make sure they couldn't wriggle through a fenced head dyke. And war was declared on goats,* their sins a voracious appetite and the damage they did to trees: for it was at this time that a sense of the need to preserve woodland began to emerge.

Even though the number of pigs was now prescribed, other livestock – cattle and sheep as well as goats – caused damage to trees and trampled their young shoots. The levels of such damage kept pace with the growth of human population. But land that had been stripped of trees by cattle provided excellent sheep grazing, and,

---

* There were so many court summonses in the Derwentfells around the turn of the century that it seems goats were outlawed, while in Borrowdale the idea became to restrict their number severely: a tenant allowed two goats for every 12s. of annual rent. Winchester, *Harvest of the Hills*, p. 104.

slowly but surely, tracts of woodland were transformed into moor and fellside.[25] Not only are sheep close croppers of grass, they extract the minerals from the soil, transferring it to their wool.[26] Both of these processes inevitably cause land erosion, as the leaching of minerals from the soil is not compensated for by the small volume of manure they produce compared to other farm animals. So, for the first time, references to the enclosing of coppice woodland to protect it from animals start to appear. In 1454, two fellside enclosures were created by the Percy agent on the western side of Derwentwater to protect the wood for use in the Newlands valley,* where there was some lead and silver mining mid-century.[27]

The basic woodland rules in most manors were that 'underwoods' (hazels, willows and alders) were available to the tenants, but that 'woods of warrant' (ash, oak, holly, crab apple and birch) were the property of the lord, their use subject to the tenants' need to repair their tenements, heat themselves and feed their animals in winter. They provided for the latter by 'croppynge', lopping off young branches (particularly ash) for winter fodder; the manor of Derwentfells had been taking croppynge fees for 'topped' and 'cropped' ash trees since the late thirteenth century.[28] And, as Wordsworth would later record, little was wasted: ash trees were planted in rows along the field borders and their branches 'strewn upon the pastures; and when the cattle have stripped them of leaves, they are used for repairing the hedges or for fuel'.[29] Holly was good too. In the 'forest areas', the overlord could grow trees on his tenants' land and – everywhere – only the lord could sell any timber. However, respect for woodland remained a minority concern, the continued production of charcoal, using slash-and-burn methods, exacerbating the damage being done to the area's stock of trees and forest.†

---

* One of these enclosures was called Catbelclose, which calls into question the local tradition that Catbells, the much-loved, double-peaked mountain on the western shore of Derwentwater, was renamed by tourists in the late eighteenth century in honour of the last wild cats found in England on its Newlands slopes.
† While the Percy steward ensured that the Braithwaite tanning mill closed in the same century it had been started, the farmers at nearby Thornthwaite, in Curwen land, continued as farmer/tanners until the end of the sixteenth century.

Records for the Percy lands in Allerdale below Derwent begin in the mid-fifteenth century and provide a glimpse of how the fisheries had been developed. By 1483 we read that the fishery of the Derwent was let to Sir Thomas Curwen,[30] who became responsible for the oversight 'of all and singular traps in the said river of Salmon ... for taking them at the forbidden time and ... at any season for those obstructing it with net, kidels, or other contrivances or engines'.[31] The right to fish the good rivers was now strictly regulated. But the rules attached to them – rather like today's riparian fishing tickets – brought real benefits for owners of land on the banks of rivers. The value of the Braithwaite length of the riverbank was assessed as about one twenty-eighth of the whole. However, the relative democracy of 150 years earlier had vanished, partly because the river had been overfished[32] and, later, because the landowners who took over from the monks saw things differently.

The number of cottagers at Braithwaite had fallen sharply; several cottages already lay decaying and untenanted in 1437 and, a hundred years later, just three remained.[33] What help there was for the poor came primarily from the abbeys, the townships (organised through the church) and from the lords of the manor, but little improved for the landless remaining in the Parish. However, the number of legal complaints relating to the rights of cottagers suggests that many of them managed to own farm animals and to graze them, whatever the regulations said.[34] And the Newlands copper mines would also have offered a potential source of extra work. As for Keswick, the town survived the late-medieval decline after the plague. At Greystoke, only a single burgage appears to have remained.*

Parish beliefs

While the select vestry at the church was the lynchpin of governance and education in the late medieval Parish, the church itself was the essential binding agent. Pivotal as the central meeting place (along

---

* The other four surviving Cumberland market borough towns by 1500 were Carlisle, Kirkoswald, Cockermouth and Egremont.

with market day), it was also an actor in the great moments of people's lives. Common festivities, common worship – and common
laughter and gossip – held the far-flung community together. And
by the fifteenth century it is more likely than not that the church
was aided by all five of its outlying chapels.

Originally, the chapels would have been licensed to the community through the bishops of Carlisle for the sum of around £4
raised from the local people, either through a rate on their land
or a charge for their church seats – a practice well established
by the mid-1400s. Only Thornthwaite, where the Curwens had
built a chapel within the Parish soon after they had cleared the
land granted them by Alice, has a safely documented early date
of around 1240,[35] no doubt because the overlord was civil. Canon
Rawnsley believed that the other chapels were probably founded
in the fourteenth century,[36] despite there being no official records
until the sixteenth. And, since the sixteenth century was a time
of great religious upheaval, it does seem more likely that the existence of the chapels was only then being registered, rather than
that there were new ones being built. John de Derwentwater had
been granted a licence to build a chapel c.1366[37] but there is no
evidence that it was carried through,[*] and the other chapels lie in
the Thirlmere valley, at Wythburn, in Borrowdale, at Rosthwaite,
and in the Newlands valley, at Littletown. Between them, the
Crosthwaite chapels of ease make up more than a third of all those
with 'ancient stipends' in the old, and large, Carlisle diocese.[38]

Wordsworth had a particular affection for the chapels and loved
their architecture. 'The religio loci is nowhere violated by these
unstinted, yet unpretending, works of human hand. They exhibit
generally a well-proportioned oblong, with a suitable porch, in some
instances a steeple tower, and in others nothing more than a small
belfry, in which one or two bells hang visibly.' His words remain an
almost perfect description of the belfryed chapel at Wythburn as
it is today. Even though it is substantially a 1740 rebuild, it is even
more unpretentious than the other chapels, since it has no porch at

---

[*] It stands at the foot of High Rigg, between the Vale of Wanthwaite and the
Vale of St John.

all.* It was a particular favourite of Coleridge's son, Hartley, who praised its simplicity:[39]

> Humble it is and meek and very low,
> And speaks its purpose by a single bell;
> But God Himself, and He alone, can know
> If spiry temples please Him half so well.

Since the chapels were the only communal meeting places for parishioners closer than the market town and the Parish church, they became the heart of their districts and townships. But only St Kentigern's had a licence to bury (and sometimes to marry) and all the chapels' parishioners continued to pay their tithes to the vicar of Crosthwaite.

The practices of Celtic Christianity had long been abandoned by St Kentigern's church, but old pagan beliefs – Celtic, Anglo-Saxon and, particularly, Norse Irish – co-existed with Christian ones in the customs of the Parish. The oldest pagan practice we know of was Beltane,[40] shared by all the old Celtic parts of Britain. In a ritual that was redolent of ancient defences against predators and the dangers of the dark, every May Day cattle were run through fires ('needfire' in Cumberland) to cure them of disease before they left for the new grass.†

The 'needfire', which was moved on from one community to another, was heaped up with damp turf and fuel to create 'plenty of reek'[41] to fumigate all the cattle. Chaos frequently ensued, as was witnessed by a full-blown ceremony in Westmorland as late as 1840.[42] The fires were built of rowan wood, uniquely effective as cure and charm, perhaps because of the trees' bright red, fire-like berries. And rowan was used, too, to stir the cream, to prevent the bewitchment of the churn and make the butter come good;[43] it was placed on doorways to ward off evil, and provided the necessary wood to make a plough run true. Rowan, holly and

* A chancel was added to the chapel at Wythburn in 1872.
† A deputation went from house to house to check every other fire had been extinguished.

yew were planted next to farmhouses to ward off evil spirits – a proximity that can still be seen today.

The term long used for the sick animals in the Parish was 'elf-shot', from the Anglo-Saxon belief that a sudden, supernatural malady was caused by elves shooting the sufferer full of arrows,[44] but most of Crosthwaite's spirits and fairies were of Norse origin and were frequently malevolent. 'Hob Thross',* 'a bodie a'owre rough',[45] acted like an irate poltergeist unless you left a bowl of porridge or buttermilk out on the hearth, in which case your household chores would be finished in recompense. The barguest acted as a Lake Counties banshee, and boggards or boggles (Norse *boig*)† abounded.[46] Pigeon feathers were believed to stop the coming of death. When a person died, a messenger was sent to 'tell the bees', and the hives were often decorated with black ribbon, a practice common to Cumbria, East Anglia, Ireland and Scandinavia.[47] A 'waiting' or 'waking' party kept a vigil by the corpse through to the day of the funeral to keep away any evil spirit wanting to enter the body. Sometimes a plate of salt was placed on its breast for extra protection, while a table of refreshments, usually alcoholic, lightened the mood.[48]

The 'gheist', a spirit distinct from the body, which often appeared to a person who was soon to die – in which context it was called a 'fetch'[49] by the seventeenth century – was universally respected in Cumbria.‡ These spirits had a Christian connection; they were in some ways tangible, if ethereal, souls. The 'gheist' door of a house was on its north side and was to be opened when someone died, to let their spirit depart.[50] At St Kentigern's a small door was built in the north wall,§ probably to let the devil out at baptism.[51]

Behind everything lay the devil, the terrifying subject of many a medieval sermon and a stark reality to the people. The church ratified instances of possession but provided the remedy of formal

* Jack i' the Hob outside Cumbria.
† Another theory banishes the Norse origins of 'boggle' and attributes it to 'bugge' (bogey), fourteenth-century Middle English.
‡ In the Parish, it was claimed that by looking at yew trees you could see the moment the spirit passed from the body.
§ This door was rediscovered by Scott in 1845, its original date unknown.

exorcism, then still a part of baptism. Sprinkled holy water and the sign of the cross were seen as ubiquitously effective, proof of the church's powers to cast the devil out. On the continent, witches had come to be considered devil worshippers, who had made a pact with the devil, and, as such, were rigorously hunted. However, the English Catholic Church appears to have remained immune to the idea and throughout the country apparently only insignificant punishments were handed down for witchcraft before the Reformation. Before the English church seriously tried to spell out the difference between a spell and a prayer, everyone knew the church's magic was best. There were liturgical rituals for all occasions: blessing houses, crops, cattle, marriage beds or the sick, dealing with sterile cattle or driving away thunder. And the quarterly service of excommunicating all thieves, murderers and enemies of the church was seen as vital protection for the Parish.[52]

When a person died, the number of times the church bells tolled indicated the sex and age of the deceased. The corpse was carried to the church (either on a sledge or strapped to the back of a pack-horse)[53] along strictly demarcated corpse roads, complete with 'resting stones' for the coffin along the way. For long journeys the funeral bread was distributed to the bearers before the procession started,* but usually the burial was followed by the 'arval', a feast to honour the spirit of the dead not to refresh the mourners, usually consisting of ale and 'havers', a type of oat bread. In the doorway of the house a bowl of sprigs of evergreen box was placed on a table covered by a clean white cloth, and each mourner took one in remembrance and as witness to the belief that the corpse's spirit lived on.[54]

Drink was built into the social life of the valley, playing a part in nearly every public and private ceremony. At birth, the child's head was washed with alcohol, the custom of 'weshin't bairn's head', which allowed the father to make merry with his friends – and by the end of the seventeenth century the drink of choice on such occasions was rum. Some believe that rum butter became the first thing to pass the baby's lips, a ceremonial welcome to the

* One and a quarter for each man, a quarter to be eaten at each stop.

new spirit.[55] If so, a taste for the hard drinking that took place at 'merry neets', shepherds' meets and, later, hunting parties, was clearly inculcated early.

At weddings, the instinctive urge of the isolated parishioners to break free from the shackles of a hard-working life and have a good do was given full licence. Usually, the whole local community was bidden to attend, or 'lated', the bridegroom's party riding around the villages for several miles around, inviting all.[56] Afterwards, the congregation raced on horse or foot back to the house, where the victor received a ribbon from the bride. A white cloth was placed on the bride's head, and the bridegroom broke the wedding cake, a thin currant slab, over her head before passing the pieces around. Mounds of food and drink were worked off with wrestling, leaping contests and foot races for both sexes, and as the day drew to a close the bride sat in state with a large plate on her knee, on which the guests piled their gifts – often, usefully, money. Finally, the couple retired to bed and an earthy bedding ceremony involving the catching of the bride's discarded stocking – no decorous bouquets here – provided a clue as to whose marriage would be announced next.[57]

The hill farmer traditionally killed his fattest sheep for Christmas, and its mince was 'made rich with fruit and boiled in the ventricle of the animal',[58] launching the celebrations at breakfast, while the season continued with feasting and dancing till after the Twelfth Day, for all, including the servants. The medieval church understood the patterns of time in the lives of agricultural workers: seasons of unrelenting work followed by festive pauses before the next period of labour. By ensuring that the moments of change coincided with a saint's day – Martinmas, Michaelmas, Lady Day, and so on – and a holiday, the church skilfully underlined its intimate connection with the crucial moments in people's lives. Like almost every annual fair in England, Keswick's greatest market fair, held on 22 July, was in honour of a saint – Mary Magdalene.

A wide range of customs were associated with the great festivals of the church. On Collop Monday – the Monday before the start of Lent – the remaining 'collops' of dried and salted meat were eaten, and Shrove Tuesday followed hard on its heels. On Carling

Sunday – the fifth Sunday of Lent – softened peas fried in butter was the expected fare. On Good Friday it was considered 'almost profane'[59] not to eat Fig Sue, a bread posset, made not with the usual curdled milk – Good Friday being a fast day – but with ale, figs, treacle and nutmeg. (The use of figs was prescribed because fig wood was believed to be the wood used for the Cross.) Pace eggs enlivened Easter all over the Lake District as eggs were decorated with flowers and dyes from scraps of material, then sealed with onion skins and boiled extremely hard. Traditionally they were displayed, used as conkers or raced down a hill, as happened at Latrigg on Easter Monday.

Overall, the parishioners saw the church as their protector, its rites and festivals interwoven with their way of life. They knew from the mass that the priest could change the character of material objects and that it worked 'like a charm upon an adder'.[60] But, since no one could alleviate illness effectively then, many a cure accessed help from all quarters; the beloved Latin of the services as well known and rationally incomprehensible for most of the people as the incantations of any hocus-pocus. And the church authorities did not much object to their doing so.

But it was not to be long before the parishioners' instinctive sense of divine protection, a crucial counterbalance to the toughness of their working lives, was to come under assault.

A New Church and the Reformation

T HE ORDERLY PROGRESS of the fifteenth century had been somewhat undone since the outbreak of the Wars of the Roses in 1455. But after the Battle of Bosworth in 1485, Henry VII, the first Tudor king, brought an end to the divisions, despite the odd 'pretender' receiving Scottish support during his reign. However, in 1513, four years after the accession of his seventeen-year-old son as Henry VIII, Anglo-Scottish relations took a more serious turn. While Henry VIII was campaigning in northern France, James IV of Scotland invaded Northumberland and border service was called upon by the lords of the manor. At the bloody Battle of Flodden, the English annihilated the Scots army; James IV, much of his nobility and some ten thousand men were killed.

The commander of the English cavalry was the exceptional soldier Thomas Dacre, and his friend Sir John Radcliffe, long-time Sheriff of Cumberland and the head of the Derwentwaters, led out the men of Keswick, along with his other tenants, to battle.* Later details of the force of the Derwentwater Parish tenants record '90 able men, 20 furnished with steelcoats or jacks [padded tunics for light armour] and caps, bows and arrows or bills – 40 with only a bill or lance or staff, the rest with nothing'.[1] Thirty men without a weapon of any sort: an evocative illustration both of the continuing toughness, danger and poverty of life for many of the Parish and the necessity to respond to the call of border service.

---

* There is no contemporary source for this, but it has always been considered true, which – given Sir John's close relationship with Dacre, whom he made his executor and the guardian of his heir – I accept.

The Derwentwater name had changed to Radcliffe three generations earlier, when the sole heiress, Elizabeth, married Sir Nicholas Radcliffe,* 'thus elevating him to the higher ranks of the landed gentry'.[2] Radcliffe had been knighted at Agincourt, and – despite being a younger son – 'because of his wife's rich inheritance and impressive social contacts [he] soon came to occupy an important place in the north-west'.[3] He was probably buried at the eastern end of the south aisle of St Kentigern's, which he had endowed as a chantry dedicated to Mary Magdalene.[4]

Around 1460 their son, Thomas, moved the family to an island close to the eastern shore of Derwentwater, which became known as 'Lord's Island', while the family's usual title was expanded to include 'of the Isle'. Thomas's younger son, Edward, would marry Anne Cartington, a Northumberland heiress, and start a new family line; Edward's son in due course to inherit Dilston from his grandmother there. Sir Thomas's overcomplicated will (apparently seeking to disinherit his eldest son) did considerable damage to the Derwentwater holdings for much of the next hundred years, long after Thomas and his wife, Margaret Parr – from Kendal and the aunt of Henry VIII's final queen – were buried in the Norman church of Great Crosthwaite in 1495. Their effigies, 'of the best English alabaster', lie on an altar tomb in the church's Radcliffe chapel.

It was their grandson Sir John Radcliffe, the local hero of Flodden,[5] who became the major benefactor, and almost certainly the instigator, of a great rebuilding of St Kentigern's. Donations are regularly recorded by his wife, Dame Alice,[6] and a date of 1523 emerges in a document from the Braithwaite court, in which the bailiff, Edmund Stanger, duns three men from Watendlath for the 12d. ox tax required 'for the building of the church at Crosthuate', a major tax for all the parishioners.[7] Just four years after his call to rebuild, in 1529,[†] Sir John joined his ancestors in the church, lying in a monumental tomb of Kendal limestone topped by a sepulchral brass, one of few in Cumberland dating from that period.

---

* From another family whose forebears were pre-Norman.
† It seems the date on the brass, 1527, is incorrect. See Thompson, 'The Derwentwaters and Radcliffes', pp. 288–324.

His will ordained that 'a priest should yearly say mass, and sing daily for his soul and the soul of his wife before the altar of Our Lady of Pity, in the church of Crosthwaite, until lands should be given or purchased for the finding of a priest to serve the said chapel of Our Lady for ever'.[8] Dame Alice would bequeath £140 to endow the salary of the chantry priest, to pray for her husband's soul and 'all Christien soules... in the chapel of Keswyke' on week-days and 'in the parish church of Crostwayte' on Sundays and holy days. In 1535 a major valuation of church property captures Sir John Clerke in the job; living in a cell at Monk Hall, his post was endowed by the rents from eight tenements close to the church in 'Brathmyre'.[9]And, as late as the nineteenth century, the south chapel of St Kentigerns, was still referred to as the Derwentwater or Lord's Chapel – or the Magdalene chantry.

In this immense rebuilding, St Kentigern's assumed the basic shape that we know today. Built, as Robert Southey said, in an age when durability was key, the 47-yard-long church 'is a large, unor-namented, substantial edifice, with buttresses, battlements, and a square tower; and having stood for centuries, by God's blessing it may stand for centuries to come ... Though the vale of Keswick owes little of its beauty to any work of man, the position of its Church is singularly fortunate. It stands alone, about half a mile from the town, and somewhat farther from the foot of Skiddaw ... there are ... none perhaps in any part of the kingdom which forms a finer object from the surrounding country.'[10]

In accordance with the fashion all over the northwest of England at the time, the new church was built with a clerestory, two new aisles down the length of the nave supporting the requisite high-level windows, the vast majority of which are unchanged today. The overwhelming first impression upon entering the church is of an uplifting sense of light and space. And history.

The north aisle lay well within the old nave, while the wider south aisle used the old south wall* and the Norman chancel arch was removed. The roof was leaded – it would last, leaking, until

---

* The chapel at the east end narrowed.

1812 – and the floor was beaten earth.* A large, heavy oak bar – still used today – slides into sockets in the walls on either side of the principal doorway, a formidable obstacle to forcible entry, and probably in use since the sixteenth century.[11] The outside of the church was copiously limewashed. The 56-foot tower, the first to adorn St Kentigern's, was built north of the centre of the west end of the church, with deep walls. For Southey, it looked 'Upward fixedly, / Like stedfast hope beneath some careless wrong' and it opens to the nave through a high pointed arch, whose apex is the height of the tie beams of the roof, revealing the huge Tudor western window behind it. The belfry carried four bells. And it was probably Sir John Radcliffe's widow, Dame Alice, who graced her husband's 'chantry' by placing the Radcliffe arms and a lovely depiction of a woman in fifteenth-century dress, representing Mary Magdalene, in the stained-glass window nearby.

After her husband's death, Dame Alice moved to live with her brother, a canon at Salisbury, but she hung determinedly on to the lands her husband had left her during her lifetime, while her husband's nephew and appointed heir upon her death, another John (the son of Sir John's sister Anne) and the Dilston Radcliffes (in the shape of Edward's son Cuthbert) continued the fight initiated by Sir Thomas's will. The eventual 1540 agreement between them gave John just a portion of the old Derwentwater lands, the bulk of their land around Thirlmere, and Tallentire.[12]

Alice took her duties to the people of the old Derwentwater lands seriously. She left 'to the poore people in the Northe within my lordship ... twelve months mynde ... in sherts and smocks of canvas' (to the value of £10),[13] and forgave all her tenants half a year's rent. She also added 40s. to the church works at Crosthwaite, and the same sum to the chapels at St John's in the Vale and Wythburn, along with £10 to each chapel and £10 to their poorer parishioners to be paid by her nephew out of a debt to her which

---

* The aisle pillars are octagonal and plain but 'the height of the bases and pillars is strangely irregular and suggest that the builders did not wish to disturb an uneven floor', which covered a miscellany of the dead, the unearthed leaden coin of Stephen's reign indicating that the space had been used for burial since the church's inception. Eeles, *The Parish Church*, p. 4.

she otherwise cancelled. That she left just 20s. to the works of Salisbury Cathedral,[14] where she is buried in one of England's great tombs, underscores her place in the long line of wealthy individuals who, having left the Parish, still cared enough about it for the rest of their lives to want to continue to help it.

'The Northern tragedy'

The Reformation, often described as 'the Northern tragedy', severed beliefs of the Crosthwaite parishioners, which despite the periods of war, famine and plague, had been gradually evolving in an unbroken line. And once Henry VIII's desires and Thomas Cromwell's genius unleashed it, the Parish became intimately, and painfully, involved.

As the first king in Europe to repudiate papal jurisdiction, Henry VIII's new position was endorsed by Parliament in the 1534 Act of Supremacy, making 'the King, our Sovereign Lord, his heirs and successors ... the only Supreme Head of the Church of England on earth', and the income from clerical benefices that had previously gone to Rome was swiftly transferred to the Crown.* In 1535, Cromwell organised the *Valor Ecclesiasticus*, a survey of church finances in England and Wales, and ordered a visitation of the monasteries. The Cistercians were at a low ebb spiritually, their founders' edicts long lost to sight. Far from living lives of quiet spirituality free from the tumult of the world, the abbots – having gained the same privileges as the great feudal overlords – spent their lives full of the same preoccupations of court and state.

There was certainly something to reform but also, as contemporaries stressed, much to keep: 'The abbeys in the North gave great alms to poor men and laudably served God ... they built bridges and highways ... and wherever they were situated in mountainous and desert places, they provided horse meat and man's meat to

---

* Through the establishment of a Court of First Fruits and Tenths. That is to say, the first year of a cleric's salary in a new post and a tenth of his income for the rest of his employment.

strangers and beggars of corn.'[15] And in the Parish their wool-marketing expertise had much improved the lives of the hill farmers.

Almost immediately after Cromwell announced the visitation, two lawyers, Drs Richard Layton and Thomas Leigh,[16] wrote asking to oversee the North, claiming, no doubt rightly, that they had 'familiar acquaintance within 10 or 12 miles of every religious house, so that no knavery can be hid from them ... friends and kinsfolk are dispersed in every place ready to assist if any stubborn or sturdy carl proves rebellious'.[17] Thomas Leigh, locally considered to have been one of the Leighs of Isel Hall just northwest of the Parish,* was actually a cousin of the family, and it was Layton, born at Dalemain, near Ullswater, less than 10 miles from the Parish, who sent a chasing letter. 'I should advise you to set forth the King's authority as Supreme Head by all possible means. There can be no better way to beat the King's authority into the rude people of the North ... They are more superstitious than virtuous, long accustomed to frantic fantasies and ceremonies, which they regard more than God or their prince, right far alienate from true religion.'[18] For which much thanks.

The pair have always been considered the pre-eminent bullies among Cromwell's agents. They were part of the small cabal that decided to include cases of 'sodomy' and 'incontinence' (the latter usually indicating masturbation) in their enquiries.[19] Layton switched into Latin for the salacious bits of his reports and seemed to get both unusually frequent and the most remarkably detailed sexual confessions.[20] Leigh had previously been reported for his own 'incontinence' and pugnaciousness and was found to be a 'sower of discord'.[21] Nevertheless, the couple were among the most efficient of the Visitors, travelling a thousand miles through the North in the winter, a prodigious feat in the sixteenth century, inspecting 120 religious houses.[22]

The 1535 inventory of church finances revealed how badly the Carlisle diocese had suffered through war and plague.† But it also

---

* At Dalemain.
† Several livings had been lost since 1291. Yet the diocese was still home to the four lowest livings in Cumbria, each raising between £1 and £2 a year in good times and nothing in time of war.

illustrated how extremely well the Parish had been doing since the mid-fifteenth century, recording the vicar's income as £50 8s. 11d., a remarkably positive relative change. In 1291, thirty-three other Cumbrian parishes had more highly rated livings; now there were just three, of which two, Greystoke and Kendal, were considerably worse off than they had been earlier,[23] while the next-door Brigham living (the parish that included Cockermouth) had fallen from £80 to £20. The average annual income from the Crosthwaite vicar's tithes, £3 from hay, £4 from calves and £31 from wool, fleeces and lambs, underlined both the general success of farming in the Parish and the recent, now vital importance of sheep; the whole picture providing irrefutable evidence that the Parish had been far less damaged by the travails of the fourteenth century than those outside the core Lake District.[24]

The vicar was recorded as John Herynge (the first to be named on record since Sir Thomas de Eskhead), who must have been involved in the great rebuilding of St Kentigern's, since funds were still coming in for the works fourteen years after he was named in the inventory. Mysteriously, his name is omitted from the current roll of vicars in the church, which resumes with John Radcliffe in 1547, an omission without any accompanying legend, due, perhaps, to there being no record of Herynge's starting date. However, to omit the name of the earliest vicar of the Tudor church in which you stand seems curious, to say the least. Even more so given that John Herynge's tithes apparently reached the highest relative value of any recorded over the ensuing 300 years of the history of Crosthwaite Parish.[25] Nevertheless, because of the troubles, Herynge's vicarage and glebe were valued at only 4s.

Unlike his father, Henry VIII had never bothered to venture to the North, the area being much neglected; the Archbishops of York had not even been *in situ* for twenty-two years after 1507,[26] and the area had hardly any notable evangelical preachers. So, the response north of the Trent was immediate when the Dissolution of the Lesser Monasteries was ordained in April 1536. Wild rumours flew around: some parish churches would be closed; no one would be allowed to eat white bread, pigs or capons without a licence.

In the Northwest, the outrage about religious change was almost equalled by the strength of agrarian grievance, largely caused by the landlords' extreme reaction to a sharp rise in prices in the early sixteenth century after 150 years of price stability. Along with a new Tudor ordering of the state and a shift in relationships, the unexpected inflation had prompted almost all landlords to introduce a substantial fine on the death of lord or tenant to accompany, or at times to replace, the more traditional, almost nominal, sum of a penny in silver,[27] a 'God's Penny'.* This must have caused considerable Parish distress. The process had started in the Percy estates in 1498–9[28] and the annual Percy income from their Cumberland lands *trebled* in the ten years between the early 1520s[29] and the early 1530s. Outside the Parish, this exponential rise was more common later in the century, and fines of ten times the annual rent became normal among the private landowners.

Inevitably, a great wave of litigation about landownership and rights (initiated by both tenants and landlords) began to roll forward, which would eventually result in a clear legal acceptance of the customary tenant's freedom to sell or let his land.[30] But the immediate result was to expose the crucial difference between manors with 'customary' and those with 'arbitrary' fines. Customary fines were fixed, the sum already settled, and the more common arbitrary fines – the fines that the landlords were beginning to exploit – are well illustrated by the Derwentwater contracts. Around the time of the Pilgrimage of Grace they state that 'at any time of transmission of possession either of the lord or tenant' (i.e., when either the landlord or tenant died, or when the tenant 'selleth or giveth away his tenement in his life time'), the tenant would pay 'such reasonable fine … as the lord and he can agree'[31] – phraseology that inaccurately implies that tenant and landlord had an equal negotiating strength at that time.

At Derwentwater and Castlerigg, Dame Alice's new husband had appointed a tough steward to her manor, a man called Middleton, who entirely broke the easy landlord/tenant relationship previously encouraged by Sir John, for which Dame Alice sued him. Demanding full entry fines and evicting tenants at will

---

* The term 'God's Penny' was used all over Europe from the sixteenth century.

were the main charges and, in one case, it appears that Middleton had every intention of seizing her tenant's land himself after the tenant had been illegally put 'out of the property by force'.[32] Despite this early support, by 1601 the Derwentwater tenants would claim that they too were being charged fines of nine or ten years' rent.[33]

*

The first outbreak of real English resistance to the Reformation occurred around Michaelmas (29 September) when the harvest was in. The date heralded the main season for the renewal of leases and payment of rents, so money was in the mind, and in 1536 Michaelmas coincided with the news filtering out that it had just been legislated that all parochial saints' days were to be celebrated on 1 October, whatever the local tradition. The residents of Dentdale (then in the West Riding of Yorkshire but now in Cumbria's far southeast) slaked their outrage by solemnly banding together to swear an oath to defend both abbey and church, a practice rapidly taken up all over the North – as was their identification of Cromwell as the villain: 'if we had him here we would Crum him and Crum him that he was never so Crumwed'.[34] Almost immediately, unrest broke out in Lincolnshire. Recently suppressed monasteries were restored and a process began of forcing Cromwell's northern supporters, including John Leigh of Isel and Sir John Lamplugh (whose family had some land in Borrowdale), to take the Pilgrim's oath of loyalty. On occasion, things went further, as in the case of Thomas Leigh's cook, who was hanged.[35]

In Yorkshire, Thomas Aske, a gentleman and – like Cromwell – a lawyer at Gray's Inn, proved to have the ability to weld the mobs of commons together and turn uprising and grievance into a 'Pilgrimage of Grace' or, widely forgotten, 'a Pilgrimage of Grace for the Commonwealth'.[36] A large force of rebels occupied York and captured Pontefract, causing triumphant assemblies for the commons. While these certainly intimidated the nobles and the gentry (and the forced oath-taking continued apace), from the start both groups had 'actively failed to resist' the revolt – allowing its possibility and strength – as they shared in its distrust of the government. So, the Duke of Norfolk, in command of the royal forces, found his troops outnumbered by almost five to one, and on 27 October he called for a parley. Had battle been joined, the rebel forces would surely have prevailed, yet, once the duke had promised to forward the pilgrims' demands to the king at the beginning of November, Aske naively agreed to a truce.

The demands included several reforms to landlord–tenant agreements, above all the establishment of 'tenant right', to underline the view that the obligations of border service remained (some argue became)[37] a legal quid pro quo for hereditary rights. Some state that this was the first time the phrase 'tenant right' was recorded, but the phrase was certainly in use in legal documents at the Derwentwater court between 1532 and 1538. Two Derwentwater tenants claimed in their court depositions that 'after the custom of the countrie called tenant right there used tyme out of remembrance' they were obliged to 'be all tymes redy ... ageynst [the king's] enemies the Scotts'.[38]

In early December, the king offered an agreement that no more abbeys would be dissolved, that those suppressed would be restored, a parliament would be called at York, and a free pardon granted to all those who had taken part in the rising. Tenant right was not mentioned but a maximum of two-year arbitrary fines was offered. This seemed acceptable to most and the rebels' more dramatic demands – that Cromwell be handed over to the people, the heretical bishops dismissed and papal jurisdiction restored – were not pursued. So Aske led a delegation of northern gentry to join the court at Greenwich Palace for the Christmas festivities.[39]

His call to arms had come late to the Northwest and the Northwestern rebel army, consisting largely of the commons and monastic tenants, which had only just mustered, were forced by his decision to disband, reluctantly. When the deadline for summoning the parliament to York passed and Cromwell remained in post, the commons – quite wrongly – began to question Aske's loyalty.[40]

Now there were attacks on tithe barns in Cumberland, and the commons of Westmorland made it clear to a gentleman who was prepared to help their cause* 'that they would admit no gentleman to their Council, as they were afraid of them'.[41]

However, by then, the northern gentry and nobility had generally lost what support they had had for the revolt and in January 1537 there had been a largely leaderless attempt to take Hull. The next month, some six thousand commoners mustered to attack Carlisle and the negative side of the splendid independence shown by the commons of Westmorland quickly manifested itself. In the leaderless revolt, some seven hundred were slaughtered in a rout outside the city. And the two risings' breach of the peace provided the excuse for the withdrawal of all the king's concessions, along with his pardon.

Robert Radcliffe, 1st Earl of Sussex,† was charged with ensuring retribution upon all connected with the Pilgrimage in the Northwest, and the king instructed him that 'a good number of the inhabitants of every town, village and hamlet, that have offended' should serve as examples of the effects of incurring the wrath of the king, setting their heads and quarters in all prominent places 'as they may be a fearful spectacle to all other thereafter'.[42] The abbots and monks from the monasteries that had supported the uprising were hanged, drawn, quartered and displayed for treason. One of the first three houses to suffer this fate was Whalley in north Lancashire. So, unsure that a treason charge would hold in Furness, it was there that the Earl of Sussex treated the abbot, Roger Pyle, to a parley. Surrounded by decaying lumps of flesh, the abbot was persuaded just to *give* Furness to the king, along with its great flocks of sheep, salmon fisheries and smelting manufactory near the abbey.[43] Crosthwaite Parish was losing a significant landlord, protector and merchant-in-chief.

The next monastic surrender was Lewes Priory, seven months later. Cromwell wanted to acquire it quickly for his son who was about to marry, so he purchased it by offering permanent pensions for all the unemployed monks.[44] Purchases of almost all large

* Lord Darcy, who had come over from Yorkshire.
† Who sprang from a successful junior branch of the same family that had married into the Derwentwaters, appointed either despite, or because of, his potential local loyalties.

monasteries over the next two years followed this pattern; only the Furness monks had never been offered pensions. Again, it was the North that suffered most. By 1539, lead from the monastic roofs was already improving the stock of royal bullets, just as bell metal was beginning to improve the royal guns (and the timber from monastic forests would soon launch a reborn navy), and a significant new bill gave the king the right to establish new bishoprics, and therefore cathedrals. Then, to span the country, six more cathedrals were created from monastic abbeys, their only realistic source.

In Carlisle, the friary church of St Mary became the Cathedral Church of the Holy and Undivided Trinity, the prior becoming its first dean. This continuity of personnel was common in all the new cathedrals, and inevitably led to the continuation of the old cathedral tradition of beautiful music and chant. The daily choral singing of Divine Office was, for the first time, open for the public. Thus, a flavour of ceremony and the 'beauty of holiness' was to remain alive within the new Anglican religion.[45] This too was unique in Protestant Europe, as was the English Protestant church's claim to apostolic succession.

At the end of 1539, Thomas Leigh visited Durham and desecrated St Cuthbert's shrine and body, still uncorrupted after 850 years. Upon the king's orders, the now decaying body was laid to rest, while the booty, including a great emerald of fabled price, was seized. Only the magnificently illuminated Lindisfarne Gospels, our greatest artistic inheritance from the Northumberland monks, survived these depredations.* It would eventually find a resting place in the British Museum in the eighteenth century.[46]

Catholicism remained the legal religion of the country and the mass still embodied Christ throughout Henry's reign. After his death in 1547, had his more Protestant son, Edward VI, lived longer, it is possible that the cathedrals might have suffered the

---

* The Durham Priory Church of Our Lady and St Cuthbert became the Cathedral Church of Christ and the Blessed Mary the Virgin, but in 2009 St Cuthbert's dedication was restored: the cathedral today is the Church of Christ, Blessed Mary the Virgin and St Cuthbert of Durham, a witness to the North's strong connection with its own history.

same fate as those in Scotland and been ruined or turned into parish churches. But as it was, that overwhelmingly English phenomenon, the monastic cathedral, became the heart of the new Anglican Church of England.

Tudor centralisation

Henry VIII had found it intolerable that his authority, universally feared south of the Trent, needed the approval of a Percy or a Dacre to hold sway in the North, so he recreated the old Council of the North after the Pilgrimage, intending to replace the power of the feudal lords. Sir Thomas Percy was executed for his part in the rebellion and his brother, the 6th Earl, already distraught at the execution of Anne Boleyn to whom he had been engaged, left all his estate, including the Parish lands, to the crown upon his death in 1537. However, after Henry unwisely ordered Thomas Cromwell's execution in 1540 – his beheading took place on 28 July, the day the king married Catherine Howard[47] – the power of the Council never really took hold. And the old feudal relationships continued to remain little affected during the reign of his son Edward VI (r. 1547–53) who, along with Archbishop Cranmer, established an unadulterated Protestant Reformation.

The epistles and the gospels were to be read in English, the recently modified Latin mass was abolished, clergy were permitted to marry and, two years into the new regime, Cranmer's *Book of Common Prayer* was made the legally universal form of worship. The first sentence of his Preface spelt out elegantly the underlying justification for the Reformation: 'There was neuer anything by the wit of man so well devised, or so surely established, which (in continuance of time) hath not been corrupted.'[48] Written in a wonderful period for the English language, Cranmer's dignified, sonorous prose has resonated with English speakers ever since, his phrases, like Shakespeare's, still a living inheritance.

However, for the Parish congregation, used to dialect far removed from Cranmer's literary English, the new words were probably as incomprehensible as the Latin of the pre-Reformation mass, while losing the accreted magic of more than a thousand years. So, initially, there was unlikely to have been much in the new prayer book for the Crosthwaite parishioners to cleave to. During the first year of its use, Edward's commissioners stripped plates, jewels and ornaments from the parish churches. Cumberland hid as much as it could but the churchwardens and the Eighteen Sworn Men of St Kentigern's proved more orthodox than many, confessing to three silver chalices, vestments of velvet and white silk, large numbers of candlesticks and more, while keeping its real wealth a parochial secret.[49]

After Edward's early death in 1553, Queen Mary's restoration of the 'old religion' greatly relieved the county; of the almost three hundred burnings and executions in her five-year reign, not one victim lived in Cumberland or Westmorland.[50] She also passed the majority of the Percy hereditary estates, including their land in the Parish, back to the family. This period of relative peace for the Parish was not to last, however, for in 1559, once Elizabeth I ascended the throne, her Act of Uniformity finally established that the Reformation was here to stay. And, on the very same day the bill was passed, visitations were ordered to the North to enforce the use of the prayer book. The queen had deftly changed her father's title of 'Supreme Head of the Church' to 'Supreme Governor ...' but even so, and even though the visitations had initially left the acceptance of royal supremacy up in the air, nearly a third of Cumberland and Westmorland's clergy absented themselves and 'were pronounced contumacious'.[51]

A year later, the Bishop of Carlisle reported that all was serene, except for one layman, Lord Dacre, and one body of people, 'the priestes, wicked ympes of antichrist, for ye most parte very ignorante and stubborne, past measure false and sotle: onlie feare maketh them obedient'.[52] And obedient they now were when he administered the oath of allegiance. However, the Scots, who had embraced a more radical form of Protestantism, soon rocked the Northern boat. The Archbishop of York considered that those priests who fled the Scottish Reformation did 'more harm than any other would or could in dissuading the people of the North' from accepting the Anglican settlement.[53] But he failed to foresee the effect on his laymen once the Scots forced the Catholic Mary, Queen of Scots to abdicate in favour of her son and she fled to Cumberland's shores in 1568.

Unrest culminated in the Rising of the North, the context for Wordsworth's *White Doe of Rylstone*, one of his two poems that reintroduced Alice de Rumelli and the Boy of Egremont. The Rising, also known as the Revolt of the Northern Earls, was launched in the Northeast at the end of 1569 by the earls of Northumberland and Westmorland. Their only new demand, in an otherwise predictable list, was that Mary should be freed from the aristocratic imprisonment Elizabeth had ordained and be placed back on the Scottish throne. The response to their call to arms was magnificent, because, it was said, of 'the olde good-wyll of the people, deepe grafted in their harts ... In truth the Percies, the Dacres and the Nevilles were lords of the hearts of the North countrymen'.[54] This was perhaps true, but it was also the case, as Elizabeth's secretary of state William Cecil had been warned, that 'There be not in all this country ten gentlemen that do favour and allow of her Majesty's proceedings in the cause of religion'; equally, 'the hearts of the commonalty' are 'altogether blinded with the olde popishe doctrine'.[55]

However, the earls were unfathomably dilatory. Once Thomas Radcliffe, 3rd Earl of Sussex – following in his grandfather's footsteps by heading north to administer the king's justice – had gathered his army of reinforcements and marched out to battle, the Rising simply collapsed. In Cumberland, Thomas Howard, 4th Duke of Norfolk, had placed every bet he had on the Dacre inheritance and it was in 1569 that he won the triple. He had secretly married Elizabeth Leyburne, the last Lord Dacre's widow, in 1566 (the year of Dacre's death), and when his new wife died seven months later in childbirth, Norfolk was granted the wardship of her four young children. On 17 May 1569 the nine-year-old Baron Dacre (George) died and, with extraordinary speed, on 19 June a specially convened court ruled that – despite Thomas Dacre's will specifying that he left his estate to his son and his brothers – the Dacre title had lapsed and the Dacre land should be shared between the three daughters.

Leonard Dacre, the children's uncle, who had presented his livery as 6th Baron Dacre, was ordered not to assume the title.

Whether the court did or did not know that Norfolk had engaged
the three daughters to his sons is not clear – but it was a surprising
ruling. Dacre, the historian William Camden reports, 'stomached it
much that so goodly inheritance should fall to his nieces'; frustrated
and angry, he returned north, seizing Greystoke and fortifying
Naworth,[56] having apparently warned the queen of the imminent Rising, in which his presence had been expected. Then, the
Rising defeated, Dacre switched sides again early in 1570, when
all seemed settled. Calling him a 'cankered suttill traitor',[57] the
queen sent Lord Hunsdon to reel him in. Answering the famous
rallying call 'A Daker, a Daker, a read bull, a read bull', a force of
3,000 Cumbrians – including some fierce fighting women – rose to
support 'Dacre's Raid'.

The fight took place near Carlisle, so, despite the old Parish links,
Crosthwaite parishioners may have been absent when, according to
Hunsdon's report, Dacre's 'footmen gave the prowdyst charge on
my shott that I ever saw'.[58] Nevertheless, after a strongly contested
battle, Dacre was defeated and fled, but the many prisoners taken
were, surprisingly, forgiven, after the intercession of Lord Hunsdon.
Perhaps Cecil saw the rebellion as a personal clan battle between
the Dacres and the Howards, and, despite executing the Duke of
Norfolk in 1572, thought the frequently Catholic Howards would
provide a strong buffer against energetically Presbyterian Scotland.
The cry of the Dacres was never again to come to the defence of the
North, Flodden forgotten.

Elsewhere, retribution for the Rising was more savage than
ever, and the North was finally bled into submission, allowing a
change from a medieval to a more modern centralising system of
governance. The whole country was badly short of money and in
the North there were far more itinerant poor, after real population
growth and the two uprisings, so Cecil decided to re-establish the
Council of the North in his own, very different mould. This brought
its governance, including the Northwest – as Carlisle had joined the
original sittings of the Council in the Northeast[59] – under central
control for the first time.

The rest of England had long moved on from the feudal system,
and now the people of the North too, who had been defending

theirs almost as passionately as religion, were to be governed no longer by their ancient rulers, but by royal servants.

The loss of the chapels and changing landlords

The general chaos and alarm of the Reformation was exacerbated in the Parish by the scale of the land changing hands, a process that continued long after the Dissolution. In some areas, landownership was, at least initially, fairly clear. The Percys' ownership of lands in the Parish remained virtually untouched by the whole process, despite having been briefly forfeit to the crown, while ownership of the extensive Furness land remained with the crown until the seventeenth century. The lands owned by Fountains Abbey[60] had also passed to the crown, but Henry VIII had sold their land in Borrowdale, including Watendlath, to Richard Graham,* along with what must have been a very considerable holding in Braithwaite, valued at £22 6s. 0d. For the king's sale of the Fountains land surrounding Monk Hall (primarily the vill of Crosthwaite given by Alice II, including a rent-free Monk Hall and Vicar's Island) to John Williamson, in 1541–2 was only valued at 11s. 8½d.[61]

The main branch of the Williamson family – who would be described in 1675 as an ancient gentle family[62] – lived at Millbeck, a mile or so north of Keswick, where their land bordered some of the old Fountains estate. After the Reformation, the Williamsons had begun to add an extensive range of Elizabethan buildings to the west side of their old pele tower. When finished, towards the end of the reign, Millbeck Hall consisted of a long northern wing with 4-foot-thick walls facing a stream whose force gave the area its name, and ended, past a fine mullion-windowed dining hall, with a large barn. A splendid door with plainly chamfered sides and a magnificent heavy inscribed lintel makes it plain that Nicholas Williamson was the final builder and that the family did

---

* The deeds read as if this included twenty tenements and a mill at Stanethwaite, but since this is not a known area of Borrowdale, it may have referred to Stanthwaite near Uldale, north of Bassenthwaite.

not bear arms.[63] Since a Nicholas Williamson is named as one
of John's tenants, and since, along with two Radcliffes and two
Jacksons, John's wife and a Miles Williamson were major tenants
in the Brathmyre chantry lands in Great Crosthwaite in 1540,[64]
land which marched with the Fountains land, and since we know
that John sold Vicar's Island in 1560, it seems safe to presume that
he too was one of the Millbeck Williamsons and used his profit
from the island sale to glorify the family house.

The heir to John Radcliffe's diminished territory, his daughter
Dorothy, had married Leonard Dacre's younger brother Francis, so
her husband was engaged in his own byzantine, thirty-year-long
inheritance dispute – about the rights to the old Dacre land and
honours. The fight would involve the Howards, the Lowthers, the
crown and religious conversion. Soon after Leonard's failed revolt in
1570, Francis must have thought money would be more useful than
his wife's diminished inheritance and in 1574 the couple sold their
Thirlmere lands.* Francis was popular locally and it was largely
as a result of the 'concerted resistance against the Howards by the

Thirlmere Bridge crossed the lake at its narrowest point. Braithwaite's
Wythburn to its south, Leathe's land to the north.

* They also sold Tallentire to the Fletchers.

Cumbrian tenantry' – in his support – that he briefly 'entered into possession' of his hereditary lands. Soon afterwards a new legal commission would discredit his claim and, having left the country without permission, Francis would find himself outlawed.

The Parish land around Wythburn went to a Westmorland family, the Braithwaites of Warcop, and the manor of Legburthwaite and the 'free fishery in the water of Thyrlemere' to the Leathes family.[65] From now on, any generic legal complaint from the Derwentwater tenants would be drawn against a Braithwaite and a Leathe,* along with the Radcliffes.[66] The sale also meant that now only the Dilston Derwentwaters owned Parish land, in the form of Sir George Radcliffe, Cuthbert's son. We will see that, living primarily away from the Parish, he found an unusual way of dealing with this when business demanded his presence there.

Shadowing the change of landownership and landlord, the Parish uplands were still technically encumbered by the complications of the unique Cumbrian baronial forest legacy, which allowed the inheritors of the original Norman landlords to sell the old forest lands (hence the ability of the Derwentwaters to sell in Thirlmere).[67] There were still only two major Lake District landowning families who had lived in the area since Norman times: the Derwentwaters, who owned their land before the Norman baronial system came into play (and whose senior branch, as we have seen, were beginning to live mainly outside the area); and the Le Flemings of Rydal and Coniston,[68] who were thought to be descended from William the Conqueror's sister, and whose landownership in south Cumbria was established before Furness Abbey arrived on the scene.

The baronial uplands system was entirely without manorial middle men – who were able to step in between the tenant and his overlord – so there were no manors whatsoever to sell in the Parish uplands. Only lands in the valleys originally given

---

* By 1787 Legburthwaite was recorded by Clarke, the Penrith surveyor, as having 'ten tenements all arbitrary which together yield about £8 p.a.'. He reported the Wythburn tenancies as all customary 'except one [either enfranchised or (unlikely) freehold] at the Waterhead, the owner of which is obliged to keep a stallion, a bull, and a boar, for the service of the tenants'. Clarke, *Survey of the Lakes*, p. 118.

to Fountains and Furness abbeys were available to be manori-
alised, unless an overlord sold – a rare event at this time. So,
the changes in the ownership of Parish land after the Dissolution
had absolutely no relationship to the still-debated rise of new
gentry in much of the rest of England. Newlands and Borrowdale
were gentry-free, and the long-standing Williamsons of Millbeck
Hall (and Lowthwaite House in St John's) held just a fraction
of the land of the 90-square-mile parish. So the Lake District
as a whole, and Crosthwaite Parish in particular, was exempted
from the arrival of any new gentry between the mid-sixteenth and
mid-seventeenth centuries.*

Attendance of the new Anglican Church had been made legally
mandatory by Edward VI, and every child was considered to be
born into it. Elizabeth had introduced a 12d. absentee fine, which
rose to £20 by 1581,[69,70] but her hierarchy was fairly unconcerned
about the attendance of the poor. Archbishop Grindal, from
Cumberland, stressed in 1571 that 'especially householders' must
keep the regular Sunday injunction. Yet there remained an assumed
identity of society and the new church, 'common prayer' emphasising both the social solidarity of the community itself, and the
church's solidarity with it. And the Anglican ecclesiastical courts
acted as society's moral enforcer.[†]

More generally, England had been the only European country
that had previously banned the translation of the Bible[‡] and for the
Elizabethan and Jacobite English, the Bible proved to be a post-
Reformation revelation. For, in the words of G. M. Trevelyan, which
remain as true as when they were written, with the 'monopoly of

* The notable exception in the Lake District was the Fletchers, who were traditionally from Wasdale and were first documented in St Bees parish register in
1546. They moved to Cockermouth, made a fortune in trade in the sixteenth
century and invested in land, branches of the family buying several manors
around the area including Tallentire from the Derwentwaters, Hutton in the
Forest and, in our parish, Wythop and the Warcop land in the Parish, in the
Thirlmere Valley.

† Their remit included all forms of private morality and the ultimate sanctions
included humiliating forms of public penance and excommunication, the latter,
at its most extreme form, involving total social and economic ostracism by the
rest of the community.

‡ In 1407, as part of the suppression of the Lollards.

this book as the sole reading of common households ... while the imagination was kindled, the intellect was freed ... for its private study involved its private interpretation. Hence the hundred sects and thousand doctrines that [would] astonish foreigners and opened England's strange path to intellectual liberty. The Bible cultivated here, more than in any other place, the growth of individual thought and practice.'[71]

However, the development that had the more immediate impact on the Parish was the complete breakdown in the wealth of the chapels, with which the late medieval church had served the isolated populations of its dales and fells. Before the Reformation there had been sufficient provision for the maintenance of a celibate priest, but the combination of inflation, the loss of the monasteries (from which so many priests came) and new clergy with families to support meant the cupboard was bare. At the beginning of Elizabeth's reign, Archbishop Parker had acknowledged the tragedy and issued an 'Order for serving Cures [benefices] now Destitute': chapel readers were to be appointed to read the services of the day, along with the homily and litany, but never to christen, marry, administer Holy Communion or preach.[72] In the same year, the Bishop of Carlisle reported on his chapels to William Cecil: 'Either must these places be wholly unserved, and so the people grow from ignorance to brutishness, or else such must be tolerated as will be entertained for five marks or £4.'[73]

This was an optimistic sum for the Parish, which only the originally seigneurial chapel at Thornthwaite could provide. Newlands' £2 15s. was nearer the Parish average and, even so, two of the chapelries had to raise an extra 2s. for every pound of rent due to fund their reader, the other three having sufficient church stock left from their ancestors' generosity to pay for one. For some time, the readers' salaries were supplemented by drawing up bonds, wills and conveyancing for the people of their valleys. But, fundamentally, it was the natural resourcefulness of both parishioners and readers that made the bankrupt system work; with 'whittlegate' and 'harden sack'. That is, the reader was given food and board in various local farms, taking with him his own 'whittle', a knife, as few would own a spare, and was also given clothing of coarse, homespun hemp or flax cloth that had been soaked in water and beaten with 'a battling wood' to make it more tolerable to wear: harden sack. At Wythburn, the chapel reader enjoyed the extra 'goosegate', the right to pasture geese on the slopes of Helvellyn.

Maintaining a centre for the hill farmers was a vast improvement on an empty chapel, an improvement that might include teaching the congregation's children to read and write in the church. This all needed organisation, and around this time chapel wardens were appointed, creating their own smaller vestry governance. There were five, for instance, at St John's in the Vale, who collected the fire tax that was due twice a year. But it was all a far cry from the old priests of the chapel, well enough paid to look after themselves, and preaching and administering the sacraments.

Another improvisation, even more unusual than whittle-gate, is captured in the Parish records, which had started early for Cumberland, in November 1562. They describe one of the two instances of a 'handfast marriage' discovered in the Carlisle diocese, a strange, unexplained and brief change to marriage habits in the North. 'Janet (Fysher) allegeth yt about Whitsonday last the said Leaonard (Bowe) was handfast to her ... by worde fit for yt purpose vix: heare I Leonard takes ye Janett to my handfast wyef ... and so they kist and this was before a great number of people.'[74] These marriages were practised on both sides of the border, and Walter Scott[75] has it that, at least on the Scots' side, they signified that 'we are man and wife for a year and a day – that space gone by, each may choose another mate or, at their pleasure, may call the priest to marry them for life'.

If these accounts are accurate, this was an astonishingly radical arrangement. But why not change immemorial practice, if every-thing was being changed around you in ways you did not like? At the same time at Threlkeld, the register of marriages recorded both the 'formal contracts of marriage' and the 'sureties for the payment of 5s to the poor, by the party that draws back';[76] both changes a mixture of the radicalism and conservatism that is one of the long-running fascinations of Cumberland.

*

While the Reformation had caused wholesale changes through-out the whole of Britain, there would be general agreement that 'the heartless manner in which it was carried out in the North left the land and people' in its immediate aftermath 'poorer in both material and spiritual things than it found them'. In the Parish, in particular, it left five chapels without a priest between them for almost 200 years. Much has been written about the damage done to the North by the violence that accompanied the Reformation here. Often the tone seems somewhat sentimental today: Henry 'found the north poor, and he robbed it of the only treasure it possessed in the wealth of the abbeys. He found it backward and nearly destroyed the only civilising influence at work there, the Church. He found the people cherished, among many faults, a few rude virtues, truthfulness, personal honour, fidelity to family and friends. He made no serious efforts to reform the faults, but he did his best to eradicate their virtues.'[77]

The words of the Misses Dodd above are perhaps uncomfort-ably sweeping, ad hominem and patronising in tone for today's taste. But, to rephrase them, the inevitable effect of a great break-down of cherished feudal and religious allegiance and the seismic economic shift created by the loss of the great monastic landlords and employers was clearly transformational and, even ignoring the eruptions of violence and implacable punishment, must have been painful and bewildering. As must have been the loss of pro-tection from evil spirits; the loss of the help from the saints when you lit a candle; the loss of the colour, the ornament and the great processions you were used to, which blessed your work and saved your cattle; the loss of a place where you might get food in hard times, and the loss of sacraments in your chapel; above all, the loss of the Church's magical properties to protect and cure *you*, exorcism (abolished by 1550), along with the miracle of the Mass (transubstantiation).

Yet for the new Protestant church, the devil remained if any-thing more powerful than ever. This was to prove an uneasy combination.

The Crosthwaite Ruling, Mining and Elizabethan Life in the Parish

I N 1571, AS public religious dispute generally calmed, dissent avoiding the spotlight, an internecine struggle at St Kentigern's culminated in 'certain church wardens'[1] reporting to the bishop that the Reformation had not taken full hold in the Parish. This was a pernicious time to have raised such a complaint, as a year earlier the pope had called on all good Catholics to rebel and had excommunicated the queen. Up until then, the intention of Elizabeth and her councillors had been to establish religious peace rather than religious truth, her restored English Prayer Book carefully worded so as to be acceptable to Protestant and Catholic alike. Now, hedged about by new fears, the attitude had changed, and the unequivocally Protestant catechism and Thirty-nine Articles were added to the prayer book.

Bishop Barnes had already determined on a general visitation. Now, with a royal commission, he armed himself with extra coercive power by including Henry Lord Scrope of Bolton, Lord Warden of the Marches. The commissioners' subsequent judgment, the Crosthwaite Ruling, was later described as 'one of the most extreme documents of the reformation period'.[2]

The true wealth of St Kentigern's, hidden from the Edward VI inquisition, was uncovered:[3] 'Two pixes of silver ... one cross of cloth of gold which was on a vestment ... three handbells ... xxix brazen or latyne candlesticks of six quarters long ... sepulchre clothes, the painted clothes with pictures of Peter and Paul and the Trinity', and much more. The commissioners' 'command decree' was that all were to be sold 'and put away effectually before 1st December next' by the churchwardens and the Eighteen Men, along with 'all and every such popish reliques and monuments of superstitions and idolatry as remained'. Other lists of 'vestiments ... tunicles ... chestables [chasubles]' belonging to the Parish church and chapels were ordered to 'be defaced, cut into pieces', and made into cushions and a covering for the pulpit. Everything sold or destroyed was to be replaced with a regulated number of simpler and cheaper items, the monetary surplus was to be used for the Parish, and a full account of all these proceedings was to be submitted to the vicar, three of the Eighteen Men and the three churchwardens by 6 December.

There was to be no communion service at the burial of the dead, 'nor for any month's minds, anniversaries, or such superstitious uses'.[4] Services, holidays and bell-ringing, and 'any concourse of idle people to the church', were forbidden on the Wednesdays in Easter and Whitsun weeks, and on the feasts of the Conception, Assumption, and Nativity of our Lady, and on prohibited saints days; St Kentigern, as Robert Southey would point out, was treated as one of the saints who was still to be respected because of his supposed blood royal. But Keswick's annual market day had to be moved from the now prohibited St Mary Magdalene's day, 22 July, to 1 August. And, while many saints' days remained, inextricably combined with the change of agricultural seasons and rent day, most were no longer holidays. Finally, it was stipulated that 'none thereafter should pray upon any bead, knots ... papisticall and superstitious Latyne primers, or other like forbidden or ungodly book'.

The charges to 'detect and present' evil livers, etc. and the injunction to ferret out and report anyone not adhering to the new rules had an unpleasantly inquisitorial tone. The vicar, the curate and the churchwardens were to oversee the new rules and to 'diligently and circumspectly inquire hereof from time to time and duely to present without favour all offenders',[5] who, if found guilty, would be fined or imprisoned. Permission (after all but the prohibited services) for the old mixed community meetings outside the church to continue – passing on official news about loss of stock and learning more from pack-men and itinerant pedlars – was the only cheerful thing in the whole document.

The way the Parish governed itself was to be the heart of the Ruling. It appears that it had been in the throes of a civil war, and that a break in the unity of the Eighteen Men underlay the original complaint, which had been taken out against the parish clerk, Gawen Radcliffe, and his supporters.[6] The complainants believed that the group had greater power than was just and were ignoring the proper and fair distribution of the Eighteen Men throughout the Parish. And it is likely that they also believed that the parish clerk had been living too high on the hog.

Gawen Radcliffe, who farmed at Monk Hall, was the grandson of old Thomas's youngest son, Nicholas, and had already unsuccessfully sued Sir George Radcliffe of the House of Derwentwater upon the latter's inheritance of the title and lands of the Dilston branch of the family (after the death in 1554 of his father, Cuthbert). Gawen may well have felt almost equally chagrined that, while it was entirely acceptable to owe rent to the monks, it was quite beneath his dignity, once the new circumstances forced him to do so, to pay rent to a mere neighbour. And he wanted compensation from somewhere so that he could continue to assert his status.

In the midst of 'the biggest transfer of wealth from one section to another section of the population that the country had ever known', the confused state of Parish landownership inevitably created disputes. As the Eighteen Men tried to steer a course through the maelstrom, their usual reliance on ancient custom and 'good neighbourhood' may have proved insufficient as a guide. The amended oath of duty laid down by the royal commission certainly contained an implicit criticism, ruling that they were 'to enjoy and exercise so full, large, and ample authority as heretofore they by lawful and laudable custom either have *or ought to have had and exercised*' (author's italics).[7] They were required 'to faithfully administer the office, the stock and the money accruing', and produce full accounts for audit by their successors and the vicar before they left office.

The commissioners also took a long hard look at the funding of the school. They found that the endowed money was by then 'not fullye sufficient'[8] to support 'a learned and industrious schoolmaister' and ordered that his stipend should be raised. Accepting that, from time out of mind, every Parish firehouse (dwelling) had paid 2d.[9]

for the wages of the parish clerk, who also received fees for burials, christenings, etc., and 'certain benevolences' (of lambs, wool, eggs and such like), the commissioners judged that he was overpaid. From now on, the Eighteen Men were to collect the tax for the school and the schoolmaster and pay Gawen Radcliffe 46s. 8d. a year out of it.

'The husbanding of the said stock' – and its use for the school – the commissioners 'wholly and utterly leave and refer to the said 18 men from time to time, as to their discretion shall seem most behoveable to the said school'.[10] Nevertheless, in response to the original complaint, they required that all the Eighteen Men's decisions be taken by the majority and also decreed that they should no longer be the sole selectors of their successors. Appointments were to be sworn in at three o'clock on Ascension Day, immediately after evening prayer, and the electors were to be the vicar; Sir George Radcliffe of the house of Derwentwater, knight, and now Lord Warden of the Eastern March but, surprisingly, not a commissioner; the receiver of the Queen's portion of the mines; the bailiffs of Keswick, Wythburn, Borrowdale, Thornthwaite and Brundholme; the Forester of Derwent Fells; the retiring Eighteen Men; and the churchwardens; or as many of the named people as were present. The vicar or (presumably if he were absent) the oldest of the Eighteen Men was to have the casting vote.[11]

So, the select vestry was no longer to be run as a self-perpetuating oligarchy and the list of selectors was clearly intended to make sure that the Eighteen Men properly represented all the main areas of the Parish. If anyone was elected and refused office, they would not only forfeit forty shillings, which would be added to the school funds, they would be either suspended from attendance at church or excommunicated, at the vicar's discretion. This was not to be a job anyone would escape from or take on lightly.

The whole episode provides a fascinating insight into the governance of the church and Parish. The Eighteen Sworn Men had been responsible for local taxation and education for as long as people could remember, and recently, as the Elizabethan parliament had begun to lay down regulations for the maintenance of roads and so on (areas previously untouched by central government), vestry governance had become a recognised legal force. After more than 150 years, the select vestry, governing by immemorial custom, had come out of the closet. The statutes assume that their chosen men were 'the most substantial inhabitants', acting on behalf of the whole parish, just as they did when forming manor court juries, although, bizarrely, the system of the select vestry itself was without any statutory basis whatsoever. However, as the 1821 'Parliamentary Report into English charities for the education of the poor' attests,[12] referring to the Ruling, Crosthwaite Parish 'was then and is still governed' by the Eighteen Sworn Men.

The Parish or Petty Constable now had to report to the vestry, which was charged to appoint men to oversee just about everything. 'Hedge-viewers', soon joined by 'swine-lookers', had already been introduced to Keswick by 1555, but the toughest and most unpopular post, created that same year, was the Surveyor, responsible for roads, lanes, bridges and drainage ditches. Theoretically allowed to call on all employers to supply labourers for two weeks each year, he usually found the help did not materialise.[13] Given the small population of Crosthwaite's vast Parish – just some thirteen to fourteen hundred people in 1563 – these were jobs that would probably have come around more often than anyone liked, although they may have been encouraged by the cheery perks of ale, bread and cheese, and later pipes and tobacco, when the select vestry decided to meet at one of the Keswick inns.[14] The inns were carefully chosen by rotation, the move a well-judged part of the evolution of a remarkable tradition.

Crosthwaite's select vestry had arisen unusually early, forced to innovate to get what help it could as it tried to deal with the ordering of its vast Parish and absentee landlords, and its first major task had been enabled by the large school endowment. Many Cumberland Elizabethan parishes had absolutely no church stock of any kind, which underlines what a rare gift that had been.

Life on the land

Underneath the reshaping of the religious life of the area, the fundamentals of ordinary hill farming continued to evolve. The shape of the landscape and its patterns of vegetation bore witness to the long reign of the monks, having been changed for ever by grazing cattle and sheep.

To ensure that the commons would still support the hill farmers, the old rule of 'levancy and couchancy' (the tenant only allowed to graze the number of animals on the commons that he could keep through the winter) prompted yet more by-laws. Sheep from outside the manor were barred;* the tenant could neither overwinter his animals in another manor, and then bring them back to the commons in summer, nor buy in fodder in the winter to supplement his own resources. Nor could he lease his lands to other farmers yet retain his rights in the commons. This basic principle, combined with the old principles of ancient custom and good neighbourhood to solve disputes, remained the guiding lights of hill-farm management.

The hill farmer's basic flock, grazing rights and 'sheep-heaf' on the fell had to be handed over to his heirs upon his death, belonging to the farm rather than the tenant. This is still the case today. And by the sixteenth century, sheep marking had already become highly sophisticated, the marks, like the basic flock, linked to the farm rather than the tenant. Permanent marking, by then compulsory, involved cutting or holing the ear in some way – often with different patterns on each ear; the most dramatic cropping, of both ears, was reserved for the sheep of the lord of the manor.[15] 'Smit' marks, smeared in tar or 'ruddle', natural red ochre, on the fleeces helped identification from a distance.† And in due course, other animals became similarly accoutred; a hundred years later the pigs in Keswick would be given ear marks 'that everyone may know their owne swine'.[16]

Like their farmers, the 'heaf-gangin' Herdwicks were incredibly tough, capable of living and lambing above 2,000 feet, sustained in the snow by sucking their wool for its oil and eating the parasitic fleas and insects for protein. Like migratory birds and salmon, the

---

* Except for an old agreement with some Hawkshead farmers, connected to the baronial past, that allowed them to use the high ground above St John's in the Vale, Castlerigg and Wythburn.

† In Borrowdale, black graphite from the wadd mines was used from its sixteenth-century discovery until around the 1830s.

LUG-MARKS FROM THE 'SHEPHERD'S GUIDE,' 1819.

1	Fold bitted	2	Slit	3	Cropped or stoved	4	Forked
5	Shearhalved	6	Halved	7	Key bitted	8	Punched
9	Ritted	10	Twice ritted	11	Sneck bitted	12	Stove forked

Some of the long-used lug-marks, as recorded in
the 1819 *Shepherd's Guide*.

sheep always returned to the precise area from which they first
came, each ewe introducing her lambs so they too became 'hefted'
to their own particular bit of open mountain and fell – the sheep-
heaf. And to protect them, primarily from scabies, and waterproof
the wool before the days of sheep dipping, the sheep were 'salved'
by hand, sometimes in special salving (or sarving) houses,* towards
the end of October. Using a mixture of tar and lard or rancid salt
butter, the salvers pulled the wool apart to anoint the skin, the
warmth of which melted it sufficiently to run all over its surface.
It was a laborious, messy process, a good smearer managing only
between ten and twelve sheep a day; soon professional salvers
('scab doctors') were travelling the district from farm to farm.[17]

The sheep also provided work for the women and extra income,
as Wordsworth describes:

'Every family spun from its own flock the wool with which
it was clothed; a weaver was here and there found among

---

* There is still a converted salving house in Rosthwaite in Borrowdale.

them; and the rest of their wants was supplied by the produce
of the yarn, which they carded and spun in their own houses,
and carried to market, either under their arms, or more frequently on packhorses, a small train taking their way weekly
down the valley or over the mountains to the most commodious town.'[18]

Carts were primitive and rare, built without wooden bottoms,
ends or sides; 'sonks' (green sods), attached with hay or straw
bands, provided the usual saddle; leather harnesses 'regarded as
effeminate and furthermore as a rather vulgar display of wealth'.[19]
Sledges transported loads on the steeper fells, as they did into the
twentieth century, and towards the end of the sixteenth century
the Parish began to assume the patchwork appearance that is still
visible today. The courts had ordered the replacement of the old
dry hedges with living hedges of common hawthorn and black-
thorn, briars and withies (wands of willow), and the practice of
building walls, or stone-sided banks, to delineate field boundaries
had begun.[20]

By now the Lake District 'forests', including the Derwentfells,
were largely divided into townships of much the same size as those
outside 'the forest', local governance becoming pragmatic. Peat, for
instance, had become more important,* and by now particular areas
of peat moss ('rooms') in the waste – as well as areas of bracken
known as 'dalts' – were ascribed to individual tenant holdings. And,
once the peat room was exhausted, the tenant could enclose and
reclaim the land, moving on to the next plot of uncut peat, further
into the moss. By the end of the sixteenth century, larger enclosures
began to make an appearance in the Parish. These were 'stinted' –
that is, the tenant bought the right to graze a specified number of
animals upon the land, to avoid potential overgrazing. The enclosure provided the known benefit that the ensuing concentration
of dung provided more nutritious grass† but also gave the tenant

* With the loss of woodland caused by the Elizabethan mining.
† The pasture closed on 1 March to allow the grass to grow and opened again
on 1 May.

an extra freedom. If he did not have enough livestock to fulfil his quota he could take in 'foreign' sheep, for a fee, up to his numerical limit.[21] The rent payable on stints was assessed by 'cattlegate', that being the amount of land required for grazing a cow, which could be exchanged for one horse or between five and ten sheep.[22]

The Derwentwater customary tenants at Castlerigg were the first to experiment[23] with stinting, in 1591, when they extended the small intakes in the borderline land to create one large pasture. Fifteen years later, most of the fells at the Wythburn end of Thirlmere were divided into ten named 'steads', larger enclosed blocks of farmland and fell. These steads rose high up the Helvellyn range as far as the watershed, 'where heaven water divideth',[24] the cost an extra rent at the rate of 4d. per cattlegate. And each stead was overseen by another new official, known as a 'grassman'.[25] The Wythburn rules were strongly upheld, a 'jury' meeting, held fairly regularly in the chapel, to administer them.[26]

Better than in any prose, the rhythms of the hill farmers' year were captured by the 127 stanzas of William Dickinson's poem *Memorandums of Old Times,* in *Cumbriana*.[27] Christmas was a time of feasting, which kept up until well into January, and in late April and May it was lambing time:

> If yance [once] they git milk and can wander about,
> They care not for frost nor for snow;
> For its plenty of suckle 'at gars them git stout,
> To skip, and to lowp, and to grow.

In July, after sheep washing – 'Now gedder in t'sheep and wesh them in't dam/ And swing them and sop them in t'watter' – came clipping time. This was a season of supper-feasts, when the drink flowed and traditional clipping songs were sung, after which it was time for home and a repeat performance for the next day:

> To help a good neighbour at his merry meetin',
> A heall country side to employ
> In housin' and clippin' wi' much friendly greetin'
> For clippins are meetings o' joy.

In August came haymaking, with early starts and late nights:

> *Now mowers cant work through t' middle o' t' day,*
> *For t 'bitin o' clegs, and for heat;*
> *So they snoozle some hours on t' new gitten hay*
> *And mak't up by workan at neet.*

September was the time to gather in the harvest, which 'endit like meast other things' with a thanksgiving feast. By October there was a sufficient lull to let the children go back to school and make time for shepherds-neets and merry-neets.[28] Then help was needed with salving.

The mining boom

The Parish, then, was not an area that you would expect to find at the centre of the first English manufacturing company,* the Company of Mines Royal.[29] Both its mines and its forge were later described by a local clergyman, Thomas Robinson, in a significant essay of 1709, as 'the most famous at that time in England, perhaps in Europe'.[30]

Robinson described Daniel Hechstetter, the German master miner and smelter who oversaw the operation, as 'a man of great learning as well as judgment in metals and minerals' and his family became much involved in the Parish. Having prospected the area, he arranged for some forty to fifty other Bavarian miners to join him in 1565 but, going home to his family in Germany that Christmas, he became ill. When he returned in October 1566, he discovered,† to his considerable anger, that local tensions had boiled over and led to the murder of one of his miners. Restoring control, he soon found that a quite different level of local opposition had been developing at the same time.

---

* That is, the first English company formed for the manufacture of an article (copper), as distinct from companies formed for trading purposes.
† From Daniel Ulsted, who had been in charge in his absence.

Sir George Radcliffe* had inherited Keswick and its surrounding land twelve years earlier, and after renting the miners some suitable land by the River Greta at Brigham, just northeast of Keswick – for the oddly small sum of £10 and an annual rent of a shilling[31] – he returned from whence he came.† His wife, Catherine, remained living 'on the Isle' and, from 1566, oversaw her husband's Parish estate.[32] Quick to be involved, she had immediately protected the murderers' ringleader, 'that naughty man Fisher', and the next two years rang with complaint about her. William Cecil, Queen Elizabeth's secretary of state, was informed: 'We cannot occupy these mines quietly so long as my Lady has possession and rule of the town. For she is the cause of all hindrance and unquietness to us.' It was even suggested that the queen might 'make some exchange with the Lady Radcliffe for this Lordship of Keswick'[33] or that the company might take the lordship over themselves.

However, all the local landowners proved to be a problem for the miners. They bought and sold treed land in hope of future profit and operated an informal cartel to maintain and increase timber prices.[34] Some even had a link with one or other of the newer shareholders in the Mines Royal company.‡ But the most powerful Parish landowner, Thomas Percy, who had become the 7th Earl of Northumberland when Queen Mary restored the Percy land to the family, and on whose Newlands land most of the mines lay, had never been invited to join the twenty-four eventually chosen.

Hence, when work started, in 1556, on the important Goldscope mine deep in the valley, with its double vein of lead and copper, Percy's men had forcibly stopped the miners removing the ore – on the grounds that they were trespassing, and the minerals belonged to their master. The company articles§ included the proviso that

---

* Who inherited the Dilston Radcliffe land in 1554 from his father, Cuthbert.
† It is possible the papers went to him and he never visited.
‡ For instance, Lady Pembroke was the sister of Katherine Parr and thus the niece of Sir Thomas Radcliffe's wife, Margaret Parr.
§ The Company of Mines Royal was only finally incorporated in 1568, but its articles had long been worked on.

the queen had 'first claim on nine-tenths of all gold and silver at a favourable rate, royalties on the copper'[35] and when Percy went to court in spring 1568 it was wrongly judged. The majority decision was that the mines contained more precious metals than copper and lead, and were therefore the property of the queen. Later that year, a disgruntled Thomas Percy was waiting on Mary, Queen of Scots.

Eighteen new mines had been identified and Cecil was informed in June, just after the trial, that the Germans could get as much ore from one miner in the Parish mines as they could get from ten men working the mines back home.[36] So, the boom boomed. The next year, 1569, Catherine, Lady Radcliffe cooperated with the company to the extent that she sold 150 oaks, 300 ashes and about 800 birches (just from 'Barrow Park')[37] but, with neighbourly support, she demanded top price. It had become clear to the Mines Royal shareholders that no local aristocratic cooperation was forthcoming, whatever the agreement might say. Couldn't those Northerners *ever* understand that to do as Elizabeth I requested was the better part of valour?

However, there had been reasons for the original local antagonism. A piece of Newlands land, for instance, was reported to be 'clean wasted and burnt with the water that descendeth from the Ure gotten by the Duchmen',[38] and by 1569 the miners had become well insulated from the local population after John Williamson sold them Vicar's Island 'full of trees like a wilderness'[39] for a hefty £60.[40] The Bavarians set to work there, building a miscellany of useful things, from a brewery to a dovecote to a pigsty, while also planting an orchard of apples and pears nurtured by manure carted over the ice in winter from the Radcliffe stables.[41] Everything clearly worked well since, between 1570 and 1584, over 5,000 ounces of silver were extracted from the Keswick mines. More importantly, the mines produced significant amounts of copper (1,250 hundredweight in 1570). The metal had become ever more essential – to manufacture arms and strengthen warships – as, after Elizabeth's excommunication that year, Philip II of Spain had appointed himself the strong right arm of the pope.

SORTING THE ORE: the two masters on the left are trying the "streak" on the touchstone. From Munster's *Cosmographia*, Basel, 1552, a copy of which was among the books at Keswick at this time.

In 1571, Daniel Hechstetter brought his family with him to live in Crosthwaite. And the year after that Lady Radcliffe must have succumbed, either to him or to the general success, as she made a reasonable agreement to lease the court house in Keswick to provide a storehouse for the miners. Brigham Forge was the centre of this hive, offering accommodation, bathhouses and smithies, its six furnaces responsible for all the smelting. Packhorses brought down the ore from the fells, some to go to the western Derwentwater shore to be ferried across the lake. Other loads went to Greta Bridge, although the miners would complain to the

JPs about both its 'state of decay' and its complete inaccessibility during any flooding.[42]

The furnaces were powered by water from the Greta* and charcoal, woodcutters and charcoal burners descending on the fells around Crosthwaite, as they would do for the next 300 years wherever they were needed in the Lake District. Creating their own clearings and camps, they built their wigwam-like charcoal kilns, sending up wispy smoke signals. Eventually, wood would be imported from Ireland[43] and coal brought from Workington,[44] although it proved to be a less effective source of energy for the purpose. As early as 1571, no fewer than fifty-three men had been regularly engaged in carting peat to keep the fires burning.[45]

The heroic endeavour of the miners themselves emerges from Robinson's 1709 survey of Goldscope, God's Gift, the most productive mine of all. 'We found the vein wrought three yards wide and twenty fathoms deep above the grand level, which is driven in a hard rock a hundred fathom, and only with pick-axe, hammer and wedge [in a method described on p.119] the art of gunpowder not then discovered.'[46] A report in 1600 described a newly erected waterwheel, the water 'brought along the side of the mountain almost 1,200 yards, in wooden troughs made of planks' and then carried twenty-eight fathoms deep into the mine, where it cascaded onto the wheel.[47] The skills were prodigious.

Each ton of ore smelted consumed half an acre of trees,[48] often from the forest of oaks, holly and ash on the lower fellsides in the Parish, and soon the available bark from the felling and charcoal production created a leather industry in Keswick, causing comment about the number of tanners and shoemakers that dwell about the town.[49] In an area once almost entirely covered with forest, wood was becoming a jealously guarded commodity. The Parish was changed indeed; most lastingly, perhaps, by the changes in its people. For, as the miners began to employ locals to sort and crush the ore, antipathy melted away. When local labour was used to lay the foundations of another waterwheel, for instance, carpenters were paid 10d. a day for ninety-one days of cutting the axles, and

* Through a mill race still traceable today.

drinks worth 1s. 6d. were offered to the farmers who helped carry them to the right place.[50]

The Parish registers record the Bavarian presence from 1562 to 1614, including some forty Anglo-German marriages in the nineteen years from 1565. The groom, almost invariably, was described as a 'Dutchman' (clearly the simplest translation of Deutschland) and the brides included three Atkinsons, three Fishers and two Youdales. This influx of new blood was, perhaps, responsible for a mini population boom, the estimated population of the Parish in 1590 being at least a third higher than it had been less than thirty years earlier.[51] But the moment that really confirmed the Germans' complete integration into the Parish was when, soon after the turn of the century, Daniel Hechstetter the Younger became Foreman of the Eighteen Men.

*

The Parish mineral boom also extended to 'wadd', the local name for graphite (known historically as plumbago). First mentioned in the Parish as useful for drawing in the time of Henry III (1216–72), it had also been used to brand sheep by the Furness monks, under the name of 'sheep odde', a term said to derive from the word 'woad'. Traditionally, however, wadd was first discovered by a Parish shepherd in the sixteenth century after a large ash (or oak) tree was uprooted in a storm near the last inhabited place on the route to the great Sty Head Pass: Seathwaite, 'the clearing in the sedges',[52] in far Borrowdale. In 1555 two royal commissioners surveyed 'the Comon of Setower [Seatoller], where the wad-hole lies',[53] some thousand feet and more above Seathwaite, and recommended a 13s. 4d. annual rent. This was nearly seven times more than was recommended for the salt well at Manesty, on the west side of Derwentwater.

Mined wadd had long been stored in William Braithwaite's barn in Seathwaite,[54] but it wasn't until 1607 when a twenty-one year lease was bought by the brothers Daniel (the younger) and Emanuel Hechstetter, and John Williamson, an armourer from London, that the mine really became alive. That year, over 170,000 pounds of graphite were sold.[55] The armourer was involved because the essence of wadd is that it is fireproof and easily worked, and it had therefore become a crucial component of the inside of the castings for bomb shells, shot and cannon balls. Impure graphite, mixed with other elements, was not particularly rare, but graphite from the Seathwaite mine – the only high-grade graphite in the world – was especially solid and uniform. Soon, another commercial use was found for it. Sawn into sheets and cut into thin square strips, which were then wound in string and pushed into tubes, rudimentary crayons were produced (pencils did not yet exist). Held in the claws of metal holders called porte-crayons, they became known as 'crayons d'Angleterre', put together in both the Netherlands and the other Low Countries.[56]

This was the heroic era of the wadd miners, the legendary 'Old Men' (the approving local name for the early miners) who,* mining without gunpowder, cut an 80-yard hand-chipped horizontal level and then tunnelled down more than 120 feet. Cutting through hard wet rock, they used the 'stope and feather' method: the 'feathers' were two 6-inch pieces of thin iron, flat on one side and rounded upon the other, about half an inch broad, and the 'stope' a similarly sized tapering wedge of iron. First a hole was bored in the rock and the feathers were placed in it, flat sides together and parallel with the cleaving of the rock; the point of the stope was then inserted between them and driven in with a hammer until the rock was rent in two. And again, and again, and again.[57]

There are many local tales of the drinking and fighting Old Men, who usually lodged around Seathwaite Farm, the wettest inhabited place in England, leaving only for familial or uproarious Saturday nights and Sundays. The stories include great smuggling legends, partly because, unlike slate, wadd was an easy substance to handle, only needing washing and grading. Worth £24 a ton[58] in 1631, Seathwaite wadd had become the most valuable commodity in the Lake District, a temptation indeed. According to Parish

* Some gunpowder had been supplied to the Germans as early as 1571, presumably for mineral hunting or defensive purposes.

lore, the Old Men forced a surface hole above where the wadd lay, marked the spot, blocked it off with waste material, and told the overseer that the supply had been mined out.

The Parish had a monopoly on its hands, which was to last almost 300 years. Once pencils began to be manufactured (the first one was documented in 1683), English pencils from the Parish – or pencils filled with imported English graphite from the Parish – dominated the trade until the mine was truly worked out in the mid-nineteenth century. Tradition has it that Keswick was 'making pencils' in the Elizabethan period and may even have invented them, but there are no known records of pencil manufacture in Keswick until much later.

The customary tenants

The numbers of customary tenants properly equipped for border service was considered to have dropped dangerously since 1536, tenancies 'reduced rather to pasturing of cattle, than the maintenance of men of service'. Broadly attributed to excessive arbitrary fines and the unruly character of the times, which had left some houses and households ruined, it was also considered that 'in some parts the tenants and the inhabitants themselves had diminished their own strength, by dividing their houses and farms, which were meet only for one able householder and family'. If so, this would have been technically illegal, since a core part of the basic agreement for customary tenants was that their land could be left to only one person (with good provision for the widow), as this was considered to aid their prosperity.

Strenuous efforts were therefore made to reverse the process and the Elizabethan courts, made distinctly aware of the need to preserve military protection for the border by the government, became 'unreservedly placed on the side of the tenants', and decreed that arbitrary fines should be 'reasonable'; which in law became a maximum of two years' current rent. And after the widespread support for Dacre's Raid, a specific argument about Cumberland tenant farmers had been attached to an Act of Parliament.

Discussing how rebellion could be avoided, it resolved that 'The fines being certain, the landlords will force them to have horses and arms in readiness, whereas now … They are so excessively fined they lack necessaries to nourish them for strength in service'.[59] The danger of rising arbitrary fines was, for the moment, assuaged.

This was the time when the use of the phrase 'tenant right' became virtually universal throughout the Lake Counties, and from now on both Parish tenant and landlord could, if they chose to and could afford it, refer their cases upwards from the manor court to the central courts of equity and common law.

In 1570 the crown briefly took control of Thomas Percy's land and commissioned a survey:

> 'Albeyt the Countrey consist most in wast grounds and ys very cold hard and barren for the winter, yet ys yt very populous and bredyth tall men and hard of nature, whose habitaciouns are most in the valleys and dales where evry man hath a small porcion of ground; which, albeit the soyle be hard of nature, yet by continuall travellys made fertile … for their greatest gaine consists in breeding of cattle which are no charge to them in Somer by reason they are pastured and fedd upon the mountains and waste … They have but little tillage, by reason wherof they lyve hardly and at ease … liable to endure hardness when necesseyte requiryth it.'[60]

The last phrase was probably a reference to the capacity of the tenants to stand up to border service and the phrase 'very populous' seems to reflect a normal contemporary viewpoint, but one wonders why sheep avoided the gaze of the servants of the crown.

In 1572 the Percy lands were returned to Henry, the 8th earl, after his brother's execution that year and Newlands valley and the Derwentfells resumed the stability of Tudor landownership denied most of the rest of the Parish. A 1578 survey listed over thirty 'customary tenants' in the valley, their tenements, with only a few exceptions, still identifiable today.[61] Apart from the usual provisions spelled out below at Borrowdale, the tenants were also constrained from digging peat and harvesting bracken outside specified times of year.

The ancient customary obligations in the Parish were spelt out particularly clearly in the Customs of Borrowdale, declared in 1583. The tenants were described as 'customary tenants [who] enjoy the ancient custom called tenant-right paying yearly for the same the rents accustomed to the lords of the said manor ... [and they] shall be ready at the bidding of the Lord Warden of the Western Marches, to serve at their own costs, namely as horsemen in summer and footmen in winter' – presumably conditions in winter were too boggy or icy for the horses. They paid a nominal fine, 'on change of the lord 1 gods penny', unchanged for what seemed like eternity, but 'at their death or on change or alienation of their holdings one year's rent'.[62] This fine is the lowest I have found recorded in the sixteenth-century Parish. Since the land had reverted to the crown, presumably a crown agent, with little local knowledge, had accepted it.

In all, the levels of freedom enjoyed by all the Parish customary tenants remained extraordinary compared with most land workers in the rest of the country. This freedom was further enhanced by the absence of new gentry and the fact that, with no chapel priests, the Parish was far too large for any effective ecclesiastical governance. This relative freedom from the power of the priest was common in the Lake District; for instance, large swathes of its uplands, once Copeland Forest, were quite detached from their mother church on the coast at St Bees. So, authority from above, from any source, except in time of border war, remained most unusually absent. This freedom, with its double-edged sword of responsibility, equally underlined the need for the tenants to organise their own governance, in which the Eighteen Men played a critically important role.

So independent-minded and so entirely distinctive was the indigenous culture of the area that when tourists and new landowners arrived there in the late eighteenth century, they soon found a new use for an existing word to describe its farming inhabitants – 'statesmen'. This was the word that Wordsworth would choose too, to emphasise the good neighbourhood and brotherliness in times of trouble that existed between the poorer and better-off fell landowners.

However, statesman society was neither as static nor as classless as other romantics may suppose; families rose, fell and sometimes rose again with considerable speed. A small minority of hill farmers with larger farms or more than one tenement even received rent from other tenants, exercising the right of the customary tenant to lease their land. But, not being substantial landowners, they didn't lord it over their neighbours.[63] The Stangers of Ullock, near Portinscale, provide a good Parish example. Hereditary foresters of the Derwentfells, symbolised by its 'horne tipt with silver hanging in a greine soilke string', from 1437 to the end of the sixteenth century, they were soon running the local Percy corn mills as well. We saw Edmund Stanger, acting as bailiff, chasing up the money for the Tudor rebuilding of St Kentigern's too and their farm of about eighty-five acres,[64] the same size as the farms of two kinsmen nearby, stood in marked contrast to the average Parish hill farm of less than twenty.[65] These Stangers stayed at Ullock until the mid-eighteenth century, still yeomen. Then the richest branch moved out, some away from the North entirely and others into different parts of Cumberland; although other Stangers and some Stanger land remained in the Parish.

At the other end of the scale, a 'husbandman' in the Newlands valley paid 8s. 6d. annual rent for a tenement house, two barns, a chamber house and four separate pieces of land of between 1½ and 6 acres, along 'with sufficient common pasture'.[66] Most husbandmen had even less land and some began to add a craft to supplement their subsistence farming – in Borrowdale, often wood-turning.[67] But, except in times of famine, usually caused by the plague, the self-sufficiency of the farmers now varied from adequate to comfortable. And, while the lowland holdings were usually substantially larger than the old forest holdings, probate evidence towards the end of the sixteenth century surprisingly suggests that hill farmers had become slightly better off than their lowland neighbours, presumably because the wealth of potential grazing on the common fell lands was now particularly valuable as sheep had come to the fore.[68]

Angus Winchester's analysis of thirty-seven Parish inventories from Thornthwaite, Braithwaite and the Newlands Valley between 1578 and 1590 records twenty-two tenants holding under £40, twelve holding from £40–100 and three with over £100[69]. Elsewhere he gives us some interesting detail about the stock holdings there between 1566 and 1590.[70] Four-fifths of the hill farmers had between one and three horses, the level higher throughout Cumberland than the rest of England because of potential border service, and everyone had some sturdy black longhorn cattle. Six farmers had between thirty and forty cattle each, the herds nevertheless averaging between eleven and twelve, including five or six milk cows. And the concentration was upon breeding, as with the male sheep, and selling on young bullocks to the lowlands to fatten up. No one had a goat, and four tenants kept cattle only (unless the inventories had failed to include the flock tied to its land).

Nevertheless, the mainstay of the majority was Herdwick sheep.[71] Most of the sheep farmers held a stock of under a hundred, and the average flock size was less than fifty. Nine had between one and two hundred, and a similar wealthy minority (this time five tenants rather than six) had large flocks of over two hundred – John Birkett at Thornthwaite* had 480, with six horses and thirty-seven cattle.[72] In Derwentwater in 1601, according to Francis Radcliffe,[73] six Parish tenants held 'two hundredth sheepe at the least'. It was from the ranks of these larger farmers that the Eighteen Men would often emerge.

Since the late 1950s it has become common practice for academics studying the Northwest and the Lake District to describe all its inhabitants (except for what gentry they can find) as 'peasants'. Quite apart from instinctively baulking at this description, for both familial and political reasons, I do not believe that, from the late sixteenth century on, the term can be ubiquitously justified either in the Lake District or the Parish, even if divided into 'upper' and 'lower' peasants as has sometimes been done.[74] The hill-farming community was by then an independent, self-regulating society, the wealthier of its members, the new substantial dynasties, creating the distinctive social character of the district they also helped

---

* The stock was recorded upon his death in 1582.

administer. For this fast-emerging group, an earlier academic description of a 'rural middle class of yeoman farmers' seems to me nearer to the mark.*

The poor

The population level of the Parish, along with neighbouring Greystoke, was exceptionally low, even by Cumberland standards.† Nevertheless, the parishioners had been faced with a growing problem of poverty (outside the mining area) as the medieval feudal tradition of lord and community supporting their poor had not proved strong enough to cope with the steady population increase since 1450. Edward VI's government had tentatively addressed the problem back in 1552, ordering every parish to officially record the number of its poor. The churchwardens and select vestry were prompted after Sunday service 'to gently ask and demand of every man or woman what they, of their charity, will be contented to give weekly towards the relief of the poor'.[75]

The Elizabethan government, and Cecil in particular, had been fearful of disorder and rioting, particularly when the numbers of vagrants grew after the Rising of the Earls, which many had supported. The Council of the North believed the beggars to be rogues, 'spreading false and seditious rumours' and disseminating messages 'from the late rebels to trouble the quiet of the realm'. Orders were sent out that all suspected should be 'punished with severity and celerity'.[76] These strictures coincided with a grotesque campaign of whipping ordered by the Privy Council, in which the vagrants were beaten until they reached the parish boundary and

* See MacFarlane, Alan (1984), 'The myth of the peasantry: family and economy in a northern parish' from Smith, *Land, Kinship and Life-cycle*, p. 343 for the growing distinctions between the lives of the Cumbrian customary tenant and the European 'peasant', and peasant societies generally. The phrase 'a rural middle class of yeoman farmers' was approved by Winchester. Winchester, *Landscape and Society*, p. 62.

† Despite upland Cumbria being considered in 1600 to be 'heavily populated, barely able to support their population', all but the self-sufficient farmers were dependent on grain from outside. Winchester and Crosby, *The North West*, p. 41.

were imprisoned, or even hanged, if they repeated the offence. This brutal campaign was to last for three years.

At the same time, bouts of famine hit the county. The first had begun in 1577, when the inland transport of grain was rigidly prohibited throughout the country. 'Divers justices of the peace and other gentlemen from Cumberland and Westmorland' sent a petition to Parliament, 'declaring the scarcity and the necessity of corn in the counties',[77] but their pleas elicited scant response. However, answers to the government's enquiries about action taken against vagrants during the whipping campaign revealed to them the prodigious numbers of poor and impotent, and from then on they attempted to organise food for all at times of famine.[*]

So, during the famine of 1587, the government set out elaborate orders to create juries (in the Parish, the Eighteen Men would almost certainly have provided the body) whose task it was to survey how many people there were in each household and how much corn they had. They could retain only as much as was necessary to feed themselves and to have corn left over for seed. The rest was to go to Keswick market, where the jury and the Justices of the Peace were to try to ensure that the corn was sold at moderate prices. They were also to use 'all good means and perswasions ... that the pore may be served of corne at convyent and charitable prices' and to see 'that the maymed or hurt soldiers and all other impotent persons be carefullye seene unto to be relieved'.[78]

Justices of the Peace (JPs) had been around since the fourteenth century, their oath of office including the words 'in all articles in the King's Commission to you directed, ye shall do equal rights to the poor and to the rich after your cunning wit, and power'.[79] But their role had been transformed by the Tudors, who introduced nearly 60 per cent of the 303 statutes that required their attention, aiming to ensure that the recently introduced government quarter sessions would take full control of local government. The JPs were mainly taken from those members of the rising county gentry (often MPs) who had a minimum income of £20 from their lands, and from the

---

[*] The concept of the deserving and undeserving poor had already been articulated in 1563.

clergy; the government usually avoiding the seriously land-rich lest it gave them too much power.

Therefore, in much of the country, the JPs' role as magistrates had both cemented the power of, and helped define the social position of, the new gentry. In practice, the sons of magistrates were often chosen to follow in their fathers' footsteps. However, the Parish, once the Williamsons of Millbeck had moved to London and let their Parish land,[80] was left virtually without gentry, only the Leathes, intermittently in Legburthwaite, and the vicar. So it was to be a long time before the technical new power of the JPs had any serious impact on Crosthwaite, or on its main manor courts.

When the 1587 orders were reissued to the Eighteen Men and the JPs in 1594, as famine loomed again, the government noted that they had previously done 'much good for the stay of y dearthe and for y relieving of y poore'. The evidence from Crosthwaite is less supportive: the sharply rising numbers of burials recorded between 1586 and 1589 had provided clear evidence of famine. However, the deaths registered are largely for Keswickians, and it seems that the hill farmers and their labourers, with their own, albeit diminishing, supplies of food, did better. Whether the vestry simply did not remove enough from the farms or there was just not enough to go around remains unclear.

Just five years after the reissue of government orders for famine control, the whole of the North was struck by plague throughout 1597–8. Not knowing how it was caused, people tried to fight back by creating methods of disinfection, as attested by the 'Plague Stone' at Penrith and 'Web Stone' at Armboth Fell in the high fells between Thirlmere and Derwentwater.[81] These stones contained holes that, in times of plague, were filled with disinfectant, probably vinegar. Money would be placed in the holes and – suitably disinfected – taken in payment afterwards.* The average number of Parish deaths per year around that time was thirty, but the 1597 church records starkly report a terrifying 267, with eighty-four more in 1598. And

---

* J. Fisher Crosthwaite reports the legend that the Keswick people would lay their produce down at 'Cuddy Beck', a stream that causes problems today when flooding is a risk, while money was placed in the stream to be cleansed. Grant, *The Story of the Newlands Valley*, pp. 41–2.

it is likely that these numbers were less than the total, as many may have been buried in the fells, their families and neighbours unable to do more.[82] At Penrith, indeed, the vicar recorded those dying of plague with a P and those buried in the fells with an F.

The second prong of the government's response to the growing poverty was to pass a series of new laws consolidated into an over-arching Act in 1601 that would form the basis for poor relief in England for the next 200 years. Making provision for the poor a local responsibility, the Act placed all the burdens on the parish. Work was to be provided for the unemployed and apprenticeships and health care were to be offered to every orphaned or indigent child. Houses of Correction were to be built for beggars and vagrants. JPs and, where there was one, the select vestry were to appoint an Overseer for the Poor, who was given authority to raise higher compulsory rates.

In Crosthwaite, two Overseers of the Poor were appointed annually by the vestry. The Poor Law had called for four overseers, and for their selection to be given the imprimatur of at least one JP; and it is unclear whether the Parish ignored the second ruling as well as the first. The overseers, as the only Parish officers bound by civil law, could use the services of the petty constable – which was the underlying strength of the 1601 Act. So, working with the Eighteen Men, the overseer set and collected the new poor rate and oversaw the distribution of benefits.

An unanticipated consequence of the introduction of the poor rate was that it hardened each parish's heart about the numbers of the poor for whom they were responsible, and the Parish manor courts soon homed in on new offences to try to lessen their number. The law required the Parish to assist four groups, including those hired for a continuous period of 365 days. So, most single labourers were now hired from the end of Michaelmas week to the beginning of the next Michaelmas to avoid the new responsibilities. Pressure on ratepayers to accept the poor as temporary labourers led to their frequent use by the surveyors to work on repairing the lanes and bridges, and prosecution for 'taverning' was extended to subletting landholdings, letting land to people outside the manor and the building of cottages without land.[83]

While the church was still universally held to be the only place for men to approach God to beg for his intercession in the event of natural disasters, like plague and famine, the great and bewildering loss for the parishioners remained the removal of the church's seemingly magical properties to protect the individual. The argument given when exorcism had been outlawed was that the power to cast out devils had been an especial gift to the early Christian church and was no longer necessary in a time of established faith. So, words and charms had been declared powerless unless God chose to heed them, finally establishing the distinction between a prayer and a spell. Man's immunity from witchcraft was drastically reduced – he was reliant now on faith alone.

So, the ordinary parishioner inevitably turned to using 'wise women and cunning men' to find stronger ways of making magic. Haemorrhage, ague, jaundice and toothache were all widely treated in the Lake District by various scriptural texts written on scraps of paper by the initiated.[84] Chunks of incantatory Latin prayer and words from the English translation of the Bible were essential elements of the cure. Everything became jumbled up: one moment prayers were said, then a magic brew of 'draught ale without Hops'[85] mixed with dried gosling's intestine was drunk. And as things continued – inevitably – to go wrong, the cures notwithstanding, belief mushroomed in the power of the black, ill-wishing witch.

Nearly thirty years after the Reformation began in England, an Act of Parliament of 1563 had made witchcraft a capital offence, which it remained for another 130-odd years.[86] And there appear to have been more trials in England under Elizabeth I, in the forty years after the act was passed, than in the whole of the rest of the period put together; the vast majority of prosecutions provoked by alleged acts of damage to people or their animals.

What was happening to create such fear and insecurity in the Crosthwaite Parish? The ancient custom of good neighbourliness and charity towards the poor had been much buffeted by the growing number of the poor and the reframing of their care as a specific Parish responsibility. Wool-gathering, the pastoral equivalent of gleaning, which had long augmented the incomes of the poor, was prohibited by the Derwentfells court. This meaningless, vicious and unenforceable move starkly demonstrates the change of attitude from earlier days, when the poor around Derwentwater were allowed to fish freely in waters belonging to the monks. And, as the clergy and folk memory still spoke of charity, the parishioner was caught between resentment and a sense of obligation, and reactions to this tension could be harsh.

Throughout England, the reaction to the religious changes of the Reformation had added an extra element of suspicion and unpleasantness to local life. Even though, in time, the Poor Laws would prove to be a step forward, they caused a shift in attitude to the poor that, when combined with the religious changes of the time, constituted a fundamental attack on the essential human need for social solidarity.

However, at the same time, Elizabeth's abhorrence of religious enthusiasm spared England the vicious confessional wars that scarred continental Europe. Protestants, beginning to be called Puritans by the end of her reign, had accepted her settlement but had every intention of changing it. Catholics, finally forced to choose in 1581 when it became a treasonable offence to be a Roman Catholic, had largely become Anglican, facilitated both by the traditional liturgy of Communion Service in the Prayer Book and the traditions of the old monastic abbeys that had become cathedrals of the Church of England. Such 'high' Anglicans were viewed as Catholics by the Puritans and as Protestants by Rome.

The different origins of the two groups making up the Elizabethan church would ignite the next century and resonate throughout the history of the Church of England.

Customary Tenants, the Civil War and the Commonwealth

By the last quarter of the sixteenth century, the reivers had become the 'Broken Men', virtual outlaws under no one's control. Kidnapping, particularly of cattle, to demand ransom had become widespread, and the reivers had also demanded tribute in the form of goods or livestock in exchange for immunity from their raids, 'there called Black Maile'. When the tribute was paid in the form of hard cash, 'black maile' became 'white maile' ... paid in silver,

Thomas Allom's romantically exaggerated picture of Scottish reivers, led by the Grahams, in battle near the top of Honister Pass.

vulgarly (but improperly) styled quit rent. A law was passed to beef up the legal remedies against both these forms of extortion to little effect, but in 1603, when James VI of Scotland ascended the English throne as James I, he promised peace for the North. However, as he made his way to London in the 'busy week', marauding Scottish reivers of the Graham family raided as far south as Penrith, seizing five thousand cattle and doing nearly £7,000 worth of damage to property,[1] in an attempt to stop the two countries uniting.[2]

Not amused, the king promptly renamed both sides of the borders the Middle Shires and placed them under the jurisdiction of a royal commission, governing the whole area as a crown colony.[3] And three years later the Graham clan was deported to Ireland, including the Grahams in Borrowdale. A county keeper, with twelve men, was appointed to hunt down thieves and bring them to justice, and areas to be watched included Keswick.[4] Borderers 'except gentlemen of high rank and respect' were prohibited from carrying weapons and, this time, the border quietened down.[*] However, the union of the crowns would nearly prove the parishioners' undoing.

Two years before James's accession, large fines had become a problem again for some Derwentwater tenants; a Dowthwaite, a Mosse, a Hodgson, a Wilson and two Graves took the issue to the High Court, making the old argument that excessive fines prevented them from being suitably prepared for border service.[5] The Derwentwater defence had implicitly accepted the validity of their case by suggesting that, far from arresting Robert Dowthwaite for not paying his fine, they had charged him because he had taken timber from woodland that by custom belonged to his lord. So, along with the flurry of sixteenth-century court cases that had

---

[*] But the practices of the peoples on either side of the border continued to diverge. Easter had just begun to be celebrated on different dates in the two countries, as though the Synod of Whitby had never happened. The logical Scots had accepted the Catholic 1582 solution to the vagaries of the old Roman calendar. The English did not do so until 1752, which must have caused endless irritation and muddle about the dates of dispatch in the legal documents on the border. MacCulloch, *A History of Christianity*, p. 683.

established hereditary tenancy, arbitrary fines broadly remained more controlled than they had been in the first half of the century too. However, once the new king had made the point that without border service the old hereditary tenancies were invalid, both the arguments that had been made by the tenants and the assumptions that lay behind them became instantly irrelevant.

For the tenants, this was a potentially fatal twist in their struggle with the landlords, as the landlords seized upon the king's suggestion, trying to change their tenancies from customary to leasehold. A series of dramatic struggles ensued. The most depressing submission I have come across came from the tenants who lost to Lord William Howard of Naworth in 1610: 'We whose names are underwritten are content freely to yeald and give over all challenge to Tennant right, beseeching your Honour to be so good as to let us have our tenements by lease for such a number of yeares as our heirs shall have no cause to say that we are unnaturall parents.' Yet in Greystoke, in a tussle with Howard's brother, the Duke of Norfolk, the estatesmen won, 'the tenants never submitting but continuing their Tenant Right Estate'.[6] The Percy tenants in the Parish also succeeded in retaining their customary rights.

With the clear bias of the landowning class, Bishop Snoden of Carlisle told the king, when he visited the city in 1617, that all over the diocese tenants were disputing the effects of the potential new land changes:* 'the vulgar people are subtill, violent, litigious and pursuers of endless suites by appeales, to their utter impoverishment and ... find admittance of their most unreasonable appeales, both at York and London, for which these higher courts deserve to be blamed.'[7] Whether reasonable or unreasonable, the tenants' arguments were undoubtedly subtle. They turned the implied quid pro quo of their Elizabethan disputes – tenant right in exchange for border service – on its head, now arguing 'that they held their lands and tenements by customary estate of inheritance, descendible from ancestor to heir, by

---

* He attributes the state of his parishioners 'to the nature of the soile and the quality of the air (like in Norfolk)' – the same quality of mountain air claimed by Victorians to be the foundation of the inhabitants' strength and independence.

the payment of customary services and not by Border Service'.[8]
In Cumberland, just the very north of the county, Howard and
Graham border land, became leasehold.

Henry Robinson, the previous Bishop of Carlisle, had assessed
his diocese just before James came to the throne, some thirty years
after the Reformation was fully accepted in the North. 'The poorer
sort are generally willing to hear, but pitifully ignorant of the foundations of Christianity ... many of them without all fear of God,
adulterers, thieves, murderers,' he complained.[9] '...this woefulness
comes principally of the weakness and carelessness of the minis-
try.'* Robinson's lament about the clergy presumably excluded his
brother, who was Vicar of Crosthwaite, one of the more 'peaceful
parts' of the diocese, where the bishop admitted there were 'some
clergymen of very commendable parts'.[10] But, between them, the
bishop and his brother had caused quite a Parish stir in 1614.

The Eighteen Men had dismissed the schoolmaster, hardly an
unusual course of action, but this time the schoolmaster, with the
support of the vicar, had refused to budge, and, after a two-year
stalemate, the bishop had weighed in. Using his power as a Justice
of the Peace, he sent thirteen of the Eighteen Men to prison, accus-
ing them of refusing to obey *his* order to keep the schoolmaster in
place, and failing to look after the money effectively. The bishop
and vicar appear to have been trying to get their hands on the
endowment money too, so the parishioners swiftly sent a petition to
the crown under the suitably alarming heading of 'Misemployment
of Charity Money'.

The commissioners were the great and good of the Lake District,†
so the absence of Francis Radcliffe, Sir George and Lady Radcliffe's
heir, born in the Parish, is notable. While he had married a rich
Northumberland heiress[11] and spent much time away from the

---

* In 1629 things had not much improved, Bishop White's visitation record-
ing 'never a doctor of divinitie nor advocate, but eleven or twelve licensed
preachers, three or four bachelors of Divinitie and eight double beneficed men'.
Bouch, *Prelates and People*, p. 254.
† Sir William Hutton of Hutton Hall, John Le Fleming of Rydal Hall, Henry
Blencowe of Blencowe Hall, John Lowther of Lowther Hall and George
Fletcher of Tallentire.

Parish, Francis had also been punished three times for being a recusant (a practising Roman Catholic who illegally refused to attend the services of the Church of England) both in Northumberland, where he largely built Dilston Tower, and on 'the Isle'. And in 1616 he was in serious trouble again, which provides the most likely explanation for his absence. For when he became the first Radcliffe/Derwentwater to be made a baronet, in 1620, his official style was 'Francis Radcliff of Darwent Water, co Cumberland, Esq'.[12]

Accompanying the commissioners was a jury of 'Good and lawful men of the said County of Cumberland', including a Radcliffe, a Williamson, a Wrenne and two Graves – suitable names for the cause of the Eighteen Men, who themselves included five men with the same surnames. Although this doubling up from the more successful tenant families was far from unusual, the bishop and the vicar must have blenched. And the subsequent 1616 decree, having described how both bishop and vicar had 'pretended to have the power of placing the master',[13] referred back to the 1571 decree and made it quite clear to them both that they had no power whatsoever over either the schoolmaster or the school funds; nor would they have in the future. The judgment went even further, comprehensively forbidding any and all ecclesiastical interference with running the school or its monies.* This was startling as, by the mid-sixteenth century, it is generally said that no one could teach in the Carlisle diocese without authority from the bishop.

Then, in another seemingly radical change from the old decree, with its careful list of the powerful who should be part of the appointment process, a process in which the vicar was to have the casting vote, the commission ruled that neither vicar nor bishop possessed 'any power or authority in the election of the said eighteen men'. While this judgment may appear to be intended to buttress the independence of the Eighteen Men, it appears that the old decree had already lost its force, as the jurors swore that 'by an ancient custom' eighteen men were yearly elected by '...the preceeding eighteen

---

* Here is the width of the decree's prohibitions: 'The Bishoppe and ordinarie of the Diocesse, his Commissary nor Chancellor nor anie other Eclesiasticall Ministers have not of right had anie other interest power or authoritie' over running the school, other than that of the laws of the realm.

sworne men'. So, it seems Crosthwaite's select vestry had again become a self-perpetuating oligarchy, and had effectively defended that position. Also, the job of the 'taskers' was fully spelled out for the first time: once appointed by the Eighteen Men (probably annually), they were to collect the fire tax due throughout the Parish – and now they were also to take an oath on Ascension Day.

The fire tax is another sign of the efficiency of the Eighteen Men's governance, in place nearly a century before the government's imposition of a hearth tax in 1662,[14] and the school stock was an acceptable £148 2s. 3½d.[15] But something murky seems to have been going on again behind the scenes and several well-known men were to repay the money in their charge by the next Easter. The commission also attempted to tidy up behaviour by ordering receipts for all rent charges. Nevertheless, it was a thoroughly Cumbrian ruling, supportive of education and clear about, indeed enhancing, the independent rights and powers of the Eighteen Sworn Men.

The great post-Reformation redistribution of lands had rumbled on. In Borrowdale, the Grahams had, intelligently or desperately, sold their Fountains land (primarily Watendlath and Stonethwaite) to Sir Wilfrid Lawson of Isel before their enforced Irish exodus; an exodus that Lawson had been in charge of, as the convener of the Royal Commission governing the border in 1606. Then, after James I sold all of the Borrowdale Furness land to two London entrepreneurs[16] seven years later, Sir Wilfrid had quickly bought Seathwaite from them.[17] The next year, 1614, he bought St Herbert's Island from the Percys and when, that November, the Londoners sold all the rest of their land to thirty-eight named farmers, Lawson headed the list recorded in the Great Deed of Borrowdale – most of the others coming from upper Borrowdale. The family would now thread through the story of the Parish right up to the end of the nineteenth century.*

The main purchasers of the lands affecting the wadd mines were Charles Hudson from Borrowdale, William Lamplugh, from nearby

---

* Sir Wilfrid's landholdings in Cumberland were largely due to his marriage. The Leighs, long of Isel, had done particularly well out of the Reformation grab for land and were cousins of one of the two bullying commissioners. Thomas Leigh had left the estate to his wife, who, upon his death, married Wilfrid, and she, in turn, left her estate to him.

local gentry, Jonas Verdon and Daniel Hechstatter of Rosthwaite,* whose mining lease was entirely unaffected.[18] Then the Borrowdale manor had been added to the sale, for which the Great Deed laid out a utopian future hierarchy 'for the apportionable benefit of themselves and the rest of the tenants of the Manor'.[19] The deed also included the misleading heading of 'Freeholders of Borrowdale', to whom it equally misleadingly conveyed all 'Wastes, commons, stinted pastures...' and 'all the Court's perquisites, demesne lands ... services of court ... each tenant according to his share, acting jointly for all the tenants mutual benefit'.

At one level the Great Deed can be read as a wish list, the seigneurial side of the agreement – as had been the case in the Customs of Borrowdale of 1583 – again evincing a lack of local knowledge. The 'freeholders' had misled themselves about both their status and their rights, which, in turn, led to historians misinterpreting the Borrowdale tenancies for over 300 years.† In fact, a later Wilfrid Lawson (Sir Wilfrid's great-nephew), whose local authority underwent a rapid increase during the Commonwealth, successfully used his power to become de facto (even before the Civil War) and, after a time, de jure, their Lord of the Manor. And, despite their aspirations, the tenants' efforts, in the cold light of reality, were to be directed merely at hedging his power, by having fixed rather than arbitrary fines. They fought and went to law, but even in this they failed.‡

In 1615, the Williamsons sold Monk Hall estate to Agnes Le Fleming of Rydal and Coniston, who used the name of her son, John, then head of the family, on the deeds. Between them they made three separate purchases, of Monk Hall, Edmund Mill etc,§

* Another thirty-two were minorly involved.

† The bound Court Books of the Lawsons' manor start in 1716 and were only released to scrutiny in the last quarter of the twentieth century. Johnson, 'Borrowdale, its land tenure', p. 66.

‡ The Lawsons' 1656 records show 'several suits depending in the High Court of Westminster and in the Court of Chancery of Oliver Lord Protector' on the issue.

§ The name may explain the purchase, as a generation earlier a Thomas Fleming had married Mabel, Edmund Radcliff of 'Munckhall's' daughter, although neither of their children had lived long enough to inherit. Fleming, *The Memoirs of Sir Daniel Fleming*, p. 46.

'divers tenements in Brathmyre in the Parish of Crossthwaite' and then more lands and tenements within the Parish of Crosthwaite.[20] The eight tenements farmed within the Brathmyre manor to provide the salary of the chantry priest just before the Reformation had fallen to the king after Edward VI proscribed the chantries. They were then redistributed via a London scrivener, Thomas Brende,[21] and an old deed seen by the lawyer Joseph Broatch at the beginning of the last century, which included a reference to some land 'at Bristow Hill within the manor of Brathmyre', then referred to the 'Homage Jury at the Manor Court holden at Monk Hall, Keswick, Daniel Fleming,[22] Lord'.[23]

So the Le Flemings had also purchased the obscure Brathmyre manor, a manor virtually never mentioned. However the tenants of the original Brathmyre chantry lands included two Radcliffes, two Williamsons and two Jacksons[24] (see page 92), so it seems likely that some of the original Monk Hall estate – that is, the ancient Fountains land sold to and by John Williamson – was co-terminus with the manor.

Agnes and John then executed another flurry of Parish land purchases, in the midst of which, in 1619 John[25] conveyed Monk Hall to Agnes for life and entailed it for his younger brother Daniel, his son William and their heirs, to whom, in due course, the main estate also fell.* Upon his marriage to Alice Kirkby, in 1632, William had 'made Monk Hall habitable',[26] considerably improving the house: vestiges of 'a moat and a square building' remaining on view a hundred and fifty years later, when the house had reverted to a 'small farmhouse'.[27] And the couple moved in with their son, another Daniel, who was baptised at Crosthwaite just a few days later, in July 1634. In all four Le Fleming brothers were christened at Crosthwaite and Daniel went to the grammar school,[28] 'first under Mr Wheelright and then under Mr Radcliff'. In 1640 the family moved away to Skirwith-Hall in Kirkland, until

---

* Upon the deaths of Agnus and John, in 1633, the main Estate had gone to John's fourteen-year-old son, William, who died before he reached his majority, leaving his two sisters extremely rich, 'being worth above £10,000 apiece' (Fleming, *The Memoirs of Sir Daniel Fleming*, p. 66) and the estate reverted to the other William, son of Daniel.

the whole Estate came through, although they continued to receive the tithe of ten marks from the vicar of Crosthwaite previously due to the monks.[29]

The original Monk Hall estate lay mostly in the township of Great Crosthwaite[30] and, while the precise details of its expansion may be difficult to decipher,* the extent of the Le Flemings's Monk Hall Estate, by Daniel the younger's majority, is both clear and significant. Spreading out to the west from the original Fountains land in the immediate vicinity of Monk Hall (where much of the land, including Bristow Hill,† surrounded St Kentigern's) the Estate incorporated High Hill and the Howrahs; one of Southey's favourite places, where looking at the church, with Skiddaw lit by a midsummer sunset, he contemplated the weight of time and eternity. The bulk of the new land was north of the Greta however, running southeast from Monk Hall. It covered what is now upper and lower Fitz Park, the old Station Hotel, and two hilly fields north of the station.[31] In the northwest it incorporated a small field in John Williamson's Millbeck Hall estate called 'Chantry Close', which also provided income for the chantry.[32] This Estate would remain with the Le Fleming family, virtually unchanged, until the last quarter of the nineteenth century.

*

When James I came to the throne in 1603, prices were around four and a half times as high as they had been in 1500, while Cumberland and Westmorland became the two poorest counties of seventeenth-century England. For the Parish, the first quarter of the century was particularly tough – in many ways. After the ravages caused by the mining industry, there was little wood left, and parishioners, like many throughout the Lake District, were reported as using 'Peats, Turffe, Heath, Furres, Broome, and such like fuell for firing, where they may be gotten, yea, and Neats‡ dung'.[33] Only

---

* When Monk Hall was sold in the nineteenth century, to make way for a cottage hospital for Keswick, no archaeological or antiquarian work was done.
† On which the vicarage sits.
‡ Ox or cow dung.

Wythburn had been exempt. Typically passing a by-law in 1606 that allowed the tenants to fell any underwood they chose outside the head dyke, this was rigidly upheld.[34] In 1622, with prices for wool at their lowest for fifty years, and the price of corn still high across the North – and thought 'like to increase as the year growes on' – hunger stalked the Parish. A year later another great mortality crisis struck, this time afflicting only the Northwest of England. Grim to relate, burials at St Kentigern's were at almost as frightening a level as in 1597, rising by five times to 256.[35]

During those years the parishioners had also been in a very different fight for their lives. In 1620, King James had proclaimed that crown estates would be let for 'Fine, or improvement of rent, by indenture onely',[36] an act later described by Dr Richard Burn, co-author with Joseph Nicolson of the first history of Cumberland and Westmorland, as 'one of the most flagrant exertions of despotism that is to be met with in English History'.[37] And given the extent of crown land there after the Reformation, this could have spelt the death knell for hereditary tenancies, the key to the unique culture of the Lake District and the Parish.

For the first time, different groups of tenants began to organise together to fight back, and in 1623 there was a surprising and extremely positive change in Castlerigg and Derwentwater. Sir Edward Radcliffe, who had inherited the estate following the death of his father, Francis, in 1620, was to have an energetic first ten years buying much new land – most significantly for his estate, the mining manor of Alston in northeast Cumberland.[38] Presumably unconvinced by the king's attempts to outlaw hereditary tenants, and only too aware of the tension and disturbance caused by the manors' recent exercise of their arbitrary rights – or perhaps simply because he did not want unnecessary distractions – Sir Edward decided to offer his tenants a deal.

In the indenture of 1623 he 'declared, covenanted, concluded, condescended and fully agreed ... for a final end to all controversies'[39] to accept the fixed ancient rent, and four times that sum upon the death of the lord or the tenant in exchange for £1,441. The fines would be 'constant ... for ever' and were purchased by sixty-three named tenants who raised the money between them, for which their descendants owed them much thanks.* This was an unusual move for the seventeenth century, and an important one.[40] The Victorians would call it 'enfranchisement', which it was emphatically not, for many feudal obligations remained. For instance, the more prosperous tenants were to provide two horses 'between Mayday and the Feast of St Andrew the Apostle to carry corn, peat and hay' within a 12-mile radius of his land. And the vast majority of the manor's tenants owed an annual hen, sometimes on demand, sometimes on a specified date.

Sir Edward and his two brothers had made a generous deal. But the actions of the sixty-three tenants, who had paid an average of around £23 each, were notably brave, for in 1623† there was little evidence that King James would fail to get his way and eventually abolish all hereditary tenancy on Cumbrian crown land, which would have had untold consequences. That he did not was partly due to his death but largely due to a remarkable, self-funded, seven-year fight by the tenants in Kendal. Originally, they had been much encouraged by a local vicar who declared 'That, having peaceably enjoyed their tenements so long, it would be hard that some greedy eagle or devouring vulture should violently pull them out to miseries'.[41] This was a somewhat dangerous attack, as it could be argued that he was describing the king, and the tenants decided it was safer to attack landlords generally. A play performed at Kendal Castle raucously took up the cudgels: 'And when our ancient liberties are gone / They'll puke and poole and peele us to the bone.'[42]

Eventually, his lawyers having compiled a list of the tenants' more dramatic attacks, the king instructed the Star Chamber, the very heart of government, to sue them for libel and incitement to violence. The tenants may have been nervous about the tone of their

---

* It is impossible at this distance to equate this fairly with the 1583 Borrowdale one year of current rent, but the fact that it was worth paying a considerable sum to achieve this end emphasises the utopian aspect of the Borrowdale agreement.

† Without evidence, motives are impossible to attribute, but there remains a possibility that both the Derwentwaters *and* their tenants, with John Bankes's help, consciously undertook the deal to avoid the potential damage to the tenants from the king's actions.

Remonstrance against the landlords – by unjustly turning them into 'tenants at will', their landlords intended to 'pull their skins over their ears, and bray their bones in a mortar, to enrich them ...' – but they stood their ground.[43] And once a significant witness – an aristocratic landowner's seventy-five-year-old steward – had submitted that inheritable customary tenure did indeed precede the practice of border service,[44] the case moved to the King's Bench.

There, in 1625, just after James's death, the judges, loath to create unnecessary disturbance in still-troubled times, finally ruled – in the interests of 'absolute peace' – that the tenants had customary estates of inheritance. The Kendal tenants had saved* the statesmen. This was the moment when a new strong cultural dividing line was drawn between the Northeast and the Northwest of England. While some customary tenants remained in the lands belonging to the Bishop of Durham in County Durham and Yorkshire, all the Northumberland tenants lost whatever heredi-tary claim they had had. Thus, the late eighteenth-century romance with 'statesmen' was purely focused on the counties of Cumberland and Westmorland.[45]

One effect of the new certainty was to strengthen the confi-dence of the Eighteen Men. The corn tithes from the Parish had long been kept by the crown, acting as rector, but Charles I sold them on to some London merchants who made a quick profit[46] by selling them on 'to certain parishioners of Crosthwaite as trust-ees'†,almost definitely the Eighteen Men. They, in turn, parcelled the corn tithes up 'for the convenience of selling them to each person who was able and willing to purchase his own tithes' and able to fulfil the covenant that he and his heirs would 'forever thereafter... keep in good and sufficient repair his or their shares of the chancel of the church'. This necessary provision would in due course be a cause of much trouble; but the whole exercise was a powerful expansion of the role of the Eighteen Men, as they con-tinued to try to maintain order.

---

* Although Charles I reversed the Star Chamber's position on tenancies in 1639, the Commonwealth soon swung back to the 1625 position, and the reinstatement of hereditary tenancies was later confirmed by Charles II.
† Subject to an annual fee – farm rent payable forever of £14 6s. 8d.

The Parish witnessed other positive developments at this time too. 'Clay daubins' had gradually begun to take over from the peasant huts of the early Middle Ages. The main timbers were suitably shaped dried oak branches, braced together in pairs into a cruck shape, with cross beams at the thin ends to create the required strength, and the building of these new houses was a communal, neighbourly performance that took at most two days. On the appointed day, neighbours and friends, bringing their own tools and food, dug, cut and mixed the clay and straw material to create the walls (in many cases using stone rubble instead) and 'dabbed' or 'daubed' it on. The early versions of these houses maintained the old medieval central hearth, but gable-end fireplaces were increasingly favoured. The new owners feasted their friends and workmen, and everyone danced on the new clay floor to beat it in, as celebrated by 'the Cumberland Bard' Robert Anderson:[47]

> We went owre to Deavie's clay daubin,
> An' faith, a rare caper we had,
> Wid eatin, an drinkin, an dancing,
> An rwoarin and singin leyke mad.

Also, the Newlands mines provided employment again. They had come to a standstill by 1597 for want of funds, but in 1604 James I had granted a new charter to the Keswick Company, its directors including Daniel Hechstetter's two sons, Emmanuel and Daniel. Sir Francis Radcliffe, Sir George's son, had done far better than his father, and signed up a twenty-one-year lease for £63 6s. 8d. for his Derwentwater land housing Brigham Forge.[48] While the operation never approached the boom conditions of its early years, it was reported at the beginning of the century that 'about 500 persons dwelling near about the works are enriched by this means to the great benefit of the country'.[49]

At the wadd mines, John Bankes was on his way to becoming their leading owner. Born in 1589 to a father of some local standing,[*] Bankes was one of the grammar school's most remarkable

---

[*] Married to the granddaughter of a Hassell. *Oxford Dictionary of Biography*.

students. A contemporary description had him being 'of honest parents, who perceiving him judicious and industrious, bestowed good breeding on him in Gray's Inn, in the hope he should attain preferment, wherein they were not deceived'.[50] As a lawyer, Bankes initially worked mainly in the North of England, often for Lord William Howard of Naworth.[51] He would certainly have had better negotiating resources than anyone else in the Derwentwater manor and may well have broached the subject of arbitrary fines with one of the Derwentwaters. And, since he was known to be dubious about any legal rights attaching to border service,[52] he would have been sure to have advised his old neighbours to accept Sir Edward's 1623 offer.

Some fifteenth-century Bankes family grants from the crown of 'the black lead mine' at Borrowdale had been renewed under the seal of James I.[53] Their origin is doubly startling: that a Parish customary tenant then had the wealth and desire to have purchased the rights, and that either the crown or Furness Abbey allowed it.[54] The year before the 'enfranchisement', John and his Hechstetter father-in-law decided to increase their holdings by buying the Lamplugh and most of the Hudson Borrowdale land connected to the wadd mine, all purchased at the Great Deed.* And, although John was to become a southern MP in 1624, soon making his name as a parliamentarian, the very next year he took over half his brother-in-law's share.

The Hechstetters were gradually selling out, and by 1634 most of their Keswick affairs had been wound up, their surname no longer ever again to grace the list of the Eighteen Men.[55] Bankes had become one of a group that took over their mining lease and even though his portion seems to have been a quarter at that stage, the Bankes family were immediately treated as pre-eminent and[†] in 1638, upon the death of one of the early shareholders, Bankes purchased his holdings, to bring the family proportion of the lease up to 50 per cent.

---

* Charles Hudson and William Lamplugh were the two other 'gentlemen' besides Lawson listed in the Great Deed of Borrowdale.
† Initially, his most important co-shareholder remained Charles Hudson from Borrowdale, despite the Bankes's purchase of much of his land.

For 'the free-holders' of the Great Deed, the whole exercise must have been extremely frustrating. One exemption to the sale had been recorded in the Deed – 'the Wadholes on Seatoller Common and elsewhere in the Manor's commons and wastes and the power to work the same',[56] presumably due to the Bankes family grants. But why would those with grazing rights on Seatoller Common, home of the high 'wad-hole' where the workings were at this period, not be due royalties or compensation of some sort? The legal answer lies in a 1597 judgment that merely gave 'the freehold-ers'[57] personal-use rights for the wadd. Some of the tenants sensibly decided to accept the status quo, soon buying into the 1632 lease for a somewhat hopeful 3,000 years.[58] Others grumbled and eventually became litigious, and the issue rumbled on, unsettled, until the last quarter of the eighteenth century, when it appears that the Bankes family effectively bought the tenants off.

Civil war

Charles I's accession in 1625 was the most settled for some 200 years. But the seeds of future conflict were already planted in the difference between the king's interpretation of Anglicanism, based on what he saw as the divine right of kings, and the aspirations of the growing middle class who were beginning to dominate Parliament.

When, four years after his accession, King Charles began his eleven-year period of rule without Parliament, Bankes staunchly supported him. By 1634 he had become Attorney-General, and his lawyer's classic three-day-long argument in support of the king's right to raise ship money in times of danger (thus avoiding the need to recall Parliament) had relied entirely on historical precedent.[59] This was a good legal argument, but also perhaps reflected his early experience in the Parish of the validity of 'ancient custom'. There, an obligatory mandate had been sent to the vicar[60] and the eighteen jurors in 1637, ordering the tenants who farmed the endowed school lands to provide some real collateral to prove they could afford to pay the rent. There may have been other concerns too, as the mandate also called for instant adherence to each and every ruling of the 1616 decree 'under a penalty of £50', a very substantial amount of money.

However, the change from 'men' to 'jurors' in describing the Eighteen Men reinforces both the sense that they did their best to sort out Parish squabbles without going to court and the closeness of their relationship with the courts. Financial management continued to tighten up and public peace over school issues would now prevail for more than a hundred years. The country was not to be so lucky, although Bankes consistently tried to mediate between king and Parliament. He also became extremely rich, thought to earn an extraordinary £10,000 a year,[61] and had bought the Corfe Castle estate in Dorset in 1635.*

Three years after Bankes's great speech, rioting erupted in Scotland when King Charles tried to introduce a new Book of Common Prayer to the Scottish church. His father, James, had successfully controlled the General Assembly in Scotland and the episcopacy had returned north of the border; Charles had been crowned in Edinburgh with full Anglican rites. Now innumerable Scots signed a covenant in support of their reformed religion and in 1638 a General Assembly was held for the first time in twenty years. Both prayer book and bishops were outlawed, resulting in 'the example par excellence of a church exercising discipline in society'.[62] By the middle of the century, 'the Scottish clergy were to become responsible for one of the most statistically intense witch persecutions in Europe, introducing sleep deprivation as a form of questioning, as they strove to maintain their iron rod of control over behaviour'.[63]

When civil war loomed in January 1642, Bankes, now Chief Justice of the Common Pleas (and still believing that 'if we should have civile wars it would make us a miserable people'),[64] stayed in London after the king had left. Parliament, unusually, endorsed him, as they continued to when he joined the king in York. As the war took hold, Bankes remained in post, accepted by Parliament, while his wife Mary, at Corfe Castle, was attacked by the

* His son would later rebuild the wonderful house of Kingston Lacy nearby.

Parliamentary forces. Supported initially only by her daughters, her servants and a force of five men, she withstood two famous sieges, heaving stones and hot embers from the battlements and, it is said, managing to kill and wound more than a hundred men. The next year Sir John's property was seized 'even to his books',* but he continued to act as the king's Chief Justice, at Oxford, until his death in December 1644.

Cumbria had been broadly royalist at the start of the war. Wilfrid Lawson (whose father had inherited Isel) had been knighted, aged thirty-one, in 1641 and in the spring of 1642 had been collecting voluntary contributions for the king. But once the parliamentary and Scottish troops had combined and taken York in 1644, Sir Thomas Glennam, its governor, retreated to Carlisle, and Sir Wilfrid took 'a rascall route'[65] and became a parliamentary colonel, leading the attack on Carlisle – while his father, at Isel, continued to send money to the king.[66]

With the early help of provisioning from the royalist gentry and clergy in the area, Glennam defended the city for eight months in one of the most terrible sieges in English history. The garrison lived off horsemeat, then cats, dogs and rats;[67] the cathedral plate was melted into coin; and even the city charter was sold to make clothing.[68] When Carlisle finally capitulated, after the Royalists were defeated at Naseby in June 1645, the heroism of its inhabitants was acknowledged by a surrender, 'upon as honourable conditions as any that were given'.[69] Nevertheless, the Puritan impulses of the Parliamentarians were soon in evidence, as the chapter house and six bays of the cathedral nave were demolished.

Even before the king's defeat, Sir Edward Radcliffe[†] had been much harried, having to pay fines for cleaving to his Catholic faith. Still legally described as 'Sir Edward Radclyffe of the Isle of Derwentwater',[70] he had had to borrow £1,200 from his wealthy wife 'at my house in Cumberland ... in my great nesassatye', in 1642.[71] Lord's Island,[‡] then, was staunchly royalist in the war,

* Bankes and three other judges had ruled that some members of both Houses of Parliament were guilty of high treason.
† Like his father before him.
‡ Islands apparently seen as a relatively safe space to live in times of war.

while just a few wavelets further south, St Herbert's Island, under Sir Wilfrid Lawson, was staunchly parliamentarian and was used as an ammunition dump. Disturbance threatened to ruffle the waters of the lake after a quixotic midnight ride by one of the defenders of Carlisle Castle.[72] He had been expecting to be given access to St Herbert's Island in order to blow up the ammunition dump, but on arrival at Derwentwater's southwestern shore, at the foot of Catbells, he found all the boats on the lake drawn up on the island. He had been let down, and his noisy demands for surrender were silenced by hoots of derisive laughter echoing over the water.

Lawson allowed himself time away from the siege at Easter 1645 to join in taking Lord's Island and attempting to demolish the Derwentwater home.[73] While still described in a legal document in 1653 as 'a mansion', it was certainly in ruins by 1707,[74] and local tradition has it that the site was twice plundered for stone to build Keswick's moot hall. One significant local royalist damaged, the parliamentary colonel moved on, via Langstrath and the high fells, to damage the other, plundering the Le Flemings's Rydal Hall, which was probably tenanted. William Fleming was living at Coningstone Hall, having been heavily fined for fighting for the king, and Daniel was just eleven. By midsummer Lawson was serving on a significant parliamentary committee and, according to an opponent, levied great sums of unauthorised money, imprisoned those who would not comply, and subsequently kept all the money for himself and his colleagues.[75]

In the wider world, the king, following a further series of royalist defeats, was imprisoned, the Puritans appearing to be unequivocally in charge. But in 1648, after Scottish Presbyterian alarm that Charles's imprisonment would result in power for the religious 'independents' they abhorred, a deal was done, and a 15,000-strong army rose for the king in Scotland. In April, in a brief flurry of successful campaigning, the Royalists regained Carlisle and, in August, laid siege to Cockermouth Castle, the solitary parliamentary stronghold in the district, destroying the western part of it. But within a month their fire was doused as all the royalist castles in the region were razed. Carlisle, one of the last two royalist cities of England to hold out, finally surrendered in October.

In the Parish, the destruction of the mines and the great Elizabethan forge of Brigham has always been regarded as the work of the Roundheads.[76] By 1671 Sir Daniel Fleming, looking at the ruins of the forge, was lamenting that 'tho these smelting houses within memory were so numerous as this looked like a little towne yet now there is not one house standing'.[77] All that was left of the prodigious German industry on Vicar's Island was a 'little ruined house'[78] too. While there remains no contemporary evidence of the sacking,[79] the passage of parliamentary troops from Penrith to Cockermouth in 1648 makes it more than likely, as do the several leaden musket balls found embedded in the old 4-inch oak door of St Kentigern's, and the defaced faces and mutilations of the Radcliffe tombs. In 1787 James Clarke stated[80] that at the sacking most of the miners were either killed or drafted into Oliver Cromwell's army. Whether or not this is true, it must have been a particularly grim time for the people of the Parish.

The Commonwealth

The war over, on Tuesday, 30 January 1649, King Charles was executed. The start of the Commonwealth, England's eleven-year experiment in republican government, caused little excitement in the Parish. The English parishes were divided into a loose federation of various sects, predominantly Independents and English Presbyterians, involving a massive reorganisation,[81] but it was not until 1653 that the 'Commissioners for Propagating the Gospel in the Four Northern Counties'[82] appointed James Cave, pastor of the Keswick Congregational Church, as an itinerant preacher at the Crosthwaite chapelries.[83] In contrast with the schoolmaster's annual pay of £12 12s., Cave received an exorbitant salary of £104, the money to be collected from various rents.[84] An end was announced to services for marriage and baptism, and for the next four years Justices of the Peace officiated for local births, marriages and burials.*

* However, in some circles, after the judicial marriage, the Book of Common Prayer was later used in well-attended drawing rooms. See Fleming, *The Memoirs of Sir Daniel Fleming*, p. 74.

A year earlier Sir Edward had forfeited his estates to the Commonwealth, for the treasonable offence of being both Catholic and royalist. However, since he had placed all his estates in trust, all that could be sold off was his life interest. Nevertheless, he was the recipient of an outburst of local sympathy, being described forever afterwards as 'loyal Sir Edward'. Then, in 1654, the portentously named Committee for Ejecting Scandalous, Ignorant and Insufficient Ministers and Schoolmasters in the Four Northern Counties at Penrith, removed twenty-one clergy from the Carlisle diocese. But at Great Crosthwaite the change of vicar seems to have arisen from natural causes when the second post-Reformation Radcliffe vicar was appointed that year, and the Eighteen Men gave refuge to the evicted vicar of Cockermouth, Robert Rickerby, by appointing him schoolmaster.

They can also be witnessed, along with the churchwardens, ordering the sexual segregation in the church.[85] The right to a pew was purchased, and could be sold or bequeathed, in the customary way, but at Crosthwaite rights were needed in two sections, 'the women's forme' and 'the man's forme'. This was quite a common Lake District practice, one which would surprise Wordsworth, but a contemporary justification claims that Noah's Ark set the precedent: 'There is a tradition that as soon as ever the day began to break' Noah and his sons would recite prayers to the Lord, while 'the women answered from another part of the Ark, Amen, Lord.'[86] Lord, Amen.

However, it must have been yet another exhausting and bewildering period, and from it emerged the Quaker George Fox. A weaver's son and a religious genius, '[Fox] took most delight in sheep, so he was very skilful with them: an employment that very much suited his mind in several respects, both for its innocency and solitude'.[87] And 'In a few years [he] was almost universally accepted as the sovereign pontiff of Cumberland' – or, more accurately, Cumbria, the birthplace of the Quakers.

Fox came to Cumberland in 1653, the same year as James Cave, fulfilling a vision experienced a year earlier on Pendle Hill in Lancashire. His revolutionary message, the last and strongest trumpet of a radical English religious tradition, was that of the early disciples, that the power of the Lord was over all and, once experienced, would produce love and truth. Universities, then, were irrelevant, as were the 'steeple houses', falsely built to contain the word, and much of the business of the courts. Fox would make no oath. The Quakers followed Christ's teaching in the Sermon on the Mount: 'Let your communication be, Yea, yea; Nay, nay: for whatsoever is more than these cometh of evil.' Their word was to be relied upon, unlike the frequently dishonest speech they heard under oath.

For the Quakers, since man responded to God internally and directly and found his own truth, even the Scriptures were secondary to direct communication with the Word that was 'in the beginning' (a serious heresy at a time of scriptural fundamentalism). Responding to God involved courage and moral strength, qualities Fox had in spades. In the middle of 1653, his ideas had seemed to coincide with those of a majority of the Commonwealth's most revolutionary Parliament, which, at that levelling moment, not only favoured abolishing tithes,* but also did consider abolishing universities – a terrifyingly authoritarian idea to modern sensibilities. But for a man such as Fox, who believed everyone could preach the word of God, a university education for preachers was as redundant as an established church.

However, Fox was too late, as a more pragmatic approach quickly became dominant in Parliament – how, for instance, was state religion to be financed? – and government moved away from its earlier positions. The Quakers were persecuted because they were true revolutionaries in an age in which the English Revolution was rowing hard back to shore.

Fox's message of the supremacy of a direct relationship with God was perfectly made for those who disliked the authoritarian organisation of the Commonwealth, with its tearing down of maypoles in spring ceremonies and its abolition of Christmas on the grounds that it had no biblical justification. It was made too for the hill farmer: anti-establishment, relying on individual

---

* Several local Cumberland priests, desperate not to lose their tithes, proved not to be above making up scandals about Fox to urge on the magistrates.

experience and judgment, but mindful of neighbours and, above all, doughty.

'Great threatenings',[88] Fox tells us, came out of Cumberland. And at his first great meeting in and around Brigham, Cockermouth's mother church, 'all the country people came in like unto a horse fair, and there came above a thousand people',[89] some from the Parish. Having exposed false Christian practice and teaching 'since the apostles' day', Fox writes, 'I did declare the word of life to them for about three hours and all was still, and quiet and satisfied.'[90]

Moving on to Carlisle, Fox was soon arrested by the magistrates for blasphemy and heresy, charges that, from his own descriptions, he had courted, with what, to a modern ear, sounds like an almost pathological absence of humility (although Carlyle's more benign description,[91] 'an enormous sacred self-confidence', may be a fairer reflection of the self-belief necessary for the missionary). Rumours spread that he would hang, an outcome supported by Sir Wilfrid Lawson, then High Sheriff. The gentry, 'great ladies and countesses', priests, and 'a company of bitter Scottish priests and Presbyterians, made up of envy and malice',[92] flocked to question Fox at the gaoler's house. Then, as the assize court moved on, he was thrown into the dungeons with the reivers who were 'exceeding lousy ... one woman almost eaten alive by lice'.[93] The gaoler 'beat Friends and friendly people ... as if he had been beating a pack of wool'.[94] Fox was beaten too, when he refused to dance before a fiddler who was brought in to bait the preacher but found himself drowned out by Fox loudly singing for the Lord.[95]

Alarmed by the prospect of a young man being put to death for his religious beliefs, MPs wrote to Lawson and the magistrates, but by that time Fox had already been released. As he made his way from Caldbeck to Greystoke, his lieutenant, William Dewsbury, 'declared truth at Portingskell', close to Crosthwaite church. For Fox would write, with evident satisfaction, 'And about this time many of the steeple houses were empty, for such multitudes of people came to Christ's free teaching and knew their bodies the temple of God.'[96]

Prophecy was rampant during the Commonwealth generally, thanks to the encouragement of private revelation, its association with radicalism long apparent. But the ordinary parishioner was still looking for the usual protection against animal and human disease. It may be that the espousal of Quakerism locally – both in the Parish and more widely in Cumberland – was driven by the feeling that, exorcism having long since been flung on the scrapheap, direct communication with God might have the strength to protect them.

The Commonwealth was a time of moral austerity and self-denial. Fasting, which had been forbidden in 1604 unless authorised by a bishop, became a necessary accompaniment to petitionary prayer; Fasts and Days of Humiliation frequently ordered by the government at times of crisis. Breaking the daily pattern of labour to enjoy a 'good do' amid the hard work of the agricultural cycles was now dangerous; everything might be being observed and reported. And many of the Puritan sects felt that they were living at the climax of human history, awaiting the Second Coming. It was the *heat* of the varieties of Puritanism that must have shocked.

So, when Oliver Cromwell, the first man to have defeated both Scotland and Ireland,[*] died in 1658, Parliament squabbled with the army and – in the apparent absence of strong governance – the people's dislike of the strait-laced reforms of the various Puritan administrations boiled over. With the Restoration of the monarchy two years later, the Anglican Church, the episcopacy (in Scotland too), maypoles and Christmas all returned without a drop of blood being spilt. The ejected vicars went back to their livings, and most of their supplanters were removed.

At Keswick a five-man commission deposed the scandalously over-remunerated pastor James Cave, who, under the terms of the Five-Mile Act of 1665, which penalised Nonconformists, would be banned from the centre of the Parish (a banishment still marked today by a large stone on the Keswick–Grasmere road in St John's

---

[*] Incidentally giving an early boost to cattle droving down from Scotland as the border taxes had ceased.

in the Vale). George Larkham, the Commonwealth minister of Cockermouth, wrote angrily on 31 May 1660, 'Rex Carolus was proclaimed at Cockermouth, with great triumphing of many wicked men' – and was forcibly evicted.[97] The leader of the 'wicked men' was Daniel Fleming, now lord of the whole Le Fleming Estate, who was in Cockermouth at the time and, in his words, led a deputation of other gentlemen to 'proclaim in Person his Majesty most joyfully... on ye Market Day, in full market'.[98] Married to Barbara, the eldest daughter of Sir Henry Fletcher, Baronet of Hutton, the couple were living at Rydal, where they celebrated the Restoration with two raging bonfires outside the gates.

Crosthwaite's schoolmaster, Robert Rickerby, returned to his old living at Cockermouth and loyal Sir Edward resumed possession of his estates. All that had been sold by the treason trustees was returned,[99] but he was worn out by the time of the Restoration 'with the weights of care and the infirmities of age' and died three years later. With his son, he had successfully bought back his life interest in his estates, the family emerging in surprisingly good shape. His will bequeathed his wife some land, in consideration of her loan from Lord's Island in 1642, and made her his executor.[100] 'I having great reason to do so, and more than ordinary motives, especially for what at my motion and persuasion I got her to pass away her present right to ... lands in Yorkshire ... which, if she had denied, as many would, our whole state (as the times then were) had been in great hazard to have been lost.'*

In the words of the historian Diarmaid MacCulloch, the clergy were 'newly aggressive against Puritanism after their sufferings ... much more out of step with the continent-wide reformed ethos than they had been before the war'.[101] Cranmer's *Book of Common Prayer* was revamped again and now 'excluded many Protestants who before the civil war would have found a home within the national church'. In particular, the English Presbyterians were

---

* Further north in Cumberland, Charles Howard from Naworth, having 'conformed' to the Church of England and supported the Commonwealth, was appointed High Sheriff of Cumberland and bought Carlisle Castle the year after the execution of the king. Later he became Baron Dacre and Earl of Carlisle.

labelled Dissenters. So, while the vast majority of the country settled back happily into the Elizabethan church settlement, the foundations were laid, for the first time, for permanently organised nonconformity. Although the penal laws were less rigorously enforced after Charles II's Declaration of Indulgence of 1672, the die had been cast.

In the Carlisle diocese, the bishop found his churches to be in better condition than he had feared. And when George Fox (who had previously returned to Cumberland to proselytise and confirm in 1657) came back for the third and last time in 1663, he was courting some danger. Sir Daniel Fleming, 'one of the fiercest and most violent justices in persecuting Friends and sending his honest neighbours to prison for religion's sake',[102] was offering the vast sum of £5 for anyone who apprehended Fox – a good year's wages. He would hound Roman Catholics too. Sir Thomas Braithwaite, who had inherited the manor of Wythburn, would first receive a letter from the magistrate in 1667, desiring an account of all arms in his possession and requiring a vow to hold them for the king's service. A year later his rapier and carbine were seized by the constables,[103] as also, finally, was his land, his estate being sold to the extremely considerable Fletchers of Hutton Hall, Sir Daniel's in-laws.

Fox, however, avoided capture. In his last visit to the Parish he had 'a glorious precious meeting' at Derwentwater, where the wife of an old friend sent her apologies for her husband, whose horses were all employed 'upon some urgent occasion'.[104] Later he visited Hugh Tickell near Keswick and then went on to Legburthwaite to stay the night with Thomas Laythe (Leathes),[105] who was soon to be imprisoned for nine days for refusing to answer, on oath, a question about the payment of tithes. A year later, Hugh and Anthony Tickell were both excommunicated for the same offence.[106]

In all, the Quakers had had an enormous effect in the Northwest, but in the Parish it was a quickly diminishing one. In 1665 Hugh Tickell, 'once it pleased ye Lord to bestow worldly riches on him',[107] had built a Quaker meeting house in Keswick with his own money. In 1681 the diocese excommunicated five Roman Catholics and

twelve Quakers for non-attendance at church, a crime now theoretically involving a heavy fine or imprisonment. But by 1730 there
were only four Quaker families out of the five hundred families in
the Parish. And soon the Quaker meeting house at Keswick was
empty, becoming the premises for a new school for girls in 1820.

Parish Charity, Mortgages and the
Last of the Derwentwaters

C UMBERLAND HAD REMAINED extremely poor throughout
the Civil War and the Commonwealth. In 1657, the tax
assessment for the whole county had been £92 11s. 4d. –
exactly the same as that for the city of Exeter. In 1644, 50 per
cent* of households in the Langdale Valley had been exempt from
hearth tax[1] and Lake District pauperism remained a major factor
after the Restoration, with large numbers of landless. The threat
of reiving from the borders had, if anything, magnified, Charles II
passing an act 'preventing ... theft and rapine upon the Northern
Borders of England', as the activities of the 'lawless and disorderly
moss-troopers had increased since the time of the late unhappy
distractions'.[2] Elegantly put.

Since the Keswick mining boom was over, there was little to
exempt the town from this general poverty, although the leather
industry was making strides by the end of the century, when
a number of small businesses powered by the Greta began to
emerge too.[3] Only wadd had one of its high days and holidays;
new workings had produced well over a hundred tons of superior
wadd for a decade in the 1640s and 1650s and one of the two
big finds in the 1660s produced a magnificent 158 tons, with
the price rising fivefold since the first decade of the century, to

---

* I have not found any useful figures for the Parish; however, in similar terrain
at Hawkshead, just north of Coniston, the proportion of households exempt
from the tax was 33 per cent.

£100 a ton,[4] by 1671. By that time, a mutual policy had developed between merchant and mine. The wadd merchants, centred entirely in London and Newcastle (presumably because of their large ports), wanted to keep prices for the unique product high[5] as they developed their trade, and at their instigation – usually by contractual demands – a policy of planned mine closures was agreed. This proved to work well for the mine owners too, but for the Parish worker, of course, it made for intermittent employment.

The higher prices also meant that general theft – unknown earlier apart from the individual efforts of the 'Old Men'[6] – was becoming a serious problem* as local scavenging of the mine waste became a new way to make extra money on the side, a successful night's graphite-stealing being more financially rewarding than a week spent working on the farms. Locally, wadd was now used as a remedy for colic, and easing 'the Pain of Gravel, Stone and Strangury ... first they beat it small into meal, and then take as much of it, in white wine or ale, as will lie upon a sixpence ... It operates by urine, sweat and vomiting.'[7] Unpleasant. But, nationally, the profit from wadd still came primarily from casting weapons, and its later use as blacking became the curse of every housewife and housemaid keeping cast iron up to scratch.

In 1678, a national effort designed to help the wool trade was first recorded in the Parish. It had always been the custom to bury a deceased body in linen but now it became illegal to bury a corpse in anything other than wool, unless a penalty of £5 was paid to the church. This curious law remained in force until 1814 and had become necessary because of an earlier government prohibition on wool exports – a law energetically evaded in the North. No fewer than fifty-four riding officers (an early, itinerant form of customs officer) were sent to Northumberland, Durham and Cumberland to enforce the prohibition. While they managed to seize 105 packs of wool, a further 236 packs destined for export were said to have

---

* The Bankes family took the responsibility for the day-long journey from the mine to Keswick, after which its protection became the responsibility of the merchant.

been 'rescued from the officers' – evidence of a good northern sense of fair play![8]

Meanwhile, in the battle between customary tenants and landlords, fights about arbitrary fines raged again in the Percy lands. Matters came to a head with a confrontation that began in 1672, when there was talk of an arbitrary fine of *five* times the current rent,[9] more than double the usual Elizabethan sum. A year before the Percy issue came to court, a judicial ruling of 1677 established, as Queen Elizabeth had held, that the legal definition of a reasonable fine[10] was two years' improved value* and, perhaps with that in mind, when it did come to court, a 'reasonable' fine was again judged to be the only one that could be imposed.

The tenants of Braithwaite and Coledale also began to assert themselves. They winnowed as before 'the farmer under the necessity of waiting for a natural wind, sufficiently strong to blow the chaff from the grain... very often had to take it to some eminence at a distance, where the breeze was more certain'.[11] But, to Lady Percy's outrage, they now refused to take their oats and bigge (barley) to the Percy corn mills for grinding, thus avoiding the tax of a fourteenth share of the grain value. Twice she summoned the tenants to court, and twice the courts rebuffed her.[12]

Then, around 1682, new problems arose. The shortage of wood was still badly damaging the Parish, and again and again the records show statesmen asking to be allowed to use timber to make good a bridge, prop up a house, and so on.† Five tenants, who had jointly purchased or inherited the Braithwaite corn mill on a £10 p.a. repairing lease, were clearly desperate. 'Your petitioners have ... done all that within them lyes, to keep the said Millne in repair, but she, being soe old a building ... and become soe very crazy ... it is not possible to support her without re-building for that the walls will not admit of any patching or reparacon.' They

---

* Lord Nottingham's judgment, in which he said this had stood for over a hundred years and should continue to do so.

† Wythburn alone had no problems as, in 1606, an official ruling stated that the tenants could fell any underwood for firewood or other use as long as it was outside the head dyke.

went on to entreat the Somersets (Lady Elizabeth Percy, daughter
and heiress of the 11th Earl of Northumberland, had married the
Duke of Somerset in 1670) either to repair the mill or to give them
the money to do so themselves, 'so that she may not suffer from
want of timely care'.[13]

The right to cut peat in the manor wastes became much more
controlled throughout the Parish during this period. Turf was
not only the most commonly used fuel but was also used for the
undercover of thatched roofs, for mending walls and for the foundations of 'hay mows', where they prevented damp from rising
and spoiling the hay. Limits were now agreed by the courts and
the Eighteen Men on the time of year, usually May or June, when
digging was allowed; each manor creating its own legal start
date and the amount of time allowed, at times only a day.[14] And
turf-cutting rights were now allocated according to the size of the
individual landholding below the head dyke. The Eighteen Men
also appointed 'mosslookers' to move cutters away from areas that
lacked a really large peat bed, usually every seven years, while new
by-laws attempted to limit environmental damage, giving a chance
that 'the turbarrey may growe again'.[15]

Since the beds often lay a good distance from the farms, their
cutting involved dragging sledges through farmland on 'turfways'.
These paths to the large peat beds reached far back into history,*
as did the old Viking driftways leading to their sheep-heaf or
sheilings. Much augmented by the early hill farmers, some of the
turfways were now as wide as 40 feet.[16] The Tudor road maintenance system had taken firm hold in the Parish by the start of the
seventeenth century and a few paved and occasionally metalled
roads were added to the old network of mining roads† as, over
time, the continual use of pack-ponies had made frequently used
routes virtually impassable. Several of the passes in the Parish had
also been improved and some of them reconstructed.[17] The great

---

* Like the one crossing Threlkeld Common on the way to Ullswater, starting
from St John's in the Vale. Both driftways and the turf ways became meticulously delineated.
† In Newlands Valley and the high-country Mines-Royal roads from Grange
to Honister.

Sty Head Pass (with its branch road to Esk Hause) was rebuilt as a causeway – the only Lake District pack-pony route to be so built for virtually its entire distance.[18] For these passes *were* roads, the routes of shepherds and pedlars on foot and gentry and visitors,* and the old saw that the ancient routes were contoured with care for least exertion – unlike their modern variants – seems to hold good.[19] By the end of the seventeenth century the multiplicity of bridges and the difficulty of local terrain for road building and maintenance was acknowledged as it had been ruled that the Parish was to be exempted from the repair of public bridges, 'because they repair so many of their own'.[20]

Styhead Pass, still the only direct link between Borrowdale and Wasdale.
Scafell Pike on the left.

* Much of the Sty causeway has been obliterated by time, weather and the walker, but the narrow defile above the gate in the wall above Stockley Bridge (through which every modern walker's variant route has to pass and which, it is suggested, once provided a checkpoint for packhorses) gives a clear view of the old causey, which, with care, can be spotted right up to Styhead tarn, at times elevated and ditched on either side. The branch pony-track road, at the top of Sty, to Esk Hause also reveals bits of its causeyed past.

The opposite view; Styhead Pass from Scafell Pike.

Before the end of the century, bracken became one of the new crops carried over the rebuilt passes. Long used as winter bedding for stock, a substitute for straw as thatching material and at times for fuel, bracken had begun to be harvested as a cash crop, as the growing use of potash in glass and soap now made it a profitable export.* This created a new problem for the Parish. When was the best time to harvest bracken? The ideal time to burn for potash was early in the season; thatching needed midsummer stems, cut or pulled before they lost their rigidity, and bedding required the dry brown bracken of autumn. The Eighteen Men and the courts inevitably chose necessary domestic use over profitability and almost never favoured early cutting, and a profusion of new rules and regulations sprang up. With a few exceptions, one could only mow with a scythe 'on bracken day' – and for one day only per household.

Wythburn, as always on the side of the tenant subsistence farmers, passed a by-law in 1677 that unequivocally denied the

---

* The alkaline content of fern ash, a good source of potash, had long been used locally, mixed with tallow as an effective, if primitive, way of washing wool.

potash producer his best time. 'No tenant or occupier within Wythburn' might 'mow' for bedding or burning before Michaelmas (29 September), while 'pulling', selecting whole fronds for thatching, was forbidden until after St Bartholomew's Day (24 August), unless the bracken was needed to clothe a new building, in which case pulling was permitted throughout the season.[21] Braithwaite's ruling, in 1690, that the cottagers were to wait to cut until three days after they had declared their Michaelmas mowing season open – by which time the prime crop had probably already been cut – raises another issue. The rights of cottagers were being squeezed throughout the Parish. In 1686, Castlerigg tenants were even fined for passing on to cottagers peat that had been legally cut.

One antidote to the poverty and religious trauma of the times comes, perhaps surprisingly, from a register of deaths. It reads to the modern ear like a hoot of delight at the demise of Puritan earnestness, but that may be a misreading. It certainly bears witness not just to the strength of Lakeland legends and tradition but to the nature of life itself in seventeenth-century Lakeland.

STOCKLEY BRIDGE.

Stockley Bridge, in Borrowdale, by William Green. This typical packhorse bridge carried the track to Sty Head.

Deaths taken out of the Register of Lamplugh* from Janry ye
I 1658 to Janye ye I 1663.[22]

Of a five bar gate, stag hunting	4
Crost in love	1
Broke his neck robbing a hen roost	1
Knocked on ye head with a quart bottle	1
Frightened to death by fairies	1
Bewitched	7
Old woman drowned upon trial for witchcraft	3
Led into a horse pond by a will of the wisp	1
Overheat himself at a house warming	1
Vagrant beggars worried by Esq. Lamplugh's dog	2
By ye parson's bull	2
Etc. etc… Old age	57

It was well known that the fairies specialised in misleading travellers, and a man who lost his way would often plead that he had
been led astray by a will o' the wisp. But, by then, fairies were
mostly ascribed a role akin to that of school prefects. The Cavalier
poet Robert Herrick instructs and warns:[23]

> *Wash your pails and cleanse your dairies;*
> *Sluts are loathsome to the fairies…*

That doesn't sound too serious, but witchcraft was a different
matter. The number of court trials for witchcraft had dropped since
Elizabethan times, and the Lamplugh registers add to the evidence
that suggests the people of Cumberland had been taking witch trials,
with their virtually inevitable conclusion, into their own hands – and
there is no reason to assume Crosthwaite Parish was any different.

After the Restoration, diocesan parishioners were still taken to
task and punished 'for going to witches and wizards, as is reported
by common fame or his own relacon'.[24] Indeed, everyday life

---

* Lamplugh is on the cusp between the Lake District and West Cumbria; it is
also a well-known local name and a 'Lamplugh' bought a good swathe of land
in Borrowdale.

continued to be much hedged about by moral legislation from the
restored Bishop's Court in Carlisle. The sabbath was to be observed
so strictly that individuals were punished for 'spreading manure',
'entertaining drinkers', 'carrying corn before 3 o'clock in ye afternoon', 'for suffering cards to be plaid in his house', or simply for
'quarrelling on ye Sabbath'. In 1686 Thomas Spedding and John
Gaskell were presented to the courts 'for prophaining the Lord's
day by playing att football'. And there was never a day when 'being
a common and pfane curser or swearer' was acceptable. All this
strictness was presumably reported largely by the churchwardens
and the Eighteen Men.*

Nonetheless, the instinctive response of the Parish to the troubles of the first sixty years of the century – the extremism of
the ideas that had been swirling around and the rampant poverty
– had created a far more reliable counterweight than the punishments of Bishop's Court. Its own response – a burst of local
charitable giving to the poor throughout the seventeenth century[25]
– was both humane and remarkably sure-footed. Many had left
or given money, often with specific requests, such as the forty
shillings annual interest on the monies donated by Thomas and
Agnes Williamson for the poor of St John's and Castlerigg, which
was to buy in 'mutton or veal at Martinmas yearly when flesh
might be thought to be cheapest [and] ... laid out in Fleshmeat
(pickled, hanged and dry'd) for their Relief in stormy Dayes in
Winter: That they may not, in such weather, be forced to hazard
their Lives in seeking of a dayly support.'[26] Practical and imaginative. And necessary – it wasn't until 1810 that it was decided that
the time had come to change the provision of meat into money.[27]

The vicar, Mr Lowry, successfully fought some recalcitrant
executors of a trust for £30 10s. *Plus ça change.*† Thomas Grave

* A 1691 case at Braithwaite illustrates an accusation of slander. Four people
were presented for 'saying that Thomas Wrenn's servant man was in bed with
the wife of the said Thomas Wrenn' and one of them was additionally summoned for adding 'that the wife of Thomas Wrenn would need drowne herself
in Cocker' [the river].
† Although it is worth noting that this was achieved by the vicar, who was
meant to have no power over either the stock or the Eighteen Men.

bequeathed sufficient money to purchase freehold land helping
131 poor people in 1821; Peter Youdall 'gentleman' bequeathed £4
10s. rent p.a. from his land in Essex, specifying 2s. for the person
'who brings the money out of the South'. Hugh Tickell, the Quaker,
willed that all of his trustees should be Quakers but left his money
split two-thirds for the poor of Cumberland and one-third for the
poor of the Parish. His will was made with no restriction of creed
but the Cumberland trustees, all Quakers, used his charity for their
own, as, in the early days, when the legacy provided £6 a year for
the Parish, did Crosthwaite. Once no Quakers resided in the Parish,
Tickell's Parish largesse was passed to the trustees of the poorhouse,
who were by then the Eighteen Men and the vicar. In 1821 it is
recorded that the money was distributed to 156 people.[28] Many
small bequests made much mention of cows, and about a hundred
years later ten such bequests were amalgamated to purchase a turnpike ticket, a rock-solid investment, offering 4½ per cent interest.

Before the end of the century, the school received its second
endowment, from Edward Grisedale, 'a Taylour in London', and
it was generous enough to raise the schoolmaster's salary from
£10 2s. to £16 2s.[29] The school had had an exceptional century.
We know of its role in Daniel Fleming's education, and the other
student who had joined John Bankes in reaching national heights,
Sir Joseph Williamson (a country clergyman's son), was his exact
contemporary. Daniel received some extra Crosthwaite education from 'loyal Mr Sanderson',[30] in 1648[31] and it may be that he
arranged that Joseph would go free to the same college by becoming Daniel's 'servitor' – a university version of the public-school
'fag'. Despite this, the couple became lifelong friends and corre-
spondents, matters of more national interest often interrupted by
talk of the Williamson and Le Fleming Parish lands.

Contemporaries considered Joseph Williamson 'a pregnant
scholar', 'a most ingenious mons'ir', and born at Millbeck Hall[32]
– which seems unlikely but not impossible.* However, he was defi-

---

* It is more likely that he lived at New Hall (now Skiddaw Lodge) on the
north side of Vicarage Hill when he lived in the Parish. Wilson, *The history &
chronicles of Crosthwaite Old School*, p. 20.

nitely involved with the family's landholdings. As secretary of state in the Restoration and the second president of the Royal Society, Sir Joseph was one of the rare scions of Cumberland to be buried in Westminster Abbey. John Bankes, of course, corresponded not only about his absentee land but also about his mines. This was quite a trio from a school with a catchment area of two thousand people living in a poor, cut-off, 90-square-mile Parish with five priest-less chapels.

It was John Bankes who bequeathed the greatest continuing legacy the Parish ever received for the poor. Shortly before his death, he had purchased a Keswick orchard and its tenement,[33] and his will had ordained that the houses on his 'two tenements [in Keswick] with the close, orchard and ground adjoining' should be pulled down and replaced by a workhouse 'to be kept and maintained for ever for the setting of poor people to work'. He also left £200, and a £30 p.a. endowment, funded by the rents from his 'enfranchised' and other tenements in the Parish. His intention was to provide enough wool, flax, hemp and iron, etc. for work to commence and, along with profit from the work, enough money to be used for 'support of a certain number of widows, impotent old men and women and blind', and to fund apprenticeships for the children of the poor. His named trustees were instructed to act 'with the advice' of the Eighteen Men.[34]

It would be charitable to suggest that the fact that most of Bankes's plans were not carried out for some thirty years after his death was due to the effects of the Civil War,* but there was clearly more to it than that. When, in 1672 the parishioners, probably the Eighteen Men, took the case to the 'commissioners of charitable uses' to put things right;† it emerged that the £30 p.a. endowment had lapsed, in part because one of the trustees, Roger Gregg the elder, had purchased the land. In order to ensure payment of the

---

* A time that probably included a long period before John Bankes's will was accepted.
† The original trustees had been George Dalston, Ralph Bankes, Richard Tolson, Christopher Blencowe, Joseph Hechstetter, Richard Gregg and Richard Tickell. That number was reduced to the heirs of three of them. 'Report of the Commissioners, p. 74.

endowment, it was ruled that property owned by his heir – and by any other old trustee who failed to pay – was to be seized.* A total of £255 9s. was to be repaid and six new trustees, including the vicar, were appointed. They were always to be Crosthwaite parishioners, and their task – with the aid of 'the eighteen sworn men of Crosthwaite', churchwardens and overseers – was to execute the provisions of the will.[35] No major complaint was ever raised again, and, although the date of the building of the workhouse is not known, it was quite a house, 'very commodious and substantial',[36] complete with two splendid chimneys, 'square up hauf way and round th'other'– the kind so admired by Wordsworth.

For James Clarke, a late eighteenth-century Penrith surveyor, it was the only really decent building in Keswick, 'Capable of lodging a much greater number of paupers than the parish contains'. The timber, 'prodigiously massey and strong', came, he thought, from Monk Hall, although local tradition favoured the old Derwentwater house or the 'Dutch huts' on Vicar's Island.[37] The Bankes's bequest, for all born within the Parish, was to transform the life of its poor for nearly 200 years. With the help of an intervention by Robert Southey, when the state moved the responsibility for their provision to Cockermouth in 1834, it would continue to help some of the Parish poor right through to the time of Canon Rawnsley at the end of the nineteenth century.

Proportionally, the endowments raised by the people of the Crosthwaite Parish before 1700 were quite exceptional in comparison with the rest of Cumberland,† a fact recognised by Bishop Nicholson in 1702: 'no parish in the diocese has so great a fund for support of the poor as that of Crosthwaite'.[38] I find myself awed both by the charitable achievements of St Kentigern's Parish and by what they indicate about its prolonged sense of coherence and community.

---

* Hechstetter appears to be the other guilty name but perhaps was too grand to mention.
† See Parson and White, *History, Directory and Gazetteer*, (Cumberland Charities), pp. 32–36, for 1821 report.

Putting money to use

In 1685 the whole country became full of disquiet again, as James II, a Roman Catholic convert, came to the throne. However, this suited loyal Sir Edward's son Francis, and another Catholic, who had once been taken into custody as a recusant and was one of the largest landowners in the North of England.* He lived in great style, largely courtesy of his father's land purchases – most of the fortune coming from the Alston mines – and the extra land acquired from his mother, supplying his wife and eldest daughter with a yearly clothing allowance of £200 each.[39] An ambitious man, he had attempted to marry his eldest son, Edward, to the daughter of Charles II in 1672 and, after the succession of James II, had finally succeeded in achieving the lesser ambition of marrying Edward (then aged thirty-one) to Lady Mary Tudor (aged fourteen), Charles's youngest illegitimate daughter.

In 1678–81, Charles II had seen off attempts to exclude his brother from the succession, a process that had furthered the development of Britain's two-party system. The king had been befriended by the Tories,[†] while the Whigs[‡] had tried to exclude James from the succession. However, in 1687, when James II tried to shore up his new position by proclaiming a general Declaration of Indulgence, which suspended penal laws against Roman Catholics and Dissenters alike, he was reliant on the support of the Whigs. The declaration was welcomed by English Nonconformists, but vehemently opposed by most Anglicans. And in Cumberland the clergy largely refused the order to read the declaration from their pulpits.

The king's fate was sealed later that year, when he produced a son with his Catholic second wife, Mary of Modena, thereby disinheriting his two Protestant daughters, Mary and Anne.[§] In the

---

* Francis had succeeded his father in 1663, and in 1679 copied him by putting his estates in trust, the same year he was taken into custody as a recusant. His release required the payment of a large £5,000 fine and his own version of the 5-mile rule: promising to stay within that circumference of Dilston.
† A Protestant nickname for Irish Catholic bandits.
‡ Nicknamed after Scottish cattle thieves.
§ Charles II had insisted on their being brought up as Protestants.

last days of 1688, following the arrival in England of an army led
by Mary's Dutch husband, the staunchly Protestant Prince William
of Orange, James fled the country. But not before he had created
a baronetcy for Wilfrid Lawson, purchased in 1688, the year of
his death, and an earldom for his niece's father-in-law, Francis
Radcliffe, who became 1st Earl of Derwentwater, Baron Tyndale
and Viscount Radcliffe and Langley. Briefly, Derwentwater became
the chief title of the family again.

The Parish had other things on its mind. While real poverty for
the landless and bare subsistence farming for the smaller tenant
were still endemic, the tenant class as a whole was becoming slightly
better off, beginning to rise above literal subsistence levels. This is
illustrated by an excellent analysis of some probate inventories in
rural Cumbria between 1661 and 1690.[40] While 21 per cent of the
inventories were worth over £100, the average small yeoman, with
an inventory of less than £40,[41] had one or two cows and a surplus
of oats, which could give him an income of £2–£5, except in a year
with particularly bad weather. His sale of surplus wool, or yarn,
could provide another £2–£3 and most of the hill farmhouses had
a dairy and could keep haylofts reasonably full for use in the harsh
months of February and March.

As a result of this possibility of modest earnings above subsistence
level, and the new sense of security on the border, the statesmen,
revolutionarily, had started to save – and to borrow. According to
the inventories, the wealth of around a third of hill farmers now
lay over 50 per cent in credits.[42] While some farmers borrowed just
enough to cover the price of buying a cow or some sheep, there
was significant investment in new buildings – farmhouses and extra
shelter for overwintering livestock – and mortgages raised on existing or new land.

This new use of, and confidence about, money was probably
the greatest innovation in the history of the customary tenant,
and their lives began to have much greater possibility. But there
was a downside; families could be exposed to fixed interest rates
at times of falling prices and, with the stakes heightened, were in
real danger if the breadwinner died young or suffered a prolonged
illness.[43] So, for many tenants, poverty and risk remained close

companions. A family might hang on through a run of bad weather or animal disease, but a mistaken investment might lead to debts of such a size that on the death of the head of the family the land might have to be sold – the ultimate defeat for any farmer. Indeed, an eighth of the four hundred people studied in the analysis of probate inventories died substantially in debt.

Nevertheless, the inventories show that the itch to do business and invest, both for those on modest incomes and for the better-off, had become almost universal. Many of the poorer or land-poor hill farmers were already supplementing their income by specialising in an extra craft (maltster, tanner, woodmonger, miller, smith, butcher or baker); but now some of them would begin to make additional money through astute moneylending and commerce as well. This, too, was an extraordinarily radical change.

These evolving financial circumstances may, in part, have been responsible for an increased emphasis on cattle (a more expensive purchase) in the Parish after the mid-century. Sheep still mattered, although Thomas Denton probably exaggerated somewhat in 1687[44] when he observed the tenants of both Mungrisedale and Borrowdale growing 'wealthy by their great flocks of Sheepe depasturing upon those high mountains'.[45] For the emphasis on cattle was real. Prompted by the removal of border taxes under Cromwell, the larger landowners had already begun to purchase highland cattle and sheep from Scottish drovers on their journey south, to be part fattened on their estate. Then, in the 1660s, a ban on the import of Irish livestock energised them to expand the trade and, along with the lowland gentry, they amalgamated their leasehold farms to provide overwintering.[46] In time, the better-off statesmen decided to try to follow suit.

They received a relative bonus in the 1690s, when land tax was introduced throughout England. This proved a heavy burden for small landowners further south, the generally nominated figure being 4s. in the pound. In the Lake District, however, perhaps owing to Cumbrian parliamentarians' stressing the general poverty of the area,[47] the tax assessments for the customary tenants worked out closer to 9d. in the pound.[48] By this time Keswick had become a magnet for the Parish poor and the town's parishioners went to court to ensure that the inhabitant of Newland and Borrowdale paid their fair shares.[49]

This new relative wealth was a necessary condition for 'the great rebuilding' of Cumbria, which lasted from the Restoration, when the border finally seemed secure, up until around 1740, when it seems demand was satisfied.[*] Throughout the Parish, many of the old cruck-framed, rubble, clay, or turf-walled houses began to be replaced with the long, low, local-stone Lakeland farmhouses that we know today. Frequently adorned with the date of the building, these houses have been well described as 'the outward expressions of the developing character and experience of the entire dale communities'.[50]

There were two standard patterns. One was a single building divided internally between house, barn and byre; the other had separate outbuildings. And houses of both types were usually split into the living area or 'firehouse', which might include the farmer's bedroom, and the 'down-house', often open to the rafters, where the work was done and the fuel stored. The house lofts, reached by a ladder, were used as a dormitory for the children and servants and the lofts of the outbuildings (when built) mainly for storing wool, while the barns and byres helped with overwintering. In later, superior houses, a stone staircase was included. Many houses had cylindrical chimneys, and almost all had white roughcast exteriors for good weatherproofing.

A great hearth occupied most of one wall, and its huge hood hung about 6 feet off the floor. Here the family gathered, warmed themselves and smoked their meat. It was said that the Cumbrian yeomen considered a well-stocked chimney to be the most elegant furniture with which he could adorn his house, but today it is the often elaborately carved settle on the wall opposite the fire that is coveted. 'Hallan drop', black sooty liquid pouring down the chimney in bad weather on to dried meats and chilly humans, provides a necessary antidote to any developing perception of cosiness or ease, and probably explains why so many men used to sit with their hats on when by the fire.

It is thought that the average house would have taken one to

---

[*] The fact that wool prices dropped at the mid-century may also be relevant.

two years to build and would have cost the profit of five average seasons, a major reason for the credit market.[51] But this was the moment for the hill farmer to build. The combination of the sense of security from peace on the border (soon to be interrupted), the rise of credit, the buoyancy of animal prices, accompanied by level and falling prices of grain in the first half of the seventeenth century, and a rock-solid sense of security of tenure, meant that investment in a house that would last for generations, to be left to or sold by the family, was becoming the usual choice for those who could afford it. Despite the extra risk, this change palpably represents another dramatic improvement in the statesmen's life, their new homes a far cry from the old 'clay daubins'.

Some hundred years later, these 'mountain cottages' lay at the core of Wordsworth's sense of the unity of man and nature in the Lake District:

> 'The dwelling houses, and their contiguous outhouses' are frequently distinguished by roughcast and whitewash, 'which, as the inhabitants are not hasty in renewing it, in a few years acquires, by the influence of weather, a tint at once sober and variegated ... Roofed with slates ... rough and uneven,[*] so that both the coverings and sides of the house have furnished places of rest for the seeds of lichens, mosses, ferns, flowers. Hence buildings, which in their very form call to mind the processes of Nature, do thus ... appear to be received into the bosom of the living principle of things.'[52]

Wordsworth also had strong feelings about the larger buildings in the Lake District that imposed themselves upon nature, rather than incorporated themselves into it, but he loved the Brownriggs' Parish house. The family had been renting the old Williamson house at Millbeck, the Millbeck church pew transferred to them in 1634 by 'Umfraye Williamson, gentlemen of New Hall'.[53] But in 1677 they had built Ormathwaite Hall nearby, in an area Brownriggs still farm

---

[*] Because they were hewn before the art of splitting had been discovered.

Joseph Wilkinson's drawing of a Braithwaite cottage is an example of
similar cottages seen all over the Lake District.

today.* This did not mean, by the standards of the time, that the
Parish had suddenly acquired some extra gentry – the most widely
accepted sense of 'landed gentry' remained those with a country
estate who were never required to work actively, except in an administrative capacity on their own lands. Until that definition expanded,
it could apply only to those who ultimately owned the land and never
to a customary tenant. It was the tenants who went to London, as we
have seen, like the absent Williamsons and the Bankes's descendants,
who leased their Parish land and became gentlemen at this time.

The view towards the end of the seventeenth century was that the
Parish had 'No great gentry hereabouts but many substantial monsires'.[54] The Wrens of Castlerigg† provide an interesting example of the
social shifts within the Parish then. Sir Thomas Radcliffe had released
some Derwentwater demesne land in the last quarter of the fifteenth

---

* Sometime before 1800 the Brownriggs had purchased Millbeck Hall as well.
Taylor, Manorial Halls, p. 149.
† Wrens lived all over the Parish – it is said that they were the primary tenants
of *thirteen* farms.

century and one tenant, Gawen Wren, had been enfranchised,[55] but his family were still serving as stewards for the Derwentwaters in the mid-seventeenth century. They had built up an estate of four farms[56] and had a long tradition of giving money to help the Parish. Then, the social fluidity of the Commonwealth had allowed another Gawen, known to all as 'the Justice Wrenne', to become a JP, a post usually restricted to members of the gentry. His estate was valued at a startling £835 upon his death – half of it in credits, in the new fashion.[57] Yet his son Gawen still described himself as a yeoman, and the lovely, simple crest of wrens on his memorial in St Kentigern's was entirely unauthorised.[*] Other 'monsires' can be spotted once St Kentigern's 'quire' was opened up for burials in 1670, a practice that continued until the space ran out sixty-six years later.

The first to be so honoured was Richard Williamson from the leased Goosewell Farm on Derwentwater demesne land, one of the oldest farms in the Parish; yet he was the only Williamson buried there, underlining the move of the main branch of the family to London. Also buried in the quire were an extraordinary twenty-five Wrens (some from Chappel-House, Borrowdale), nine Leathes (the lords of Legburthwaite), eight Brownriggs, five Jacksons and Bankes, and two Fishers, Allasons, Wilsons, Wilkinsons, Howes, Mosses, Buntings, Gaskarths and Birkheads all followed – representing the major families of the Parish.[†] The Leathes, consistently given the title of gentry in the directories interested in status, were always given the prefix of Mr., but Richard Williamson, the Brownriggs, Gasgarths, Jacksons, Bankes and Fishers never sported the prefix. And the title itself was a fluid one, which at that time could denote a gentleman, a status en route to gentleman or, on occasion, simply a choice; and two[‡] of the twenty-five Wrens had chosen or achieved the title in 1695 and 1725.[58]

* His son, the third Gawen, married a granddaughter of Sir Daniel Fleming, and did become a 'gentleman', Winchester, '"Pure Commonwealth"?', p. 95. The history of the couple's heirs, if they produced any, is not known.
† And one Wharton, Rabye, Wood, Walker, Fletcher, Wallas, Taylor, Radcliffe, Ritson and Richardson.
‡ Perhaps the Gawen mentioned above, who had become a gentleman, and a child of his.

There are two interesting omisions in the names of the great and good buried in the 'quire'. The omission of any Stangers who, as we know, had been for some time by far the richest landowners in the Percy lands of the Parish, is particularly curious. Then, none of the original nine Graves families who took part in the 1623 'enfranchisement' received the burial honour although they still peopled the Parish. The clue to *their* absence may lie in a 1792 will in which Leonard Grave, a banker in Lombard Street left Dale Bottom, High Row, and Beck House to Leonard Grave, Gentleman of Islington.[59] So, the most successful branch of the family could have left the Parish by the time the quire burials took off. The many Graves that stayed continued to play a significant part in its business and were frequent members of Eighteen Men.

So the Parish remained free of the 'new gentry', as did the Lake District, until the advent of the different social circumstances of the 1780s, although it did acquire some new neighbouring gentry. The Earl of Derby had built the large and splendid Mirehouse on the eastern side of Bassenthwaite Lake in 1666, selling it two years later to Roger Gregg, along with its estate, which includes the Brundholme woods in the west of the Greta valley and several fells. The estate has stayed with the family ever since, passing by gift and inheritance to the Speddings, who live there today. But, more generally in Cumberland and Westmorland, gentry would be leaving rather than joining the area during the eighteenth century.[60] And while some of the Radcliffes/Derwentwaters, the Norman Parish gentry, remained, the last recorded date of a Radcliffe burial at the Lord's Chapel in St Kentigern's seems to be 1691,[61] so the Parish relationship with the Derwentwaters was already on the move before it was violently severed from its most important, more than seven-hundred-year-long, now aristocratic connection.

The last of the Derwentwaters

When James II's eldest daughter, Mary, and her husband, William of Orange, took the throne offered by Parliament, their coronation on 11 April 1689, some clergy remained Jacobite. The body of the Church of England, however, grudgingly agreed to tolerate Protestant Nonconformists and, unlike Roman Catholics or Unitarians, allow them their own preachers and places of worship. In the Parish, Bishop Nicholson reported, near the end of William and Mary's reign:

'The Quire wants Glaseing and Care to be taken with the Roof; and yet, with all its imperfections, it is in a better state than could well be expected where so many are at ye charge … From the same unfortunate Cause comes that Multitude of Seats which crowd up the whole Chancel, even to the very sides of the Communion-Table: which has no Rails about it, nor is (hardly) an inch above the Floor. The body of the Church is very uneven in its pavement; occasioned by the frequent burying there, and the little (or noe) care that's taken by those that break the ground … And the same neglect has occasioned the spoiling of a great many Seats.'[62]

So, while there was a real sense of the church fabric reflecting nearly two centuries of religious and political turmoil, there remains a sense of the essential importance of the church to its Parish. The floor, chaotic and uneven as it was, reflected the number of burials in the church. The year before the bishop's visitation, in 1702, he had confirmed 'four hundred young persons' there, an extraordinary number out of a total Parish population of around two thousand, even when confirmations only happened every three years and the previous bishop was said to have been extremely lax.[63] More widely, the Anglican Church was rising from its post-Commonwealth doldrums, on the way to becoming almost universally popular again when Mary's sister Anne, a strict churchwoman, ascended the throne on William's death in 1702.

Two years after her accession, Queen Anne, truly remarkably, wiped out the financial apparatus that had accompanied the Reformation, revoking the royal tithing, and calling upon Parliament to pass an Act under which the money would be used to augment the salaries of the poorest livings. Much of Henry VIII's heist may have been squandered, but from 1706 livings below £50 began to be augmented by Queen Anne's Bounty. The chapels in the Parish now had a chance of being saved. By the end of Anne's reign, two societies had been launched, the Society for Promoting Christian Knowledge and the Society for the Propagation of the Gospel (both of which were still thriving energetically in Victorian times), and church services had become much more frequent.

Politically, all had been much more uneasy. James II had died in exile in 1701, the year before Anne's accession, and over in France the thirteen-year-old James Francis Edward Stuart had been recognised as king of England and Scotland, renting some jewels for his coronation crown. In England, Parliament passed an Act of Settlement that barred all Roman Catholics from the monarchy and ruled that Anne's 'heir presumptive"* would be Sophia, Electress of Hanover, followed by her Protestant heirs. But three years later a Scottish Act of Security legalised the Scots' right to make their own choice of royal successor, whether Protestant or not, creating a clearly dangerous position for the English, given the long history of the 'auld alliance' between Scotland and France. England threatened to cut trade and free movement between the two countries, unless the Scots entered negotiations leading either to the repeal of the Act of Security or to political union.

The Westminster Parliament enacted their Articles of Union in July 1705 and, after a labyrinthine battle waged with money and power, the Scots finally enacted their own acceptance that the two countries should be 'United into One Kingdom by the Name of Great Britain'[64] in the Union of Scotland Act on 16 January 1706. It is said that the bells of St Giles' Cathedral in Edinburgh rang out with 'Why should I be so sad on my wedding day?'[65]

Meanwhile, in the Derwentwater family, Edward and Mary had separated, and in 1702 their children, upon the request of James II's widow, had been sent to the Stuart court in Paris. James Radcliffe – who would become in 1705 the 3rd Earl of Derwentwater – was thirteen, slightly older than his kinsman, the 'Old Pretender', and their intimacy and James's sense of loyalty were to define his

---

* Her last surviving child had died in 1700.

James, Earl of Derwentwater, still 'our earl' in the
Keswick Vale as late as the mid-twentieth century.

short life. In 1709 the young earl was granted a licence to return
to England* and quickly became well known for his rather unusual
relationship with his tenants, which seems to have been a remarkably generous one. The following description, by the novelist and
historian Tobias Smollett, a staunch Hanoverian, is just one of
many: 'An amiable youth, brave, open hearted, generous, hospitable and humane. He continually did offices of kindness and good
neighbourhood to everybody as opportunity offered; and the poor,
the widow, and the orphan, rejoiced in his bounty.'[66]

The earl paid one long visit to the Parish, staying in Keswick at
the Queen's Head, in the year of his arrival in 1710, but was soon
away from the North for two years while the Dilston house was
rebuilt, returning in triumph in 1714. This was the same year as

---

* Somewhat surprisingly, since two years earlier (while much of the English
army was fighting the French in Europe under Marlborough), he had been on
a captured French boat sent to Scotland to capitalise on disaffection about the
passage of the Act of Union.

the death of both Queen Anne and the heiress presumptive, whose eldest son, George, for whom English was his fourth language, was offered the throne – irrefutably a gift from Man and Parliament, not God, as over two score people had a closer hereditary link to Charles II than the new king. George wasn't popular; a scornful song about turnip heads was soon passing from inn to inn. But the Jacobites missed their vital moment. And a year too late, the Scots gathered in support of the old line and proclaimed the exiled Stuart prince James VIII of Scotland.

The legal remedy of *habeas corpus* was suspended, and Curwen, along with one of the Howards who had remained Catholic, was confined in Carlisle. However, a clerk in the secretary of state's office warned James Radcliffe, who escaped into hiding among his tenants for the next month. All around him the Catholic gentry were being summoned by the Scots, and eventually, having asked the magistrates what he was accused of and receiving no answer (and, traditionally, shamed into action by his pious Catholic wife, who was said to have thrown down her fan, demanding his sword in return), James, aged twenty-five, and his nineteen-year-old brother, Charles, returned to Dilston, prayed and marched out on 6 October 1715 with a small troop of his retainers.[67]

> *For the Radcliffe hath spoken*
> *The Radcliffe hath broken*
> *The chains the usurper hath made,*
> *And never was seen so gallant a maien*
> *As he mounted the Stuart's cockade.*

Once the rebels reached Penrith Fell, the Cumbrian militia, mostly armed with scythes, billhooks and pitchforks, prudently decamped.[68] For, although 'the posse commitatus of the two counties with 12,000 to 13,000 men' had all been summoned, 'they found themselves unable to bring a single man to measure swords with the insurgents: ... The affections of the people had been strongly interwoven with the ancient monarchy ... and such feelings are not easily eradicated.'[69] The Jacobites, some seventeen hundred men, entered Penrith, collected £500 in 'taxes' in the

name of James III, and sat down to the supper prepared for the
Bishop of Carlisle and the officers of the militia. Meanwhile, a contingent went off to Lowther Hall to raid the cellars and declared
the quality of the wine and ale excellent.[70]

The predominantly Catholic rebels chose a High Anglican MP,
Thomas Forster, as their general, to avoid religious dispute, but he
proved a poor choice. At Preston, having barricaded the streets and
suffered relatively small losses in the fighting, he disastrously failed
to defend the bridge over the River Ribble and, after the arrival of
new government troops, decided to capitulate, against the Scots',
and probably James's, wishes. That decision taken, the earl offered
himself as one of the two hostages, later saying, on oath, that he
chose to give himself up 'lest the capitulation might have proved
insufficient'.[71]

Seventy-five English nobles and gentlemen became prisoners,
along with four hundred other ranks, who were to be transported
to America; the Scottish prisoners numbered over a thousand. The
two Radcliffe brothers and the other leaders were sent to London;
James to the Tower and Charles to Newgate Prison. James's wife
set out immediately on horseback, some 300 miles, in appalling
conditions – 'The season was so severe, and the roads so extremely
bad, that the post itself was stopped … the snow … generally above
the horse's girth'.[72] Indeed, a number of the prisoners, who were
walking, died owing to the severity of the conditions in the hardest
winter for thirty years.

Many pleas for mercy were lodged on behalf of Lord
Derwentwater, by his wife, his friends and his peers. The House
of Lords asked both the government and the king for clemency
just the day before the execution. But the best argument had come
from the earl himself, addressing Parliament a fortnight earlier: 'I
have confessed myself guilty, but, my lords, that guilt was rashly
incurred, without any premeditation, as I hope your lordships will
be convinced by one particular. I beg leave to observe, I was wholly
unprovided with men, horses, arms and other necessaries, which,
in my situation, I could not have wanted, had I been party to any
matured design.'[73]

And that, of course, was true. The nobility of the North

had had generations of experience of how to raise armies, Derwentwater's tenantry were numerous and widely spread, yet James went to war with just his personal retainers from Dilston. While this may well have stemmed from a semi-conscious desire not to expose more people to the risks of his own loyalties, one cannot prove it. But, as the earl said, 'my offence was sudden and my submission early'.[74]

Three times he was offered clemency if he rejected the Catholic faith and acknowledged George as the rightful king of England; three times he refused: 'as inconsistent with honour and conscience'.[75] Some were saved, Lord Derwentwater was not, and London became agitated. King George supported the Whigs, having quickly judged the Tories to have proto-Jacobean sympathies. And, fearing James's combination of Stuart blood, wealth and popularity, Walpole's government denied the clemency plea from the Lords, merely granting the substitution of death by beheading for the original sentence of hanging, drawing and quartering.

The earl wrote five rather wonderful letters in his last few hours, full of love and concern for others;[76] two of the five to his wife, 'My dearest worldly treasure'. He is even funny to Charles, about whom he is clearly very worried. His religion is central. As he said on the scaffold: 'I die a Roman Catholic; I am in perfect charity with all the world.' And he finished with a political point, 'If that Prince who now governs had given me my life, I should have thought myself obliged never more to have taken up arms against him.'

Soon, bareheaded, he repeated three times 'Dear Jesus be merciful to me', the third time in a loud voice, the agreed sign for the executioner's axe. A spectator reports, 'the vast multitude really seemed to give a groan not unlike the hollow noise of the sea at a distance'.[77] The day was 24 February 1716.

'A good death' can be a manufactured thing for someone with a sense of theatre, but I find the twenty-seven-year-old remarkable, and certainly some chemistry transformed his death into the realms of poetry and legend. Perhaps it was his innate honour: [78]

> He left a name at which the world grew pale,
> To point a moral, or adorn a tale

Perhaps it was the death of the title and later the line:

> With me, the RADCLIFFE's name must end
> And seek the silent tomb:
> And many a kindness, many a friend
> With me must meet their doom…
> But when the head that wears the Crown
> Shall be laid low like mine,
> Some honest hearts may then lament
> For RADCLIFFE's fallen line.

Or perhaps it was the sense that he was not a natural spiller of blood or trampler of the downtrodden. In a letter to a neighbour, asking him to look after the horse that had been his favourite, when he escaped capture by living with his tenantry – the grey upon which 'Lord Derwentwater rode away' – he wrote, 'GOD send us peace and good neighbourhood, unknown blessings since I was born'.[79] Or, perhaps, it was just that old affection in the North for Catholicism and the Stuarts. Whatever created the feeling, it lasted for generations.

James was seen as a martyr, and healings were supposed to have taken place for those who touched his heart, kept by its entrepreneurial London embalmer. And famously 'The Red Streamers of the North', the *aurora borealis*, shone dramatically as his coffin reached County Durham on its way to Dilston. The sky flamed with bursts of orange and red, brilliantly set off by luminous aquamarine, tinged with blue, a sight said never to have been seen before in Northumberland. And the lights must have caused much astonishment, fear and excitement in the Parish too, as, well over a hundred years later, when a similar phenomenon occurred, the people said nothing of the kind had been seen since 'Lord Derwentwater's Lights'. In the mid-twentieth century, the earl was still referred to in conversation by one of the hill farmers in the Derwentwater valley, entirely unselfconsciously, as 'our earl'.[80] Today, the lights are still talked of, but with an educated knowledge that perhaps speaks of other things.

*

Given Cumbria's enchantment with story and legend, surprisingly little attaches to the Derwentwaters until their final flourish, when it was given full rein. It was said that Lady Derwentwater escaped from Lord's Island during the 1715 rebellion and climbed a vertiginous fissure just south of Walla Crag on the northeastern side of Derwentwater, clasping her jewellery and plate, to use them to save her husband. En route, she dropped a white handkerchief, 'clearly seen' over a century later; a touch of white paint providing a useful tourist enticement.[81]

Since James Radcliffe's wife was at Dilston and the old Derwentwater house on the island was uninhabitable, it is, perhaps, a strange tale, but a much embellished one. Local tradition describes sentries posted on all the roads;[82] some tell of a chest of treasure sunk in the lake, others of an apron full of money, which scattered as the apron strings broke. The fissure up which Lady Derwentwater theoretically escaped is still called the Lady's Rake today.

This legend, like the distant earlier ones we have encountered, may have some basis in fact, given the mid-nineteenth-century discovery of thirty-four silver pennies from the reigns of Edward I and Edward II, not surrounded by any fragments of a container, and the discovery of a silver coin in 1769 in a similar position near Lady's Rake. This suggests either the reinvention of a much earlier story or the eighteenth-century country imagination confusing stories about the Radcliffes during the Commonwealth with what was still alive in their minds: the knowledge of how James's wife had pleaded, and pleaded again, for her husband's life.[83]

In sober fact, James's wife and their only son, John, went to live in France and in 1719, after a long court battle, John was awarded a life interest in the Derwentwater estate, to the government's disgust. The Countess of Derwentwater had tried to keep in touch, writing to find out what had happened to a particular servant, only to be told: 'I did hear he was transported and is dead.'[84] And in 1722, a year before her death, aged thirty, she was still trying to look after Derwentwater estate, discovering from her man of business: 'The Leases are safe come from London to my hands, but I am much afraid several of them will not be executed by the Tenants – considering the fall of Lands again and no trade, and the scarcity of money … its thought that several hundreds of Tennants will be broken.'[85]

John Derwentwater died eight years later, aged nineteen, in 1731,[86] and the government remained implacable, soon after his death passing an Act of Parliament to keep the estate in the king's name and in 1735, arguably illegally, granting its revenues to Greenwich Seamen's Hospital. There was, however, some compensation for the customary tenants. They had refused to pay a fine upon James's execution in 1716, on the grounds that 'the next lord, the King, had gained the manor through violence, specifically head removal'.[87] Then,* taking advantage of the fact that in law the king never dies, they waltzed past the death of George I in 1727, until a 1739 law was passed to deal with this, and the unenfranchised were finally caught in 1760, upon the death of George II.[88]

---

* Despite the instruction 'the tenants to pay fines on the death of the king, as if he were a private person'. Nicolson and Burn, *The History and Antiquities*, p. 79.

Chapels, Oaks and Wadd

I N 1723, ALMOST a hundred years after Parish customary
tenancy had been confirmed by the Star Chamber, the old Percy
tenants had taken an enormous step forward. The Somersets
had gone too far again. Fines had been 'Exhorbitant and unreasonable exceeding two or three more years value',[1] and 'in places
where the ancient rent is low' demands came in for between sixty
and a hundred times the old annual rents. The estate had recently
forced their tenants to pay heriots 'for Tenements not heriotable
by any particular or Speciall custom', increased the heriot fees,
and 'endeavoured to compel the Tenants to pay distinct heriots for
every parcel of a Tenement'. So this time, it was not just the general
fine that was contested at the manor court, but all forms of landlord exploitation of the norms.

Like the Kendal tenants, who had successfully defeated the abolition of customary tenancy, the Percy Cumberland tenants entered
into a 'Strict and Solemn Combination and Confederacy ... to stand
by and Assist each other with Mutual Contributions of Money
and all other ways and means of Assistance.'[2] Somerset's steward
bemoaned that, of the 1,500 tenants on his lands, 'there was only
150 who had the wisdom and justice enough to submit to his Grace's
undoubted right'.[3] The court ruling ordained that the general fine
and all else should be reasonable, and this time, revolutionarily,
the steward realised he was beaten and the ruling held. A glorious
moment for the Parish statesmen on the old Percy land, as the backbone of solidarity they had inserted into their sense of community
had changed everything. This proved the last time the issue of arbitrary fines was raised at the Percy manor court.[4] Fifty years later

– long after the Somerset title had been overtaken by the creation of a new title, the Earl of Egremont,* and passed, through the female line, to the Wyndhams – the Egremont steward upheld the 1677 judgment.

In the old Derwentwater manor, the customary rents were far lower, four times the old customary rent, because of the 1623 indenture. In 1738[5] only Widow Wren, Widow Watson and Gawen Wren paid more than £1 a year, the maximum rent for a shop in Keswick, still in the doldrums between mining and tourism. The number of customary tenants had risen to 108, a sharp rise from the sixty-three who had originally bought them their freedom from arbitrary fines.† This indicates that the average holding had become smaller, probably largely owing to familial sharing of land or marriage, but also probably because of some sales of land. And the papers show just sixteen tenants paying arbitrary fines in the manor, paying the legally acceptable two years' current rent.[6] They also show that a large number of both kinds of tenant had bought themselves out of their various feudal service commitments by paying a small annual fine. And that the Derwentwaters still owed the Le Flemings an annual 6s. 8d. 'for the Mill-Dam'.[7]

So, all the Parish customary tenants were now free from worries about unfair rents, the four-hundred-year battle finally over. Their cohesion had originally been helped by family groupings of land, but as this diminished over the centuries, shepherding, the governance of the Eighteen Men, and learned habit, or 'ancient practice', had upheld the force of community as before.

The 1723 ruling coincided with a good period for the hill farmers generally; the price of corn had remained fairly stable after 1690, while the price of sheep had doubled. And the study of Cumbrian probate inventories (encountered in chapter 7), which also covered the years 1721–50,‡ shows that the benign economic conditions had had a very favourable impact: the average value of individual

---

* Reuniting part of the Parish land with the title of its original owner.

† Some on adjacent land to the owners' customary land, others presumably on land thought insignificant back in 1623.

‡ By which time, the Parish population was some 2,280, i.e. five hundred families multiplied by Cumberland's average family unit then.

inventories had risen by 75 per cent over the period.[8]

By then, the majority of the mortgage agreements appear to have been intended to provide for the farmer's children once the core farm had passed on to the main heir. Statesmen were now beginning to leave real money to all their children for the first time, and it was usually scrupulously divided equally between sons and daughters. To protect the interests of youngest children, in the event of their not receiving their money at the due time, they were sometimes given bequests in the form of land. And, occasionally, mortgages had been specifically raised either on the family land or on new land bought for the child to earn a living. Usually, however, it was left to the heir and executor to carry out the bequests and provide patrimonies for his siblings out of his new estate.[9]

As a result, it is estimated that, once interest on loans and other overheads are taken into account, the average yeoman farmer's annual profit virtually disappeared, providing just £1 or £2 a year over a thirty-year period, in the early eighteenth-century.[10] Things could potentially get tougher as the money left to support children was to grow substantially, rising from an average sum of £76 in 1750–55 to £154 just twenty years later[11] – the money not being divided between more children, but more of it going to each child.[12] Another change stood out from the inventories: the tenants who had joined the better-off by starting to purchase and overwinter 'black' cattle (the Cumberland name for the Scottish drovers' stock) had made markedly more than those who lacked the initial capital to buy them, providing an extra reason why more than half the wealth of the average hill farmer still lay in credits.

Another effect of the new practice of mortgaging and borrowing and lending money was to exacerbate the growing differential between the top and bottom of the statesman class.* The number of inventories worth over £100 had risen from 17 per cent of the total to 40 per cent, while the percentage of those leaving under £40 had only dropped from 46 per cent to 31 per cent.[13] And in the

---

* The average estate of the better off moved from £144 to £287, and from £20 to £23 for the poorer between the two periods. This differential had widened most dramatically after 1721.

broadly equivalent parish of Hawkshead there was a stark doubling of the differential between the top and bottom rungs of the yeoman ladder. The Hawkshead analysis also shows that the number of tenants specialising on their craft, rather than using its income to help their farming business, had doubled and left an average inventory of more than £60, 50 per cent higher than well over a third of the total sample.[14] For every winner there was a loser, and the poorer were in relative, if not absolute, terms poorer still. Despite this, and partly because the fairly sparse opportunities for expenditure aided the natural instinct of the landowner to accumulate capital, stock and land, the customary tenants continued to live a homogeneous, profoundly traditional life. Personal wealth appears to have affected aspirations and the old frugal way of life surprisingly little.

So, the mutual identification of rich and poor hill farmers broadly remained, and there was no sense yet of any revolutionary changes to land management either. The absolute relationship between the number of stock you kept through the winter and the number you could graze on the commons remained a fundamental law, and care was taken to ensure that the system remained robust. There was no sense of change either in the deep involvement of the Parish in its governance. Some even suggest that select vestries now controlled the functions of the manor courts, functions they had been quietly absorbing in the previous two centuries.[15]

Nevertheless, with a monetary differential of more than ten times between the top and bottom groups of parishioners, the age-old story of mutual solidarity was beginning to sound stretched. Signs of a declining belief in traditions of local governance might have been spotted at Braithwaite manor court as early as 1698, when one J. Birkhead, unless he got sworn in within the next ten days, was to be punished for refusing the office of Constable.[16] By 1755 some of the Newlands 'turnmen' (those due to take their turn in court) just didn't turn up, apparently preferring to pay the 5s. fine.* Given the historic power of both the manor courts and the yeoman solidarity controlling them, this was a crack that could have

* And their common absences continued, even though the fine had risen by nearly eight times by 1817. Grant, *The Story of the Newlands Valley*, p. 94.

consequences. And retrospectively it becomes clear that 80 per cent of all the cases taken to the manor courts in Cumbria in the eighteenth century had been already recorded by 1750.

Thomas Christian and Queen Anne's Bounty

In the country at large, the Hanoverian monarchs continued to favour the Whigs, who, in turn, appeared more interested in the church's relationship with the state than in religion itself. And intellectuals who embraced the Age of Reason and the Scottish Enlightenment found enthusiasm intolerable. Before the half-century was over, Bishop Butler of Bristol and Durham, sounding almost like a beleaguered clergyman of a rather later era, agonised that 'It is come, I know not how, to be taken for granted by many persons that Christianity is not so much as a subject of inquiry ... it is now at length discovered to be fictitious. Accordingly they treat it as if in the present age this were an agreed-upon point among all people of discernment, and nothing remained but to set it up as a principal subject of mirth and ridicule, as it were by the way of reprisals for its having long interrupted the pleasures of the world.'[17]

In the Parish, two eighteenth-century vicars had extraordinarily wide connections in the area. Thomas Tullie was descended from Thomasine Hechstetter, a member of the family who had once been at the heart of the Elizabethan mining boom, and Dr Tullye of Keswick,[18] and so was perhaps already bonded to the Parish. Before he became vicar of Crosthwaite in 1710, he had rebuilt the family house in Carlisle, which as Tullie House still stands, much enlarged, as a focal point of the city today.[*] The governance of Crosthwaite church remained largely unchanged, save in one respect: since 1700, there had been three churchwardens rather than two, presumably to cover better the growing population.

Six years after he became vicar, Tullie assumed the position of Chancellor of the Diocese of Carlisle, a job that by then included the role of archdeacon.[19] He would resign from the former role a

---

[*] Since 1893 it has housed the Tullie House Museum and Art Gallery.

decade later, so that it could be given as a lucrative wedding gift to
John Waugh, his twenty-four-year-old intended son-in-law. Young
John subsequently ran the diocese, allowing his father, the bishop,
to enjoy a life in London, far from his yeoman origins.* But St
Kentigern's was extremely lucky in Tullie's replacement, Thomas
Christian BA, who became vicar, aged thirty, in 1728.

Despite Crosthwaite's living being one of the better paid – oddly
those most subject to the besetting eighteenth-century clerical sin
of pluralism† – Christian stayed solely with the Parish until his
death in 1770, an unusually long run. His great-great-grandfa-
ther had been buried in the chancel of St Kentigern's in 1648, the
Parish records describing him as 'of the old family of Christian,
of Miltown, in the Isle of Mann and Captain Lieutenant to the
royalist Sir Edward Radcliffe at the time of the civil war'.[20] Loyal
Sir Edward. But Thomas's father had moved the family to the
manor and estate of Ewanrigg on Cumberland's west coast, subsequently expanding its hall and its lands and developing a coal
mine. In 1732, soon after Christian arrived at Crosthwaite, his
first wife, Elizabeth, who had quickly produced two daughters,
died at the age of just twenty-one, probably succumbing to one
of the epidemics of smallpox and cholera that were then rampant
in Keswick.

Hugh Walpole describes the conditions of the time in his novel
Rogue Herries[21] (1930), set in eighteenth-century Cumbria: 'In the
minor streets and "closes" the cottages, little houses and pig-sties
were thronged very largely with a foreign and wandering population … crowded with foul middens and encroached on by large
open cesspools, pig-sties and cow-sheds. The refuse stagnated
and stained the air and tainted the soil…' the 'stink' described
by Walpole still overlaid by the distinctive smell of raw hides and
curing leather. Shockingly, Christian's second wife, Jane, died –
aged twenty-three – in 1736, only four years after the death of his

---

* Waugh was the last of four local yeomen's children to become Bishop of
Carlisle (between 1598 and 1723). His predecessors were Bishops Robinson,
Potter and Smith. The other local bishops came from the gentry.
† Pluralism was the holding of more than one – often considerably more –
ecclesiastical office simultaneously.

first wife, while giving birth to their son John. It was not until he married for a third time that Thomas Christian found a wife – Emma, born in 1710 – who would survive him.

In the midst of the personal tragedy of Elizabeth's death, the vicar had been fighting a long battle with his parishioners to reclaim tithes that were his by right. The old Crosthwaite curate maintained that the parishioners had defrauded the previous two vicars of tithes throughout their tenures. Lowry, the vicar whose diligence had augmented the Crosthwaite fund for the poor, had not been prepared to fight, despite his son's promptings, for 'he, being of a peaceable temper and having many children to provide for, and the precarious state of his health ... thought it most advisable to decline ... contesting his rights and to take what he could get quietly and peaceably for the sake of his family'.[22] Clearly, Christian's case was a gamble, and Chancellor Waugh tells us that, during his 'long and tedious lawsuit to recover the right of wool as tything', had he not 'happily prevailed at last ... he had been ruined by it'.[23] It was a young man's battle, and presumably Thomas Tullie had been too busy and too rich to need to take it on during his tenure.

The case started formally on 30 March 1732 and lasted until at least late 1734,[24] and Thomas Christian brought it against ten farmers from all over the Parish (except the Thirlmere valley): three Graves, three Hodgsons, two Wrens, one Wilson and, surprisingly, only one Fisher. It had been agreed by all that the 'Parishioners usually tender and deliver the wool by weight ... without the said Vicar or his farmers seeing the nine parts thereof, which is and always was, tendered without sight or view'. This rather Christian view of the honesty of others on the part of earlier vicars turned out, as Thomas had expected, to be myopic.

William Dover, one of the two yeomen chosen to represent Newlands and Portinscale, admitted that he 'verily believes that many of the parishioners (if they be not honest) may impose upon and defraud the Vicar', and William of Swinside, Gentleman, married to a Fisher and inheritor of a flock of around three hundred sheep, admitted that a relation of his frequently told him that the clippers were ordered by the parishioners 'to set out and sever the

Hogg wool from the rest of the other wool and take out some of the best fleeces'. This ties in with an example of malpractice identified by Waugh,[25] the arbitrary replacement of tithes on hog wool by a general 10d. payment per lamb (and, curiously, 11d. in Borrowdale).*

When Christian eventually won the case, it seems that the farmers thought it was a 'fair do'; Waugh records that 'Mr Christian is regular and exact himself and notwithstanding the suit on good terms with his parishioners'.[26] This says a great deal about Christian and about the continuing basic neighbourliness of the Parish; for the fight was significant financially, potentially doubling his income in a good year for wool from around £100 to £200, the living valued at £146 on average per annum.

This gave Christian enough security to build himself a new home, 'a very neat convenient living',[27] which still stands today on Vicarage Hill, Keswick. He describes it in precise terms: the 'Vicarage house is 20 yards in front, at the last end ... is a Barn, Stable and Cow House 16 yards in length, on the south and east sides there is an orchard and garden containing one acre and a half.'[28] All the buildings, except for the cow house, were covered with slated roofs, the slates held in place by 'mutton bone' pegs. The new vicarage must have been a replacement for an older building, since 'a long-forgotten well, of very ancient construction, and in perfect condition'[29] was discovered in the 1950s, when a floor collapsed. The glebe field, created when the gift of the vicarage moved to the Bishop of Carlisle in the thirteenth century, remained with the vicarage until both were sold towards the end of the twentieth century.

The Eighteen Sworn Men had now invested most of the school stock in land. They invested £85 in 1695; then, in 1702, £123 in an estate of around 36 acres in Great Crosthwaite estate; and, in 1730, £113 in a 13-acre estate at Wanthwaite in St John's.[30] In the church, Christian tried to remedy some of the failings recorded by Bishop Nicolson at the turn of the century. We learn from a survey

---

* Hogs (or hoggs) are sheep older than lamb but technically before their first shearing.

of the year 1749, conducted by John Waugh, that the communion table, which had been unrailed and stood hardly an inch above the floor, was now 'railed and raised'. However, Waugh continued: 'the chancel is not in sufficient repair, tho' the Impropriators have promised to set about it but they are so many and so litigious that they are not entirely brought to do what [they] ought ... Many other inconveniences remain and are like to do so.'[31] It seems that the effects of the Reformation were still felt in St Kentigern's.

Nevertheless, there was a great, healing, clerical change in the Parish as, at last, the chapels became beneficiaries of Queen Anne's Bounty. In most of England, the appointing of lay readers had died out fairly quickly after its introduction under Elizabeth and there had been no trace of them at all in Lancashire south of Furness. But in the Lake District proper the inadequate system struggled on for nearly 200 years.[32] Things moved more quickly once Sir Daniel Fleming's fifth son, George, became bishop in 1734, aged sixty-seven, and five years later the bishop could report that only the chapels in Great Crosthwaite Parish and one other were still solely served by readers. And, as he was only too well aware, these chapels were particularly cut off and therefore especially in need; 'none can require it more were the salaries sufficient for their maintenance'.[33]

The Parish housed both the worst-endowed chapel in the whole diocese, at Newlands, and the first chapel to be augmented in the diocese (in 1719) at St John's in the Vale, long before Bishop Fleming's time. At Newlands, the Elizabethan reader's salary of £2 15s. a year was actually *lower* 180 years later,[34] but after the Bounty eventually came through, the living became worth the dizzy sum of £22 a year in 1777.[35] At St John's, the Revd John Gasgarth, who came from a long-standing local family, had given the chapel £200, which had immediately been matched by the Bounty. And rather generously, Thomas Tullie had given his right of the gift of the living to the Gasgarths (a right later purchased by the Lonsdales) and the parishioners, the right to be exercised in alternate years.

Three years later, thirty-seven parishioners of St John's gave another £100 on the condition that whoever served the chapel as deacon would teach all the children reading, writing and arithmetic and the boys, 'should it be thought expedient', Latin and

Greek. The lessons were to be free[36] and, if the incumbent chose not to do the job himself, he forfeited £5 out of his annual salary.* In time, the school house – 'a small stone building by the church' – was built.[37] By 1732 the chapel joined the third of the diocese that employed a perpetual curate and the Reverend Isaac Robley, a Queen's College graduate, could, at last, restore some of the sacraments to his parishioners. But even then the job came with no fixed abode, the curate initially living outside the chapel's boundaries. And in 1773 the incumbent, John Wilson, refused to teach without a fee, a precedent that his successors would follow.[38]

The other four Parish chapels gradually came to be served by deacons in holy orders, still only qualified to read the prayers and homilies of the Church of England. So, initially, the improvements may have been marginal, as Robert Southey described in his *Colloquies*:[39]

> '...because there would have been some injustice and hardship in ejecting the existing incumbents [the readers], they were admitted to deacon's orders without undergoing any examination. The person who was thus reader, as it was called at yonder Chapel in the vale of Newlands and who received this kind of ordination, exercised the various trades of Taylour, Clogger and Butter-print maker.'

However, the fact that the readers and deacons of the chapels were so often local men prolonged the absence of outside authority in the Parish and must have helped the cohesion of the central vestry. The steep decline of the chapels since the Reformation had been reversed. Whatever the weaknesses of the system, as centres for the regular exchange of gossip and necessary information about stock by the inhabitants of these small, far-flung communities, the chapels were significantly strengthened. And by 1750, when all the

---

* And, at exactly the same time in Borrowdale, the parishioners had been giving their own money to try to raise enough for a cleric who would conduct, as Newlands did, a free school at the west end of the chapel. This was a common practice in the Lake District, 'sometimes to the scandal of the authorities who found the communion table inked and so forth'.

Parish chapels had been augmented by the Bounty,[40] they could at last again enjoy the traditional festivities that accompanied the sacrament of christening and, in some chapels, marriage. One of the great iniquities of the Reformation had finally been redressed.

The felling of the Derwentwater oaks

In 1745 the Jacobites threw their hat into the ring for the last time, in what was to be the final Anglo-Scottish war, and the Parish farmers in the Crosthwaite valley drove their cattle through the jaws of Borrowdale for safety.

This time there was no Derwentwater to lead the rebellion. Charles, the titular fifth earl, had been barred from the title on the legitimate grounds that he was under sentence of death. Famously escaping from Newgate prison dressed as a woman, he had fled to France, where he had seven children and indefatigably sought justice for his eldest son, who was to become the 4th Earl of Newburgh upon his mother's death and should, legally, have inherited the Derwentwater title upon his father's disqualification. But Parliament, adamantine and presumably fearful, passed yet another special statute, this time to legislate that those born abroad were unable to inherit. When Charles tried to join the 'Forty-Five, his French ship was captured before it landed. The following year, he became the penultimate person to be beheaded in England, displaying 'great serenity and calmness of mind', despite, or perhaps because of, being 'dressed in scarlet faced with gold, a gold laced waistcoat, and a white feather in his hat'.[41] His rackety life was to become the subject of many a historical novel.

Without him, quite unlike the rising of the 'Fifteen, only thirty years earlier, the Stuart prince had picked up little support as he marched south. Since the area had, for so long, supported the Stuarts, this might seem surprising. But just as Cumberland's support for Catholicism was finally demolished by excess slaughter, it seems that the execution and banishment of the Derwentwaters created a similarly pragmatic feeling that the Stuarts were now an ancient, and lost, cause. And after the Jacobite defeat at the bloody

Battle of Culloden in April 1746, the revolt was finished.

The 'Forty-Five exacted a heavier death toll than the 'Fifteen; as many as two thousand rebels were slaughtered at Culloden. Others were hunted down and taken to Carlisle, where a randomly chosen 127 were tried for treason, almost all found guilty and executed within the county. The heads of two Macdonald lairds were placed on the Scotch Gate, where they remained for years, and the heads of two English Jacobite officers were returned from London to hang on the English Gate.[42] The general feeling in the county was that 'the executing of too great numbers is shocking',[43] and there was considerable discomfort. Nevertheless, the border with Scotland had not enjoyed a single period of fifty years' peace since the arrival of the Normans, and this proved to be the last time Carlisle was ever in the front line of attack; Cumberland and the Parish would never again be fought over by hostile forces.

In Scotland, the English 'pacification' of the Highlands began, a violent attempt to destroy its clan system, much aided by the Scottish landowners' decision, a little later, to clear the glens for sheep, as Scotland became 'colonised for wool'.[44] But in the Parish, a different line was drawn with its past. Charles Radcliffe's eldest son, James, claimed his title and estates under common law upon his father's death, but once he wanted to marry in 1749, he officially acquiesced to his estates' income going to Greenwich Hospital, in return for a £30,000 recompense for himself and his siblings.[45] Some 11,000 acres of land, half of Derwentwater lake, and Keswick south of the Greta were to be lost to the Derwentwaters for ever, as the crown and Parliament finally won their thirty-four-year legal battle, fought by fair means and foul.

The fewer than a thousand acres of old Derwentwater demense land provided the hospital with the vast majority of its Parish income; in 1738, the rent roll would show the receipt of £233 6s.1d. from seventeen tenants (ignoring the Keswick shops and some quarries all let for £1 or under), compared with £32 11s. 6d. from the 108 customary tenants and £19 1s. from the forty-one burgage tenants.[46] The original Greenwich survey had complained that the 'hedges are all in bad Repaire' and 'the Land it Selfe ... verry poor and no Lime to be had but at a verry great expence'.[47] But coppices thrived all over the estate, as they did throughout the Parish, and there was much wonderful wood, which, after the clearance at the time of the mining boom, was now mature and ripe to be sold, a decision taken the next year, in 1739.* However, it took almost ten years[48] for the sale of a twelve-year licence to cut timber to come through to the Spedding brothers, who were leading a bid from the Whitehaven wood merchants, trying to feed the growing fleet. And the main shareholder, James Spedding, who also purchased Armathwaite, immediately applied to tenant Castlerigg Farm in order to oversee operations.

The past of the parishioners had been intimately connected with 'the lovliest grove of large oaks', about 27 yards tall, 'all of equall hight and bigness', at Crow Park[49] on the north shore of the lake. Eighteen acres of oak with 'not one very crooked one amongst them ... and not even a shrub or any other tree',[50] bearing witness to their history as the ancient parkland of the Derwentwaters. Upwards of fourteen thousand trees were felled, including a willow on the Lord's Island with a girth of over 11 feet, and 'later a local farmer, Mr Scott dug out the remaining roots and ploughed the land, starting at the bottom of the rise and cutting a single ridge and furrow in a spiral'.[51] John Dalton – a friend of the writer and Whig politician Horace Walpole – having described the area as a classical paradise in his 'Descriptive Poem' of 1755,[52] apologised in his introduction for raising any false expectations about finding the 'sylvan shrine of the rural divinities wholly undisturbed and unprofaned'. Visitors, he explained, 'must be prepared to be shocked at some late violations of those sacred woods and groves, which had, for ages, shaded the sides of the mountains, and ... that lovely lake'.

The tale of the great felling was told again and again, becoming part of local lore, which cannot have escaped the attention of Greenwich Hospital. In 1748 the hospital offered new twenty-one-year leases on their demesne land, a sign of their long-term

* They valued the wood at £4,875.

commitment to its management; the 750 acres on the eastern side of Derwentwater were let as fifteen farms.[53] When the large-scale tree-feeling commenced, the hospital's policy had been to prepare the land for growing crops and to ensure that grazing animals were kept out of the remaining woodland. But the policy began to gravitate towards longer-term investment in timber and, by concentrating on planting new trees rather than coppicing existing ones, to forgo immediate rental income. By 1760 they began to improve the appearance of the lake shore and introduced mixed planting for ornamental effect. Larch, Scots pine, Lombardy poplar and willow joined the oak, ash, elm and birch trees acquired from the Derwentwaters.

The hospital's top hierarchy agreed to support the new policy of 'increasing rather than diminishing the Wood upon the Derwentwater Estate' in 1774, and another 187 acres were commandeered to grow timber.[54] Friar's Crag had already been fenced off and planted ornamentally. As tourism grew and a disciple of Capability Brown was appointed as a receiver to the hospital in 1777, the amount of ornamental planting escalated. More than a third of the trees planted on the estate before the end of the century were oaks, whereas on the hospital's less picturesque Northumberland estate the number of oaks planted was a mere 3 per cent.[55] So, the hospital clearly *did* accept that aesthetic considerations should be taken on board for the Derwentwater shoreline, for which they have never been given credit.

Twenty years after the felling began, the poet Thomas Gray described Crow Park as 'a rough pasture, once a glade of ancient oaks, whose ancient roots remain in the ground but nothing has sprung from them. If one single tree had remained this would have been an unparalleled spot.'[56] Nearly ten years after that, in the first great guidebook to the Lake District, *A Guide to the Lakes*, published in 1778, Thomas West called for wood preservation throughout the area and decried the felling on hospital land as 'the unfeeling hand of avarice'. By 1800 we find the first printed description of Crow Park as simply 'a beautiful pasture'[57] but the loss of the trees was still being lamented by writers of Wordsworth's generation. Today it is one of the few Derwentwater connections that is still talked about, and the felling of the trees in Crow Park is generally considered to be the first time the destruction of perceived beauty prompted popular protest in England.

Some have suggested that the felling was ordered because, given the Derwentwater Stuart blood, 'it was thought necessary for the public safety that every vestige of that ancient family should be removed'.[58] A key passage in the judgment to execute James Radcliffe in 1716 contained the words: ''twas evident success on your part must have forever established Popery in this kingdom, and that probably you could never have again so fair an opportunity';[59] and that would have been a major establishment fear. If there had been a Derwentwater in situ, might the defeat of the 'Forty-Five have proved a tougher proposition? Close to a thousand years is a long time to weave yourselves into the affections and loyalties of a people hefted to your land.

It seems some element of fear of the Derwentwater name lingered in Parliament long after the battle was won. For, after the two Jacobite rebellions, a journalist in a 1749 issue of *The Gentleman's Magazine* talks not of Derwentwater but of 'Keswick Water', as did another article that year describing a flood.[60] As late as 1837, J. M. W. Turner named his painting of the lake, doubtless with no conscious motive, 'Keswick Lake, Cumberland'. While the scholarly Thomas West believed Derwent Town to be the original name for Keswick,[61] it seems the name Derwentwater, once universal, had, for a time, become forbidden or taboo.[62]

This was a seismic change for the Parish. Probable builders of a pre-Conquest church and certainly the chief patrons of the church's Tudor rebuilding, the Derwentwaters and the Radcliffes had played an integral part in the development of Crosthwaite's church, parish and vestry. Their fourteenth-century arms and their fifteenth- and sixteenth-century tombs, memorial brass and stained glass still bear witness to this today. There had been several Radcliffe vicars (and paid parish clerks too) and many of their more distant relations were members of the Eighteen Men; some have appeared in our story. Peter Crosthwaite's meeting with the last of the Derwentwaters, Anthony James, the 4th Earl of Newburgh's heir and only son, when he visited his traditional land around Keswick in 1800, provides a touching postscript to the family's story. The first Derwentwater to be British-born since the lamented 3rd Earl, Anthony James rather romantically negotiated with Crosthwaite for the purchase of an old ash armchair belonging to his family and saplings of all the indigenous trees on Lord's Island – costing him £5 in all. Once he had attained his majority, in 1778, he had applied to Parliament for the restitution of his estates, offering to pay a large annual rent to Greenwich Hospital in recompense. What he got was £2,500 a year for him and his male heirs for ever. Since the earl died childless in 1814, Parliament's deal to part him from his old inheritance had been cheap indeed, for the Derwentwater male line died with him. Their title bizarrely devolved to the descendants of Thomas Clifford, the first husband of Anthony James's grandmother Charlotte Maria Livingston.*

In the Parish, even after James's execution, there was usually a Radcliffe on both sides of the argument – the descendants of Nicholas on occasion sporting a 'Sir' or an 'Esq.' – the family having intermarried with the Fishers, the Stangers, the Williamsons, Bankes, Tickells, and more.[63] However, a 1787 survey speaks of J. Radcliffe Esq., probably a Quaker, 'a descendant of the Derwentwater family; he is the last that I know of in this country, and has no children, so that name may probably become extinct'.[64] By the beginning of the nineteenth century, there was no trace of the family in the Parish.

The great storm and wadd mining

A freak Parish storm accompanied the beginning of the destruction of the oaks in 1749, observed by the surveyor, cartographer and journalist George Smith, who was trapped by it outside Keswick for six days. The storm remained so notorious that its story was still being told in Lake District guidebooks and directories almost two centuries after the event.

On 22 August, thunder and lightning erupted with exceptional

* Loyal Sir Edward's wife.

violence behind Skiddaw, the subsequent torrential rainfall flooding the land between Derwentwater and Bassenthwaite Lake for almost a week, rendering the roads to Keswick impassable. On what began as an extremely hot and sultry day, the inhabitants of Wanthwaite Vale in St John's started to hear a 'strange buzzing noise, like the working of the maltmill, or wind at the tops of trees, for two hours together', a Keswick correspondent wrote a week later.[65] The valley was enveloped in darkness as the storm passed overhead and crashed into the mighty Wanthwaite Crags on its eastern side. 'To the noise of thunder, was added that of the cataracts'[66] as a mile of precipitous fell 'was covered in an instant, with one cascade of roaring torrent ... sweeping all before it'.[67] Legburthwaite Mill and its kiln was swept away in five minutes flat, one millstone never found and the other carried 'some hundred yards' away by the cataract, laying 'waste to a great tract of arable and meadow land which will for the future be forever spoil'd, being as deep in some places as the tops of trees', one of George Smith's party observed.[68]

Legburthwaite Mill, once it was reconstituted, placed in a somewhat over-romanticised context.

The storm did great damage to the parishioners' livelihoods, as the gravel and sand, as well as rock 3 to 4 yards deep,[69] covered their land, the Keswick correspondent recorded. He saw far-flung rocks, one with a circumference of 36 feet, which the inhabitants of the valley estimated were 'larger than a team of ten horses can move'.[70] As far away as Armboth on the western side of Thirlmere, George Smith tells us, parishioners had moved through thigh-deep water from house to barn to the tops of their hay-mows for safety; some clung to trees, 'every moment expecting that the trees to which they had fled ... should be torn up by the roots, and the hay overturned by inundation'.[71] All the while, 'the most terrible thunder and incessant lightning that was 'ever known'[72] continued remorselessly.

Appearing less fearsome to us – used as we are to television coverage of worldwide natural disasters – the descriptions of the storm read to contemporaries like a domestic Armageddon, hence the longevity of its fame. 'The inhabitants', we are told by George Smith, 'were scarcely less astonished and terrified, than they would have been at the sound of the last trumpet and the dissolution of nature.'[73] 'The first man to map the Cumberland Fells',[74] Smith became the first cartographer to provide any detailed maps of the Parish. This is notable because, in the wider Cumbria, it took almost another forty years before even the educated began really to understand the topography of the Lake District. The centrality of the Scafell–Gable range – the nub of Wordsworth's imaginative description of the whole Lake District – was not recognised in print until the very end of the eighteenth century.*

George Smith had been waiting to visit the wadd (graphite) mines in Borrowdale, only the second outsider on record to do so. The first visitor, Bishop Nicholson in 1710,[75] reported that the deepest vein of the 'old men' had been opened up the year before, but had been ruined by 'pilfering interlopers'.[76] By the time of Smith's visit there were reports of as many as forty lights dotted about the workings in the high fells at night, as thieves scavenged.[77] Smith saw eighteen in daylight himself, including some girls, working away in 'the principal heap of rubbish ... within a pistol shot' of the miner's

* In the 1799 reprint of West's *Guide*.

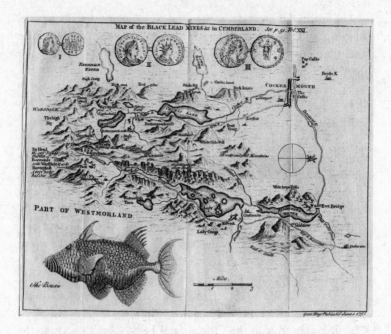

George Smith, the first man to map the Cumberland Fells, charts the
placement of the Parish wadd mines here.

lodge;[78] and he is today notorious for his claim that the poorer
inhabitants of Keswick lived mainly by 'stealing or clandestinely
buying of those who steal, the black lead, which they sell to Jews,
or other hawkers'.[79]

In 1750, the year after Smith's visit at the time of the great
storm, John White, whose job it was to guard the mine, was waiting
in the mine house with his musket and pistols charged, having
heard rumours of trouble. A mob surrounded the mine house and
announced that they would kill him unless he sat tight. A few days
later, given a friendly warning to make himself scarce, White sur-
reptitiously enlisted six men to help him and barred the door. The
raiders managed to clamber on to the roof, tore off the slates to
make a hole to fire through, and wounded one of White's men. But
when the gang's leader was mortally wounded in the ensuing fire-
fight, the rest fled. As did John White, frightened of being accused

of murder, until Henry Bankes, then the mine's owner, vouched for his and his men's innocence and a full pardon was received.[80] The story hit the national press, and George Smith's account of his visit was duly published in *The Gentleman's Magazine*.

In the same year John Spedding reported a more sophisticated local attempt at theft, as the steward William Hetherington,* 'with subterraneous wickedness', was discovered to have enterprisingly tunnelled in the opposite direction from his claim, reaching both the upper level and the guardhouse some 40 feet below.[81] A little later, when two miners were brutally attacked with cudgels and thrown down the shaft in broad daylight, Henry Bankes had had enough and started to lobby Parliament.[82] So, in 1752 an Act was passed threatening a public flogging, a year's hard labour or transportation for illegal entry into the mine or for any theft of wadd. Five large slate boundary stones were positioned, warning of trespass, the ones below the common inscribed J. Bankes Esquire, 1752.†

Commercially, the policy of keeping stocks high and sales measured had worked brilliantly for the mine owners. So its theft had become even more irresistible[83] and, in reality, the smuggling from the mixed spoil by the poor, which earned the smugglers around 6s. to 8s. a day, did little real harm to the market. The practice wasn't going to stop anyway, whatever the threats. So, by the time William Gilpin, doyen of the picturesque movement, wrote about the mines, he described the toils of the scavengers as 'honest gains'.[84]

However, large-scale theft, whether by the mine's employees or by organised gangs, was entirely different, and it is said that, by the 1760s, £1,000 worth of illegally sourced wadd was being traded each year.[85] Temporary houses had been built on top of the shafts that were already being worked and miners were searched after

* Sent to Carlisle on trial, he was nevertheless reinstated.
† On the common, they read Shepherd 1752. John Shepherd had long had the mining contract for that land but two years later there would be a major fracas, when his grandson was discovered breaking into a Bankes mine. The Shepherds subsequently sold half their lease to several speculators with no northern connections.

each shift. By 1778, the year of a massive new find, the mines produced in total 32,536 pounds of first-class wadd, and there were nearly as many overseers as miners, the guards being paid as much as, or more than, some of the best mineworkers.[86] And yet this was the year when the low wadd hole suffered one of its first attacks by an organised gang. Bridgett Birkett, one of the two leaders, was caught by one of the new, better-paid guards from Buttermere, and the wadd was eventually traced and returned to the depths of the mine for safety.[87]

Unlike the old copper mines, the Seathwaite wadd mine had really strong local connections. The Dixon family had been associated with it from the early days,[88] and Thomas Dixon, who had been one of the two to recover the stolen goods in 1778, had lived all his life at Seathwaite (as had his wife) and duly became the steward. Moving to the new Bankes steward's house,* with a good view of the mine, he would later bequeath the position to his son and then his grandson. The Hudsons, too, had long had a financial involvement with the mine, and the Joplins, Fishers, Birketts and Braithwaites had bought into the lease back in 1632, while others, like the Scotts and the Hodgsons, had done more private deals. But connections could sometimes be on both sides of the fence. Which was the difficulty.

People knew that Joseph Fisher from Keswick traded in the black market† but didn't expect him to acquire £1,000 worth of wadd and take it to London to sell.[89] Then, when a trusted miner was discovered in the process of stealing £300 worth of wadd,[90] there was real shock when his fellow workers were stripped and another four of them were caught black-handed too. But wadd fever had reached such a pitch by then that, when some of the precious stuff was found on Vicar's Island (where it had been left behind by the Germans), there was talk of draining Derwentwater in search of more fabulous wealth.

*

---

* This is still in place today.
† Thought to be so called because of the black stain left on the hand as wadd was exchanged.

Ferociously tough work was also available at the Honister slate quarries, the most productive in the Lake District. The first extant documentary reference to the quarry is dated 1728, but it may well have started hewing its famous green slate – still providing cladding for so many local houses and landmarks today – a while earlier. The quarry was located in the south of the Parish, in the wild country at the top of Honister Pass. Many of its workers were inhabitants of the Parish too, some of them living in primitive huts on the slopes of the lowering crags around the mine, others walking long distances to work. The miners transported the hewn slate by muscle and sledge along narrow paths and scree. They boasted that the vast chambers they had hollowed out in the mountains would hold the population of a large city. The classic description of their work was written almost 140 years later by Eliza Lynn Lynton, daughter of a Crosthwaite vicar, but the miners' labours can hardly have been any easier before:[91]

'...It is simply appalling to see that small moving speck on the high crag, passing noiselessly along a narrow grey line that looks like a mere thread, and to know that it is a man with the chances of his life dangling in his hand ... he sets himself against the perpendicular descent, and comes down the face of the crag, carrying something behind him – at first slowly, and, as it were, cautiously; then with swift step, but still evidently holding back; but at last with a wild haste that seems as if he must be overtaken, and crushed to pieces by the heavy sled grinding behind him ... and now he draws up by the roadside – every muscle strained, every nerve alive, and every pulse throbbing with frightful force. It is a terrible trade – and the men employed in it look wan and worn, as if they were all consumptive or had heart disease. The average daily task is seven or eight journeys, carrying about a quarter of ton of slate each time.'

Yet the toughly bred labourers survived – and some flourished. One of the quarrymen is said to have walked to work from Seathwaite, returned home to wash and change, then run, via the Langstrath valley, almost two thousand feet up to Esk Hause, before plunging down into the Langdale valley to join a party. Having danced his socks off, he returned home again and then went off back to work at Honister the next morning. As the Borrowdale vicar who reports this story points out, while it initially seems like fable, once one remembers the marathon fell races, still fiercely competitive today, it seems more possible.[92]

Work was equally harsh in the slate quarries at the top of Skiddaw. Having flaked off the fissile slate there, quarrymen would carry it down the mountain and, according to George Smith again,[93] 'each man carries as much as would load a Cumberland cart'. Walking upright, with a sort of hod upon his shoulders to accommodate the slate, the quarry worker would use his sure mountain feet to get himself and his extraordinary load safely down the mountain, and then make his way back up again, for some more quarrying and carrying.

So, there were other ways for the parishioners to make a living, if they found that their land was unworkable after the great parish storm of 1749. But these ways too were tough.

Enfranchisement and the
Christian Family

T HE RELATIVE RISE in hill farmers' wealth – which was to
survive the cattle plague of the 1750s virtually untouched
– had irritated the landlords. With relatively stable or fixed
rents in the Parish, they were searching for a way to turn this to
their own advantage. In the South and most of the rest of the
country, where leasehold tenancy had displaced all other kinds of
tenure by the beginning of the century, the landlords, with strong
government support, had moved aggressively and successfully from
the traditional sense of landownership as 'a limited and not always
saleable right in things'[1] to a new sense of exclusive property rights.

They had dammed rivers for fishponds and enclosed forest with
traditional wood-rights for the commons to make parks, subsequently allowing their new herds of park deer to trample the local
crops. Vigilante groups had energetically resisted, provoking, in
1723,* the most 'viciously repressive' English legislation for 400
years. The so-called Black Act authorised the death penalty for
more than fifty poaching 'crimes'. This was a greater number of
capital offences than the entire criminal code of any other European
country;[2] and soon the use of the ultimate sanction would starkly
underline the government's new stance.

The poaching laws' effects reached the Parish too. In the sixteenth century, some Keswick men had hunted on the western side

---

* The year that the old Percy tenants in the Parish had finally won their hun-
dred-year battle about rents.

of Derwentwater, 'with bows and arrows and hound and horn, certain wild animals called Fallow deer',[3] and got off with only a fine. But after the passing of the Black Act no one dared even bag a pheasant, their only remaining weapons sabotage and irony. So, the Cumberland hill farmers did their best to denude their county of game for the upper classes, destroying grouse and partridge eggs with ease and brio: on one occasion they did even better and sent an ironic present to 'a public meeting of qualified gentlemen in an adjoining county of 2000 partridge eggs, carefully packed'![4]

Timber and land

Cumberland landlords, meanwhile, intuited that the burgeoning process of industrialisation might allow them also to assert exclusive property rights, whatever their landownership agreements with their tenants might say. Since wood had become a vital prop (in two senses) to support the growing commerce of the west coast, they began to switch their search for extra profit to timber. The scarcity of wood had been a problem in the Parish ever since the mining boom, but, while landlords had been tough, they had stayed approximately within the rules – according to which underwoods were the property of the tenants and woods of warrant the property of the lord, as long as he allowed, upon request, the tenants to carry out necessary home and farm repairs and building. But now the landlords began to display an insouciant disregard for *where* the timber came from.

Around 1755, all thirty tenants in the Newlands valley banded together to send a 'Remonstrance' straight to George, Earl of Egremont:[5] 'We and our Predecessors have from time Immemorial claimed the timber and other Trees growing in the Hedges of our Customary Estates ... and have Loped them, or cut 'em down for our own Proper Use or Uses without the Stop or Molestation of any Former Lord thereof, or their agents.' And they had also claimed 'the Superfluous Branches of the Lord's Timber trees, or take of the Coppice Woods' immemorially. So they were now 'greatly surprised' to find themselves fined for such activity. They continued: 'We flatter ourselves that your Lordship have had the Custom represented in a False Light.' And they concluded, with a good Cumberland sting in the tail, please 'stop such Rapacious Proceedings in Future', so we can avoid having to go to law.

The tenants of the thirty customary holdings in the next-door manor of Thornthwaite had grown accustomed to using or selling the hedgerow trees without permission.[6] Once the Greenwich Hospital acquired the manor in 1735, it did all it could to quash this practice. In one case, it stopped the payment of £6 12s. 6d. to Thomas Jefferson, the incumbent of All Saints Cockermouth, for the sale of some coppice wood on his tenement to a Keswick clogger. The parson argued that surely he should not receive worse treatment from them than a 'Roman Catholic lord' but eventually gave in to avoid prosecution. When the issue was finally tested at law in the 1770s,[7] it was eventually ruled that the hedgerow trees belonged to the tenant,[8] but Lord Egremont appeared unmoved. For, in the same decade, his steward raised more than a year's rent[9] from all his leasehold farms by selling his tenants' underwoods and brushwoods to the proprietors of the Ellenfoot furnace. His tenants continued to claim the whole lot was theirs, as did Sir Wilfrid Lawson's tenants in Bassenthwaite, after Lawson had sold 'all the timber on their estates' to 'a company of Iron dealers' for making charcoal.[10]

In 1777, customary tenures covered two-thirds of Cumberland land and an even greater percentage of land in the Parish.[11] Some argue that the relationship between tenants and landlords in the Parish remained essentially feudal, as it was 'based upon the extra-economic extraction of the surplus from the direct producer by the feudal lords'[12] (in the form, for instance, of boon days and annual hen-giving).* However, the theoretical socio-economic status of the customary tenants was in practical terms irrelevant – as long as they remained jurors. For, having learnt the strength of solidarity, they could make sure that they prevailed in the legal fights between tenant and landlord.

* The common post-Marxist definition.

So, while the battle for timber continued, as no court decision wavered from the principle that the tenants had certain rights in respect of woods of warrant and control of the underwood, not only did they never lose their rights, they had the upper hand. Feudal the system may or may not have been, but, quite unlike almost all of the rest of the country, the tenants en bloc were the most powerful force at the courts. By the end of the eighteenth century, they had begun to compete with the landlords in the timber market for themselves. Both county and Parish remained very particular places.

By the 1760s, turnips and clover had made their belated entry into the Parish. Clover has the important capacity of replacing nitrogen in exhausted soil, and turnips helped enable the cows to withstand the winter: 'generally kept in the house night and day during winter, except while at water'. Milk and fresh meat became potentially available all year round, enlivening the old diet of the salted and the smoked. And now, once their cream had been taken off to make butter, the farmers' families could keep back some milk, perhaps to make 'blue-milk cheese' – or sell it fresh to the cowless. However, many tenements remained small, their sheep flocks numbering as little as eight or ten. And in Borrowdale life went on throughout the century much as it had for the previous hundred years, enlivened by an annual ritual drinking session to inaugurate the 'King of Borrowdale' at the Miner's Arms in Rosthwaite. Sally Youdale, the so-called Queen of Borrowdale, born in 1768, brings the time and the place vividly alive:

'There was no wheeled thing in Borrowdale in my youth, we used to caryy o'nag back. We had peat and sticks but no coal. People were very particular about going to chapel and afterwards met in t' chapel garth for news. Joss Harry came frae t'Watendlath with his dog. [Worth a mention as the dog continued his regular attendance at chapel long after his master had died.] ... Snow on t'fell tops till midsummer ... There were fiddlers and fellows for t'Christmas dance; servants, statesmen's sons and daughters were aw alike. We had chimney hams, bacon, mutton; rows of breet pewter plates ont'dresser. Weddings to Kurk o'nag's back.'[13]

This good-humoured description of the socialisation that kept life bearable offers a counterbalance to an angry (anonymous) Cumberland writer of 1766, much quoted in the twentieth century, who made everything sound pretty bleak as he bitterly rehearsed the unrelenting toughness of the life of the average tenant farmer.[14] Thanks to the mountains and the local climate, he wrote:

> 'the middle of February is our winter, and the farmers must have out half of their straw, and two thirds of their hay at that time, or their stock perishes. We cannot turn out horses and cows to grass till the beginning of June, at which time the grass begins to be fit, and after the winds and incessant rains over the winter ... the land is kept so cold and spongy that we cannot sow oats before April, bigge before June and ... our lands, with the vast quantity of manure that we must employ, more than is necessary south of the mountains, cost one-third at least more to till ... and does not produce half the crops...'[15]

There were 10,000 estates in Cumberland, he claimed, ranging from £10 to £100 a year, and 'These petty landowners work like slaves; they cannot afford to keep a man servant, but husband, wife, son and daughters all turn out to work in the fields; they wear wooden shoes, shod like a horse's foot with iron.' Their diet is 'whey, turnips, oatmeal bread, oatmeal and water ... and they work very hard upon this diet; they breed many children and ... when they grow up they post away to happier climes, and make you very good servants'.[16]

This is a polemic. Fish, which the writer entirely ignored, were still both plentiful and admired; the poet Norman Nicholson felt 'that the eighteenth century looked even on Derwentwater primarily as a gigantic fish-pond'.[17] Salmon still spawned in the Greta as well as Derwentwater,[18] where trout were fished in April and May, and in Bassenthwaite Lake pike and perch could also be had. The parishioners' diet was actually 'oat cake, buttermilk and whey, ale, fish and whatever they could produce from the land'. Also, as we will see, genuine enfranchisement had begun to be offered in the old Percy lands in the Parish. And Arthur Young, who was to become Secretary of the Board of Agriculture, would paint a very different portrait in 1768,[19] although admittedly he took no notice of the smaller farms.

The number of sheep in flocks around Keswick, he reports, ranged from 100 to 1,000, and profit from each sheep varied from 4s. to 6s., of which a shilling was for the wool (3–4 pounds per sheep) and the rest from lambs, among which losses could still be considerable. He adds that the sheep stayed on the commons in both winter and spring.[20] However, Young confirmed the relative rarity of farm labourers in Cumberland, describing a 70-acre farm, worked with only the help of one boy and a maid, and a 240-acre farm employing a man, a boy, two maids and two labourers. The maid was expected to brew, bake, milk and make butter and cheese, and was paid between £3 and £6 a year; but she and the boy, who appeared to earn closer to £3 than £6, lived in and were fed. As did the man, who would be the chief farmworker, ploughman or shepherd and earned between £9 and £14 a year;[21] all wages appear to have risen quite healthily since the first twenty years of the century.

The labourers, however, seldom lived at the farm, although they were often provided with food, and were usually still hired at either the Cockermouth or Keswick hiring fairs, held every Whitsun and Martinmas. Virtually never employed for as long as a year, essentially for reasons of Parish tax, they earned between 6d. and 10d. a day. The boys 'in brand new suits of green and red, given to them by their parents, stood with straws in their mouths as a sign they wished to be hired as "lads"';[22] by sixteen or seventeen they would graduate to labourers. Like the permanent employees, many of them will have been children from large yeoman families, where there was insufficient employment on the home farm.*

Young reports that manuring remained common throughout the Parish; there were still no beans, 'very few peas', the wet climate being unsuitable, 'and as little rye'.[23] He also describes

---

* For at least two centuries, their forebears had left home to find work, their parents choosing to employ extra labour when necessary. See MacFarlane, 'The myth of the peasantry: family and economy in a northern parish' from Smith, *Land, Kinship and Life-cycle*, pp. 343–7.

how turnips were cultivated, although this seems a decade or so early for their general introduction, when they became almost universally used in the reasonably sized landholdings for feeding and fattening sheep and cattle, particularly in winter. And potatoes were now part of the regular diet. There were two methods of cultivation. The first method, which, on balance, was considered less productive, was the 'lazy-bed method', in which you placed your tubers on top of manured grassland and then dug trenches, throwing the earth up over the tubers. In the second, the land was ploughed, then 'well dunged' before the tubers were placed 1 foot deep in alternate furrows. The land was then hand-weeded, aided by one run-through with the plough in the unplanted furrows, and an acre thus prepared yielded a crop of between two and four hundred bushels.

However, the hand-weeding may not have been too laborious, as the fields were still pretty neglected – witness the cheerful lines of William Dickinson:[24]

> No cleaning of land, no picking of weeds;
> Let everything prosper that can:
> For all plants were sent to ripen their seeds
> And make themselves useful to man.

Horses still bedecked the view as, based upon ploughing an acre a day with two or four horses, the hill farmers reckoned that twelve horses were necessary to manage a hundred acres. Depending upon their means, and the size of their holdings, they used different methods to achieve this. Many dealt with their land themselves, involving an intermittent capital outlay of £7 for a cart for two horses or £5 5s. for a one-horse cart, each horse costing around £6 10s. a year to keep. Alternatively, a cart and a horse were hired for a day for 3s., or the ploughing was bought in at a cost of between 5s. and 6s. an acre, the payment for labour much the same as for the horse and plough. The cattle were still long-horned, their average yield six gallons of milk a day. The cows were brought down to the valleys in winter, the calves now allowed to suckle for two months.

It is estimated that, by 1750, around 80,000 head of cattle were crossing the Solway plain annually on their way south, and the richer statesmen, who had joined the trade of fattening Highland cattle and sheep, needed more access to grazing on the commons to benefit seriously. Initially, they just took as much as they could. A typical Keswick court complaint was raised about a man who rented land outside the manor to grow hay and then, having already illegally fed his increased stock through the winter, brought them back illegally to graze, 'to great Abuse and Oppression on the Commons'.[25] This was only legal on stinted land, never on unenclosed commons. And the fundamental significance of the issue was that it would insidiously damage the whole manor court system, the fulcrum of the combined customary tenants' power.

We have previously considered the possibility that the emphatic widening of the monetary gulf between the richest and poorest statesmen between 1660 and 1750 would, in time, damage the age-old solidarity of the class. And pondered whether the expensive new statesman habit of leaving monetary legacies to all their children might exacerbate the situation. However, not only had the mutual community interests of the statesmen, represented in the Parish by the Eighteen Men, never been seriously dented before, it had been responsible for their success in the centuries-long battle with the landlords about rent. And it appeared to be on the verge of achieving the same result in the battle about timber. Yet, since a growing minority of the better-off wanted to exploit the commons, and the juries were usually the principal tenants, no one tried hard to stop them, with consequent damage not just to the 'order of the commons' but to the traditional cement that had for so long bonded the tenant class together.

Both the courts' legitimacy and its effectiveness were significantly undermined, even though for some issues they remained thoroughly useful. Good examples of that are the two restrictions added to turf-cutting etiquette at Braithwaite. In 1764 it was ruled that no one was to carry turf away from Raveling Moss 'until they have first worked or contributed their share of the expense towards repairing of the way leading from the said moss to the Turnpike road',[26] a good old-fashioned ruling. And twelve years later, all were required to 'drain the water off and ... bed the peat pots well', to mitigate the danger of stock stumbling in waterlogged holes.[27]

The export of potash boomed – 'some thousand loads'[28] of bracken from the Lake District now passing through Lancaster every year. This exacerbated the old tensions about the times for cutting, since many tenants would have wanted to profit from the new market. Keswick had tried to be even-handed, ordering that no one was to 'cut any green bracken to burn to ashes'[29] without the jurors' consent, allowing at least the possibility of profit from good potash, while the emphasis in the Braithwaite court in 1766 remained on preserving bracken until it was dry enough to be harvested for bedding even though an increasing use of slate for roofing was leading to a diminished need for bracken thatch. Thus, once alternative sources of potash began to decimate potential profits from bracken at the end of the century, the need for vigilant bracken legislation evaporated, although using old bracken as litter continued in the Lake District and the Parish until the middle of the twentieth century.[30]

That happened naturally, but the sense of the loss of the courts' legitimacy and usefulness, once they had been induced to favour the greed of the richer tenants, is illustrated by the dramatic drop in the number of cases taken to court. As we have seen, *80 per cent* of the eighteenth-century cases presented to the courts were taken in the first half of the century.

Enfranchisement and turnpikes

In the underpopulated Newlands valley, a new issue arose to underline the growing disparities of wealth. There had always been regular changes of tenements and homes among the age-old community of Fishers, Graves, Scotts, Thwaites and Bowes (joined by the Dovers at the end of the sixteenth century),[31] depending on the success and longevity of the individual hill farmers, and sale documents often covered an astonishing array of unspecified 'houses, buildings, gardens, yards ... woods, underwoods, moores, mosses; Sheep Heafes, Commons, Pastures and Turbage'.[32] Then, at the beginning of the eighteenth century, several other families[33] had moved to the valley, prompting, in time, a significant rise in land disputes between neighbours.[34]

In the midst of these disputes, in 1759, a revolutionary offer was made in all the old Percy lands: tenants were given the opportunity to purchase land on a freehold basis – this was true enfranchisement and (unlike the 'enfranchisement' of 1623) was actually described as such at the time. With the now thoroughly monetarised market, many of the larger Newlands tenants seized their chance. In year one, there were two valley enfranchisements,[35] while at Keskadale a new owner, John Hudson of Loweswater, paid £150 to purchase and enfranchise 70 acres of high summer grazing. A year later, several more enfranchisements were achieved by Newlands men, including two Fishers.[36] The cost was eight years' market rent, slightly less than a third of the market value of freehold land.[37] Egremont, retaining not just his mineral rights but future control of any land that might be required to exploit a new find, offered a 4 per cent mortgage for a maximum of ten years. And, as in Derwentwater and Castlerigg well over a hundred years earlier, the enfranchised continued to pay the increasingly nominal sum of the 'ancient yearly customary rent ... to be ever after paid as free rent'.[38]

Surprisingly to the modern eye, the woodland of enfranchised property was always sold separately, the newly enfranchised given first offer 'upon fair and reasonable terms'. These terms were defined after two separate valuers (albeit both employed by the Egremonts) had priced the wood, at 10 per cent less than the market price, plus 5 per cent (usually) to compensate the original owner for loss of future profit. However, mortgage terms were not on offer for woodland, and since its value could only be raised once the wood had been cut, large areas could prove difficult for the yeoman to purchase.[39]

This is best illustrated by the case of an enfranchisement at Fawe Park on the western lake shore of Derwentwater, one of three such that took place in the first year. Fawe Park, 'which had a great deal of very good timber' in 20 acres of parkland, proved a complicated transaction[40] for the purchaser, William Stanger,[41] who paid £200 for 75 acres had required a 'loan' of £600 from the Egremonts to pay £963 for the wood. Four years later, half of this sum had been repaid, along with the 4 per cent interest on the whole, presumably from sales of the timber.[42] Sufficient remained, however, for Thomas Gray to comment on the beauty of Fawe Park fifteen years later.

The new owner of the wood was free to enclose it, should he wish, and the ratio of price per acre and the price for the wood varied substantially depending upon the quality of both, as is demonstrated by the other two enfranchisements on the western shore that took place in the first year. John Fletcher, a carpenter at Waterend, paid £80 for 44 acres, including quite a stretch of shoreline, substantially more than the £40 for 50 acres at Manesty at the southern end of Derwentwater, paid by Thomas Gillbanks; although the price of the wood, which seems to have been principally oak coppice in both lots, was approximately the same in each case, at around £145.[43]

Enfranchisement was a major new stage in the evolving story of the Parish hill farmer, allowing potential future change in both landholding and status, as, once the fines on alienation* no longer applied, the burden on the sale and purchase of land was substantially eased. So, it would become easier for a buyer to become a landed proprietor, building up an estate peopled with tenant farmers, who, as in the South, had no personal stake in their land. In Newlands properties began to change hands more frequently, and outside purchasers started to buy. Two of them had old valley names:[44] Mary Scott, a spinster from London, bought Mill How tenement in 1778; and a decade later, William Harryman, Gentleman, also from London (whose family were one of the new arrivals in the valley at the beginning of the eighteenth century), invested in a house and two cottages in Portinscale.[45] More locally, a Keswick innkeeper bought a house at Braithwaite, two tenements in Littletown and several small dales 'above the beck'.[46] The age of buying a property as an investment *and* as a second home had arrived.

Like the recent misuse of the manor courts, this was a major shift from the homogeneity of the past. Some of the poorer Newlands

* Transfer of land.

customary tenants, whose forebears might have originally drained the valley, may well have sold some or all of their land as a combination of the vagaries of the market for wool and a greater survival rate of children – which meant more mouths to feed[47] – proved the final straw. And since the remaining customary tenants still carried out some of their historic obligations (although they were often exchanged for money by then), the new distinction between the enfranchised and the customary tenants underlined the starker difference between the richer and poorer statesmen.

Later, enfranchisement would be regarded as the necessary prelude to enclosure, for reasons the Egremont steward ruminated upon[48] when the process started. Without enfranchisement, he worried, if the commons were enclosed, his tenants would be bound to improve their freehold lands in the enclosure at the expense of their tenements, where some of their earnings went to the lord of the manor. By 1831, enfranchisement was on offer in the bulk of the Parish.[49]

John Thornton's *A turnpike near Keswick*. The man on the horse is William Green, an artist Wordsworth admired for his authenticity.

All this change in the statesmen's lives coincided with the revolutionary arrival of the turnpike trusts, the first deliberately planned network of roads in England since the Romans.* Privatised trusts were set up by Parliament for each road, to be financed by payment from travellers at toll-bars or gates; and in 1761 a Turnpike Act took charge of the road from Kendal – via Ambleside, Dunmail Raise, the Parish and Whinlatter – to Cockermouth. Once the Keswick–Penrith road was turnpiked too (its conjunction with the Kendal road at Keswick, soon to be acclaimed 'the grand rendezvous of tourists'[50]), the way was now open for pioneers.[51]

But since the settled population almost invariably walked and used packhorses for trade, they could complain, as John Wren from Threlkeld did, that since, from their point of view, 'all the roads and bridges between Penrith by Keswick to Cockermouth are in very good repair', a turnpike could just 'prove a way of oppressing the country and bubbling them out of their money and Labour about Highways'. He concluded 'the poor Commons like not turnpikes'.[52] And, indeed, the turnpikes did mean that more tasks and responsibilities were heaped on the 'poor Commons' in the Parish, without much immediate benefit. Only the wealthiest of Parish yeomen used carts for transport.

The Braithwaite road-building papers of 1769–1859[53] show how the system worked in Newlands, and indeed the Parish generally. Repairs were winter jobs, usually undertaken in February, with a last-minute rush in October when the accounts were due. Each inhabitant with lands rated at £50 or over was 'liable to provide statute labour upon public highways for six days, with two horses and carts'; the richest having to provide two 'able men therewith each day', rather than the one ordained for the rest. And those who kept 'a team, a draught or plough', whatever their estate, were also due to provide six days' labour and two men.

Tenants with lands rated between £3 and £30 – a seemingly random group, which included a Radcliffe (who was also the

* The state of the roads had slowed the movement of the king's troops in the '45.

turnpike surveyor), a Banks, a Stanger and some labourers – 'were each liable to provide six days' labour with one able man each day'. Twenty-five of the villagers owned or tenanted land, five were labourers. If you didn't want to work yourself but would rather pay for it to be done by someone else, you had to announce this at St Kentigern's on the first Sunday of January. In 1769, almost half of the Braithwaite men did so. And the church came in useful again when the projects were 'let out', being 'cried' (for 10d. by the town crier) twice at the church and once at Keswick.

By the 1790s, the accounts reflect the structural alterations to the narrow packhorse bridges, originally built with no, or very low, parapets to accommodate the width of the panniers; but by then widened, with higher sides to protect wheeled vehicles. Post-chaises were introduced, carriers' carts and wagons and then stagecoaches. And by the time mail coaches had joined the throng,* the Braithwaite accounts were considerably more haphazard, and included a fee of 'half a galaine of gaine [gin]' for some bridge work. Not that the Eighteen Men objected; they duly approved the accounts and passed them on to the Justices of the Peace and by 1829 held regular meetings on the issue, introducing the word 'ratepayers' to their minutes for the first time in 1838. For the relationship between the JPs and the Eighteen Men prefigured in the Elizabethan Poor Laws had developed into a permanent intertwining of Parish and secular governance, with the JPs acting as a backstop.[54]

The arrival of the new turnpike roads and the first reasonably accessible entry to the Parish and the Lake District was a change that was to prove as transformational to the social conditions of the Northwest as the centralising policy of the Tudors had been to its political life.[†]

---

* In the 1790s.
† Only one visitor is known to have travelled extensively through the Lakes before the 1770s: the great Methodist preacher John Wesley, who in all made twenty-six long journeys there.

The Parish and the Christian family

In the Parish, the vicar and the Eighteen Men had shared a long, mutually equable period, ever since the court case between them had ended in 1735. Ten years later we discover, from an agreement to change the administration of the Bankes charity, that the Parish had 'lately been subdivided into several divisions', each having 'its own officers and maintaining its own poor',[55] which appears to have given rise to a number of disputes. To avoid these, and so that 'the said benefactions might be applied to the mutual advantage of the whole Parish', as Bankes had intended, it was decided that the Eighteen Men would resume their old responsibility of adjudication along with the incumbent vicar.[56] Since Christian was the only person who had been and remained a trustee, this move is likely to have been his and emphasises a sense of mutual trust.

In 1764, a small house was built close to the school for use of the schoolmaster, who was described in the deed as the 'Continuous School Master'. The building had been authorised by the 'Eighteen Governors or Trustees for the Free School'.[57] This is not just an interesting 'or', it also illustrates a new title for the 'eighteen sworn men', the usual legal description, and it was one that was to be used ever more frequently.

Under Christian, in marked contrast to the enthusiasm and wholesale conversions of George Fox a century before, the Parish remained untouched by the evangelising influence of the most effective preacher of the age, John Wesley, founder of Methodism. Wesley returned again and again to Whitehaven and Cockermouth in the 1740s and 1750s, and had some real success there, as well as at Carlisle. But despite passing through Keswick many times, he is not known to have preached there and had little impact on the Parish. Preaching at Lorton, a little west of Crosthwaite Parish, he recorded in his Journal for 15 May 1759 that his congregation 'found God to be a God of both hills and valley, and nowhere more present than in the mountains of Cumberland'.[58] For me, Wesley had the Cumbrians right, but the fact remains that he inspired little contemporary enthusiasm for Methodism in rural Cumberland.

Christian also oversaw more significant changes to the status of his chapelries. The greatest and most surprising step was taken not long before his death when, in 1765 and 1767, Borrowdale and St John's chapels were granted the right of local burial, a right they had never before enjoyed in their entire history. As we learnt earlier, it was because of the extreme need, during the great plague of the fourteenth century, for locals to bury their dead at Grasmere chapel – rather than traipse all the way to Kendal – that the chapel had been redesignated as a Parish church.

In the same year that Borrowdale got its burial ground, Christian had one last fight with the Eighteen Men. The usual complaint was raised, that the schoolmaster, this time Harrison, then the Newland's curate, did not give enough time to the school. The vote of the Eighteen Men split half and half, and 'the vicar had great influence, (so) as matters stood, was able to retain the curate as schoolmaster'.[59] The Reverend Christian, however, had not taken the usual Cumberland stubbornness and relish for battle properly into account, despite the experience of his early energetic court case. The defeated nine set about quietly lobbying those they intended to elect to the body of the Eighteen Men the following year and, winning their support, drew up a legal bond with their names pledged to call for the dismissal of the master and get a full-time replacement. Christian's appointments were not always judicious; in 1746 he had given the Thornthwaite curacy to Thomas Addison, who during his fifty years' tenure supplemented his earnings by working as lawyer and doctor as well as priest, and who '(as is said) fought Cocks and smuggled'.[60]

The chancellor, Waugh, had his own views on the Eighteen Men. While he was entirely clear that it remained their legal right to 'place and displace the master at leisure', he was distinctly dubious about the wisdom of the system: 'They are Tyrants annually – and no master is like to continue long there.'[61] And, taking the ninety years from 1664, after the church records became completely regular again after their Commonwealth break, there were indeed ten schoolmasters in the first twelve years of the period. However, after that, there had been some good runs of seven and twelve years among the more frequent two years, including a period of sixteen years with *two* licensed schoolmasters.* In the time of Waugh and Christian, Thomas Wilson stayed for fourteen years from 1732, while others stayed for an average of three and a half years. And the results were pretty good. Only one person in the Braithwaite road accounts couldn't write, just making his mark to record receipt of his money.

All these schoolmasters had still benefited from the ancient tradition of 'cock-penny'. While Crosthwaite's schoolmaster may have been in less need of it than his equivalent in Millom – who lived off an unchanged Elizabethan salary of £16 until 1782[62] – when Peter Harrison took over at Crosthwaite in 1850, his salary had to be adjusted for its loss.[63] Each year on Shrove Tuesday, the pupils had been allowed to conduct a cockfight at the south end of the school ground, for which privilege they paid the master his penny, or a gift. However, these playground cockfights eschewed the slashing and killing of the adult version of the sport, referees calling a winner before excessive blood was spilt. The principle behind the practice, according to Arthur Young, was that 'learning effeminated and softened the mind too much and therefore these cruel sports were permitted to harden … feelings and encourage a martial spirit and ferocity of temper'.[64] An entirely unlikely explanation for pupils leading the tough lives of the dales and the fells.

The Parish had been lucky to have had an enlightened and well-connected eighteenth-century vicar. One feels that the Reverend Christian's forty-two-year tenure as vicar of Crosthwaite was both well fought and well spent. He was well served, too, by the even longer tenure of Nicholas Graves, Parish clerk for fifty-six

---

* A particularly notable headmaster, Alexander Naughty, had spent three years at Crosthwaite in 1703, and remained a neighbour of the Parish (and Christian for most of the time) for fifty-one years, after Lowther nominated him to succeed his father as vicar of Threlkeld. Famed as a classical scholar, Naughty was more notorious locally for his way of life. 'He lived in a most homely and slovenly fashion, never tasting any food better than Brown Bread or Oatmeal, which he seasoned with a little salt, and boiled in his only pan, which was never washed … His dress was the meanest in the Parish, he wore wooden clogs, had a high-pitched feminine voice and in later years imbibed freely of intoxicants. Nevertheless, was a great and learned man.' Wilson, *The history & chronicles of Crosthwaite Old School*, p. 23.

years. At the centre of everything, Graves kept an inn at Keswick, where the Eighteen Men often deliberated, as captured in the church records. Their foremen usually still bore the old family names we have become familiar with, but in the last thirty years of Graves's tenure they tended more often to come from families living closer to St Kentigern's than in the past.[65]

Certainly, the fabric of the church was decaying during Christian's time, as money had never been forthcoming from the landholders considered responsible for the chancel roof since the Reformation. But he had a good relationship with his parishioners, including, it seems, his generation's yeoman-made-good-after-he-left-the-Parish, Edward Stephenson.[66] Baptised at Crosthwaite, well before Christian's time there, in 1691, and with a well-off father by local standards, Stephenson had joined the East India Company and become President and Governor of Bengal in 1728 at the age of thirty-seven. A grand moment. But thirty-five hours after learning of his appointment, he discovered that, due to the slowness of communication between London and India, another had been appointed direct from London – to whom Stephenson then formally handed over the keys of Fort William and the job. There was nothing dishonourable in all this, but, unsurprisingly, Stephenson left the company the next year and returned to England, after twenty years away.

By then a rich man, he acquired some fine property in the North, a London house and an estate in Essex, but first he returned to Keswick where he bought and leased some attractive land in the Parish, primarily at Manesty and Stable Hills, opposite Lord's Island. However, the bizarre circumstances of his brief gubernatorial tenure must have rankled, as Stephenson named the house he built in Keswick[67] during his short sojourn there 'Governor's House'. And, upon his death in 1768, two years before Christian, the inscription on the large stone slab just below the altar steps, covering his splendid new family vault, included the words 'Esq.' and 'Governor of Bengal'. His body returned from London to the land of his forefathers, his legacies included £50 to Christian, described as '*clerk*', and £20 for a local woman, who was to mourn – seemingly a modern substitute for the chantries of old.

Christian left his successor a new house and a more secure financial base. And the church, cared for and administered in a manner that would have been impossible had he fashionably added many other livings to his name, had remained central to the governance of the Parish; a Parish much enhanced by the saving and quick development of the chapels, as they moved towards being able to marry and baptise.

His life had been a religious and humble one, compared to many of his remarkable family, who provide a good illustration of the industrial development of the west coast. The vicar's younger brother had married Bridget Senhouse, whose family founded the coastal town of Maryport in 1748/9, in support of their own and others' growing coal-mining businesses. At Ewanrigg, his eldest brother, John, had continued to develop the family coal mine, and his grandson John became Christian's most significant relation locally. Marrying his cousin Isabella, the sole heiress of Henry Curwen of Workington Hall, who owned the Workington coal mines, John changed his surname to Christian Curwen.*

The Workington mines competed with the, eventually, larger Lowther mines at Whitehaven and between them they drew workers from all over Cumberland. In due course, the Lowther mines would stretch a mile under the sea, their miners naming two particularly steep descents into the deepest pit in England, Hardknot and Wrynose, after the two Lake District passes.[68] And it was these mines that proved to be the main draw for the pioneer tourists, mesmerised by gases escaping through long pipes far out to sea, where they were fired and consumed 'in perpetual flames'.[69] Industry, as yet untainted, provoked a celebration of man's ingenuity. Thus, when he wasn't lamenting the loss of the Derwentwater oaks, John Dalton wrote of its power to change 'the face of nature / THESE are the glories of the mine! / Creative Commerce, these are thine'.[70] John Christian Curwen's influence, though, spread far further than the Workington mines. Called 'the father of Cumbrian

---

* Readers may remember that the Curwens had owned Thornthwaite since the late twelfth century and that the family crest is one of those on St Kentigern's fourteenth-century font.

farming',[71] he was a pioneer of estate management and farming technology, developing remarkable early schemes for employee health and pension provision (at times to his own financial disadvantage) and the first agricultural shows.

Finally, Thomas Christian's sister, Mary, married Edmund Law, who was Thomas's clerical next-door neighbour at Greystoke (so Thomas probably introduced them) and became Bishop of Carlisle in 1769, just before Thomas's death. The couple's sons provide another illustration of the mobility of Lakeland society. Their Law grandfather had been a country curate and schoolmaster, who walked 4 miles each way to work for over forty years, whatever the conditions, 'all this for a pittance of twice ten pounds a year. If this be not earning a living hardfully there can be no such thing in this world.'[72] Yet three of them joined their father in the Upper House; and four members of a family unit in the House of Lords over two generations, all achieved under their own steam, is, if not unique, extremely rare.

One of Christian's great-nephews, however, was mostly considered disreputable; a certain Fletcher Christian, who caused something of a stir with his mutiny against Captain Bligh on the *Bounty*. He was named after his mother's wealthy family, the Fletchers, but it was his mother, after some family profligacy, who faced the threat of a debtors' prison. Upon her husband's and father's deaths she had fled back to the Isle of Man with her children, to live off a small pension provided by the richer Christians.[73] This, presumably, explains why Fletcher's brother, Edward, the brilliant legal scholar, taught briefly at Hawkshead grammar school, when William Wordsworth was there. Eccentric himself,* Edward eventually became the first Downing Professor of the Laws of England. He had, with knowledgeable sympathy, represented the Wordsworth family in their protracted battle with Lonsdale to win back the money owed their father; for which the Wordsworths expressed tangible gratitude when William's uncle

---

* One of several Cumbrians who were perceived to have a problem with their clothes and, in Edward's case, consequently never succeeded in court as a barrister. Turner, *Fletcher Christian: Some Facts, Some Fallacies*, p. 16.

and brother became the two main witnesses to record the testimony of Fletcher's fellow sailors about Bligh's behaviour on board the *Bounty*.

It has been said, in the context of the wealth and industry of West Cumberland, that 'The histories of the Senhouse, Curwen and Lowther families admirably illustrate the abundant and aggressive energy of the region during the eighteenth and nineteenth century.'[74] Two of these families bore the same inheritance as Crosthwaite's eighteenth-century vicar, who lies at rest with some of his family in two Georgian tombs directly outside the east end of St Kentigern's. And, while his families' industrial feats may have drawn the pioneering tourists, it was now time for Thomas Christian's Parish to be 'discovered'.

Part Two

Great Crosthwaite Parish Appreciated, 1769–1834

The Lake Poets in the years 1804–1806

The Lake District Opens Up

F ROM THE 1780s onwards, Parish summers were enlivened by the somewhat perplexing arrival of tourists, although a trickle of pioneers had been visiting the easily accessible lakes and the west coast mines, to explore and research, ever since the 1750s. The tourists' dramatic crossing of the treacherous sands of Morecambe Bay underlined the difference between their usual European travels to places whose cultural roots they shared and their discovery of this strange isolated part of England where the 'dialect [was] for some harder to understand than French or Italian'.[1] 'Nature' became the key soon after 1769, the year Thomas Gray, one of the most admired poets of the day, revisited the Lake District.

Gray came upon his 'Vale of Elysium' (the Keswick valley) from Penrith and left the Parish via the new turnpike from Ambleside, 'in some little patches not completed yet, a good country road',[2] the road that made his tour possible. He stayed in Keswick every night he spent in the Lake District, and his description of his journey is considered seminal to the evolution of both the Romantic movement and the Lakes. In 1775, the landscape artist Joseph Farington followed him with the specific intention of painting all of his views, and the poet's route was followed by Girton, Turner and innumerable others. Gray's favourite views* would be transformed, in Thomas West's *A Guide to the Lakes in Cumberland, Westmorland and Lancashire* in 1778, into a series of numbered 'stations', which offered especially striking views and were perfect for painters. Stations – a word consciously chosen for its religious

---

* Along with those of some others.

connotations – would become a late eighteenth-century passion, while West's *Guide*, the first, outstanding, guidebook to the Lake District, 'institutionalised the picturesque tour of the Lakes'.[3]

Crosthwaite became an established viewing point. Gray had loved the view from Thomas Christian's vicarage, which he had seen two years earlier, and on the third day of his tour, 2 October 1769, almost as soon as he had arrived in Keswick, the poet 'straggled out alone to the Parsonage, fell down on my back across a dirty lane with my glass open in one hand, but broke only my knuckles; stay'd nevertheless, and saw the sun set in all its glory'.[4] Two days later he was back again, this time arriving to stay with the elderly vicar. 'I got to the Parsonage a little before Sunset, and saw in my glass a picture, that if I could transcribe it to you, and fix it in all the soft-ness of its living colours, would fairly sell for a thousand pounds. This is the sweetest scene I can yet discover in point of pastoral beauty.'[5] Join this description with his description of Grasmere, 'in one of the sweetest landscapes that art ever attempted to imitate',[6] and it is almost as through Gray was collecting pictures.

The vicarage view, also one of Wordsworth's four favourite places from which to admire Derwentwater,[7] needs a little dream-ing to imagine today, since, as there were then far fewer trees, the view stretched not just to the lake but to Castlerigg's stone circle. And unlike us, Gray is not really looking at the magnificent range of mountains but at the vale, the fields with their sheep, the lake, and the soft immediate hills – pastoral beauty – and he is using an eye trained by the Arcadian tradition of Virgil, Spenser's *Shepheardes Calender* and the fashionable paintings of Claude Lorrain, all cele-brating a utopian idea of the innocence of the life of the shepherd, untainted by the more worldly.

Gray's 'glass' was, of course, the Claude glass, named after the painter, which greatly aided the later picturesque tourist in 'framing' the view he was turning his back on, accentuating its tonal qualities.* Were one to feel the view would be more pictur-

---

* Gilpin had introduced his concept of the picturesque the year before Gray's tour of the Lakes in the first edition of his, originally anonymous, *An Essay on Prints*.

esque in moonlight, a coloured slide inserted into the glass would oblige. John Christian Curwen even modified the octagonal Claife Viewing Station on the shores of Windermere upon this principle. The windows of his upper room had green glass (for a spring view), yellow (for the warmth of summer), orange for autumn leaves, blue for winter, and purple to give the sense of an impending storm. Moonlight he eschewed.

In the Parish, the best-known story against Gray concerns his firmly stopping at the old Furness settlement of Grange, refusing to go through the jaws of Borrowdale, where the river Derwent meanders and rushes past the eastern side of Castle Crag, the apparent full-stop at the southern head of the lake. Having seen huge fragments of rock left from a rockfall that had completely blocked the path three years earlier, and perhaps being mock-heroic to amuse his correspondent,* he referred to the avalanche conditions of the Alps: 'those passes ... where the guide tells you to move on with speed and says nothing lest the least agitation should loosen the snows above'.[8]

There was no valley road into Borrowdale in the late 1760s, hardly even a path, and that little more than the rocky bed of the river. Until 1842, the packhorse road travelled up the eastern fells to Watendlath and then down again to the valley on the other side of 'the jaws'. George Smith, recounting his journey to the wadd mines twenty years before Gray's visit, had thought Grange to be 'our ne plus ultra' and then, having discovered the river bed, 'was obliged many times to alight'. Once he was through the jaws, he added, 'We turned from this fearful prospect afraid even of ourselves.'[9] So, Gray's refusal to move on hardly merits the scorn and psycho-analysis visited upon him by academics who, with little knowledge of the terrain, have taken local reactions at face value. Certainly, along with all his contemporaries, Gray was no mountaineer, nor even a hiker. Gray went for walks.

On one occasion, however, Gray proved to be decidedly gullible

---

* Gray's journal was primarily written for his friend, Dr Wharton, who was ill and so could not accompany him, and the poet posted his entries to his friend daily to help him feel as though he was partaking in the experience.

when he took on trust the local information that 'all access here
[to Seathwaite, which Gray had not in fact seen, since it lies in
far Borrowdale] is barr'd to prying mortals ... only there is a little
winding path ... for some weeks of the year passable to Dale's men;
but the Mountains know well, that these innocent people will not
reveal the mysteries of their ancient kingdom'.[10] Or, more likely, in
true Cumbrian fashion, the parishioners had no intention of risking
the possibility of competitive sightings of smugglable wadd. Also,
as late as the 1798 edition of Thomas West's *Guide*, there is no
mention of any of the mountains in the central Scafell–Great Gable
range. So academics as well as tourists must have been bamboozled
by locals protecting their livelihoods.

Other stories ring true. Gray talked with a farmer in Borrowdale
who had been chosen the previous year to be the one let down on
a rope to the ledge on Eagle Crag to destroy the eggs in the nest,
'the people above shouting and hollowing to fight off the old birds,
which flew screaming around but did not dare attack him'.[11] By
then, eagles were recorded in only four spots in the Lake District,
two in the Parish, Gray's Eagle Crag (near Stonethwaite), where
John Housman, one of the few contemporary writers about the
Parish who was a native of Cumberland, tells us that their 'carnage'
during the breeding season still took about one lamb a day in
1800,[12] and on Eagle Crag above Thirlmere.

Gray's *Journal* utterly transcends his occasional gullibil-
ity, overflowing with fascinating observations from the eye and
responses from the heart. The poet reflected the distinctions of the
new interest in aesthetics launched by Edmund Burke's *Enquiry*[13]
in 1757: 'Beauty' representing gentle, pastoral views, suggesting
ease and safety,* and the 'Sublime' representing vast, raw, unmediated natural power, creating 'horror', a word whose meaning
soon changed from a visceral distaste or aversion to awe.† And
Gray shared the aesthetic of the time, fusing the writerly and the
pictorial, but his primary response to our valley was, for me, a

---

* Which Burke thought caused pleasure through their link with man's fundamental instinct to propagate.
† Which, in turn, owed its fascination, Burke thought, to prompting the universal instinct for self-preservation.

religious one. He had been made aware of Keswick as a destination by a 1753 letter of Dr Brown[14] (a local Cambridge-educated clergyman and William Gilpin's tutor), whose favourite spot was the Keswick valley, 'a vast amphitheatre, in circumference above twenty miles', and of Brown's analysis that 'the full perfection of Keswick' would 'require the united powers of Claude,* Salvator and Poussin'.[15]

However, the Reverend Brown brought something else to his experience as well: 'This accumulation of beauty and immensity tends not only to excite rapture but reverence; for my part I make an annual voyage to Keswick, not only as an innocent amusement, but as a religious act.'[16] This, I suspect, provided the clarion call that seduced the cautious Gray, who had most explicitly expressed his own religious reactions to landscape when he first encountered mountains in the Alps with Horace Walpole in 1739. In a complete break from the aesthetic standards of the day, Gray found that, for him, the mountains did not repel but proved transcendent: 'Not a precipice, not a torrent, not a cliff, but is pregnant with religion and poetry ... There are certain scenes that would awe an atheist into belief without the help of any other argument.'[17]

I think Gray felt similarly in the Crosthwaite valley; in the evening, watching 'the solemn colouring of night draw on, the last gleam of sunshine fading away from the hilltops, the deep serene of the waters, and the long shadows of the mountains thrown across them, till they nearly touch'd the hithermost shore ...'[18] or, in bright daylight, 'beneath you, and stretching far away to the right, the shining purity of the Lake, just ruffled by the breeze to show it is alive, reflecting rocks, woods, fields and inverted tops of mountains, with the white buildings of Keswick, Crosthwaite church and Skiddaw for a background at distance'.[19]

Writing of a simplicity, directness of response and truth that

---

* Claude's vision is imbued with nostalgia for an imagined vanished past, but he painted outdoors and brilliantly captured the effects of light, presenting ideal landscapes and harmony between man and nature. Poussin's studies of mythological figures in landscapes stressed the order and majesty of nature, a perspective that has been compared to Milton, while Salvator Rosa's wilder romantic vison, peopled with bandits, was to find its echo in Byron.

pointed the way towards Wordsworth and the redemptive function of the link between man and nature.

Gray was an influential arbiter of taste, and his *Journal* circulated among the educated until it was published in 1775, after his death, and then picked up, along with extracts from Dr Brown, by the publishers of the second edition of Thomas West's *Guide* in 1780. The much-travelled West, a Jesuit priest from Furness, also saw the landscape in religious terms, but his language has none of the emotional immediacy of Gray's. His prescribed viewing stations included all of Gray's and he intended his work 'to encourage the taste for visiting the lakes', although his compass remained narrow, simply following the better roads. He assured his readers that 'the inhabitants partake nothing of the ferocity of the country they live in, for they are hospitable, civil and communicative ... Every cottager is a narrative of all he knows'[20] and tempted artists from the Grand Tour by knowing references to (and contrasts with) the scenery of the Alps and the Apennines.

West had been persuaded to write by Dr William Brownrigg of Ormathwaite Hall, a Crosthwaite parishioner, prompted by 'his passion for the improvement and notoriety of Keswick'. One of the scientific theorists who had helped to enable the mining boom, Brownrigg, having started his career in Whitehaven as a surgeon, had become a famous chemist. Judged the second most important[*] scientist to be born in Cumberland,[21] he was the first to write of choke-damp,[†] argue for mine ventilation and investigate gaol fever. His book on the failings of salt manufacture attracted the American Benjamin Franklin, who came to stay at Ormathwaite and demonstrated in Derwentwater his experiment into the effect of pouring oil on to troubled waters.

West awarded three more 'stations' around Derwentwater than Windermere and 'the garden of Crosthwaite vicarage' was Station VIII – for James Clarke, in his 1787 guide, 'the grandest view for the artist of any in the country'. However, while West accompanies

---

[*] The first is John Dalton.
[†] A mixture of unbreathable gases left in the mines after the oxygen has been removed from the air.

Gray's description with a good one of his own, he has a criticism: 'Whoever takes this view from Ormathwaite, in a field on the western side of the house, will be convinced of Mr Gray's loss in want of information. For the very spot he stood upon there is in the centre of the foreground, and makes a principal object in the pastoral part of the picture he praises so highly.'[22] We don't know whether Gray went to Ormathwaite Hall or not (although most early visitors did), but West was surely repaying Dr Brownrigg with an elegant compliment. Which would no doubt have pleased him as, once he had taken over the Hall in 1760, he had expensively converted a coach house to a laboratory, built several outbuildings, and bought Millbank Hall. Having taken out a mortgage from Rowland Stephenson of £3,200 in 1780 (later topped up with another £1,400) he was near bankruptcy seven years later, and received £8,000 from his nephew, in return for promising to leave him the house.[23]

West's *Guide* remained in print for over fifty years and, just five years after its first publication, the cartographer Thomas Kitchin reported the difference it had made to Keswick, which, 'though a poor village, receives great benefit from the resort of gentry to see the romantic lakes and mountains that surround it'. By then there had been a step change from the fact-finding early pioneers, and showmen had begun to enhance the 'visitor experience' and turn it to their financial advantage. Responses would surely be heightened by loud noise reverberating off the mountains, creating the aural sublime sharpened by a frisson of horror: so, to oblige, six brass cannons mounted on swivels were brought in on the Duke of Portland's four-oared, ten-seater barge.[24]

In time, at the magnet of the Lodore Falls, at the southern end of the lake, disembarking visitors from the boat were not only greeted by a small cannon on arrival but had the choice of two cannons to fire themselves, a 4s. one and a 2s. 6d. one. The choice was clear, as Robert Southey's Don Manuel sardonically described later: 'when one buys an echo, who would be content for the sake of saving eighteen pence, to put up with the second best, instead of ordering at once the super-extra-double-superfine?' He was right; the smaller cannon soon rusted away from disuse.[25]

St Kentigern's already had its own aural sublime to welcome

the tourists. In 1767, when the four church bells were in need of attention, the Parish rate was increased[26] to allow them to be taken down, repaired and then triumphantly rung, as large quantities of ale were consumed in celebration. But the work done must have been flawed as, eight years later, a major church appeal raised £196 – a considerable amount – to recast the old bells and create two more, and a tentative sort of change-ringing was first heard in the valley.[27] Peter Crosthwaite, one of Keswick's most enterprising citizens, then living in St John's in the Vale, took his children out into a field every Sunday to listen to the new bells before continuing to chapel.[28] And as the change-ringers became more expert, Southey would find the voices of the bells 'the most affecting and the most exhilarating of all measured sounds', 'Wooing to happier thoughts / Than all the songs and viols in the world'.[29] They resonate too through Hugh Walpole's *Herries Chronicles*, where they warn, mourn, comfort or cheer the whole valley at regular intervals.

*

Perhaps the most colourful and cheerful scene in the entire *Chronicles* celebrates the famous Keswick regattas of the 1780s. These were the brainchild of Peter Crosthwaite and the 'off-cum' Joseph Pocklington, and the spectators were mostly Cumbrians, who tend to love a good do. So, at one level, the whole glorious day fitted in with the monetary charity that the – otherwise eccentric – Pocklington dispensed to the poor of Keswick and Borrowdale.

Peter Crosthwaite, a student at the Parish grammar school, came from Dale Head, Thirlmere, some 6 miles away over the high fells.[30] But from 1735, and for about another 150 years, his family also farmed the Monk Hall lands owned by the Le Flemings, so Peter may have spent his weekdays closer to the school. His father, Robert, was a foreman of the Eighteen Men.[31] After working as a mariner with the East India Company for seven years,* Peter had briefly returned to Keswick in 1765 and become engaged to

* After some rather cursory training in navigation from Governor Stephenson.

Hannah Fisher before leaving for Northumberland as a customs officer. When he returned in bad health in 1779, he briefly lived and rested in St John's and then, in 1780, moved to a larger house in Keswick,[32] to begin a multifaceted new career. His meteorological records were good enough to be used by the early scientist John Dalton;* he campaigned for pure water (sinking a well and providing a town pump) and created a well-built, zigzagging tourist path up Latrigg, the Keswick fell at the east end of Skiddaw.[33]

It was in 1781 that he first became involved with Joseph Pocklington and devised Keswick's first purpose-built tourist attraction, Museum House. It advertised 'two of the best landscape mirrors such as Mr Gray used at the Vicarage garden'[34] and a Cabinet of Curiosities, the contents of which ranged from a chicken with two heads to a straw hat belonging to one who had sailed with Bligh on the *Bounty* (a local friend of Fletcher Christian's?). This was augmented by a collection of musical stones, covering two octaves.† Not quite in tune, these were bars of hornfels, metamorphic rocks that Crosthwaite had dragged out of the River Greta, on which he would bash out 'God Save the King'. Elsewhere, two barnacles from the bottom of Captain Cook's ship vied for attention with Pocklington's resplendent giant turnip, 38 inches in circumference. Much of the collection consisted of Crosthwaite's trophies from his time in the East India Company, and the later Captain Wordsworth room was dedicated to treasures from afar collected by Wordsworth's elder first cousin, John. They included an 'Albatross from the Cape of Good Hope' with a reported 10-foot wingspan.[35]

Crosthwaite's method of soliciting trade created a lot of local antipathy. He set his chair among some carefully angled mirrors and when a carriage or potential customer hove into angled view, he would thump his drum in time with the museum's barrel organ, while his wife ran upstairs to strike the 16-pound Cantonese gong,

---

* Whom we shall meet later.
† This started a Keswick tradition, and three more sophisticated versions were made. The Richardsons created one in 1840 and performed three times for Queen Victoria, the Tills created theirs in 1875 and took it to America, after which the Abrahams made one that could be used to promote Keswick.

which, we are told, sounded like a cathedral bell and, on a fine day, could be heard 4 miles away.[36] *The Cumberland Pacquet*, the Whitehaven weekly paper, listed the visitors, and by 1793 a grand '1540 persons of rank and fashion' were thus seduced into the museum.[37] They had been charged a shilling to explore, but, wisely, Crosthwaite allowed 'Country People' to get in at half price. His museum, despite much wasted venom with a local competitor, mainly dispensed by Crosthwaite, flourished under the auspices of his family for just over a hundred years.

Despite its eccentricities, Crosthwaite's museum was very well regarded, considered by an expert contemporary[*] as 'the most capital [museum] North of the Trent',[38] while a modern study of the period rates it as 'one of the finest museums in the provinces'.[39] The star exhibit – perhaps the most exciting Iron Age artefact in England – the late Iron Age, scabbarded, Embleton[40] Sword, decorated with enamel in a red and yellow chequerboard design, topped with a beautiful bronze hilt, was only held by them briefly. Only discovered in the early-to mid-nineteenth century, Peter's grandson sold it to the British Museum, for £32, to join the Lindisfarne Gospels, when he closed the museum in 1870.

Derwentwater had already become far more widely known in the decade before Crosthwaite opened the museum. Arthur Young had made the first recorded circumnavigation of the lake the same year as Gray's visit – and had been bewitched. Seven years later, William Gilpin (another Cumbrian clergyman), the master of the school of picturesque painting, wrote that 'a circuit round [Derwentwater] naturally suggests the visionary idea of improving it. If the whole lake belonged to one person a nobler scene for improvement could not well be conceived.' His manuscript, *Observations on Several Parts of Great Britain, Particularly the Highlands of Scotland, Relative Chiefly to Picturesque Beauty, Made in the Year 1776*, slowly circulated – as had Gray's – among the educated, but neither work prompted the two major local landlords, Greenwich Hospital and the Egremonts, to sell off parcels

---

* Sir Ashton Lever, who had accumulated one of the most important natural history collections of the time.

of their land to strangers. However, Arthur Young's ecstatic, if less well-expressed, response, published in 1770, had certainly been absorbed locally, and the smaller unenfranchised tenants of Egremont land adjacent to the western shore – conscious of potentially higher land prices in the future – shrewdly (and successfully) petitioned the 3rd Lord Egremont for a second round of enfranchisements in 1776.[41]

It is also possible that Gilpin's siren call to rich landlords in search of a landscape had reached as far as Joseph Pocklington; certainly, Wordsworth later expressed the view that Pocklington's probable temptation had been 'to be a leader in a new fashion'.* For, although Pocklington had first visited Keswick the year before Gray, he made his permanent move ten years later, in 1778, buying a farm at Ashness and Vicar's Island[42] in a complicated transaction from Miles Ponsonby. The son of a wealthy family from Newark in Nottinghamshire, who had inherited a fortune in his twenties, Pocklington's purchase cost a mere £300,[43] only 50 per cent more than the cost of the new bells for the church. The island was mainly corn land with 'a few sycamores ... covering a hovel'. Cutting down the trees and leaving the island looking like a 'treeless whale-back',[44] Pocklington constructed on its top a fine classical house† surrounded by a shaven lawn – the centre of the view from every direction.‡ The house was originally admired by all and sundry, as were Pocklington's distinctly more dubious sham 'tourist attractions' that gradually came to litter the island.

Three early editions of West[45] judged that, with Pocklington's 'improvements', the island had become 'one of the most beautiful spots', and it was to be[46] the centrepiece of the attractions once Joseph Pocklington and Peter Crosthwaite joined forces in 1781. Following on from the earlier regattas arranged by John Spedding

---

* In his first letter on the Kendal–Windermere Railway.
† The design anticipates several villas built at the end of the century around Windermere, including Brathay Hall and Storrs Hall.
‡ This was the essential cause of Wordsworth's disgust with the 'alien improver'. The site of the building was exposed 'like an astronomer's observatory... on the island's highest elevation', its builder's intention to dominate nature rather than build in congruence with it.

of Mirehouse at the eastern end of Bassenthwaite Lake, they
launched on 28 August the initial Derwentwater regatta, a blend of
country fair and grand spectacle, with a prize of 7 guineas for the
winning boat. Competing with one of the worst rainstorms seen
in Keswick for years, the first regatta was almost wiped out, but a
year later all went spectacularly well.

King Pocky's new paradise.

The event lasted all day, and the *Cumberland Pacquet* reported
that the marquees stretched along the edge of the lake for 400
yards. A truly extraordinary array for the small population of
both town and Parish. And for the races 'the sides of the mountains were clad with spectators, and the glassy surface of the Lake
was variegated with a number of pleasure barges ... tricked out in
the gayest colours and glittering in the rays of the meridian sun'.[47]
The boat-racing was accompanied by foot races, a sweepstake for
swimming horses (towed out to the middle of the lake on a raft,
which was then sunk), and various other entertainments and side-
shows – plus a feast for the gentry. As night fell, 'a string of lamps
stretched from the waters' edge to the town and the day ended
with fireworks and a dance'.

The exuberant set piece of the day was a mock naval battle orchestrated by Peter Crosthwaite, who had experienced ship-to-shore fighting, and as 'Admiral' Crosthwaite's forces, assembling behind the cover of Friar's Crag on the northeast side of the lake, attacked Pocklington's island, noisy battle commenced. The island's nine-pounder cannon had been packed with moss and damp rags to ensure maximum impact, and the *Pacquet* records 'a terrible cannonade ... on both sides, accompanied with a dreadful discharge of musquetry ... being echoed from hill to hill ... All nature seemed to be in an uproar.' The battle was apparently heard as far away as Appleby, the county town of Westmorland. No tingles of horror here, this was your full-blasted Armageddon.

Pocklington was governor and commander-in-chief of the island, and each year there was an ever grander succession of stewards, eventually including the Le Flemings, the Howards and the Lawsons,[48] to moderate excessive realism. French horns were added to the cacophony of cannons and guns – musical interludes already standard fare for the intervals between battles. Each year the invaders, armed with sword and musket, reached the island, were initially repelled, and then landed. Bodies fell to the ground, as smoke shimmied the view, and vast quantities of beer and beef were consumed. Indeed, in 1783 the ale caused a hitch, as the two men appointed to negotiate the capitulation of the island had 'unfortunately sacrificed so liberally to Bacchus' that they were unable to speak.

The regattas caused a considerable stir in Cumberland and became one of the highlights of the county's sporting and social calendar. The *Pacquet*, doing its job, even suggested that, were they more universally known about, Keswick would become the most popular resort 'in the kingdom'! While it might appear that more sophisticated tourists were unlikely to find the regattas to their taste, one such thought a visit would have proved useful for Milton: 'Had the poet who described the battle of the Gods seen Regatta-day at Keswick, it would have very much enriched his muse for the subject.'[49]

The man responsible for the regatta boats was Rowland Stephenson, who had acted as steward in 1782, as did his son

Launching some tourists to Lodore Falls and Rowland Stephenson's
Low Door Inn.

Edward the next year. A London banker who had inherited his uncle Governor Stephenson's Parish lands, Rowland had acquired a small estate around Lodore upon the death of its Whitehaven owner in 1780[50] and quickly developed the Lodore Falls and promoted Low Door Inn. This was twelve years after the governor's death and his purchase was presumably prompted by the burgeoning tourist possibilities of Keswick but, again, may have been a response to Gilpin.

Five years later, Pocklington became Stephenson's next-door neighbour, buying the Barrow estate,* the land in between the edge of the hospital demesne lands and Lodore, from a Mr Robley, where he built a lovely new house (now a particularly beautiful youth hostel). There he shaved off the branches of an oak, whitewashed it, and shaped it into an obelisk, aiming for 'a ghost tree', which would shimmer in moonlight. 'So Art beats Nature',[51] Coleridge would scornfully reflect. Pocklington, a generous employer, had always been on the look out to give money to

---

* Mr Robley was possibly related to St John's first perpetual curate.

the poor of Keswick and Borrowdale and provided yet more work by building a carriage road from Barrow to Keswick at his own expense, before he moved into his new residence. The island then came into its own as the perfect stage set for the drama of the annual battles, while, at Barrow, Pocklington decided it was time to compete directly with his neighbour by exploiting the water-fall in the woods behind the house. Having diverted the route of the river to double the waterfall's height to 108 feet, he renamed his new home Barrow Cascade Hall. To ginger up the gothic mood, he added a white castellated hermitage and advertised for a hermit, to be paid half a crown a day on the condition that for seven years the applicant would talk to no one and would neither wash himself nor cut his nails. Nobody applied for the job.[52]

Pocklington, however, had achieved his ambition, as the *Cumberland Pacquet*[53] quickly acclaimed the effect of Barrow Cascade as 'greater, and more astonishing, than that of the long-celebrated Fall at Lowdore'. Like Peter Crosthwaite, Pocklington was a brash and effective self-promoter, and the pair had boosted each other's ambitions. Crosthwaite had launched his museum just a few days after the first regatta and the next year had created and produced Derwentwater's first useful tourist map. This spurred Pocklington on to get his own plans and draw-ings of his island buildings engraved. The accompanying text of his first engraved print claimed that he had 'discovered' the stone circle or Druid's Temple on his land, adding that 'This is sup-posed to be the most compleat and last built Temple in Europe'.[54] The locals reported that 'the master had those stones set up ... but the Lake is always knocking em down'.[55] Undeterred, or perhaps impressed, when Crosthwaite advertised his revised map of Derwentwater (along with maps of Windermere and Ullswater) for sale in 1783, he included a plan of Pocklington's island and its various 'attractions'.

Crosthwaite's maps, a charming and 'revealing memorial of this second stage of Lake travel',[56] focused on the lakes (with occasional depths), roads (several impassable), mines and springs, West's stations (the later maps including a few of Crosthwaite's own) and landowners. The names of the vicars, or inhabiting curates of

The great and the grand relax before Pocklington's much enhanced
Barrow Falls. The man silhouetted halfway up the falls
demonstrates their size.

St Kentigern's – the church was illustrated on every map – changed correctly when necessary, while Monk Hall was ascribed to the Le Flemings (even though Crosthwaite was probably born there) rather than the tenant. Similarly, the Lake poets at Greta Hall would be ignored in favour of the owner, Mr Jackson.[57] The museum sold all Pocklington's engravings, and Crosthwaite's maps – which always featured Pocklington's new buildings – were very successful; by 1789, 4,450 sheets of paper were ordered for them.[58] Pocklington would supply William Hutchinson with a run of 800 engraved prints of his drawings for his 1794 *History of Cumberland* too – and was favoured with Volume II's only double folding plate – but the entrepreneur's most long-standing tourist draw came after the purchase of some land south of Lodore, in places adjacent to Barrow estate, in 1788.

The land included the Bowder Stone, already notorious, being the only illustration, other than St Kentigern's, to adorn Peter Crosthwaite's 1784 map of Derwentwater. A giant, erratic stone balanced improbably on a relatively small edge, 'like the roof of a house reversed',[59] the stone was to be Pocklington's final tourist creation for the Lake District. Quickly embellished with his usual bravura, along with some somewhat rickety ladders, this time he successfully included the human element, hiring an elderly lady in a new cottage to 'lend the place quaint atmosphere'. Pocklington had become both a creator and a collector of classic picturesque sites and his sense of the significance of his land permeated the guidebooks.

The Lodore Falls, 'the Niagara of England',[60] remained the indisputable tourist diamond. The Bowder Stone, first described as 'much the largest stone in England, being at least equal in size to a first-rate man of war' – it is 11 yards high and 21 yards long – was described in the same terms in every guidebook for the next hundred years. Yet it was Pocklington's Parish swansong. From 1793 the address on his prints had become his newly built Nottinghamshire home, and in 1797 he sold the island for £2,000 to General Peachy – who became a close friend of Robert Southey – and left the area entirely. Barrow House estate, complete with its sheep-heafs and stints, twenty cattle grasses in Wythburn and nineteen in Borrowdale, remained in his possession. As did Ashness and Watendlath Farms, two fields near Rosthwaite,[61] and last but not least, pew rights in Borrowdale church. In 1853, his heirs* would sell everything to the new owner of Barrow House, S. Z. Langton, for £12,000.[62] But the motive for Pocklington's departure from the Lake District is not on record.

*

The last of the outsiders to revolutionise the land structure of the Parish at the end of the century was Lord William Gordon, and the story behind his entrance upon the scene in 1781 makes it almost inevitable that he did so in direct response to Gilpin. Coming from a tribe that 'Maun be baith brave and gay',[63] Gordon's early history was almost as scandalous as that of the poet Byron,† and it took a very long time before the court allowed him to purchase his first post, Deputy Ranger of St James's and Green Parks. Potentially redeemed, he had already entered the House as a Scottish MP when his younger brother, Lord George, plunged the country into the anti-Catholic Gordon riots in 1780. Suddenly looking like the safer of the 4th Duke of Gordon's two brothers, William now acquired the heiress he needed to assuage his debts. Problematically, though, The Honourable Frances Ingram-Shepheard had been a ward of court since the death of her father and, although her guardians approved the match, the guardian's court did not, because of the couple's marked disparity of fortunes.

Ever bold, the gay Lord William Gordon ignored the ruling, returning successfully to court in 1781 with a pregnant bride, who was to come of age the following year. The couple flourished, his post as deputy ranger suiting them both. Aware that any long-term

* Now married into the Senhouse family.
† He had eloped in 1768 with his married cousin Lady Sarah Bunbury, a favourite of George III, after she had had his child. However, once her notorious divorce began, the couple split up and William retired abroad accompanied by his dog, vowing never to return. So, when he did, he had a lot of ground to make up.

success required being favoured by the Regent, the couple lavished money on both their London house and on Green Park. By December it was being said that 'there is not anywhere ... a more agreeable Display of Taste' and, equally fast, Gordon agreed to purchase the 44 acres of Waterend estate on the western shore of Derwentwater, which had been enfranchised at the earliest possible moment, in 1759.

Frequently described as a wedding gift from his new mother-in-law, the project was in fact entirely Gordon's* even though it is far from clear he had ever been to the Lake District. But Gilpin's manuscript, with its seductive Derwentwater challenge, had been dedicated to Queen Charlotte and was well thumbed at court, and Gordon's landscaping taste had become his claim to restorative fame. The motive for his purchase seems clear, a choice underlining what Derek Denman, whose research into Gordon has reintroduced him to the Lake District, has called 'the unique public English garden model that Derwentwater had become'.[64]

Gordon immediately obtained estimated prices of the other landholdings along the western lake shore.[65] The woodland at Fawe Park, the second largest wooded estate, had recently been bought by John Fisher, who had almost wholly cleared it in three years, no doubt, in part, to finance his purchase.[66] The largest area of wood, in the Brandelhow estate, had been acquired by Robert Baynes, the Egremonts' Cockermouth steward.[67] Putting a sitting tenant on to the customary land, he applied to enfranchise his tenement and bought some five thousand numbered trees, valued at over £750.[68] He too started to cut and replant. By 1781 there was little old timber left along the shore[69] and, having agreed to purchase the Waterend estate and its farmhouse for £1,400 (along with an adjacent smaller freehold and customary estate at Parkside), Gordon then paused – as he often did – for three years.

He finally completed in May 1784, having employed Thomas Benson, the new Egremont steward,† to act for him. However,

---

* Waterend was to become the only one of his three main houses that he owned himself.
† Robert Baynes's son-in-law.

he had baulked at Benson's report of the re-estimated prices, sometime before 5 March, which he found 'excessively unreasonable'. He continued, 'I shall not think any more about ... them'[70] – but, ever changeable, in May he sent his own man of affairs, James Oliver, to the Parish. Two small customary 'intacks' adjacent to Swinside were swiftly purchased from 'Mr Radcliffe' for £110, although the wood remained the property of Lord Egremont. Meanwhile, the enfranchised owners of Hawes End and Brandelhow were apparently in the process of doubling their asking prices.[71]

By July, as Oliver was negotiating for Brandelhow, the richer Pocklington swept in with a higher offer and, whatever Gordon's recent view of the prices, the new Parish landowners were on the brink of a profitable battle of the titans, Benson reporting that Pocklington 'seems determined to purchase on any terms ... and I am told means to lay out £10,000 in Purchases near the Lake'.[72] Gordon gritted his teeth and agreed to match Pocklington's offer of £1,600 for Brandelhow, despite Oliver's lower valuation. This was another characteristically bold action on his part: not only did Gordon have less accessible money than Pocklington, his purchases would have been meaningless, in terms of his ambitions for the western shore, if he did not manage to acquire the Hause End tenements between Waterend and Brandelhow, and Westray, a freeholder there, was refusing to sell (see map, p. 248).

However, if there was one thing that Gordon, as a courtier, understood, it was the power of higher status. So, September saw Lord and Lady William Gordon and Lady Irwin, Lady William's mother, attending dinner with Pocklington and his guests on the island,[73] and a surprising entente was born, Pocklington withdrawing his bid for Brandelhow. The western shore was to be Gordon's. Pocklington marked his stopping point by building his first lakeshore home, Finkle Street House, at the southern end of Portinscale in 1785.[74] In the same year, having recently purchased Fawe Park from John Fisher, he sold it on directly to Gordon for £1,500, quite ignoring the Egremont steward.

By 1787 Gordon had secured the missing Hause End and Parkside tenements, negotiating with the recalcitrant Westray's executors.* And by then he had enfranchised the land and bought the wood where necessary from his London friend and neighbour, Lord Egremont; so he now held the freehold and wood of all the western lake shore south of Portinscale.† And three years after that, his one-floor summer abode facing Derwentwater Bay, essentially a pavilion with three bays, was finished: 'a sweet and solemn retreat', where the lake 'washes its very walls'.[75]

Designed in part to provide a picturesque view for those looking across from the eastern side of the lake, Gordon's house also gave a politically pleasing bow to the Prince Regent's creation of Brighton Pavilion. It was surrounded by pleasure gardens, which in due course developed into 58 acres of picturesque woodland,[76] visited and admired by every well-bred tourist. Peter Crosthwaite's grandson recalled the process: 'There was only one large forest tree on that side of the lake at the time, but Lord William planted it with ... every variety of wood. Many miles of gravelled carriage and foot walks ... all trimly kept, and free from anything to mar its beauty.'[77]

The process of thinning the trees and shaping the woods, an essential part of creating a picturesque landscape, was carried out energetically for at least two decades, and in 1779 Gordon added Castle Crag to his estates, to save a picturesque site from becoming defaced by quarrying.[78] Although Gordon took less care towards the end of his life[79] (he died in 1823), he was a distinguished pioneer, pointing the way to the high picturesque. He had little interest, however, in the working needs of his tenants. Two of the properties he had acquired, Low Hause End and Brandelhow – the latter with its flock of 125 hefted sheep – maintained their farmhouses, but Parkside and High Hause End lost theirs and several other houses fell into dereliction. Once 'social romanticism' had brought the plight of the tenants to the fore, some of Gordon's aesthetic descendants treated their tenants with consideration. Gordon, however, removed his as necessary.

* It is likely that Gordon smoothed the path for Pocklington's purchase of Old Park farm from Greenwich Hospital that year, along with their permission to build stables on it to serve his island.
† Gordon had attempted to go further by offering for Manesty, but Rowland Stephenson chose to stay put.

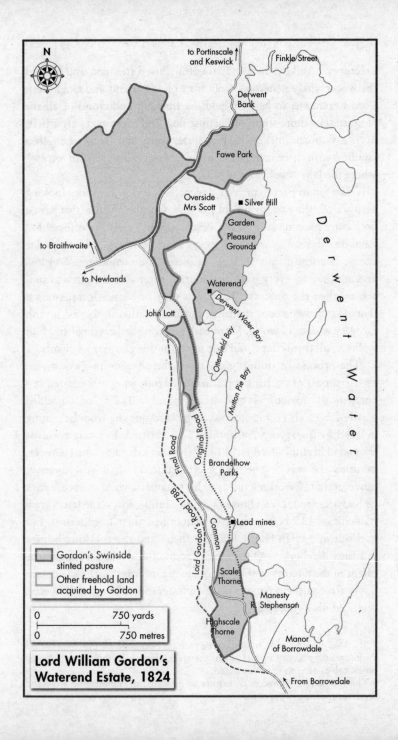

N

to Portinscale
and Keswick

Finkle Street

Derwent
Bank

Fawe Park

Overside
Mrs Scott

Silver Hill

Garden

Pleasure
Grounds

to Braithwaite

to Newlands

Waterend

John Lott

Derwent Water Boy

Otterfield Bay

Mutton Pie Bay

D
e
r
w
e
n
t

W
a
t
e
r

Brandelhow
Parks

Final Road

Original Road

Lord Gordon's Road 1788

Common

Lead mines

Scale
Thorne

Manesty
R. Stephenson

Highscale
Thorne

Manor
of Borrowdale

From Borrowdale

Gordon's Swinside
stinted pasture

Other freehold land
acquired by Gordon

0		750 yards
0		750 metres

**Lord William Gordon's
Waterend Estate, 1824**

His successful acquisition of so much land presumably led Gordon to imagine that all his tenants had their price, an assumption that prompted his one major failure. He developed the idea of diverting the western shore road from the north end of Catbells to Manesty and raising it to 200 metres above sea level, a plan Gilpin had expressly suggested,[80] and which would give breathtaking views.* The scheme was supported by both Stephenson and Pocklington, who gave money to help build the road, and Gordon's steward was immediately instructed to offer extra money to the smaller tenants at the quarter sessions to get them on board too. Then, of course, Gordon went ahead anyway. His work on the terrace was thoroughly approved by a tourist in 1787,[81] who believed it 'vies with the magnificence of a Roman work' and offered that the road 'when finished, will present a scene almost rivalling the beauties of the opposite shore'.

The locals, however, had other ideas; they thought the road too steep and too risky. Gordon thought this 'must be a joke in a Borrowdale man'[82] and offered to deal with the problem by building a protective wall. He authorised more money to persuade the recalcitrant, combining the bribe with the threat that he would not offer a penny to repair the decaying current road. But the people of Borrowdale and Portinscale stuck to their guns, and a compromise third road evolved, considerably higher in places than the old road but avoiding the really steep climbs. This was probably the first time the democracy of the Lake District had thwarted a major plan from a new landowner in the Parish; but it would not be the last.†

The conflict between the landowners' interests and those of the smaller statesmen, with their 2-acre closes used mainly for coppicing or occasionally coaling wood, was real. And, inevitably, one or two had tried to exploit the process, 'Mr Radcliffe' and Daniel Fisher both trying to sell their small 'intacks'[83] to Gordon, while simultaneously cutting their wood, a process that was quickly

---

* Gordon presumably hoped to enclose the commons below the terrace for landscaping.

† This road, one of the most beautiful in the Parish, is now tarmacked and the lower local road is rapidly becoming a track.

stopped. But what is really striking is that every other land purchase of Gordon's[84] was made either at the end of the tenant's
productive working life or soon after his death. These tenants were
clearly loath to leave the land they had worked on all their lives, but
their children thought the offered price too good to resist,[85] which
it probably was, and that they could farm elsewhere equally well
but more cheaply.

*

While this change was in progress, the aesthetic concerns of the
flood of visitors to the Lakes and the Parish were changing too.
A taste for the picturesque, 'the interregnum between classic and
romantic art', first introduced by Gilpin anonymously back in
1768,* the year before Gray wrote his *Journal*, had begun to sweep
through the middle class.

And what was admired changed too, as the incomers' landscaping efforts had not always met with the guru's approval. Over time,
Gilpin's savaging of Pocklington's 'miserable and tasteless' ornaments on the island entirely transformed the previously general
praise reflected in Thomas West's guides. There was indeed much
to mock: not just the 'druid temple' modelled on Castlerigg, 'a few
round stones set in a circle like boys playing at Marbles',[86] but a
small fortress complete with cannons and a boathouse disguised as
a Westmorland chapel. However, the guides' editors, perhaps sensible of the monetary and marketing good Pocklington had done for
the Parish, held back and only cast aspersions upon King Pocky's†
excesses in 1796, when he had virtually left the scene.

Gilpin had defined the gap between Burke's 'Beauty' and
'Sublime' as that kind of beauty 'which would be effective in a
picture'[87] and, while he accepted the possibility that nature worked

---

* In his popular and frequently expanded *Essay on Prints*. However, although
Gilpin toured the Lake District in 1772, and his manuscripts were widely dis-
seminated to, among others, Thomas Gray and Horace Walpole, they were not
published until 1786.
† The soubriquet was first used by Coleridge and gained considerable currency.

on 'a vast scale, and, no doubt, harmoniously, if her scheme could be comprehended',[88] he found this irrelevant. Mere humans should use nature simply as a starting point, and then improve it, to make a harmonious picture. So, while Gray responded to Blencathra as he saw it,* a mountain 'whose furrowed sides were gilt by the noon-day sun, whilst its brow appeared a sad purple, from the shadows of the clouds as they sailed by',[89] Gilpin found it simply disagreeable – it formed 'whimsical, grotesque shapes', he said – and dismissed it. Similarly, any socio-economic comment was without his compass, his ragged peasants simply picturesque additions to a re-landscaped scene.

His rulings for picturesque paintings included an emphasis on the foreground, as 'the basis and foundation of the whole picture',[90] and on shade, which 'should greatly overbalance the light'. Suitable views were to be rough and asymmetrical; ruins preferred to buildings, wilderness to gardens – the opposite of Burke's pleasant pastoral 'Beauty'. This was an English take on the emerging European Romantic movement, which, despite a joint fascination with the effects of light, was itself far more full-blooded, following Rousseau in its spontaneous response to nature and emotion. A response that, in England, had to wait for Wordsworth.

After the publication of Gilpin's *Observations on the Mountains and Lakes*[91] in 1786, picturesque tourism in the Parish largely took the form of collecting the right views, for, as its author had predicted, 'the pleasures of the chase are universal'.[92] Gilpin's 'little rules' had become an early form of aesthetic political correctness and, once learnt, were faithfully followed by picturesque travellers and artists alike. Their vocabulary – and the schematic outlook it expressed – reads foolishly and repetitively today and prompted Jane Austen's sarcasm at the time. Norman Nicholson, the twentieth-century Cumbrian poet and writer, despite some real appreciation of Gilpin, found the movement rebarbative: 'In the Picturesque, the only creative act is that of man himself, a small, mean, self-satisfied manipulation of an abstract landscape.'[93]

---

* 'Skiddaw's sister, whose western feet touched the Parish', which Gray called, as many do, Saddleback.

Nevertheless, the impact of the picturesque aesthetic on the Lake District and the Parish was enormous. It would combine with the demise of the Grand Tour – following the French Revolution and the wars that ensued – to unleash the final and largest wave of the first tourist invasion of the Parish.

The Ignorance of Strangers and
'William Wordsworth of Windy Brow'

B Y THE 1790S, Keswick's premier position as a tourist destination had been established, and in 1795 Greenwich Hospital
invested in improvements to the shops and some nearby buildings in Main Street.* Occasional tourists began to branch out from
the centres of Keswick and Ambleside – the Hon. Mrs Murray, for
instance, after her visits in 1794 and 1796, achieved the title of 'the
First Lady of Quality to cross Honister Pass'[1] – but on the whole,
the pioneering exploratory spirit of the earlier tourists had gone.
As tourists began to arrive in force – helped, since 1781, by the
regular horse-driven coach services across Morecambe Bay, which
provided an illusion of greater safety – their trips became somewhat more routine; suitable for holidaymakers searching for what
they had already read about.

The response of the parishioners to this new phenomenon can
best be illustrated by the underlying irony of their name for the
picturesque tourists, 'the Lakers': 'laking' or 'laiking' being the
dialect word for 'playing' and, more particularly, for children
playing.[2] A good example is a report of a 'poor unrefined rustic'
pouring scorn on a tourist who had bought a plot of land near the
Grasmere shore and paid far too much for it. He was 'a neat nacky
man like, and thinks it a *fine diversion* to look at the water coming

---

* Lord William Gordon, Rowland Stephenson and about forty others had petitioned that The Shambles, an abattoir, should be moved elsewhere. Denman,
'John Housman, and Cumbrian identities', *CW3*, xii, p. 123.

down the fells, when there's a flood like, and that's all *he* has for his money'.[3]

It wasn't just the locals – who had at times played with Gray and were originally apparently bemused by all the entirely unexpected attention – who thought it all a bit silly. In 1798 *The Lakers*, a satirical three-act comic opera starring a lady botanist planning to write a gothic romance, added to the scorn. The Parish, of course, was at the heart of the opera, its history providing the heartbeat. 'I think I shall lay the scene of my next upon Derwentwater ... make St Herbert to have murdered a pilgrim who shall turn out to be his brother ... Horror is to be piled upon horror.' As the authoress examines the landscape through her Claude glass, she puts the finishing touches to her picture: 'I have made the church an old abbey, the house a castle' and 'have put in the foreground the single tree they ought to have left standing'.[4]

The new visitors' tours, usually following Gray's route, encompassed the whole Parish. Derwentwater, the Vale of Elysium and Borrowdale remained the biggest draws, but St John's in the Vale had been put firmly on the tourist map too, after the publication of Gilpin's *Observations* in 1786, which recounted the story of the mighty storm of 1749. So, the statesmen soon joined the Keswickians in looking for ways to make extra money from the curious visitors, their children opening gates for carriages and competing as guides.

Skiddaw was the greatest mountain draw of all the mountains in the Lake District – mainly because it could be conquered on horseback – and once West's guidebook included a description of a 1795 ascent with a 'guide and with horses accustomed to the labour' by the feted author of *The Mysteries of Udolpho*, Ann Radcliffe, the sense of possibility conjoined with 'awe' was heightened. The best-selling novelist of her day, Ann Radcliffe – who wrote far better than is suggested by the pastiche comic opera, which was thought to star her – starts off prosaically. As her horse tops Latrigg, she records the sight of 'that part of Keswick which separates the two lakes, and spreads a rich level of three miles ... immediately below; Crosthwaite church nearly in the centre, with the Vicarage rising among trees',[5] lying just below the 'grounds of Dr Brownrigg'. Her emphasis both upon the church and upon acquaintance reflected an interest that was virtually universal then; the church thronged with summer visitors.

But hovering just below the surface of Mrs Radcliffe's portrait of the church in its familiar setting are the first intimations that Crosthwaite Parish church might lose its centrality within its Parish, prefiguring the seminal movements of power from Church to State in the nineteenth century. As we know, the status of the land surrounding the Parish church was particularly obscure after the Reformation. The land sold after the chantries were abolished was later described as 'situated, lying and being in Crosthwaite and Brathmyre'.[6] Subsequently, an Elizabethan court case had described some tenants 'of the *manor* of Crosthwaite [author's italics]'[7] while most of the Le Fleming land acquired from John Williamson in the early seventeenth century was described as lying within 'the vill of Crosthwaite'.[8] And we know that Sir Daniel Fleming's manor was named Brathmyre. Since both manor titles appear to refer to the same land, this might be explained by the whirlwind of legislation about land change causing the Elizabethan court case to simply mistake the name of the Brathmyre manor for Crosthwaite, because of its greater fame. Or, conceivably, both were small manors; Crosthwaite manor spreading southwest from its land by the church and Brathmyre smaller and more central, spreading southeast.

The dispute that led to the court case mentioning 'Crosthwaite manor' was about 'the common of turbary and pasture in Brundholme',[9] which lay on the north and west of the Greta. The manor, first mentioned as such in 1437,[10] was part of the Northumberland estate passed to Henry VIII.[11] Sold on before the estate returned to the Percys, the area became far more significant during the Elizabethan mining boom,[*] as a part of the manor lay on the opposing bank of the Greta to Brigham Forge, and more active ownership probably lay behind the Elizabethan court case.

Most of this information was passed on by the first of the new directories that accompanied the opening up of the Lake District,

[*] Witness the Crosthwaite Ruling of 1571 when its bailiff had been named as overseer, rather than, as would have been conventional, the bailiff of Newlands, with its chapel.

published in 1777 by Nicolson and Burn. Joseph Nicolson, responsible
for Cumberland, was steeped in local knowledge and scholarship,[12]
and his eldest brother, Thomas, had been vicar of Crosthwaite for
a year between Tullie and Christian in 1727.[13] The directories vary
considerably in their reliability,* but the next one, the *History of the
County of Cumberland*, collated and in part composed by William
Hutchinson,[14] and largely written in the 1790s, is also reliable in the
main.[15] Using the Nicolson and Burn text for much of its history,
including Brundholme manor, it has a full description of Crosthwaite
Parish. But it ceases to mention Brathmyre.

That the manor which had surrounded the Parish church was
no longer deemed significant by the turn of the nineteenth century
(not long after the use of the manor courts had rapidly diminished)
makes it clear that major change was already in the air by the time
the Lake Poets first arrived in the Parish.

The loss of knowledge in the directories after Nicolson was
partly caused by the new 'experts', whose frequently ignorant
views were absorbed by tourists and fellow 'experts' alike. These
were visitors to whom the history and evolution of the closed area
of the Lake District was, of course, unknown, since their visits to
the area were far too brief to allow them to make any serious study
into the 'hows' and 'whys' behind their immediate observations.
And their mistakes did real damage, although few admitted it as
openly as did Hutchinson's agricultural writer when he renounced
his 1793 published descriptions of Bewcastle (close to the Scottish
and Northumberland borders) in 1796:

> 'We cannot depart this country [borders] without acknowl-
> edging that in our description of Bewcastle, we were led into
> several errors, by the asperity in which correspondents in-
> dulged their pens, when they contributed their information.
> We have been happy to find ... that the general character of
> the inhabitants ... greatly differ from the shade which was
> thrown over them; that they are humane, courteous, and hos-

---

* For example, Mannix and Whellan, *History, Gazetteer and Directory*, assigns
the lordship of Brundholme Manor to a man buried over thirty years earlier.

pitable; and, perhaps, from not having too great a share of erudition, the more honest. We have to lament, in common with other county historians, that, in the multitude of communications, from the liberality, and sometimes officiousness of strangers, we have been subject to be misled, when we had to speak of districts not well known to us ... in the above instance we felt ourselves greatly hurt, by conveying censure where we should have given praise.'[16]

Unsurprisingly, the writer, Housman, was a rarity; he both came from Cumberland and was not a member of the gentry.

Admittedly he does not name-call any other experts, but Arthur Young, for instance, appeared to be blissfully unaware of how the unique tenancy system worked; his glib idea[17] that all would be much simplified if the landlords increased the rent* would have produced a hollow laugh on one side and quiet glee on the other; that battle had been fought. James Clark, the surveyor from Penrith, said that 'the church of Keswick (properly called Crossthwaite Church) is dedicated to St Cuthbert';[18] and Thomas Pennant produced the howler† that it was not long since the income of the Great Crosthwaite vicar 'was five pounds per annum, a goose-grass [the right of grazing his geese on the commons] a whittle-gate ... and lastly, a hardened sark [i.e., a shirt of coarse linen]'.[19] Such mistakes could never have been made by anyone local; all divorce the Parish and its church from their quite extraordinary past.

One assumes that Thomas Tullie or Thomas Christian, on £146 a year, would have been merely amused by the ignorance of an 'off-cum'. However, it is difficult to imagine Christian's reaction to the entry into the Parish of Richard Watson, the Bishop of Llandaff, who burst upon Brundholme as lord of the manor shortly after Christian's death. He presumably acquired the manor from the Hassells of Dalemain. Also a Cumbrian, Watson provides a richly theatrical example of the pluralism eschewed by Christian. The son of a Westmorland schoolmaster, Watson arrived at Cambridge

* Thereby forcing enclosures.
† After his visit in 1772.

with 'blue worsted stockings and coarse mottled coat',[20] clothing long remembered there. And he then lived a supremely confident life, avenging himself on those who had patronised him.

He moved on from being an unpaid professor of chemistry (having never read a book on the subject nor witnessed a single experiment) to the 'richest professorship in Europe',[21] that of Cambridge Regius Professor of Divinity, in 1771. Watson tells us that he 'reduced the study of divinity to as narrow a compass as I could, for I determined to study nothing but the bible ... scorning all else as the opinions of mere men as little inspired as myself'.[22] A decade later he had sixteen livings and an income of £5,000 a year, curates on £20–£50 per annum dotted here and there to help fulfil his duties. Moving back to the Lake District in 1788, six years after he had become a bishop, Watson built Calgarth Park on the shores of Windermere, where he lived the life of a country gentleman for the next thirty years. His time was principally spent, he tells us, 'in building farmhouses, blasting rocks, and enclosing wastes, in making bad land good, in planting larches'. He continues in this self-satisfied vein: 'I recovered my independence, set an example of spirited husbandry to the country and honourably provided for my family.'[23]

At Brundholme he no doubt enjoyed his status, but initially the financial benefit will have been small, as by 1795 all the tenants were enfranchised, a move started before Watson's time.* Money would come through, however, twenty years later, when the commons of Brundholme (more than half the acreage of the manor) was enclosed. It was divided primarily between the bishop, John Spedding and Brownrigg's heir – his nephew Sir John Benn Walsh, Bart – whose immediate family never returned to live in the Parish but who still owned land there as late as the 1980s. According to legend, Watson had never visited his bishopric of Llandaff; in reality, he *did* go there every three years to officiate at

* The process there offers an interesting illustration of the suspicion with which some small landholders approached the idea, as records remain of eight admittances to 'customary tenancies' upon the death of the owner – at just the time when the tenant might be most likely to think of buying enfranchisement – between 1771 and 1781.

confirmations, but as a general rule he asked those who wished to be ordained to come to him at Windermere. A prolific writer and a natural polemicist, the bishop had written a famous *Apology for the Bible* in response to the influential radical Tom Paine, causing George III to observe that he was not aware that the Bible needed apologising for.

Like most of his compatriots, including the prime minister, William Pitt, Watson had felt sympathy and some excitement at the fall of the Bastille in 1789, seeing it as a first breach in French absolutist governance.

Enter the revolutionary poet

In 1793 Wordsworth was to write a famous letter, *A Letter to the Bishop of Llandaff on the Extraordinary Avowal of his Political Principles*. He was then a young man of twenty-two, staying in the Parish, supposedly filling in time between Cambridge and 'vegetating upon a paltry curacy' once he reached the age of ordination the following year. Born in the grandest house in Cockermouth's main street, Wordsworth had lost his thirty-year-old mother just before his eighth birthday. Five years later his father died intestate, and William and his four siblings became homeless. They lived on what they could glean from the two uncles who administered his father's largely bankrupt estate, which was owed the enormous amount of £4,625 by their father's employer, Sir James Lowther, the 1st Earl of Lonsdale, who declined to pay. The two main Lowther estates, at Lowther and Whitehaven, had come together for him through inheritance, and 'Wicked Jimmy's' consequent campaign to control the parliamentary seats of both Cumberland and Westmorland, 'Lonsdale's Ninepins', was ruthlessly aggressive. He did not seem like a man who would change his mind, yet until, and if, Lowther's money came through, there was no chance whatsoever of Wordsworth living a life of gentlemanly independence.

He had spent the previous year, 1792, in revolutionary France, where he had fallen in love with Annette Vallon, and his child

(whom he had never seen) had just been born.* But when he had
arrived there in November 1791, even though his age and circumstance must surely have meant that he would be susceptible to
– and probably badly in need of – a transcendental cause, he didn't,
in any real sense, engage. After pocketing a stone from the rubble
of the Bastille, he observed himself 'affecting more emotion than I
felt'.[24] For his real emotions remained entwined with the land and
land workers of Cumberland, which:[25]

> *Retaineth more of ancient homeliness,*
> *Manners erect, and frank simplicity,*
> *Than any other nook of English land.*

But Wordsworth, along with his strong familial sense of injustice, had a highly developed sense of the injustice society meted
out to the poor, so it seems inevitable that he would eventually
catch the radical mood and believe 'Devoutly that a spirit was
abroad … [which] should see the earth / Unthwarted in her wish
to recompense / The industrious and the lowly Child of Toil'.
Justice and reason would triumph and there would be 'better,
days / To all mankind'.[26] Once caught, the poet was completely
swept away:[27]

> *Bliss it was in that dawn to be alive,*
> *But to be young was very heaven.*

Alive with revolutionary fervour, along with falling in love – a
sudden double unleashing of a young man's passion – once the
French declared war on Austria in April 1792, Wordsworth saw the
volunteer patriot army as martyrs, marching to war 'like arguments
from heaven'.[28] And the savage repression of the counter-revolution
in the Vendée, the September Massacres in Paris – some 3,000 royalists were taken out of prison and murdered – all this could be
accepted as part of a sometimes painful journey to the new world.
So, as Wordsworth returned to England in search of a livelihood at

---

* These facts were not generally known in Wordsworth's lifetime.

the end of the year, he was full of love for humanity and convinced that now it was no longer just the English Lakes that could show man how to live: 'Not favoured spots alone, but the whole earth / The beauty wore of promise.'[29]

Earlier that year, English support for the Revolution had been gingered up by the publication of Part 2 of Thomas Paine's *Rights of Man*, calling America as witness to the possibility of republics that worked *for* the people; but the September Massacres, before Wordsworth's return, had abruptly changed the general mood in the country, a change violently underlined by the execution of Louis XVI on 21 January 1793. Llandaff's short piece deploring the execution was published nine days later,* appended to an earlier sermon, 'The Wisdom and Goodness of God in having made both Rich and Poor' (the rich could help the poor, the poor could learn patience).[30] Watson now said, 'of all forms of government ... a republic [is] the most oppressive to the bulk of the people' because of 'the tyranny of their equals'.[31]

Wordsworth chose to attack him, out of a large potential field, because Watson was from Westmorland, had a liberal reputation, and Wordsworth had previously defended him; so Watson was trebly traitorous. Just before Wordsworth wrote, in February or early March, he had been shaken to the core by France's declaration of war on Britain on 1 February – an occurrence he had intellectually anticipated but not allowed himself to believe in:[32]

> No shock
> Given to my moral nature had I known
> Down to that very moment – neither lapse
> Nor turn of sentiment that might be named
> A revolution, save at this one time.

The letter, 'written by a Republican'[33] at a 'period big with the fate of the human race',[34] was incandescent and ad hominem:

* The day when the church held services commemorating the 'martyrdom' of Charles I.

'Your lordship very properly asserts that "the liberty of man in a state of society consists of his being subject to no law but the law enacted by (the) general will of the society to which he belongs".[35] You approved of the object which the French had in view when in the infancy of the revolution they were attempting to destroy arbitrary power and to create liberty on its ruins. ... It is with indignation I perceive you "reprobate" people for having imagined happiness and liberty more likely to flourish in the open field of a republic than under the shade of a monarchy. You are therefore guilty of the most glaring contradiction. Twenty-five million Frenchmen have felt that they could have no security for their liberties under any modification of monarchical power. They have in consequence unanimously chosen a republic. You cannot but observe that they have only exercised that right in which by your confession liberty essentially resides.'[36]

As for Llandaff's 'attempting to lull the people of England into a belief that ... they have already arrived at perfection in government',[37] Wordsworth retorts: 'our penal code is so crowded with disproportionate penalties and indiscriminate severity that a conscientious man would sacrifice in many instances his respect for the laws to the common feelings of humanity.'[38] He had, he says, no respect for the legislators, 'statesmen whose constant object is to exalt themselves by laying pitfalls for their colleagues and their country'.[39] He then adds the radical observation: 'If there is a single man in Great Britain, who has no suffrage in the election of a representative, the will of society of which he is a member is not generally expressed; he is a helot in that society.'[40]

And Wordsworth had one last barb to unleash: 'The friends of liberty congratulate themselves upon the odium under which they are at present labouring; as the causes which have produced it have obliged so many of her false adherents to disclaim with officious earnestness any desire to promote her interest ... Conscious that an enemy lurking in our ranks is ten times more formidable than when drawn against us ... we thank you for your deserting.'[41]

For all the bravado, it is possible that Wordsworth never tried to publish his letter to the bishop. He would certainly have been arrested if he had published under his own name, and even *sub rosa* it would have made life tricky with the uncles and ruined his standing in any court case against James Lowther. However, since the government brought charges of sedition against several booksellers and publishers that year, it is equally possible that Wordsworth *did* approach a publisher, who found discretion to be the better part of valour.

It was to be an agonising eighteen months for the poet. 'Britain opposed the Liberties of France',[42] and in France 'thus beset with Foes on every side / The goaded land waxed Mad',[43] as the Terror was launched in the autumn of 1793. Wordsworth's justification of violence to the bishop had, typically, used an analogy with nature. 'A time of revolution is not the season of true liberty … The animal just released from its stall will exhaust the overflow of its spirits in a round of wanton vagaries, but it will soon return to itself and enjoy its freedom in moderate and regular delight.'[44] But 'soon' was to cease to be an appropriate word.

He found himself 'At enmity with all the tenderest springs / Of my enjoyments',[45] loyalty to the cause undermining the bedrock of his instinctive beliefs. His old faith in history and poetry failed, and Wordsworth's revolutionary hope for the future, foreseeing 'the man to come parted as by a gulph / From him who had been'[46] entirely contradicted his settled belief that 'the child is father to the man'. Even his response to nature, if *The Prelude* is to be believed, had a new barbarism. Losing his earlier reverence and identification, his response became 'an appetite' for the 'wider empire for the sight', unmediated by reflection;[47] 'more like a man / Flying from something he dreads than one / Who sought the thing he loved'.[48] And, while nature's power diminished from a core inspiration and home to merely a refuge, Wordsworth had nightmares about the Terror for years after it had finished: 'Such ghastly visions had I of despair and tyranny.' He was left with 'a brain confounded, and a sense / Death like, of treacherous desertion, felt / In the last place of refuge – my own soul'.[49]

The next year, 1794, Wordsworth spent more time in the Bishop of Llandaff's manor in the Parish than anywhere else. His school friends had helped him to avoid the mockery the bishop had suffered at university by urging him to replace his clothes, as their cut and material marked him out as an uncouth northerner and therefore an object of amusement.[50] The previous year, his old school friend William Calvert, whose father had been the Duke of Norfolk's steward at Greystoke (a similar job to Wordsworth's father's) and whose family had lived in the Parish since the integration of the German miners in Elizabethan times, had sent him an extremely gracefully worded invitation to accompany him upon a trip, from which Wordsworth travelled to Salisbury Plain. This can only have been prompted by an enlightened sense of fraternity, as Calvert must have been only too aware of Wordsworth's extraordinary fall in status.* He had no money and no home, but rare talent, and Calvert clearly felt he deserved practical support.

Wordsworth had then spent Christmas visiting his more accommodating uncle, Richard, in Whitehaven. He also spent time with the Calverts and another old school friend, John Spedding, who lived at Armathwaite, a fine house situated at the northern end of Bassenthwaite Lake. Soon afterwards, Calvert – who had joined the Duke of Norfolk's Regiment of the Militia rather than going to university – would offer Windy Brow, his Latrigg farmhouse, to William and his sister Dorothy, whom William had not seen for over three years. The siblings had spent extraordinarily dissimilar lives after the first six years of Dorothy's life, when she was sent away from home upon her mother's death. The boys had lived first with their father and, upon his death, with their maternal grandparents in Penrith but had experienced happy times at school in Hawkshead, where they lodged in term time. Hawkshead grammar school, which occupied a grander and more recent building than Crosthwaite's, appears to have been an excellent place of education. The Calverts, local to the Parish, were pupils there, as was John Spedding, close by at Armathwaite.

Meanwhile, in 1778, Dorothy had arrived to live with her

---

* The help is frequently attributed to a desire to enable William to practise as a poet but, as John Worthen argues, this destination was far from inevitable at the time, and retrospection has perhaps generally made too much of this.

mother's cousin, Elizabeth Threlkeld, whose progressive Unitarian household in Halifax had offered her both security and love. There, she spent a whole nine and a half years entirely separated from her own family, not even being invited to her father's funeral or on Christmas Day (which was also her birthday). Until, in 1787, aged fifteen and a half, she was summoned back to her grandparents, to make and mend shirts for her brothers and perhaps to help with her grandparents' haberdashery shop.

This was the first time the surviving members of the immediate family had been together since their mother's death and those few summer weeks were a profoundly significant moment for all of them. For Dorothy, the reality of her father's illness and death, let alone the family's subsequent impoverishment, from which her contented Yorkshire life had shielded her, became traumatically real, just as her long absence did for her brothers. And their pain was reinforced by the scornful behaviour of members of their grandparents' household, unpleasantly underlining the children's position as dependants. No wonder the siblings huddled together, trying to work out what their finances might be, and no wonder Dorothy wrote to Jane Pollard, her intimate confidante from Halifax, who was to remain a lifelong friend: 'Many a time have Wm. J. C. and myself shed tears together, tears of the bitterest sorrow, we all of us, each day, feel more sensibly the loss we sustained when we were deprived of our parents, and each day do we receive fresh insults ... of the most mortifying kind.'[51]

The school holiday over, Dorothy was alone again, her grandfather dying at the end of the year. She was helped by a new friendship with Mary Hutchinson, the daughter of Penrith's tobacco merchant, whose family had been similarly orphaned and split up a few years earlier. But she was saved by her uncle William Cookson, who tutored her when he came back to visit his mother, while courting his future wife, who lived at Penrith. After their marriage, in 1788, Dorothy was scooped up to live with the couple in the Rectory at Forncett in Norfolk. She was as happy in their evangelical and conservative household as she had been in the very different household at Halifax; the only 'home' in which Dorothy was ever unhappy was her 'grandparents'.

In 1790 William had joined her at Forncett for his Christmas vacation from Cambridge. And this real time together had had to sustain her for the next three years because, once Annette had ceased to be a secret within the family, the Cooksons banned William from visiting. Despite her new income of £4 a year[52] from the money left her upon the death of her Cookson grandmother, Dorothy now thoroughly understood that she would have to live with one of her brothers. She adored them all, but William, the closest in age, some twenty months older than her, was her choice. And, despite the separation, the plan to live with him had grown into an inhabited and flourishing dream for them both, sufficiently grounded for William to have told Annette about it, and for Dorothy to write to Annette the moment she knew of her existence, expressing her delight at sharing a home with her in future.[*]

How genuine this feeling was between the two siblings is impossible to know; they corresponded, and Dorothy read and commented upon William's draft poems with an astute and protective eye, but, in any usual sense, they hardly knew each other. And there were large apparent differences of view. While William was in France, Dorothy had revelled in three months spent at Windsor, after her uncle had been appointed a canon there.[†] She was enchanted by everything, treading 'upon Fairy-Ground' as she walked with royalty upon the terrace. She said of King George III in a letter to Jane Pollard, 'I am too much of an aristocrate or what you please to call me, not to reverence him because he is the Monarch more than I would were he a private Gentleman.'[53]

William and Dorothy planned to arrange a 'chance' meeting in Halifax at Elizabeth Threlkeld's house in mid-February 1794 (a month Wordsworth, still depressed, had greeted with the observation 'I have been do[ing] nothing and still continue to be doing nothing.').[54] Their plan succeeded and they spent six weeks together; a time happily extended by William Calvert's offer of

---

[*] William expressed his longing to Dorothy for the time when he could live with 'that sympathy which will almost identify us when we have stolen to our little cottage'.
[†] They stayed in a grace and favour apartment in the cloisters of St George's Chapel.

Windy Brow, which they travelled to in April. From Kendal, the two siblings walked 18 miles to Grasmere, setting off again the next morning to walk the final 13 miles to Latrigg. For the rest of their lives, as Dorothy discovered her 'wonderful prowess in the walking way',* they saw this journey as a pilgrimage. 'Home' was the Lake District, so this was a literal homecoming. At Windy Brow, Dorothy loved Peter Crosthwaite's terrace path on Latrigg's slopes and was entranced by the view of 'the vale of Elysium as Mr Gray calls it'.[55] Cooking their own food and living very cheaply, mainly on milk and potatoes, she extended their stay again – to much family disapproval.

William had published two poems, with inauspicious timing, in the month of the French king's execution, both criticised and analysed by Dorothy and her younger brother, Christopher. One was *An Evening Walk, Addressed to a Young Lady, From the Lakes of the North of England*, mostly written during Wordsworth's time at Cambridge, and now the pair talked together of it, as he began a major revision, eventually almost doubling its length. The original poem had presented Dorothy with her lost heritage, complete with its customs and legends, as the poet traced a walk from Derwentwater and 'the roar ... of High Lodore' over to Grasmere and Rydal and on to 'my Esthwaite's shore'.† By the end of the revision, Dorothy had become William's 'beloved companion' on the walk,[56] a person whose mind and eye quickened his own profound response to the natural world.

For, while still pained by the cruel evolution of the revolution in France, with all that implied about the nature of mankind, Wordsworth's mood had been infinitely lightened by Dorothy's response to nature. This was a role she was to fulfil for the rest of her sentient life. And the developed *Evening Walk* introduced the poet's sense that accessing universal beneficent energy from the natural world, while available to all, could only be achieved by those with a heightened sensibility – like Dorothy.‡ So their six

* As she excitedly told Jane.
† The lake closest to his school at Hawkshead.
‡ 'Yes, thou are blest, my friend, with Mind awake / To Nature's impulse.'

weeks in the Parish were spent happily, creatively and productively, as they worked, walked, explored and occasionally visited, spending three days with the Speddings, and appreciating 'the friendliest attentions' from Raisley, William Calvert's younger brother,[57] who was not, however, in good health.

A sketch of William Calvert by his wife, Mary. His family had moved to the Parish from Bavaria during the Elizabethan mining boom, its members frequently numbering among the Eighteen Men. The Calverts were gentry by the nineteenth century, and William was a close friend of both Wordsworth and Southey.

And something else, more important, happened. Before they had even arrived at Windy Brow, the two of them had bought a notebook and Dorothy began another lifelong habit and gift: of copying out her brother's work, beginning with our earliest draft of 'A Night on Salisbury Plain'. The process was redemptive for her;* she was determined that her brother should write.

* She had found a way to fight the 'painful idea that one's existence is of very

> *... now speaking in a voice*[58]
> *Of sudden admonition like a brook...*
> *She ... preserved me still*
> *A Poet, made me seek beneath that name*
> *My office upon earth, and nowhere else.*

Wordsworth had been given a renewed sense of purpose and destiny, a potential escape from his depression, as he became 'thy Poet'. This was Dorothy's preeminent gift and the time spent together in the Parish sealed their bond, which could now be written about with no literary artifice:[59]

> *No separate path our lives shall know*
> *But where thou goest I shall go*
> *And there my bones shall rest.*

As the poet and biographer Lucy Newlyn has written, after 1794 there was nothing Wordsworth wrote that did not imply Dorothy's presence 'as listener, commentator, and potential contributor'.[60] The future wasn't written in stone, however, and William's immediate life continued to be primarily political, despite Dorothy's attempts to lure him away, but during their six weeks together in the Parish, an aspiration, a goal and a prophecy of creative genius, which was to be fulfilled, was undoubtedly born.

William took Dorothy to stay with Uncle Richard in Whitehaven, visiting the Calverts, and possibly the Speddings, before rejoining Dorothy and her cousins on Morecambe Bay in late July. Walking across the sands, thronged with pedestrians and carts and wagons catching the tide, he hailed one of the travellers, asking if there was any news. There was: Robespierre was dead. 'Few happier moments have been mine / Through my whole life than when first I heard ... forth-breaking on those open sands /... A hymn of triumph.... / They who with clumsy desperation brought / Rivers

little use', a predictable response to her dependent life. Letter to Jane Pollard, 2 September 1795.

of blood ... swept away! / Their madness is declared and visible.'[61]
Wordsworth's faith was renewed:[62]

> ... In the People was my trust,
> And in the virtues which mine eyes had seen,
> And to the ultimate purpose of things
> I looked with unabated confidence.

He felt certain now that the Republic's 'triumphs be in the end /
Great, universal, irresistible'.

In that moment, he must have felt fully healed from the anxiet-
ies and torments of the past eighteen months; liberated by casting
Robespierre as the villain, a perversion of the revolutionary ideal.
Wordsworth was later honest enough to admit to the visceral attraction of Old Testament justice; finding 'something to glory in, as just
and fit' in the 'rage and dog-day heat'[63] of the Revolution. But in
October, as the French army became random aggressors, preferring
looting to starvation, the pendulum must have swung back again
– a common reaction among English republicans. Wordsworth
may have initially discussed this with the sickly Raisley Calvert, to
whom he returned in September, as politics were again at the front
of his mind. But he found him 'worse than when I left Keswick, but
a good deal better than he had been some weeks before':[64] Raisley
was displaying the classic up-and-down symptoms of tuberculosis.

The young man had earlier offered, remarkably, to share his
income with William. Now, feeling weaker and planning to go
abroad to escape the Lake District winter – taking William to
look after him – he changed his financial offer to a legacy of £600,
naming William in his will as 'William Wordsworth of Windy
Brow'.[65] The poet later wrote that Raisley's wish was to 'set me
above want and to enable me to pursue my literary views or any
other views with greater success or with a consciousness that if
those should fail me I would have something at last to turn to'.[66]
This wasn't just the gift of a thoughtful friend or a poetic acolyte;
it was surely the gift of a friend who shared Wordsworth's views
on the world.

Raisley's brother William was away with his regiment in

Tynemouth, which suggests different political affiliations, but he nevertheless responded with warmth and generosity when Wordsworth wrote describing the circumstances – including his need for money to accompany Raisley on the trip. As did Richard, Wordsworth's elder brother, albeit with more irony, when he agreed to stand surety that William's legacy would not be sequestered by Uncle Richard's widow, upon the debts owed to her husband for paying for his nephew's education.

When Raisley found, just as they were about to start the journey, that he simply could not travel, he increased the sum left to Wordsworth to £900, with the added instructions that the money was to be used to purchase annuities for himself and 'so much ... as to him will seem meet' for Dorothy, whom he had obviously both admired and felt concern for in April. While Raisley's generous provision for the Wordsworths, and the thought that went into it, bears strong similarities to the formidable charitable gifts of past parishioners – indeed, the Calvert forebears had taken their turn among the Eighteen Men – it was a rare thing for a young man to do with the blessing of his family. And the two Williams were to remain friends for the rest of their lives.

By early November 1794, Raisley was in such pain he could not 'bear the fatigue of being read to'. Wordsworth's sustenance from both nature and the Lake District, which Dorothy had helped to revive, became severely dented again. 'Cataracts and mountains are good occasional society, but they will not do for constant companions,' he wrote. Although he added, 'This is a country for poetry it is true; but the muse is not to be won but by the sacrifice of time, and time I have not to spare.'[67]

So, following Raisley's death on 9 January 1795 (less than two months after he had turned twenty-one, the age that legitimised his will), Wordsworth paid a quick visit to Dorothy and then rushed back to London to join the fray. Once there, he joined a circle of some of the most significant radicals of the day, centring on the radical philosopher and journalist William Godwin. His aim still to change the world, Wordsworth soon became far more involved with Godwin's philosophy. Losing much of his hope for the French Revolution, as the revolutionaries 'had become oppressors in their turn', he gave up his intensely felt faith in the 'general will' for Godwin's sense that individual rational judgment was the be-all and end-all. Briefly, he felt a sense of superiority and purpose as he delved to 'abstract the hopes of man / Out of his feelings, to be fix'd henceforth / For ever in a purer element'.[68]

Dorothy considered his way of life 'altogether unfavourable for mental exertion',[69] as her brother desultorily looked to journalism, and even began to describe her hopes of living with William to Jane Pollard as 'airy dreams'.[70] Who knows whether the promise of their time in Windy Brow – about half Wordsworth's poetry written over the ensuing two years belonged to their few weeks there[71] – would have been fulfilled if William had not been offered another rent-free house, Racedown, near Broadwindsor in Dorset.

Arriving at the end of September 1795, the couple's twenty months there, before Coleridge's advent in their lives, was not, on the surface, a productive one: there were six-month lulls, as Wordsworth wrote nothing new. Realising what he must have been subconsciously suppressing, that Godwin's extreme rationalism in no sense accorded with his own temperament,* Wordsworth lost his recent foothold on his rock-climb away from revolutionary fervour and 'Yielded up moral questions in despair'[72] as the two 'Gagging Acts'[73] of 1795 came into force, eroding the freedom of speech that had been enshrined in the 1689 Bill of Rights. By 1796, however, he was clear that Godwin's creed† merely provided 'a sophism for every crime'.[74] Yet, as he still floundered, his creativity and humanity stirred.

Underneath everything, and a crucial prerequisite to rebalancing the agony of his conflicted feelings about the Revolution, Dorothy's particular capacity for natural observation, with its spontaneous combination of a sense of wonder and joyful lyrical intensity, allowed William to look again at nature and re-enliven and rejustify his childhood faith in its unique power to

* Godwin wrote, 'everything understood by the term co-operation is in some sense an evil'.
† Well described by Southey after a similar loss of faith two years earlier, 'the fundamental error' of Godwin's philosophy was 'that he theorises for another state, not for the rule of conduct in the present'.

unlock the visionary and the sublime.* The healing had begun. In Dorset, the couple lived extremely carefully. William could not even afford a London newspaper but, as Dorothy wrote early on to her confidante Jane,† 'We are both as happy as people can be who live in perfect solitude. We do not see a soul.'[75] An interesting remark for a woman bringing up a young child, Basil Montagu, for which Basil's widowed father paid the Wordsworths a vital £50 a year.[76] The couple's assumptions that Raisley's bequest would be sufficient to allow them to live successfully, if frugally, as all had hoped and some still say, were wide of the mark. The poet was not to be self-supporting until he was forty-three, half a lifetime later.[77]

Raisley's money had been loaned out at 9 per cent and it seems that William and his elder brother, Richard, had naively but confidently expected to be able to get the same annuity rates, despite their lack of securities. However, the roughly £500 available in 1796 would have actually generated only some £30 a year at the market rates the Wordsworths were likely to achieve,[78] clearly far from enough to make William and Dorothy financially independent.‡ Once he realised this, William foolishly loaned the bulk of the money to two friends, one of them Basil's father, some of it on a promised 10 per cent interest. The results of these loans would – as might have been expected – turn out to be disastrous. Deeply aggrieved by the financial situation created by their father's death and James Lowther's dishonesty, the Wordsworths as a family had a bad habit of making mistakes with money.§ Perhaps this was why William fostered the general belief that he and Dorothy were

---

* He would write, in *Tintern Abbey*: '...In thy voice I catch the / Language of my former heart, and read / My former pleasures in the shooting lights / Of thy wild eyes.'

† Who had recently married the Yorkshire flax manufacturer John Marshall, later to take over the old Derwentwater lands in the Parish.

‡ Interest rates were extraordinarily variable then. Looking at the various Parish charities in 1821, three used the safe 4½ per cent from turnpikes and tolls. And one individual offered the same rate, while the three other individuals offered 10 or 11 per cent.

§ They gambled considerably on a financially successful result for John's first voyage as captain.

living on Raisley's inheritance, although it was not until 1804 that
the poet felt secure enough in his achievements to finish his public
poem of thanks to him:[79]

> CALVERT! *it must not be unheard by them*
> *Who may respect my name that ...*
> *If there be aught of pure, or good, or great,*
> *In my past verse ...*
> *To think how much of this will be thy praise.*

By then, Wordsworth had written much of his greatest poetry.
In part enabled by Raisley's legacy, the promise of William and
Dorothy's stay at Windy Brow had been fulfilled.

The Parish Encountered
by the Lake Poets

W HEN WORDSWORTH LEFT the Parish to go to London
in 1795, its population was more than 3,000, having
risen by over 30 per cent in less than forty-five years;*
the population of Penrith, around 4,000, offers a useful local comparison. And almost half of its population had been released, after
some 230 years, from having to undertake the arduous journey to
St Kentigern's to have their children baptised, since all the chapels
had begun to baptise again (and some to marry). The balance, in
1793, had been forty-two children baptised in the chapels and forty-eight in the mother church.

The 1790s was a decade during which religious debate had
come back to the fore. On one side lay both atheism and deism,
a rationalist belief in one God and the hope of an afterlife after
the exercise of necessary morality in one's lifetime; and on the
other, and in direct opposition to both, the new evangelism.
Unequivocally supporting biblical Christianity, the evangelists
believed that revelation, not reason, was central and that the vital
redemption from original sin could only be achieved through
faith; their central experience of conversion followed by a constant monitoring of behaviour.

This emphasis upon individual salvation and man's essential
'depravity and guilt' chimed with the growing sense of the depravity of events taking place in France,[1] offering rigid self-control

---

* The English population, as a whole, had risen even more.

as a corrective to the emotions that the revolution had originally prompted from many in Britain.[2] Their validity was now seen to have been entirely undermined by the path the Revolution was taking. The movement was strong in Cumberland, for, despite John Wesley's antipathy to Keswick and his broad failure to stir the Cumbrians, he had had the effect there of spurring a particular growth of evangelical sentiment among the Anglicans of the area.

The outside preaching, the enthusiasm so disliked by the mid-eighteenth-century church and – possibly above all – the emotional directness of the hymns favoured by the evangelicals had generally stirred and converted people in a way in which the metrical psalms of the Anglican Church had quite failed to do. The leader of the evangelical revival in Cumberland, Isaac Milner,* had become Dean of Carlisle in 1792 – traditionally, the last dean to wear a wig. Several thousand people came to hear him preach, one of them saying, 'I have seen the aisle and every part of it so thronged, that a person might have walked upon the heads of the crowds.'[3] Milner dominated the city and the diocese. With local Nonconformists, he started the Carlisle Auxiliary to the British and Foreign Bible Society, the Church Missionary Society, and the Church Society for Promoting Christian Knowledge. Under his evangelical influence, a century that had begun, during the reign of Queen Anne, with the arrival of the first Christian missionary associations in Cumberland came full circle.

The apparatus that would become an integral part of the Victorian church was starting to take shape. Nonconformism had not yet begun its steep local ascent, however. In 1793, the number of pledged Nonconformists in the Parish had tripled from fifty years earlier, but they still numbered only forty-five families.[4]

The 1790s was also a decade when events in the wider world – in particular the war with France – had a real effect on the Parish. In 1798 the Eighteen Men were required to ask every male parishioner aged between fifteen and sixty whether he was

---

* President of Queen's College, the usual Cumbrian connection.

willing to fight,* while the vicar was expected to explain government plans and calm the people's fears. Then, in March the
next year, Jacobin certainties began to be undermined when
Napoleon conquered Switzerland, abolishing its cantons. Talk of
an invasion swept through Britain, and an Irish rebellion against
British rule, ineffectually supported by a small, mistimed French
landing, resulted in the imposition of martial law there. A severe
Lake District winter freeze combined with July floods to seriously
to affect the price of oats; but the old statesman resilience had
remained firmly in place, the pragmatic solution of many parishioners being to turn to making turnip bread.[5]

In 1800, the year that two of the Lake Poets made their homes
in or next door to the Parish, twin Acts of Union were passed in
Dublin and Westminster, and Parliament became directly responsible for Irish affairs. Roman Catholics made up about five and a
half million of the Irish population, a number equal to more than
a third of the population of England and Wales.[6] Catholic emancipation, in Pitt's view, was the logical next move, and the king's
opposition to it was the main reason for his resignation as prime
minister in early 1801. The issue was, and became for some time,
a cause of fierce debate; one in which all three Lake Poets were
passionately involved.

Agriculture still employed more than a third of British workers
and provided around a third of the national wealth,[7] and in 1793,
the year after the war with France had started, the Board of
Agriculture was created, with Arthur Young as its secretary. In
the context of a country whose output had already started its revolutionarily sharp rise to 2 per cent annual growth,[8] its aim was
to boost production and enumerate the advantages to be gained
from modernisation and enclosure. Young, for instance, found the
amount of untouched but, in his view, potentially cultivatable moor-
land between Keswick and Penrith 'melancholy to reflect on', for 'a
waste acre of land is a publick nuisance'.[9] Behind this development
lay the beginnings of the utilitarian movement, which represented a
danger for minorities. The currency of utilitarianism is happiness,

---

* Because of the Defence of the Realm Act, passed on 5 April.

difficult to assess, and for Jeremy Bentham, one of the doctrine's leading exponents, its only *measurable* form was money.*

Young immediately sent two commissioners to Cumberland, John Bailey and George Culley. Their first and second reports, *General View of the Agriculture of the County of Cumberland*, in 1793 and 1794, along with two other detailed accounts, gives an interesting slant on the world the poets would encounter. We have already met John Housman's *Topographical Description* and *Descriptive Tour*, both first published in 1800, and Hutchinson's *History of the County of Cumberland*, published between 1793 and 1797. The *History* is full of quoted comment from others, including some work of Arthur Young from 1768.† Hutchinson also employed the younger Housman to 'visit every parish'[10] to, in particular, cover agriculture – soil, produce, wages and cultivation – and these parts of the book form some of the most valuable material today. But it is Hutchinson himself who offers a charming description of the middle-ground views of the Keswick valley from the town: the nearest valley 'was covered in yellow corn; the rest clothed with wood ... little valleys of cultivated land presented themselves in the openings and windings of the mountains, and small enclosures and three groves of oaks stretch up the steep skirts of several hills from the brink of the water'.[11]

Vicar's Island was covered in corn too,‡ while St Herbert's Island was wholly covered in trees. And on the west of the lake, the cultivated shore, with strips of corn dissecting the meadows, rose slowly up to the feet of the fells. At the opening of Newlands Valley, you could spot little cottages among 'verdant enclosures, intersected by

* 'It is from his money that a man derives the main part of his pleasures; the only part that lies open to estimation.' Quoted in Simpson, *Wordsworth's Historical Imagination*, p. 80. Southey had a 'Benthamish compound epithet' for this philosophy: 'metaphysico-politico-critico-patriotico-phoolo'. Letter to Bedford, 1 October 1820.

† The date printed by Hutchinson in 1758 but may have been a misprint for 1768 as Young would have been only seventeen in 1758 and the report of his tour was published in 1770.

‡ The emphasis on the yellowing corn in the Crosthwaite Valley is surprising to a modern observer, as self-sufficiency in cereals has long ceased to be a local ambition.

growing fences and little coppices of wood, while ... the cattle and sheep, depasturing, climbed the steeps'.[12] Oats were planted once a year, and barley twice, the former produced 'in pretty good perfection'[13] throughout the Parish. It appears, however, that turnips were not used as extensively as they could usefully have been.

The land running from Crosthwaite to Bassenthwaite Lake was praised as being 'loamy, very deep and fertile', followed in quality, according to Housman, by the land in St John's and Thornthwaite. He described Borrowdale soil as the most sterile in the Parish.[14] Cows, according to the commissioners,[15] averagely produced 7 or 8 quarts of milk 'at a meal', 5 pounds of butter a week and some skimmed milk cheese for home consumption. Both they and Housman thought the butter first-class, the commissioners reporting that, having been placed in firkins and sold to dealers, some 30,000 pounds of it was sent out of the county annually.[16] And there was a larger variety of sheep now, Blackface and Silverdale the two main breeds joining the traditional Herdwick.

Housman reckoned there were more than 30,000 sheep in the Parish, 9,000 of which were in Borrowdale,[17] and that the number was rising. All of the sheep (whatever critics from the South might say) were of a good size, the largest of them being bred in St John's in the Vale. They were salved in October or November, the 'salvers' still itinerant, and 4 quarts of tar and 16 pounds of butter were required to salve thirty-five to forty sheep. The best lambs, those who survived the butcher's cull, tended to sport particularly long fleeces, with 'a rough pile at the top'.[18] This was doubly beneficial, as it proved effective cover in winter, repelling rain and snow with a good shake, and fell off before shearing time.

When it comes to information about winter stock, Housman and the commissioners complement each other. The former[19] reports that 'The sheep are kept upon the moors in summer, and frequently in winter; they are, however, brought down into the enclosures during inclement seasons where they are fed with hay, which the shepherd carries upon his back to the flocks, sometimes even to the heights of the mountains'.[20] The commissioners add that the young sheep were kept back after salving in the intakes, or enclosures, where they cropped either grass or stubble. These enclosures were

either saved specifically for the young sheep or became available
when the cattle were housed at the approach of winter. The rest of
the sheep usually joined them in the enclosures if snow was fore-
cast, when much hay was dispensed.[21] Young's stockholding detail
colours in the picture for the larger Parish holdings. He describes
a 100-acre farm owning 8 horses, 10 cows, 20 young cattle, 400
sheep and 4 fatting beasts; and a 70-acre one owning 4 horses, 8
cows, 200 sheep and 2 fatting beasts.

All Young's examples enumerate twice as many horses as 'fatting
beasts',[22] but buying and selling 'black cattle' remained a thriving
business (see p. 182), even if this was an unevenly spread truth in the
Parish. By this period, large numbers of Scottish cattle were being
driven into Cockermouth market, an easy source for our parishioners. In *The Two Drovers*, Walter Scott has a good description of
the work of the Highland drovers, in bonnet and plaid, who would
head the slowly moving cattle through the Parish on their journey
south, right up until the arrival of the railways.* The drovers would
sleep with their stock, sustained by onions, handfuls of oatmeal
'and a ram's horn filled with whisky'. To be any good at the job,
they were 'required to know perfectly the drove roads, which lie
over the wildest tracks of the country, and to avoid as much as
possible the highways, which distress the feet of the bullocks, and
the turnpikes, which annoy the spirit of the drover'.[23] So the drove
road from Cockermouth to the Parish avoided the roads close to
Bassenthwaite Lake, taking a more direct route through the fells
well south of the water.[24]

The Cumberland hill farmer's diet was now more varied than
the labourer in the South, who lived on a never-ending regimen
of dry bread and cheese. Game remained subject to the Black
Acts, but cheaper fuel meant more soup, and potatoes were now
often made into hash enhanced with small amounts of meat,
'Cumberland tatie pot', as the farmers began to keep back more of
their mutton and beef than before.[25] However, according to one
expert,[26] the diet remained deficient in 'greens' and still wasn't

---

* The railways killed the market for the fairs as the dealers began to travel the
country and buy 'out of the byre'.

good enough to resist the winter 'ague'. For Housman, by the turn of the century, the old simple diet was being ousted by tea and butcher's [fresh] meat: 'Tea is now not uncommonly the breakfast of the farmer and his wife: even the wives of mechanics often feel their stomachs too delicate now-a-days, for the digestion of hasty pudding and boiled milk [porridge].'[27]

Parish farm labourers' wages, by the last quarter of the eighteenth century, had gradually become more similar to those in the rest of England, but they hadn't risen much. In 1794 Hutchinson stated that the benefit of the commons was such that a hill farmer could raise his family on an income of £6 a year,[28] while the commissioners and Housman disagreed about the level of wages. Housman reports that both harvesting and mowing grass paid the same wage in the Parish as forty years earlier (1s. and 2s. a day respectively) but with the additional provision of food. And although women still only got a shilling and beer at harvest time, men now got meat as well.[29] The commissioners, while reporting slightly lower wages in the county as a whole,[30] consider them to be already high, which they assume was to compensate for intermittent employment. They describe a working day of six in the morning to six in the evening and believe that women were both paid and fed at harvest time. Housman and the commissioners agree, however, that the wearing of home-made clothing remained a clear distinction between Cumberland's labourers and those in the South.

Agricultural improvement was the new passion,* so the commissioners, almost inevitably, called for more drainage, the reclamation of peat bogs, planting larches, and so on; mostly good suggestions were the money available. But they also found things to admire: the 'remarkably well built' houses looked both neat and comfortable, which was 'particularly pleasing and presupposes a stranger with a favourable idea of the cleanliness of the inhabitants; an idea which he finds well-founded, on further investigation'. Their delight in this even prompted a Wordsworthian moment, as they noticed how each house was different, 'everyone

---

* Witness the George Stubbs portraits of enormous newly bred cattle outside country houses.

building according to what he thinks most convenient for his stock and situation'.[31]

Cumberland mole-catching elicited their praise and admiration too: it was 'the most excellent practice, for every parish to let the destroying of their moles for a *term of yeares*, for a yearly sum',[32] leaving scarcely a molehill to be seen in enclosed ground throughout Cumberland! And the commissioners considered the universal use of single-horse carts to be so sensible that they listed their benefits with the intention of persuading other counties to take them up.[33] Some drains had been laid 'with great art'[34] too and, partly due to the single-horse carts, the roads 'are in general very good, both parochial and turnpikes'.[35]

The age-old Lake District sleds, still in use in the early twentieth century.

Since our last encounter with Parish farming and shepherding, at the beginning of the second half of the eighteenth century, the all-wooden 'tummel cart' had made its unsteady entrance. The commissioners report a recent improvement for those who now used a wheel with a nave and spokes turning round a fixed axle, making them more manoeuvrable.[36] And the labour-intensive, home-made wooden ploughs – drawn by both animals and humans – were soon to be changed for iron ones. But for transport in the hills the parishioners still used, as they had done for so long, the wheel-less sleds joyfully described by Wordsworth – just as they would into the twentieth century on some of the steepest ground. They also continued to winnow as before. In 1786, seven years before Bailey and Culley's *General View*, parishioners were still described as carrying their hay home bundled either side of their horses, 'for they make no stacks'; manure was similarly transported, even through the streets of Keswick, steaming in wicker baskets.[37] And the push-plough (or breast-plough), an exhausting device pushed by chest or thigh, still did good service stripping turf well into the nineteenth century.[38]

There were, of course, good reasons for all this – the innumerable small landholdings, the frequently steep, infertile, stony land in the Parish that would prove a challenge to any new machinery, and the toughness of stock and labour, half of which the commissioners must have semi-consciously discounted. Writing that same year, Andrew Pringle, the agricultural commissioner Young had sent to Westmorland, observed with fastidious, and hilariously sexist, distaste: 'it is not uncommon to see sweating at the dung-cart, a girl, whose elegant features and delicate nicely-proportioned limbs seemingly but ill accord with such rough employment.'[39] But he makes the point that, had commentators chosen to report on the lives of the agricultural poor as well as on high society, they would have realised that it had always been so – even in that Mecca of good manners, pre-revolutionary France.

The commissioners were even more widely 'disgusted', objecting to women – 'many under twenty years of age, with as fine forms and complexions as ever nature bestowed on the softer sex' – driving any cart at all; especially since they 'rode in so awkward a manner behind the cart-saddle'.[40] Housman, who spent more time than the others on ordinary life, had the right idea. He reckoned that any girl in Cumberland could reap more corn in a day than the average labouring man in the South,[41] and that their lives working on the farm made them 'alert, hardy and industrious' and 'excellent wives for men in the same station'.[42]

The financial security of parishioners had long been significantly boosted by home wool manufacture, carried out mainly by women and children; and men were able to fall back on work in the mills and quarries. So hill farmers and labourers were much less likely to need parish relief than their counterparts in the South, and we know that, in relative terms, the Parish made extremely good provision for their poor. The Eighteen Men – still the core of local governance and order, despite the weakening of the courts' role to conserve the commons – raised, in conjunction with the overseers, an exceptionally low poor rate for the time, 9d. in the pound (it was as high as 2s. in Penrith). Also, in contrast to farmers in much of the rest of the country, the war years (1792–1815) were good ones for the Parish hill farmers; the selling price of butter went up by a third and of mutton by well over a third, and the price of beef doubled before the turn of the eighteenth century. And, as food prices continued to rise, any surplus food the Parish could produce was going to be particularly profitable.

Away from Cumbria, the real wage for artisans fell by around a quarter during the war years in London and the maladministration of the Poor Law and the paucity of its provision proved to be a major cause of riot, even though England's poor rates had risen from over £2 million in 1785 to £15.3 million in 1802.[43] The main trigger for rioting south of the Lake District, however, had been a lack of affordable food,* usually brought about by a rise in the price of wheat bread owing to bad harvests or excessive levels of export.† Again, the Parish was largely immune from these problems, as wheat was still only used for high days and holidays. 'Time and again',[44] northern MPs had expressed their utter lack of interest in its price – on occasion placing a pair of Cumberland clogs and a Northumbrian barley loaf on the Speaker's table, to let Parliament know that some of its definitions of poverty simply equated with everyday life back home. There was no more money for taxes.

---

* No fewer than nine national food riots had exploded during the eighteenth century; in all of them, agricultural workers had played a relatively small part.
† In 1795 there was a riot in Carlisle against Liverpool traders who were exporting grain.

So when, inevitably, apart from making a small number of sensible, viable suggestions for agricultural improvement, the commissioners scorned all the Parish's conservative, well-tried methods of farming, there was little buy-in from the statesmen, probably particularly offended by the comments about their 'barbarous' lack of care concerning the most effective rotation of crops and their thoughtlessness about improving their stock.[45] The commissioners also lamented that threshing machines, drills for sowing the various kinds of grain and horse hoes had not yet found their way into the district. These comments, though, quite ignored the fact that the labour-saving effects of threshing machines had the disadvantage of creating more winter unemployment on the land, which both the Parish and the Eighteen Men were always anxious to avoid. So the tone of a drinking song of 1777, still sung at annual Cumberland dinners in London for those who had profitably moved away from their hill-farming backgrounds, may represent well the local reaction to the commissioners' disapproval:[46]

... Yet something we owe to our atmosphere keen;
Our minds, like our bodies, are vig'rous and hence
That boast of our countrie, strong masculine sense ...
The sons of refinement reproach us in vain,
'Tis our pride that our language and manners are plain,
Old Bess thought them courtly, and so they were then
'Ere nonsense and ton made monkies of men.

The Board of Agriculture's 'sons of refinement' brought the word 'statesman' to official notice. Although Bailey and Culley are often credited with being the first to do this (in their second edition), it was actually Pringle who first used the word, entirely unselfconsciously – and at least five times in his 1794 edition – as a simple way of differentiating the statesmen from farmers; the former were considered landowners, the latter renters. This introduction was to prove a significant moment, heralding the common early nineteenth-century perception that Lake District hill farmers were in some way special – different from all other similar groups in England. The word was used elsewhere in England, but it took on this particular flavour only in the Lake District and, after 1800, soon swept into the mainstream through the much reprinted Housman. It then acquired its permanent status through Wordsworth, whose specific use of the word, to encompass all proprietors who worked their own land, we have seen. His essential point was to underline the similar histories of those with the smallest and largest holdings – the 'peasants' and the 'yeomen' – and to call for society to maintain the smaller as well as the larger.

Ever since then, this use of the word 'statesman' has created controversy. Twentieth-century Marxists tended to equate the Parish yeoman with the Scottish and Irish peasantry as the victim of capitalist forces, hence their general use of the word 'peasant' for both the poor and the wealthy Parish hill farmer. Even today, some writers speak of the statesmen facing a choice between paternalism and progress. Yet, as we know, a statesman/customary tenant, unless he was criminal, could not be thrown off his land; his rents were fixed and he was free to mortgage or rent his land, sell it or leave it to his eldest child. So, in reality, certainly from around 1730 onwards, a landlord's decision about whether or not to exercise paternalism could only be exercised on leased land, which, in the Parish, largely lay in the Greenwich Hospital's old demesne land and the east Derwentwater shore. There, Joseph Pocklington, paternalistically, did like to keep people in work, although Lord William Gordon, after all his purchases on the west side, would certainly have pleaded not guilty.

Initially, the attitudes to the statesmen in the previously complementary descriptions of Parish land we have been examining tended to divide fairly strictly along class lines. Housman was devoted to 'the spirit of investigation and improvement, in that most useful of all arts, *Agriculture*',[47] but saw himself as a bridge between the land worker and the gentleman agriculturalist. In his words, 'To be ignorant of the manners and customs of the fashionable world, is wholly inexcusable in those who have an opportunity of acquiring such knowledge; but to be ignorant of low life, is a mark of imprudence, or of the meanest sort of pride, in the gentleman, and almost of criminality in the statesman, the legislator, and the magistrate.'[48]

Cumberland-born and 'brought up in country employment', he had been sent – as a 'remarkably faithful and intelligent person' – to cover much of England for Sir Frederick Eden's three-volume 'history of the labouring classes in England', published in 1797 as *The State of the Poor*.[49] This work, along with his indeterminate class status, make Housman's observations particularly valuable. In his 1795 tour for Eden, he endorsed the capacity of the Cumberland man to avoid poor relief, a Cumberland labourer earning 'nearly as much' as one in Hertfordshire but 'from his superior economical skill and care' having comparatively 'insignificant' expenditure. 'The peasant of the North is as intelligent, as ingenious, as virtuous and as useful a man, as his less provident neighbours ... probably far more contented and happy, than the South-country labourer, who is for ever receiving, and for ever wanting, assistance and charity.'[50]

Housman had a strong and well-informed relationship with the statesmen. He described them as 'the happy people who inhabit the peaceful dales, shut up among the mountains, where labour and health go hand in hand'.[51] He also stressed the age-old Cumberland peculiarity, caused by its ancient system of land tenure,[52] of a relative lack of distinction between employer and employed, well expressed later by William Dickinson in his poem *Memorandums of Old Times*:[53]

> ... o' fare't alike – beath maister and man,
> In eatin' and drinkin'or wark;
> They turn'd out at morn and togidder began
> And left off togidder at dark.

Housman's feel for the small farms that still dominated the Parish was almost Wordsworthian: 'Property is very much divided in this county, and most of the little farmers cultivate their own small estates which gives them an air of independence and constitutes a principal trait in their local character.'[54] While his first point is a fact and his second an opinion, together they present a fascinating contrast to Arthur Young, the commissioners' employer, who exactly represented his class and had oddly reported[55] 'No small estates' around Keswick and flocks rising from one hundred to one thousand. It appears that he simply did not *see* the innumerable smaller holdings and flocks of the Parish; presumably his political view had dimmed his sight.

However, Young's views were well reflected by the new 'experts'. In their view, all the smaller statesmen stood in the way of progress. For Hutchinson, enfranchisement might change matters, as arbitrary fines and boon service were responsible for both perpetual impoverishment and 'indolence'.[56] But, along with his fellow middle-class local chronicler James Clarke, author of *Survey of the Lakes* (1787), he was generally full of disapproval, convinced that 'these base tenures greatly retard cultivation'.[57] Both 'lamented' the joint policy of Greenwich Hospital and Lord Egremont of not selling Parish land to 'people of fortune', believing that should they do so, 'the country would be considerably improved and enriched'.*[58]

Only Pringle addressed the statesmen's position with any grace. Reporting on the number of small statesmen who had had to sell their land, he wrote: 'It is difficult to contemplate this change without regret, but considering the matter on the scale of national utility, it may be questioned whether the agriculture of the country will not be improved as the landed property becomes less divided.'[59] Bailey and Culley were less nuanced on the matter: 'customary tenure is allowed, on all hands, to be a great grievance and a check to improvement'.[60] Their proposed solutions were a scheme to ensure universal enfranchisement along with enclosure of the commons; longer leases for renters, allowing improvement to make economic sense for the farmers; and a change to the tithe computation, to tax 'natural produce of the land' rather than 'the capital employed in the trade'.[61] Housman felt equally strongly about tithes (90 per cent of which were still paid in kind in Cumbria generally) and short leasehold tenancies.[62] *Pace* the universal enclosure of the commons, much of this was sensible and achievable.

---

* An example of such 'enrichment' was graphically provided by the eastern shores of Windermere, which had virtually no public access before the coming of the National Trust.

By the time of their 1797 edition, Bailey and Culley started to reflect the common emotion engendered by the word 'statesman', away from Wordsworth: a sort of patronising romantic admiration that had at least some relationship with the old Arcadian artistic viewpoint. Having begun by stating their fundamental belief – 'To the small proprietors, Agriculture, we presume, is little indebted for its advancement' – their tone becomes slightly more respectful, albeit still condescending:

> 'These "statesmen" seem to inherit with the estates of their ancestors their notions of cultivating them, and are almost as attached to the one as the other: they are rarely aspiring, and seem content with their situation, nor is luxury in any shape an object of their desires; their little estates, which they cultivate with their own hands, produce almost every necessary article of food; and clothing, they in part manufacture themselves; they have a high character for their sincerity and honesty; and probably few people enjoy more ease and humble happiness.'[63]

The improvers' universal opinion that the statesmen were backward, resistant to change and their tenancy a curse quite ignored the dramatic change we have witnessed. 'The great rebuilding' that followed the Restoration was tangible proof of the marked increase of disposable wealth some had enjoyed and bore witness to the introduction of borrowing and mortgages and an escalating desire for the statesman to leave all his children as well provided for as he could. Subsequently, the successful battles in the Parish over arbitrary fines had bettered the lives of all, so that, by the nineteenth century, when the practice of renting considerably widened, the customary tenants held many of the leases.[64] However, as we know, during this process of change, the statesmen had become a far less homogeneous group, with an ever-growing differential between the wealth of the groups at the top and bottom of the class.

An article by a Cumberland correspondent of *The Gentleman's Magazine*, written four years before the publication of Bailey and

Culley's first report, but presumably unread by the commissioners, reflected the situation far more accurately: 'Things are now assuming a new appearance ... The rust of poverty and ignorance is gradually wearing off. Estates are bought into fewer hands; and the poorer sort of people remove to towns, to gain a livelihood by handicrafts and commerce.'[65] Wordsworth believed that between 1770 and 1820 the number of freehold[*] statesman tenures was halved, and the size of the holdings doubled.

Since the commissioners were passionate believers in both size and enclosure, they would doubtless have approved.

Wordsworth's use of the word 'freehold' was an undoubted mistake, if a witness to his sense of the reality of customary tenure. When he paid his salute to the Kendal fight that saved the tenure, without which he considered 'these Landscapes would have wanted the greatest part of the most interesting ornaments which they do to this day possess', he was absolutely clear: 'I allude to the partition of the Country into small estates, and all those unaffected graces which arise out of that arrangement of property chiefly held by customary tenure.'

So, while Bailey and Culley had clearly come to feel a half-conscious approbation of the independence and self-sufficiency of the average statesman's life, their observations significantly misinterpreted the context and, in fact, should have been written partially in memoriam. Statesmen had weathered tough times before, but for some of them the eighteenth century had proved too extreme. Newlands' tenants had had steady rents and fines ever since 1723 but lacked the great advantage of the majority of Derwentwater tenants, whose ancestors had bought them the currency of the paltry old fixed rents. So the Newlands tenants were more vulnerable and, as we have seen – a decade before Wordsworth thought conditions began to damage his statesman ideal – the influx of richer tenants to the valley at the *beginning* of the eighteenth century had soon led to excessive disputes about boundaries and some original tenants having to sell their ancient land.

* See footnote on p.330.

The disparity between the richer and poorer tenant had then been exacerbated by the arrival of enfranchisement. And, while the monetised and mortgaged property market and the better child survival rate had been revolutionary, as with any revolution, this had created both winners and losers. For some in Great Crosthwaite Parish, the eighteenth-century changes had had a major and tragic effect, as land farmed for generations by the same families was lost. Entirely ignored by Bailey and Culley, this was a tragedy that Wordsworth was to universalise.

*

Keswick, for Housman, was 'a small but neat and pleasant market-town, and, in general, well-built',[66] the houses adorned 'with whitened walls and blue roofs';[67] he was probably used to the pigs and the insanitary conditions. Hutchinson, who had had an unpleasant experience in Keswick with his younger brother in the 1770s – staying with 'a drunken and soporiferous Innkeeper' with a 'small share of natural intelligence' but 'much impertinence'[68] – was less enchanted. He goes on to describe the market, while suggesting, oddly, that there is 'little appearance of trade' in the town.[69] On 30 March 1787 it had been publicly announced that 'The Inhabitants of Keswick and the Country round have come to a unanimous Resolution to make Keswick a Perpetual CORN MARKET for all kinds of Grain': wheat and barley were to be found at the lower marketplace, oat, rye, peas and beans at the upper. And, apart from selling the finest butter, the weekly Saturday market, Housman tells us, was 'chiefly for woollen yarn (spun in the adjacent dales), a variety of fish from the lakes, and the finest mutton in the kingdom',[70] an accolade Hutchinson was happy to endorse.

By then, of course, the tourist business was in full swing. Even if neither of these count as 'apparent trades', and even if Hutchinson doesn't mention the 'eighty pairs of looms' generally working by the Greta,[71] he does comment on 'the manufactory of coarse woollen goods, carpets ... and some linen which occasions great resort on the market-day'. He also mentions the building of a new

cotton mill.[72] The town was clearly emerging from the doldrums
of the middle of the century, when it had been described as 'much
inferior to what it was formerly', although, having lost its leather
works to Settle in Yorkshire, it still hadn't regained the bustle of
its mining heyday. However, by now Keswickians used 'mostly
coals' for their heating, after the introduction of a powerful steam
engine on the west coast in 1780 had speeded up production.*
There was even a tiny coal mine in Borrowdale, at Riggs Head.
But the rest of the Parish outside Keswick, and the valley's inhabitants, continued to use peat.

The grammar school remained the only Parish school mentioned in the early nineteenth-century directories until 1816, when
a Keswick National School for girls was established, and generally things had been ticking over smoothly. The facilities were still
quite primitive, although three privies were now available for the
hundred-odd students. Nevertheless, 'complaints were made that
the corners were used by boys and girls alike for want of better
arrangements,[73] and benches thrown out of the church, for age
and collapse, were seized upon as an improvement for the school
seating and wobbled on the old cobbled floor'. The headmaster, the
Reverend William Parsable, who was also the curate of Newlands
and was to become a friendly acquaintance, at least, of Southey,
coped with all this by being a strict disciplinarian. And in 1801,
the year after the poets' arrival, the situation would boil over.[74]

That July, Napoleon had been spreading rumours of new invasion plans and local volunteers were gamely drilling in the fields
around Keswick at Spooney Green. Boredom and absenteeism are
said to have been running high at the school, frequently causing
'Peppery Bill' to lose his short temper and administer plentiful
punishments. Complaints reached the Eighteen Men from the
parents, but 'the Trustees were as flayte [frightened] of him as
were the scholars'.[75] A first. Then William Slack, who had leased
Monk Hall, was told by his niece[76] that her brother had been badly
flogged and decided to take the law into his own hands. Marching
down to the school to demand an explanation, he didn't like what

---

* By 1792 the west coast exported over 295,000 tonnes, mainly to Ireland.

he heard and picked up Peppery Bill by his neck and trousers and threw him out of the schoolroom. A crowd gathered and quickly grew.

This was an undoubted breach of the peace, and the vicar, Isaac Denton, also being a magistrate, was forced to report his friend, who landed up in a two-day trial at Lancaster. A coach transported 'several parishioners, a teacher, and some of the older scholars' to court,[77] where the display of Peppery Bill's torn shirt won the day, costing Mr Slack a reported £200 fine and £700 for costs, gargantuan sums, which I assume are exaggerated.[78] But whatever the cost of his punishments, Slack's reception in Main Street, once he got home, must have provided some consolation, for he was cheered by the parishioners from both sides of the street, all the way back to Monk Hall. Parsable flourished too. Having left the school and started a private one of his own, he soon became the licensed curate of Borrowdale as well as Newlands, and then a vicar.

All in all, though, life for most had been improving again, and Housman's splendid 1800 cameo of Cumbrian revelry in his *Descriptive Tour* no doubt portrays a typical Keswick night out for miners, townsfolk and farmers alike, a few hundred yards from the Coleridges at Greta Hall:[79]

'In their dances, which are jigs and reels, they attend to exertion and agility more than ease and grace ... No order is observed, and the anxiety for dancing is great ... the young men, busied in paying addresses to their partners, and probably half-intoxicated, forget who ought to dance next; a dispute arises; the fiddler offers his mediation in vain; nay the interference of an angel would have been spurned at: blood and fury! It must be decided by a fight, which immediately ensues.

'During these combats ... the weaker part of the company ... get upon the benches or stand in corners, while the rest support the combatants, and deal blows pretty freely among each other; even the ladies will not infrequently fight like Amazons in support of their brother, sweethearts or friends.

At length the fight is over and the bloody-nosed pugilists and unfeathered nymphs retire to wash and readjust tattered garments, [then] disperse into different public houses; and the encounter, which generally commences without any previous malice, is rarely again remembered.'

Not a bad spirit for the poets to encounter.

13

Wordsworth and Coleridge Settle
in the Lake District

ON 20 DECEMBER 1799, five and a half years after William and Dorothy's first experiment in living together at Windy Brow, they returned 'home' to the Lake District, to live at Dove Cottage in Grasmere. Their time of wandering, in soul as well as body, was past. William was unequivocally a Poet; his chief subject, from now on, whether autobiographical or exemplary, one that beat with the Parish's living heart.

William and Dorothy Wordsworth's first home of their own at
Town End, later to be known as Dove Cottage.

In June 1797 Samuel Taylor Coleridge had literally bounded into their lives, as he cut across a field and leapt over a gate; a time forever remembered as the jumping-off point for an *annus mirabilis* for both poets. Coleridge's deep desire for emotional connection – 'Better to die, than live and not be lov'd'[1] – led to passionate friendships and hero-worship, lived through with an intensity, a desire almost for possession and fusion, that perhaps sowed the seeds of their eventual dissolution. A need caused, he believed, by leaving home as a child ''ere my soul had fix'd / Its first domestic loves'; and hence through life he was doomed to 'Chasing chance-started friendships'.[2]

At Alfoxden in Somerset, where the Wordsworths had moved to be nearer the Coleridges, all three fell into instant sympathy. Their growing friendship had the effect of finally healing Wordsworth's loss of confidence, largely already restored by Dorothy's extraordinary personal response to nature – spontaneous, particular, direct – which had gradually moved him on from the long unproductive months to the beginning of his work on the poem 'The Ruined Cottage'. Before the end of the year, he would acknowledge her importance to his rebirth: '...in thy voice I catch the / Language of my former heart, and read / My former pleasures in the shooting lights / Of thy wild eyes.'[3]

During a year of communal creativity, words, lines and ideas shared, energetic walking spurred all three of them on. On a November walk, Coleridge talked of *The Ancient Mariner*, a poem whose lines were to be almost entirely his own, although Wordsworth played a big part in the poem's evolution,[4] suggesting that the mariner should have committed some crime – indeed, that of killing an albatross. This thought may have been prompted by his cousin's kill at the Cape of Good Hope, by then residing in the Captain Wordsworth room in Keswick museum. And the poem can be seen as a prime example of the attempt, later disavowed by Wordsworth, to marry in their *Lyrical Ballads* Coleridge's desire to give the supernatural an everyday reality with Wordsworth's ambition to infuse ordinary reality with a power equal to that of the supernatural.

The son of an Anglican clergyman, Coleridge had rightly

described Wordsworth a year earlier[5] as 'at least a *Semi*-atheist', while he was a passionate Unitarian at this time, believing Christ was the son of Joseph, and therefore fully human. This inspired his sense of the essential 'oneness' of the universe, nature and man harmoniously linked together by the all-present God; and this sense of God as present within nature, as its pervasive life force, much influenced Wordsworth. But it wasn't until January 1798, as Coleridge left Somerset to try his hand at being a Unitarian preacher, that Wordsworth encountered the white heat of creativity.

There were physical signs of all depression lifting, as he radically changed his habits. For years he had spent the mornings in bed, rising at midday, but now, Dorothy reports, he 'gets up between 7 and 8 in the morning, for he is fully convinced that the relaxing tendency of lying in bed so many hours' was 'destroying capacity for vigorous effort of intellect or will'.[6] Instinctively, it seems, at the same time he reached towards the Cumberland of his childhood for new material. His poem 'The Old Cumberland Beggar', which he 'observed* and with great benefit to my own heart when I was a child',[7] embodies lives lived in the Parish and the Lake District generally. An old beggar, known since childhood, has throughout his life walked the same long, exhausting rounds to the same people in the same communities, hoping for food and water. A useful, not a useless, life, said Wordsworth, for it provoked a pattern of small good deeds from those who sustained him, which constantly refreshed their humanity and self-worth:[8]

> ... *And thus the soul*
> *By that sweet taste of pleasure unpursued*
> *Doth find itself insensibly disposed*
> *To virtue and true goodness.*

---

* *The Fenwick Notes*: an autobiographical and poetic commentary Wordsworth dictated to Isabella Fenwick over a six-month period between January and June 1843.

Wordsworth prays that the beggar be allowed to continue along his way, rather than end his days in the workhouse:* 'As in the eye of Nature he has lived / So in the eye of Nature let him die!'[9]

'The Pedlar', written in February/March 1798, is more significant.† A first stab at masked autobiography, it was the final proof of Wordsworth's poetic rebirth, introducing a Cumbrian statesman, the subject of much of Wordsworth's great poetry, a man '...born of lowly race / On Cumbrian hills...' who went to a school that was the 'Sole building on a mountain's dreary edge', used what books 'the rustic vicar's shelf supplied' and, from the age of nine, started to shepherd his father's sheep. Often returning alone 'to his distant home' in the dark, in awe and fear:[10]

> So the foundations of his mind were laid.
> In such communion, not from terror free,
> While yet a child ...

There is reference to the Coleridge-inspired 'one life of things', but the pedlar's access to it was virtually pantheist. He 'did not feel the God, he felt his works'.[11] '...In the mountains did he FEEL his faith / There did he see the writing';[12] Wordsworth's provocative words 'the God' transferring the power of the creator to the creation.[13] The poem also includes one of those passionate, visceral evocations of the power of nature in the Lakeland landscape to shape, and possibly undo, the mind, passages to which any aficionado will thrill with recognition and awe. For me, Wordsworth faces its implications here better than anywhere else – and with considerable bravery. As the pedlar tended his father's sheep on the tops:[14]

---

* Wordsworth would continue to stress the need for independence throughout his life and, as late as 1835, wrote that it was better for 'ten undeserving' to be assisted rather than that 'one morally good man, through want of relief, should either have his principles corrupted, or his energies destroyed'.

† Wordsworth worked on the poem, intended to be part of 'The Ruined Cottage', until 1804, when he decided it was too long and thought of publishing it separately. The Pedlar eventually morphed into the Wanderer, the main character of *The Excursion*, and ceased to be Cumbrian. The 1799 *Pedlar* was first published as a separate poem in 1969 by Jonathan Wordsworth, and he republished it in 1985, along with *Tintern Abbey* and the 1799 *Two-Part Prelude*.

> *... the clouds were touched*
> *And in their silent faces he did read*
> *Unutterable love. Sound needed none,*
> *Nor any voice of joy; his spirit drank*
> *The spectacle: sensation, soul, and form,*
> *All melted into him; they swallowed up*
> *His animal being; in them did he live*
> *And by them did he live – they were his life.*

A child can lose himself altogether in 'the other' yet return to himself, but once the pedlar was twenty 'he was o'er-powered / by Nature', eventually content only when he found a sublimity, an ecstasy of communion, akin to Plato's world soul, that could never, in sanity, be constantly accessed. The awe-full, overwhelming, animal, childlike response of fusion with nature, in which the soul could escape its human confines, was an experience so powerful that the pedlar had to leave his homeland – just as Shakespeare's Lear needed protection from the storm lest he go mad.

Leaving his source of the eternal and choosing the emerging benefits and safety that the adult Wordsworth now perceived of a gentler, restorative response to nature, the pedlar was 'Happy, and quiet in his chearfulness'.[15] Yet his early ecstatic communion remained the foundation of his moral being. For, having once been subsumed by ineffable love, now 'His heart lay open' and 'the talisman of constant thought / And kind sensations in a gentle heart / Preserved him'[16] in a less moral world.

Wordsworth had finally tapped into the mainspring of his poetic power. 'His faculties seem to expand every day ... and his ideas flow faster than he can express them,'[17] Dorothy reported happily. From now on he mixed the autobiographical with poems about the poor, which allowed him (for instance, in 'The Idiot Boy') to reconnect with humanity and to develop the adult ethical standpoint to complement his new response to the natural world, one rooted in a connected community life of human empathy, sympathy and harmonious working with nature. This was the life he believed he had witnessed at Hawkshead but had then discarded for the Revolution, and one that he was soon to ascribe as particular to the Cumbrian statesman.

In the magisterial poem *Tintern Abbey*, which closed the two poets' *Lyrical Ballads* of 1798, Wordsworth states his new credo as a poet and a man. He distances himself from physical communion with nature by giving his old feelings to Dorothy. And although he maintains 'I cannot paint / What then I was,' he admonishes the passion of his younger self as morally unsuitable, for it was 'all in all'.[18] Remembering his anguish about the French Revolution five years earlier, he leaves passion behind and searches for serenity,[19] resigning political consciousness to quietist understanding of 'The still, sad music of humanity'.[20] And yet, at some mystic/religious, Coleridgean level, everything is married in a joyful fusion:[21]

> ... *And I have felt*
> *A presence that disturbs me with the joy*
> *Of elevated thoughts; a sense sublime*
> *Of something far more deeply interfused ...*
> *A motion and a spirit, that impels*
> *All thinking things, all objects of all thought,*
> *And rolls through all things. Therefore am I still ...*
> *... well pleased to recognise,*
> *In nature and the language of the sense,*
> *The anchor of my purest thoughts, the nurse,*
> *The guide, the guardian of my heart, and soul*
> *Of all my moral being.*

Here the poet stands, his guilt about Annette and his daughter, about the course of the Revolution, almost biblically subsumed under his vocation and the life he shares with his sister. His use, in line 112, in the passage about Dorothy, of the words 'For thou are with me'[22] is a clear allusion to the words of Psalm 23, 'though I walk through the valley of the shadow of death, I will fear no evil: For thou are with me.' This stance is underpinned by Wordsworth's reiteration of the more pragmatic insurance of his rediscovered moral code: '...that best portion of a good man's life / His little, nameless, unremembered acts / Of kindness and of love.'[23]

This was an *annus mirabilis* indeed, but something darker was forever to taint it. Soon after Coleridge had bounded over the gate, he wrote of Wordsworth, to Southey, '[He] is ... the only man, to whom *at all times and in all modes of excellence,* I feel myself inferior,'[24] surely an excessive reaction from a poet at the height of his powers. And in the muddles, conscious and unconscious, of joint creative endeavour and an intended merger of aim and ambition, Coleridge offered – and Wordsworth eagerly accepted – an impossible gift.

For Coleridge handed over to his fellow poet his own cherished scheme of a highly ambitious philosophical poem incorporating man, God and the world, to which he had suggested he would dedicate twenty years of reading and thought. Yet he knew Wordsworth had to earn money, that he discovered truth 'by intuition rather than by deduction', or even reading, and that there was 'a clinging to the palpable'[25] in his non-autobiographical work. These are not the traits of a pure philosopher. It was Coleridge, not Wordsworth, who would have been better equipped for the task – if indeed anyone could bring it off – had opium not debilitated him. Nonetheless, the concept fitted Wordsworth's sense of the great role of the poet, and he seized upon the idea. For the rest of their lives, as the impossible project never came to pass, both poets – and even Dorothy[*] – thought of Wordsworth as having at some level failed, a sentiment entirely at odds with the huge burst of energy given him by Coleridge's approbation in that famous year.

In the autumn of 1798 William, Dorothy and Coleridge travelled to Germany, leaving Coleridge's wife, Sara, at home with their children, and the months they spent there would underline the difference between the two men. Some weeks spent in Hamburg reinforced William's belief that 'moral happiness' was likely to disintegrate under urban pressure, and he and Dorothy, anyway unable to afford to live there, escaped. Away from Coleridge, Wordsworth was again swept along by a surge of creativity. Prompted by recurring memories,[26] he soon began work on the unplanned blank-verse *Two-Part Prelude*.[27] He was now strong enough to re-experience to the full his passionate, wild boyhood, fleshing out what he had

* And later his wife, Mary Hutchinson.

hinted at in *Tintern Abbey* with 'extraordinary sensory immediacy'[28] and creating some of the most resonant stories ever told.

In almost all of them Wordsworth is largely alone, an 'orphan' ... 'Fostered alike by beauty and by fear',[29] primal responses for a child living within the Lake District. But here, and only here, Wordsworth juxtaposes these breathtakingly vivid scenes with the 'fructifying virtue' of the famous 'spots of time' sequences, describing the poet's quintessential memories (mostly laid in childhood and linked to the deaths of his parents). Demonstrating through them the value of fear in imprinting memory, he considers its experience a vital gift of a mountain-country childhood. For, by recalling our own quintessential memories, 'our minds – / Especially our imaginative power – / Are nourished and invisibly repaired'.[30]

> For the soul –
> Remembering how she felt, but what she felt
> Remembering not – retains an obscure sense
> Of possible sublimity ...

And the experience of fusion with nature in childhood, as explored in 'The Pedlar', became a core part of the end of the new *Two-Part Prelude*, which incorporated twenty-two of its lines.[31]

> From Nature and her overflowing soul
> I had received so much that all my thoughts
> Were steeped in feeling. I was only then
> Contented when with bliss ineffable
> I felt the sentiment of being spread
> O'er all that moves, and all that seemeth still
>
> ... for in all things
> I saw one life, and felt that it was joy.

This reincorporation of his birthplace into Wordsworth's fundamental moral and creative vision also embraced the value of hard physical work and sport as part of the ideal of a beneficent community. He remembered the schoolboys of his youth who decided on summer afternoons 'To beat along the plain of Windermere / With rival oars...' as they passed infinite beauties and pregnant mysteries.[32]

> ... In such a race,
> So ended, disappointment could be none,
> Uneasiness, or pain, or jealousy;
> We rested in the shade, all pleased alike
> Conquered and conqueror. Thus our selfishness
> Was mellowed down...

Their arrogance was tempered by the grandeur of what they saw around them, the majesty of nature and the mountains gradually producing in the boys the quality attained by the pedlar, 'A quiet independence of the heart'[33] that allowed the danger of potential submersion within the awe-inspiring sublime to modulate into a calmer sense of harmonious beauty, in which God and nature remained indistinguishable – but were gentler.*

Written in magnificent blank verse, and a work of exceptional originality that broke with all known convention, *The Prelude* would not be published in any version until after the poet's death. Coleridge was to create an original phrase for this new form of poetry, 'psycho-analytical understanding'.[34]

The Lake District and the Parish become 'Home'

At the very end of 1799 William and Dorothy installed themselves in Dove Cottage, a move that had been almost intuited rather than consciously decided upon, and their new Grasmere home was to become the cottage of the siblings' long-held dreams. Wordsworth immediately began to lay claim to his new territory. On Coleridge's first Lakes tour he had commented that 'In the North, every Brook, every Crag, almost every Field has a name – a proof of greater Independence and a society more approaching in

---

* The verse Wordsworth circumspectly deleted from his draft had 'god' twice in lower case.

their Laws and Habits to Nature'.[35] In his *Poems on the Naming of Places*, Wordsworth started to give places new names based upon shared associations with, or complementary characteristics of, members of his own circle.

Coleridge felt in his bones that Wordsworth 'will never quit the North of England – his habits are more assimilated with the Inhabitants there'.[36] As indeed they were. So, when he learnt of a rentable house that had just been built in Crosthwaite, called Greta Hall, he took the plunge in July 1800. Standing atop a small hill between Vicarage Hill and Keswick, the house, Coleridge wrote to Godwin, is 'of such prospect that if, according to you and Hume, impressions and ideas constitute our Being, I shall have a tendency to become God'.[37]

Castle Crag blocked the 'jaws of Borrowdale' and Coleridge's view of the valley. Seen here from the nearby village of Grange.

Later, on the day his heavily pregnant wife Sara and their adored son Hartley joined him at their new home, Coleridge stood in his study and communed with the view: 'From the Window before me there is a great Camp of Mountains – Giants seem to have pitched their tents there...' Then, stepping out of the window on to the 'leads' of the roof,[38] in the sunset, he celebrated 'the most fantastic mountains that ever Earthquakes made in sport, fantastic, as if Nature had laughed herself into the convulsion, in which they were made'.[39] And, hard upon his arrival, he was off in the fells, running, loping, jumping, incessantly exploring and glorying in what he saw – and trying to capture both the sight and sensation in words; the Parish prompting some of the best, and most original, descriptive writing about the Lake District mountains ever created.

The house had been built by William Jackson,[*] a successful carrier, a new career inaugurated by the turnpike roads. Jackson became the model for the character of Benjamin in Wordsworth's *The Waggoner* (1806), the poem that introduced us to Dunmail Raise. His 'stately wain' and horses were stabled close by on High Hill, the route between St Kentigern's and Keswick, and ran to Kendal and Lancaster.[40] And although, as Coleridge relates, 'he got all his money as a common carrier, by hard labour, and by pennies and pennies',[41] his tombstone at St Kentigern's sports a coat of arms (probably unauthorised). It is likely that he came from an upwardly mobile statesman family connected to the Jacksons of Armboth Hall – over the old bridge in Thirlmere from Dale-head Hall. He was, Coleridge continued, 'one instance, among many in this county, of the salutary effect of the love of knowledge – he was from a boy a lover of learning'[42] and had amassed a considerable library.[†]

Jackson had created a fully furnished gentleman's house at the front, with smaller accommodation at the back for himself and his housekeeper, Mrs Wilson, who was to become a nanny to the Coleridge children. In front of the house lay a field and an enormous garden (nine-tenths of it a nursery), while at the back lay an orchard, from which the grounds ran down to the River Greta, loved by all the Lake Poets. Full of the silver gleam of salmon and trout, and with an unusually quick rise and fall, the Greta was far noisier in the days before its larger stones were removed for

---

[*] Peter Crosthwaite's mysterious instructions to the engraver of his 1794 map had been to 'replace Crosthwaite's Observatory' – an illustrated structure on his 1788 map, of which there is no trace – 'with Mr. Jackson's Greata [sic] Hall'.

[†] At least as large as Thomas Poole's, said Coleridge.

building.[43] It became the poets' 'Loud Lamenter'. And, one way and another, Coleridge was caught: '…my Glass being opposite the Window, I seldom shave without cutting myself. Some Mountain or Peak is rising out of the Mist, or some slating Columns of misty Sunlight is sailing across me so that I offer up soap and blood daily, as an Eye-servant of the Goddess Nature.'[44]

Within a fortnight of his arrival, the three friends had walked upstream to visit a beloved old grass bench near Windy Brow, and all three rebuilt it, as Coleridge joined in honouring this crucial beginning to William and Dorothy's story together and published a poem in celebration.* This compliment was almost immediately repaid by Wordsworth, writing his *Inscription* to St Herbert's Island, a place seen clearly from the Coleridges' new house, and later comparing the creative closeness of the two poets to that of the two saints.[45] A second volume of *Lyrical Ballads* was planned, and it seemed the poets' collaboration was to be as intertwined and fruitful as before. Indeed, they were to be constantly in contact with each other for the next three and a half years – except when either of them was away from home – and they shared eighty-one days of Coleridge's first six months in the Lakes.

The Coleridge family

The Coleridge family, largely minus its legal head, were to stay in Keswick at Greta Hall for twenty-nine years. Hartley was nearly four when he arrived, and was deeply loved by his family, but his upbringing, true to the freedom and wildness of the Rousseau model, taught him the opposite of self-control. He was clearly spoilt, as Coleridge, possibly unconsciously, realised.† Nevertheless,

---

* Signing himself off as 'VENTIFRONS' (a Latin interpretation of Windy Brow) for publication in the *Morning Post*, his message was overtly Christian, creating an analogy between building 'the seat of sods' and a place in heaven. Newlyn, *William & Dorothy*, p. 118.

† 'A little child, a limber Elf, / Singing, dancing to himself / A faery Thing with red round cheeks… / Which fills a Father's Eyes with Light! / And Pleasures flow in so thick and fast / Upon his Heart, that he at last / Must needs express in Jove's Excess / In Words of Wrong and Bitterness…'

he became much loved locally and would remain so throughout his rackety life.

Sara Coleridge had endured the agony of losing her second son, Berkeley, to smallpox while her husband was in Germany, and her hair, one of her beauties, had fallen out in handfuls. After cutting it short, she wore a wig for the rest of her life.[46] She had suffered, too, in the *annus mirabilis*, child- and washing-bound and entirely excluded from the joyful, creative threesome. Before she married, she had read and discussed Mary Wollstonecraft's *Vindication of the Rights of Woman* with Coleridge. She was, he declared, 'a woman of considerable intellect'.[47] But Dorothy, far from exercising her brother's evolving ethic of everyday kindness and good deeds, had been unfriendly and dismissive, declaring Sara to be 'deficient in organic sensibility'.[48]

Once they were in Keswick, though, most of 'the neighbouring families' visited.[49] The Coleridges already knew William Calvert, now retired from the militia and building the grander Greta Bank nearby. Their other visitors included 'a Colonel Peachy who lives in the Summer in a very beautiful house on an island in the Lake Derwent Water ... a Mr Spedding and his wife and her unmarried sisters, all young persons, seem to be an agreeable family – and they live here all year. The Revd Mr Wilkinson; Mr Losh etc....'[50] The vicar, Isaac Denton, must have been away, but two years later we catch a glimpse of Coleridge at dinner at the vicarage from Sophia Thrale,* who confided to her diary: 'There was Company to dinner, among them a Mr Coleridge who struck me as being remarkably clever, unfortunately a provincial dialect, but is a most brilliant converser and very entertaining.'[51]

James Losh, brother of a school friend of Wordsworth and an early adherent of Southey's original ideas for Pantisocracy,[52] (see p. 348) was the radical lawyer primarily involved with Edward Christian's committee considering the evidence of the sailors who had returned from the *Bounty*.[53] The Speddings, nearby neighbours from Bassenthwaite Parish, were, of course, good friends of

---

* A wealthy brewer's daughter, who was to bring the equivalent of £2.6m to her marriage to a member of the Hoare banking dynasty.

Wordsworth, and although Coleridge cattily describes the unmarried women as 'chatty sensible women, republicans in opinion, and just like other Ladies of their rank, in practice', the Misses Spedding were to become Sara's main local friends over the next three years.[54] And soon the Peachys became good friends of Southey.

William Brownrigg had died just before the newcomers arrived and his absentee heir was to rent out Ormathwaite. The original tenants, the Reverend Wilkinson, an enthusiastic amateur painter, and Brownrigg's niece Mary were already living there, as they had looked after her uncle in his old age, and Wilkinson's sermon on envy had been much referred to in Peter Crosthwaite's notebooks. The couple became friends of all the inhabitants of Greta Hall but soon departed for a rectory in Norfolk, to be replaced by Lieutenant Ponsonby, presumably one of the many children of the Miles Ponsonby of Haile who sold Vicar's Island to Pocklington through the right of his mother, Dorothy née Wilson. 'Mr Wilson of Ashness' had bought Vicar's Island in 1681 and Dorothy had inherited the Wilson estate, including Ashness and Watendlath.[55] This creator of the estate is likely to have been a 'Mr' Wilson of Keswick, one of the rare 'Misters' buried in the quire, upon his death in 1695.

The Lawsons still held their land in Borrowdale, although their main seat had moved from Isel to Brayton (near Aspatria, some 18 miles away from the Parish). Coleridge was soon granted the full run of Sir Wilfrid Lawson's 'princely' library, and they became friends. Like many of the local gentry, Thomas Stanger-Leathes of Dalehead Hall, close to the eastern shores of what is now Thirlmere, was frequently absent and would spend only the summers in the Lake District, although his family remained much attached to their estate. There are no records of Lord William Gordon or Rowland Stephenson meeting Coleridge. Joseph Pocklington had left the area altogether, Barrow House being 'only inhabited by servants', until Southey reported, in 1818, the Ponsonbys moving in on a low rent but with promised house improvements,[56] their Pocklington link maintained even if the heritage of the main branch of the Parish's Wilson family had become obscured.

Whatever Sara's natural inclination for local society, however, the next three years were largely taken up with family trouble, although all seemed well when she gave birth to Derwent in September 1800, helped by her younger sister, Southey's wife Edith, who was staying with them at Greta Hall. Coleridge wrote, with pride, 'My wife was safely and speedily delivered of a very fine boy on last Sunday night – both he and she are as well as it is possible that Mother and new born Child can be. She dined and drank Tea up, in the parlour with me, this day – and this is only Wednesday Night! – There's for you.'[57] But Derwent quickly developed bronchitis and threw convulsive fits, the shock of his illness prompting his father to turn, belatedly, and somewhat frantically, to some of the journalistic work he had taken on to boost his flagging income.

The Dove Cottage circle had expanded. Mary Hutchinson, Dorothy's friend from Penrith who had stayed with the Wordsworths for six months at Racedown in the 1790s, had brought her sister Sara with her to Dove Cottage, and both had become part of 'the gang',* all carving their initials together on a large rock, their 'Rock of Names', near the road through the Thirlmere Valley.† Coleridge was already infatuated with Sara when, by the end of September, just two months after he had arrived at Greta Hall, he had fought his way through to finishing the second part of Christabel; the first part was already set up in type as the poem was planned to end Volume II of Lyrical Ballads (notwithstanding the apparently wholeheartedly agreed decision that the two-volume edition should carry only Wordsworth's name).

The second part of the unfinished Christabel was as long as the first and introduced a gothic Lake District as the setting for the tale, the opposite of Wordsworth's 'perfect home'. After Coleridge read it aloud at Dove Cottage, both Wordsworths were 'exceedingly delighted with it',[58] according to Dorothy.‡ Yet two days later, on 6 October, Wordsworth said it was not to be included in the new volume, and suggested publishing separately a discordant combination of the finished poem with a finished 'Pedlar'.

Many trees have been sacrificed to scholarly disagreement about

---

* Coleridge's amused description.
† About halfway between the two houses, where they often met.
‡ The next day, after a repeat performance, 'we had increasing pleasure', she reported.

the motive and justice of Wordsworth's decision to drop the still-unfinished poem, with critical sympathies fairly evenly divided between the two poets. The facts are few: all of the published Volume II consisted of new Wordsworth poems. In later life, Coleridge certainly came to resent the events, including his name not being used for the first volume, but by then he was ill, subject to paranoid nightmares. *Christabel* was to have a profound influence on the next generation of Romantic poets – its eventual publication by John Murray, in 1816, was prompted by Byron – and its tone bears little relation to the Wordsworth poems; in Volume II Wordsworth published a footnote to *The Ancient Mariner* elaborating its defects and informing his readers of the author's offer to put it aside, a note unseen by Coleridge before publication; some outstanding Coleridge poems, including early ones such as 'This Lime-Tree Bower my Prison', were overlooked. On publication of the second edition of *Lyrical Ballads* at the very end of the year, Coleridge promoted the volume with might and main; but, perhaps in part because of the effects of a legitimate feeling of grievance, he fell ill shortly afterwards.

For the next seven months Sara devoted herself to nursing him, and sometime in the spring the opium dose was increased by the use of the notorious Kendal Black Drop. Even though Jackson had waived the first six months' rent, the couple were sunk in debt – they even owed £25 to Keswick tradesmen – and Coleridge retreated to a higher plane. Claiming to feel scorn for worldly things, he also became contemptuous of most of his old friends, still entirely enmeshed with 'the gang', as some time that spring his infatuation with Sara Hutchinson turned into obsession. The loving pride in his wife expressed in his letters of September 1800 had changed by April 1801 to public contempt. Whatever his prenuptial protestations about the rights of women, Coleridge now claimed 'blue stockingism'[59] destroyed the far more important wifely virtue of 'the desire to please',* and the avowed Christian so forgot himself that he misused Christ's words on the cross: 'Father forgive her!

---

* He wrote: 'The perfection of every woman is to be characterless … Creatures who, though they may not always understand you … always feel you and feel with you.'

She knows not what she does.'[60] For not knowing her place, Sara became persecuted by a man who could lose all control.

Scarred by her own family's fall from middle-class grace to near bankruptcy in her adolescence, Sara was naturally prickly and defended herself with a quick temper, swiftly puncturing the polished, calculatedly light manner she had affected in homage to her youth in Bath. Yet there is something marvellous about her. Life had already been tough for her, as it continued to be, but, throughout it, her favourite seal for her letters pictured a chirpy cricket and the motto *Toujours gai*.[61] A type of stoicism quite foreign to the statesmen or the Wordsworths, maybe, but stoicism all the same.

In October 1801, after nine years of intermittent fighting, the preliminaries for peace were signed between Britain and France, giving rise to surprise, joy and celebration on all sides. A month later Coleridge sought his own peace, withdrawing from the coldness of the northern winter to travel alone to London to work at his journalism and, he hopefully told Southey, to practise 'self-discipline'. He would return north at the end of February 1802, first visiting Sara Hutchinson at Gallows Hill for eleven days before proceeding on in March to Keswick and his wife,[62] who became pregnant again by the end of the month. The Wordsworths stayed at Greta Hall for a week at the beginning of April, during which Wordsworth shared the opening stanzas of his wonderful 'Ode: Intimations of Immortality', lines he had only just composed at Grasmere.

Taking up the loss of the 'celestial light' of a child's fresh soul he had mourned in *Tintern Abbey*, Wordsworth was now asking the question 'Whither is fled the visionary gleam? / Where is it now, the glory and the dream?' Coleridge was caught by the verses, and after an all-night conversation between the two poets, mostly about their own lives, immediately started his own response, an unpublishable letter to Sara H, the very next evening. There were inevitable connections to Wordsworth's words in 'the Letter', but this would prove to be the pair's last poetic dialogue. Coleridge had his reason for despair and the loss of inspiration at the ready: an unsympathetic marriage, 'my coarse domestic Life has known No Habits of heart-nurturing Sympathy'.[63] By the end of April,

Wordsworth had read an early draft of Coleridge's 'Letter', tracing a path from 'when like an own Child, I had to JOY belong'd'. This quality had long stayed with him, allied to hope, through 'distress' and 'misfortune', but now, Coleridge wrote, 'I am not the buoyant Thing I was of yore'.[64] This narrative may have provided the impetus for Wordsworth to begin to tackle his own unanswered question, for he worked hectically on his first draft of 'Resolution and Independence' that month – the first, and surely the greatest, exemplar of his poems that express the admiration and self-admonishment that can be prompted by observing the life and character of poor land workers. Having described his own visitation of sudden depression during a morning walk, he continues with his magnificent description of meeting a stoic leech-gatherer:[65]

> ... *not all alive nor dead,*
>   *Nor all asleep – in his extreme old age:*
>   *His body was bent double, feet and head*
>   *Coming together in life's pilgrimage.*

This was an adult 'spot of time'. And its message, surely for Coleridge as much as himself, was clear, resonant and to be internalised: 'I could have laughed myself to scorn to find / In that decrepit man so firm a mind.'[66]

1802 was a significant year for the poet. Shortly before it began, he and Mary Hutchinson had agreed to marry, and in June the family had received the glorious news that 'Wicked Jimmy' Lowther was dead and his debts were to be paid by his cousin and heir, Sir William, the family in due course receiving the sum of £3,825. So there would be money to live on. And since the Treaty of Amiens had finally been signed in March and the English could safely visit France again for the first time in almost a decade, William and Dorothy travelled there in August to agree a financial settlement with Annette and to meet his daughter, Caroline, before William married Mary in October.

Meanwhile, Coleridge had been swithering. He even described rare moments of regretting the birth of his 'Angel children' as the ties that bound him to his pregnant wife in his Letter. Inevitably, the marital relationship reverted to its painful pattern[67] and it was not long before Coleridge suggested a separation and, after his wife's vehement reaction, fell violently ill. Sara, 'shocked and frightened beyond belief',[68] finally resolved to appear mild and act with submission, realising that 'nothing but tranquillity keeps him tolerable, care and anxiety destroy him'. Between June and October, Coleridge would write, 'At home all is Peace and Love'.[69]

Yet by July Coleridge had begun to turn 'the Letter' into his famous 'Dejection: An Ode', in part expressing his central fear that he had both lost his distinctive, holistic imagination and was divorced from any sublime response to nature, which 'This, William! well thou know'st / Is that sore evil which I dread the most / And oft'nest suffer'.[70] Yet Coleridge's unWordsworthian gothic reaction to the Lake District in the second part of *Christabel* had become internalised in the new poem as, fleeing 'Reality's dark dream', he listens to the wind whirling around Greta Hall:

> ... What a scream
> Of agony by torture lengthened out
> That lute sent forth! Thou, Wind, that rav'st without,
> Bare crag or mountain-tairn (sete), or blasted tree,
> Or pine-grove wither woodman never clomb.

This quite different perception of nature and the Lake District had been building as Wordsworth had expanded his sense of nature as teacher in his new poems, and so can be read as conscious, or unconscious, antagonism.

Nevertheless, Coleridge felt so well that summer that he extended his claim to making Lake District history by becoming the region's first recorded rock climber, adding to his achievement as the first unguided fell-walker to conquer the tops. He was in his element. So, it was a cheerful Coleridge who, on 1 August, stripped a besom stick of its twigs, scattering them all over the kitchen floor to accompanying domestic protest, and sallied forth at half past twelve for the first eighteen-mile leg of his walk, supported by his new walking stick. A shirt, a cravat, two pairs of stockings, a book of poems by the German writer Johann Heinrich Voss, a little paper and half a dozen pens were safely packed away, along with a 'natty green oil-skin' in his knapsack.[71] The poet had been planning his nine-day 'circumcursion' for some time; it was to be more than 100 miles in length,[72] and would require Coleridge to ascend well over 10,000 feet, frequently on improvised routes off shepherd's piste – scrambling his way up vertiginous routes on stony ground.

Scafell lay at the heart of the tour, Coleridge reaching its summit on Day Seven, and the mountain offered him the defining experience of the entire walk; as he told Southey, upon his return: 'Of all earthly things which I have beheld, the view of Sca'fell and from Sca'fell (both views from its own summit) is the most heart-exciting.'[73] He wrote to Sara Hutchinson[74] from the summit, 'O my God! what enormous Mountains there are close by me ... And here I am *lounded** so fully lounded that tho' the wind is strong, and the clouds are hastening hither from the Sea ... and we shall certainly have Thunder – yet here (but that I am hunger'd and provisionless) I could lie warm, and wait methinks for tomorrow's Sun ... I must now drop down, how I may, to Eskdale...' Via Scafell Pike, he decided. Any fell-walker today will tell you that there is no direct route to Scafell Pike from Scafell but Coleridge, reckoning the ridge down to Mickledore looked like a pretty direct descent, took it. Today called Broad Stand, the route is used for rock climbing and – again, any expert will tell you – Coleridge was lucky to be alive by the time he reached the bottom of it.[†]

But he *loved* the experience, and he subsequently wrote Sara H. one of the classic descriptions of mountain adventure:

> '... now I came (it was midway down) to a smooth perpendicular rock about 7 feet high – this was nothing – I put my hands on the ledge and dropped down – in a few yards came to just such another – I dropped that too, and yet another, seemed not higher ... but the stretching of the muscles of my hands and arms, and the jolt of the Fall on my Feet, put my

* A local word for 'sheltered'.
† Two climbers died after falling from Broad Stand in 2017 and 2018.

whole Limbs in a Tremble, and I paused, and looking down, saw that I had little else to encounter but a succession of these little Precipices.

'...So I began to suspect I ought not to go on, but then unfortunately tho' I could with ease drop down a smooth Rock 7 feet high, I could not climb it ... the next 3 drops were not half a Foot, at least not a foot more than my own height, but every Drop increased the Palsy of my Limbs – I shook all over, Heaven knows without the least influence of Fear, and now I had only two more to drop down ... but of these two the first was tremendous, it was twice my own height, and the Ledge at the bottom was so exceedingly narrow, that if I dropt down upon it I must of necessity have fallen backwards and of course killed myself.

'...I lay upon my Back to rest myself, and was beginning according to my Custom to laugh at myself for a Madman, when the sight of the Crags above me on each side, and the impetuous Clouds just over them, posting so luridly and so rapidly northward, overawed me. I lay in a state of almost prophetic Trance and Delight – and blessed God aloud, for the powers of Reason and the Will, which remaining no Danger can overpower us! O God, I exclaimed aloud – how calm, how blessed am I now – I know not how to proceed, how to return, but I am calm and fearless and confident – if this Reality were a Dream, if I were asleep, what agonies I had suffered! What screams!'

After his long rest on the ledge, Coleridge made the jump safely – how he did so, without a rope, we are never told. But he did it.

Then, finding the cleft down Mickledore scree – today used by climbers as their first pitch in ascending Broad Strand[75] – he realised he wouldn't get 'wedged in' if he skewed his knapsack round to his side. Reaching safe ground as the storm clouds were 'coming in most tumultuously', he decided, at least, to give up his attempt on Scafell Pike and set off down the steep track to Eskdale in a state of exhilaration.[76]

On one level, reading the whole passage, I have never found

better writing about the physical sensation of tough climbing in the Lake District. Joy and excitement leap off the page, the tone reminiscent of much of Wordsworth's brilliant writing about his own boyhood experiences in the Lakes. Yet this was the man who was also creatively engaged in 'Dejection: An Ode', 'one of the best accounts of depression in literature'[77] – the view of the American academic Martin Corner, with which I concur.[78] Far from just a loss of buoyancy, Coleridge here describes the loss of all feeling and a weight that precludes any full response to nature or his own mind:[79]

> A grief without a pang, void, dark and drear,
> A stifled, drowsy, unimpassioned grief
> Which finds no natural outlet, no relief,
> In Word, or sigh, or tear.

> ... each visitation
> Suspends what nature gave me at my birth,
> My shaping spirit of Imagination.

The ode, just like 'the Letter', uses the word 'joy' (six times) to describe the primary human response to (and with) nature. It was also the emotion Coleridge most frequently expressed when he wrote about fell-walking.[80] Perhaps the heady exertion of the mountain adventure could be seen as representing a manic phase, the 'fix', the only way to feel fully alive, which the pedlar knew would be, ultimately, his undoing. There is no sign here of the hard-learnt Wordsworthian lesson of moving to a more restorative relationship with domesticated nature; nor any heeding the message of 'Resolution and Independence'. Coleridge veers from ecstasy to despair to a complete absence of feeling. He doesn't record taking any laudanum with him to the mountains, so perhaps it was that freedom, combined with the adrenaline rush of the experience itself, that allowed his outpouring of spirit.

If so, it was not to last. The last few months had been an unhealthy, conflicted time both in Coleridge's personal relationships and within himself. In the month of the publication of the second edition of the *Lyrical Ballads*, Coleridge had described himself as 'a kind of Metaphysician',[81] and two months after their publication he had written, in a letter to William Godwin, 'the Poet is dead in me ... If I die, and the Booksellers will give you any thing for my Life, be sure to say – "Wordsworth descended on him, like the [GREEK 'Know Thyself'] from Heaven; by shewing to him what true Poetry was, he made him know, that he himself was no Poet."'[82] By the autumn of 1802 Coleridge had two versions of 'Dejection: An Ode' ready to publish, one addressed to Lady (Sara Hutchinson), another to Edmund (Wordsworth). He chose to publish the Edmund version in the *Morning Post* on 4 October, William and Mary's wedding day, which was also the seventh anniversary of his own wedding – an apparent hex on the marriage he had always encouraged. A week later he published an anonymous epigram mentioning Annette's name, in what can only be seen as a veiled threat to Wordsworth.[83] The hopes of the two poets for an Alfoxden in the Parish had not materialised.

The Statesman Poet and Historian

WORDSWORTH'S NEW POEMS in the second volume of *Lyrical Ballads* often illuminated the ethic first established in the still-unpublished 'Pedlar' – and magnificently realised in 'Resolution and Independence': humble admiration for, and implicit admonition from, the ordinary man, who accepted suffering with stoicism and dignity as part of life in the natural world. Written in the simplest literary language available – intended to be 'the very language of men' and to capture a naked republican truth rather than distance it with 'poetic diction' – Wordsworth placed his characters in a landscape described by Juliet Barker as 'defiantly Lakeland'.[1] He stressed too that the characters he wrote about were based on real people, and believed that his use of plain biblical English would lessen the danger of words distorting, for the reader, the essential truth of his characters' feelings, thoughts and actions.

Wordsworth eschewed also the paternalistic sentimentality of the prevailing artistic view of land workers and the poor. His fundamental reason for writing about them was that he felt that, by closely observing those engaged with nature itself, we can see more clearly 'the primary laws of our nature'. For the land worker, close to natural rhythms and cycles, 'our elementary feelings exist in a state of greater simplicity' than for those whose elementary feelings are obscured, or even lost, in a whirl of town and industry. Wordsworth's new theme, then, was 'No other than the very heart of man', and while he presented his cast in a 'spontaneous overflow of powerful feelings',[2] his essential capacity to be, in Coleridge's words, 'a spectator *ab extra*, feeling *for* but not *with* his characters'[3] remained.

The poet wrote only one promotional letter for the volume, significantly to Charles James Fox, the powerful liberal opponent of William Pitt, espouser of the French Revolution and proponent of civil and religious liberty – a recipient of a very different stamp from the Bishop of Llandaff. The letter characterises the statesmen as 'small independent proprietors of land ... men of respectable education'[4] who 'show how deeply the spirit of independence is, even yet, rooted in some parts of our country'.

The letter to Fox, which is in some senses a perfect sequel to its predecessor, put forward an entirely different central idea: Wordsworth sent it 'solely on account of the two poems in the second volume' – 'The Brothers' and 'Michael' – that most embodied it. The quality he had identified in Fox that made him the ideal recipient of the letter was that he 'felt that the most sacred of all property is the property of the poor' and the statesmen's 'little tract of land serves as a kind of rallying point for their domestic feelings... a fountain [today the word would be 'source'] fitted to the nature of social man from which supplies of affection, as pure as his heart was intended for, are daily drawn'. It was to this man, not the revolutionary, that Wordsworth directed his argument that industrialisation and mismanagement of the poor was inevitably leading to the destruction of independent domestic life. 'No greater curse can befall a Land,' the poet warned.

Wordsworth had now spent a year living in the area that had provided him with his original sense of moral order. His levelling instinct unbowed, he had moved on from abstract notions of political virtue to something more local and more human, a passionate re-engagement with his own perception of individual people, their lives and land, their joys and hardships, and now their experiences of war. At the heart of the two poems he picked out for Fox was a strong sense of attachment to both ancestral land and family, along with experiencing the tragedy of loss; feelings, of course, deeply interfused with the poet's own experience.

Wordsworth was not only a supremely perceptive witness to an existence that is sparsely recorded, at a time when the number of families working wholly or partly on the land in the Lake District fells and valleys was far larger than today, he was also fighting to ward off the potential curse of poverty destroying their way of life. Consciously memorialising both individual statesmen and this life, he tells Fox that these poems are not just an act of homage and love, but written in 'reverence for our species'. And, bringing to mind 'ancient custom', the old phrase used in the laws that had governed the management of the Parish, he argues that, because the statesmen have inherited their land, they have an intimate bond with every inch of it; it is the 'tablet' upon which their domestic affections 'are written'.

A note about the statesmen attached to 'The Brothers' reveals,[5] for me, the essence of his attraction and admiration. The quality, born of their stoicism and empathy with the cycles of nature, of which '[T]here is not anything more worthy of remark', he wrote, was '...the tranquillity, I might say indifference, with which they think and talk upon the subject of death. Some of the country churchyards, as here described, do not contain a single tombstone, and most of them have a very small number.'* Yet the statesman remembered. As the priest describes in 'The Brothers', 'We have no need of names or epitaphs, / We talk of the dead by our fire-sides ... / The thought of death sits easy on the man / Who has been born and dies among the mountains.'[6]

Leonard, one of the two orphaned brothers of the poem's title, then continues the priest's thought: 'Your dalesmen, then, do in each other's thoughts / Possess a kind of second life'[7] – a gift that Wordsworth too bestowed, as he returned home and translated fireside memories and stories into poetic record.

'The Brothers' germinated from an account Wordsworth and Coleridge had heard in Ennerdale, while 'Michael' is based on the true story of an ageing shepherd of that name and was the first tale told him by Ann Tyson, his beloved Hawkshead landlady, while he was at school. Both poems record everyday statesman life. The 'homely Priest of Ennerdale' of 'The Brothers' '...sate / Upon the long stone-seat beneath the eaves / Of his old cottage ... / Employ'd in winter's work', while about him members of his family busied

* A subsidiary reason for the old attraction to the Quakers, who always bury anonymously.

themselves with carding and spinning wool. In 'Michael', the shepherd's wife – 'a comely matron' – has a particularly productive workplace:[8]

> ... *two wheels she had*
> *Of antique form, this large for spinning wool,*
> *That small for flax, and if one wheel had rest,*
> *It was because the other was at work.*

Michael often carded the wool for her, and they ate their supper of soup, oatcakes, home-made cheese and skimmed milk, sitting in a room dominated by the large – and, in the Lakes, virtually universal – chimney piece, 'Which in our uncouth country style / Did with a huge projection overbrow / Large space beneath.'[9] Michael had always sheared the sheep on a stool under the 'clipping tree' near the house, to shelter from the weather. In 'The Brothers', the shepherds were clad in 'country gray', a cheap mixture of natural white and black wool, which avoided the expense of dye. This was brought to national prominence by the popular song 'Do ye ken John Peel with his coat so gay', whose original wording ran, 'Did ye ken John Peel wid his cwote sae gray'.[10] Skiddaw grey was much manufactured in the Parish, and Peel's use of it is made emphatically clear in a later hunting song, celebrating his forty-year career as 'sportsman and brother':[11]

> *No broadcloth, nor scarlet adorned him*
> *Not buckskins that rival the snow*
> *But of plain Skiddaw grey was his raiment,*
> *He wore it for work, not for show.*

The two poems also bring alive the statesman's sense of community. According to the priest in 'The Brothers', 'To chronicle the time, we all have here / A pair of diaries, one serving, Sir, / For the whole dale, and one for each fire-side.'[12] Both refer to children who are looked after by their communities: in 'Michael', a parish boy is sent off to find his fortune, with money collected at the church door and a basketful of pedlar's wares. Having grown 'wondrous rich', the former parish boy 'left estates and monies to the poor' – like so many in the Parish – and even 'at his birth-place built a Chapel'.[13] In 'The Brothers', the school attended by Leonard and James – the two orphan boys – 'was distant three short miles', and they 'could write, aye and speak too, as well / As many of their betters'.[14] It could be Crosthwaite grammar school the poet is describing. The boys' animal spirits and the joy they take in their surroundings parallel the intense pleasure that Wordsworth himself took in the Lake District landscape and could, of course, apply equally to the Parish schoolchildren: 'Like roe-bucks they went bounding o'er the hills', playing 'like two young ravens on the crags'.[15]

Both poems bring alive the essence of the statesmen's experience and reflect Wordsworth's sense not only of the antiquity of their connection with the land but also his fear that their numbers were fast shrinking. The couple were 'The last of all their race' (as people often were in Wordsworth's writing), the eighth generation of a family with a cottage and a 'few green fields':[16]

> They toiled and wrought, and still, from sire to son,
> Each struggled, and each yielded as before
> A little – yet a little …

But, despite these modest circumstances, 'their hearts o'erflowed the bounds / Of their inheritance'. The boys had been brought up by their grandfather, Walter Ewbank, 'this good old man', whom they 'truly' loved. Upon Ewbank's death, both Leonard and James become destitute:[17]

> The estate and house were sold, and all their sheep,
> A pretty flock, and which, for aught I know,
> Had clothed the Ewbanks for a thousand years.

The elder of the two, Leonard, went to sea, like John Wordsworth, in a bid to make enough money for the two brothers to start again, even though 'His soul was knit to this his native soil' and he was only 'a very Stripling, twelve years old'. James, the younger, pined and started to sleepwalk, as though in search of his brother, but found happiness, as the community 'took him to us':[18]

> He was a child of all the dale – he lived
> Three months with one, and six months with another;
> And wanted neither food, nor clothes, nor love.

Whittlegate – when priests moved from house to house to find sustenance, taking their own cutlery with them – was not only for clerics!

Then double tragedy strikes. The news arrives that Leonard has become a slave to the Moors on the Barbary Coast, and James 'had gone forth among the new-dropp'd lambs, / With two or three companions whom it chanc'd / Some further business summon'd to a house / Which stands at the Dale-head'.[19] Waiting for his friends to come back, the boy fell asleep on the heights of Proud Knott, near Pillar in Ennerdale. His companions were unable to find him upon their return and when the child had not turned up by the next morning, all the neighbours searched. Change and danger in the mountains were constant possibilities, demanding cooperation: '...a sharp May storm / Will come with loads of January snow, / And in one night, end twenty score of sheep / To feed the ravens.'[20] This time, too, the search ends tragically – with the discovery that James has sleepwalked over the edge of the mountain and fallen to his death.

Leonard returns home from captivity, with joy but in some trepidation, only to hear from the priest the tale of his brother's demise – a method the poet uses to distance us from any mawkish sentiment. Until this moment, every character in the story has been true to the Wordsworthian/statesmanlike ethic of mastering trouble and enduring adversity – the grandfather to the very last 'had the lightest foot in Ennerdale' – but on hearing of the loss of his family and its ancestral land, Leonard can no longer face the prospect of staying in his ancient home. 'So he relinquished all his purposes'[21] and fled, becoming a grey-haired mariner, a wanderer at sea.

*

'Michael' is the foundation statesman poem and the Wordsworths' first year at Grasmere had added its own layers to the story. Prefiguring the sacramental act of the poem, William, Dorothy and John, their beloved sailor brother, had walked to Grisedale Tarn, the legendary repose of Dunmail's sword, to say their goodbyes and lay the foundation stone of a fishing hut on the tarn's shore, as a pledge to their joint futures when John came back from sea.[22] This connection may have been unconscious, but the next connection was clearly not. Soon after Wordsworth discovered Coleridge had not finished *Christabel*, he went with Dorothy in search of Michael's old sheepfold at Greenhead Gill, in the Helvellyn foothills. They found it on 11 October, and Dorothy recorded it was 'falling away' but 'built nearly in the form of a heart unequally divided'.[23]

The poem is also topographically exact: Dove Cottage had once belonged to Michael's family, along 'with some fields and woodlands on the eastern shore of Grasmere'.[24] And its story was seminal for Wordsworth: 'The earliest of those tales that spake to me / Of Shepherds, dwellers in the valleys, men / Whom I already loved'[25] as ' a rambling school-boy'. Until he heard Michael's story, he had experienced the shepherd's presence ... 'in his own domain' of field, fell and mountain: 'As of a Lord and Master; or a Power / Or Genius under Nature, Under God, / Presiding.'[26] Gradually, as the influence of the tragic strength of the tale took hold, this love expanded. Empathy had led the poet:[27]

> ... *on to feel*
> *For passions that were not my own, and think*
> *At random and imperfectly indeed*
> *On man; the heart of man and human life.*

He feels admiration for a life that left a husband and wife '...neither gay perhaps / Nor cheerful, yet with objects and with hopes / Living a life of eager industry'.[28] This lies at the core of Wordsworth's original moral message, the essentially good human life imposed by nature's power in a mountain world, and the necessity – turning into desire with the benefit of landownership – of hard work within

1. Sir John Bankes in full rig as Chief Justice of the Common Pleas.
His charity for the poor of Crosthwaite Parish and his wadd
mines both transformed lives and added much wealth for
more than three hundred years.

2. The Wad-Mine House captured by
Joseph Wilkinson in 1795, the era of
the 'Old Men'.

3. The Arms of The
Company of Mines Royal.

4. A view of Rosthwaite, Borrowdale, from the pony track up to Watendlath. Another general view of the Parish.

5. Turner's luminous painting of travellers arriving in Lancaster, after crossing the treacherous Morecambe Bay Sands.

6. The Regatta Battle between the forces of 'Admiral Crosthwaite' and Pocklington in full swing on the Island.

7. The new bells of St Kentigern's offered a descant to the recently imported canons, their shots echoing from fell to fell.

8. Joseph Farington's view of Skiddaw and Derwentwater from Brandelhow. The land would become the first major Lake District purchase for the National Trust.

9. William Calvert's Windy Brow, the first place that William and Dorothy Wordsworth lived together, by Joseph Wilkinson.

10. Dr Syntax. Thomas Rowlandson's popular take on the English search for 'Picturesque Beauty'.

11. *Wanderer above the Sea of Fog* by Caspar David Friedrich. The essence of German Romanticism.

12. Benjamin Robert Haydon's more philosophical take on English Romanticism, painted in response to a Wordsworth sonnet written on a climb up Helvellyn when he was aged seventy.

13. Sir Thomas Lawrence's romantic portrait of Southey in 1828, the year before his *Colloquies* were published, a work its author considered 'autumnal'.

a cooperative community. After being temporarily enraptured by the prospect of a new revolutionary start for all mankind, the poet passionately reclaimed his original moral stance. He taught himself, once again, to live according to the stern values of the statesmen, perhaps reinforced by guilt at having temporarily abandoned them. Indeed, he wrote 'Michael' shortly after meeting the ancient leech-gatherer, whose stoicism became the poet's bulwark against depression and self-pity.

Wordsworth had fought hard to produce a worthy poem to end the second volume of *Lyrical Ballads* and believed his Hawkshead landlady's story, '...though it be ungarnished with events / Is not unfit, I deem, for the fire-side / Or for the summer shade.'[29] Michael was an exceptional man: 'his bodily frame had been from youth to age / Of an unusual strength'; 'his mind was keen / Intense and frugal.'[30] And he was an exceptional shepherd, 'prompt and watchful more than ordinary men', and prepared to attend to the needs of his flock whatever the weather: 'And truly at all times the storm, that drives / The Traveller to a shelter, summoned him / Up to the mountains.'[31]

The following lines are a hymn to his and his peers' life and work:[32]

> and grossly that man errs, who should suppose
> That the green valleys, and the Streams and Rocks
> Were things indifferent to the Shepherd's thoughts ...
> So many incidents upon his mind
> Of hardship, skill or courage, joy or fear;
> Which like a book preserved the memory
> Of the dumb animals, whom he had saved,
> Had fed or sheltered, linking to such acts,
> So grateful in themselves, the certainty
> Of honourable gains; these fields, these hills
> Which were his living Being, even more
> Than his own Blood – what could they be less? had laid
> A pleasurable feeling of blind love,
> The pleasure which there is in life itself.

There is joy unconfined in Michael's love for his son too – '…that instinctive tenderness, the same / Blind Spirit, which is in the blood of all'. A joy that develops as the boy grows and joins his father in his work; Michael and his son 'were as a proverb in the vale / for endless industry'.[33] Wordsworth continues:[34]

> …why should I relate
> That objects which the Shepherd loved before
> Were dearer now? that from the Boy there came
> Feelings and emanations, things which were
> Light to the sun and music to the wind;
> And that the Old Man's heart seemed born again.

Unnecessary to relate to the statesmen, that is, but a lesson for others.*

Michael had stood surety for a nephew whose business had gone wrong, and, as so often since the introduction of money and mortgage to the statesmen's lives, his finances became unstuck, and he stood to lose almost 'half his substance'. His heart briefly failed him. But 'As soon as he had gathered so much strength / That he could look trouble in the face',[35] he felt he would have to sell patrimonial land and began to rail against fortune. But he quickly stops himself – ''Twere better to be dumb than to talk thus.'[36] And his solution echoes 'The Brothers'. 'Our Luke shall leave us, Isabel,'[37] he tells his wife, to restore the family fortune with the help of a kinsman; an action that Michael is determined will deliver his ultimate goal, that the 'land shall be free / He shall possess it, free as the wind that passes over it'.[38]

Isabel faces despair too, as she watches over her troubled husband's sleep, and '…could see / That all his hopes were gone'. She tells Luke he must not go, 'For if you leave thy Father he will die'. Luke, who is proud and delighted with his new role, makes light of her fears, and she too 'Recovered heart … and all together sate /

---

* One only has to read of James Rebanks's relationship with his grandfather and father in his autobiography to understand that this is the eternal key to continuing hill-farming life. Rebanks, James (2015), *The Shepherd's Life: A Tale of the Lake District*.

Like happy people around a Christmas fire'.[39] Facing up to trouble and recovering heart were two more Wordsworth/statesman fundamentals. There is one sacramental act to perform before the parting. Michael takes his son to the valley above Greenhead Gill and, probably for the first time, speaks of his love to his tearful son, repaying '...a gift which I myself / Received at others' hands'.[40] Before he goes, Luke must lay the cornerstone of a sheepfold, which Michael will then build for Luke, in communion with his spirit, as 'Thy anchor and thy shield'[41] in a differently dangerous world:[42]

> an emblem of the life thy Fathers lived
> Who, being innocent, did for that cause
> Bestir themselves in good deeds.

This was Wordsworth's now profound belief.

The ending is inevitable and briefly dealt with. Away from the Lake District, in 'the dissolute city', Luke succumbs to temptation and is forced to 'seek a hiding-place beyond the seas', presumably to escape his creditors. So Michael is left beyond rational hope. He had earlier asked God to forgive him if he judged 'ill' for Luke in deciding he should leave home. Yet Wordsworth tells us – and the words sound almost like the incantation of a learned principle – 'There is a comfort in the strength of love / 'Twill make a thing endurable, which else / Would break the heart.'[43] Since the poem remained particularly significant for Wordsworth long after the agony caused by the death of his own children, perhaps the principled words are there simply to provide comfort for the stoic. A heroic life may *not* be undone. Perhaps too, having lost his principles to the Revolution and subsequently recovered them, Wordsworth had no space left within him to question further.

He appears to be prioritising the love of land over the love of a child – just as Michael's decision seemed to do. Describing the balance of this agonised choice in a letter to a Racedown friend,[44] he describes the choice as lying between 'the parental affection, and the love of property, landed property, including the feelings of inheritance, home and personal and family independence'. These qualities were, for Wordsworth, essential for a good life; a prime begetter of 'the quiet independence of heart' so central to his ethic. This good is rarely experienced today; its loss was vast then. And for Michael, perhaps, the idea of his son potentially living his life on land that was not his was insupportable. The shepherd endures the desolation created by his decision to send Luke away and continues to tend his sheep and his land for seven more years:[45]

> And to that hollow Dell from time to time
> Did he repair, to build the Fold of which
> His flock had need. 'Tis not forgotten yet
> The pity which was then in every heart
> For the Old Man – and 'tis believed by all
> That many and many a day he thither went,
> And never lifted up a single stone.

Isobel dies three years after her husband; the land goes into 'a Stranger's hand', and soon only the clipping tree and the heart-shaped, unfinished sheepfold remain, as witness to the tragedy and the long tenure of Michael's family. Until, that is, Wordsworth gives the story a 'second life', which has extended now beyond local firesides for over two centuries; immortalising his own, as well as Michael's, connection to Greenhead Gill and so offering compensation for the broken bond between father and son.[46]

*

The two poems were presented to Fox as 'written with a view to show that men who do not wear fine cloths can feel deeply'.[47] Like 'The Pedlar', they 'embodied a coherent and unified vision of man and nature which had been tested and found firm by a man searching not only for poetry but for a basis to his life'.[48] But there seems little chance that Wordsworth's fundamentally puritan ethic would have resonated with an aristocrat – and something of a libertine. And indeed, Fox had little germane to say. But Wordsworth never claimed what he was due. That, by accident of life, he had become a virtually classless person and, by accident of birth, found himself among a class of men who are 'now almost confined to the north of England':[49] independent, ancestrally landed workers of respectable education. A combination which allowed him a revolutionary, authentic identification with his subjects, statesmen facing adversity.

The drives and morals of the statesmen he knew would have been 'inconceivable' to those, like Fox, 'who have only had an opportunity of observing hired labourers, farmers, and the manufacturing poor'. And they are equally inconceivable for many today, who believe Wordsworth's language and level of thought was way above his subjects' station (exactly the opposite of the contemporary criticism that his language was too plain). But it is we, the educated,[50]

> ...men adroit
> In speech and for communion with the world
> Accomplished, minds whose faculties are then
> Most active when they are most eloquent,
> And elevated most when most admired.

who often, with 'vulgar eyes', mistake the quality of the souls of 'lowly and obscure' men, deaf to their 'tale of honour'.

Wordsworth's writing examined sensibility. Leaping over the wall of articulation and finding that 'Words are but under-agents of their souls',[51] he refreshed his and our understanding of *égalité*, applying it to the interior life of Everyman. His fusion with the soul of the statesman, as rooted in the inhabitants of the Parish, uniquely reasserted the reality and worth of the common people.

Fox was unlikely to have been the most sympathetic recipient of this splendid letter – but the feelings and thoughts it expresses have echoed down the centuries.

The statesman historian

The 'demise of the statesmen' is a subject that has been much discussed for over 200 years. As late as the last years of the nineteenth century, Hardwicke Rawnsley, who had a natural affinity with farmers and shepherds, would often refer to having a crack with an old man, one of the last, late-lamented 'old statesmen' still alive. By the twentieth century, the demise was almost universally accepted (if not defined), its causes disputed and probed, as the directories from 1829 onwards apparently provided a statistical basis for the chronology of decline.[52]

The common contemporary and twentieth-century argument stresses the period after 1815 as the key to the loss of the statesman numbers. In contrast, Wordsworth's organic view of the land and the land worker and his intimate knowledge of the Lake District prompted, as we have seen, a quite different judgment about the state of hill farming during his lifetime: it was that between 1770 and 1820* the number of freehold statesmen halved, while the size of their holdings had doubled.[53]

Wordsworth's view was certainly believed locally. Almost as soon as he and Dorothy had arrived back in the Lakes, a neighbour had told Dorothy that 'in a short time there will only be two ranks of people, the very rich and the very poor, for those who have small estates are forced to sell and all the land goes into one hand'.[54] The Lowthers had long been the most voracious indigenous purchasers of Cumberland and Westmorland land.† After various enclosures (see chapter 17), they are said to have purchased twenty-seven manors from their enfranchised tenants, essentially to acquire their mineral rights rather than to carry out agricultural 'improvement'.[55] And it has to be said that Wordsworth would engage in a small amount of land manipulation of his own, purchasing an estate in Little Langdale, in order to create six small freeholds to garner more votes for the Lowthers for the 1818 election.[56]

An underlying part of Wordsworth's sense of the history of the

---

* Until 1835 Wordsworth had changed the language in two places in every edition of the *Guide* to keep 1770 as the date that the perfect balance of the statesman's life began to shift, ever more dangerously, but in the 1835 *Guide*, mistakenly, or with revised thought, the date technically changes to 1780. In 1770 freehold was sufficiently rare that Wordsworth must have included customary tenants, whether enfranchised or not, underlining his strong sense of the element of ownership in the statesman's relationship with his land.
† Some suggest the comment was more local – about the Le Flemings.

statesmen was his belief that there had been a connection between many Lake District customary tenants and their land 'for more than five hundred years'. The Victorians, excited by new discoveries about England's Viking past, wallowed in the idea, but twentieth-century academics largely found the concept foolish; for some, it contradicted their view of history. Others went further and denied that customary tenants had an inherent connection with their family land in the Lake District,[57] others asserted that it was decidedly unusual for any yeoman family to stay in the same landholding for more than two generations.[58]

In the Parish's old Derwentwater manor, that was certainly not the case. The names of those 'enfranchised' by the Derwentwaters in 1623 included nine Graves, four Gaskarths, Crosthwaites, Wrens and Wilsons, and three Bankes, Hodgsons and Dowthwaites – all names still present in the 1851 census.[59] A branch of the Graves family is documented as having lived at Dale Bottom in the Naddle valley for at least 350 years,[60] with another at Burns Farm from the end of the 1500s until well into the 1800s.[61] However, the most successful branch of the family left to make their fortunes in London in the eighteenth century, continuing to hold their land but leasing it out.[62]

In Thirlmere, the Leathes, who had bought the manor of Legburthwaite in 1557, stayed at Dale-head until the land was acquired by Manchester Corporation in the last quarter of the nineteenth century. And the reservoir the corporation created also put an end to the Dowthwaites' long tenure at the Green[63] (with its iconic position in front of Castle Rock),[64] the family having arrived there some time before 1564.[65]

So, discounting the Leathes, as they were gentry, we have already noted that three families farmed the same land in the Castlerigg and Derwentwater manor for over 300 years, and both the Gaskarths at High Bridge End[66] at Legburthwaite and the Hodgsons in the Naddle valley at Causeway Foot (a small dairy and sheep farm) joined the Graves at Burns by staying put there for 275 years.[67] Two more Derwentwater tenures spanned 200 years,[68] one of them soon leased to tenants;[69] five spanned more than 150 years;[70] and another two lasted more than a hundred years.[71]

Green Crag, later called Castle Crag. The Dowthwaites lived at its foot
in 'The Green' for at least 300 years. Vikings were said to hide there during
the tenth-century battles and it was the site of Walter Scott's enchanted
castle in *Bridal of Triermain, or The Vale of St John*. One of many examples of
ancestrally held land in the Parish.

Many of these families will have lived on their small farms long
before we have written references for them, and innumerable others,
not listed here, can be found that equally, if less dramatically, overturn
the 'two generations only' assertion. Away from the Derwentwater
Manor, the richest branch of the Stangers of Ullock, near Portinscale,
as we have seen, stayed in the Parish's Percy lands for over 300 years,
whereas in Newlands just under a quarter of the seventeen holdings
were held by the same families between 1578 and 1780, and more
than a quarter between 1633 and 1780.[72] So, the twentieth-century
claim that it was 'rare' for more than two generations of one family to
farm the same land, and that no local value was attached to longevity of possession – in apparent disproof of the Wordsworth sense of
statesman history – is simply not borne out in the Parish.[*]

* What evidence there was seldom came from the central fells.

The Derwentwater manor, however, does not support Wordsworth's belief that the number of buildings 'that go to decay or are destroyed' was good evidence for the halving of statesmen numbers, as only three appear to have been abandoned between 1770 and 1840. It did, however, add some substance to his complaint about the 'wealthy purchasers, who ... erect new mansions out of the ruin of the ancient cottages', the main culprit being his good friend William Calvert, who built Fieldside House[73] on the western edges of Castlerigg, awaiting the permanent return of his daughter Mary and her husband.[74] More seriously, there is little evidence of such a heavy loss of the smaller tenancies in the Parish during the period, despite Wordsworth's strong sense of it. Twentieth-century writers dramatically extended his argument by claiming that there was such a loss of the smaller farms that they were virtually wiped out.

Some applied the small-farm definition to those under 20 acres, others (presumably assuming that any smaller holding had already disappeared) to those of between 15 and 40 acres.[75] The crystal-clear information from the 1851 census in Thirlmere invalidates this claim in the Parish context: eleven farms there held 40 acres or fewer, compared to seven of their somewhat larger brethren. While 60 per cent of Cumberland farmers held fewer than a hundred acres in 1851,[76] in Thirlmere (ignoring the lord of the manor) the figure was 100 per cent,[77] reminding us of the pro-tenant legislation that was constant throughout Wythburn's history.

The landholding pattern in the rest of the Derwentwater estate was fairly consistent with the Cumberland average, but even so there were six other farms smaller than the size thought to have survived. So, with no untypical pattern of abandonment and the untypically large number of small landholdings in Thirlmere, the Derwentwater manor quite clearly does *not* fit the twentieth-century argument that the smaller farms had virtually vanished. The manor also demonstrates the problems at the other end of the scale, where twentieth-century writers variously impose a limit to a statesman's or yeoman's holdings of 100 or 150 acres: seven*

* Eight including the Leathes who were, indeed, gentry.

Derwentwater farmers held farms of 100 acres or more, two of those holding over 150.*

Two other issues, unmentioned by Wordsworth and many twentieth-century commentators, will have affected the consolidation or loss of statesman land. The marriage of customary tenants often brought together holdings that allowed some younger sons to create new autonomous holdings, a process presumably abetted by the new mortgaging for the children's future. And emigration must have had an effect too. Parish church records from 1600 to 1750 indicate a fairly consistent excess of births over deaths, despite an apparently stagnant population.[78] And the emigration inferred from this (usually then within England rather than abroad)[79] would suggest some consolidation of smaller tenements.

It is said that throughout England emigration 'had been virtually continuous in peacetime since the early eighteenth-century',† and, in Cumberland, it tended to follow the trading voyages from its west coast – and a few former parishioners found their way to America and the West Indies. In the swell in foreign emigration from the 1830s, the Parish seems to have particularly favoured Canada and the United States, where six instances of the name 'Keswick' can be found. But the process only really took off after the mid-nineteenth century, quite outside Wordsworth's timescale, with a surge in the emigration of labourers. Between 1861 and 1900 it is estimated[80] that, on average, 3.5 per cent of Cumberland men and 2 per cent of Cumberland women (with higher percentages in the core Lake District and, one must assume, the Parish) were emigrating each decade.

Almost all endorse Wordsworth's belief that the primary cause for the loss of statesmen was the demise of home wool-spinning. By the late eighteenth century, knitting was a financial help to the larger statesmen as well as the smaller home-spinners,‡ profitably taking up their shepherd's spare time – even while they were tending sheep. And

---

* Some of these may have been leased.

† Baines, D. *Migration in a Mature Economy*, Cambridge 1985, p. 46. Quoted Shepherd, *Across the Oceans*, p.13.

‡ Women spinners could earn 3s. a week, knitters 2s. 6d. and children about 2s. at this time. Bouch and Jones, *A Social and Economic History*, pp. 265–70.

Lake District probate evidence from the last half of the eighteenth century suggests that, in the smaller holdings, a married labourer's wage could be more than doubled by the work of his family and that the value of the agricultural element in the deceased's estate was only 44.2 per cent.[81] Wordsworth's statesman poems illustrate this everyday normality, and in 1800 Housman could still say, 'The Cumbrians are almost all manufacturers in miniature.'[82]

The poet considered the cut-off point to be 1820 but home-spinning and weaving did not entirely cease even after the mid-century, only passing its tipping point by the twenties. As we will see, the Dover woollen factory, a major Parish employer, was still going strong into the 1850s, and a smaller woollen mill at Stair in the Newlands valley only *started* just before 1810. In the 1830s, when Wordsworth considered that all was finished, employment at Stair reached its peak, supporting eight families. And, after the poet's death, the 1851 census shows at least five families still gained their livelihood from the mill, along with six of Thomas Williamson's seven children, aged from seven to twenty-two. So, while the loss of the home-spinning and wool-manufacturing market had certainly seriously affected the lives and well-being of many of the Parish hill-farmers, the timeline does not corroborate Wordsworth's; his view of the speed of the loss was too fast.

However, had any untypically significant changes in the shape of landownership taken place in the Parish between 1770 and 1829? There must have been proportionally far more changes when the area was undergoing and then recovering from the scourge of the fourteenth-century plagues, and considerable change during the inferred emigration between 1600 and 1750. By the early eighteenth century, when the wealth of the better-off local families began to grow faster than the wealth of their land-poorer brethren, we saw changes in the Newlands valley.[83] However, while three Newlands farms appear not to have been owner-occupied in 1641,[84] the number had only risen to five over the next 150 years, still leaving two-thirds of the seventeen Newlands holdings farmed by their landholders in 1796.

With one large exception, the same process of small land changes continued throughout the Parish. Between 1796 and 1829 the numbers of parishioners paying the lowest level of land tax markedly rose, while the middle level, paying between 4s. and £1, dropped noticeably more than those paying the Parish maximum.[85] It was the middle that was being squeezed, the changes usually still not about anyone losing all their land but selling some to provide marginal additions for the better-off.

The notable exception to this general Parish pattern was the wholesale changes of landownership around the Derwentwater shore between 1770 and 1800, which had usually taken place on the death or retirement of the tenants, many of whom had already enfranchised their land. This process had coincided with a doubling of the average amount bequeathed to statesman children during the previous twenty years.[86] Lord William Gordon and Joseph Pocklington had picked a good time to go shopping.

Perhaps unsurprisingly, as one of the very few writing about the changes in the statesmen's lives who had spent the majority of his life among them, Wordsworth was the only person to emphasise that period as the key to understanding the decline in the number of statesmen – rather than taking the general view that the crucial period was post-1815. This intuition has been backed up by the recent research of C. E. Searle, one of the two modern writers that I have found most helpful with regard to Parish detail, for his analysis demonstrated that the customary tenants in the central Lake District area owned the same percentage of the land in 1829 as they had in 1800.*

So, three clear Parish facts emerge from this period. The evidence conclusively demonstrates the very considerable length of time that many of the customary holdings had been owned by the same families, and the continued existence and economic viability of the smaller landowner as late as 1850. It also shows that the twenty-five years up to 1800 witnessed the greatest change of landownership in a short time ever recorded in the history of the Parish – resulting in a significant reduction in the number of statesmen holdings.

It comes as no surprise that Parish reality fails to reflect what is considered the general Cumbrian pattern.† However, it is the Parish

---

* For more detail of this analysis, see Appendix 1.
† See Appendix 1 for more.

that lies at the heart of the land and the people that Wordsworth was writing about; those who lived their lives in a community 'whose constitution had been imposed and regulated by the mountains which protected it'.[87] And it is time the Lake District and the hill farmer were placed at the centre of the argument.

Reading and thinking over many years about the work of those scholars and historians who had written about the customary tenants, I had assumed that – despite the inevitable differences in use of terms, dates, figures and sources making it difficult to discern a clear pattern – the virtually universal concentration on the years between 1815 and 1850 as crucial to 'the demise' was correct. Once I had learnt more about the Parish, however, I came to the view that the mixture of scorn and bemusement directed at Wordsworth's analysis of 'the demise' was simply missing the point – namely that, although the poet had many relations who lived on the fringes of Cumbria, he was not talking about Cumbria in general but about the core Lake District. And in the Parish at least, the 'traditional', anti-Wordsworthian view of the timing of 'the demise' did not appear to hold good.

However, as I looked more closely at the sources, the basic contradiction I had been failing to reconcile suddenly resolved itself, and I realised that the prevailing argument might well be wrong in a much broader sense. C. E. Searle had analysed two things, in different places, that, when put together, suddenly made a pattern. Firstly, his analysis of the records indicated that, in 1800, 42 per cent of his central Lake 'Dome' land was owned by the 'peasantry',* which had always seemed impossible to reconcile with the assertion that two-thirds, or 66 per cent, of the land in Cumberland was held by customary tenants in 1794 (the estimated figure in the first agricultural commissioners' report).[88] Had that amount of change happened in six years, contemporaries would have been unable to miss it.

Testing the veracity of the commissioners' estimate, Searle's second elucidation went back to the solid research of one of the most influential Lake District historians, Joseph Nicolson of

* See Appendix 1.

Nicolson and Burn. Analysing the two-thirds of manors for which Nicolson and Burn gave tenures,[89] and taking a conservative guess that half the number of the, relatively few, mixed tenure manors were customary, tells us that 77 per cent of Cumberland land was held by customary tenants in 1777.* An unavoidably approximate figure perhaps, because of the manors missing from Nicolson and Burn's survey, and because we do not know the relative proportion of customary holdings in the mixed manors, but as precise a judgment as we can be offered from the data available. This more than justifies the commissioners' sense of the large amount of land they believed to be customary; indeed, they may have used Nicolson and Burn's work to make their estimate, but it was a retrospective guess and the landholdings were starkly different by 1800.

THE DECLINE OF THE STATESMEN IN THE LAKE DISTRICT

(from C. E. Searle's research†)

	Lake dome and Parish		Lake fringes		Cumberland	
	Percentage land held by customary tenants or peasant proprietors per cent	Reduction over period per cent	Percentage land held by customary tenants or peasant proprietors per cent	Reduction over period per cent	Percentage land held by customary tenants or peasant proprietors per cent	Reduction over period per cent
1775	77		77		77	
decline	35	45.5	42	54.5	44	57.1
1800	42		35		33	
decline	0	0	0	0	3	10
1829	42		35		30	

* Nicolson and Burn, *The History and Antiquities* described 210 of the 325 manors surviving in Cumberland and Westmorland at that time.
† See Appendix 1.

These figures[90] accord well with Wordsworth, as the dramatic fall in the amount of land held by Lake District customary tenants in the last quarter of the eighteenth century, 14 per cent a decade, coincided with the time of all the land changes around Derwentwater. Had there been a consistent pattern of reduction between 1775 to 1829, it would have been 6.5 per cent a decade.

Modern historians of land-use and tenancy in Cumbria, in the long period when the decline/demise was taken as fact, all looked to Blamire's evidence to the Select Committee in 1833 (see page 494) as their primary guide and so consider that the dramatic reduction had taken place post 1815. But it was not until 2007 that David Uttley attempted to enumerate this belief, researching the well-populated Leath Ward (which includes Penrith).[91] His work was based primarily upon the numbers of customary tenants, rather than the size of their landholdings, and his discovery that they constituted 27 per cent of the ward's landholders in 1913[92] was really significant. Based upon his work I have concluded that a conservative estimate of the numbers of Parish customary tenants just before the First World War would seem to be somewhere over 30 per cent (see page 502).

Accepting, of course, that there is no direct correlation between landholdings and the people who held them, Uttley originally appears to ascribe, without referring to any specific evidence, the entire loss of 376 customary tenants between 1780 and 1829 to the fifteen years between 1814 and 1829.[93] This is a surprising nod to a general tendency he queries[94] but[95] underlines the fact that, to the best of my belief, no commentator other than Wordsworth lays any stress on the last quarter of the eighteenth century as a major factor in the decline, and that he has been entirely ignored – as have the implications of Searle's work, despite other evidence from it having been frequently referred to by his fellow scholars.

Taking into account all the available sources I have considered, a strong sense emerges that the entire numerical debate about 'the demise' up to the end of the nineteenth century, largely concentrating on the 1815–50 losses, (after which the number of small grazier farmers held remarkably steady) was based on a false premise. This is unequivocally true of the Parish and maybe so more generally, since the percentage losses between 1777 and 1800 were larger in the Westmorland 'fringes' of the Lake District.

The context for ignoring Wordsworth's perceptions is a combination of the contemporary class-based reports of the 1790s we have already examined and the vituperative tenor of the political debate about landholding in Britain after the end of the French wars, which we will explore later. Also, Wordsworth never fully explained his brilliant intuition, although, in a more general way, he largely attached the blame for the crisis on the loss of income from home manufacture, the new gentry and the new buyers of land. He set almost all his statesman poems some time before the French wars, never telling us of a wealthier purchaser (statesman or not) being able to buy hereditary land for any general economic reason; it simply occurred when, for personal and familial reasons, mortgage and debt became terminally damaging to the seller – as in 'The Brothers'. Michael's tragedy is to face the debt mountain twice, once as a result of his own decision, and each time standing to lose half his land. No new gentry or new buyers of land press either issue.

One interestingly provocative interpretation of this absence of an up-to-date explanation is that, once Wordsworth had returned to live in the Lake District, he semi-consciously placed his poetry in the past (with the exception of *Home at Grasmere*), to avoid the complexity of what, practically, to do about the present.[96] This theory comes from David Simpson's *Wordsworth's Historical Imagination*. Simpson had read widely and his book is full of fascinating insights into Wordsworth, but he quite misinterpreted the nature of customary tenancy.* He argues, for example, that 'if Michael's father had been a freeholder, he might have mortgaged...'.[97] Somehow, despite good research and thought, he had not grasped the unique quality of a customary tenant's absolute ownership of his land unless he was found guilty of a criminal act. And that therefore, as we know, customary tenants had been mortgaging land since the end of the seventeenth century.

* See Appendix 1.

Pastoral tenant farmers walking home with their stock.

I have raised this because the basic misconception, from which much follows, gained heft after Simpson's school of criticism charged Wordsworth and the Romantic movement generally with betraying or distorting history. So the underlying misreading of customary tenancy, among writers who have not seriously studied the subject, is still widely perpetuated today, and this matters – while a proper understanding of the subject would mitigate many criticisms of Wordsworth.

There are, I suspect, two different proximate causes for the common lack of comprehension. Firstly, it seems very difficult for people to grasp the truth about customary tenancy unless they have a context for it. Since these conditions were not found elsewhere in any other large areas of the country, the initial reaction is that the customary tenants *cannot* have had the rights that Wordsworth described (and we have explored). Similarly, 'mortgaging' seems to be consistently misread, the assumption being that the practice inevitably involved banks and large landowners, which it frequently did not. There were no accessible banks when mortgages first started to festoon the inventories of hill farmers, a situation that scarcely changed during the eighteenth century, when mortgaging became ever more general. The statesman's loans and credits were largely to other statesmen – either full-time land workers or land workers who practised another trade on the side – work for lawyers not bankers. Indeed, for a statesman, lending money became a well-trodden path to an eventual change of class for the successful.

Wordsworth's reputation has suffered from this misinterpretation of historical truth. It has also obscured the great difference in customary tenure holdings that we have witnessed between 1775 and 1800. That is a change of real significance to the history of both land use and the history of the customary tenant in Cumberland but, since it is not commonly acknowledged, credit for Wordsworth's brilliant intuition has yet to be granted.

The Lake Poets

O N 6 OCTOBER 1802, two days after their wedding, William and Mary Wordsworth arrived back at Dove Cottage. Bedrooms were exchanged, but otherwise there seems to have been no obvious disruption to the previous routine. William now had two regular amanuenses, and Dorothy had help with housework.[1] Now that he was married, Wordsworth would occasionally travel to Keswick by cart, albeit a dung cart 'wi' a seat-board in t'front, and a bit of bracken in t'bottom, comfortable as owt'.[2] When Coleridge, returning home from a seven-week jaunt around the country, came to visit the new couple on Christmas Eve, they had news for him: his daughter, another Sara, had been born – prematurely – the previous day. John, their own baby, was born in June 1803, six months later, also prematurely, and Dorothy, who had stopped writing her journal at the beginning of that year, began her career as a splendid aunt.

The month after John was born, an admirer offered Wordsworth some land at the foot of Skiddaw in the Bishop of Llandaff's manor in the Parish.[*] A prominent Laker, Sir George Beaumont was a talented amateur artist and an energetic patron of the arts. He had been introduced to the Lake District by his friend Joseph Farington in the 1770s and had been spending the summer with his wife in the Jackson part of Greta Hall. Once he observed the two poets talking together, he had become convinced of the necessity of

---

[*] The bishop was soon to enter the same circles as the Lake Poets, Southey meeting him three years later and finding him reasonably acceptable as he had as little time for the doctrine of the Trinity as Southey did.

bringing 'these two geniuses' closer together.[3] Having previously purchased two small fields at Applethwaite, a lovely twenty-minute walk towards Skiddaw from Greta Hall, he generously offered Wordsworth the deeds of the property in mid-August.

The poet's eventual reply, two months later,[4] was a curious one: he said he loved the idea but added – truthfully – that he doubted Beaumont's dream could come to fruition, because he could not afford to build and, anyway, it seemed likely that Coleridge would leave the country 'for his health'. However, rather than simply rejecting the offer, Wordsworth suggested he might be a steward of the land with liberty to plant and improve, with a view to building on it later.[5] But if he eventually found he could not 'pitch his own tent there', he would restore the land to Beaumont, to offer to 'some worthy person' who could. These were complicated conditions; in particular, when and how would Wordsworth finally know whether he would or would not be able to build there?

It may be that Wordsworth's suggestion was prompted by a desire to avoid the apparent rudeness of an outright rejection of such a magnificent offer; equally, he may have felt that it was just too good to pass up entirely. Landownership would turn him into a fully-fledged freehold statesman, with all the personal freight that involved, and enable him to vote, for the first time in his life. We will never be sure of his motive, as Beaumont's graceful and undoubtedly welcome answer was 'plant it, delve it – and build upon it or not, as it suits your convenience, but let me live and die with the idea the sweet place, with its rocks, its banks, and mountain stream are in the possession of such a mind as yours'.[6] His gift of his own painting of an imagined cottage nestling there was hung over the Dove Cottage chimney piece, and Wordsworth later wrote to his benefactor, 'There is not a day in my life in which that exquisite little drawing of yours of Applethwaite does not affect me with a sense of harmony and grace, which I cannot describe.'[7]

More than forty years later, in 1848,[8] something happened that indicated that the poet's reply *was* fundamentally driven by a desire to have the land. New to the Parish, a Dr Leitch had purchased a small plot of land between the two Wordsworth fields, planning to build a cottage there, as he loved 'the mingled sounds of the church

bells and the running brook which blend there, perhaps more musi-
cally than anywhere else in the whole valley', and believed a home
planted there would refresh a spirit 'weary both with bodily pain
and the burden of this unintelligible world'. These words, in Leitch's
case, were far from a cliché. He had just retired to Keswick after a
long and painful battle, probably with tuberculosis,[9] which had left
him, in Thomas Carlyle's words, 'frightfully disfigured in face'.[*]

Derwentwater and St Kentigern's from Applethwaite by Henry Gastineau.
Wordsworth loved this view and bought a print.

He only wrote to Wordsworth to check that he did not want to
build on the land himself, after his own purchase, and the poet's
reply was distinctly disingenuous: 'If your intention was to fix the
site of your cottage upon the ground bounded on both sides by my
property, I certainly should feel much obliged by your selecting
some other spot, and one that might interfere as little as possible with the prospect and character of the Dell.' The building of

* Leitch was to do great good in the Parish and in 1849 was sufficiently
confident there to buy Derwent Bank, Pocklington's considerable house in
Portinscale.

an adjacent mill, 'which impaired much the privacy of the Place', had previously upset William, but the deed had been done before he knew of the plan. And, unable to prevent the building, he had promptly transferred the land to his daughter Dora, when she was 'a frail feeble monthling'.

Fifty pounds, plus fees, to the worse, Dr Leitch did the decent thing and assured the poet that, since those were his feelings, he would find it 'impossible for me to entertain the idea of building a cottage there'. He imagined he might be able to sell the land back to the two statesmen who had been granted it as compensation for the loss of their share of the commons when the mountain had been enclosed. And since they didn't really want to sell, Leitch said, probably accurately, 'I daresay [they] will take it back again on very easy terms – so I hope you will not consider me at all in the matter.' Or perhaps Wordsworth would like to buy? With the agreement of his son-in-law, Wordsworth did, and soon afterwards a cottage was built. The land had become his patrimony, and, like any good statesman, he intended it to remain in his family. But, unlike the subjects of his poetry, the veneration in which he was held by 1848 allowed him to override the usual effects of land purchase.

Beaumont's picture continued to be cherished by the Wordsworths throughout their lives and, ten years after accepting the gift, William wrote a sonnet for him about 'this favoured land'. In the correspondence with Dr Leitch, the poet wrote of having 'a sacred feeling' for it. Just as the Parish had launched William and Dorothy's living together at Windy Brow, two small fields within it provided sustenance and, as they moved on to grander things, a permanent reminder for the couple of their original idea of the place for a perfect home.

Enter the Southeys

A month before Wordsworth became a Parish landowner, on 7 September 1803, the twenty-nine-year-old Robert Southey and his wife Edith arrived at Greta Hall, in an attempt to recuperate with family members from the bitter grief they had suffered on the death of their baby daughter, their first child. A year earlier, Southey's letter to his old school friend and benefactor Charles Wynn, four days after his mother's death, had described his 'very strong' feeling on seeing the dead body that there 'could have been no world for the dead'.[10] Briefly – and I think for the only time – Southey had lost his belief in an afterlife. He needed swiftly to find a means of containing his emotions, and 'it required thought and reasoning to recover my former certainty, that as surely we must live hereafter, as all here is not the creation of folly or chance'.[11] The alternative would have been impossible to bear, and this rediscovered certainty was Southey's ultimate resource for the rest of his life.

However, he remained haunted by the fierce danger of love and loss, his usual means of controlling his emotions entailing throwing himself into his work, the company of friends, or his books. And, as he later confessed to his brother Henry, 'I cling to [my books] with a comfortable feeling that it is the only safe form of attachment, that they are my friends whom there is no danger of losing, who must survive me.'[12]

The couple were soon joined by their dependants, Edith and Sara's widowed sister, Mary Lovell, and her fatherless son,* as the domestic name for the house changed from Greta Hall to 'Aunt Hill'. And despite Southey's comment the day after he arrived – 'no symptoms of root striking here'[13] – they were to remain there for the rest of their lives. A scholar, who kept his old friends, had a strong sense of fun and loved children, Southey was also shy and forbidding, as he well understood, writing (when he had planned to go to London with Edith to start his legal studies), 'I shall live a secluded life in London, probably without making another friend ... The repellent coldness of my manner will protect me from any acquaintance for I cover the milk of human kindness with as rough an outside as a cocoa nut.'[14] But, in time, the Parish evolved into Southey's sanctuary. He would import his own famous 'Lakers' each summer and become the great expert on Parish history; and, after his appointment as poet laureate in 1813, he became a prime tourist attraction in himself.

* Mary's husband, the poet Robert Lovell, had died of a fever in 1796.

His seminal relationship with Coleridge had begun in a spirit of revolutionary fervour in June 1794. Southey was still a student at Balliol and, as he wrote upon Coleridge's death, that meeting 'fixed the future fortunes of us both'.[15] Two years earlier, Southey, mainly through his friend James Losh, had been on the fringes of Edward Christian's commission of 'passionate abolitionists', investigating the captured *Bounty* mutineers, three of whom were hanged that October. Along with other revolutionary sympathisers, Southey romanticised the mutiny as a symbolic storming of the Bastille and began to think emigration was the logical response to English political repression.[16] His meeting with Coleridge turned that spark into a 'hallowed Fire', as the couple 'planned a utopia of our own upon the basis of common property – with liberty for all – a Pantisocracy – a republic of reason and virtue',[17] to be set in America, the new republican utopia. Coleridge's new word came from Greek and meant 'equal government by all' – like the governance of the commons in the Parish.

'The leading Idea of Pantisocracy is to make men necessarily virtuous by removing all motive to Evil',[18] and it was partly in reaction to the Terror in France that year that it gathered sixteen recruits. The economic plan was that each man would invest £125 and 'labour two or three hours a day, the produce of which labour would, they imagine, be more than sufficient to support the colony...' Both poets believed that love of family was founded on chastity and led to a love of mankind, which Coleridge, at least, saw as leading to a love of God[19] – and it was almost part and parcel of the scheme that Southey and Coleridge had married two sisters, Edith and Sara Fricker. But, despite Southey's working with heart and soul to raise the money, reality diminished the possibilities. America became Wales, the number of men became five,[20] and for Coleridge the utopia of Pantisocracy turned into the merely banal idea of becoming 'Partners in a petty Farming Trade'.[21] However, he stuck with it. But although the imagined costs per man were reduced to £60,[22] even that could not be found.[23]

As Coleridge later described, the project had been a 'gradually exhausted balloon of youthful enthusiasm'.[24] And his and Southey's relationship was to sour, at times very badly. They remained connected in the public mind, largely through the attacks on both of them by the conservative weekly *Anti-Jacobin* from late 1797 onwards. The newspaper's satirical masterpiece was Gillray's brilliant pull-out cartoon, 'New Morality', published in 1798. This depicted both Coleridge and Southey with large asses' heads kneeling to sort out a flow of books, cascading down from a 'Cornucopia of Ignorance'. *Joan of Arc*, Southey's radical epic, which the writer Charles Lamb claimed 'is alone sufficient to redeem the character of the age we live in from the imputation of degeneration in Poetry',[25] was shown stuck in his pocket. Wordsworth, the oldest of the three poets, was not then in the public eye, but Southey's waspish review of *Lyrical Ballads* was soon to anger him as much as it did Coleridge.

Away from the cartoons, it was the women who eventually kept the two men together, and Southey's support and generosity to Sara on her son Berkeley's death,[*] asking Sara and Hartley to stay, was to prefigure the pattern of mutual support that developed between the two sisters at Greta Hall. And, as new babies were born – another seven over time for Edith – relationships mended. The Southeys lived mostly on the ground floor, where the whole household met for breakfast in a room they christened 'Paul' and dined next door in a room named 'Peter'.[26] Southey also took over one of the two first-floor drawing rooms as his study, library and inner sanctum, a place to which only his wife was admitted without invitation.

Always neatly dressed, almost as soon as he arrived Southey began to impose order on the somewhat chaotic household, developing his rigid habit of allocating each time of day to a different activity. At this time, the morning was for reviewing, in the afternoon he would either 'read or doze', and the evening was for his writing,[27] although later he wrote poetry before breakfast, added a constitutional walk and dealt with correspondence at the end of the day. As the critic and essayist William Hazlitt wrote,[28] 'he passes from verse to prose, from history to poetry, from reading to writing, by a stop-watch'. By the end of October, he had sent his brother a lyrical description of the Parish landscape, which 'tempts me to take far more exercise than I ever took

* He arranged the child's funeral.

elsewhere', adding, 'I have therefore seldom or never found myself in stronger health.'[29]

By 2 November Southey persuaded the Coleridges to troop down to St Kentigern's for the official christening of all three of their children and he strode off to church every Sunday, usually incorporating the Howrahs into his walk. In the summer he would invite visitors into his blue square family box pew, in the south end of the chancel, just in front of the pulpit.[30] A tall figure, he appeared to tower over the congregation once he stood up, unconsciously displaying, according to the sexton, 'aw wunderful heed of hair, neah better hereabout'. He became a sight to see in his own right, as the eleven-year-old Ruskin on a family holiday would later affirm, in confident doggerel:

> Next morning, the church how we wished to be reaching!
> I'm afraid 'twas as much for the poet as preaching!

Once the service was over, he continued:[31]

> We looked, and we gazed, and we stared in his face;
> Marched out at a slow-stopping lingering pace;
> And as towards Keswick delighted we walked,
> Of his face, and his form, and his features we talked.

A similar trip to see Wordsworth at church had left Ruskin far less impressed.[32]

It is said that, lifting his face to the Lord and shutting his eyes, Southey seemed to be the 'devoutest of the devout all through the service', until, that is, the vicar – Isaac Denton until 1820 and then James Lynn – climbed the pulpit steps. Once the text on which the vicar was to preach was given out, Southey was no longer so easy to spot, putting his head into his hands and generally making it clear that 'the subsequent proceedings interested him no more'.[33] He later sat, observed Lynn's extremely clever daughter, Eliza, 'in a state of rigid indifferentism', having 'done his duty to God and the Establishment ... to the sermon, which was purely personal, he openly refused to give his attention'.[34]

The pews of the church that welcomed Southey were, Eliza continues, 'the familiar old cattle-pens of every size and shape, wherein the congregation sat in all directions'.[35] The private pews were all situated in the aisles and the chancel, and, to Southey's amusement, since those that paid for them were responsible for them, they were often painted 'a decent white, or divine blue, or any other colour, from time to time, that taste might dictate'; to outdo a neighbour, he surmised. The free benches were positioned in the nave, still with men on the north side and women on the south, and the huge minstrels' gallery was a sight to behold. Sloping sharply up and filling the west end of the nave, it mirrored Skiddaw's full-stop to the Crosthwaite valley. Once singers and musicians were called into action by the sexton sounding his pitch pipe, the congregation would turn their backs to the altar 'to face the music'.[36]

That Southey loved the church we have seen in his fine and moving descriptions, his love of the bells, and his rediscovery of its patron saint and only begetter, St Kentigern. But the church hardly presented him with its best face in his early days. The intransigence of the parishioners responsible for the old leaden roof hadn't budged since the Reformation and the top of the fourteenth-century window was obscured by the plaster ceiling – a gap between them permitting a colony of birds that inhabited the roof to join the congregation.[37] The wind whistled through the roof-holes and, in places, 'the rain gained unchecked admittance',[38] making choosing the place for one's pew a necessarily strategic exercise. The Derwentwater effigies, which moved Southey, lay close to the church entrance, the stone-seated porch itself 'old and crazy'.[39]

None of this can really be laid at the vicar's door but it does seem that the brothers Denton (Isaac had taken over as vicar from his brother Henry after a six-year term, in 1786) had failed, quite extraordinarily, in their duty of care. The glazier had been taking out the old stained glass, pane by pane, 'to repair' over time, but had quite failed to return them. Instead, he created small coloured glass boxes, which he sold or gave to his family, until finally only the three pieces described earlier remained in the windows, as they do today.[40] While it is not really clear how much good old glass there was in the church, it is difficult to understand the Dentons' apparent disregard. And an equally curious incident reflects far better upon secular Parish organisation than clerical.

Isaac Denton must have had a period of absence, as, certainly by 1790, a curate, the Reverend A. Allason Esq., was living at the vicarage.* He came from a substantial Keswick family and, from 1785 to 1792, had been purchasing and then enfranchising bits of land to accompany what he had inherited from his father. The land, then called Greta Side Estate, lay within the great bend of the Greta where Southey lived, and ran west–east from Crosthwaite Road to the end of the old Keswick burgages.† However, from 1790, Allason appears to have been blithely selling the same land to two purchasers, William Jackson, Southey's landlord, and Robert Richardson, who was concentrating on building up water-powered businesses on the riverside. Then, in 1793, the Reverend Allason was certified as having been a lunatic for the previous seven years, a period during which he 'did not enjoy lucid intervals so that he was not capable of Governance of himself or his Estates' – or presumably, of St Kentigern's or the Parish.[41]

Both Jackson and Richardson refused to pay the rent and other monies owed while their ownership of Greta Side Estate was under dispute. The great and good of the Parish eventually judged that Richardson would own the land and hinterland at the town end of the river, where he had already begun his businesses, while Jackson had the rest of the land and the glory, once he built Greta Hall, of the estate being renamed the Greta Hall Estate. But Isaac Denton and the churchwardens seem to have quite simply ignored the whole situation.

The Dentons came from an old Cumberland family. They had lived in their family home, Warnell Hall, from the mid-sixteenth century until 1774, when Isaac's father had sold it on to James

* Crosthwaite's Derwentwater map of 1809 mistakenly still placed Allason at the Vicarage. It would have been amusing to read Southey on the subject had the two actually overlapped.
† The southern boundary after Greta Bridge is less certain but probably then continued from the river along Main Street.

Lowther.* So perhaps the Denton children were just used to decay, which might explain the glass but hardly the mad curate. Or perhaps their ignoring of both problems was simply an extreme example of Southey's main indictment of the vicar – laziness. If so, it was both egregious and slightly surprising for, despite their lackadaisical approach, the family had clearly come to love Keswick. The Dentons introduced a parochial library to the vestry; two of Isaac's daughters would move, in due course, to Greta Lodge, becoming Southey's next-door neighbours; his eldest son, William, farmed in the Parish; while his son Henry, retiring to Keswick from London, lived there for forty years. Subsequently becoming a JP, Henry was a generous, and somewhat radical, supporter of Parish needs, arguably striking the first blow of what would later become the footpath wars on Latrigg, and leaving £500 to the grammar school. So the Parish would come to have good reason to like the Denton family.

Exit Coleridge

Before the Southeys arrived, the Coleridges had already agreed that 'S.T.C.' should winter abroad 'for his health', and he duly left en route for Malta to spend his 1803 Christmas with the Wordsworths. There, high in the fells above Grasmere, Wordsworth read aloud to him the second book of *The Prelude*, Coleridge immediately recognising the transcendent power of this 'divine Self-biography'. And Wordsworth, inspired as always by his praise, wrote the next three books of *The Prelude* at extraordinary speed – over the next ten weeks.[42] Once he had done so, he realised he had neither finished nor faced the challenge Coleridge had offered; to illuminate the feelings of those who had once wholeheartedly supported the French Revolution but now recanted.

Southey, hardly knowing anyone in Keswick then, found himself missing Coleridge. In January he stayed with Sir Wilfrid Lawson,

* The sale of Warnell Hall took place six years before Henry became Crosthwaite's vicar and was part of Lowther's successful campaign to buy up, and then lease, landed estates and manors throughout Cumberland and Westmorland, largely in order to control the parliamentary seats.

the 10th and last Baronet of Isel, where the famous Lawson library helped to improve his mood, as did the company. 'I met there some good sturdy politicians and talked more to my heart's content than I had done many a long day. Our politics here are very different from what they were in the West of England, I do assure you that it would be a source of some pride to me were I a Cumbrian by birth.'[43] Then, in April 1804, Edith May was born. By now, Southey had gained sufficient comfort from being surrounded by solid and immutable mountains that his recent lingering sense of 'the instability of human existence'[44] was easing, and that spring found him receiving 'a deep joy' from the Parish landscape, 'for which nothing else could compensate'.[45] Nevertheless, he would soon write that his hope of Edith May's continued survival 'God knows is of all dreams the one which I least venture to indulge'.[46]

Southey had become a strong swimmer, and he spent much time 'on and in' the lake. He often took the children with him on these excursions and included Jackson and Mrs Wilson in their picnics (probably to take care of the cooking). All were warmed by building their own fires. By the summer, he was making his own company, throwing himself into entertaining Lakers and, surprisingly, helping to organise a subscription ball at Keswick's summer theatre. Sara Coleridge bloomed in her husband's absence, whether 'in society' in the Parish or as an 'assisting hostess' to Lakers at Greta Hall. Life was gayer. And her invented language, 'Lingo Grande', weaved its way through the house, one of her 'FUNNY THINGS', according to Hartley.[47] She and Southey bantered, and he teased her, later describing himself as sitting 'under the shadow of Mrs Coleridge's nose'.[48] She was becoming both much liked and admired.[49]

In 1804 the Wordsworths' beloved daughter, Dora, was born and the poet found his answer to the loss of the 'visionary gleam'. The internalised joy and wonder of the child still offered the possibility of hope and joy but was quietened now by an acceptance of mortality. But, in February 1805, the death of his beloved brother John, drowned at sea, shattered their whole family. This was Wordsworth's first significant adult experience of death and its effects would be profound. Southey immediately wrote offering to visit as soon as he and Dorothy felt they would derive any benefit from his company.[50] And the warmth and shared grief of his visit, along with some practical help he offered afterwards, transformed the possibility of the poets having good feelings for each other.

While the Coleridge thorn kept pricking away at more intimate connection between the two other Lake poets for some time yet, grief and loss were to remain an entirely unadulterated bond between the two neighbours for the rest of their lives.

That spring also saw the publication of Southey's epic *Madoc*, concerning the legendary exploits of a medieval Welsh prince who flees to America, which he had started when he was in the throes of Pantisocracy. It was particularly close to his heart, but the reviews were mixed. The *Imperial Review* described it as 'the second heroic production in the English language, the first being Paradise Lost',[51] but many mocked the poem for its use of Welsh and Aztec names. As early as March, Southey was losing his own confidence in the poem, admitting, probably for the first time, that 'he was a good poet but a better historian'.[52] He was to make no real money from *Madoc* either, and afterwards would not write a single line of poetry for more than three years.

There was no good news about the war either, which had resumed the previous year. In May Wordsworth joined the Ambleside Volunteers, drilling twice a week, along with 'the greatest part of the Men of Grasmere'.[53] Generally, volunteer numbers had soared – not least because joining their ranks brought exemption from the militia ballot – but Southey could report only eighteen in the Parish,[54] although Dr Leitch would soon set up his volunteer corps of 'Skiddaw Grays', their worn flag still in St Kentigern's today. However at the end of the year there *was* a cause for rejoicing: Nelson's great naval victory at Trafalgar on 21 October. On 29 November, decreed as a day of general thanksgiving for the victory, Keswick was warmed up with ox roasts, bell-ringing and drink, after prayers at church.

Wordsworth, in 1806, reflecting on his brother's death in Elegiac Stanzas, finally rejects his old and cherished 'Poet's dream', enabled by a 'heart that loves alone/Housed in a dream, at a distance from its Kind!' and 'welcomes fortitude and patient cheer',[55] pointing to a new and determined regulation of emotion in his work. The previous year he had been putting together the

last three books of the *Prelude*, work which introduced the magnificent 'Snowdon' passage, showing that he could still write about
the past at his untrammelled best. He could though, perhaps no
longer have written the Ode. But he both felt and understood its
significance and, for the rest of his life, gave it pre-eminence in
his published work. In his 1807 *Poems, in Two Volumes* it was
the culminating work and, in later editions, generally set in a
different typeface.[56]

In August, Coleridge's ship arrived back in English waters
and lay in quarantine as Sara bombarded her friends with the joy
of the news of his arrival.[57] While Southey had begun to worry
that 'Greta Hall will no longer hold us',[58] as Edith was pregnant
again, Sara remained ecstatic. So were the Wordsworths, who had
decided, soon after Coleridge's departure, that they missed him so
much that upon his return 'we shall go wherever he goes'.[59] And
although they had then not heard a word from him for a whole
year,[60] William immediately cancelled his trip to the Borders and
Walter Scott to be at home for Coleridge's arrival.[61]

He would have gone to London, as Coleridge appeared to be
lingering there, but was afraid they might miss each other on the
road, as Coleridge seemed incapable of any firm plan, for he was in
a far worse condition than he had been on his departure some two
and a half years earlier. Yet, despite the evident decline in his health
that had taken place while he was away from his family, the poet
announced almost immediately that he must either part from his wife
or die.[62] For two and a half months he kept his distance from the
North, telling all his friends, but not his wife, about his intentions.

In early October, Southey's son Herbert was born, breaking
through the poet's fatalistic self-restraint since the death of his
infant daughter, as he was finally able to give his love to a child
without emotional inhibition. But the baby had been born into
a maelstrom. By the end of the month, Coleridge had eventually
been forced by his friends to go to Keswick. His journey crossed
with the Wordsworths in Kendal, on the way to spend their winter
in an estate farmhouse near the Beaumonts' seat at Coleorton in
Leicestershire, and all three of them were equally shattered by
Coleridge's appearance. Bloated in both face and body, he was

almost unrecognisable. Dorothy wrote, 'Never never did I feel such shock as at the first sight of him, he is utterly changed.'[63]

Travelling on, complete with an invitation to join the party at Coleorton, Coleridge arrived at Greta Hall to be greeted by excited, expectant children and wife, only to demand a divorce. Sara's entire future was at stake, and she fought. Initially, dosing up, Coleridge was adamantine, but time gentled things, and by 24 November, to Southey's great relief, he agreed to a friendly separation – and departed for Christmas.[64]

Before his first brief visit to Greta Hall in 1800, Southey had written to Coleridge to say that his – Southey's – affections were 'ever returning to rest upon you. I have other and dear friends, but none with whom my whole being is intimate – with whom every thought and feeling can amalgamate.'[65] His view had now changed completely: 'His habits are so murderous of all domestic comfort that I am only surprised that Mrs C is not rejoiced at being rid of him, [he] besots himself with opium, or with spirits, till his eyes look like a Turk who is half reduced to idiotcy by the practise – he calls up the servants at all times of night to prepare food for him – ... does nothing which he ought to do, and everything which he ought not.'[66]

The Wordsworths were far more confident, William characteristically believing that 'If anything good is to be done for him, it must be done by me',[67] and Dorothy that 'If he is not inclined to manage himself, we can manage him'.[68] At Greta Hall, however, Southey held the couple responsible for Coleridge's ruination. For, whether it was opium addiction or marital incompatibility, when Coleridge 'complained of his itch' they 'helped him scratch, instead of covering him with brimstone ointment, and shutting him up by himself'. Fundamentally, Southey believed, 'Wordsworth and his sister are of all human beings I have ever known the most intensely selfish', for they subjugated everything and everyone to the cause of burnishing William's reputation. Coleridge's role had been just to act as a sounding board for his fellow poet, 'to be in fact the very rain and air and sunshine of his intellect',[69] a role he would play at Coleorton.

Wordsworth had risen to Coleridge's parting challenge before he left the country – to catch the feelings of those initially in love with the French Revolution, only to recoil as it pursued its course – and had finished the thirteen-part *The Prelude* the previous year. And it was as 'The poem to Coleridge' that he read it through the evenings of the twelve days of Christmas* to the three women and Coleridge, sitting around the fire. As the last line finished – to silence – Coleridge found himself 'in prayer': 'Ere yet that last strain dying awed the air / With steadfast eye I viewed thee in the choir / Of ever-enduring men.' It was, for him, the first (and, for many, still the greatest) poem ever to have taken on the 'high theme' of 'the foundations and the building up / Of a Human Spirit'.[70]

Coleridge later expressed moments of acute pain at Coleorton. But he was still determined to live with the Wordsworths and wrote to his wife on 7 February. The crisis over the divorce having apparently passed, Sara received the letter from her husband equably – until she opened it. Would Southey be leaving Greta Hall? In which case, Coleridge wrote, he intended to return there with the Wordsworths in tow. Knowing that, if this were to happen, she would have to leave her home, Sara rushed to Southey with the letter in high anxiety and Southey instantly made up his mind not to allow it. 'That be hanged for a tale!'[71] he said and decided he would stay in Keswick indefinitely with his family.

Having considered the house 'half-finished and half-furnished',[72] he immediately set about to change matters. 'Everything is to be made decent, and my study beautiful,' he wrote to his younger brother Tom.[73] He would paper 'the parlour with cartridge paper [and] have the abominable curtains there died deep blue', fringe them and buy a carpet and white curtains for his study. More importantly, he wrote that 'I look at the Lakes and Mountains with more delight because the thought of leaving them is no longer in my mind'. *Most* importantly, Southey was going, at last, to round up all his books and ship them to Whitehaven: 'Think of the joy it will be to arrange my books, to see them altogether, and worship them every day.' He would never have been firmly rooted at Greta Hall without his books.

His extraordinary library was to become both the centre of his

* Plus one.

life and the centre of his work, which even two of his three severest
critics had to acknowledge had extraordinary range and scholarship. Hazlitt conceded that 'no other man in our day (at least no
man of genius) has led so uniformly and entirely the life of a scholar
from boyhood to the present hour';[74] for Byron, he was 'the only
existing entire man of letters' of his time.[75] So, by 1807, the Parish
had a star, now firmly settled in its midst.

The Lake Poets

The year 1807 was also when Southey published his first popular
prose publication, *Letters from England*, purportedly the observations of a Spanish tourist, Don Manuel, out of whose mouth
sprung many of Southey's sardonic observations on the Parish. It
also included the first of his portraits of industrial poverty: 'The
dwellings of the labouring manufacturers are in narrow streets and
lanes, blocked from light and air ... crowded together because every
inch of land is of such value that room for light cannot be afforded
them ... a great proportion of the poor lodge in cellars, damp and

Don Manuel comments on the particular shape of Lake District cart wheels,
which he had only seen before in Spain.

dark, where every kind of filth is suffered to accumulate, because no exertions of domestic care can ever make the homes decent ... hotbeds of infection'.[76] These words are a remarkable anticipation of Engels, an element of Southey's writing that is often ignored.

Don Manuel's success led to the firm decision on Southey's part to concentrate on non-fiction. Poetry, when it returned in mid-1808, was relegated to the briefest of his daily slots – before breakfast. History was the thing, he told Walter Scott that September. He added, rather chillingly, that he was 'more disposed to instruct and admonish mankind than to entertain them'.[77] And he explained his choice frankly to his fellow poet Walter Savage Landor three years later: 'It is more delightful to me to compose history than poetry ... as to an employment which suits my temperature. I am loth to ascribe this ... to any deficiency of power, & certainly am not conscious of any; – still I have an ominous feeling that there are poets enough in the world without me, & that my best chance of being remembered will be as an historian.'[78] From 1807 on, Southey had hoped above all to become historiographer royal,[79] like the poet Dryden before him.

His *Life of Nelson* is still in print today and Nelson's modern-day biographers pay due homage to it. In 1961, when his tomb in Crosthwaite churchyard was in need of repair, the Brazilian government paid the costs, in gratitude for the significance of his three-volume *History of Brazil* (1810–19). When he came to write his history of the Peninsular War, Wellington lent him all his personal papers.[80] Yet Southey's scholarly writing was dwarfed by his journalism, the main source of his income. He had been a prodigious reviewer from the start, and, in 1809, would launch himself into current affairs, chronicling the year for the *Edinburgh Annual Register** and writing essays for the *Quarterly Review*. As a result of that work, some today see him as 'a missing link in the development of English Conservatism between Burke and Disraeli'.[81]

For Wordsworth, a man striving with every sinew to remain fully alive to nature and its relationship with man, and wary of too

* A job he would continue to do for the next four years.

much book-learning, Southey's new ambitions were unimaginable; the difference given almost physical substance by Southey's protective protest that having Wordsworth in a library was 'like letting a bear into a tulip bed'.[82] But, ironically, 1807 was the year the literary critic Francis Jeffrey introduced the concept of 'a certain brotherhood of poets who have haunted for some years about the Lakes Of Cumberland' in the October edition of the *Edinburgh Review*. He had described the three poets as a 'new school' earlier, in 1803, before Southey arrived in Keswick – his commission for the new *Edinburgh Review* being to 'barbecue a poet or two'.[83] Picking out Wordsworth as one of the sect's 'chief champions and apostles', this had marked the moment when Wordsworth moved into the public eye alongside Coleridge and Southey.

Jeffrey had been at one with the earlier Gillray 'New Morality' cartoon and decried the 'perverted taste' of these 'followers of simplicity' as not only foolish but actually damaging to the fabric of society by attempting to undermine the authority of its poetic tradition. Underlining the link with Gillray, the theoretical subject of the review was Southey's *Thalaba*, even though the essence of Jeffrey's criticism had 'no particular allusion to Mr Southey, or the subject before us, he appears to us to be less addicted to this fault than most of his fraternity'.

The occasion for Jeffrey's 1807 attack was the publication of Wordsworth's *Poems, in Two Volumes*. What reviews there were had been relentlessly savage, but Jeffrey, despite his own invective – 'If the printing of such trash as this be not an insult to the public taste, we are afraid it cannot be insulted' – was somewhat more balanced, acknowledging the 'originality, pathos and feeling' in some of the collection.* His association of the 'new school' with the Lake District would become a pearl without price for Lake District tourist trade but, for the three poets involved, it was both ignorant and demeaning. Originally it was amiably – or perhaps ironically – dismissed by Coleridge, who suggested to the Beaumonts that the concept was merely based on astonishment that 'three professed

---

* The poems that he believed had denied the prescriptions of the 1800 preface to *Lyrical Ballads*, which he pilloried. *Edinburgh Review*, October 1807.

poets, in every respect unlike each other, should nevertheless take pleasure in each other's welfare – and reputation'.[84] But, as the attacks continued remorselessly, anger and hurt grew and all would, in time, wreak their revenge.

In truth, the tag permanently damaged only one thing: Southey's posthumous reputation, as it emphasises the strand of his writing that least resonates today. And, away from Jeffrey's bile, the *personal* similarities of the Lake Poets were indeed remarkable. All had a capacity for depression and different solutions for dealing with it. All suffered for periods from bouts of illness or hypochondria and from stress, although Southey was much freer from it for a long period of his life in the Parish, and only Coleridge became addicted to opium. All had genius and aspired to, and believed in, their own capacity for greatness. All thought deeply, and had a strong philosophical and moral bent, which, by now, *pace* Coleridge's behaviour towards his wife and family, stressed the importance of domestic affections as well as trying to 'force into notice the situation of the poor, and to represent them as victims of the present state of society'.[85]

All of them had married women whose position in life had been radically changed by the deaths of their fathers; none of them came from safe homes, and all had been, or felt, orphaned or abandoned when young, which Wordsworth undoubtedly was. Coleridge's father had died when he was eight and, as we have seen, he felt he had been sent away from home before 'his soul / Had fix'd its first domestic loves'.[86] Southey spent most of his time between the ages of two and six with a maiden aunt, with whom he shared a bed, and whose temper was such that he lay stock-still beside her, lest he should wake her, for anything between three and five hours each morning. That 'these were, indeed, early and severe lessons in patience' seems a pretty mild response, perhaps mellowed by the release he had found when visiting his grandmother's house, where he could run wild.[87] Southey had written before his marriage, 'Keen as my relish is for the pleasures of domestic life, I have experienced them but little.' So, all three were in thrall to the need for harmonious homes.[88]

Equally, all of them were constantly beset by financial worries. From early on in their lives, they found sponsors who admired their talents sufficiently to offer them a regular income, which soon proved insufficient.[89] Only Wordsworth publicly expressed his gratitude. While they all relied upon handouts, at first only Southey made serious efforts to provide for himself and those close to him, by throwing himself into his prodigious journalistic endeavours. As he characteristically observed, 'it was well we should be contented with posthumous fame, but impossible to be so with posthumous bread and cheese'.[90]

All had been caught up in the fire of enthusiasm for the French Revolution and republicanism, when, as expressed by Southey years later, 'Old things seemed passing away, and nothing was dreamt of but the regeneration of the human race'.[91] All changed their view, Coleridge at alarming speed, and Wordsworth earlier than Southey, who could still declare in 1809 that he was and would always remain a Jacobin.[92] Just two years earlier, Thomas De Quincey had been distinctly alarmed, on his first visit to Greta Hall, to discover in casual conversation that both Southey and Wordsworth thought Britain would never come good until the royal family was 'expatriated'.[93] But all of them now were reconciled to their new reality:[94]

> Not in Utopia – subterraneous Fields, –
> Or some secreted Island, Heaven knows where!
> But in the very world which is the world
> Of all of us, – the place in which, in the end,
> We find our happiness, or not at all!

Similarly, all three of them had at one time considered being clergymen, although for some time Christianity was central only for Coleridge. However, they would each find a personal faith by the end of their lives. Southey, the pillar of Crosthwaite church, had rejected the doctrine of the trinity and the concept of original sin before he went up to Oxford.[95] Once there, while professing that both church and state were 'rotten at heart ... and should be hewn down and cast into the fire',[96] he objected to Voltaire because 'the man who destroys religion deprives us of the only substantial happiness'[97] – simultaneously exhibiting conflicting strands of fundamental belief.

Southey loved his Uncle Herbert, an Anglican clergyman, and

might have followed his path in a different world, as he believed 'in Christ Jesus as the true teacher' and derived 'my best hopes from that belief'. By the time he had settled in the Parish, he had begun to inveigh against Methodists, who, he said, 'deaden the moral feeling, and defile the imagination', 'have a system of confession more fatal in its moral consequences than the Popish',[98] and held to the shocking idea of eternal damnation.

Wordsworth had a lifelong affection for the village church and its part in the community and a strong sense that Christian morality was essential for a well-lived life. But it was not until the winter of 1807 at Coleorton that he first regularly attended church.[99] The poet had captured the truth of his previous life and had become a happily rooted family man; church may have seemed a natural part of this (and he may also have been influenced by his wife). As his faith began to stir, Grasmere church, 'the last Central Home', began to feature ever more clearly in his (and Dorothy's) writing and lives,[100] allowing the possibility that as Wordsworth's Christianity grew, his poetic inspiration waned. It could also be argued that, later, after the deaths in infancy of two of his children, his religion was primarily a source of comfort, until it deepened in his old age. But, however he accessed it, Wordsworth always had a passionate sense of 'the other'.

On the burning religious issue of the day, Roman Catholic emancipation, again all three felt as one. Essentially, for Southey, the problem with Catholicism was that 'They will not tolerate'* and were pledged to work for the downfall of the established Church of England. He saw the entire history of the Anglican Church as the gradual, but vital, emergence of a saving bulwark against the ravages of Roman Catholicism and Protestant fanaticism. He believed the conjunction of church and state and the 'Common' prayer of the church held society together, and was 'inseparably ... connected with the best interests of the country'.[101] And the poets' position on Roman Catholicism had become a Tory principle – 'No Popery', the slogan of the 1807 election.

---

* Feelings reinforced by his brief time as the private secretary to the Irish Chancellor of the Exchequer in 1800.

Southey and the Parish, and
New Establishment Positions

T HERE WERE MANY aspects of Parish life away from St
Kentigern's that, while they corresponded to Wordsworth's
childhood, were hardly going to seduce Southey. One such
activity, a dogged display of bodily strength, was the ancient art of
Cumberland wrestling. From 1818, however, the Carlisle ring was
closed for four years, and Crow Park in Keswick became 'the gathering ground of the most important wrestling in the North', so it
would have been difficult for Southey to miss it entirely.[1] We know
that hunting, which often featured in Wordsworth's poetry, did not
appeal to Southey, who was far from being a robust countryman.
Indeed, in Scotland, he had refused to join Sir Walter Scott's party
for salmon spearing, on the grounds that it was a cruel sport. And the
only time we know that he followed the hunt, he wrote to one of his
oldest friends asking for his pity, '*miserere mei*'.[2] However, the excitement and drama of the local meets and the sight of man and hound
raking up and down the fells cannot have entirely passed him by.

Fox hunting on foot was a key element in Lake District life,
originally simply a practical necessity rather than a sport. All sheep
owners had been expected to pull their weight when it came to
dealing with foxes, an obligation backed up in 1690 with a 'paine'
of 12d. in the old Percy lands should they fail to do so.[3] Organised
hunts began to emerge soon after the mid-eighteenth century, introducing a unique Cumbrian system of drag hunting,* in which the

---

* Unlike today's use of the word for following an artificial scent for sport.

hounds were walked in line in the valleys to pick up the scent, while in the South the hounds start from a covert where a fox is known to lie. It sometimes took hours for the pack to pick up the stale scent left after a fox's night-time visit for food but, once caught, the hounds were unleashed and the hunt proper began. Dogs and men followed the trail on foot into the high fells.

Southey would have known all about the dates of the meets, announced – along with the stock auction dates and 'jobs to let' – by the churchwardens immediately after the church services[4] (and the churchwardens were still paying a bounty for dead eagles and foxes too).* In his time, hunting in the Lake District was – as it remained – an entirely classless activity, and the 'great grey foxes' of legend were still there to be caught; the largest kill ever reported, of a fox weighing 26 pounds, occuring at Pocklington's Bowder Stone as late as the nineteenth century.[5] More importantly, there was a great step forward with the introduction of trencher packs, the most celebrated of which belonged to John Peel (who was born the other side of Skiddaw from the Parish, at Caldbeck).† Peel was called out by farmers near and far, but, since his passion for the hunt meant he was always short of money, many of his hounds, the 'trenchers', were kennelled and exercised free at farms other than his; although not, one suspects, his favourites, Ranter, Royal, Briton and Bellman.

Two small hunting packs were kept in Keswick, one by a Mr Mayson and the other by Mr Slack of Derwent Hill,[6] and, before the off, Peel's Blencathra Hunt would visit two Keswick inns: the Royal Oak, where today a marvellous stained-glass window memorialises the events, and the Pheasant Inn, just west of Monk Hall. For the big meets, having risen at four or five, Peel would blow on his horn until all his hounds arrived – some so eager that they were known to have jumped straight through the windows if the door was shut. Later, at his fabled drinking celebrations at the end of the

---

* Back in 1723, they had missed a trick when some Keswickians had thought cub hunting might turn out to be profitable. But on a payment of only 1s. per cub but 3s. per fox, this rather intelligent form of pest control naturally stopped.
† The Revd Lynn's other living.

day, the mask (head of the fox) was dipped into the ale before the carousel began.[7] Yet, when he spent the night before the hunt with a neighbour, John Woodcock Graves, spent the night before the hunt with Peel, and heard his host's mother singing 'a very old Rant called Bonnie (or Cannie) Annie', as Graves spontaneously wrote out the words of the famous hunting song 'D'ye ken John Peel' to accompany the tune; while Peel smiled 'through a stream of tears which ran down his manly cheeks'.[8]

*

In February 1808[*] another Southey child was born, Emma, named after her godmother, Emma Peachy. Southey was unusually sanguine about the girl's arrival when he wrote to his Bristol friend, John May:[9] 'About an hour ago Edith was safely delivered of a daughter the child is a very fine one, & God be praised, every thing as yet promises well.' Sixteen months later, however, Emma died after a brief illness.

The Spanish revolt against Napoleon that spring had reawakened the radical in Southey. Its sister revolution in Portugal called for British support against the Franco–Spanish troops sent to quell it, and the French troops suffered their first defeat of the Peninsular War. However, when the Convention of Cintra was signed at the very end of August, the troops were allowed to withdraw, still armed and complete with plunder, and returned, either by British ships to France, or to Spain, thus endangering the Spanish freedom fighters. All three Lake Poets were enraged, and Southey and Wordsworth[†] planned a county address 'to appoint a day of national humiliation for this grievous national disgrace'. When the interests of William Lowther, Earl of Lonsdale, torpedoed their plan, they were incandescent.

* The year Southey started to build his steppingstones across the Greta to supplement the old wooden bridge, which had nearly killed Coleridge's two-year-old daughter, Sara, when she fell between its rails into the water.
† With John Christian Curwen, William Calvert, John Spedding and 'Mr Mathews of Wigton'. Wordsworth subsequently wrote a long, angry pamphlet on the subject.

'Nothing could be done,' Southey wrote to Humphrey Senhouse, 'except making some of Lord Lonsdale's "merry men" hold up their hands in public against opinions which they had freely expressed in private. In fact, there is as little (political) independence in the country now as there was during ... the feudal system, and the dependence is now of a dirtier kind.'[10] Lowther was also a powerful and influential member of a class Southey despised: 'our nobles [who] enjoy all the advantages of their rank in this age, without any of the dangers which former environed it. Their rivalry with each other expends itself at elections, where they bleed in purses instead of person...'[11] An exercise Wordsworth, rather than Southey, was to find himself intimately involved with.

Nevertheless, Southey was only too happy to approach Lowther the following year, when he was drawn to the idea of becoming the steward for the old Derwentwater estates. The job paid £700 a year and he imagined it 'would please me well, in so much as it would give me the power of preserving the woods and improving both the property and this beautiful place by planting'.[12] He began to lobby energetically, with Walter Scott on the case, but when his former school friend Grosvenor Bedford told him that the current steward was 'employed for seventeen to eighteen hours out of every twenty-four, together with his first clerk',[13] reality kicked in. Southey's interest evaporated in an instant, and he wrote back to Bedford, 'so much for place-hunting'[14] – although, in truth, his lobbying and networking were only to grow as time went on.

It was in 1809 that Southey started to be 'historiographer to Mr Ballantyne' for the *Edinburgh Annual Register*, and the annual salary of £400 allowed Greta Hall to be much improved that year and the roof fixed. After Jackson's death in September,* Southey had rented the whole house for the first time and it was to be the complete 'Aunt Hill' who joined in as the Parish exploded in jubilation on 25 October 1810 – not because of any good news about the interminable war, but to celebrate George III's Golden Jubilee. It was a good do. Debtors were released from prison; there was an amnesty for deserters who agreed to return; Southey helped an

---

* Mrs Wilson was invaluable for the children and remained.

amateur poet pen an appropriate ode, *Ego et Rex meus*;[15] and St Kentigern's bells competed with the sounds of regattas – which had made a return to the Parish, albeit in more muted form. However, the bells were outclassed – not only by the hymns sung from the top of the tower but also by the cannons dragged up there to wake the Skiddaw echo. Unperturbed, the tower withstood the shock. Two years later the rotten lead on the church roof was finally stripped off and replaced by slates, the first of a number of botched jobs.

By now, Southey had become a real part of the Parish and the wider Lake community. He was on good terms with schoolmasters and got on well with Jonathan Otley, the statesman watchmaker and geologist. His servants were attached to him, and he had made some good new friends among the gentry. Outside the Parish he was close to the Speddings and Humphrey Senhouse from Maryport, who had a fine library and would travel with Southey on occasion. Within the Parish, Calvert had always been a close friend and he was joined by General Peachy, with whom Southey often played whist in the evenings,[16] and, in due course, Lord Gordon at Waterend.

Southey had good relationships too with the Sunderlins, who rented Pocklington's house in Portinscale, now called Derwent Bank, and the Ponsonbys at Ormathwaite. The only members of the Parish gentry with whom I have found no mention of him having a relationship are William Slack (still famous for dealing with 'Peppery Bill') and his wife Mary. They had built a lovely house, Derwent Bay, at the northern end of Portinscale. Later vulgarised by Victorian 'fortification', it was originally long, narrow and much windowed, but with more floors than Gordon's original 'Pavilion'. The family, sporting a crest that included a snail to denote deliberation and perseverance, were to stay there until 1935.[17]

Generally, this was a time when the gentry were becoming seriously alarmed. Napoleon's Continental System, together with real poverty, had severely affected the country. As early as 1806 there had been reports from Lancashire[18] that 'Weaving of all denominations are falling rapidly and a universal gloom hangs over the lower class of people'. In time, some were throwing acid on the cloth of factory looms, and frame-breaking and major protest began to spread all over the industrial north. Major rioting broke out in mid-1811,[19] and as early as March that year Southey, hyper-vigilant about the 'many-headed beast',[20] had tasked local JPs to take steps to put 'some check to the outrages which almost every night are committed in Keswick'.[21] Someone had broken into one of his outhouses, and he mentioned a fire at Monk Hall, where a barn, several outhouses, 700 bushels of corn and a quantity of timber had gone up in flames, an event significant enough to make *The Gentleman's Magazine*; not that anyone attributed it to arson.[22]

At the turn of the year, Percy Bysshe Shelley came for a brief stay in Keswick. Southey greatly enjoyed his visit in January 1812, but Shelley despaired of the changes that had taken place in the older man's political views. Nor did the younger poet think much of the town: 'In fact my friend at this Keswick, tho the face of the country is lovely the people are detestable. The manufacturers with their contamination have crept into the peaceful vale and deformed the loveliness of Nature with human taint.'[23] The young man had both saved a baby from the Greta, and subsequently been told it had been discarded by a factory worker because it was illegitimate, and also appears to have been knocked out after opening his front door to some ruffians;[24] so it was a fair point.[*] Perhaps in part it was this that persuaded Southey to load up 'an old Spanish fowling piece to keep up the courage of the family' that month and order some pistols and a watchman's rattle from London.[25] He reckoned these precautions would be worth sticking to for some time.[26]

By then, more than ten thousand people in Lancashire were unemployed.[27] The saboteurs, now calling themselves Luddites, had begun to organise themselves, drilling and marching like the volunteers, and, in response, machine-breaking was made a capital offence in February. Byron declared the law 'barbarous' in his maiden speech in the House of Lords, while Wordsworth, now convinced that the regeneration of society was a lost dream

---

[*] However, his subsequent criticism is surprising: 'The debauched servants of the great families who resort contribute to the total extinction of morality. Keswick seems more like a suburb of London than a village of Cumberland.' After all, this was the winter.

and that industry dehumanised its workers, wrote, 'If much firmness be not displayed by the government, confusion and havoc and murder will break out and spread terribly.'[28] Southey warned of the dangers of 'the sinking down of Jacobinism from the middle to the lower ranks' in the *Edinburgh Annual Register* that year. A growing fear of 'the mob', seen as distinct from 'the people', had moved all three Lake Poets to conservative positions.

Broadly, though, Keswick was little affected by the troubles of the industrial north and a letter from Southey to William Peachy in January 1813 (the month in which the Southey establishment finally took to Cumberland clogs, 'the wisest of fashions') gives a fine flavour of middle-class entertainment in the locality: 'Yesterday we had a grand entertainment at Derwent Bank. Lord Sunderlin ... caught hold of the players ... just as they were packing off from a most unsuccessful campaign in the town ... and Miss Barker* ornamented the room with festoons of evergreens and artificial flowers, which had a very pleasing effect. Ours you know is but a scanty neighbourhood at all times – the good-natured old Lord however invited every person with whom he had any intercourse – and we mustered about fifty persons besides some dozen or score of children to see [the play]. The company were in good humour and the players, never perhaps having been either so well paid or so well fed were in good spirits. The upstairs entertainment concluded with God save the King in full chorus. We then went down to a cold supper ... This has been a great event in our little circle.'[29]

Southey's letter, having reported that all his chickens had been stolen, also reported some more serious matters in Carlisle, where many of the workers were immigrants from Ireland or Scotland. He held his political opponent John Christian Curwen to be partly responsible for this; the latter imported Irishmen to Workington in such numbers as 'to render some precautions necessary',[30] since

---

* The first of Southey's two great female friends and intellectual companions, Miss Barker lived from 1812 at Greta House, which became a social centre. Their relationship of twenty years was apparently distanced after Southey's son Herbert died in her arms. What is now Scafell Hotel was being built as a home for her but, running out of money, she went abroad.

the Irish immigrants were 'bringing down our peasants, to their level'. And Southey wasn't averse to a little scandalmongering to sharpen his point, having written gleefully to John Rickman three months earlier: 'There is a secret history about Christian Curwen. He would have carried his election hollow, if he could have faced the stories ... The country at this moment rings with scandal about him & the Bp of Llandaff's daughter, the truth of this *scandalum magnatum* ... is pretty vile by a letter of Christian Curwen to a neighbour of mine – in which he confesses to impudence but vows & protests innocence as to anything farther.'[31] A few years later Southey wrote, in another letter to Rickman, that Curwen had had no money to spare for the election since he was 'kept always poor by the innumerable bastards he has to support – this is actually the case'.[32]

Southey had a new neighbour that year. James Stanger, who having made a fortune as a city merchant in London, had bought some land on the other side of the track from the vicarage and was building what was then called Dove Cote at Lairthwaite, which now provides the old heart of Keswick school. Stanger had married a distant cousin, whose brother Christopher from Whitehaven, also a friend of Southey's, was a London doctor, and whose sister, Mrs Crothers, also lived in the Parish. James's considerably younger brother, Joshua,[33] born in 1801, was to marry Mary Calvert in 1824, so either the Stanger brothers' parents had returned to Keswick with James or he was looking after Joshua himself. Both James's family and that of his wife had their roots among the senior statesmen who had farmed for so long at Ullock near Portinscale; some local connection had clearly remained, as the family again became decidedly visible in the Parish.* James was to become both an admirer and a close friend of Southey's.

---

* The *Oxford Dictionary of National Biography* describes Christopher as born in Whitehaven from a family who had for several centuries owned estates near Keswick. Those who remained in the Parish included, in 1758, one Stanger who had recently sold 70 acres in Newlands to John Hudson, and another who held 75 acres at Fawe Park.

The poet laureate and *The Excursion*

Coleridge had consistently failed to pay either the rent or the taxes for his part of Greta Hall, or to send anything towards the support of his family – except for a bonus £100 in 1812, a quarter of the takings from a successful play[34] – but Sara's half of the Wedgwood annuity had greatly helped. However, by the end of that year she had found out that the annuity itself had been halved and realised that, humiliatingly, as Southey said, 'the whole of what' she received 'would now have to be spent on the two boys'.[35] Southey soon appreciated that, even though he thought Sara was less 'disposed to be anxious' than any other woman he knew, the worry 'keeps her awake at night'. By 1813, as well as being in financial trouble himself,[36] Southey was beginning to be concerned about Sara's health.*

However, thanks to a chance meeting in 1812 with Walter Savage Landor, who shared his interest in the Peninsular War, Southey was writing poetry purposefully again. He had avoided Landor at Oxford, finding his manner and consciously unpowdered hair excessive, but after they had met in Bristol in 1808 and discovered their political trajectories through the French Revolution had been extremely similar, they had become both lifelong friends and each other's defenders. Towards the end of 1811, when Grosvenor Bedford had suggested to Southey that he should allocate more time to poetry than his pre-breakfast slot, the reply had been emphatic: 'Why man you might as well advise me to set up a carriage, buy an estate and build a house upon it.'[37] But in 1813 all changed as Landor generously offered to fund the printing of any poetry that Southey wrote.

That same year, Southey learnt that he was to be offered the post of poet laureate. Walter Scott had turned down the post and recommended Southey, to whom he wrote encouragingly, 'I am not such an ass as not to know that you are my better in poetry though I have probably but for a time the tide of popularity in my

---

* A year later, in a letter whose privacy he stressed, Southey was asking his old friend Grosvenor Bedford for any money he could afford, 'for it is low water with me'. A debt owing to him had not been repaid and he had had 'for some time a serious extra increase of expense thrown upon me'.

favour.'[38] Southey considered the position potentially degrading, as its reputation was at an all-time low. However, since the job of historiographer royal that he hankered after was not available, he intended to take the post and use the £90 annual fee to help fund an insurance policy for his dependants.[39] As he was waiting in London for the offer to come through, it emerged, somewhat surprisingly, that Parish tentacles had reached as far as the laureateship.

Lord William Gordon entered the stage and Southey's rather scornful description of events to Edith makes one wonder whether he was aware of Gordon's dramatic early history: 'It is not a little amusing to discover when anything friendly is to be done by men in power, how many are desirous of having a share in it ... Today I saw Ld Wm Gordon, & was not a little surprized to learn that the whole affair of the Laureateship was left to him! Lady W^m is sister to the Marchioness of Hertford, – the appointment is in the gift of the Marquis & so as it was to be given to me Lord W^m is to have the credit of giving it. All this is comical enough. However he is a very good natured man, & has taken the trouble of calling upon me three times to tell me this, & it costs me nothing to say I am much obliged to him, which is all he wants: & when you see him which you will do before my return you may say the same.'[40]

A few days later, when Southey was still waiting for confirmation, he was far less insouciant about Gordon's power of patronage, actually searching him out to 'endeavour to hurry this appointment by a simple notification that I certainly do not intend to wait for it. As long as my own affairs keep me in town, well; but they are not to suppose that I will submit to be detained here for the Marquis of Hertford's pleasure, or anybody else's. They ought to know that in accepting the office I am conferring a favour rather than receiving one.'[41] But when he was actually appointed,* Southey rushed off a 'choice verse' to Edith, which began: 'I have something to tell you which you will not be sorry at,' and ended: 'Keep this I charge you as a precious gem / For this is the Laureate's first poemm.'

His first official poem, a New Year ode entitled *Carmen Triumphale, for the Commencement of the Year 1814*, included the

---

* At eight o'clock on 5 November 1813.

lines: 'In happy hour doth he receive / The Laurel, meed of bards of yore, / Which Dryden and diviner Spenser wore...' While Southey's sense that the office would bestow no credit to him remained, he believed that he had negotiated conditions that would allow him freedom from any sense of being a poet for hire. He resolved to use his national role to comment on public affairs and turn the post into something worth aspiring to. This was soon shown to be naive on his part. The Parish, however, simply delighted in the new fame and standing that their neighbour had acquired. When he arrived home at Greta Hall, his daughter Edith and her friend Mary Calvert proudly crowned him with a wreath of laurels.[42]

However, within less than two months, the government censored *Carmen Triumphale*. The original, which Southey had submitted to the Master of the King's Music,* had called for the French to rise up and assassinate Bonaparte and 'take vengeance' for themselves and mankind. But all references to a call to arms were cut, as Southey's first composition as poet laureate became for him '*Carmen Castratum*'.[43] The next year's ode would suffer the same treatment, as the poet's praise of George Washington – risky while the country was still at war with America – was struck out too. Both incidents of censorship were grist to the mill for those who relished the stark contrast between the government job and Southey's earlier radical beliefs. And the literary battle had had a national echo chamber ever since the Conservative *Quarterly Review* (Southey's mouthpiece since 1809) had been created in response to the Whig *Edinburgh Review*.

Southey had already written there that the press was 'inflaming the turbulent temper of the manufacturer and disturbing the quiet attachment of the peasant to those institutions under which he and his father have dwelt in peace'.[44] But once he, along with Coleridge, called for censorship, he had earned the undying enmity of many of his fellow intellectuals, who launched what would become a new tradition of making fun of the poet laureate.

---

* The laureate's poems were, in theory, intended to be set to music and performed at court, but this notional practice was ignored throughout Southey's laureateship.

*

Wordsworth got a salary in 1813 too. He had written to Sir George Beaumont, acknowledging that 'whatever sacrifice it cost me, a considerable portion of my time *must* be in some way or other devoted to money-making',[45] and Beaumont's friend Lord Lonsdale offered him the post of the Distributor of Stamps for all of Westmorland and much of Cumberland. Once he had identified the perfect clerk to deal with the financial side, John Carter – who stayed with him for the next thirty-seven years,[46] gardening and joining his secretariat on the side – the work did not overburden him. However, work it definitely was, which Wordsworth took seriously.

He was, at this time, trying to put his life in order. The poet remained in a state of profound shock, and what turned out to be ineradicable grief, over the deaths of two of his young children, Catharine and Thomas, the previous year. He had again trusted Southey with the truth, writing 'I loved the Boy with the utmost love of which my soul is capable, and he is taken from me ... O Southey feel for me!' He wrote to Coleridge too, who wrote a gnomic reply promising to visit, but never came.[47]

Lonsdale had also sent Wordsworth £100 in January – the first evidence of an annuity that had originally been refused but was accepted reluctantly, but with grace, after the children's deaths. This made it possible for the family to move to Rydal Mount in 1813, where they would stay for the rest of their lives and which they deeply loved. But more income was needed for the family. At this point, Wordsworth had published no poetry for six years, and time suddenly didn't feel infinite. So, despite his loathing of publication, he agreed that it was time to brave the printer's ink for all his unpublished work. Dorothy was 'most thankful ... for the MSS (with the constant revisions) were in such a state that, if it had pleased Heaven to take him from this world, they would have been almost useless'.[48] And, to her joy, Wordsworth wrote fast and furiously.*

* Although in due course keeping a large amount of the new work private or reshaped for separate publication later.

The plan was to start with *The Excursion*, which would consist of some nine thousand lines in nine books (or parts), incorporating work written over sixteen years, including much of 'The Pedlar' and 'The Ruined Cottage'. Wordsworth's first public attempt at a 'Great Poem' – the only work of substantial length published in his lifetime – would, the family felt, at last expose the critics' empty charges of puerility and vulgarity in his poetry for what they were. First planned out in 1804, *The Excursion* was to be, and was presented as, a major part of the overarching idea of *The Recluse*, which would now start with *The Prelude*, originally conceived as an introduction. With a remarkable lapse of literary–political judgment, if with some familial acumen, Wordsworth dedicated his poem to the 'illustrious Peer' the Earl of Lonsdale, as a token 'Of high respect and gratitude sincere'. William Lonsdale was a very different man from 'Wicked Jimmy' Lowther, his third cousin once removed, being far more civilised, and said to have 'restored some fairness to the Cumberland voting system'. But, to Whig critics and Wordsworth's old political associates, the dedication simply underlined the irony of the poet's new position as a government tax inspector.[49]

Seldom read today, by the mid-1830s *The Excursion* had been reprinted four times and had sold more copies than any other volume of Wordsworth's poetry, despite[50] an initial critical blast. William Hazlitt's[*] review in *The Examiner* in August 1814, which both highly praised and sharply criticised, introduced a permanent strand of literary Wordsworthian debate, crystallised by Keats's brilliant description of Wordsworth's 'poetical character' as 'the egotistical sublime' four years later. And Hazlitt's criticism – 'All accidental varieties and individual contrasts are lost in an endless continuity of feeling; like drops of water in the ocean-stream. An intense intellectual egotism swallows up everything ... as if

---

[*] Hazlitt, born in 1778, led the attacks on the changed views of the Lake Poets. He had stayed with Coleridge and Southey, who helped him escape to Wordsworth's home after Hazlitt's behaviour with a local woman had raised a male posse of revengers. An admirer of Napoleon, Hazlitt's favourite topics were the restored European despotisms and the Lake Poets, by whom he was felt, among other things, to have betrayed confidences.

there were nothing but himself and the universe' – earned him Wordsworth's permanent enmity.

Francis Jeffrey went in for the kill in the *Edinburgh Review*.[51] His famous opening line, 'This will not do', ushered in a thirty-page review, packed with malice. Much of Jeffrey's review, to use one of his words, is 'silly' – for example, his objection to the concept of the pedlar – 'a person accustomed to higgle about tape' – as a character. But there were some palpable hits in the attack on Wordsworth's 'salutary truths'. Not only were these expounded 'at far greater length, and with more repetitions, than in any ten volumes of sermons we have ever perused', they were either known to all or so obscurely expressed as to be incomprehensible. And, at times, in the philosophical conversations between the four main protagonists of the poem (the Poet, the Wanderer, the Solitary, the Pastor), Byron's foolish dismissal of Wordsworth as 'a dull disciple' of Southey's school[52] makes brief sense.

However, 'The Wanderer' (a revised version of 'The Pedlar', based on an inhabitant of Scotland rather than of the Lake District) and 'The Ruined Cottage', written a year earlier at Racedown, introduced the whole work. One of the great poems about human suffering, 'The Ruined Cottage' is less starkly tragic than in earlier versions but still includes, like 'The Pedlar'/'The Wanderer', magnificent, transcendent passages, often considered the highest expression of the great old Wordsworth lesson of the unity of nature and man. They received their due from Hazlitt, who wrote that 'In power of intellect, in lofty conception, in the depth of feeling, at once simple and sublime, which pervades every part of it ... this work has seldom been surpassed'.[53] But he added that it was nine years since the poet had written, 'My hopes no more must change their name, / I long for a repose that ever is the same',[54] and the critic saw signs of exhaustion, which he attributed to the constant striving necessary for the originality of Wordsworth's poetry of the mind.

The battles with self that duty had imposed, after experiencing agonising family loss, must have contributed too. And the brilliant early passages about the ecstasy of communion with nature are, at times, treated as almost improper here, to be put away, for the peace of community. 'The Wanderer', for instance, deadens the previously central message of the great personal danger of an adult consciously searching for a permanent experience of the bliss found by feeling entirely 'outside' oneself. Now it offers analogies with the Swiss and the Savoyards.

The effect of incorporating those early works into this 'philosophical pastoral poem'[55] necessarily delays the passages that reflect the family's eight years of churchgoing, such as in the lovely passage describing conscience in Book 4: 'As God's most intimate presence in the soul, / And his most perfect image in the world.' And Book 4 looks both backwards and forwards in the poem, introducing 'regions consecrate / To oldest time', which the Pastor, introduced in Book 5, would people with 'narratives of calm and humble life' from Lake District statesmen towards the end of the poem. For me, in this juxtaposition of Christianity and nature, the old immediacy of connection is often overtaken by a desire to teach and save, and the Christian message and solution, loved afresh by the Wordsworths, feels somewhat 'learned' here, having little of the richness of a George Herbert or a Gerard Manley Hopkins, poets who spent their lifetimes exploring and interrogating the relationship between the Christian and his God.

For while expressing the profoundly comforting sense that[56]

> *One adequate support for the calamities of mortal life*
> *Exists – one onely; an assured belief*
> *That the procession of our fate, howe'er*
> *Sad or disturbed, is ordered by a Being*
> *Of infinite benevolence and power;*
> *Whose everlasting purposes embrace*
> *All accidents, converting them to good.*

There is little of the central Christian message of salvation. Some believe[57] that Wordsworth was trying to *write* himself into his changed/changing beliefs here, others that he had become a Christian stoic, an acceptable description of Southey's position. But, while there is a strong sense that the poem's injunctions to the individual to be pious, dutiful and reverent connect primarily with the needs of a healthy society, it is important to take account of the difficulty for twenty-first-century writers to fully inhabit nine-teenth-century religious belief, itself inevitable a response, in part, to the everyday normality of child mortality.

Hence, taking the poem as a whole, the comment of Wordsworth's friend and admirer, the lawyer Henry Crabb Robinson, that the poet's religion 'would not satisfy either a religionist or a sceptic',[58] was very much to the point. However, a key passage for Wordsworth, the one he hopes 'my readers will remember', is an uplifting song of praise from the Pastor to his God at the end of the poem, delivered after a heart-stopping passage describing the sunset. Then, as the Pastor shares the tales of the Lake District statesmen, he again brings alive Wordsworth's old lesson, the estimable life full of 'small, unre-membered goods', which brings its own peace. These tales ring as true as ever and are frequently moving, adding the beneficial effects of the statesman's sense of freedom and autonomy from the wider world of greed and profit to the poem's universal message:[59]

> ... *Earth is sick,*
> *And Heaven is weary, of the hollow word*
> *Which States and Kingdoms utter when they talk*
> *Of truth and justice. Turn to private life*
> *And social neighbourhood; look we to ourselves;*
> *A light of duty shines on every day*
> *For all ...*

For the Victorians, duty resonated, as did the poet's calls for England, like the Pedlar/Wanderer, to aim for an even keel. And, while the poem is an early commemoration of imminent victory (the long war with France on the verge of ending), the victory would only be final if England were to reassert its old strengths of self-confidence, duty and love of church and village community. The poem's fervent patriotism, early praise of empire and emphasis on duty and religion combined to ensure that the Victorians would take *The Excursion* to their hearts. Charles Kingsley's reaction, after reading it with tears and prayers, was this: 'To me he is not only poet, but preacher and prophet of God's new and divine phi-losophy – a man raised up as a light in a dark time.'[60]

The aristocracy, gloriously lampooned twenty years earlier in Wordsworth's letter to the Bishop of Llandaff, are now, assuming they play the better part, essential to the poet's enlightened order. This is the first public glimmer of a train of thought that culminates in the damning evidence of Wordsworth's 1818 election addresses for Lowther – natural perhaps given his parental background, but surely a betrayal of the essence of his great poetry. However, the late Victorian publisher's preface to an 1892 edition of *The Poetical Works of Wordsworth*,* which duly included *The Excursion*, claimed its volume was 'indeed complete, with the exception of "the Prelude" ... which is not generally considered equal to his former poems'. Within a decade this judgment would look foolish as, around the turn of the century, the birth of psychoanalysis and a search for the numinous in a less religious age – William James's 'natural religion' – led to *The Prelude* becoming seen as Wordsworth's greatest achievement.[61]

Today, *The Excursion* is read as one of the two primary texts that illumine Wordsworth's deep, instinctive, ecological insight. Four years earlier the poet had already expressed the essence of today's green ideal in his nascent *Guide to the Lakes*,[62] that 'the hand of man ... is incorporated with and subservient to the powers and process of nature'.† And part of the message of *The Excursion* is to teach man to wed himself to 'the green earth' as his 'living home', as the poet laments the loss of the 'green margin on the public way',[63] of seeing people 'breathing fresh air, and treading the green earth'.[64] Then, in Part VIII, he lambasts the manufacturing spirit, which has spurned man's vital task of being 'earth's thoughtful lord' and has produced:[65]

> *Such outrage done to nature as compels,*
> *The indignant power to justify herself;*
> *Yea to avenge her violated rights,*
> *For England's bane.*

* Published by Frederick Warne.
† This was an insight Lake Poets shared – witness Coleridge's 'The finest edge, into which a meditative mind of a Contemplator was ever ground, is but the back of the Blade of grass in comparison with the Subtlety of Nature'.

John Ruskin's dark prophesies in *The Storm-Cloud of the Nineteenth Century* and his argument that 'the fundamental material basis of political economy was not money, labour and production but "Pure Air, Water and Earth"'[66] extended this idea, but he always saw Wordsworth as the person who had best brought the profound interrelationship between man and the earth to the fore: he was 'the keenest-eyed of all modern poets for what is deep and essential in nature'. In the words of the Wanderer at the opening of *Book IX* there is,

> *An active principle*
> *In all things, in all natures, in the stars*
> *Of the azure heaven, the unenduring cloud.*
> *In flowers and trees, in every pebbly stone*
> *That paves the brooks the stationary rocks,*
> *The moving water and the invisible air.*
> *Whate'er exists hath properties that spread*
> *Beyond itself, communicating good.*

Even more importantly for Ruskin, *The Excursion* not only re-expressed that profound connection – but portrayed man as an *intrinsic part* of nature, and in his Modern Painters quotes the passage from Part V where the landscape, with 'mists flying, and rainy vapours', bids a man to 'Be a Presence or a motion – one / Among the many there'. Part of an experience that belongs to nature and to the man alone.

And this sense may have contributed, in part, to Southey's passionate defence of the poem. Declaring his 'full conviction' that posterity would rank Wordsworth with Milton, he ridiculed Jeffrey's claim to have written 'a crushing review', retorting: 'I despise his commendations and I defy his malice. *He* crush the Excursion. Tell him he might as easily crush Skiddaw.'[67]

The End of the War and
New Battle Lines

I N APRIL 1814, two months before *The Excursion* reached the
bookshops, Napoleon had abdicated and been exiled to Elba. For
Dorothy Wordsworth, it was 'like a dream'. The war had lasted
most of her adult life and now 'peace, peace – all in a moment'.[1] But
the peace proved to be short-lived. In February 1815 'the patron
saint of farmers'[2] escaped from Elba – and Parish and Cumberland
farmers and labourers continued to profit from high prices.

During Napoleon's exile, Southey had published *Roderick, the
Last of the Goths*, a fierce epic of 7,000 lines set in the eighth
century, at the time when the Moors were expelled from northern
Spain. He had started writing the poem many years earlier and,
perhaps because its patriotic appeal found a contemporary echo,
it became the most successful of his epics and romances, with
three editions appearing within eighteen months and five by 1818.*
Byron, much to his credit (as a battle between the radical new poets
and the newly conservative Lake Poets for the country's future was
already in the air), said publicly that he had found it 'as near perfection as poetry can be'.[3] Southey's previous epics had included some
endnotes, but in *Roderick*, reflecting his move towards becoming a
serious historian, there were a hundred pages of notes 'thick with
extracts from Spanish historians'.

However, the force of Jeffrey's contempt for *The Excursion* –
his twelve-year attack having reached a critical mass and become

---

* Pratt, Fulford and Packer, *The Collected Letters*, Introduction to Part 4.

common currency[4] – had shifted Southey to a new position. Southey had been particularly irritated by the concept of 'the Lake Poets' since he had written only once about the Lake District (and that pseudonymously),* his great epics having always been set in the past, but now, in response to the widely publicised disdain enveloping Wordsworth, he decided to add his own weight to the concept, as a badge of honour and fraternity. He would incorporate the Lakes (and his view, via *The Excursion*, that the area could offer 'a moral way of life that set a standard for the rest of society')[5] into his major poetry as, simultaneously – in line with his sense of being the poet laureate – he would also now incorporate the present day.

Enclosures and a Parish bonfire

Meanwhile, in the Lake District, the Greenwich Hospital had continued to invest in tourism. In Keswick the Old Shambles was cleaned up, which Southey thought 'much improved' things.† By 1813 the town's distinguishing feature, the whitewashed and somewhat alpine Moot Hall, had been built on the site of the old courthouse, its ground floor available for local markets. The new building, probably built in part with yet more Derwentwater stone transported from the 'Isle', and still incorporating the bell and the weathercock of the old Derwentwater House, was considerably larger. Four years later, the hospital appeared to regret the expenditure, their surveyors revealing that they considered Moot Hall to be an extravagance: 'A building upon much less a scale, and at less expense,' they declared, 'might have answered every requisite purpose, and if it had been made of a lighter construction, it might have been equally useful as well as ornamental to the town.'[6]

Then, in 1814, the hospital and Lord William Gordon had taken the first steps in the Parish enclosure movement. Gordon gained some 160 acres of stinted pasture from the enclosure of 203 acres of Swinside (see map on p. 248). Southey had expected him

---

* *Letters from England: By Don Manuel Alvarez Espriella.*
† By 1818 the abattoir would be demolished.

to achieve more. In one of his gossipy letters, he wrote of Gordon's property being about to be 'prodigiously increased by an inclosure ... of all the fells between Derwent and Buttermere'.[7] This larger claim, though, had been rejected by Parliament. The hospital, meanwhile, enclosed the 1,273 acres of Thornthwaite Common,[8] which, owing to its late-seventeenth-century sale, had fallen into the old Derwentwater manor just too late for the tenants to be included in the general Derwentwater 'enfranchisement'. And as there was no demesne land, the Curwens never having lived in the Parish,* all the tenants were customary.[9]

Unusually, the hospital decided to enfranchise all their tenants at the time of the enclosure, without charging the usual 30 per cent of the land value. In exchange, the hospital received 782 acres of commons adjacent to the 116 allotted to them by the Act – their intention being to plant trees in the entire area, the origins of today's Whinlatter Forest. In fact, they planted slightly less than half of the area, having had to sell off some of the better land to help pay for walling. And, as planting costs were high, they let the remaining unplanted land for grazing,[10] mostly to the old customary tenants, who had done well from their free enfranchisements. Unsurprisingly, a survey in 1817 indicated that the hospital's actions had not been profitable; its conclusion that 'no advantage will be derived to the Hospital's Estate by an Inclosure of Castlerigg and Derwentwater common'. There, the hospital started to enfranchise the unfranchised too but took the usual fee.[11]

The next major Parish enclosure, 3,488 acres of Brundholme Common, followed a year later.† As we know, Brundholme had, unusually, four major landowners, two of whom were relatively recent, and they had probably pushed the case for enclosure and successfully sold the idea to the majority of smaller landholders, creating a flurry of change in small plots of land between Millbeck and Applethwaite. The Le Flemings sold land to Brownrigg's heir and

---

* Although four years earlier the Hospital had gained a small estate at Beckstones after the tenant, Hannah Grave, was convicted of felony.
† I have taken the current Victoria County History (VCH) figures, rather than the slightly smaller ones in Tate, 'A Handlist of Enclosure Acts and Awards', pp. 175–87.

William Calvert acquired another 125 acres, most of Latrigg becoming part of his estate. Vicar Lowry lost 'a Right to some Brackens on Latrigg' but kept 'a Rood of Moss for Peats' elsewhere[12] and apparently Wordsworth took up his bit of the commons. No more of the 14,421 acres of Percy lands in the Parish were enclosed, and the vast majority of Borrowdale's 18,663 acres remained unenclosed too. The Castlerigg and Derwentwater enclosure, which would enclose far more land than the other Parish enclosures combined, was not to be created until 1848.[13]

The expert collator of all the centrally recorded Cumberland enclosures, W. E. Tate, was much struck by two primary differences between the Cumberland deeds and the others he had studied. Firstly, there was the survival of baronies and manors 'long after they were virtually extinct further south'. In the Dacre/Howard lands of Greystoke and Gisland, the term 'barony' was still used in the Acts of enclosure, and the Honour of Cockermouth remained proudly standing too. Every single Act of Parish enclosure referred to its manor, and also illustrated the second point that surprised Tate. He had expected the use of the phrase 'The township and parish of X' in the Acts to refer to a coterminous administrative unit, as elsewhere, whereas the Parish enclosures, as in much of Cumberland, described 'the township of X in the manor of Y in the parish of Z'.[14]

All Cumberland enclosures, whose purpose was primarily to privatise wasteland and commons for pasture, would have been impossible without the instigation (or active or passive agreement) of the majority of customary tenants. As a result, all over the county stone walls began to snake up the fells from the valley, the stones wherever possible sloping outward and downward to guide the rain run-off and so keep the insides of the walls dry.[15] They were often built by skilled itinerant drystone-wallers, who generally tested the completion of their work by 'taking a leap at it with both feet'.[16] The walls provided shelter for sheep in bad weather and incorporated vertical clear-cut joins, to indicate whose responsibility it was to maintain a section of a common wall,[17] as well as 'hogg-holes' to allow the yearlings through. These structures provided, in C. E. Searle's words, a new 'landscape of individual and absolute control'.[18]

A Lake District 'hog hole', to allow the yearlings
through the new enclosure stone walls.

As so often before, the whole process was in dramatic contrast
with the South, where, far from turning common land into private
pasture, the emphasis had been on enclosures bringing pasture back
into more productive arable and mixed farmland – and so threatening the livelihoods of village communities. And in the South the
smaller landlords had more often than not been entirely ignored
in the enclosure bills passed by Parliament, the enclosures themselves fiercely and bitterly resisted by the commoners.* However, in
Cumbria, it was generally agreed that the stock was semi-starved,
as the commons were becoming threadbare, owing to the practice
of overstocking by many of the larger landowners, yeoman or no.
For many, enclosure appeared to be the answer.

Larger landowners, because of the extent of their holdings, had
the option of fencing off extra land from customary use and fully
exploiting it. The far greater number of small landowners across the
region could only hope – as was eloquently expressed by the tenants
in Wasdale-head, another area deep in the Lake District – that
enclosure would 'enable such as the parties as are desirous to avoid

* There may be some similarities between Cumberland and the other upland
communities in England but this seems not to have been fully explored yet.

all Abuses in future ... to enjoy in Quietness and Without oppression their respective Interests'.[19] This was language redolent of old decrees from the Eighteen Men. And indeed, the illegal exploitation of the commons by the larger statesman landowners, which had led to so many court indictments, did fall away. However, the smallest landowners' interests were still often damaged, as, although their enclosed land was allocated strictly proportionally, the legal costs, combined with the costs of fencing, walling and extra liming, were often out of balance with the benefits accruing from a small extra patch of distant commons.

So, just as Dr Leitch described in Applethwaite when he was negotiating with Wordsworth, the smallest landowners frequently, if at times reluctantly, sold out. One problem had been well expressed by a Quaker in 1812, who worried about 'those that have a little of their own, yet from the pressure of the times, though industrious, can hardly make ends meet. A cottage and two or three acres give them credit, they pay taxes...'[20] And, for them, the commons 'is a resource ... in time of difficulty' to avoid throwing 'cattle away at fallen markets'. A small patch of land not adjacent to your own, which required expenditure, was hardly going to help. For the relatively small numbers of landless, always ignored by the directories, the enclosure of the commons was insupportable. William Pearson, a local friend of Wordsworth, admitted regretfully that 'there was one party who had a right, a privilege on these commons ... whose claim was entirely forgotten – this was the poor labourer, (or cottager) who could have kept a pony, a sheep or a cow upon the commons'.[21]

In all, 18 per cent of the Parish was to be enclosed.

*

Finally, on 21 June 1815, Wellington's aide Henry Percy, who had travelled in his blood-stained uniform without stopping, brought the news of the total victory of Waterloo to London. The following month, Mrs Denton, wife of the vicar of Crosthwaite, died of cholera after just three days of illness; the Parish (including Robert Southey) was 'much shocked', all unaware of the danger 'until the last'.[22] However, the usual celebrations were rolled out for the victory, although this time they were mixed with mourning and collections for the wounded and bereaved.

Notwithstanding, Southey and Wordsworth determined that Napoleon's overthrow would be celebrated in a style like no other. A great bonfire was set up on the summit of Skiddaw and Southey chose a day for it to be lit – only for the event to be rained out. More vexing, local vandals then set fire to and scattered the bonfire.[23] But these setbacks would be overcome, and on 25 August 1815 the summit of Skiddaw received an influx of distinguished visitors. 'Never, I believe, was such an assemblage upon such a spot,' Southey said proudly, taking Herbert and Edith May. Derwent Coleridge arrived from over the Raise with all his schoolfellows from Ambleside and was disgusted to find that they were too late for the climb, while his sister Sara was enraged and tearful to be told that she was too delicate for it, 'protesting she could perform the thing with greatest ease'. Wordsworth brought Dorothy, Mary and their eldest son, John; James Boswell arrived with Lord Sunderlin (aged seventy-seven) and his wife.

Southey provided an enthusiastic account of the proceedings: [24] '...some of our neighbours, some adventurous lakers, and Messrs. Rag, Tag, and Bobtail made up the rest of the assembly. We roasted beef and boiled plum-puddings there; sung "God save the King" round the most furious body of flaming tar-barrels I ever saw; drank a huge amount of punch; fired cannon at every health with three times three, and rolled large blazing balls of tow and turpentine down the steep side of the mountain. The effect was grand beyond the imagination ... our bonfire fairly put out the moon.'

For Southey, the final defeat of Napoleon was one of England's finest hours and this was a consciously patriotic feast. There was just one slip-up, which he recorded with some glee: 'When we were craving for the punch a cry went forth that the kettle had been knocked over, with all the boiling water ... The persons about the fire declared it was one of the gentlemen; they did not know his name, but he had a red cloak on; they pointed him out in the circle. The red cloak (a maroon one of Edith's) identified him; Wordsworth ... had committed this fatal *faux pas*, and thought to slink off undiscovered. But as soon as ... I learnt ... I went round to all our party, and communicated the discovery, and getting them about him, I punished him by singing a parody, which they all joined in: "'Twas *you* that kicked the kettle down! 'Twas you, Sir, you!"'

The pure rum that Messrs. Rag, Tag and Bobtail were left with had its due effect, and the party's retreat was marked by a track of fire, pitch and abandoned tarred ropes. But from below all seemed serene: 'seeing the company descend by the light of torches had a most uncommon and beautiful effect', Mrs Coleridge wrote.[25] Everyone survived the eight-hour jaunt unscathed, and the anxious waiting party sent up fireworks and a fire-balloon on their return to Keswick a little after midnight. Such a heroic feat, of course, made the newspapers, *The Cumberland Pacquet* reporting that this was the first time that carts had reached the top of Skiddaw. And the next week *all* the children were able to go to the Sunderlins' celebratory illuminations at Derwent Bank on the other side of the lake. Sara Coleridge noted comfortably that there was 'a great deal of good company'.[26]

The war was truly over.

Shifting perspectives

The unrest in the country between 1815 and 1819 is considered to have been closer to erupting into serious violence than at any other time during, or after, the period of the French Revolution.[27] In Lancashire, the 1803 wages of the weavers and spinners had dropped two-thirds by 1818, their poverty compounded by the enactment of the 1815 Corn Law. This kept the price of corn artificially high, by ruling that no foreign corn could be imported until the price of England's corn reached 80s. a quarter, with results that Southey foresaw: 'Was there ever such a blunder as to quarrel with the people about *Bread*!'[28] Wordsworth, with his permanent bias towards the rural poor, was the only Lake Poet to support the Act, as did the poets' new friend William Wilberforce, although both thought the price was fixed too high.[29]

Tourists enjoying Castlehead, the fulcrum of the Greenwich Hospital
battles, and one of Southey's favourite views.

Since the price of Cumberland wool remained at the high levels
generated by the war years until 1819, the Parish initially seemed
exempt from the general pain. However, the seeds of inevitable
trouble had already been sown in the Greenwich Hospital estate. The
average acreage of the fifteen tenanted farms had long since dropped
from 50 acres to 35; the estate's new vision being to increase rather
than diminish its area of woodland, and actively to improve its long-
term value by planting. Another 220 acres of woodland had been
planted by 1805, a time of economic optimism in the Parish, and, in
part to compensate for the investment, the hospital had emphatically
raised the rent it charged to its tenant farmers. They had been advised
that 'all the farms [about Keswick], except perhaps the farthest, will
no doubt be readily let for the accommodation of the inhabitants
and at better prices than farmers (merely as such) could pay'. The
old closes were divided and the old wood cut and cleared, the aim
being to create drained and cultivable land for the Keswickians. The
fifteen farms were expanded to twenty-five, averaging 19 acres each.
Ominously, all the new leases had been shortened so that they would
each expire at the same time, in 1822.[30]

Roughly simultaneously, the managers of the hospital estate both forbade any cutting in Castlehead, except for fully grown interspersed timber, and aborted the receiver's plans to cut down 592 oaks[31] that were visible from the lake, their decisions complementing the recent changes in land use on the western side of Derwentwater. Now a wood would no longer be sold in its entirety for felling; trees would be sold one by one, for timber. The aesthetic benefits of retaining woodland in this way were good for tourism but not for income. So, while the hospital's gross rental receipts leapt forward during the war years despite their renting out less land (Parish rents doubling between 1805 and 1815), the estate's net rental income had fallen substantially,* because of the cost of planting and more careful felling. After the war, rents dropped elsewhere in the Parish: for instance, in the three estates let out in Wythburn to provide income for the chapel there, the rent fell between a quarter and a third in the years from 1814 to 1817.[32]

By 1817, even the hospital surveyors acknowledged that their land was let out at its full rack rent.† While the high rents appeared to be sustainable for many of the smaller Keswickian units, the larger farmers of Stable Hills and Goosewell Farm both gave notice to quit. This painful period in the manor lasted until around 1820, and would be criticised by Parliament, in part causing the appointment of a new Secretary to the Hospital in 1819. Southey, in an article about the poor away from the Parish in the *Quarterly Review* of 15 April 1816, was also scathingly critical about what had happened elsewhere to 'the small farmer, or the yeoman, who had his roots in the soil – this was the right English tree in which our heart of oak was matured ... But old tenants have been cut down with as little remorse and as little discrimination as old timber, – and the moral scene is in consequence as lamentably injured as the landscape.'

Then, just one day after the article's publication, Southey and his home were assailed by a tragedy that was nearly to break him:

---

* From almost 90 per cent in the 1790s to 50 per cent by 1813.
† The term then meant the full value of the land.

the death of his beloved son Herbert, aged only nine. The very next day Southey sent the letters he had written Herbert to his son's god-father, Grovesnor Bedford, for preservation[33] and later even had to ask him for help to pay for the funeral.

A letter he had written a year earlier, brimming over with paternal pleasure and pride, shows his delight in his son. He had chosen to be Herbert's tutor and told of his son's precocious progress; Herbert knew as much Greek, at the age of eight, as one might expect from a fifteen-year-old. 'But there has been no cramming,' he added. 'His lessons are short and easy, and made almost as much a matter of sport as of business. No child can possibly offer fairer hopes.'[34] And, as his son lay dying, the poet's only desire was for a time when his family would all be together, in a place where 'happiness is permanent, and there is neither change nor evil'.[35] A belief in heaven and the afterlife firmly embedded in him again, after the brief, terrifying lapse following his mother's death.

A year later, Southey went further, saying he was only able to bear his grief because 'the way before me cannot be very long, – & there is the Gate of Heaven at the end of it. – Neither of my parents got beyond fifty. – I am in my forty third year.'[36] This was a thought he often returned to in the next few years and Dorothy Wordsworth worried about him for a long time: 'He works so hard, and looks so delicate, that one cannot see him without some anxious thoughts; and, resolute as he is, he will forever feel his bitter loss. It comes on him heavily at times and he has not the boyish glee he used to have.'[37]

The month after Herbert's death saw the publication of Southey's significant laureate poem *The Poet's Pilgrimage to Waterloo*. He had travelled to the battleground with the artist Edward Nash in 1815 and, true to his new position of welcoming rather than scorning the label of 'the Lake Poets', he used Skiddaw – 'Majesty serene ... the bulwark of this favoured plain' – and the domestic harmony of his life in the Lake District as symbols of 'the nation's covenant with God'.[38] Southey continues:[39]

> *And we did well, when on our Mountain's height*
> *For Waterloo we raised the festal flame,*
> *And in our triumph taught the startled night*
> *To ring with Wellington's victorious name,*
> *Making the far-off mariner admire*
> *To see the crest of Skiddaw plumed with fire.*

In his Proem to the poem, Southey beautifully describes his joyous return to his family, thereby establishing his authority to 'indict the revolutionaries and warmongers who have destroyed these virtues in Europe'[40]: 'Life hath no purer deeper happiness,' he wrote – above all the sight of his boy, 'Waving his hat around his happy head'.Those lines must have seemed unreadable so soon after Herbert's death, as, perhaps, would Southey's prayer for himself:[41]

> *Scoff ye who will! but let me, gracious Heaven,*
> *Preserve this boyish heart till life's last day!*
> *For so that inward light by Nature given*
> *Shall still direct, and cheer me on my way,*
> *And brightening as the shades of age descend,*
> *Shine forth with heavenly radiance at the end.*

The darkness was not helped by the times. Both Southey and Wordsworth were sharply aware of the pain and danger of post-war life outside the relative peace of the Lake District; they also remained deeply concerned about the poor, as well as alarmed about the mob. Their fundamental fear, as spelt out by Southey to a former school friend, was this: 'For some years I have believed (and most reluctantly believed) that we are hurrying towards a Revolution, which according to all symptoms will not be less bloody nor less destructive than what has been witnessed in France.' He promoted the new, and at the time radical, suggestion of state spending on infrastructure as part of the solution, expanding on the idea in a letter to his neighbour William Peachy, who had been out of the country for a while: 'You will find much distress in the country. No folly was ever greater than to cry for retrenchment ... A customer of 50 millions having suddenly left the market. Can stupidity go further than to recommend spending less in remedy? So instead of paying them as soldiers you must support them as paupers; and you have driven them into the mob instead of the ranks.'[42]

There were deep divisions in the country, not just between the rich and the poor but also, by then, between the landed gentry and the manufacturer. The political campaigning of the time became violently inflammatory, in one of the most overtly political periods ever for British writers. Virtually all the major poets and novelists made an appearance on the public stage,[43] fighting for different post-war futures; the essential human distinctions in this commentariat initially (with one exception)[44] being age and class.

The older, 'conservative' side, having lost their faith that the human race was to be reborn, were determined to hold on to the best elements of the past, winnowing things down to their ideal form and aiming to keep society's conscience alive. So, having witnessed the destruction of a historic church in France, the 'bards of orthodoxy' did everything they could to try to protect and enhance their own. On the other hand, the more aristocratic 'radicals', such as Byron and Shelley, too young to have experienced the French Revolution at first hand, celebrated a cult of joyous sexuality as their expression of freedom, and espoused humanism rather than religion, attacking the Lake Poets for supporting a 'politically reactionary Christianity'. They equally rejected the way of philosophical solitude for a poet, scorning it as 'narcissistic, cowardly or immoral',[45] rather than spiritual and contemplative as Wordsworth believed it to be.

This literary battle had been heightened by the new quarterlies and monthlies, joined in 1817 by William Blackwood's *Edinburgh Magazine* (later known as *Blackwood's Magazine*), a Tory answer to the *Edinburgh Review*, which echoed their policy of publishing vindictive – and saleable – reviews of contemporary writers. And there was some cross-dressing as the reformist, humanist *The Examiner*, started by the Hunt brothers (in no way aristocratic) in 1808, had fully acknowledged Wordsworth's early genius by 1813.*

---

* Leigh Hunt had been imprisoned for seditious libel in 1810–11 and found himself reading Wordsworth's poems, which quite undermined the assumptions he had made after the universal critical drubbing of *Poems, in Two Volumes*. He commissioned Hazlitt's review of *The Excursion*.

Hunt professed that no writer since Spenser and Milton had seen further into 'the sacred places of poetry' than Wordsworth, and that he was 'the greatest poet of the present'.[46]

The younger aristocratic poets had originally been much influenced by Wordsworth too but felt he had betrayed his original genius. As Byron* had said economically in the year of *The Excursion*'s publication, 'Wordsworth – stupendous genius! Damned fool!'[47] Two years later, Shelley's sonnet 'To Wordsworth'[48] recognised his genius as 'the Poet of Nature', feeling and loss, a man who, 'In honoured poverty' wove 'Songs consecrate to truth and liberty'. But no longer, leaving Shelley 'to grieve / Thus having been, that thou should cease to be'.[49] So it was that, broadly, when the genius of the Lake Poets was first publicly recognised in print, it was by the very people who were violently attacking their more conservative position about post-war current affairs, so the trio were now besieged from both sides.

In 1816 Wordsworth had found occasion to vent his feelings about Jeffrey, whom he compared to Robespierre[50] – a spleen originating in the common knowledge that Jeffrey had actually *liked* the *Lyrical Ballads*, writing to a friend around the time of publication: 'I have been enchanted with a little volume of poems, lately published, called "Lyrical Ballads", without an author's name.'[51] Walter Scott described the situation well: he had seen Jeffrey in private 'weep warm tears over Wordsworth's poetry' despite in print mounting 'the Scorner's chair' to aid the *Edinburgh Review*'s sales – which, in turn, would help to promote the journal's progressive political agenda.[52] Coleridge had been crafting his own response to the success of Jeffrey's populist rewriting of literary criticism since 1814. And his inaccessible but important two-volume *Biographia Literaria*, published in 1817, introduced a new standard by which poetry could be professionally judged – imagination.

However, despite Byron's unstinting praise for *Roderick*, and despite Southey's useful suggestions about improving the life of the poor and his stark portrayal of industrial poverty – and, ironically,

---

* Bryon's 3rd canto of *Childe Harold's Pilgrimage* was even considered to be plagiarism by Wordsworth on occasion. See Bate, *Radical Wordsworth*, p. 422.

precisely *because* of his frequent forays into the public space –
Southey took the main brunt of the radicals' attack; his assumption
of the role of moral instructor of the nation too tempting a target
for the opposition to ignore. So, when Southey publicly espoused
Edmund Burke for the first time, and slapped his glove in the face
of electoral reform in October 1816, dismissing its adherents as
'some weak men, some mistaken or insane ones, and other very
wicked ones',[53] a few of his former radical associates retaliated by
publishing the following year his – previously unpublished – radical
play of 1794, *Wat Tyler*.[54]

Wat Tyler can be read today as 'New Testament' dramatic
history[55] but Southey at the time acknowledged it as a 'piece of
sedition'.[56] In a careful letter to Peachy (a general, after all), he
dismissed the play as the work of his twenty-year-old self, written
in just three weeks and submitted to a publisher (then in Newgate
Prison) who had ignored it, and which, he, Southey, had never
bothered to enquire about again. Yet, when he now tried to injunct
for unauthorised publication, he was denied on the grounds 'that a
person cannot recover in damages for a work which is in its nature
calculated to do an injury to the public'.[57] As *Wat Tyler* sold some
60,000 copies, more than any of his other works, his enemies' bile
overflowed; Hazlitt was like a terrier, and 'apostate' remained the
cry, as the recent tradition of making fun of the poet laureate rose
to new heights.

Contrary to the vituperative claims of his attackers, Southey
had refused to apologise for, or deny, his early Jacobinism far
more consistently than either of the other two 'Lake Poets', never
entirely giving up hope of their bringing about radical change until
the Jacobins joined forces with Napoleon – 'for I would fain have
believed that with all their dreadful errors, they set out with noble
principles'.[58] So, when the 'slander' of apostasy was repeated in
Parliament, and William Smith fulminated against 'the settled,
determined malignity of a renegade', Southey wrote an open letter
in response in early 1817.[59] He had, he said, always aimed at 'bettering the condition of all the lower classes' and still desired 'a
greater equality in the condition of men' – positions he would continue to champion for the rest of his life. All he could be charged

with, he said, was that 'as he grew older his opinions altered concerning the means by which amelioration was to be affected ... as he learnt to understand the institutions of his country, he learnt to appreciate them rightly, to love, and to revere them, and to defend them'.*

At the same time, Southey wrote a much quoted private letter to the prime minister, Lord Liverpool,[60] whose government had recently suspended the legal remedy of *habeas corpus* – just as Pitt's government had in the 1790s, then endangering the Lake Poets and their friends. Often used as primary evidence for judging Southey a straightforward reactionary, the letter reveals that his views actually embraced both sides of the debate; the connecting theme being the provision of aid to the poor to enable them to have decent lives and thus avert the danger of mob rule. It expressed his concern that the repeal of *habeas corpus* had not immediately been used 'to place the chief incendiary writers in safe custody', restating his point that, while twenty-four years earlier the spirit of Jacobinism had influenced men 'in my sphere of life ... [it] has disappeared from that Class and sunk into the Rabble; – who would have torn me to pieces for holding those opinions then; and would tear me to pieces now for renouncing them'.

The army, Southey went on, was the only bulwark preventing the revolution of the industrial masses, yet weekly, daily, the revolutionary press 'was read aloud in every Ale House where the men are quartered', while soldiers were as prone to contagion as any other group. 'You must curb the Press, or it will destroy the constitution of this country.' So far, so reactionary. Yet this was only half the argument of the letter – a fact discovered by the diligence of Lynda Pratt and Ian Packer as recently as 2016. Southey's

---

* Similarly, when Southey tried to imagine himself back into the time of the Reformation, he wrote: 'My own belief is this, – that if in those dreadful days I had been a young man, I should have courted martyrdom for the reformation, – if an elderly one I should have suffered it for the sake of the establishment: - in the first case youth hope and ardour would have made me overlook all the immediate evils and dangers of the change; in the other, the good would have appeared too doubtful and remote, the evil so certain and immediate, that I should have thought it better to die than to assist in the work of destruction which was going on.' Notably, in both cases he saw himself as being a martyr.

position was in fact far more nuanced; he ended with a suggestion that the state should use the 'great moral Steam-Engine' of Robert Owen and others to give land to disbanded troops and sufficient aid to get them started, 'then giving them a life-hold interest in the ground upon an equitable rent'. The broad span of his views is clear: while William Cobbett, for instance, would have abhorred any action advocated in the early paragraphs of the letter, he would have warmly supported the land-aid scheme, a practical extension of the general argument Southey had made to Peachy.

Southey later offered an eloquent explanation of his early radicalism, as the creation of 'a republican spirit, such as may easily be accounted for in a youth whose notions of liberty were taken from the Greek and Roman writers, and who was ignorant enough of history and of human nature to believe that a happier order of things had commenced with the independence of the United States and would be accelerated by the French Revolution'.[61] When, as a mature adult, he celebrated the Spanish uprising against Napoleon, he wrote not just that 'at length a national resistance had been aroused against this iron tyranny' but, more tellingly, that 'Young men understood now by their own emotions how their fathers had been affected in the morning of the French Revolution'.[62]

But, in the midst of writing his 'tender epistle to William Smith' and trying to injunct the publication of *Wat Tyler*, Southey feared he might lose his home, as a result of the travails of his current landlord, Tolson, a commission agent from Liverpool who, by April, was in gaol for debt.[63] In the usual Lake District hotchpotch of landholdings, a small part of the estate was customary, owing fines of £33 on the death of the king or changing proprietors, but most of it was now freehold, and Tolson's debt theoretically allowed his property to be sold off for reparation.[64] Southey intended, with Wordsworth's help, to make a proxy bid for the house and land despite departing, in late April, on an extensive European tour – a 'change of air, scene and circumstance is almost necessary for me'[65] – that he had planned with Humphrey Senhouse ('the only Cumberland Gentleman whom I have found with a love of things which deserve to be loved').[66]

On his return in mid-August, Southey found out that Greta Hall had been auctioned in June and bought by Isaac Fisher, a London gold and silver merchant and a scion of the Fishers who had, ever since the Great Deed, been substantial Borrowdale landowners. Southey's proxy bid had been beaten and, while his only comment on the matter in six weeks of correspondence was 'I am not sorry, being in no condition to purchase estates', he would say later that he had not been 'well used about it'. His initial reaction had been to feel encouraged, as Fisher 'talks civilly and promises largely'.[67] But Fisher then died, before the legal complications over the land- lord's debts had been sorted out, leaving Seathwaite Farm and the remarkable sum of £50,000 to John Fisher of Seatoller House in Borrowdale.[68] Tolson somehow or other held on to Greta Hall for the rest of Southey's life and, as part of the deal, Southey paid his rent to the mortgagee for a period.[69]

Altogether, this was a typically muddled and complicated Lake District property negotiation, but Southey was duly refreshed after his nightmare year by his extensive tour. He had known he needed to escape, but, as early as June, had written to Bedford that his spirits 'will be better when I am at home again'.[70] For it was living in the Parish with his loving family – and the comfort of his library – that had fundamentally sustained him amid the storm of personal attacks and destabilising political events. Back at Greta Hall, follow- ing a business trip to London or one of his longer excursions, 'For some time I was idle for very happiness, – the mere being at rest – of knowing that I had not engagement of any kind, but that where I slept, there I should breakfast, and that where I breakfasted there I should dine and where I dined, there I should drink tea, sup and sleep ... a pleasure of which it seemed I could never have too much.'[71]

And the old sense of neighbourhood lived on, witness the Parish creation, in 1818, of one of the six Lake Counties savings banks introduced immediately after the Act allowing them. Their func- tion was to accept the small deposits of the working man, which would have been too small for an ordinary bank (not that Keswick had such a thing then) to bother with, and to offer a higher level of interest on their savings than they could have secured pri- vately. For Southey they were the most 'beneficial institution[s]

... devised since the foundations of civilized society were laid', in part because he felt that, by encouraging the working class to save for their old age, the banks would help to counter radicalism and 'prove a strong bulwark for property in general'.[71] In Keswick the not inconsiderable sum of £6,000 had been deposited by 1829, a sum that 457 depositors would have more than doubled less than twenty years later.[72]

At St Kentigern's the dean had praised the 'entirely' new common seats in the nave in 1817, and in 1818, just six years after its rebuild, the roof was fixed again as it had been 'on the point of falling in';[73] so everything would have been more comfortable. This was all positive action, which had Southey's full approval. But the dean's rather surprising judgment, *before* the roof had been re-fixed, that it 'is now a very superior Church – complete in all respects and may contain near 1500 persons'[74] indicates that standards were still pretty low. But the school – if the Cumberland headmasters' reports in an 1817 survey of endowed grammar schools, designed to help the government embrace an enquiry into the 'Education of the Lower Orders', are to be believed – was shown to be exceptional in an entirely new way.[75]

To start with an apparent weakness, just six pupils were then taught Latin and Greek, but I suspect that this was a source of considerable local pride. The teaching of Latin and Greek was part of the definition of a grammar school, but Crosthwaite was the only Cumberland school to offer a figure; several spoke of 'very few' pupils, and one admitted to having none 'at the moment'. It is safe to assume that Latin and Greek did not feature on a school's curriculum if its master was paid 'not exceeding £4 a year', while it is likely that, proportionally, more pupils studied the two subjects in schools in large towns. The specialist classics schools – pre-eminently Great Blencow – were, of course, a different matter.

Attendance at the other Cumberland grammar schools ranged from twenty to thirty (thirty in Penrith) to seventy to eighty at Wigton, several describing a marked drop in numbers during the summer quarter when the scholars are 'irregular in their attendance especially during the hay and corn harvest'. That was no doubt true in the Parish too, but attendance at Crosthwaite school was in a league of its own – 'at present 260 Scholars upon the Books'.[76] While the phrase 'upon the books' suggests Crosthwaite was putting a typically competitive spin on the figures, the level of attendance was clearly dramatically higher than at any other school. And not only did Crosthwaite grammar school teach the largest number of children, the Eighteen Men paid their headmaster £80 a year, the highest wage in the county, and also employed an undermaster, who was paid £30 – more than the headmasters of Cockermouth and Penrith.

The only known sketch of Crosthwaite grammar school a decade before its re-build in 1829.

A number of other schools had boarders and/or gave private tuition, which would have augmented the headmasters' income. And several had also at some time lost most, or even all, of their endowments, a fact the 1817 survey's collator comments upon throughout England; St Bees,[77] for instance, had land 'supposed to be worth at *least* £8,000' but revenue of 'less than £100'.*

---

* This issue would be raised by the Select Committee for the Education of the Poor, who discovered that the school had leased some valuable mineral rights to the Lowther family, back in 1742, for 867 years for only £3 10s p.a, The Earl of Lonsdale was a governor of the school . *Morning Chronicle* 21–23 September 1818.

So, the effects of the particularity of the Eighteen Men's rule of
Crosthwaite school – no gentry and no vicar ever involved – and
the long-time Parish community effort and involvement with the
school had produced, relatively, quite exceptional results; at the
same time, it remained the only Cumberland grammar school of
any size that was genuinely free for every child that attended. This
evidence raises the question, for the first time, of whether it was
the particular *form* of Crosthwaite grammar school governance –
despite the overcrowding and the poor amenities (there were only
three privies for the entire school, for example) – that allowed it to
serve its Parish children best.

These were the things that warmed Southey about his home, but
Edith, aged forty-four, became pregnant again during an outbreak
of typhus in the Parish.[78] In February 1819 she endured a dangerous breech birth, which left her both physically and mentally
exhausted after the arrival of their second son (who was to be their
last child). Southey named him Cuthbert, publicly because he liked
'genuine English names'; privately, and disturbingly, he admitted
his choice had been prompted by the saint's relationship with St
Herbert and his own loss.[79]

Tom, his younger brother, was to arrive the following month,
with six children and six Devonshire cows, to pursue his fortune
– with 'all the help that I could muster'[80] – in 30 acres of the
Newlands valley, living at Emerald Bank on Newlands Beck.[81]
Southey anticipated the event with relief: 'it will very much increase
my comfort, and draw me out very often to bathe in the beck below
the house, where there are some of the finest basons [i.e., basins]
in the country.'[82] Once the family arrived, he found that, proud
as he was of the health and strength of the growing Cuthbert, he
was bested: 'four of his Newlands-cousins are young Ogres – absolute Killcrops'[83] and two months after their arrival Southey was
still expressing unalloyed pleasure in having his brother's family
close by. He wrote to Grosvenor Bedford, 'It is a good thing for me
that Tom is so near', and told him the house was just 'a gunshot
from' the delightful beck they had so enjoyed bathing in.[84]

Soon, however, the family needed more support, which the
recent diminishment of the previously safe annual royalties from

Roderick was making it very difficult for Southey to provide. By June 1820 Edith was becoming exasperated by their straitened circumstances, a mood that her husband's reply presumably did little to improve: 'you must well know that when my brother is in want … I cannot but assist him to the extent of my power … I must do as my Mother would have wished me to do, had she been living.'[85] This was a learned principle for Southey. The only solution he and his youngest brother, Henry, could see was for the family to emigrate, although neither saw much chance of that happening. And indeed, Tom's family stayed in Newlands for several years, taking lodgers, but proving fairly unsuccessful farmers. Their next three children were all baptised at the chapel and in 1825 Tom is even recorded as a chapel warden.

Throughout these years, Robert Southey continued to enjoy swimming in the beck – 'He was just a girt watter dog … he was terrible fond of bathing thereaway, belaw t'Emerald Bank'[86] – and often took his visitors with him. These probably included some Cambridge undergraduates who, by the end of the 1810s, had started to visit the Lakes with their dons 'in flights to study in the long vacation'[87] and usually gained access to Greta Hall. This new influx had created an original Parish nomenclature, as, muddling up College and Collegian, the locals settled on the clearer 'Cathedral' as a term for the students; a bill was sent, for instance, to an undergraduate lodged with Southey's gardener addressed to 'Mr Clarke's Cathedral'. And the word stuck.

In the wider world, Luddite protest had turned political. The county of Lancashire, with its array of new industrial towns, had only two MPs, while in the country as a whole over half the *c*.610 MPs were returned by 154 owners of rotten or closed boroughs.[88] Anger had been steadily growing, and, on 16 August 1819, a protest meeting of up to 70,000 at St Peter's Fields in Manchester was violently dispersed, resulting in at least fifteen deaths in what became known as the 'Peterloo Massacre', an ironic reference to the decisive victory over Napoleon four years previously. Southey, believing 'it is the direct and undisguised object of those demagogues … to bring about revolution by force', maintained the situation required 'the adoption of restrictive measures to … curb the audacious spirit

14. Jonathan Otley.
A Parish man.

15. Coleridge's wife, Sara.

16. Crosthwaite Vicarage after Lynn had enlarged it. Painted
by Canon Gipps's rather remarkable daughter, Lucy, whose work
was commended by John Ruskin.

17. Derwentwater quay. Sara Hutchinson 'could not have believed an engraving could have given the quiet and solemn feeling inspired by such a [twilight] scene'.

18. William Westall's Keswick in 1820, his aquatint creating a triangle between the whitewashed Crosthwaite Church, a particularly white sheep and snow-covered Skiddaw. Eighteen years later the foreground would have been dominated by Marshall's new church, St John the Evangelist.

19. John Marshall, millocrat and great benefactor of the Lake District and the Parish.

20. Jane Marshall, Dorothy Wordsworth's intimate friend from childhood.

21. The wool-drying barn at Millbeck, as depicted by Joseph Flintoff. The painting also shows the Georgian home of Daniel Dover, which was later taken over by the artist.

22. South Window of Southey's Study by Caroline Bowles, 1841.

23. John Lough's effigy of Southey in St Kentigern's. In 1879
the Dean of Westminster, A. P. Stanley, described the poet as 'the genius
of Keswick, almost as exclusively as Wordsworth is of Grasmere and
Rydal – or as Shakespeare is of Stratford-on-Avon'.

24. William Westall's engraving of Greta Hall, then surrounded by trees.
The artist had spent one winter 'lodged' at the bottom of Southey's garden.

25. Keswick Main Street in 1870, captured by John Brown, a local painter and
decorator. In the far left-hand corner, serenaded by the strolling player Jimmy
Dyer, John Fisher Crosthwaite looks away while the 'noted pig keeper' John
Glaister puffs on his pipe.

26. Beatrix Potter reimagined her sketch of St Herbert's Island as Owl Island for Squirrel Nutkin's boating adventure in 1902.

27. A rare portrait of Canon Rawnsley by his wife Edith, who had exhibited at both the Royal Academy and the New Watercolour Society in London before turning her attention to the Keswick School of Industrial Art.

28. A later watercolour of the National Trust Executive Committee meeting on 15 April 1912, agreeing the acquisition of Blakeney Point, by Thomas Matthews Rooke. Canon Rawnsley, perhaps not offering his full attention, takes a central position but, Octavia Hill was in reality too ill to attend.

29. Photographer Joe Cornish captures the dappled light on Rawnsley's memorial to John Ruskin on Friar's Crag, land that the National Trust, in turn, bought as a memorial to him.

30. *Thirlmere*. A fine example of the changing artistic responses to the Lake District in the new century, by Paul Nash.

31. Today's Herdwicks remain hefted and imperturbable.

of blasphemy and treason … much as we deplore the necessity for such measures … as the indispensable and only means of saving the country from the worst of all evils'.[89] Revolution in England was now his most fundamental fear.

When George III died in January 1820, Southey began to revise his opinion of the Prince Regent, now George IV. He saw him as another 'beleaguered object of radical hostility' and said he was prepared to 'wear the King's colours'. The year started well for Southey, as he received an honorary degree from Oxford, raising one of the two largest ovations (Wordsworth would have to wait for the Victorian Age to receive his). John Keble, a future leader of the High Church 'Oxford Movement', and soon to be hailed 'the first man in Oxford',[*] found Southey a delight; the poet, he noted, 'left a most excellent name behind him, for his kind unassuming manners, with everyone who had been in his company for five minutes'. When his *Life of Wesley* was published that same year, it received the approval of several bishops, and Southey began to be seen as an Anglican sage.[90] The Bishop of London considered the book 'an important service to our ecclesiastical history',[91] steering a careful course between 'seducing people to Methodism by setting its good points in too alluring a light, & of wounding religion by treating its extravagancies & follies with too much levity'.

But the early 1820s would be another bruising time for Southey. The younger romantic poets had long been taking potshots at the Lake Poets, half obscured by publishing anonymously, which Southey publicly ignored. However, at the beginning of 1821, the literary side of the political battle about England's future caused not just an attack on reputation but an actual death. In 1817, its year of first publication, William Blackwood's *Edinburgh Magazine* had included in its October edition an anonymous attack on what 'Z' called the new 'cockney school of writers', describing James Leigh Hunt as 'a man of little education'.[92] Three years later, John Scott, a close associate of Leigh Hunt and his friend John Keats, had

---

[*] The only man to have an Oxford college named after him who was not either a benefactor or a saint.

launched *The London Magazine* and, in the November edition, hit back with a full-scale onslaught on 'Z'; he then continued the battle with two more articles stridently decrying Blackwood's conduct.

In February 1821 an illegal duel ensued between Scott and a representative of 'Z' and, before the end of the month, Scott was dead. Wordsworth, writing to Henry Crabb Robinson, commented that 'I do not recollect any other English Author's dying in the same way' or so 'foul' a time, which promised 'no good to the Republic of Letters or to the Country'.[93] This was the poisonous atmosphere of ad hominem attacks and counter-attacks when, in January, Southey had added some lines to his official requiem for George III, *A Vision of Judgement*, just as it was about to go to print. The lamb had turned lion, and Southey included a coruscating attack on an unnamed 'Satanic school' of poetry, whose 'diseased hearts and depraved imaginations'[94] had torpedoed his proud claim of 1807 that any father could safely entrust his child to modern poetry 'without apprehension of evil'.[95]

Enough now has been seen of Southey's life to introduce Thomas Carlyle's brilliant, instinctive analysis of him. They met when Southey was approaching sixty. Lurking beneath Southey's delight in children, his sensible attitude to money, his formidable work ethic, his generous acceptance of responsibility for others, his good manners and his self-control, his frequent iciness in public coexisting with a sense of domestic fun, Carlyle finds an exceptionally tightly wired nervous sensibility. 'In his eyes especially', according to Carlyle, 'was visible a mixture of sorrow and of anger, or of angry contempt, as if his indignant fight with the world had not yet ended in victory, but also never should in defeat.'[96]

A few days later Carlyle asked whether the poet knew De Quincey, who Southey believed had proved a traitor to the hospitality offered him by the Lake Poets when he referred to Coleridge's opium habit in print. In answer to the question, Southey erupted like a volcano, his face 'as I looked at it had become of slate colour, the eyes glancing, the attitude rigid, the figure altogether a picture of Rhadamanthine rage, – that is, rage conscious to itself of being just'.[97] Southey knew he had overstepped social bounds and went out of his way to be agreeable for the rest of the evening, during which Carlyle observed 'the singular readiness of the blushes; amiable red blush, beautiful like a young girl's when you touched genially the pleasant theme', but noticed too that, on occasion, the 'serpent-like flash of blue or black blush'[98] briefly returned, if something unsettled him.

Carlyle the historian asked himself:

'How has this man contrived, with such a nervous system, to keep alive for near sixty years ... How has he not been torn to pieces long since, under such furious pulling this way and that? He must have somewhere a great deal of methodic virtue in him; I suppose too, his heart is honest, which helps considerably ... I reckon him (with those excitable blue blushes and those red) to be perhaps the excitablest of all men; and that a deep mute monition of conscience had spoken to him, "You are capable of running mad if you don't take care. Acquire habitudes; stick firm and adamant to them at all times, and work, continually work."'[99]

Southey knew that work was his salvation – 'Whenever anything distresses me, I fly to employment, as many fly to battle'[100] – and he consciously built up his rigid habits to counteract the 'melancholy I never yield to'.[101] But the older he got, the more he would react to attacks and public events with an immediate, emotional and often hysterical response, prompted by his overarching fear of revolution; a fear that could distort his settled beliefs, and create contradiction or violent reaction.

The Arrival of Eliza Lynn Linton
and the 1820s

ISAAC DENTON HAD died in 1820, to be replaced by a new vicar with a tribe of children who naturally came to enjoy picnics and other excursions with the Greta Hall contingent. The vicar himself, however, was to become one of Southey's *bêtes noires*.[1] Brought up in Kent, James Lynn had married the young daughter of the Dean of Rochester, Samuel Goodenough, despite the Goodenough family's considering themselves better born than the Lynns. However, once Samuel had become Bishop of Carlisle, he brought the Lynns with him, appointing his son-in-law Rector of the partially mining Parish of Caldbeck in 1814.

With a beautiful rectory and a good living, for the rector was also the lord of the manor, Caldbeck (John Peel country) was nevertheless a tough parish, 'where the people were half savages … not a school of any kind was in place'. There were seventeen public houses in a village of just three hundred people,* and this extraordinary number of inns had its effect: no one ever 'tried the experiment of sobriety … Not a man would have held himself justified in marrying before the woman had proved her capacity for becoming a mother', and 'Saturday night fights came as regularly as the Sunday-morning shave'.[2]

The parishioners of Caldbeck were used to a local priest who fought, drank and ploughed energetically and was said to be more

* Compared with Keswick's thirteen and a population at least seven times Caldbeck's.

punctual for the fights than for the chapel. Lynn had had to marry his curate about three weeks before the couple's baby was born. So he found that his efforts to admonish and improve were generally ignored, as 'the men swore at him and threatened to do him a mischief if he did not hold his noise … and the women jeered him for a Molly who put his nose where he had no concerns'. 'Thus the heart was taken out' of the new vicar, who decided the better part of valour was to check on the honesty of his tithes.[3] This made far more sense to the parishioners and, as Lynn checked them out perfectly genially, it was decided that he 'was a good 'un of his kind', after all.[4]

When the bishop added the living at Crosthwaite to that of Caldbeck in 1820, the tough family critic[*] thought the Parish was 'Eden' compared with Caldbeck, attributing this to the influence of the 'resident gentry', the school and the Eighteen Men, but also to '"statesmen", or peasant proprietors, who owned no master and were no man's hire'. This gave them 'a great deal of honest moral courage and sturdy personal independence', which made the Parish as a whole far less 'ferocious and uncouth' than Caldbeck.[5]

Underneath, however, the critic felt the parishioners were equally drunken and immoral, a view confirmed later by a particularly effective curate in 1836: 'With all the love that I bear them, which is very great, I must say that amidst many excellent and amiable persons there are interspersed as many dissipated characters as I have ever known in proportion to the population. I mean in respect of drunkenness. Easter week was a most riotous Season, in that respect and in cockfighting.'[6] The combination of an unusually high level of literacy and a higher than average level of illegitimacy in the whole area has been much commented upon. Living-in farm servants, technically well paid, but with half their wages paid in kind, were at this time as common as labourers (still subject to the twice-yearly hirings) and were usually not allowed to marry. So, saving up and delayed marriage was a necessity for any sort of a better life, and as late as 1851 the county census shows a higher than average proportion of unmarried people, both male and female.

---

[*] Lynn's youngest daughter, of whom more anon.

However, there is a marked difference between the story of an uncouth Parish curate from one of the chapels and that of the Caldbeck priest, just related. All the curates at Crosthwaite were St Bees' men now, the critic said, from the theological college that had been founded by Thomas Christian's nephew, Edmund Law.* The first Anglican theological college, and famous across the North, St Bees was still said to supply more candidates for ordination than any other in England and Wales in 1870. Our critic claimed that in the Parish many of the St Bees' men were quite drunken, but the story concerns one of them at dinner at the vicarage during the bishop's visitation. Asking his lordship casually whether he would like some cabbage, the curate proceeded to carve him some using his own knife and fork, with which he had already 'eaten generously'.[7] Quite a venal sin really.

By the time the Lynns moved in, Edward Locker had been appointed secretary at the Greenwich Hospital; an unequivocally positive change, both for the Parish and Southey, if not for the hospital pensioners.[8] Somewhat revolutionarily, Locker believed his duty was to support the tenants and the hospital's beneficiaries equally;[9] he even invoked the spirit of the Derwentwaters, 'the liberal spirit of a great Landed Proprietor'.[10] In 1821 his recommendations were threefold: a programme of investment in the hospital's Lake District holdings; that the receivers 'be immediately authorised ... to offer ... relief to Tenants, instead of depriving them of their leases' when they were 'oppressed by the low state of the Market'; and, finally, the preservation of the Derwentwater woods, which, he said, 'constitute the great ornament of KESWICK, and as the inhabitants derive most of their income from strangers, who visit this beautiful scenery, they would be seriously injured if the noble woods were cut down...' This was an extension of the hospital's wood-conservation policy, but Locker predicted that the annual thinning of the trees would earn £1,000 a year.[11]

The actual net income made from the wood in the seven years between 1823 and 1830 was a mere £877 6s. 5p., so something was clearly wrong with Locker's expectations – or the execution

* Before he became Bishop of Chester.

of his policy. Nevertheless, for the first time, someone in the role of secretary had gained unequivocal control of policy management for the estates; and Locker's views aligned with Wordsworth's and Southey's – and had the all-important support of the Lowther family.[12] His intention, possibly because the surrounding customary tenants had more freedom, was to create tenants 'much superior to those holding leases under other great proprietors in the north of England'. In order to achieve this, Locker needed to create work. So work was made, with Southey taking an active part in deciding what infrastructure would be particularly useful. By 1825, the receivers were left with no real way of harvesting mature timber without Locker's personal approval; it seemed inevitable that Parliament would become involved again.

Following the government's examination of the educational provision for the 'lower orders' in 1821, a parliamentary report into 'the English Charities for the Education of the Poor' was produced. This report, which confirmed that the '18 sworn men' still governed the Parish, tells us that the 2d. Parish tax for education appeared to have ceased early in the eighteenth century, and that there was now no school stock apart from their rented land, which had been let out at public auction for nine years in 1817 for £99 4s.,[13] a small drop from the previous rent of £100 10s.[14] The schoolmaster's salary was now lower at £65, but the usher's remained the same at £30, the balance put towards a fund for repairs. It records too that the school *had* had over 200 pupils at times but 'currently averaged 120', which tends to make one query the grand total of 260 pupils 'on the books' reported by the Eighteen Men or the Crosthwaite grammar school headmaster four years earlier (see page 402).

However, the parliamentary report concluded that 'all children that present themselves are taken', and it may be that the small drop of rent in 1817, the lower schoolmaster's salary and the drop in pupil attendance (both of which still remained dramatically higher than the other Cumberland grammar schools) reflected the fact that some of the inhabitants of the Parish were falling on harder times. The price for its wool had been descending from 13s. a stone since 1819 – only gradually to rise again to 13s. in the 1870s. In 1823, the year for which we have the first surviving ledger book

for Keswick's remarkably extensive textile industry at Millbeck,* a
stone of Cumberland wool raised a comparatively paltry amount,
between 6s. and 7s. 6d. Another major change for the hill farmers
to endure. The Millbeck business had started when the corn mill
we first encountered in the thirteenth century, at the lower part of
a close called Low Rudding, had been converted into the severally
owned Old Carding Mill.

The sale of a share to the young Daniel Dover of Underskiddaw
in 1797 had marked the beginning of a considerable expansion.
A fulling mill, weaving rooms, a warehouse and press room were
built at High Rudding, complete with a pay office on the opposite side of the stream, connected by a flying bridge.[15] Then, soon
after the turn of the century, a new carding mill and 'Millbeck
Village', a row of five workers' cottages, had been added at Low
Rudding.[16] The earliest agreements for both mills are in the name
of Joseph Dover, 'woollen manufacturer of Keswick', whose
death, aged eighty-five, in 1810 had been memorialised by one
of St Kentigern's grandest tombstones. Beautifully conceived
and worked by William Bromley, one of the Keswick dynasty of
stonemasons,[17] it records Joseph's nine biblically named children,
including the youngest, Daniel, who funded it.† Five years before
his death, old Joseph had allowed some new blood, John Grave
and John Ladyman, into the running of the business, a contract
with its own nod to eternity, as the agreement was supposed to last
for 5,000 years.

The year after Joseph's death, Daniel became the foreman of
the Trustees of the Free School – in other words the Eighteen Men,
who, true to form, dismissed the schoolmaster that year.[18] By 1817,
when John Ladyman embarked on a new career as a pencil manufacturer, Daniel had become managing director of the whole

---

* It should be added that since the Parson and White, *History, Directory
and Gazetteer* describes Clark's woollen business in Applethwaite close by as
'large', rather than Millbeck's, it is possible that two such vigorous enterprises
flourished in the Parish, and we simply lack documentation on the former.
They could, of course, be describing the same place.

† The eldest son, another Joseph, became in due course the tenant at
Ormathwaite.

woollen-manufacturing enterprise, a role he continued until his death twenty-five years later. The ledger book provides evidence of the startling breadth of his business. Pennistones, a blue or indigo coarse woollen cloth, cheap and made in lengths of 600–800 yards, was an export favourite, as was kersey, a cloth of many colours, good at keeping out cold and wet and popular in Europe, both for the less well off and for clothing European armies. The wool dyeing was carried out by Daniel's brother, John, at the forge in the Richardson industrial part of the Greta Hall Estate[19] by the river.[20] And the company bought in its wool not just from the Parish and its surrounding area, but from brokers as far away as Glasgow and London, the shipments including wool that originated in Greece, Russia and East India.

The sales of the Millbeck manufactures were even more wide-spread.* The company traded with Jamaica, New York, New Orleans, Baltimore, Philadelphia, Quebec and Montreal, the Cape of Good Hope, Montevideo and the West Indies, continuing the relationships earlier established by the Cumberland ports on the west coast. That this was not all recent business is indicated by the tablets in St Kentigern's in memory of J. W. Scott of New Orleans, who died in 1811, and his brother Henry from Baltimore, who died six years later. And there are other local examples, which indicate links between Parish emigrants and their old home: for instance, six brothers[21] from Brundholme, who were all merchants in the West Indies.

Many of the export sales were in kind, the West Indies often paying in rum, sugar and coffee, while the Cape of Good Hope obliged in wine. This fine Millbeck export business was to peak in 1834 but was priced out of the market twelve years later, it seems, by the economies of scale in the new steam-powered mills and by transport costs, although it is traditionally believed that the company blanketed the army in the Crimean war in the 1850s, when we know the company's domestic sales were still holding up well.

Keswick was beginning to flourish again, reflecting a nation-wide trend away from the countryside to town, and now housed

* Thanks, no doubt, to their Liverpool shippers and agents.

Part of Daniel Dover's woollen manufactory can be seen at the far turn of the road in this view of Skiddaw from Applethwaite.

almost half the Parish's population of 4,087. A Methodist chapel
had been built in 1814, although its minister was not to arrive until
1836, and the Congregationalist chapel, built in 1803, had just
been brought alive in 1819 by the Reverend Thomas Griffen, who
started a Sunday school there that year.

By the time Lynn arrived in the Parish, his family had swelled
to include as many as eleven children, and the vicarage had to be
enlarged. A 20-foot extension was added to the house, abutting a
large terrace built out on the south side of the hill, and the house
duly provided ten bedrooms. It was cleverly designed to be consistent with the 'Queen Anne' frontage by 'cheating' the windows
inside the first floor of the extension. Nevertheless, Vicar Lynn
appears to have complained to the bishop about his two livings
more than any of his diocesan colleagues. His parishes were
generally considered two of the most beautiful in Cumberland,
but Lynn judged Caldbeck 'low' and Keswick 'unfavourable to
constitutions predisposed to pulmonary or liver complaints'.
However, the constant criticisms were no doubt largely attempts
to justify his frequent absences, as he took his family 'home' to
Rochester.[22]

Soon after his arrival, Southey gossiped that the vicar in 'the
course of his improvement has unluckily demolished the old horse-
block, which ought to have stood for ever, of Gray's station'.[23]
He then added – surprisingly, given his later feelings regarding
Reverend Lynn, 'The new vicar reads and preaches well, and fills
the Church, so much so that a gallery is talked of, and an organ.'
Southey continued in more characteristic vein, however: 'The
parishioners have created a monument to his predecessor, praising
him for his duties – to the non-performance of which this popularity must be ascribed.'[24]

Two years after the Lynn family's arrival, another remarkable
child was added to the Parish roster. Eliza Lynn (later known as
Eliza Lynn Linton) would become the incisive 'family critic' whose
views on Caldbeck and a Parish curate we have already encountered. A friend of Landor, Dickens, Swinburne and others, she was
also the first full-time salaried female journalist in England and a
famously controversial figure in the Victorian literary landscape.

Eliza had had a difficult start in life: her mother died soon after her birth, followed a year later by her eldest sister, a maternal figure who had taken over her care, which bereavements left her father somewhat unhinged. At this point most of the Goodenough family, barring Samuel, dropped the Lynns, but the bishop did his best, offering financial support, which the vicar apparently ignored. Exasperated, the bishop demanded, 'In the name of heaven what do you mean to do for your children?' To which the vicar famously replied, 'Sit in my study, my Lord, smoke my pipe, and commit them to the care of Providence.'[25]

James Lynn was true to his word. The two youngest girls were not formally educated at all, the vicar believing female education to be a reckless extravagance.[26] Indeed, according to Eliza, she was instructed 'to have no opinion of (her) own, or, if she was unfortunate enough to have one ... to keep it to herself.'[27] The family seldom had people to the house, which was stalked by a kind of hysterical emotionalism, as their father's life became 'a mingled web of passion and tears'. The children would be woken to 'the echo of his midnight prayers ... the sound of his passionate weeping mingled in sobbing unison with the moaning of wind in the trees'. This added 'an awful kind of mystery to his character', as he searched for a never-found peace.[28]

As Eliza grew up she was beaten, her father putting 'religious conviction as well as muscular energy into his stripes',[29] and locked up in a small dark cupboard under the stairs; weekly, if her adult memory was correct.[30] And, in time, inevitably, she rebelled against everything, with an intensity bred of an innate refusal to be subjugated. Once, in late adolescence, after stating an intemperately expressed republican view, she tells us, 'my father incontinently knocked me down'.[31]

But Eliza also tells us that her father was 'largely and unostentatiously generous in the parish'[32] and, for the rest of her life, she was devoted to the Lake District, the Parish, the vicarage and 'lovely Keswick'. As a young child, her love was focused on the vicarage hayfield and the two cows, 'Cushie' and 'Hornie', which she helped the cook lead back from the field to the milking byre, and the field down to 'the little brook where the minnows were'.

She would talk later of the joys of 'home views across the garden that touch the heart like the face of a fair child'.[33] And her reactions to the church bells, like Southey's and Dr Leitch's, were of pure joy: 'Such a peal! – pouring a very cascade of music thro the vale – when the wind blows gustily, sinking and swelling with the breeze in mingled passion and suppression infinitely beautiful.'[34] Indeed, as Eliza recorded, the bells were acknowledged to be 'the best in the country' and were 'the pride of the Parish'.[35]

Eliza described the Crosthwaite valley both accurately and eloquently: 'the broadest district and the most populous in the lake country ... Derwentwater lies away by itself at one end of the valley, leaving the rest free for man. So that is only part of the life of the place...'[36]: 'Derwentwater is the gem of the whole [Lake District]. Whatever there is of beauty special to the other districts is here in ripest fullness ... The Vale of Keswick is the opened rose itself, and all the other lakes and mountains are the leaves and buds ... and Borrowdale is the heart of the Rose; the inner golden recess where the bees seek their food and the butterflies their enjoyment; the point where so many lines converge, and where we rest before taking wider flight beyond.'[37] It was a full-hearted endorsement.

Eliza claimed, as an adult, that she did not understand what caused the coldness between Southey and her father. However, given how her father behaved to his children, and that his besetting sins were 'indolence and self-indulgence' – failings that were anathema to Southey – and that he apparently believed that while writing merely for pleasure and interest 'increased lustre', 'to depend for bread on one's pen was ... no better than fiddling in an orchestra, acting in a barn or selling yards of silk across a counter',[38] the reasons seem abundantly clear to an outsider. Southey judged that 'The Vicar is an unpleasant person to deal with – not in his manners, but in his course of conduct.'[39]

The new science and rebutting assassination

The Lynns' arrival coincided with the period when Southey and
Wordsworth first learnt more about a new scientific approach to the
Lake District. Adam Sedgwick had been appointed Woodwardian
Professor of Geology at Cambridge in 1818, upon which he said,
reflecting the Bishop of Llandaff before him, 'Hitherto I have
never turned a stone; henceforth I will leave no stone unturned.'[40]
Sedgwick's sister was married to the landscape artist William
Westall, whom Southey was both fond of and impressed by* – he
would become godfather to two of the Westalls' children. The
poets would therefore have the opportunity of gaining an intimate
introduction to the new science, for the professor was to become
one of the great geologists of the day. And a statesman living in
Keswick was to help start him on his way.

Previously, 'scientific travellers' to the region had just procured
individual rock specimens to contemplate, while the Parish had
produced men, primarily in the shape of Brownrigg, who applied
scientific principles to the mining industry on the coast. But now
scientific principles were applied to the land itself by Jonathan
Otley. A Langdale valley statesman, Otley was to live in Keswick
for more than sixty years, having moved there in 1791, in part
because of an offer to use Peter Crosthwaite's museum library.
Earning his living primarily by making and mending watches and
clocks, and much admired for being 'the cleverest man with his
hands hereabouts', Jonathan soon settled in lodgings up a flight of
extremely steep stone steps in King's Head Yard, a few strides from
Moot Hall – known to all as 'Jonathan's upt Steps'.[41]

As he tramped and re-tramped the mountains, Jonathan learnt
from his conversation with the miners, and thought and observed
and compared with consummate care, studying everything around
him (as, in fairness, had Peter Crosthwaite), recording his findings about local botany, meteorology, geology and minerology.
The first person properly to research and write about the wadd
mines, he also made the most detailed record of the appearances of

* Wordsworth had met him at Cambridge.

Derwentwater's mysterious 'floating island', with notes on international comparisons.[42] He constructed a rain gauge in Crow Park, to record accurate rain levels; actively supported the need for clean water, latterly seeing one of his earlier suggestions taken up; and kept tracks and paths in good order. By 1818 he had designed what was considered the 'first accurate map' of the Lake District;[43] and, unprecedently, from 1824, he recorded the level of Derwentwater each year.[44]

His claim to greatness is his 1820 paper, which was the first to recognise the threefold geological composition of the Lake District: Skiddaw Slate, Borrowdale Volcanic rock and the Silurian Slates, a classification that stands today. This was an awesome deduction from an Ambleside statesman with no formal tertiary education. But a chance encounter in 1812 with the brilliant scientist John Dalton, who was studying on the slopes of Helvellyn, had boosted his confidence. For, from then onwards, the two men would meet and discuss their work virtually every summer until Dalton's death in 1844.

Dalton came from Eaglesfield, a small village about 2½ miles southwest of Cockermouth; the birthplace of both Fletcher Christian and of Robert de Eglesfield, *the onlie begetter* of Queen's College, Oxford* (who had also endowed its eternal Cumberland link). His beginnings, as one of the seven children of an impoverished Quaker handloom weaver,[45] were as humble as Otley's; he attended school at the nearby Pardshaw Hall, where George Fox's meetings evidently still bore fruit. In 1793 he had published a textbook, *Meteorological Essays and Observations*, using his own and his friend Peter Crosthwaite's detailed observations of Kendal and Keswick. This, along with his fame as a Kendal teacher, gained him an invitation to teach at Manchester New College, recently set up to provide higher education for dissenters.[46] Here, Dalton's fascination with meteorology led to his discovery of Dalton's Law of Partial Pressures and eventually to Dalton's Atomic Theory, the first empirically based scientific theory of the atom.[47]

---

* Eglesfield named the college in honour of Philippa of Hainault, wife of King Edward III.

Otley acted as both colleague and guide whenever Dalton was back in the Lake District, and he had eventually been persuaded by the scientist to offer his papers to the Manchester Literary and Philosophical Society.* So, by the time Adam Sedgwick started his Lake District fieldwork in 1822, Otley's seminal paper had been published for two years, and the Cambridge professor also employed him as his guide. Sedgwick remarked that Otley 'was the leader of all we know of the country'; he adopted – and always acknowledged – Jonathan's 'three great divisions of the Slate formation',[48] and, as his own career took off, he used many of the Keswickian's figures and observations. And he would – consistently – recommend 'my good old friend Jonathan Otley' as 'the author of the best guide to the Lakes that was ever written',† saying, 'All Otley tells you may take for Gospel; for he only tells what he knows. He is a very clever truth-telling old man.'[49]

Otley was to say, in his eighties, that seeing each of the two geniuses he had been 'so kindly noticed by' every year had been 'one of my principal and greatest enjoyments'.[50] The stimulation of trained scientific minds, honed by peer interaction, can only have spurred him on. And both men kept in touch with him for the rest of their lives.

Sedgwick would also get to know Southey and would often delegate Jonathan to pass on his greetings, perhaps when the latter was taking up Southey's offer to use his library or mending a clock or a musical box.[51] For, although he was exceptional, in many ways Otley is a good example of what Southey saw as a typical Parish man, a product of a society he greatly admired. Treasurer of the Cockermouth and Penrith Turnpike Trust for three years in the 1820s and an evaluator for the Savings Bank, Jonathan had spent time as one of the Eighteen Men and was a loyal supporter of St Kentigern's, choosing a modest pew, next to a pillar and attending James Stanger's Bible class.[52] However, by the time Sedgwick and Southey became friends, Southey was a changed man, for the year

* To which, through Dalton's influence, he had been elected a corresponding member at the beginning of 1815. Smith, *John Dalton*, p. 49.
† In Professor Sedgwick's opinion, better than Wordsworth's. Both guides are described later.

1822, when Sedgwick took up his fieldwork, was one that would affect Southey for the rest of his life.

His *A Vision of Judgement*, the poet's frequently overwrought requiem for George III, envisaging his death as the moment for a poetic last judgment upon the events of his reign – into which he had interpolated his remarks about a 'satanic school' at the last moment – had been published in 1821. The new king, George IV, proved one of its few admirers and Southey's delight was evident. Byron, however, had already written the third canto of *Don Juan*, which, unlike the first two cantos, was to be published under his own name, and poured contempt upon the Lake Poets: 'Thou shalt believe in Milton, Dryden, Pope; / Thou shall not set up Wordsworth, Coleridge, Southey; / Because the first is crazed beyond all hope, / The second drunk, the third so quaint and mouthey.' Southey publicly ignored this – and the lines were not actually published until December 1821 – but Byron had by then not only taken Southey's 'satanic school of poetry' to heart but had become much stirred by an alleged ad hominem slander by Southey and turned to his brilliant, assassinating lampoon of Southey's laureate poem.

It was finished by the end of October, but his publisher, John Murray, chose to pass it on to another, and Byron's *The Vision of Judgement* did not reach the public until 15 October 1822. He portrayed Southey at the pearly gates starting to read a poem, when, after a few lines, the angels and devils flee in disgust, and St Peter knocks him out of heaven to fall into Derwentwater:

> He first sank to the bottom – like his works,
> But soon rose to the surface – like himself;
> For all corrupted things are buoy'd like corks,
> By their own rottenness.

Byron's portrayal of the 'poor, insane creature, the Laureate', who 'had turn'd his coat – and would have turned his skin', was unforgettable. Although many shared the critical view towards Byron's parody expressed in the October issue of the *Literary Gazette* – 'we know no language strong enough to declare the disgust and contempt which it inspires' – it was inevitable that such a well-ex-ecuted attack on the poet laureate would leave its mark on critical opinion – and on Southey himself. The impact of *The Vision of Judgement* on him was profoundly painful, and the humiliation of Byron's satire was to choke him as a poet. He would write soon afterwards, 'The love of writing poetry is departed from me'; his later bald statement to Uncle Herbert that he was 'no longer a poet'[53] acknowledging an immense personal defeat, one that, at some level, could be laid at the door of what he now thought of as 'the odious job' of being poet laureate.

No matter that by the end of 1824 all three of the younger romantic poets – the most significant critics of the work of three middle-aged Lake Poets – were dead, only Byron reaching his thir-ties. No matter that, tragically, they had no time themselves to show the effects of ageing upon inspiration. By the end of the decade, Southey could still write, 'it is in verse only that we throw off the yoke of the world and are as it were privileged to utter our deepest and holiest feelings'; he believed that only poetry, of the writing arts, was capable of improving society. Yet he had virtually foresworn it.

His response was both original and heroic and went almost unnoticed until it was uncovered by some recent scholarship.* For, once he was sure that nothing could be made of the job of being poet laureate, Southey simply went on strike. In 1822 he just stopped – completely, never writing another word as laureate right up until his death, twenty-one years later. There was a slight flurry of criticism when he produced nothing on Queen Victoria's acces-sion in 1837, but no one ever faced Southey down and made him write anything, and his regular small salary continued to be paid annually, without protest. This was his way, after nine years of trying to make the job work one way or another, of refusing to be enslaved by it, just as he had always promised himself. By the late 1820s, he had dropped the name poet laureate from his publica-tions. And when he was organising the 1837–8 complete edition of his work, he supressed some of the laureate poems and inter-spersed the others throughout the three volumes, often obscuring

* By Lynda Plant and Ian Packer.

the occasions for which they had been written – *Southey's* work, not the result of any public office. An admirable and successful bid to be his own man.

Family goodbyes

In 1820 Hartley Coleridge, at the end of his probationary year, had lost his fellowship at Oriel College, Oxford, as a result of 'intemperance'. Two years later, as Southey's confidence as a poet was being destroyed, Hartley's father realised that there was far more to this charge than Hartley had led him to believe and made plans to send his son back to the Lakes to be under his mother's eye and teach in Ambleside which, indeed, he did for some four years, until the school closed. Southey found the idea preposterous and refused to take Hartley in. 'What authority can a mother exercise over a man of six and twenty?'[54] Writing was Hartley's only resource and therefore London the only suitable place to be.

Sara Coleridge, while accepting that Hartley's effect on the diminished household of three adolescent girls and two infants would have been extremely problematic, soon wrote that she 'felt like one without plan or purpose; without hope or heart', and, for the first time in ten years, took her daughter Sara to London to see her father, in what would be a six-month stay in the South. There, her daughter shone and fell in love with her cousin, Henry Nelson Coleridge. But when they returned to the Lake District, the waspish effects of Edith's apparent depression made both Saras slightly less certain of their place in the household.

So, it may seem less surprising that, in 1824, Southey had a typical moment when his kitchen window was smashed at the dead of night – by, rather oddly, a leg of mutton[55] – and he engaged the town crier to warn that anyone found at Greta Hall at night would 'take the consequences' and face those pistols. But he was more cheerful celebrating the wedding of William Calvert's daughter, Mary, and Joshua Stanger. Mary's bridesmaids were Sara Coleridge, Isobel Curwen (the daughter of John Christian Curwen's heir, who was to have an unhappy marriage with John

Wordsworth) and Dora Wordsworth, with whom, after being sent
to board at school in Ambleside, Mary Calvert had forged a close
friendship that was to last Dora's lifetime.

Then, two years later, family tragedy struck again. All had
seemed propitious when Southey discovered, on returning from
a trip to the Netherlands,[56] that the Earl of Radnor had been so
impressed by his *Book of the Church* (1825) that he had made
him an MP by giving him a pocket borough – not that Southey
had the necessary property qualifications to take up the post;
indeed, he was never even able to cast his vote until, ironically, the
passage of the 1832 Reform Act, which he would much oppose.
Nevertheless, Keswick was 'in an uproar' when he arrived back
home, 'the people here having agreed my election is greatly to
the credit of the place'[57] and the band offered more music by the
lake for the evening. But Southey declined the offer, writing privately 'for me to change the scheme of life and go into Parliament,
would be moral and intellectual suicide'.[58] And well before the
music stopped, Southey was back at Greta Hall to make the tragic
discovery that Isabel, his penultimate child, 'the flower of a fair
flock', was mortally ill.

Cuthbert remembered later, 'It was the first time I had seen
sorrow enter that happy home; and those alternate days of hope
and fear, and how he paced about the garden in uncontrollable
anguish, and gathered all around him to prayer when all was over,
are vividly impressed in my mind'.[59] However, nothing could have
affected Southey as much as Herbert's death had done, and he
recovered. This time, though, Edith never really did; the serious
depression that then engulfed her would seldom lift and would
have a real effect on Greta Hall.

The town of Keswick continued to experience a boom during
the 1820s. Between 1800 and 1831 its population grew proportionally faster than that of any other town in the Lake Counties except
for the two county capitals, Carlisle and Appleby.[60] By 1829, a mail
coach was running daily through the town, the journey to London
taking two nights and three days. Pedlars still arrived with their
wares on fair days and holidays, but it was now the carters who
brought the most consistent flow of outside news and gossip to

the town. The 1829 Directory reported around 260 Keswick children attending 'the Church, Methodist, and Independent Sunday schools'.

Tourism was booming too. There were twenty lodging houses, the Queen's Head and the Royal Oak[61] reigned supreme among the thirteen inns and hotels, and a splendidly named coach, 'The Defiance', ran every day except Sunday from Queen's Head either to Penrith or Cockermouth and on to Whitehaven. Post-chaises and ponies could be ordered from the various inns, complete with 'intelligent guides'.[62] There were 'neat pleasure boats with experienced boatmen for the water',[63] and altogether 'the innumerable parties of pleasure, who crowd and enliven the neat little town of Keswick'[64] were pretty well catered for.

Hartley was by then declaring that Greta Hall had become a 'house of bondage'[65] for his mother and sister, which was clearly overdramatic. For when Henry Nelson Coleridge was finally earning enough for his wedding with Sara to take place on 3 September (seven years after the couple had originally fallen for each other), it was agreed that Sara's mother would leave Keswick and live with Derwent and his wife and their new baby – but she found herself surprisingly torn. Sara the elder knew that she should be with her family but was loth to leave Southey and 'this delicious country'[66] where her children had been raised, loth even to leave the Wordsworths, to whom she had become 'yearly *more* and *more* attached'.

It was a wonderful wedding. St Kentigern's was made resplendent in 'a smother of roses', the weather was fair, and the eight bridesmaids – Dora Wordsworth, the three Southey cousins and four Senhouse daughters (their father had taken over Derwent Bay while his own house was being done up) – all attended the bride, wearing roses in their hair. Sara was given away by Southey and married by the recently ordained John Wordsworth. The party returned to an elegant breakfast in Southey's study, and the couple then departed on their honeymoon (Southey accompanying them for part of their journey). The other wedding guests celebrated until four in the morning at the Senhouses' gala ball.[67] But Mrs Coleridge, who had stayed with her sisters at Greta Hall during the wedding, presumably to oversee arrangements, did not venture out.

She and Southey both hated the change, Southey reflecting that, next to a funeral, marriage was 'the most melancholy of domestic events', removing 'a beloved member of a family'.[68] In this case two; Mrs Coleridge and Southey had lived *en famille* for twenty-six years. The poet survived by giving a riot of entertainment for the thirty 'cathedrals' who visited Keswick that summer,[69] but it was an extraordinary wrench for Sara to leave her home and move south, staying with the Wordsworths en route, to make arrangements with them for Hartley's future.

When she arrived at Rydal Mount, Wordsworth clearly felt real sympathy for her, but Sara found Dorothy recovering from the first serious illness she had suffered in her fifty-six-years. Possibly a form of cholera, the affliction proved to be the beginning of her physical decline. The year before, William and his daughter, Dora, had surprisingly spent seven weeks with Hartley's father, visiting the Rhine. Dora maintained 'they get on famously but that Mr C sometimes detains them with his fiddle faddling, and that he likes prosing to the people better than exercising himself to see the Country'.[70] Wordsworth took the humbler role, 'roughly dressed ... fustian trousers, thick shoes'. He more resembled a mountain farmer than a 'lake poet', in the view of a fellow Englishman in Brussels. But on reflection this observer decided that 'his total absence of affectation or egotism' and 'something unobtrusively amiable in his bearing towards his daughter' actually gave Wordsworth the advantage.[71]

Sara had been left a legacy by Sir George Beaumont with Hartley in mind, and she arranged to send the Wordsworths regular sums of money for her son's board and lodging, plus parcels of clothes, all of which they would administer, as they too tried to keep an eye on him. Each day, Hartley was expected to come to Rydal Mount and say goodbye to his mother. But, just as he had failed to keep his promise to come to the wedding, Hartley stayed away.

What letters remain suggest that only his father's failure to return from Germany after Berkeley's death had wounded Sara more.[72] Mother and son were never to meet again.

Southey's Parish Colloquies

THE YEAR 1829 was a highly significant one for Southey in two other ways. Firstly, it was the year he lost his long fight against Roman Catholic emancipation. By 1828, tensions in Ireland had risen to boiling point, most of the British army being camped there 'to help the police'.[1] Something had to give, and Wellington's government proposed the Emancipation Bill, with the intention of avoiding an Irish civil war.[2]

The events leading up to the Glorious Revolution and its Protestant Constitution were still firmly in the public mind; the Bill of Rights 'as important to the eighteenth century as Magna Carta had been in the thirteenth'.[3] The Emancipation Act prescribed an oath to be sworn by Catholics to 'disclaim, disavow, and solemnly abjure' any intention to subvert the Church establishment or disturb or weaken the Protestant religion anywhere in the United Kingdom.[4] The pope neither approved nor condemned it, and, from the Duke of Norfolk down, Roman Catholics took the oath. Popular opinion against Catholic emancipation was strong, and George IV, who had sobbed as he signed the act, believing he was breaking his coronation oath, was closer to public opinion than the unreformed Parliament. Wellington believed that emancipation would ease Ireland's running sore, but it did not.

Southey, who had always believed that power for the Catholics in Ireland would create more violence, was distraught. He got up a petition from 'the inhabitants of Keswick' to the House of Commons, to protest, and inserted the subject into the preface of his new book, *Sir Thomas More: or, Colloquies on the Progress and Prospects of Society*, an attempt to decipher 'these portentous and

monster-breeding times'. Its publication in 1829 was the second significant public event for the poet that year; and, long planned, the
work most closely reflects his adult view of the state of the nation.
The route towards it had been a tough one, as we have seen, encom-
passing Southey's original desire to use his laureateship for the
public good and then, accepting defeat, to free himself both from
the censorship and the distorting lens the role had thrust upon him,
and be his own man. The man who wrote the *Colloquies*.

The idea had germinated twelve years earlier, when Southey
first experimented on a dialogue between himself, as a radical
youth, and Thomas More.[5] Within a year or two he had enmeshed
that idea with a description of the Parish, as living in it and learning about it, while becoming the Parish historian, was making an
essential contribution to his thoughts about, and solutions for,
society. Writing the *Colloquies* had given Southey comfort too. But
when he eventually published them, dedicated to Uncle Herbert,
Southey saw them as an autumnal work. Partly due to their long
gestation period, * they are extremely repetitive and certainly far
from perfect. But far more importantly, after a life lived during an
exceptional period of change and rancour, the *Colloquies* sum up
Southey's conclusions 'as a moral and political writer'.†

Certainty was hard to find for a man who had designed a utopia
before he was twenty and given his heart and soul to the French
Revolution, convinced that man was to be reborn, only to recoil later,
in honour, from the Revolution's terrible path. But by now Southey
was clear that his error was not the quest itself, but in 'fancying that
there is a short road' to such a radical change for society and imagining that the change could come about through the use of force.

He had said, when describing his library, 'In plain truth I
exist more among the dead than the living, and perhaps feel more
about them'; and most of his writing aimed at breathing life into
figures from the past and asserting not just their importance but
their relevance.[6] And this lifelong immersion had allowed him to

---

* In the 1823 letter to Joseph Cottle that acknowledged his love of writing
poetry was waning fast, Southey described the *Colloquies* as likely to 'go to
press in the winter'.
† Explanatory letter to Murray.

construct firm new ground to stand upon, ground from which to understand how society had arrived at its present parlous condition and to plot the course of a future path towards a time 'when men become Christians in reality as well as in name, something like that Utopian state of which philosophers have loved to dream'[7] – the essence of Christian hope for the world. Or, as he has Thomas More say, speaking as one of the dead come alive to him through study and love, 'having a clearer and more comprehensive knowledge of the past, we are enabled to reason better from cause to consequences, and by what has been, to judge what is likely to be'.[8]

Southey was proud of his conclusions in the *Colloquies* and of the basis from which they had grown, convinced that they would be important for future generations. And while hardly read at all today, they could still resonate with those whose youth coincided with the potentially revolutionary struggles during the 1960s, first for black civil rights in the United States and then against the Vietnam war. They provide much to reflect on for anyone today who has recently pondered the strength of the American constitution in the face of a presidential onslaught too. For Southey's post-war political stance had been strongly coloured by the perception that a myopia about the future on the part of a self-regarding French Enlightenment, was, to a degree, responsible for the Revolution – an occurrence that he believed had been 'more disgraceful to human nature than any other series of events in history'.[9]

Southey orchestrated his thoughts using his hard-won, systematic 'art of historical book-keeping' to annotate and re-annotate his exhaustively, and exhaustingly, collected encyclopaedia of historical knowledge. First, he told his brother, take separate foolscap quarto books for each subject to be covered, including one to describe the geography of the action; read the longest book on the subject to establish a chronology, keeping a margin to detail sources after each paragraph, and only write on one page. Split the opposite page two-thirds to one-third, the larger portion for all the changes that further – and further – reading will cause you to amend or expand upon the original, and the smaller section for your own evolving thoughts.[10] Read half a dozen books at once, so you never get tired of them, and cherish and record each small bit of colour or surprising detail that engages you and make up an index to retrieve them – and *never* rely on someone else's footnote, check yourself, and see what strikes you.

Then, once he had done the bulk of his research, Southey would give himself a period of simply reading widely, recording only those perceptions that threw light on the subjects that already interested him – and on which he had already started notebooks.* This whole process reflected what writing about history meant for Southey: a 'granular antiquarianism'[11] of colour and detail to attract and ground the reader in another time, drawn together with his general historical principles and conjectures, 'the general impressions and conclusions that much reading leaves behind'.[12]

The matter of the *Colloquies* is fifteen discourses on the progress and prospects of society, the connected subjects of the title, between what are really two Southeys: Montesinos, a young, optimistic version of himself, nevertheless disturbed by current society; and the ghost of Thomas More, who, while having a more pessimistic view, keeps his utopia firmly in mind. One that was far distant from Pantisocracy but not entirely unlike the Parish, 'a small-owner republic with laws to regulate and protect but also to compel labour'[13] and the couple's debate is 'relieved'[14] by a guided tour of it. This was in part Southey's response to the frequent calls for one, but at a deeper level a hymn of thanks and praise for its beauty.

However, fundamentally, the Parish provided the locus for some of the main arguments of the book; the primacy of affection for hearth and home, the value of community and the value of gradual change – values so well represented by Jonathan Otley, and the essence of Southey's experience there. Taking the form of walks, often starting from or finishing in his library at Greta Hall, the Parish material was extensive. Some thirty pages, for instance, are devoted to Crosthwaite church and St Kentigern, and

* This system over time, after the basic architecture had been affirmed and reaffirmed, was likely to reinforce the subjective bias of the record as, without heroic self-restraint, more and more selections would be chosen to illustrate points that already interested the collator, rather than setting off in pursuit of any contrary facts or opinions that wandered by.

throughout the *Colloquies* local history is related to the linear history of the country.

The *Colloquies* also gives us Southey's most extensive description of Parish scenery, offering the work's most direct writing. Full of feeling, perception and knowledge, they provide a living spring to refresh the reader – and a descant to some of the more self-consciously antiquarian language of the discussions. The poet tells Parish and family stories, identifies perfect viewpoints and walks, worships the Greta and, highlighting the value of nature to a full human life, captures the animal joy of a child's response and the restorative capacity of earlier memories. Fully Wordsworthian here, Southey lambasts the poverty of feeling demonstrated by those who sped through the Lake District, capturing sight after sight, unconsciously reflecting the priorities of the emerging consumer class that both poets distrusted. But he warmly welcomes all who find in the mountains 'a correspondent expansion and elevation of mind'.

Fixing the Parish clearly in the eye of the reader was sufficiently important to Southey that he had, in 1820, commissioned six engravings for the *Colloquies* from his good friend and chosen illustrator, William Westall.[15] Indeed, he may even have delayed publication until he had received all the illustrations he wanted.[16] Westall had had an adventurous youth, having been chosen, aged just eighteen, a year after he had become a probationer at the Royal Academy, to be the landscape artist for an early circumnavigation of Australia under the patronage of Sir Joseph Banks.* He made his first visit to

William Westall in an etching by William Daniell, based on an original portrait by his Royal Academy contemporary George Dance.

* Having sailed with Captain Cook, Banks was one of the most powerful men in science in Europe and sought material to classify the flora and fauna.

the Lakes in the winter of 1811 and returned to Keswick for part of every winter until 1820. The artist is said to have bumped into Lady Beaumont in a painting shop in Keswick and had been introduced to Southey and his circle by 1816. Early the next year, Southey was encouraging Westall to get on with his *Views of the Caves in Yorkshire* and urging John Murray to publish them.[17] By the summer, the artist, 'a man much to my liking', was lodging at the bottom of Southey's garden,[18] the only companion for the family that winter, as both he and Southey worked flat out.[19]

The resulting Yorkshire engravings Southey thought 'wonderful specimens of ingenuity and I dare say a great deal better than if he had understood the process of aqua-tinting engraving better when he began – for by blending them in some cases with the soft ground, and heightening it with the graver in others he has produced all that could be desired, in a way which would puzzle a mere mechanic to understand, and with all the freedom and originality of his genius – which is of a very high order'.[20] Wordsworth must have felt the same, as the engravings inspired three sonnets 'suggested by Mr W Westall's view of the caves in Yorkshire', the first time that Wordsworth's writing was prompted by a mechanical print. He uses the solidity of the 'frozen moment created by the artist'[21] to draw moral lessons; in Malham Cove, imagining the genesis of 'this semicircle profound' to be the giants who rebelled against the immortals in Greek myth, and – seeing that as a grand, but unfinished work – meditates through 'thought's optic glass'* about the futility of human ambition.[22]

From the 1770s artists had begun to focus on landscape, rather than just using it as background for portraits or classical or religious paintings, although originally the work had only been available in small, expensive print runs, usually aimed at antiquarians or natural historians.[23] But at the same time there was a revival of the woodcut, and in 1775 the introduction of the aquatint. This process introduced the possibility of light and shade to the old

---

* A subsequent change from the original 'Truth's mystic glass', which plays on upturning the old picturesque habit, exemplified by Thomas Gray, of using the Claude glass to alter the view.

techniques of dots and lines, and soon combined with improved printing and papermaking techniques (particularly in the 1810s)[24] to allow larger print runs of books with illustrations, priced at levels available to the middle class. Views – with a capital 'V' – were becoming democratised. The first for the Lake District was Joseph Farington's *Views of the Lakes*,[25] twenty engravings illustrating Gray's chosen viewpoints, published in book form in 1789. And the first poet to be illustrated with views etc., was Robert Bloomfield's *The Farmer's Boy* in 1800, which was wildly successful – the publisher, Longman, trebling the number of illustrations between the first and eighth edition in 1805.[26] This revolutionised the market; one soon joined by Burns and Cowper. And the accessible pricing meant that, as tourism grew, prints of places had overtaken prints of natural history and historical ruins in popularity.

Sketch of Sir George Beaumont and Joseph Farington painting a waterfall, by Thomas Hearne. A servant, or the artist, looks on.

The Lake Poets inevitably despised what Southey called 'picture books for grown children',[27] snippets of verse subservient to the illustrations. They equally despised the books' consumers; the sort of visitors, following the current 'migratory habits of the opulent classes', to the Lake District 'whose enquiries are mainly directed to find out what is not necessary for them to see';[28] and, of course, sales of their poetry were hardly likely to bring illustrated publishers rushing to their door. But at the new annual exhibition of the Society of Watercolours, the Lake District had risen from being the subject of one painting in 1805 to sixteen the following year, by artists who included J. M. W. Turner and Thomas Girtin.[29] While William Gilpin's desire to find the 'picture' in the landscape was justified, for him, by his sense that Joseph Farington had already portrayed the District accurately,[30] Girtin seems never to have visited at all, drawing on earlier sketches, such as Beaumont's *Borrowdale*, for inspiration. Nevertheless, the area soon became second only to Wales in popularity and, in purely commercial terms, it made sense for both poets to consider the idea of illustration for themselves.

After his Yorkshire engravings, Westall turned his attention to the Parish. In 1820 he published *Views of the Lake and of the Vale of Keswick*, for which Southey supplied an introduction gratis, as he thought that 'our scenery will for the first time be treated by a man who can do it full justice'.[31] And after publication, he declared that the *Views* 'gave the illusion of presence as never before in reproduction'.[32] Carefully accurate, their brilliance is shown in the contrast between the effects of cold, late-afternoon Lake District light in *Skiddaw*, a picture that nevertheless editorialises with the use of an extraordinarily sharp white for the sheep and Crosthwaite church to create especial attention, and the quite different effect of light in *Keswick Lake from the East Side*, set on the Keswick's Derwentwater quay. For Sara Hutchinson, 'the view of Derwent Water in twilight is above praise ... I could not have believed that an Engraving could have given the quiet and solemn feeling inspired by such a scene'.[33]

Montesinos's and More's reflections as they walk are often prompted by Parish views, but Southey intended his new commissions from Westall for the *Colloquies* to underline the area as a special place to be visited and learnt from,[34] rather than one that

Derwentwater, Bassenthwaite-Water and Skiddaw from Walla Crag by William Westall.

simply offered beautiful scenery. So, even though he is in no doubt that Westall's engravings 'have in them that which is common to poetry and painting',[35] he encourages the reader or tourist to take a deeper view than the pictures by themselves allowed[36], inviting them to move through the picture frame and engage in the joyful 'rough scramble up a rocky stream' with the children and earn the view. Upon arrival you would see: 'The water, the rocky pavement, the craggy sides, and the ash tree, form the foreground and the frame of a singular picture' – the picture you must break out of to experience the view. 'You then have a steep descent, open on one side of the lake, and on the other with the wood ... reaching to the shore [and] a distance of water, hills, and remote horizon, in which Claude would have found all he desired, and more even than he could have represented, had he beheld it in the glory of a midsummer sunset.'[37]

Southey tells Westall in a letter that the introduction of Claude to the description is intended as a compliment to his engraving on this page – *Derwentwater, Bassenthwaite-Water and Skiddaw from Walla Crag* – (which it no doubt was), but it was also designed to make the invitation to the reader or tourist irresistible and break out of the picturesque into full engagement. For Westall's remarkable engraving is not just of the view, but of Southey, the viewer, viewing it, visually reinforcing his Wordsworthian teaching – not just of the benefits of healthy walking, but of the chance to free oneself from the moral and spiritual diminishment of modern industrial life by fully experiencing the sustenance offered by a real engagement with nature.

*

Thomas More had been woken from the dead by Montesinos's constant thought about life in the age just before the Reformation, which both peripatetic philosophers thought the best period England had ever produced for its labouring people. As Southey writes, the 'feudal system had well-nigh lost all its inhuman parts, and the worst inhumanity of the commercial system had not yet shown itself'.[38] Villeins had been freed or had 'emancipated themselves' during the ravages of the Wars of the Roses,[39] and the monasteries were still there. 'None were beneath the notice of the priest, nor placed out of the possible reach of his instruction and his care,'[40] and the poor could still be relieved by charity and church.

But it is the disasters that followed that really drew the two men to that period, for each believed that he lived, or had lived, 'during one of the grand climacterics of the world'.[41] In More's case, the Dissolution, 'in every way injurious to the labouring classes'[42] – a prime reason for the religious Risings – disastrously intermingled in much of England with the effects of the Tudor sheep enclosures, when, as More said in his *Utopia*,[43] 'sheep began to devour men and fields and houses'.* Thus, 'a trading spirit ... gradually superseded the rude but kindlier principle of the feudal system: profit and loss became the rule of conduct'.[44]

---

* The passage also says: 'whereas the art of fleecing the tenancy was in its infancy and could not always be practised with the same certain success.' An excellent summary of Parish history.

While his contemporaries believed depopulation was the main scourge of the enclosures, for More (and Montesinos) the real disaster was the creation of outcast 'vagabonds', the men thrown off the land. And Southey's philosophers believed the numbers of these outcasts – men with little option but to prey upon the society 'which had so unwisely as well as inhumanly discarded them'[45] – to be unprecedented.* Thus, the march began, very slowly for the hundred years until the travails of the Civil War were over, of the evil of a 'vagrant and brutalised population': the 'process ... of raising a manufacturing populace and converting peasantry into poor was ... begun'.[46]

Now, in this second climacteric, the process was 'fast approaching its consummation'.[47] Montesinos, the Parish man, compared the Elizabethan enclosures to the 'extinction of small farms',[48] as his current example of the dangers of the move from feudal to commercial values. And he poured scorn on the consistently aristocratic post-war governments, their worst sin being to have allowed fast change without proper thought for the consequences. More fundamentally, he claimed that the word 'outcasts' was out of date; the poor and dispossessed were now so numerous that they 'have become a caste'. And a caste dangerously entwined with the popular enthusiasm for the 'levelling system of democracy': a hybrid of many forms that threatened, through government weakness and mob strength, to dismantle the 1689 Bill of Rights; the Protestant constitution sacred to both men as the permanent living inheritance of love and protection of country – and less than 150 years old.[49]

This essential feeling that the constitution was to be protected, rather than seen as a block to progress, was one of the crucial differences between the conservative and radical of the day. For Southey, it was a part of his adult reaffirmation of the Burkean understanding of the English nation 'as a partnership not only between those who are living but between those who are living, those who are dead and those who are not born'.[50] And he combines it with

---

* This analysis seems to ignore the effects of the fourteenth-century wars and plagues, perhaps not then well documented as Macaulay, in his review of the book, was to place the worst of the plagues in early Henrician England.

another Burkean cornerstone – 'local attachment', love of hearth and home. Burke's 'little platoon we belong to in society' was 'the first link in the series by which we proceed towards a love to our country, and to mankind',[51] as both become an extended family.

Southey's contribution to the Lake Poets' general adult reconnection with Burke was unique, for only he embodied – rather than simply described – it. Witness his Proem with its 'vignettes of familial harmony':[52] 'Here I possess ... what more should I require? / Books, children, leisure ... all my heart's desire.'[53] His children crowd and clamour around him, bursting with energy and enjoyment, and Southey is offering his own delight in his family as part of the blessings Burke describes.[54] In Wordsworth's poetry we seldom hear of his family, but in the *Colloquies* walking was familial and familiar – in the Parish – choosing favourite spots rather than exploring any faraway places. And Southey's chosen artist, William Westall, was necessarily part of his 'platoon', present at an occasion both described and illustrated with the caption *A day upon Saddleback, men, women and children, dine by the side of the tarn.* All connected. Home was a sanctuary within nature, and Southey 'blest God who had enabled me to fulfil my heart's desire and live in a country such as Cumberland'.[55]

More and Montesinos often circle around each other as they talk, reflecting both their walks and a frequent return to earlier thoughts. At times, akin to a Platonic philosopher, Southey judges by perfect forms, but there is seldom a current concrete conclusion. And More's 'Allow something, my friend, to the contradictious principle in human nature'[56] perhaps carried the freight of both the times Southey had lived through and some acknowledgment of their effects upon his own character.[57]

In his concluding Colloquy, Southey adopts Kant's argument[*] that, since nature has made man uniquely capable of reason, mankind can only fulfil its natural destiny when making full use of this determining characteristic; a process that would require universally accepted constraints upon individual and state actions.

---

[*] From Immanuel Kant's *Idea for a Universal History*, which had been recently translated by De Quincey.

Europe, Kant felt, was on the way. But it lacked real morality, a necessary condition, which should therefore be taught; one of Southey's central social ideas. His only amendment to Kant's argument was a change from his 'hidden plan of Nature' to 'the revealed will of God', and an insistence that the essence of the new education must be 'the precept of the Gospels'.

'Colloquy XV: The Conclusion' starts by describing the general curses of the age, above all the sinfulness of the nation (primarily exhibited by a weakening sense of duty and moral obligation); the destruction of religious obedience; and[58] the particularly British curse of industrialisation, which Southey had previously described as a system 'which breeds yahoos as fast as they can be bred and invents machines to throw them out of employ'.[59] But, as Montesinos finally unscrolls his roll call of hope, he praises the 'minute inquiries of the government into the state of the industrial poor', which reflected 'a general desire throughout the higher ranks for bettering [their] condition'. And he spells out his own prescription. State-helped emigration,[60] 'an improved parochial order',[61] more efficient policing, more moral, religious and constitutional education, the establishment of new co-operatives,* perhaps offered by the savings banks, and work provided by the state.

The whole curious structure of the *Colloquies* was true to its age, a synthesis of the conservative reaction to the French Revolution and a harbinger of Victorian medievalism and the Gothic Revival; but all with a radical twist. Ruskin, for one, found himself 'much pleased', when he read it in 1843.[62] And the *Colloquies* were frequently referred to in the heated national discussions about parliamentary reform,[63] a debate that had brought the French Revolution back into the forefront of the minds of intellectuals who had not experienced it themselves; Carlyle, Macaulay and John Stuart Mill all either contemplated, or actually wrote, books about it.

This was part of the context for Macaulay's 10,000-word review of the *Colloquies* in the *Edinburgh Review*.[64] But it is also

---

* The Brighton Co-operative Society looked as though it was going to put Robert Owen's ideas into effective practice. Owen visited Greta Hall and Southey admired him but regretted that he was not a Christian.

thought that the great historian consciously framed his article, with its timely celebration of Whig principles and vicious drubbing of the author, as a major stepping stone on the path to gaining a parliamentary seat, which he achieved later that year.[65] And since Southey was not only poet laureate, but the star of the opposition *Quarterly Review*, and was considered in those circles as 'the most important literary supporter of the Tories in the present day',[66] the attack had real currency.

The two men were chalk and cheese. For Macaulay, the Whig historian, history was linear, moving ever forward (as he famously said in the review 'A single breaker may recede; but the tide is evidently coming in'[67]), so his bias was always towards anything that fitted that progressive pattern. The Industrial Revolution, over the long term, and over any short period, was an unmitigated good. On the other hand, Southey, who had long been dwelling upon the idea of sheep farming as an explanation for the end of feudalism,[68] had pinpointed the pre-Reformation as the best time for the poor,* underlining the importance of the portrait of his sheep-farming Parish to the book, a shadow of a happier time. This was an inevitable red rag to a Whig, for whom the belief that any earlier time was better than the present day was, of course, anathema.

Macaulay's judgment is categorical: the work is 'an absurd fiction wholly destitute of information and amusement'.[69] 'In the mind of Mr Southey reason has no place at all'; his writing is only saved from 'utter contempt and derision ... by the beauty and purity of the English'. Much of his scorn centres on Southey's form of argument, which, had he taken Southey's admission that 'I am not one of those fastidious readers who quarrel with a writer for telling them too much'[70] as the cue for a good joke about the *Colloquies*' incessant repetition, might have fallen away. But, like all good invective, his attack contains elements of truth, such as his suggestion that the predominant cast of Southey's mind seems to be 'I do well to be angry' (reminiscent of Carlyle's later subtle

---

* He had written to Rickman about the *Colloquies* as early as 14 January 1820 and by the end of the month (28 January) was asking him for access to government files to check a detail about sheep-farming under Henry VII.

portrait of the poet). And this brings up the crucial distinction between the two men. Macaulay, born in 1800, was too young to have experienced the immediate impact of the French Revolution and its aftermath, while Southey's entanglement with it did indeed create a later problem with tone.

For, in theory, Southey's original fanatical certainty about the value of the French Revolution now completely disqualified any expression of intemperate enthusiasm. Yet he had begun to believe 'we sacrifice too much to prudence; and, in fear of incurring the danger or the reproach of enthusiasm, too often we stifle the holiest impulses of the understanding and the heart';[71] a danger when the less educated were prey to demagogues who incited exactly the previous passion for change that Southey had seen destroy a country and spill blood throughout a continent. *Of course*, Southey now thought change should be approached gradually and with care, yet, equally, he was the same man he ever had been, and his original passion for perfection and the betterment of the life of the poor gnawed away at him. The tension is evident and is, in part, responsible for the 'peculiar austerity' that 'marks almost all Mr Southey's judgements of men and actions'.[72]

But Macaulay's attacks, often witty and acute, are also economical with the truth. A particular instance is his use of the two occasions when Southey employs a Parish example to expound on industry. First, there are Southey's comments comparing the few old cottages in Applethwaite with the nearby 'Millbank Village', the five new workers' cottages at Dover's Millbank factory. This is a short passage in the seventh Colloquy but provides the longest quotation Macaulay uses in his review, and so is, presumably, either central to his argument, or considered the safest passage to attack. Southey gives a lovely, Wordsworthian description of the Applethwaite cottages and their much-loved gardens, which reflect 'some regard to neatness and comfort, some sense of natural, and innocent, and healthful enjoyment'. They are 'such as the poet and the painter equally delight in beholding'.[73] He then compares them with 'the new cottages of the manufacturers ... upon the new manufacturing pattern – naked, in a row',[74] and entirely without connection to their wider environment.

This juxtaposition carried the weight of comparing the 'effects of industry and agriculture' and asking why everything connected with manufacturers, 'from the largest of Mammon's temples to the poorest hovel in which his helotry are stalled ... present such features of unqualified deformity', all of one character, which 'time will never mellow, nor nature clothe' and 'will remain always as offensive to the eye as to the mind'.[75] On the face of it, Southey had set himself up for a fall, and without the proper context (see below), it is easy to make the comparison seem risible.

Macaulay attributed the poet's stance to a picturesque view of history, based merely on taste, making 'the picturesque the test of political good',[76] and his jibe stuck, as the *Colloquies* are still often looked at – wrongly, I think – in terms of the picturesque today.* 'Romantic history', another current description,[77] is far more robust, as it can incorporate the Romantic view of the relationship between nature and moral or spiritual improvement and Wordsworth's concept that the Lake District provides an image of 'Man, Nature and Human Life'.[78]

But, fundamentally, the form of the *Colloquies* is based upon what the two moralists see as they walk in the Parish. This must mean that the Parish itself is, at one important level, the proper, and indeed only, context, within which to judge the descriptions of it. And we know that Dover's factory was the pre-eminent industrial example of the day in the Parish and was yet to reach the peak of its formidable export business. We know too that no new residents had yet disturbed the old Applethwaite cottages,† which still perfectly matched Wordsworth's descriptions of the indigenous cottages of the Lake District, which 'clothed in part with a vegetable garb ... in their very form call to mind the processes of nature'.[79]

Macaulay asks, with heavy irony, 'Does Mr Southey think that the body of the English peasantry live, or ever lived, in substantial or ornamented cottages, with box-hedges, flower-gardens,

* Unless the term 'picturesque' is expanded to such an extent, for example anything connected with what could be a picture or in a picture.
† As we have seen in the correspondence between Dr Leith and Wordsworth.

bee-hives, and orchards?'[80] The 'body of English peasantry' is not, of course, a good description of Southey's co-parishioners, but the Parish answer is yes, many had and many did, if we are to believe Wordsworth's portrait in the *Guide* or our eyes today. And there is absolutely nothing in Southey's description, except the naming of hollyhocks, daffodils and snowdrops, all prolific in the Lake District, that is not mentioned in his fellow poet's 'representative idea of a mountain cottage in this country',[81] a description that necessarily intertwines the evolution of the cottages and their inhabitants: 'These houses have been, from father to son, inhabited by people engaged in the same occupations ... being for the most part proprietor ... at liberty to follow [their] own fancy'.[82]

This is a qualitative distance away from the assumption of consistent, universal, grinding agricultural poverty from time without end, which appears to lie beneath Macaulay's whole assault. An assumption that never underlay Wordsworth's indigenous history, and most certainly did not reflect the long period of the French wars when the Parish reality had been decidedly favourable compared to most of the rest of England.* There is perhaps no reason why Macaulay should have known this, but his notably self-serving enumeration of relative poor rates, to suggest that there was less poverty in the industrial towns than in the country, forced him to mention that in the returns for the year ending March 1828 'Cumberland alone, of the agricultural districts, was as well off as the West Riding of Yorkshire'.[83] Had he considered seriously the area Southey was describing, this should have given him pause for thought.

For it is the Parish that Southey is describing throughout the *Colloquies*; it was his living example of a better environment for the poor. Local history is a part of national history. And the Parish's old principles of ancient custom and good neighbourhood

---

* Macaulay could not have known (or indeed cared) how foolishly some of his comments would appear to those whose lives are described in the *Colloquies*. For instance, to the hill farmer, with his historical oat-based diet, the remark that 'our parish poor now eat wheaten bread. In the sixteenth century the labourer was glad to get barley.' Or the idea that the glorious future would include 'cultivation, rich as that of a flower-garden ... carried up to the very tops of ... Helvellyn', when even Latrigg had proved too high for oats.

had produced remarkable results: the levels of money given to its school and poor, all managed by the Eighteen Men, being quite extraordinary. A Whig enquiry into the state of national charities had been published in 1821, the year in which Carlisle's population was 14,531; the parish of St Bees, including Whitehaven, 19,969; Workington 7,188; and Crosthwaite 4,087 – similar to Wigton, a quarter less than Penrith and a third less than Cockermouth.[84] Yet the Parish endowments for the school and the poor were producing more than *double* almost every other parish in Cumberland. And before the end of the seventeenth century the Crosthwaite charity money had produced more than double *all* the Cumberland parishes; entirely managed, by then for around 400 years, by those whom Macaulay felt had been subsumed by poverty and, one suspects, ignorance.

Even industry was made gentle by the old Parish values. In 1829 Daniel Dover had built a Sunday school for the children of the millworkers, today the Underskiddaw Church Room, while his grandson and his wife would leave £800 for the grammar school. Throughout the 1830s the company would sell quantities of potatoes to the millworkers, probably as some form of help in the tough post-war conditions. Other industrialists, of course, spent money on charity, but whether they gave special discounts to poorhouses or would accept, as Dover did intermittently, a ten-gallon cask of double-strength gin, a quarter of mutton, a firkin of butter or a cow as payment is distinctly doubtful.[85] In all, there is tangible proof of consistent concern for, and managerial coherence of, welfare in the area Southey was describing. Macaulay patronised too liberally.

He was also inaccurate, at best, when he used the passage quoted to illustrate that Southey held no truck with 'mortality and statistical tables', the basis of his main argument against the poet. Southey's good friend John Rickman was the leading demographic statistician of the day and freely supplied Southey with the quantitative information he required for his social essays.[86] Judgments about poverty or the standard of living must consider longevity and health, as well as employment, and Macaulay admits that there had always been a higher 'mortality rate' in cities than in the countryside. But his use of the birth and death statistics (evidence that was 'far too low and vulgar for a mind as imaginative as that of Mr Southey') gave him the 'best reason to believe' that this contrast had not only 'diminished in an extraordinary degree' over the previous fifty years but, by implication, would soon become more than whittled away.[87] Yet today's statistics suggest that life expectancy, which had been steadily rising, stagnated from the mid-1820s for the next fifty years, as industrialisation became an ever more potent force.[88]

However, while Macaulay's own arguments give one little faith that statistics could not be manipulated by emotional or intellectual bias, since the end of the French Revolution probability and statistics had become seen by all as the necessary basis of future analysis. The old faith in Providence and a benevolent God had been largely lost,[89] but Southey's analysis reflected not just Parish truth but a growing split between post-Napoleonic agrarian and industrial capitalism as well. And, in time, any argument about worth would fall to his side of the argument too. Once the Dover factory ceased work in 1886, Daniel's great-nephew[90] put everything that he could up for sale, simply demolishing the fulling mill, the new carding mill and 'Millbeck Village'. The Applethwaite cottages, however, remain decidedly valuable today.

Southey had long acknowledged the possibility that industry might eventually do the working labourer some good, as 'whatever diminishes the necessity for bodily labour will be a blessing for mankind',[91] and the second Parish prompt to thoughts about industry comes in 'Colloquy XII' upon the Greta. The philosophers look down upon a large cotton mill surrounded by workers' cottages in a position that 'the founder of a monastery might well have chosen for its seclusion and beauty, and its advantage of wood and water'. The size, shape and position of the mill remind Montesinos of a convent, and when More asks whether the 'manufactory' or the convent would lead to more melancholy reflections, Southey gives an unequivocal acknowledgment that without industry Britain would have had neither the 'means or men' to have prosecuted the vital and long-drawn-out war against France and that 'this good is paramount to all other considerations'.[92] This passage is entirely ignored by Macaulay, allowing him to mischaracterise Southey as uniformly opposed to industrialisation.

Yet the matter of the clash between the two giants wasn't really about progressive and reactionary attitudes. It was fundamentally about the way Southey wished to bring about improvements for the poor, about whom he had a viscerally different attitude. Not only did he not accept Adam Smith's reading of commercial progress as part of the linear progress of society in general, he actively objected to its advocacy of *laissez-faire* and thought *The Wealth of Nations* 'a hard-hearted book'.[93] And his own calls for universal education of a moral nature, infrastructure projects to create employment and sponsored emigration, all involved state intervention and aid – the very opposite of the Whig position.

Macaulay's view was that the profit motive inevitably meant that all action was most successfully undertaken by the individual. 'Mr Southey's idol, the omniscient and the omnipotent state ... will best promote the improvement of the nation by confining themselves to their own legitimate duties ... by maintaining peace, by defending property, by diminishing the price of law and by observing strict economy in every department of the state.'* It's an argument that rumbles on today, but one can safely assume that the welfare state was not part of Macaulay's expectation of the ever upward path of the nation. Just as, today, few would disagree with the following judgment made about Southey's work in a study of *The Quarterly Review Under Gifford*: 'In a series of brilliant articles he had promoted a philosophy of social reform that greatly resembles the modern welfare state.'[94]

For many, Southey's argument about state intervention provides the key that unlocked the debate about his 'apostasy'. Not so for Macaulay, who, having one essential historical principle, preferred this in a man, whether right or wrong,[95] and upped the attack by categorising Southey as a violent ultra-Tory,† writing that he

---

* Later, Keynes argued that the utilitarian moral philosophers of the eighteenth and nineteenth century had damaged society by popularising 'a perverted theory of the state', guided by 'business arithmetic', in which the judgment of the social value of any activity was whether it turned a profit, resulting in a market that failed to deliver a host of real social goods that were wanted and would have been enjoyed.

† One description of this group was those who opposed Catholic emancipation and wished to uphold the Bill of Rights. But it does not sound as though

'passed from one extreme of political opinion to another, as Satan in Milton went round the globe, contriving constantly to "ride in darkness". Wherever the thickest shadow of the night may at any moment chance to fall there is Mr Southey.'[96] So that was clear.

With hindsight, Southey's argument, prefigured in the 1812 *Quarterly Review*, that the rapid increase in the numbers of the poor 'rendered their physical and moral condition worse at present than in any former time since the shock of the Reformation subsided',[97] may well have been the first shot in another ongoing dispute, about whether industrialisation did or did not damage the condition of the poor, Southey's position being taken in the twentieth century by historians of the far left, such as E. P. Thompson and Eric Hobsbawm. The solution he developed in the *Colloquies* to ameliorate the problem was seen by the philosopher John Stuart Mill as the 'connecting link' that joined his life and career together, a position also adopted in the twentieth century by the critic and writer Raymond Williams.[98] It was clear to both that Southey's mature attempts to mitigate the effects of unbridled market forces on the poor, by using state intervention, grew organically out of his early radicalism.

*

Soon after the publication of the *Colloquies*, Anthony Ashley-Cooper, the future Earl of Shaftesbury, who was at the start of his parliamentary career as a great Tory social reformer, and with whom Southey had no acquaintance in common, got in touch with him to offer a helpful fact, and the two started a surprisingly intimate correspondence. On Boxing Day 1829, the year of publication, Southey had written to Wilberforce, 'When I was young I was proud, presumptuous and positive. My views were clear because they were confined ... I had no misgivings, and was so conscious my intentions were right that it never occurred to me even as a possibility that my opinions might be wrong.'[99] What *work* to dismantle all that and find some basis upon which to rebuild; and

Macaulay was using the description in that limited sense.

then, in the raised temperatures of the day, to end up in a long-running, public dogfight.

Southey expressed the same point slightly differently to Shaftesbury three years later. 'I was some years older than you are now before I gained firm ground for my political opinions. They were rather feelings than opinions before that time – rather exacted by sympathy or provocation, than taken up upon enquiry and reflection, and in that state they might have remained',* wrote Southey, until he was forced to examine their foundations in his work for the *Edinburgh Annual Register*[100] and, in doing so, changed his mind about parliamentary reform. He needed to be both researching and writing in order to think rather than merely to react.

By 1833, Southey was offering advice to Shaftesbury and another new young friend, Lord Mahon, both about the passage of the bill concerned with the abolition of slavery and the so-called Ten Hour Bill aiming to reduce the working hours of children in factories. He had already sent Shaftesbury a recent Colloquy he had written† about the factory system, the reform of which was their shared passion, and had got Cuthbert, then fourteen, to sign the petition he had organised in support of the Factory Act. Its passage, in 1833, was a genuine step forward.

Up until then, the laws regulating the employment of children had only covered cotton manufacturing, and had no means of enforcement, while the new Act covered all textile factories, except for lacemaking. It also finally created a structure for factory inspectors, even if the number initially legislated for – four – was risible. Children's conditions were, at least in theory, mildly improved and included two hours' daily schooling. It wasn't as much as Southey or Shaftesbury wanted, and Parliament played the usual games. It would take another seven attempts to bring about the Ten Hour Act for all women and young people between the ages of thirteen and

---

* As Carlyle had sensed.
† With John Rickman. Southey had been protesting the cruelty of the 'hellish' factory system for some 'five and twenty years' but recent publication of a parliamentary report on child labour made him realise that 'bad as I knew it to be, I knew not the half of its barbarity till [Sadler's] Report has published it to the world'. Letter to J. W. Warter, 23 January 1833.

eighteen, which both had been aiming at and, in 1847, Shaftesbury finally achieved.

Southey had died four years earlier, and Shaftesbury wrote in his diary upon his death, 'I loved and honoured him; that man's noble writings have, more than any other man's, advanced God's glory and the inalienable rights of our race. He was essentially a friend of the poor, the young and the defenceless – no other so true, so eloquent, and so powerful.'[101] An ultra-Tory, in any sense that a modern analysis can comprehend, Southey was not; he was what became called a Radical Tory, albeit one with a rash tongue and pen – part of an honourable tradition. And he was more sinned against than sinning.

Part Three

Living in Interesting Times,

1829–74

Fields, River and Greta Hall, by William Westall. The house is atop the hill
adjacent to Crosthwaite Vicarage, close to St Kentigern's.

A Church Fracas, the
Marshalls and Guides

SOUTHEY'S *COLLOQUIES* HAD been rich in real Parish history, but the directories were reflecting a process that continued to bury it. Back in 1797, as we have seen, the Crosthwaite/ Brathmyre manor, the locus of the Parish church and the manor of the Fountains' monks was entirely omitted by William Hutchinson. In 1816, *Magna Britannia*[1] reinstated Great Crosthwaite but ascribed its ownership to the manor of Brundholme, itself described as lying 'in the townships of Great Crosthwaite [in which, the directory affirmed, stood Monk Hall, still belonging to the Le Flemings] and Under-Skiddaw'. This change had probably been fairly recent, as Great Crosthwaite and Underskiddaw were the only townships in the Parish not described in detail, which indicates some confusion or mystification. Indeed, the manor of Brundholme may have been included only at the insistence of Richard Watson, Bishop of Llandaff,* for the next directory did not mention Brundholme at all.

Parson and White, a usually reliable directory, which appeared in 1829, the same year as the *Colloquies*, relegated 'Crosthwaite Great and Little' to 'very small hamlets in the township of Underskiddaw', along with High Hill (like Great Crosthwaite, certainly part of the original Crosthwaite/Brathmyre manor)† and Applethwaite and

---

* Watson died the year *Magna Britannia* was published.
† The newly mentioned High Hill, originally Holy Hill, leads from Crosthwaite church to Keswick and borders the Howrahs on its southern side, the lands to which St Kentigern's mass christenings were ascribed. Running from the Derwent, past Vicarage Hill, to the Greta, all this land, along with Crosthwaite, was certainly part of the original Brathmyre/Crosthwaite manor.

Millbeck, which were unequivocally Brundholme territory. So the manor that gave its name to the 90-square-mile Parish, and which had included both the Parish church and Monk Hall, had now become a hamlet in a township with no inhabitants of its own.

The church had been changing too. The evangelical movement had been weakened after the French wars because of the widespread belief that the dissenters had initially supported it. And the green shoots of a new religious sense had begun to emerge ever since John Henry Newman had begun to preach in Oxford back in 1822. A search for beauty and truth and a 'sacramental sensibility' had started to spread among his undergraduates, instigating the Oxford Movement.[2] Popular sympathy for the Middle Ages had been growing too, superficially through the picturesque movement, monastic ruins no great advertisement for the Reformation, but more profoundly through the influence of the Romantic poets who Newman believed 'to be part-cause of the Oxford Movement as the human spirit yearned for new depth'.[3] And Newman, John Keble and, in time, Edward Pusey,[4] reacting against the Calvinist stress upon individual response to both God and the 39 Articles, had begun to look back beyond the Reformation and 'recover the study of the ancient fathers', disinterring and incorporating devotional treasures that the Church of England had lost.[5] This Anglican High Church religious revival was part of a pan-European movement[*] and their influence would grow as the 1830s progressed.

By the end of the decade, its adherents were named the Tractarians, in recognition of the fact that Newman and his colleagues had issued a series of tracts affirming the Anglican church's unbroken link to the ancient fathers as part of one Apostolic Catholic Church, reflecting its unique Protestant claim to practise and uphold apostolic succession. The movement was to break down because of church politics and popular misunderstanding of the word 'Catholic', but it led to a genuine Christian revival. As observed by Owen Chadwick, the distinguished historian of the Victorian church, its appeal to the English religious conscience, through the mixture of a 'stern call to discipline and self-denial ...[6]

---

[*] Mysticism became the German solution.

the poetry of heart in its hymns [and the] sacramental sensibil-ity in their worship'[7] was 'to affect the duration of the Victorian Church'.[8] The movement 'strengthened the soul of the Church of England',[9] imparting 'a new beauty and depth to the authentic traditions of English religion'. And the devotion and character of the Anglican clergy would change between 1825 and 1850, as the desire for 'the liturgy to be reverently and prayerfully celebrated [and] churches no longer left to damp and dilapidation' became the accepted normality.[10]

More mundanely, at St Kentigern's, the pulpit, pews, roof and more were sufficiently dilapidated that they all needed to be patched up again in 1829.[11] And, two years later, John Ruskin reported that the church seats, although they had been dusted, were so dirty and greasy that the girls in his party almost feared to sit down on them, in case they ruined their dresses. It wasn't until after Southey's death that the church was properly restored – in the poet's honour – for the first time since its early Tudor rebuilding. The old school building had been on its last legs too, and a special subscription had been raised to enhance the endowment and allow *its* complete rebuilding. The Eighteen Men issued instructions that the builders were to reuse some existing wooden parts of the school building, and return any that were unused to their keeping; and the new building was raised and finished during the summer holidays.[12] It was apparently a very efficient performance, despite the dean's crit-icism, in 1817, that the Eighteen Men 'are said to be as arbitrary as the great Turk' – a revelation of the long-suspected view that the clerical establishment, irked by the law, felt that the Eighteen Men didn't know their place. The dean also reported that, on his visit, the school had 200 pupils, the master was paid £65 and the assistant £25.*

There was now a stable by the main gate into the churchyard for the use of both pupils and churchgoers, separate lavatories and two schoolrooms, the smaller one housing the twenty-eight schol-ars of the upper school, which took pupils up to the age of sixteen, and the larger one for the main school, sitting over a hundred

---

* In 1833 there were definitely 200 pupils: 160 boys and 40 girls.

pupils of both sexes from the age of five upwards. These pupils included another Banks (no 'e' in the name locally by now), who was also to make a fortune in London, and 'a swarm of children from the poorhouse',[13] girls and boys of all ages benefiting from his forebear's charity. And the children were conscious of the mix themselves, old students erecting a headstone upon the headmaster's death in 1821, with the somewhat pompous but well-meaning comment that, under him, 'The school was a little world of all sorts and conditions, but thanks to the high principles and indomitable energy of the master, no ill effects came of the dissimilar circumstances of the scholars'.[14]

The established church was being badly damaged by its resistance to reform of the parliamentary franchise. In 1830, Earl Grey, having formed the first full Whig government for almost fifty years, introduced his parliamentary reform bill; when the House of Lords rejected it the following year, only two bishops voted in favour. The press pointed out that, had the other twenty-one joined them, the bill would have passed. This created popular fury; eight thousand people stormed through Carlisle and burnt an effigy of Bishop Hugh Percy. The turbulence became confused with a cholera scare affecting much of the country and when the king called for a national day of fasting and humiliation, the preachers, almost to a man, called for the betterment of the lot of the poor.[15]

Large numbers attended the two Sunday church services in the Parish, 'many attending who were not church goers'; a situation Southey believed to be generally the case in Cumberland, except in Carlisle, where the press 'has educated a rabble who are ripe for violence. They cannot be worse in any part of England.'[16] In Parliament, the Lords rejected the bill again; the government fell and was then returned, the Duke of Wellington having failed to form a Tory administration against a backdrop of violent unrest in the country. By June 1832, not a single bishop opposed the bill's passage through the Lords.

Meanwhile, Southey, who had become more active in local affairs, had agreed to be elected to a version of a local board of health.[17] His most immediate fear was the threat of cholera, which he believed was spread by vagrants travelling from the cities into the countryside. He even succeeded in getting the Keswick horse races cancelled in July 1832,[18] overcoming opposition to the move on the part of brewers and publicans. By October, he could report that, despite the arrival in Keswick of refugees from Whitehaven and Workington – where the disease 'had been most fatal'[19] – the town was free of it.

By then, Reverend James Lynn was on a five-year leave of absence, which had started some time in 1831, living in the place of his heart's desire, Gad's Hill Place, near Rochester, where Bishop Percy had previously reigned. A young, evangelical curate, the Reverend J. W. Whiteside, had been left in charge of St Kentigern's and the vicarage. Naturally strict, in August 1832 he rounded up the churchwardens after the second lesson and strode off, with his posse, to tour the public houses, intending to present their occupants to the ecclesiastical court for profaning the Sabbath. By the time he reached the Twa Dogs in Brigham, the message had got around and the pub was empty – but it was clear where the mêlée of men on the nearby Calvert Bridge had come from. A fierce lecture ensued.

The parishioners would probably have continued to live and let live, but the Reverend Whiteside did not do so. The next Sunday, he lashed out in his sermon 'with little restraint',[20] condemning the people of Keswick as ungodly and drunken, and the parishioners decided that they had had enough. The Eighteen Governors of the Free School, the Eighteen Sworn Men, quickly designed a poster to put up all over town, announcing a special general meeting of the whole vestry, or congregation, the following week. The anger behind its conclusions is palpable. It was unanimously agreed on 1 September:

'1. That the Head Master and Usher of the Free Grammar School of Crosthwaite [who must have supported the curate], are to have notices delivered to them, to quit the said school on the 1st of December next, and to give peaceable Possession of the said School to the Eighteen Sworn Trustees for the time being ...
'4. Equally unanimously agreed that the Sunday School now held in the said Free Grammar School should not be con-

tinued after the second day of September. NB. Should the
present Eighteen Sworn Trustees allow the Sunday School or
any other Institution to take Place in the said Free Grammar
School, they think it would be a breach of their Trust.'

It was also resolved that a 'small Quarter Pence' would be paid
by each pupil for the heating of the school. The sum was later
accounted for more clearly in a flyer in 1884, promoting a new
teaching method, as 6d. a year.[21]

The vestry resolution took the traditional distrust between the
vicar (or the curate in this case) and the parishioners to levels not
reached since the bishop had imprisoned some of the Eighteen
Men in 1615. And the fact that the ruling was to be enforced the
very next day, and included a strong prohibition upon the freedom
of action of the Eighteen Men, speaks volumes about the general
strength of parochial feeling. So, it must have been a distinctly
queasy Reverend Whiteside who announced the ruling from the
pulpit the following Sunday.

Southey's view was that, while he believed Sunday schools
would do no harm, he would far rather see children going to church
with their parents 'than at the heels of school-master'.[22] But he was
on the side of Reverend Whiteside, praising him 'for his courage'
in the *Quarterly Review*. Meanwhile, Sunday school continued to
take place in the church until James Stanger (described by Eliza
Lynn as 'a rich adherent of the energetic curate')[23] came to the
rescue and spent £1,000 building a Sunday school on High Hill.
The girls' elementary school moved in to fill up the weekdays,[24]
and by the end of 1833 it had eighty pupils, double the number of
four years earlier, their learning restricted to reading, writing and
plain needlework, and their parents paying 2d. a week.[25] James
Stanger produced books for a free library and played the organ
at the Sunday school, which, fourteen years later, was reported as
attracting 350 children (an impossible number for its size).[26]

The Parish, in the nineteenth century, called noticeably more
general vestry meetings than had been the case earlier; different
committees – not only the Eighteen Sworn Men – debated a range
of different subjects. For instance, back in 1813, the decision to

spend extra rates to cover the £360 needed for church repairs was announced by 'We the Minister, Churchwardens and Parishioners', although the checking mechanism was two men in each of the three main areas of the Parish (all bearing old names) who may have been some of the Eighteen Men. Another group – all farmers, and all familiar names – had met, after a public notice had been put up in 1814 to discuss raising the fees payable for destroying foxes; the price had been held for a hundred years and the animals had now become 'far more than at former periods'. Five years later, the judgment was modified so that only half the going rate was paid for foxes caught outside the Parish or during a hunt.

Enter the Marshalls

The most significant change to take place during the Reverend Lynn's five-year absence was the sale, in 1832, of the Castlerigg and Derwentwater manor to the Marshalls. John Marshall had married Jane Pollard, a fellow Unitarian – and Dorothy Wordsworth's intimate friend from her time with 'Aunt Threlkeld' – in the year the Wordsworth siblings had stayed together in the Parish. Born well off in Leeds, Marshall had soon moved the family cloth-selling concern into the new business of flax manufacturing and, by the end of the wars with France, had transformed his £7,000 inheritance into a £400,000 fortune. A workaholic, innovator and risk-taker, Marshall was long the most successful flax manufacturer in England. Having spent generously on charitable causes as well as on his family, Marshall's wealth was variously assessed on his death in 1845 at between £1.5 and £2.5 million, almost unimaginably large sums at the time.[27]

The magnate had become attracted to Keswick and the Lake District on his honeymoon and, during Jane's years of childbirth and nursing, had spent three days in 1800 touring the area in the Wordsworths' company. The 1790s had been as character-forming for Marshall as they were for the poet, and in 1793 he had come close to bankruptcy. The lesson Marshall took from this experience was that he had to be 'at the Mill from six in the morning to nine at night, and minutely attend to every part of the manufactory', aiming for 'distinction and riches'.[28] On the face of it, manufacturer and poet seem like chalk and cheese. However, Marshall's touring diary reflects both his visceral reaction to dramatic natural scenery, particularly the crags at Wythburn and Honister,[29] and his passionate interest in woodland, indicating that there was a genuine basis for a friendship between the two men. In 1807 the pair had a constructive discussion about their mutual interest in planting; Wordsworth's acceptance that there *was* a place for larch came out of these conversations. And information Marshall provided about Scottish forestry would later find its way into Wordsworth's *Guide to the Lakes*.

By 1810 their relationship had become closer. Marshall, who was worried about Jane's health – she had already borne ten of her twelve children – had decided to rent a country seat in the Lake District. Dorothy had advised them against renting Ormathwaite Hall, on the grounds that the house was small and in poor condition, so Marshall decided on Watermillock on the western side of Ullswater. Here the couple enjoyed a summer that 'answered our utmost expectations both as to health and happiness'.[30] Delighted with the area, Marshall soon purchased some land close by and began to build his own country house, which he called Hallsteads. A proud man, with an acute sense of his own worth, he had absolutely no pretensions to be anything other than he was, at the forefront of the modern 'aristocracy' of industry, popularly known as the 'millocrats'.[31] However, his plans were quite different for his children, who were to be country gentlemen, 'as well as businessmen and leaders in the development of science and industry';[32] and that required good houses.

At the end of 1831, the year in which the hospital had offered enfranchisement to those without it, Wordsworth had given Marshall an early tip-off that they were intending to sell their manor to 'some capitalist for the purpose of making it his summer residence'.[33] The income from the hospital's northern estates, which during Edward Locker's time as secretary had relied upon the Alston mines, had crumbled once the price of lead crashed,[34] so the issue of the hospital's income had come up yet again in Parliament. In 1829, the

directors and the general court were replaced by five commissioners, including the treasurer of the Admiralty and Locker. Choosing
their time well, the receivers provocatively marked trees for felling
again along Southey's walk to Castlehead, which ten years earlier
Southey had written would be 'the greatest loss that Keswick could
possibly sustain'.[35] This time the commissioners, including Locker,
referred the proposal to the Admiralty.

Their answer was almost the opposite of Locker's recommendations of 1821 – 'the wood on the Hospital Estates should be
cut down in such a manner and at such times as may yield best
revenue, without reference to the beauty of the scenery' – and it
was to change everything.

Southey's call to Locker – 'Our woods! Our woods! Come and
look at those trees from my window and judge for yourself whether
Christian charity could require or enable me to forgive such trespass as that of cutting them down'[36] – was unavailing. So, when
the commissioners agreed to consider selling the estate on 2 July
1831, Locker might well have thought this a better option than the
extensive tree-felling that was threatened.

By the time Marshall was tipped off, John Junior, his second
son and a partner in the business, was on the lookout for a grand
estate and was considering buying Lord William Gordon's.
However, it had been mostly unoccupied since Gordon's death in
1823, and the trustees, having failed to sell, had felled the mature
timber and let the farming and the cottages for income. By contrast, in the Castlerigg and Derwentwater manor, there were 300
acres of woodland and even more[37] in the hospital plantation in
Thornthwaite. Woodland was Marshall's passion, and he was not
a man to be denied. Wordsworth, too, was clear that the manor
was a better choice, that its land might be sold off 'in parcels' by
someone who 'did not care about disfiguring the Country when
he came to divide it'. This was a conservation issue for both men.
Nevertheless, the poet's suggestion of building a house, admittedly
one 'of moderate size',[38] in a field behind Friar's Crag – the only bit
of woodland on the lakeside open to the public – might have strangled Ruskin's relationship with the Lake District almost at birth.

If the hospital had not sold, their planned major cutting, a century after their post-Derwentwater cull, would probably have caused violent protest, as there was by now a far larger informed constituency. And anyone felling would surely have earned 'major maledictions of all persons who admire this spot'. So potential buyers whose interest in the estate was purely commercial were warned off, and Wordsworth and Southey both helped to ensure that John Marshall I was the only bidder at the London auction in April, when 'the enchanting Keswick estate was sold to Mr Marshall … the first and only bidder, for £30,000 guineas'.[39] Marshall benefited, as Wordsworth wrote, from the 'great mistakes' that could be made in valuing wood[40] and he quite outmanoeuvred the hospital, paying just £16,768 for it.

Wordsworth was delighted, but Southey, agreeing that the wood had sold for too little, and regretting that his relationship with Locker was no longer useful to the Parish, was warier about the outcome. With some amusement, he reported to John Rickman, 'Marshall, the cotton [sic] king, intends it to be an appanage for his son, John, the Leeds candidate, and when that son called on me not long ago, I expressed a wish that he would ornament the unsightly and swampy ground at the foot of the lake, by planting; and I said that alders would grow well there.' Rickman answered immediately that 'alders were worth only fourpence a foot'.[41] And if the memories of the twelve-year-old Eliza Lynn are correct, Southey's apparent scorn about John Marshall II was initially shared 'by the impecunious well-born' in the Parish, as they fussed 'as to the propriety of visiting him and his'.[42] There was no need for haste, however, as John Junior and, ironically, Thomas Babington Macaulay were elected to the first two parliamentary seats for Leeds.

The Millbank textile industry was still enjoying its robust export business when the first pencil factory on record, Banks and Co., was founded by John Banks at Forge Mill in 1832. The pencil business has deep roots but, owing to a loss of records and a later fire, they remain obscure. For Joseph Ladyman – he who had forged a business agreement with Millbank lasting 5,000 years (and given Hutchinson a glorious, poetic description of the structure of wadd seams back in 1792) – had left the mill in 1817 to go into pencils full-time. He was named as a pencil-maker in an 1811 directory,* and this led to his being later acclaimed 'the father of the pencil industry'.[43] Yet, while there had been general references to wadd and pencils ever since the turn of the century,† we have no idea where Joseph (or any other pencil-maker) then worked.

The early Banks pencils had been handmade, using Florida cedar for the casing; their manufacture involved a small handsaw, a hand-plane and a darning needle, and the graphite was stopped an inch or two from the end of the pencil: this was skilled work. By 1851, when the company won the prize medal in the Temple of Art and Industry at that year's Great Exhibition, it was firmly on the national stage. The exhibition was visited by six million people, equivalent to a third of the British population. A magazine article published three years later made it clear that the firm had become mechanised.[44]

A machine cut planks into thin, long, oblong strips, half the width of the finished pencil, while the operator simultaneously used his feet to operate a circular saw (placed at right angles to the strip cutter) to incise the grooves for the insertion of the lead. Then a smaller oblong strip of the same length as the first was cut, and the strips were sorted into the successfully and unsuccessfully shaped, the latter being sold to the town as firewood. The wadd, likewise sorted with extreme care, was also sawn into thin strips, of similar hardness, so that 'when they are made up it may not be found that a pencil is an HH at one end and a BB at the other',[45] and inserted into the pencil groove.

Then, in Banks and Co.'s *pièce de résistance*, a unique, pur-pose-built machine glued and rounded the long sticks, some six to eight hundred a day, before they were sent to the hand-finish-ers, who pushed them up and down between a leather board and

---

* There is a theory that since the 1829 directory reports Joshua Ladyman – not the son but perhaps the brother of John – living at Greta Lodge (part of the estate that encompassed the Forge), the Ladyman brothers may have both started their pencil works there, later taken over by Joseph Banks, who had the perfect name with which to market it. Banks's company certainly took over the Fosters' company, started sometime after his own launch by 1850, just two years later dropping the Foster name altogether.

† For instance, *Magna Britannia* 1816 reports that wadd's 'chief use now is for making pencils'.

a leather-covered roller. 'Some thousand dozen a day' were polished thus by each worker. Finally, the sticks were cut to length,
their heads finished off by a guillotine, also 'used only by Messrs
Banks', whose name was stamped on each pencil by an ingenious
tool 'which could letter 120–200 pencils a minute'. The difference
in price, and probably consistency, between these pencils and the
earlier, handcrafted ones was considerable, and Banks pencils now
sold all over the British Isles, with some overseas orders to boot.
The people employed to make them, who numbered around 130,
were said to produce 'not less than ten million pencils per year'.[46]
The factory would use wadd exclusively from Borrowdale up until
1906. But its source was to become a contentious and significant
issue once the competition hotted up.

The *Guide to the Lakes*

In 1835, three years after the start of the first known pencil
company and two years after the opening of the new school for girls,
Wordsworth published the final, revised version of his *Guide to the
Lakes*. The first version had been published anonymously twenty-five years earlier to accompany the Reverend Joseph Wilkinson's
Select Views[47] and earn him some useful money. Wilkinson,
who had by then moved from Ormathwaite to Norfolk, had con-
tacted his old neighbour Coleridge, who had passed the idea on to
Wordsworth. Once he was sure that the book would not harm sales
of the guide produced by his artist friend William Green, who had
exhibition galleries and salerooms in both Ambleside and Keswick,
and whose accuracy the Lake Poets admired, Wordsworth took on
the commission.

Dorothy had immediately seized on the idea, as she felt a guide
'would bring him more money than any of his higher labours'.[48] In
fact, the first version of the *Guide* to appear under Wordsworth's
name was not published until a full ten years later, in 1820, when it
accompanied his collection of sonnets on the River Duddon. Both
the poems and the *Guide* had been well reviewed,[49] a significant
moment in Wordsworth's fortunes, and two years later the *Guide*

was published for the first time as a separate volume, followed a
year later, after the first print run of 500 copies had virtually sold
out, by an expanded edition. This sold more slowly but by the time
of the final text in 1835, the guidebook industry was flourishing
throughout the Lake District and Wordsworth changed his previous title of a 'Topographical Description' to 'Guide'.

William Green's massive two-volume *Tourist's New Guide*
to the Lake District had appeared in 1819 and had been much
admired, but it included a copy of Jonathan Otley's brilliant map,
used without authorisation, which rankled with Otley. His own
*Concise Description of the English Lakes … with remarks on the
Mineralogy and Geology of the District* was published in 1823
and would become a bestseller. He was a careful man, and it was
not until he had made a further revision to the map for the third
edition of his *Concise Description* that Otley would admit, with
pride, that the map 'is now with confidence offered as the most
correct delineation of the district yet published'.[50] He was proud too
that 'the reader may be assured, that this is not an abridgement of,
nor compilation from the labours of others; but the result of actual
observation' – a distinction the book shared with Wordsworth's.
He had sold 6,000 copies of the *Concise Description* by 1835,[51]
the last two editions including woodcuts of the mountain ranges
of a type to be developed in the twentieth century by Alfred
Wainwright. Over the same period, Wordsworth had sold only a
thousand copies of his *Guide*.

Sales of the 1835 edition of Wordsworth improved when the poet
approached Hudson's, a local publisher with the right contacts, but
the real change in the book's fortunes came when he allowed the
publishers to include their own tourist apparatus, a task the author
considered 'very troublesome and infra dig'.[52] He had written to
Hudson's that 'my neighbour tells me that the Botany in Otley is
not arranged scientifically … It would be a decided advantage to
have this done',[53] which it duly was. But battle was really joined
with the bestselling Otley by the inclusion in the *Guide* of 'Three
Letters on the Geology of the District' by the now renowned Adam
Sedgwick. Wordsworth was only too aware of the importance of
his coup, writing to the scientist, 'It will give the Kendal lake Book

so decided superiority over every other, that the Publishers have good reason to rejoice.'[54] Indeed, the presence of Sedgwick's material was regarded as so important that not only did Hudson's fail to mention the new 'Botanical Notices' on their cover, they also gave more space there to the celebrated geologist's work than they did to Wordsworth.[55]

Sedgwick's contribution caused damage to the sales of Otley's *Concise Description* and pain to its author. But it would be five years before the subject was broached by the two friends, Otley confirming what Sedgwick already knew: 'I had rather have seen your letters in some other work than a Guide to the Lakes; as, if they augmented the sale of Mr Hudson's work, of course mine would be diminished at the same time.'[56] However, he accepted Sedgwick's explanation that the situation had come about as a result of a promise made to Wordsworth twenty-three years earlier, before he and Otley had met, and that he had received no royalties. At the same time, Sedgwick reassured Otley that he thought his *Concise Description*, which he always recommended, 'one of the best guide books ever written'.[57]

Sedgwick's comment that his brother-in-law Mr Westall 'tells me that I have almost destroyed the sales of views of which before he had made a considerable profit'[58] indicates what a beneficial effect his Letters were generally thought to have had – far more damaging to the top seller than the myriad competition that was published by then by 'almost every bookseller in the district'.[59] The elderly Otley wrote rather sadly, 'If I cannot lay claim to superiority, I can to originality. I have a laid a foundation on which others have built, and if they rise above me, I must be content to live on the ground floor.'[60] But he did more than simply survive. In 1849, his eighty-fourth year, he bravely printed 1,250 copies of the eighth and final edition of the *Concise Description*.

Three years later, he was captured affectionately by Dr Leitch[61] as he 'took his measures' at Friar's Crag:

'...carefully picking his way over the rough rocks towards his famous low water mark ... in order to "describe a new remarkable event" of the valley. [It] seemed like tradition creeping and stumbling forward to chronicle the silent births of time ... moving along, in his well-known solitary, quiet manner ... busied too in one of those careful, accurate observations for which he has long been famous ... all the sights and sounds which in this valley accompany the close of day, were in harmony with the idea of the old man ... The similitude between the hour and the man, the sunset and the departing life, became so impressive, that it was an unpleasant shock to see him slip and fall on the rock ... Fortunately, however no harm was done; the veteran first examining his hand, gathered himself up, and then with redoubled caution proceeded on his errand.'

By 1856 the elderly Otley was lonely and failing. He wrote his last diary entry on 5 August, the month in which he suffered his second stroke.[62] When Sedgwick, who was also ill, made the effort to visit him a little later, Otley was bed-bound and could no longer speak. As the two men clasped hands, the professor burst into tears, calling out as he fell on his knees, 'Jonathan, I'll pray with you.'[63]

After Otley's death, Sedgwick wrote to a friend, 'I wish with all my heart that my letters to Mr Wordsworth had been printed in Otley's Guide.' The academic geologist Professor David Oldroyd has said of the relationship between Sedgwick and Otley, 'I know of no similar case in the history of geology.'[64] His remark does credit to both men and is a reflection of the enormous appeal, for those who both knew him well and had the brain to understand his, of the 'quiet, nature-loving, God-serving Jonathan Otley'.[65]

*

Wordsworth never changed the heart of his original 1810 text,[66] which, moving on from the far smaller compass of both West and Clarke, celebrated the unity of the Lake District, embracing all the valleys radiating from the central fells and the Helvellyn range. He had admired the 'distinctness and unaffected simplicity' of Gray's response to it, at times capturing pictures, while his own illustration of a full response was, at times, to write a prose poem.

The rain-burst after which 'every brook is vocal and every torrent sonorous';[67] the mountains that 'in the combinations they make, towering above each other, or lifting themselves in ridges like the waves of a tumultuous sea, are surpassed by none';[68] the showers 'darkening or lightening, as they fly from hill to hill'.[69] He wrote of a land where the effect 'of mist or haze ... is like that of magic'.[70] And of Parish land, Wordsworth's land, he wrote, 'I do not know of any tract of country in which, in so narrow a compass, may be found an equal variety in the influence of light and shadow upon the sublime and beautiful features of the landscape.'[71]

The poet had been shocked by the taste of the rich (and usually not indigenous) new builders in the area, desolate about their 'introduction of discordant objects, disturbing that peace and harmony of form and colour, which had been preserved for so long'.[72] He was desolate too about the loss of his beloved cottages, which 'fall into the hands of wealthy purchasers, who ... if they wished to become residents, erect new mansions out of the ruin of the ancient cottages, whose little enclosures, with all the wild graces that grew out of them, disappear'. He considered the Lake District to have a unifying moral integrity, which rightly belonged to all and should override the wishes of those who were unable to respond to it. So, in the third part of the *Guide*, Wordsworth's mission to furnish the '*Minds* of Persons of taste and feeling for the landscape' expanded to include persuading the enlightened to protect the innocence of the area (or perhaps its 'humility', a word the poet often uses of its people), while equally trying to persuade those who encroached upon it to act in sympathy with the environment.

'The rule is simple; with respect to grounds – work where you can in the spirit of Nature, with an invisible hand of art.'[73] He continues: 'the like may be said of building, if Antiquity, who may be styled the co-partner and sister of Nature, be not denied the respect to which she is entitled.'[74] His essential disgust with Pocklington's house was that it was 'built on the precise point of the island's highest elevation',[75] faithful to the pre-Romantic view of aiming for domination of, rather than congruence with, nature. For, in mountainous regions, houses should be 'not obvious, not obtrusive, but retired ... to admit of [them] being gently incorporated

into the works of Nature'.[76] Often judged a Puritan, Wordsworth
had no problem with houses that called major attention to themselves as a 'principal feature in the landscape' on the fringes of the
Lake District, where there were no significant fells and the land
was undulating or flat.[77]

His prejudice against the new regimental larch plantations in
the district, 'vegetable manufactory' despoiling the vales rather
than being correctly placed in the cheaper 'barren and irreclaimable
land in the neighbouring moors',[78] derives from the same source. In
nature, and in Scottish forestry, larches grow on higher ground, and
there the 'interposition of rocks ... break[s] up the dreary uniformity
... and the winds would take hold of the trees, and imprint upon
their shapes a wildness congenial to their situation'.[79] Lower, richer
ground should be reserved for oak and ash and other deciduous
trees, including Wordsworth's, admittedly evergreen, beloved holly.

Aged fourteen, the poet had been particularly struck by the
effect of evening light upon an oak tree and, as an old man, recalled
that it was at that moment he first realised that the 'infinite variety
of natural appearances' had never really been fully addressed by
poets – and glimpsed his own future.[80] As an adult, function and
balance had become a major part of how he saw. And twenty years
after Wordsworth's death, the inventor of the word 'ecology', the
German zoologist Ernst Haeckel, defined it as 'the body of knowledge concerning the economy of nature', a phrase Wordsworth had
used in the *Guide*.

Describing the relevance of tarns within the ecosystem of the
Lake District, he had said, 'In the economy of Nature these are
useful, as auxiliars to Lakes; for if the whole quantity of water
which falls upon the mountains in time of storm were poured
upon plains without intervention ... the habitable grounds would
be much more subject than they are to inundation.'[81] The *Guide*'s
introduction to 'the economy of Nature', its view of commercial
forestation, and its author's instinctive understanding of colonisation and succession have led many to believe that Wordsworth and
the Lake District provided 'the cradle for nascent ideas in landscape conservation and environmentalism'.[82] Today, Wordsworth's
suggestions would be called an 'environmental impact assessment'.

Wordsworth also presented a history of the people of the Lake District in the *Guide*, their work and their interaction with the force and splendour of nature. This reflected his ambition to teach his readers to 'look through the clear eye of understanding as well as through the hazy one of vague Sensibility'.[83] First written at the end of the marvellous decade that gave birth to *The Prelude*, 'Michael' and the statesman poems, the *Guide* provides, in many ways, the bass notes that ground the poetry. Quite distinct from the 'theme park' some today chastise Wordsworth with having created, his work expressed his passion for the living heritage of sheep farming; profoundly viewing it as the major human intervention that had aided the beauty and utility of the area – in an almost divine symbiosis.

The Return of the State
and the Seigneur

ENFRANCHISEMENT AND ENCLOSURE were affecting the age-old pattern of landholding Wordsworth fought for, and in some cases affecting the statesmen's way of life too. Labourers (almost never described as cottagers now) still laboured, their existence frequently ignored by the directories. Usually owning a small plot of land for wintering an animal or three, they were relatively well remunerated at last, but it remained hard to move up the social scale to proper farming for many, and from the mid-nineteenth century many labourers were to move out of the area entirely. Farmers, another major class, leased the Derwentwater demesne land along with a surprising amount of other leased land in the manor, usually owned by the customary tenants who had made their fortunes away from the Parish but continued to hold and tenant their land.

We have seen the Williamsons, the Le Flemings and the Bankes leasing their land in the seventeenth-century and a Gawen Wilson of Essex, Gentleman, must have been another of their number as he was one of the signatories of the 1623 Derwentwater 'enfranchisement'. In the eighteenth-century we saw the London Graves leasing their three farms[1] and there will have been others whose lives we have not followed. The still indigenous, wealthier, customary tenants, like the Wrenns, often leased much of their land too – at the height of their local power John Fisher Crosthwaite, a Victorian historian of the area, reported that they had been the primary tenants of thirteen Parish farms. Also the Eighteen Men had purchased and leased an estate in the Wanthwaite valley, which provided one of the two main sources of income for their free school. Similarly, 'Glebe Farm' had been created in 1717,[2] to give the curate of St John's an income. And, from the early nineteenth century, as the amount of leased land expanded, farmers from other parts of the local area joined the Derwentwater tenants.[3]

Although some customary tenancies with technically arbitrary fines remained in the two great Parish estates, enfranchised tenants represented the new normality. Only Borrowdale developed differently, where, as late as the 1870s, the ratio of 'freehold(s) by enfranchisement' to arbitrary customary tenancies was merely three to two – a startling departure from the trend in the rest of the Parish, as was the Lawson definition of enfranchisement.[*] This mixture of landholding continued to be virtually unique to Cumbria, without any other large northern equivalent. However, as we have noted, after enfranchisement, land purchase became a simpler process. In Newlands we saw occasional outside investment for the first time in the 1760s – although usually by people from within the Lake District or Cumberland. Twenty years later, when wealthy outsiders first entered the Keswick valley, intent on surrounding Derwentwater with their estates, this was made possible by land freed up by the statesmen themselves.

It was not a case of *having* to sell, as had happened after the death of Michael's widow, or 'being no longer able to maintain themselves upon small farms', as Wordsworth described. It was a matter of money or lifestyle, a choice to sell land and livelihood for a price that they found irresistible. The decision, which was usually taken when the tenancy was changing hands after a death, frequently involved continuing to make the same living on cheaper

---

* Many of the original Borrowdale enfranchisements were curtailed, as they usually 'reserved' something for their lord, and, as late as 1907, customary rent could still be referred to as the 'Lord's Rent'. The Lawsons', most unusual, reservation of the rights to their rent from the 'customary grasses' on the fells was, oddly, accepted even by men like Henry Marshall and J. Fisher Crosthwaite, the latter of whom, nevertheless, described the Borrowdale tenancy as 'Lord of his Estate'. The Lawsons continued to own the grasses on Langstrath and another common in the 1920s (and vestigially later). Johnson, 'Borrowdale, its land tenure', pp. 63–72, passim.

land. Then, once enclosure became a consideration, the original tenant-holding became worth more because of the extra demarcated land on the commons, which, in turn, provided another possible prompt to sell.

Combined, these changes opened up the possibility of an irreversible change of Parish land use. For, once an outsider bought a customary tenancy, enfranchised or otherwise, he almost always employed a tenant farmer on a straight lease. Thus, the new changes would, over time, seriously weaken the overwhelming historical dominance of the customary tenure holdings in Parish land, the form of land use to which Wordsworth was wedded.

Legal changes were creating an equally large disruption to the historical statesman way of life. In 1833, Parish administration had been *de jure* separated from its 700-year history when a new Derwent division was carved out of the two baronies-cum-wards-cum-divisions, marking the first but final break with the old Norman local government structures. The new division ran from Maryport to Crosthwaite, which retained its legal supremacy over Keswick, as the old manor of Derwentwater and Castlerigg became part of a subsection of the new division named 'Crosthwaite … including Applethwaite, Braithwaite, Castlerigg, Keswick, Millbeck, Newlands, Portinscale, St John [sic], Thornthwaite and Wythburn' – a legal description that would hold into the twentieth century. The reality was that the changes of 1833 would shift control away from Crosthwaite almost entirely, although it was to take another fourteen years for this to become unequivocally clear to the Parish.

Also, in the early decades of the nineteenth century, the vestry system was subjected to considerable upheaval – for two basic reasons. Firstly, the country's poor rates had quintupled between 1785 and 1817–18, when they stood at over £10 million. Secondly, many parishes ran an open vestry system, which meant all the members of a parish could attend meetings, and in the mood of post-war nervousness about a possible English revolution, the establishment feared that these meetings could become dangerously disorderly and inflammatory. Two bills had been passed, in 1818 and 1819, to encourage the creation of new select vestries, and to authorise, for the first time, a salaried overseer of the poor whose appointment was always to be vetted and agreed by the select vestry, if one existed.

In 1820, Carlisle saw a fierce court battle to establish the relative authority of a newly set-up select vestry and a newly salaried overseer, the sessions of which were attended by between thirty and forty magistrates. The case revealed that scams were being carried out by all and sundry and feelings ran high, one overseer stating, 'We are willing to submit accounts to any gentleman, except in the character of Select Vestrymen.'[4] But, even in this new version of the Cumbrian fighting spirit, the judgment, of course, underlined the select vestries' authority and was seen, at least by Cumberland, as clarifying the matter.

In the cities there *was* considerable corruption in the system, many vestries having become more 'closed' than 'select', and yet another Select Vestries Bill went through Parliament in 1831. However, despite acknowledgment by the prime minister, Earl Grey, that there had been no complaint from rural parishes, behind closed doors the select vestries were losing the battle to the new salaried overseers. This process was hastened by the passing, three years later, of the 1834 Poor Law Amendment Act, intended to stamp out abuses of the existing system and to limit the cost of poor relief – and widely regarded today as an anti-working-class Act. More significantly for our story, it was later to be described accurately by the left-wing intellectuals Sidney and Beatrice Webb, the first to study vestry governance in depth, as 'the Strangulation of the Parish'.[5]

At Keswick, John Bankes's bequest had, of course, boosted the monies produced by the Parish poor rates, each division merely paying 5s. a month for each of their housed paupers in 1821. The charity's income was then £222 7s. 6d.[6] Although the benefactor's intention to provide a workhouse that produced some profit had fallen by the wayside once the use of machinery made that impractical, the large garden remained, providing 'wholesome air and exercise' and fulfilling the exact purpose that Bankes had intended for it. In the words of James Clarke, writing in 1787, it was 'cultivated by the poor who, in return, are supplied their vegetables from it ... and a large quantity ... are sold out of it, and the money applied to the house'.[7] By the time these words were written, the building had become 'the Great House', a relatively comfortable poorhouse, at times said to have housed up to eighty inhabitants, including whole families. And by 1821, although the money was no longer sufficient to pay for Parish apprenticeships, if a child was apprenticed outside the Parish, he went off supplied with two suits of clothes.[8]

The 1834 Act foreshadowed the wholesale removal from the Parish of responsibility for the poor. This would pass, four years later, to a newly created Cockermouth Poor Law Union, covering forty-eight parishes and overseen by fifty-eight guardians: two from Keswick and one from all the other Parish townships.[9] Parish ratepayers now elected the guardians, the weight of their votes reflecting the weight of their wealth,[10] the first absolute sign that the new Parish gentry could potentially remove power from the Eighteen Men. The guardians also appointed the 'relieving officers'. These developments were immediately and seriously damaging for the Parish poor: far from mixing with a wide social range at school, poor children were initially not provided with any education whatsoever. Writing in *The State of the Poor*, a survey of the English labouring classes, published in 1797, Sir Frederick Morton Eden was moved by a visit to a workhouse in Carlisle. The poor people of Cumberland, he wrote, 'prefer the chance of starving among friends and neighbours, in their own native village, to the mortifying alternative of being ... lodged ... in a poor-house, "the motley receptacle of idiots and vagrants"'.[11]

A specialist workhouse was built in Cockermouth in the early 1840s, on the model plan devised by the Poor Law commissioners. Families were split up, housed in male and female wards; the diet was restricted and bad, the work offered demeaning and unpleasant. Economy was the commissioners' watchword. Most of those living in the Keswick poorhouse were forced to choose between moving to the shockingly different conditions of Cockermouth or running the risk of starvation by staying in the Parish – where St Kentigern's long maintained its special pew for 'the Poorhouse'. In contrast, at Cockermouth the old Crosthwaite parishioners would endure forced Christian instruction and worship within the work-house but were forbidden to attend any church outside it. After death, their bodies, if unclaimed after forty-eight hours, were likely to be dissected for medical research and training.

A few inhabitants of Bankes's poorhouse were luckier, as Southey had managed to maintain a small refuge. The charity commissioners had sought its immediate closure once the Cockermouth workhouse was built, but he had had a word with them in 1834 and the decision was changed;[12] his official position on the local board of health bearing good fruit. When, in 1861, the state finally ordained that the building was to be closed, it was still housing eighteen people.[13] It is much to Southey's credit that he focused on the problem as, in the same year, he suffered two major shocks – and every good thing remaining from his youth seemed to be turning to dust.

On 25 July 1834, Coleridge died of heart failure – possibly as a result of his years of opium use – in the house of the physician James Gillman, with whose family he had been living since 1816. At the time of his death, it was only five years since the two Saras had left Southey's household, but in London Henry Nelson Coleridge's unalloyed admiration for his uncle and father-in-law had gradually, and somewhat remarkably, achieved a real family entente. Although Hartley was still absent, the dedication of his first volume of poems to his father had given both his parents much pleasure. In 1832, writing to a friend about the christening of Sara and Henry's second child, Coleridge had even been able to admit that 'In fact, bating living in the same house with her there are few women, that I have a greater respect and a *ratherish* liking for, than Mrs C.'[14]

Southey's first reaction to Coleridge's death was to behave like a loving friend, writing a few lines to Grosvenor Bedford in which he revealed his belief that 'the course of my life received its bias' from his first meeting with Coleridge. Finishing the thought, Southey just stopped, as though overcome, before writing a lengthy and affectionate letter to the Coleridge family. But his thoughts must have turned, as the Rhadamanthine Southey was flashing ice when he wrote to the poet Caroline Bowles, 'All who were of his blood were in the highest degree proud of his reputation, but this was their only feeling concerning him ... Perhaps no man's death has ever occasioned more of what is now called sensation – or less sorrow.'[15]

Then, two months later, the mental health of Southey's wife, Edith, changed for the worse, suddenly and dramatically; 'this morning she was perfectly insane', Southey wrote to his brother.[16] Immediately realising she needed professional help, he took her to an asylum in York, where she was violent and had to be restrained. After a few months, it was clear there was little that could be done for her, yet, 'parted from my wife by something worse than death', Southey brought Edith back to Greta Hall. 'Precisely the conduct which those who know you best, might and did expect', Joseph Cottle wrote to him from Bristol after Edith's death, just over three years later.

Just one thing that year afforded Southey some chance to indulge the glee his friends had once characterised him by – the anonymous publication of the first two volumes of *The Doctor*.* Lightly based on a narrative about Dr Daniel Dove of Doncaster, a 'flossofer', and his horse Nobs, about whom Coleridge and he used to spin stories (whose 'humour lay in making it as long-winded as possible' and each time telling it differently),[17] *The Doctor* was really a vehicle to share much of Southey's exhaustively collected encyclopaedia of arcane information – few subjects not covered. As W. A. Speck, his most recent biographer, noted, Southey's 'boyish spirits' were still on display 'at the age of sixty',[18] and he much enjoyed joining in – even prompting – the literary guessing game about the book's author. Revealingly, what has lasted is the introduction of the nation to 'The Story of the Three Bears' in print (for many, still its best telling, even though Southey's interloper was a vagrant old woman rather than Goldilocks), a tale he had long told his children; just as his most appreciated poem today is his wonderful stream of onomatopoeia about the Lodore waterfall – created in response to the children's challenge.

* Seven volumes were published, two posthumously by his son-in-law Jon Warter. This may have been an error: the Poetry Foundation judges them 'at last a grotesque parody of Southeyan garrulousness'.

And so never ending, but always descending,
Sounds and motions for ever and ever are blending
All at once and all o'er, with a mighty uproar,
And this way the water comes down at Lodore.

The battle of the seigneurs

When James Lynn returned in 1836, he found a Parish 'awakened to a high pitch of evangelical fervour' (as later described
by his daughter Eliza),[19] the Reverend Whiteside, the evangelical curate, having had rather more success than might have been

imagined. A Parish civil war, not dissimilar to the split among the Eighteen Men and the churchwardens that had led to the harsh sixteenth-century state commission, was in full spate. The new evangelicals, Eliza tells us, believed that the more conservative Lynn had, along with his predecessors (for those that remembered them), never truly preached the Gospel or told them anything about 'faith before works' or 'free will' and 'prevenient grace'. The other Parish churchgoers thought the new order extreme and the idea of evening gatherings – where prayers took the place of games and biblical exposition the place of forfeits – not just dull beyond endurance but also unseemly. And they were fairly dubious about Sunday schools as well.

When the Marshalls bought the Derwentwater and Castlerigg manor in 1832, the more traditional parishioners had proved to be the stronger party, causing the Parish revolt. The split was then institutionalised by the removal of the Sunday school from the premises of the free grammar school to a new building raised by James Stanger – after which the only move was that made by Reverend Whiteside, who would leave the Parish in July 1835. There was much to question at that time about the condition of the Parish. The vicar and the incumbents of three of the Parish curacies were non-resident, behaving like eighteenth-century vicars. Isaac Denton Junior, in charge of Wythburn, lived in Buckinghamshire, where he had been given a parish, and William Parsable, who was still in charge of Newlands and Borrowdale, mainly resided at his third living in Gilcrux.* This was a period when whatever advantage was going to come to the parish churches and chapels would be the work of laymen.

James Stanger remained one of the Eighteen Men and was a good friend of Southey, although the poet had decided by 1834 that, despite liking Whiteside personally, 'That race of Evangelicals should be called Dysvangelical preachers of ill tidings'.[20] The curate

---

* He did give £70 to each of his Parish livings and owned a house and 5 acres of land in Borrowdale. However, when he and Lowrie had accompanied the chancellor of the Diocese of Carlisle on an official visit to Borrowdale back in 1814, the chancellor had noticed that the chapel had undergone a major repair. Both curate and vicar seemed equally astonished.

must have been a fire-and-brimstone man, and the concept of hell remained damnable for Southey. Both Southey and Stanger wished to improve where they could, and Stanger had long had discussions with his friends about the lack of proper care for some of the parishioners in, or near, the eastern side of Keswick, which was improperly served because of the marked expansion of the town's population in that direction.[21]

He concluded that a chapel was essential there and, knowing that no 'person connected with the place' had 'contemplated the proposal', in late March or April 1835 he went to see John Marshall II at Headingley (in Leeds) to discuss buying some land for the project. Two years earlier Wordsworth had suggested to Marshall that Broomhill Point, some raised ground to the eastern side of Keswick, would make the perfect spot for a manor house, and John had called in the architect Anthony Salvin to draw up plans. He then made no further move. That ground would provide a good space for Stanger's chapel and Stanger was thrilled when Marshall had, as he saw it, 'met the proposition in so cordial and handsome a manner'. Assuming that it would be 'chiefly ... my own responsibility to accomplish' the new chapel, Stanger immediately got to work to solidify his plan.

However, Marshall had to retire 'from active affairs' that April, owing to the effects of a recurrent pulmonary disease, and this may have prompted some new thoughts of his own about what he would do with the land. At the Headingley meeting, he had talked of a church for 800 people, which Stanger thought 'beyond the probable requirements of the district' and would involve a very grand building indeed. These hints of an intrinsic disagreement led to the first Parish 'battle of the seigneurs', an entirely new kind of Parish fight* – although one partially fuelled by the split in Crosthwaite's parishioners. The clerical issues raised in the fight were fundamental: church or chapel, patronage, connection with St Kentigern's through the vicar or not, the bishop or not, and the religious flavour of the church's

---

* Unless you count Pocklington graciously accepting Lord Gordon as a fellow 'improver' of the Derwentwater shore.

teaching. For many years, these issues lay buried along with the dead bodies of the participants, but they might have come alive again when Canon Richard Watson used what church papers there were to describe what happened. However, in the published interpretation of them, he resorted to the time-honoured policy of simply lauding the victor.[22]

The canon implies that the idea of creating another religious building on the east side of Keswick was entirely John Marshall's. Marshall had, he said, sought local support from Mr Joshua Stanger but was then forced to go ahead alone when some 'serious differences arose' between them. As we know, Joshua Stanger had married Mary Calvert and they had not yet returned to the Parish. And, as we have just seen, his brother *James* Stanger (closely involved with St Kentigern's) had initiated the contact with Marshall, not the other way round.

By May James Stanger had clarified his proposal,[23] providing a capital sum of £3,000, made up of separate donations of £600 each from himself, Joshua, John Marshall, Abraham Fisher of Seatoller and friends, and the Reverend William Carus Wilson and Cambridge friends, the patronage to be held by four substantial evangelical trustees.* After the consecration, he wished each trustee to add £120 – or, much better, £200 – the maximum to be matched by Queen Anne's Bounty, the process that had so benefited the chapels in the past.

Once Stanger realised that Marshall did not fully support this, he offered to withdraw. 'I should much regret appearing to interfere with any decided plan,' he said, seeking reassurance from Marshall that he would move ahead quickly. His reasoning was that his own plan involved non-parishioner money, while Marshall would be living in Keswick (this was not actually clear) and could be more involved in the new church since he had no connection with St Kentigern's.

On 29 July the Reverend James Bush arrived in the Parish as

---

* He envisaged a church or chapel seating up to 450 people and costing £1,500 to build; there would be 250 paying sittings at 7s. as, he thought, 'we should not obtain a higher rate'.

Lynn's new chaplain. He had been Byron's fag at Harrow, which may have amused the poet laureate, and proved to be both conscientious and overworked, immediately addressing the difficult situation in Keswick. Both the bishop and Marshall approved his use of the Moot Hall for a regular Sunday evening service from the end of October; the congregation, Canon Watson tells us, spilling out into the market square. *This* was the genesis of a realisation, said the canon, that a Keswick 'parish church' was needed.

On 26 October, Bush wrote to Marshall to thank him for allowing his service, adding a postscript from Southey saying that 'he [had] had a communication with the Bishop' and would like to meet Marshall when he came to Keswick. And a third plan, proposed by the bishop, Southey and James Bush, began to emerge as Bush asked Marshall to withdraw his stipulation that an equal amount be raised by parishioners' subscriptions and suggested that the patronage of the new church be vested in the bishop as patron of the Mother Church.

Bush added that the bishop believed he could procure assistance from the Church Building Society with those conditions. Government support for the building of new churches had become available soon after the end of the French wars,* fundamentally because of the exceptional mismatch between population numbers and available church services in the new industrial areas – where tithes and potential pew rents were irrelevant. Also, there was a general sense that the church's teaching and care offered a crucial bulwark against a potential English revolution.† Southey had welcomed this with his usual saltiness in the *Quarterly Review*: 'Our forefathers built convents and cathedrals – the edifices we have erected are manufactures and prisons, the former producing tenants for the latter.' He and Wordsworth were, of course, enthusiastic supporters of more churches, and Southey was particularly well informed about the problems of church extension.[24] But the three churches the new commissioners built in Cumbria lay,

---

* The commissioners' churches, sometimes called 'Waterloo' churches.
† It was also thought that the paucity of churches had aided the spread of dissent.

rightly, in the far larger catchment areas of Carlisle, Workington and Kendal.

In October Stanger had repeated his offer to withdraw his own proposal as long as Marshall would assure him he would move with speed but, getting no agreement, continued with his plan. By the end of the year his estimate of the necessary expenditure had risen to £4,000, which he had duly raised, with offers of funding from Joseph Pocklington, General Peachy, Mr Spedding and Southey. By then, less than half was intended for the initial building costs, the rest prudently reserved – by one who had long wrestled with church finances – for the care of the priest and the building. Meanwhile, Marshall had been conferring with his lawyers about the best way to achieve sole patronage and, by the end of the year, had raised his offer from £2,600 to £3,000. In early January, Bush added a third request to his list: 'My Impression is that if you could draw up a plan abating somewhat of the Price of the Building and making the Income more sure than if it would be if arising largely from Pew Rents [a parsimonious suggestion] it would facilitate the measure.'

Stanger would have strongly agreed with all the proposals of Bush and Southey, while – a situation little understood by Southey and the bishop – Marshall would never have agreed either to the patronage of the new church being vested in the bishop as patron or to stint on the building. Marshall's parents were Unitarian, as he was himself, apparently, so there was scant appreciation of church financing, and the desire for a fine building was basically a seigneurial instinct. The intentions and ambitions of the two pro-ponents of the plans were quite different. Stanger was used to being the richest person in the Parish, with all the influence that gave him, but Marshall was on another level: he was a real seigneur, used to being lord of all he surveyed – his plan to build a church in Keswick apparently prompted by learning of the Derwentwaters' generosity to Crosthwaite church.[25]

However, by January, it was clear that there was no chance that Stanger would back the Marshall plan. Bush had foolishly posted an anodyne request for a subscription to support Marshall 'for the glory of God and the convenience of the town' into Stanger's letter box on Christmas Day, and Stanger had finally exploded. He informed Marshall on 5 January that he would now show his own amended plan to the bishop. He had never received the 'distinct promise' about speed he had consistently required from Marshall but had continued to remain passive until the last few days. Yet now he found that he had 'been kept in entire ignorance as to what has been going on' and – rather than the Marshall family taking on the whole project, as he had assumed – had discovered 'that urgent applications are being made to several parties [including] warm friends and promised supporters of my plan'. He was now abandoning the 'delicacy' that had made him hold back until this point and could 'no longer incur the responsibility of abandoning my plan'.

Marshall swiftly communicated the new position to Bush, who, after 'much Conversation with Mr Southey', strongly advised Marshall to send 'a plain statement of the whole transaction' to the bishop. The following lines of Bush reveal, finally, the third critical issue in the conflict: 'If all your plans fail, I shall always hold you in grateful recollection, for your Endeavour to prevent this Great Parish from the Gloom of Calvinism which hangs over it like a black cloud.' This also explains Southey's involvement. And the bishop was 'an old-fashioned high church-man',[26] so there was no possibility that he would support Stanger's rigidly evangelical plan, which he saw as 'the peculiar views of a party'. Without modification, Stanger's plan had, in reality, never stood a chance.

However, the bishop considered that Marshall's desire for a matched subscription was unlikely to be raised without Stanger's support and his potential solution is interesting. 'In case of failure', might Marshall be prepared 'to assist in the building of a Chapel of Ease'? The bishop went on to say, 'If a sufficient fund for a small endowment could be raised, a separate Clergyman might be appointed to it, who would assist the Incumbent or Curate of the Mother Church in visiting the sick and other occasional duties. The Patronage then should be in the Vicar ... and if sufficient funds could be procured for an adequate endowment it might be converted into "a District Church".'

Then the bishop simply vanished. Having spent most of January with his family at Alnwick Castle, he was briefly at Rose Castle before going to London on 1 February. So Stanger, whether he knew it or not, was marooned, and completely outplayed. In March he told Marshall that he hoped to get down to see the bishop in April, adding, with the entirely mistaken view that he still had some power, 'any proposition which I may make I shall be anxious to make as little unsatisfactory to you as possible'.

What actually happened was that, in *early* April, John Marshall himself had taken over the whole project. Once he had realised he was on his own, he moved quickly and effectively, and with outstanding generosity – a generosity that would be continued by his family, spending vastly more than the sums he had previously offered, were their equivalent to be raised by the rest of the Parish. But it was Stanger, rather than the bishop, Southey or Bush, who had read him correctly: the desire for sole patronage, with all that potentially implied, proved to have been Marshall's only essential demand.

The issues that underlay the dispute were first exposed a year after the new church, St John's, was consecrated in 1838. *Both* the churches that fell within the Marshall manor, St John's and the Thornthwaite chapel, were to be made into 'district churches' within the Parish. The area designated to St John's encompassed some 1,200 people, as Keswick's small township had been enlarged to incorporate some of the land of St John's in the Vale, so that change made sense, but the decision about Thornthwaite, which in 1831 had a tiny catchment area of 174 people, had no ecclesiastical reasoning behind it, despite its acceptance by the bishop. So the motive was undoubtedly seigneurial – indeed, no religious action in the Parish had had such an obviously seigneurial influence as the creation of St John's since the twelfth century and Alice I's choice of Crosthwaite to build her church, followed by her daughter's disposal of much of its wealth.

While one might raise the question of whether the good of the Parish itself had ever been considered in the redesignation of Thornthwaite's chapel, the immediate problem, whatever it might indicate for the future, was solved by the conditions of an endowment of £2,000 from the ever-generous James Stanger and 'Capt. Henry', the son of William Peachy's widow. Their conditions were twofold: firstly, that the larger division of Braithwaite* be annexed

* 245 people in 1831.

to the newly ordained church of the Holy Trinity, in a district to
be called Thornthwaite-cum-Braithwaite, and, secondly, that the
patronage for the new church should be shared between the incumbents of St John's and the Parish church. So in the end it was James
Stanger's sense and generosity that, despite his ultimate refusal to
support the Marshall plan for St John's, smoothed what seemed a
far less acceptable proposal into something that made some sense
for the Parish as a whole.

The Marshalls and the manor

The Marshall family had almost the same sort of effect on
nineteenth-century landownership in the Lake District as the
pre-Reformation 'great families'. And the Marshall aim – to conserve the natural scenery and increase the production of their fells
and woodland by planting – was largely achieved, even if their
tenure in the Lake District was a mere blink of the eye in comparison with that of their predecessors. Indeed, the combination of
Marshall's money, his instinctive reaction to the landscape and the
fruitful interplay between his and Wordsworth's ideas about how
best to preserve it was of lasting benefit to the area and the Parish.

While John II had had little time to plan any significant plant-
ings, he had been true to his father's principles and protected the
existing woods by entailing his estates and stipulating that a specific, highly conserving figure for wood was to remain on the estate
at all times.[27] And, as John II's younger brother Henry became the
Marshall family's representative in the Parish, his father and his
planting theories remained in total command. By 1845, £200,000
of Leeds's manufacturing profit had been spent on Lake District
property, some £10 million in today's money; well over a quarter
of it, £55,843, in the Parish.[28]

However, by and large, John Marshall I and his family took a
decidedly modern attitude to his land and tenants, and his strongly
utilitarian views were well developed by the time he acquired
Castlerigg and Derwentwater for his son. For Marshall, economic
benefit was both the prime motivation of human action and the

ultimate source of mankind's 'greatest happiness', happiness that should be distributed, as he wrote in his only published book,[29] 'to each individual such share as may arise from the produce of his own exertions'. While work was equally essential to Wordsworth's view of the statesman's life, the two men had fundamentally opposing views about society. Marshall scorned the customary management of the commons, as he believed that community worked against individualism, his primary economic driver.* Inevitably, this rigidly utilitarian attitude had meant that, in his lands at Loweswater, Marshall's attempt to enclose the commons and 'leap over entrenched customary hurdles' had ended in failure,[30] which must have come as a shock to him.

His unfettered economic relationships with the leasehold tenants of his freehold land there were much more to his taste, if not always to theirs. In a downturn, Marshall made it clear, when his steward on that estate was recommending that he lower the rent, that he was only content for his tenants to get a comfortable living 'with diligence, but not without' – and anyway kept a weather eye out for the market rent. Against advice, he harried out a tenant whose rent was in arrears, using the meaningless, age-old self-justification that 'Unless he can make his farm answer, it is better for himself that he should leave it...'[31]

This was a quite different attitude from that espoused by the old northern aristocratic landowners, best represented by the Earl of Carlisle's steward, John Ramshay, around the mid-century.† Talking about small tenanted farms, or possibly the dangers for really small customary tenants upon enclosure, Ramshay's view was that:

> 'The policy of destroying small holdings depends upon the necessities of expedience of individual cases. To carry the policy to anything like the full extent would occasion a good

---

* It could be argued that a system that in places left the lord of the manor retaining power over the trees of customary tenants, yet unable to plant and protect trees on his common, was lose-lose for a productive woodland estate: reasonably acceptable though it was for the shepherd.

† The drastic Poor Law Bill of 1834 is seen as representing this new millocrat/ aristocratic tension too.

deal of hardship and would lead to dissatisfaction. These small tenants are generally the most industrious class – They have in almost all cases been at service for a number of years – by care and saving have been able to get together as much as will start them on a small farm and as a rule they are very deserving people.'

It was virtually inevitable then that disquiet had begun to rumble in the Parish soon after John Marshall II had become lord of the manor in 1832. Just a year later, the *Cumbrian Pacquet* published a piece, under a running headline SPECIMEN OF WHIGISM, complaining about Marshall's refusal to continue the annual Keswick Races at Crow Park. The millocrat was charged with acting in exactly the way he maintained the Tories did, doing 'as he likes with his own'.[32] For, as the article in the *Pacquet* pointed out, the races had not just provided much enjoyment; 'during the festive days much money was expended in the neighbourhood', which would have helped the townspeople and hardly affected the Marshalls' ample pockets.

Greta Bridge passed from Marshall's domain in the east to St Kentigern's Crosthwaite in the west; a distinction originally conceived during the Norman administration.

The next week a letter to the *Pacquet* from 'The Old Man from his observatory on the Top Of Skiddaw' (presumably Southey) made two more complaints. The charge for guides to put a boat on the lake had doubled, and the age-old custom of the 'poorer class' drying their washing on hedges in the Derwentwater estate had been rudely shattered, as 'now their clothes are torn from the hedges and thrown into the roads'.[33] And life had indeed become tougher for Marshall's estate workers, who found their wages more than halved from the 2s. 6d. a day paid by Greenwich Hospital. It was said that, quite unlike the average Cumberland labourer of the time, they were paid so little that they 'could scarcely keep their families in bread'.[34] This was particularly shocking for the Parish as, since 1820, they had been used to the very different regime of Southey's friend Edward Locker, who as secretary to the hospital actively supported the land workers and their employment, believing this to be part of his responsibility.

However, the biggest change the Marshalls made in the Parish, their 7,000-acre enclosure, was not carried out until thirteen years after John II's death in 1836. But it was sought, I will argue, at least in part because of state changes to manorial governance made in 1828. The government had legislated that there should be formal petty sessions divisions, overseen by JPs, for all the wards, and these had ruled supreme over local governance across most of the country ever since. Even in Cumberland many manor courts had closed by the end of the eighteenth century. But in the Parish and most other upland territories they continued hence, after 1810, between 80 and 90 per cent of Cumberland manor court cases related to grazing rights.[35] So, when John II had taken over the Derwentwater manor in 1832, the petty sessions courts would not have seemed threatening to Keswick, as the town was too far from the centre of the county. However, once the new, smaller Derwent division was created, 'to bring justice, as it were, to every man's door',[36] the year after the Marshall purchase, the circumference narrowed.

At first, this had no effect, and their manor court went on as before, sitting most Saturdays at the Moot Hall, while the petty sessions court sat at Cockermouth. But, by 1847, Keswick had been ordered to establish its own petty sessions court too. From that moment on, while a joint Court Baron and Customary Court[37] would continue into the next century, to be held annually on 22 May, the regular business of the manor courts, with their customary tenant jury, was taken over by two new Keswick state courts. The first was a petty sessions court for the Derwent division that sat in the Marshalls' Moot Hall[38] and called upon two of the four JPs then available: James and Joshua Stanger, Thomas Spedding and the Hon. John Henry Curzon,* who lived at Derwent Lodge in Portinscale. And the second was a new county court of record, which, having no official housing, met monthly at the King's Arms, just as the Eighteen Men had, and arbitrated land disputes up to the value of £20, this being the sum below which a man could not be arrested prior to the case coming to court.

This change caused a seismic shift in power from the customary tenant to the landlord class.[39] It was probably the largest single life-change in the statemen's history and was certainly the quickest to take effect. It seems inevitable that this major diminution in their status would have affected the statesmen's self-regard, since – other than retaining governance over the school – their class lost the power it had enjoyed for some 450 years over all local affairs.

The date of the first Keswick petty sessions, sometime before 1847, is clearly significant in terms of the date of the Derwentwater enclosure, which was first mooted in 1842 and finally agreed in 1849. And it seems probable to me that the tectonic shift from parochial/manor governance to state governance was the primary reason the Marshalls took the action they did. Realising that it would be unwise to place much future reliance on their traditional oversight of the old democratic management of the commons, they decided, along with their tenants, to enclose a considerable portion of Derwentwater and Castlerigg land. For the tenants, extra land for themselves and common land over which they had joint control, at a time when they had lost their judicial powers over it, must have felt good.

* The fourth son of Lord Teynham, who probably arrived in Keswick after his 1829 marriage in Carlisle.

The Marshalls gained control of rather more than double their original demesne land, over which they obviously still retained control, and the tenants received a roughly similar percentage of land for their own individual exclusive control. John I's aim had always been to stint the commons (making smaller enclosures with a legislated number of animals allowed to graze), which he almost always failed to achieve elsewhere, but in memoriam, the Marshalls now stinted rather than enclosed the commons, by some way the largest part of the 7,000 acres falling within the Act.

Again, it seems obvious why this suited the tenants; stinted land largely prevented overgrazing (and had long been used success-fully at Wythburn), and continued the old, cooperative, mutually enforced management they had always favoured for pasture. Stinting avoided the costs of stricter division, which, as we have seen, could be disproportionately expensive, and sometimes ruinous, for the smaller landowners. The Marshalls' desire for stinting is far more surprising. Stints involved community, rather than individual, rule, which was against their principles, and they had no control over the land of their stints, which, like their fellow stint-owners, they were unable to usefully improve unilaterally, build on or grow wood on. Equally, it was land they could not sell, only the stints upon it being purchasable. In fact, the practice of stinting had nothing practical or ideological to recommend it to the millocrat's family.

But, for the passionate lover of Lake District land, it was another matter. The Marshall enclosure was one of several late enclosures of large amounts of fell land in the central Lake District, where it was soon discovered that little economically viable improvement would be possible. All the others were enclosed by using new, rigidly rect-angular fencing 'created on the enclosure commissioners' drawing board',[40] much of it later converted to coniferous forest plantations. In the Parish, the only such plantation that would endure was in the Manchester Corporation land surrounding Thirlmere. So the aesthetic benefits of stinting were large.

As a friend of Wordsworth said, 'Inclose the Common, and dead fences will come across the eye. If we wait till they are succeeded by thorn hedges, which we cannot see over, what will become of our prospect ... we have the lawn of nature before us, let us retain it.'[41]

In agreeing with this, the Marshalls, despite their irritation with customary tenancies, in fact conserved the 'second nature' that generations of Parish tenants, along with nature, had wrought on the land through shepherding. A landscape and life that still honours them today. Although seldom mentioned by name, Marshall played a major part in developing the nascent idea of landscape conservation in the Lake District.

The Fall: the Real 'Demise'
of the Parish Statesmen

DESPITE THE STATE'S beginning to curtail their governance of the land, around this time the Cumberland sheep
farmers' extraordinarily long-held capacity to order their
own environment took a major step forward. The first *Shepherd's
Guide, or a Delineation of the Wool and Ear-marks of the different
Stocks of Sheep on the East Fells*[1] had been published in 1817, so
that everyone could identify a stray sheep and 'restore to every man
his own'. Six areas within the Parish were included in the second
edition of the *Guide*,[2] appearing soon afterwards, which, although
still a small-scale affair, repeated the call of the first book, 'That all
stray sheep shall be proclaimed at the church on Sunday, and at the
two nearest market towns, by bellman on market days'.[3]

This proviso was dropped as the new editions got larger
and thicker and governance changed, and the year after the
Marshalls' enclosure they were co-signatories in the *Shepherd's
Guide for the West*, which published a thousand names including, for the first time, those from Castlerigg, Naddle and
Thornthwaite.[4] Then, in 1873, a giant book, incorporating all
the fell associations, listed the places of meeting for each district. Many, no doubt, carried on from the old shepherds' meets,
as they did in Thirlmere, where the meets had been held for
generations at Thirlspot (home to the King's Head pub, often
mentioned by the Wordsworths) and Dockray alternately. And
there they remained until the 2005 *Shepherd's Guide* recorded
a move to Threlkeld cricket club[5] as the hill farmers continued

to maintain order in their vast connected sheep-heafs across the whole of the district.

This new printed information was particularly important after the end of the manor courts, for much had clearly changed. The loss of the deep local knowledge provided by the ancient involvement of vestry governance in Cumberland, and the Eighteen Men in the Parish, had become quickly apparent. By 1875 it was recorded that considerably more disputes between the smaller landholders about damages – primarily concerned with trespass of stock – arose in the county court than had been known before, even though the judgements were suspect since they were made by men with little, or even no, knowledge of the ancient heaf arrangements.[6]

*

More generally, we left the long-running argument about the states-men's demise convinced, I hope, that Wordsworth's sense of the significance of the years 1775–1800, in terms of numerical loss, was an essential part of the truth, puncturing the otherwise virtually universal focus on the years 1815–50. However, his intuitive sense of what was happening to the statesmen's world he had grown up in had not been shared by those born twenty years later. William Blamire, John Christian Curwen's nephew and chairman of the tithe commissioners, born in 1790, had reported to Parliament in 1833 that '...since 1815 a greater change has taken place in the pro-prietors of small farms than any antecedent period of much longer duration ... The number [of statesmen] has considerably dimin-ished.'[7] This was an even more specific timeline than Wordsworth's and, as Blamire was the most respected indigenous contemporary expert, his judgment has always been given much weight.

However, a witness to the 1832 Poor Law Commission had reported that 'property is more divided here I suppose than in any other county in the Kingdom'.[8] And, as Searle records no loss of statesmen at all in the core Lake District between 1800 and 1830, and less than a tenth of the loss between 1775 and 1800 in the rest of Cumberland, it seems Blamire was mistaken, certainly about the Lake District; probably for the entirely human reason that he had

been a boy in the war years, when things went well, and will have
been shocked by the pain he witnessed on the land after its end –
pain that was, to him, a new thing.* So, having already relayed the
virtually unanimous reports of Cumbrian farmers to the 1832 Poor
Law Commission that their capital was 'diminishing',[9] he brought
up the problems with children's legacies. These had escalated, as
the peak average statesman's legacy to his children between 1825
and 1830 – £326 – was more than double the pre-war average.

Blamire added, 'I know of some remarkable instances where
parents have left a provision for their younger children out of
estates which have not been sold during the continuance of high
prices, which have fallen so much … as to leave their eldest sons
with hardly anything.'[10] Wills often included provisions for quite
speedy payment after the testator's death, so even a small freeholder
or enfranchised customary tenant might have to take on more debt
to be able to provide for his children's or siblings' legacies. These
legacies might in turn lead to a breaking up of land into smaller
holdings, although I have come across no clear evidence of this in
the Parish. But there *was* a change, and it is one that has been far
less talked about. Despite the post-war problems, the average customary tenant after the end of the war had a far better standard of
living than his grandfather or great-grandfather.

The numbers of agricultural labourers and farm servants
recorded in the 1841 census were strikingly high.† In the
Derwentwater manor, for example, the census revealed that all the
farmers had live-in servants, whatever the size of their holding,
even capturing a fifty-year-old agricultural labourer with five children and two servants.[11] This is a real surprise, for back in 1776
the disgruntled anonymous reporter in *The Gentleman's Magazine*

---

* The underlying conclusion of this para is necessarily true of the Parish, which
had no, or virtually no, small freeholders before enfranchisement (except some
of the Keswick burgage tenants). I would also expect that conditions would
not have been seriously different for those parishes with a preponderance of
small freeholders in a mixed landholding area.
† The census also captured a small influx of miners, as the end of the period
saw the beginning of a burst of mining development and redevelopment and
the rents from miners will have helped substitute for the loss of income from
home-working with wool.

had said, 'These petty landowners work like slaves; they cannot afford to keep a man servant, but husband, wife, son and daughters all turn out to work in the fields'; and the more balanced Arthur Young had agreed in 1822 that there were few farm labourers on small farms. So, some things, even if they were ignored by Blamire, who had not witnessed pre-war conditions, were unequivocally better for the statesmen after the war than they had been some fifteen years before it.

In the second half of the century, conditions fairly quickly reverted back to those described a hundred years earlier, family labour becoming the essential component of the workforce once again. In the 1841 census for Castlerigg, for instance, two 50-acre farmers and two agricultural labourers had employed nine servants between them. Yet, in the 1871 census, when three families occupied the same land – two farmers with 120 acres each and a butcher – they employed just three servants between them, one of the farmers relying entirely on his six children.[12] And, retrospectively, it is now apparent that, between the 1851 and 1911 census, the number of 'indoors' and 'outdoors' labourers/servants in Cumberland and Westmorland dropped by a startling 60 per cent, from 21,000 to 8,500.[13]

Since the Parish years between 1820 and 1850 also fail to provide additional evidence to support the views of contemporary commentators about the timing of the largest loss of statesman numbers (see pages 335–39), the context of their misconceptions deserves more thought. Most significantly, the whole issue of landholding after the French wars had become a curious public flashpoint in the broader fight about England's post-war future, and the Lake District held the key to one of the central arguments of the debate.

Wordsworth had always been clear that landholding for peasant proprietors was at the heart of his concern, arguing in his 1801 letter to Charles Fox not just for better treatment for the poor but for a broader definition of poverty, to allow the inclusion of property owners – the theme behind his profoundly felt early poem 'The Last of the Flock'. Strong 'domestic affections' were fundamental to his sense of the ideal conditions for human life, and he believed that they 'will always be strongest amongst men who live in a country not crowded by population, if these men are placed above poverty'. The last phrase reveals his key to saving the statesmen.

And Wordsworth had been strong to save. In 1824 he successfully opposed the enclosure of Grasmere commons in support of the needs of the fell farmers. This was appreciated. 'Ye may gar now reet up to t'sky ower Guzedale, wi'out liggin' leg to t'fence, and all through him',[14] a local builder, whom Wordsworth had taught to skate, told Canon Rawnsley. And, in 1835, the Tory Wordsworth argued that it was better for 'ten undeserving' to be assisted by the poor laws than that 'one morally good man, through want of relief, should either have his principles corrupted, or his energies destroyed'.[15]

When first articulated, Wordsworth's argument that the way of life of his small statesman proprietors had been, and should remain, uniquely beneficial for the poor chimed with various people who had been promoting the gift – or cheap lease – of small areas of land to all since the 1780s. Tom Paine and Thomas Spence, among others, had carried this idea forward, and Robert Owen resurrected it after the end of the French wars; the intention of all was to assist society by creating more self-sufficiency in food for its poorer members. In 1821, William Cobbett had pronounced 'a return to *small farms* to be *absolutely necessary* to the restoration of anything like an English community'.[16] Seven years before Wordsworth's death in 1850, after a series of particularly violent industrial protests, the Chartist Land Plan had been introduced, its intention being to help factory workers to leave the town and live independently in a cottage with an allotment of 2 to 4 acres.[17] But there was a flaw in the arguments.

Cobbett's case for small farms was badly weakened by the reality that they had long gone in most of England. And behind his argument, and that of the whole movement, lay the virtually unprovable legend of lost rights. This made Wordsworth's portrait of Lake District society central. There, the age-old rights of small landowners (customary tenants in the most part) remained. The recent reordering of society may have made their lives more difficult, but for those who were able to continue, their rights continued too, a tangible example for society to examine. This allowed John Stuart

Mill, the pre-eminent philosopher of the time, to champion peasant proprietors in his *Principles of Political Economy* in 1848, his decision to do so largely a result of his reading Wordsworth's description of Lake District statesmen. 'Cumberland and Westmoreland', Mill wrote, were the one 'part of England, unfortunately a very small part, where peasant proprietors are still common.'[18] But their existence legitimised the potential practicability of the plans of those reformers who wished to provide landholdings for the poor.

Southey's *Colloquies*, meanwhile, had launched the Lake District into the lively early rumblings of the post-war debate about whether the standard of living of the British working class was helped or hindered by industrialisation, a controversy that persists to this day. It can be claimed that he was the first to propose both that the industrial poor were more damaged than not, and that they should therefore be helped by state intervention; the Lake District battle richly illustrated by Macaulay's vituperative, highly personalised rebuttal (see pages 439–47).

For a Whig, the concept of looking backwards to look forward provoked rage in itself. Remembering the amused scorn of the late eighteenth-century government inspectors about the 'inefficiencies' of statesman farming, it isn't difficult to imagine the farming moderniser's anger, not just that winter employment was still preferred to the use of threshing machines[19] – at a time of a vastly increasing national need to feed industrial workers – but that some people actually admired such stubborn landholders. Some critics went so far as to 'advocate that the statesmen should be removed from their land'.[20] By whom, one wonders? Emotions ran high, and facts lost their weight, as they so often do in long-drawn-out political debates. Since statistical proof was then unavailable and the arguments rested mainly upon impression, this was perhaps inevitable.

So unpleasantries still peppered the debate. Blamire had reported to Parliament that Cumberland farmers still lived frugally, albeit 'now they have tea and coffee for breakfast; formerly they never had anything but porridge'.[21] Perhaps because the accusation that statesmen were living off the fat of the land would not stand up to scrutiny, and few scorned the statesmen's work ethic (as opposed to their efficiency), modernisers concentrated on Blamire's absolutely correct description of the increased legacies for children, considering the statesmen to be aping the gentry. This attack continued into the twentieth century. In a 1984 article, the historian J. V. Beckett, an expert on Cumbrian landownership, wrote that 'eighteenth-century Cumbria witnessed a deliberate search for status. Thus, the more prosperous yeoman began to imitate the habits of the gentry, entailing their estates, giving portions to their daughters, and providing jointures for their wives'.[22] Apparently, they were exercising their 'domestic affections' for no other reason than to show off.

At a time when the conditions faced by children working in factories shocked much of the nation, the Lake District statesmen were, as we have just seen, to be penalised economically if possible and, retrospectively, to be patronised – merely for attempting to look after their families. Were such critics worried, perhaps, that any continued success on the part of the statesmen – given their conservatism in farming matters and close identification with the past, combined with their care for the financial security of future generations – would undermine the core Whig belief in 'progress'?

Today, there is a deeper questioning generally of the reality of the whole twentieth-century argument about 'the demise'[23] of the statesmen. We saw the *Cumberland Pacquet* reflecting Keswick distaste about some of the actions taken by the Marshalls in the 1830s, yet a study of the *Carlisle Journal* in the years 1815, 1822 and 1833 shows that, while parliamentary papers about national agricultural distress and national unrest over corn prices were reported, no comments about a local farming crisis were ever attached.[24] Perhaps, even more significantly, there was no press outcry about the findings of Blamire's Select Committee, so relied upon today.[25] And several factors – above all, the consistent assumption that the different directories and government census-takers all used similar definitions of the words 'farmer' and 'yeoman'* – have served to undermine both contemporary and twentieth-century arguments.

A forensic modern study of eight Furness townships revealed the

* The census takers obscured the complex reality of Cumbrian land workers by sticking to their understood categories of straightforward commercial capitalist farming. The discovery of more reliable records (such as the Lawson papers in Borrowdale) has also made things clearer.

serious unreliability of both the statistics and the comparisons the studies had been based on.[26] In a comparison of the 1849 directory and the 1851 census, the latter was shown to list 30 per cent more farmers and yeomen than the directory; only half of those listed in either source could be found under the same category in both; and the median acreage of the farms included in the directory was two and a half times larger than those of the farms the directory excluded. In the Parish, according to the first genuine directory,[27] published in 1829, which distinguished between 'yeomen' and 'farmers' – in this context meaning, respectively, landowners of whatever kind and renters – about 48 per cent of Newland inhabitants were yeomen but, bizarrely, under 25 per cent in St John's, Castlerigg and Wythburn (taken as one unit).[28] When one remembers that the majority of its Wythburn holdings were 40 acres or under in 1851, and that at the turn of the century Newlands had 65 per cent owner-occupiers, the directory figures seem unlikely to be reliable.

This misreading of the statistics was often compounded by the many critics who jettisoned Wordsworth's use of the word 'statesmen', seeing its use as a Romantic affectation. The poet had created his own category muddle once, as we saw earlier (see p. 290, ft p. 330), but, essentially, the word 'statesman' had one simple function for him: to encompass all owner-occupiers below the level of the great farmers, whether they were on the breadline, a prosperous yeoman, a small freeholder, or a customary or enfranchised tenant.

'Yeoman' (with a good sprinkling of 'peasants') became the usual twentieth-century substitute for 'statesman'. But in the Parish the word is entirely absent in the 1841 census for St John's-in-the-Vale, Castlerigg and Wythburn; and it has just one mention in their 1871 census[29] – this for John Wilkinson, who farmed 210 acres,[30] which was double the acreage frequently considered the maximum of the 'statesman class' in the twentieth century. Equally absent in the records of central government and the Anglican Church, the word is also as appropriate to the world outside Cumbria and the Lake District as within it. So, for some, it meant a relatively wealthy customary tenant, usually enfranchised, sometimes not, and/or leaseholder, and/or freeholder; mix as desired. What it almost never meant was a customary tenant holding 10 or 20 acres, a key component of Wordsworth's statesman class.

It has become clear in retrospect that the number of 'grazier farmers' recorded in Cumberland in 1851 – 5,266 – remained virtually constant until 1911.[31] In marked contrast to the 60 per cent drop in the numbers of agricultural labourers and farm servants, grazier farmers declined by less than 2 per cent during the same period. Put together, these facts emphasise the lower standard of living for the statesmen after the mid-nineteenth century and suggest – as was indeed the case – that their land had a lower average acreage. In 1851 the land ratio for the Cumberland 'grazier farmers' split almost fifty-fifty between those holding 5 to 49 acres, and 50 to 99 acres,[32] with 60 per cent of farms holding fewer than 100 acres (and an even higher ratio in Westmorland) as against a national average of 22 per cent. By the 1870s, even though the 'grazier farmers' still worked 75 per cent of Cumberland and Westmorland farms, their average size had significantly decreased as nearly 77 per cent of Cumbrian farmers then held between 5 and 100 acres.[33] The frustration for us is that the relevant records only differentiate by size of holding, not between customary tenants, enfranchised or otherwise, and leasehold farms, so the golden thread running through our story is almost lost.

However, David Uttley's excellent study of the Leath ward in 2007 provides an answer for 1913, when 19 per cent of the tenancies there were customary and a further 16 per cent mixed.[34] He takes the same conservative 50 per cent split of the mixed tenancies as we did for Searle's analysis of Nicolson and Burn (see page 336), and arrives at the conclusion that 27 per cent of Leath landholdings remained customary tenancies in 1913, exactly the percentage the study provides for relevant landowners, through analysing the tithe returns. He also reports Margaret Shepherd's work identifying 35 per cent of landholders remaining owner-occupiers in the pastoral parish of Stainmore in Westmorland in 1910.[35] So the general situation is clear: the statesmen had continued farming but with less help and considerably less land.

Mutton prices rose by 30 per cent[36] during this time, and wool prices finally returned to where they had been in their wartime heyday. And when a taste for leaner joints of mutton started to emerge, the hill farmers changed their practices, adapting to a new market, and sold their lambs and wethers earlier,[37] their business now fully connected to a wider than local market. Then, in 1893, a decade after Rawnsley joined the Parish, the *Carlisle Journal* reported that large farms were in serious trouble because of the costs of labour while the smaller farmer, who could now buy small 'mowing machines and reapers... which can be fitted into the space of a cupboard in the barn' were doing well.[38] This relative success, compared with the rest of the country, continued up until 1913. Combine this with the incontrovertible evidence that the numbers of the five thousand or so 'grazier farmers' hardly varied between 1851 and 1911 and the numerical argument for a 'demise of the statesmen' should be finally laid to rest.

The Parish and the core Lake District had started the century with virtually a third more statesmen than Cumberland generally,[39] the hold of customary tenancy always stronger in the Lake District than across Cumberland as a whole, and this proportional difference is likely to have risen as modernisation grew apace in the lowlands. And, as customary tenancy seemed, ever increasingly, most suited to pastoral hill-farming, the hill-farmers had become relatively successful between 1840 and 1870.[40] So it seems safe to assume (given the 27 per cent survival of customary tenants in Leath ward in 1913 and 35 per cent in the Westmorland pastoral parish in 1910) that our Parish, with fewer original small freeholders than the Leath ward and enjoying a successful hill-farming period, would have approached the First World War with a minimum of 30 per cent of its land farmed by statesmen; 32 to 33 per cent would probably be the best reasonable guess.

However, undoubtedly something had happened to cause Canon Rawnsley at the very beginning of the twentieth century to call a man with 1,300 sheep a 'chieftain shepherd',[41] despite his refrain about having a crack with one of the last, late-lamented 'old statesmen' still alive. But this change had little to do with numbers of people and the conserving case had never rested upon statistics, which was the opposition's preoccupation. Wordsworth and Southey were fighting to save a hard-working egalitarian way of life, in which you had and took responsibility for your own life and worked within a mutually reinforcing autonomous community. Soon after the middle of the century, that description had lost much of its reality in the Parish, as the statesman class no longer had the responsibility for looking after it, even though, in the old Percy lands at Braithwaite, the final manor court verdict was not taken until 1868. By 1900 there could have been no thought of it.

It was surely this relative loss of status that was the *actual* loss that caused the lament for the exaggeratedly diminishing number – and eventual extinction – of 'the old-fashioned statesman'. In the Parish, the life the parishioners' ancestors had taken for granted was no longer fully there to live, and the statesmen held a different place in society.

A hundred years earlier, in 1750, the Parish statesmen had been in pragmatic control of all they surveyed. They provided the juries for the courts and, throughout that century, beat back every landlord's attack for profit and timber. They provided the Eighteen Men for the vestry to administer the school, the Parish taxes and the poor law, and to give guidance on the regulations of the commons. They remained robust in opposition to any interference in the administration and financing of the school from the vicar, although they had started paying their tithes more honestly. Socially, supposing this was a subject they ever thought about, since no one received 'attention or respect' from 'claims of blood or wealth',[42] there was no one to better them living in the Parish, except for the vicar and – in the summer – the Leathes family at Dale-head, whose influence did not really spread past the Thirlmere Valley. This was the life Wordsworth and the conservers wanted to protect.

But before the end of the eighteenth century the historically robust mutual identification between rich and poor statesmen had become fractured once the self-interest of the richer statesmen, who wanted more land on the commons for their black sheep and cattle trade, caused a dislocation both of the laws of the commons and the uses of the courts. The Parish may have remained more cohesive than the average, largely through the effects of the school governance, but once the Lake District was opened up, the Crosthwaite/

Keswick valley had more than its share of early new arrivals, with the power to upset the old balance.

When describing what he called 'the Romantic Settlement', the historian W. A. Collingwood wrote 'these good people, like the Vikings, first came on raids and then as immigrants'. But in Keswick the moves were almost simultaneous, as the town had by far the earliest history of any in the Lake District[43] of people moving in for reasons other than earning a living. Following Joseph Pocklington and Lord William Gordon were the Lake Poets at the turn of the nineteenth century, and the people who swam in Southey's wake. This had created yet more change, as, for the first time since the brief appearance of the Le Flemings in the seventeenth century, no gentry had actually lived full-time in the valley.

William Calvert was the first, his status established by his father's and grandfather's roles as stewards for the Howards. This was revolutionary in itself, and, after Calvert's death, his grand new house was bought by a younger son of the Speddings from Mirehouse, the first family from the established local gentry to live in the Parish. Other old statesmen families had achieved a more obviously acknowledged status by then too. In 1796, Thomas Allason, Thomas Gaskarth and Joseph Fisher of Thornthwaite, all with surnames from the 1613 Derwentwater 'enfranchisement', were each identified as 'gentleman' in a legal document.[44] And there were no doubt others.

Then two local men were individually named in the summary of the commutation of tithes: Sir John Walsh (the Brownrigg Ormathwaite heir) and Abraham Fisher Esq. The Brownriggs, who held some land in Newlands as well, had always been seen as important, but their status had markedly risen with the fame of the distinguished chemist,* his pall bearers including the three baronets Sir Wilfrid Lawson, Sir Michael Le Fleming and Sir Frederick Fletcher-Vane. However, upon his death, Ormathwaite produced just another absentee Parish landlord. John Fisher had been named as a principal landholder in Borrowdale's Great Deed, his heirs

---

* Dr William Brownrigg of Ormathwaite Hall, the second most important scientist to have been born in Cumberland (see chapter 10).

now holding land in St John's and Underskiddaw as well. And, as we learnt from Southey's attempts to buy Greta Hall, some of the tribe had moved to London and become decidedly well off; the £50,000 legacy from Isaac to Joseph Fisher – who, like Abraham, lived in Seatoller House in Borrowdale – was more than enough to produce another local Parish 'gentleman'. Although, by 1864, the house would become tenanted after Abraham died childless.

These families reflected, like the Bankes, the Williamsons and the Wrens before them in the Elizabethan and Commonwealth periods, the potential change from statesman to gentleman. But* they were not then JPs and seldom socialised with the Parish's imported gentry. James Stanger broke the mould by returning with a city fortune, rather than leaving to make one, and he and his brother Joshua, upon his return, along with William Calvert, were JPs. And then there were Southey's more itinerant friends: General Peachy, General Wade, Lord Sunderlin et al. (often taking over Pocklington houses), and the more recent Slacks and the Hon. John Henry Curzon, many of whom were JPs too. Above all, of course, there were the Marshalls.

For nearly 500 years the Parish statesmen had been welded into an age-old vestry system along with the vicar, and memories lingered of the time when they had had the local Derwentwaters as their lord, major landowner and leader in the national wars against Scotland. The new gentry could, through the vagaries of their house ownership, find themselves involved in Parish government – witness a call to appoint Southey as the surveyor of roads – but, intrinsically, it was their wealth that changed the old structures. A good example of this is when James Stanger and Henry Peachy created the Thornthwaite-cum-Braithwaite district as a condition of their £2,000 gift that allowed Thornthwaite's chapel to become a district church. Or, again, the whole impact on the area of the Marshalls' activities.

A balance for the statesmen, some aided by their new land after the enclosures, might have been found that assailed neither their self-respect nor their identity, had this not coincided with the

* With the exception of a later Abraham Fisher in 1860.

changes created by the two seismic nineteenth-century movements we have already glimpsed.

Firstly, capitalist, utilitarian thought and practice had come firmly to the fore (its rise both prompted by and improving the rapidly growing strength of national and international markets), creating a new aristocracy of industry. This was a class epitomised by John Marshall, who, typically, thought economic benefit the key to motivation and happiness. More Parish land had been bought for income, and so farmed by others than the landowners. And John Marshall was not unusual in taking great care over his rents. Rack-renting, as the phrase is used today, might be an exaggeration, but the new farmers were certainly not going to become easily and consistently better off. Nevertheless, many became wealthy enough to be able to time their entry into the market, holding on to stock until prices rose, leaving the smaller, mortgaged Parish landowner seriously disadvantaged if, to preserve any capital at all, he needed to sell when prices were low or borrow yet more to keep going.

Secondly, and most critically, the state asserted its power over local governance, imposing administrative centralisation on Cumberland again for the first time since the Tudors. And it was the specific government action of creating the new Derwent division that soon severed the umbilical cord between the Parish statesmen and the courts, the buttress of their long-held local power. The manor court system had certainly been creaking, but, as has been said, the courts 'were neither independent self-perpetuating bodies nor instruments of the lords' interest. They were tenant organisations'.[45] So, when the state ordained that Parish legislation move from statesmen's juries to gentry JPs, it wiped out most of the local power and influence of the statesman at a stroke.

The only spheres of influence that remained for them were shepherding, and for a little longer, the school. They had become 'just farmers', and farmers without any legal influence on the management of the commons or any official power to mitigate centralised regulations relating to their land. Most of their old responsibilities had been taken over by the gentry. Of course, it seemed and felt different in the Parish; the status of the statesmen had been severely reduced. As late as 1845, Sir John Woodford* wrote to the Borrowdale statesmen that since 'time immemorial' their ancestors had believed that their form of landholding was 'a valuable privilege, which proved ... the honourable and ancient lineage of [their] families, putting them on equal footing, in all respects of the old ancestral descent with some of the highest of the land'.[46] Somehow, this no longer rang true.

So, the years between the 1760s and 1874,† from the opening up of the Lake District to the eventual removal of the Eighteen Men and their governance of the school, witnessed a revolutionary change in the Parish; one that damaged for ever the old power of the better-off statesmen, who had made up the Eighteen Men and overseen the secular governance of its 90 square miles for nearly 500 years. With the intrusion of new gentry and new ways of making laws, the 1837 statement that 'the statesmen have approached much more near the common level' became simply true.[47] As it did throughout the Lake District. What was not true was the assumption that the vast majority of statesmen had simply left their land and disappeared; there had been a fall in relative status, rather than a 'demise'.[48]

And, even at 'more near the common level', members of the old statesman class could still hold their heads high. A full 200 years after the small farming proprietor had been swept away from most other areas of England,[49] the unique Cumbrian history of landownership continued to produce a unique result. In the last twenty-odd years of the nineteenth century, when the price of mutton, beef and corn started to drop as imports swelled, the demand for lamb and lightweight mutton held up and the 'backward' Cumbrian hill farmers, never trading corn but still growing sufficient oats and turnips for themselves and their stock, survived the depression years (until well after the First World War) with a success 'almost unmatched in the whole of England'.[50] In the census of 1891, their number actually rose.[51] For the Whig and the Marxist, that must have been as exasperating as it was incomprehensible.

* He would inherit Lord Gordon's old estate.
† The decade before Wordsworth registered the beginnings of a change of status and the date that the school was removed from the statesman to state control.

Friendships Were For Life and Longer

ROBERT SOUTHEY MAY have found both the dispute about
the constitution of St John's and the church's arrival in
the Parish a welcome distraction from his own, now sad,
life. Greta Hall, which had seen three families grow up there and
had overflowed with people every summer, was to be sepulchrally
quiet for nine long years. In 1834, after her return, Edith had to
be looked after, with the help of their two unmarried daughters.
Her condition was variable but always such that they could 'have
no abiding guests'. While they were helped financially the following year – Southey was given a £300 annual government grant,
after turning down Prime Minister Peel's offer of a baronetcy –
and while he had always been patient with his wife and '[her] old
unhappy habit of objecting to everything',[1] he was concerned about
subjecting the same strain upon his daughters.

He trusted in their inherent sense of duty and the mutual support
they would all offer each other. 'They keep up their spirits for my
sake, and mine are better because I have to support theirs. Indeed,
mine are equal to the demand upon them,'[2] he wrote firmly. But the
poet, always one for whistling in the wind, can only have benefited
from Parish distractions outside the house. The early foundations
of the lovely Marshall church, to be built of pink limestone from
the Eden valley, had just been laid at the end of 1836, when John
Marshall II died, at the tragically young age of thirty-nine. He
had not left any provision in his will for the completion of the
church[3] but his wife, Mary Ballantine Marshall, who had buried
her husband as an Anglican, paid for its completion and took his
place until their young son Reginald reached his majority.

Southey had written to William Peachy before John Marshall's death, happily telling him that, in response to the bishop's and Marshall's invitation, he had agreed to be one of the two trustees of the church and would appoint the second incumbent to the curacy. After John's death, Reginald Marshall's trustees understood that they would have the sole nomination for the first appointment, and thereafter make appointments jointly with another trustee, either Southey or an individual chosen by the 'pew-renters according to the subscriptions contributed'.[4] But Southey had become decidedly more anxious about his involvement. In 1837, he described the office as 'forced upon me' and was worried about the source of a sufficient endowment to support a priest and build a parsonage.[5] But he underestimated the Marshall family; a 'parsonage', also designed by Salvin, was rapidly put up, using local stone from Castlehead, with instructions that all material and labour should 'be of the best'. So, perhaps because the building costs of £1,630 were double the original estimate, it was paid for by John's sister, Mary Ann. Southey should have remembered his view of the previous year, when he told Peachy that 'nothing can be more liberal than the whole of Mr Marshall's conduct'.[6]

Meanwhile, during the building of St John's, James Stanger was improving St Kentigern's. Responding to a petition to remove the vertiginous singers' gallery at the west end and replace it with a more subdued affair for the schoolchildren, he created an organ gallery for the fine organ[7] he had donated. Reverend Lynn spruced up everything, chiselling the stone and taking the radical step of removing the interior whitewash (along with all the vestiges of previous painting, alas), which had traditionally been reapplied annually.

In early October 1837, Cuthbert Southey went up to Queen's College, Oxford, having not being accepted for Christ Church, to the disappointment of Edith May's husband, John Warter: 'I am sorry he is to be at Queens owing to the society he must now seek out of college. In his own they are mostly North-countrymen and sadly unpolished.'[8] A month later, Edith died and Southey's words to his brother Henry (with whom his daughter Kate was staying) – 'thank God she is now at rest'[9] – expressed gratitude for the deliverance of all four of them. However, six weeks later he would tell

Henry, 'I am a full ten years older than when you saw me in the summer'[10] and, with only Bertha and Mrs Lovell (the other Fricker sister) in the house, Southey felt unbearably lonely, and remained silent. But spring began to do its work and the poet made strenuous efforts, taking daily 4-mile walks come rain or shine, which he knew helped to boost his spirits.[11]

Nevertheless, on a foreign trip in August (in a party that included, as well as Southey, Cuthbert and Humphrey Senhouse), Henry Crabb Robinson* wrote starkly in his diary: 'None of us in setting out were aware of how great a degree the mind of the Laureate had departed. He had lost all power of conversation and seldom spoke.'[12] That summer, Southey had become obsessed with the idea that a marriage with the poet Caroline Bowles would set everything to rights. They had corresponded for twenty years, and the editor of their letters concluded, despite their correspondence having begun twelve years after Herbert's death, that Caroline was fixed in Southey's mind 'as a friend in darkening days, after the death of his beloved son, and when he began to step down from the heights of his life'.[13] Perhaps so. Certainly, Southey believed her care and solicitude offered the only chance of reverting to his old self.

Two months later, in October, just under a year after Edith's death, Caroline persuaded Southey to tell his children that they planned to marry the following year. He wrote to Bertha and Edith May, 'You will love her the more for having made me myself again,' and 'as far as human foresight extends, I have provided against that loneliness which I must else have felt when any farther diminution of my reduced household might take place'.[14] But these thoughts made no difference to Cuthbert. Having appeared to get on with Caroline when they met earlier, he reacted to the news of his father's impending second marriage with fury.

Southey was at home at the consecration of St John the Evangelist by the bishop on 27 December 1838, when Chancellor Fletcher read the deed from the altar declaring Mary Ballantine Marshall 'sole Foundress and Patroness'.[15] James Bush had not been offered

---

* The friend who had identified that the treatment of religion in Wordsworth's *Excursion* would not satisfy either 'a religionist or a sceptic'.

the chance to become the chapel's first curate, an appointment he had hoped for, in part because he wished to 'cut his connection' with the vicar – who had, quite extraordinarily, never paid him – but also because he had found a house for his wife at Dalehead 'in which she thrives',* and the new church would be slightly closer.† The incumbent chosen by Reginald Marshall's trustees was Frederick Myers, whose inaugural sermon lauded the beauty of the church and ended with the pledge that it should 'ever be a place of worship, a house of prayer and not preaching'.

One of the two final architect drawings of St John the Evangelist.

* She had been forced to leave the vicarage, perhaps because of the marsh, and had recovered in Buttermere.
† Bush's move away from the vicarage had been a relief to Southey, who felt the exercise, fresh air and comparative rest he would then enjoy every day, riding to and from work, would fend off the possibility of a breakdown from overwork. CRO PR 167/7/1.

Myers's fame is largely local, but he did much good. Having worked his way through the two opposing 'high' and 'low' theological schools to his own position, he had impressively turned down the larger job of vicar of Leeds parish church for the perpetual curacy at Keswick, mainly because the social views of the recently Unitarian Marshalls encompassed his own; in particular, he nurtured a desire for Christianity to be a forceful agent in challenging society's injustices. Hence, he started two schools, laid the foundations for Keswick's first public library, and organised adult lectures, debates and mutual-improvement societies. He also applied much balm to the young Eliza Lynn, who, having long plunged into the voracious reading of her self-education, 'teemed with views, disquiets, passions and questions'. Myers and his new wife, Susan, the youngest Marshall daughter, generously did all they could to calm and straighten. She always remembered their kindness to her, as she remembered Hartley's.

One thing was crystal clear to Eliza: Myers and her father were not destined to get on with each other; in fact, they hardly talked. The Myers found Lynn 'arid, unenlightened, fossilised – a leafless stick in a stagnant pool'. He found them 'unsound, fanciful, unreal – painted sparrows passing for birds of price'. And 'soon the new incumbency became as completely differentiated from the old parish, as is the frog from a tadpole. Thoughts, doctrines, modes and hours of conducting the service, all were different.'[16]

*

In March 1839 Bertha Southey married her cousin Herbert Hill Junior, a schoolmaster, and went to live at Ambleside. None of Southey's children attended their father's June wedding in the south of England. Caroline, worried about Southey's condition, called upon his brother Henry to give an opinion, unbeknown to her husband. While the diagnosis was favourable, Henry admitted that 'At present he is a very old man of his age – a year or two ago he was quite to the contrary'. The couple arrived home in August 1839, and it was only a few weeks later, on 6 September, that Southey wrote his last known letter. He lived with dementia for a further three and a half years; Wordsworth's famous final visit, almost a year after the couple had returned, perfectly captures the situation. 'He did not recognise me till he was told. Then his eyes flashed for a moment with their former brightness, but he sank into the state in which I found him, patting with both hands his books affectionately, like a child. Having vainly attempted to interest him by a few observations, I took my leave, after five minutes or so.'[17]

The next year Lynn reported that Southey was so confused in St Kentigern's that he went into the wrong pew.[18] Kate, aged thirty-one, was still living at Greta Hall and later claimed,* 'My father did not know me, twice shortly after his return he looked me full in the face and asked me, who I was.'[19] If true, that would have been a terrible shock and, unfairly, she and Cuthbert quickly adopted the idea that Caroline had trapped their father into marriage from a desire for fame and fortune. Since Southey was no longer really capable of protesting or defending his wife, the situation soon became intolerable. Southey's whole sense of family order and love of children, long witnessed in the home where 'the cheerful spirits' never forsook him,[20] was grotesquely turned on its head.

When Caroline decreed that Kate should see her father only once a week, both children briefly departed, and Cuthbert's conditions for their return (in 1840) were that the dining room should be used solely by themselves and Mrs Lovell; their father and Caroline were to be banished upstairs, and Kate was to have a short daily visit with her father.[21] When she was young, Kate, according to Eliza Lynn, had been 'famous for a certain quiet hardness which amounted to calm brutality',[22] and the children subsequently refused to communicate with Caroline; only Edith May and her husband, far from the action, supported her. By August the following year, Southey was barely able to feed himself; in February 1842 Caroline reported, 'it is almost come to *carrying* now, when he is moved from place to place'.[23] He died in his sleep the following year, apparently of typhoid, on 21 March.

* In a statement to Myers, which Wordsworth had suggested she wrote in 1840/41.

More sadness was to follow. Soon after Edith's death, Southey, in the depths of despair, had written to Cuthbert about his will, telling his son that he had made 'no estimate of my library, because if it please God that you should make use of the books ... they would be of more value to you than any sum that could be made by dispersing them'.[24] His library of 14,000 books had been a life's work, the poet's great treasure and legacy. Sir Walter Scott's son-in-law found it 'one of the noblest private libraries in England' and had understood 'that his soul was there'.[25] Yet, since Cuthbert, by now ordained, had taken the remaining aunt, Mrs Lovell, into the vicarage that came with his new living in Cockermouth, and Kate had moved to a house on Vicarage Hill,[26] they put all the contents of Greta Hall under the hammer. One of the outstanding private libraries of late-eighteenth and early-nineteenth-century England was scattered to the winds, like chaff.

James Stanger and the Parish, on the other hand, did everything that could be done to honour, rather than dishonour, Southey's legacy. Caroline wrote of the kindness of neighbours,[27] and Stanger, the poet's friend and neighbour, raised a subscription and a committee to create a suitable memorial. St Kentigern's had remained in a dilapidated state despite the many facelifts, and, feeling it would be unfit to place Southey there, Stanger offered to pay for a complete and thorough renovation before installing the memorial. With the agreement of both the parishioners and the religious hierarchy, the young George Gilbert Scott was approached. The moment his plans were in, a full vestry meeting was held, including all the tithe owners, to discuss an eccentric objection from Sir John Woodford about his proposed stone corbel head of the young Queen Victoria. The meeting found the objections 'wholly without foundation' and, with all the confidence of youth and early Victorian England, Scott boldly set forth.

The flat roof was entirely removed and rebuilt with 'best Baltic pitch pine, stained and varnished',[28] and the nave and the chancel were opened to new triangular tie beams with carved ends. Those in the chancel rested upon the new corbel portrait heads, and all the stone pillars, arch ends and window apertures were chiselled anew and left un-whitewashed,[29] so 'the natural reddish hue of the stone (was) brought to light with warm and becoming effect' and 'the plaster on the walls was tinted to harmonise'.[30] The contents of the rather surprising raised charnel house in the northwest corner of the nave were swiftly removed, the bones carefully laid to rest. And, once all the flagstones were lifted, the Parish dead who were buried in the chancel and the nave, except for the Stephensons and the Jacksons of Armboth in their deep stone vaults, were similarly moved and devoutly reinterred, followed by the careful reburial of the Derwentwater bones from the chantry.

A new south porch replaced the old, but all the memorials were returned to the walls, which Scott covered with exceptionally thick coats of plaster, some 4 or 5 inches thick in places. The stained glass was, with one exception, intended to marry with the early Tudor church; the exception being a centralised east window, carefully traced and measured to exactly replace its off-centre fourteenth-century original. The nave was newly seated with oak Gothic Revival pews. So far, so good.

But, in the urge to clear out debris, old tiles were swept away, as was almost all the church furniture. The silver cups were given to the Newlands and Wythburn chapels, and all the pewter items broken up to prevent secular use. Numerous oak benches were placed in the chancel for displaced pew-owners to sit on, but some box pews remained, including 'two formes on the north side of parish church'. The Ormathwaite seats given to the Brownriggs back in 1634 by Umfraye Williamson,[31] which, although 'elaborately adorned', were thought a bit too simple, so some 'finely carved angels' were added to perk them up[32] and there is no mention of the Le Fleming pew being altered. However, Scott gaily got rid of everything else, including – possibly – some unreliably documented 1640 carved pews in the chancel, and certainly the carved 1610 pulpit, which the rebuilt Newlands church happily seized upon.

Scott even created a typical Victorian memorial altar tomb by the Radcliffe chapel, on which he placed their brass, and then, raising the Derwentwater effigies, barbarously cut their sides off, to fit them into position under his new monument. This was Victorian confidence run wild. Less barbarously, but rather wilfully, he also created twenty new choir stalls in the chancel, despite St Kentigern's having no surpliced choir; while the now more gently sloping singers' gallery remained at the west end of the church. Surpliced choirs were becoming much more popular nationally then, and Scott, as a High Churchman, must have wanted the stalls and have overcome the very different view of his paymaster, James Stanger, the strong supporter of the Reverend Whiteside's evangelical tenure.

The church reopened in 1845, a memorial window on the south side telling its latest story; a brass plaque on the sill stated that it was put in 'by the parishioners gratefully to commemorate the munificent restoration and embellishment of this church by James Stanger, esquire'. Just as the early Tudor parishioners had been awe-struck the last time St Kentigern's was rebuilt, the early Victorian parishioners were much struck by the change; for Eliza Lynn (and the readers of her ensuing guidebook), the church had become 'the lake Cathedral'. She also refers to a good deal of local grumbling; for many people, while the new St Kentigern's was certainly grand, Scott's church felt too empty, stripped as it was of so many of the church decorations from different ages that fascinate and deepen the sense of the longevity of worship. And the new pebbledash exterior, un-whitewashed, badly diminished the old sense of the church's centrality when seen from the surrounding fells.

The treatment of the Derwentwater tomb was a considerable affront to many of the parishioners too, but the work of chiselling it into place had continued for some years, carried out by a stonemason known as 'Martin'.[33] Later, in 1859, out of the blue, a strange woman purporting to be Amelia, Countess of Derwentwater placed herself next to the tomb, put a seal on it and forbade further work. A letter (written in half-inch letters and covering both sides of a sheet of coarse paper 19 inches by 12 inches) addressed to *Mr Dover of Millbeck, Churchwarden, Crosthwaite 1859* reports that that vicar removed the seal, the lady and her seat, thereby giving 'Martin the liberty when the Lady returned back to the Tomb: to pull her gloves out of her hand and cast them back in her face'. A spirited poem generalised the affront:

> *We'll sing the Vicar the Habeas Corpus*
> *It's always sweet to us;*

Because it was made on purpose
To keep us free from Brutes.

However, the poem achieved little, as the police refused to take the church keys when the Lady offered them, after reporting that the vicar had turned St Kentigern's into a 'Den of thieves'. And the vicar, by coming quickly to remove the keys, successfully prevented the Lady's planned onward journey to give them to the Bishop of Carlisle.

Amelia continued to assert her claims (and established a talent for composing letters and pamphlets) until 1869, and her arrest; she would die in poverty. The identity of the person who gave her the keys remains a mystery as, by 1859, there was a new vicar who had made it evident that he had little or no respect for the history of his Parish and the parishioners' feelings were already raised. Indeed, the letter touched on other grievances about the Scott restoration and was clearly designed to hide the writer's identity. While it could have been written by Amelia herself, one of the angry parishioners seems the more likely author.

For an early twentieth-century architect who examined the church fabric in order to remedy some problems, Scott's restoration had been 'drastic'. Its very blankness, however, made the Southey memorial, the focus of the rebuilding, very prominent, when it was reverently placed in the south aisle. Apart from the usual legal requirement for the relevant landowners to reroof the chancel, Stanger had paid for everything, some £4,000, but subscriptions had helped him with the memorial. Its self-taught sculptor, J. C. Lough, touchingly paid out of his own pocket, if Rawnsley is to be believed, for a change of material from Caen stone to white marble, more than doubling its cost.[34] And he achieved a remarkably life-like embodiment of the poet, book in hand and clad in academic robes, reclining on a couch with tasselled pillows, his meditating face turned towards the spectator: a face Cuthbert believed to be the most lifelike three-dimensional representation of his father in existence.

The committee had approached Wordsworth to write the epitaph, and he had struggled with it, first trying a prose passage that lingered too long on the last years, those uppermost in his mind.[35] He had told one friend six months earlier that 'My verse days are almost over', but, for Southey, he turned back to poetry.* Sixteen lines became eighteen, then eighteen twenty, as Wordsworth added the lines: 'Whether he traced historic truth, with zeal / For the State's guidance, or the Churches weal.' But it was the last two lines that gave him the most difficulty; not only were there four variations, but at the last moment the sculptor was made to re-chisel them. The poet had laboured to do his friend justice, and by 9 December 1843 his son-in-law could write to Henry Crabb Robinson, 'I think it will please you.'[36]

For Wordsworth, the older man, old age had been far less harsh than it was for Southey; the two men's careers had, in some ways, followed opposite trajectories, as fame and wider recognition had come late for Wordsworth. But Mary Wordsworth had still chafed about any work that distracted from what she, even as late as 1838, still considered to be his important mission, namely *The Recluse*; had Dorothy been sentient, her feeling would surely have been the same. And it was to a relative stranger, a visiting American academic that year, that the poet himself had finally been confident enough to acknowledge the truth. Asked why he wasn't finishing the work, Wordsworth replied, 'Why did not Gray finish the long poem he began on a similar subject. Because he found he had undertaken something beyond his powers to accomplish. And that is my case.'[37] At some level, the relief of this public utterance of what, one suspects, was a long understood private truth must have been profound.

The next year Wordsworth had received his honorary degree from Oxford, where the spontaneous burst of applause from masters and undergraduates gave him intense pleasure. As did taking a tour of Lady Le Fleming's grounds in June 1840 with Queen Victoria's aunt, the dowager Queen Adelaide, when she visited him – their owner remaining firmly ensconced in her house, in uninvited umbrage. In 1842, the poet had been given £300 a year from the government by Prime Minister Robert Peel, like Southey;

---

* Touchingly corresponding with Coleridge's nephew.

this was particularly gratefully received, as Wordsworth had just managed to pass his role as distributor of stamps for Westmorland on to his son. All this had made it easy, when Peel offered him the laureateship after Southey's death, for Wordsworth to reject it on grounds of age; he added that he knew Southey's failure to produce something on Queen Victoria's accession had 'caused him not little uneasiness'. However, Peel's clever reply – that he was the sole choice of both his Queen and her prime minister, and that nothing was expected of him except for the honour of his name – changed his mind.[38]

There had been other late changes too. William Faber, briefly the acting curate at Ambleside, had wooed Wordsworth into the High Church, the movement that had secured him his Oxford degree, and urged him to purge his early poetry of pantheism. Of particular significance, this caused the poet to add the words 'My trust, Saviour! is in thy name!' to 'Salisbury Plain', his first explicit statement of belief in the redemptive power of Christ crucified, the difficult essence of Christian faith; and a belief that stayed with him.

Perhaps it was this that led to a different sort of self-examination. An 1844 letter to his friend Isabella Fenwick, describing events that left him prey 'to the remorse of my own Conscience', contained the sentiment, 'only let me believe that I do not love others less, because I seem to hate myself more'.[39] The following year he wrote again to Isabella, 'My pleasures are among Birds and Flowers, and of those enjoyments, thank God I retain enough; but my interests in Literature and books in general seem to be dying away unreasonably fast – nor (do) I much care for a revival of them … I read my own less than any other – and often think that my life has been in great measure wasted.'[40]

However, the poet Wordsworth had taken much pleasure from a grand local tea party given for his seventy-fourth birthday at Rydal Mount that year. The event was attended by some three hundred children and a hundred and fifty adults, and the tables were decorated with evergreens and spring flowers and laden with oranges and gingerbread. There was dancing on the terrace, and a decorated pace egg for each child to take home.[41] Wordsworth wrote that he wished that occasions when 'the rich mingle with the poor as much as may be upon a footing of fraternal equality' happened more frequently, lamenting that no social event had replaced the festivities of the old feudal dependencies.[42]

This was the year when Wordsworth had the last lines of his epitaph to Southey re-chiselled too.[43] He had approved of Southey remarrying, but subsequently felt that Kate was badly treated. Caroline had come to see Wordsworth as the enemy, and had not invited him to the funeral at St Kentigern's. But Wordsworth went anyway – driven over to Crosthwaite by his son-in-law – as did his son John and his seven-year-old grandson, William,[44] Southey's godchild. They joined Cuthbert, Bertha and Kate in the churchyard, the group standing apart from Caroline, Edith May and her husband. Southey's brother Henry, who had behaved well to everyone, arrived, sadly, a day late.

As Wordsworth's final version of his epitaph to Southey started its long vigil in St Kentigern's, Caroline revealed the depth of her bitterness when she said of it, 'Was ever such a miserable failure? – or anything so utterly heartless and spiritless?'[45] It was to her supporter Walter Savage Landor – who, along with John Rickman, would refuse to allow his correspondence with Southey to be printed – that she turned for a robust poetic appreciation that warmed her and, in truth, many others.* And as Parish tourists began to buy postcards not only of Southey but also of his tomb, the seventy-three-year-old Landor began his second deep friendship with someone from Crosthwaite Parish – Eliza Lynn, the vicar's daughter.

*

Eliza, who had adored Landor's *Imaginary Conversations*, provided an adulatory account of her first meeting with the poet: 'When I was introduced to an ill-dressed and yet striking-looking old man – with unbrushed apple-pie boots; a plain shirt-front, like

---

* 'In maintaining the institutions of his country / He was constant, zealous and disinterested / In domestic life he was loving and beloved / His friendships were for life and longer', 'the purest and most candid writer of his age', 'the most inventive poet', 'the most diversified', etc.

a night-gown, not a shirt ... His snuff-coloured clothes rumpled and dusty – but an old man with a face full of the majesty of thought ... and an air of mental grandeur all through, and was told that he was Mr Landor – WALTER SAVAGE LANDOR – I broke into an ardent exclamation of joy.'[46] It seems little wonder, then, that the couple became devoted friends for the rest of Landor's life. Living in Bath, after the break-up of his marriage in the 1830s, he had left his family in Italy, making over his income to them and, it is said,

Young Eliza Lynn Linton, painted by Samuel Lawrence.

just keeping a subsistence income for himself. However, he gave Eliza a whole season of balls there, chaperoning her as if he were her real father.[47] The relationship with Landor also taught Eliza something significant. Her need for an admiring and loving father figure, combined with her observation of Landor's own famously volatile temper, instilled in her, for the first time, a sense of the importance of self-restraint.[48]

Three years earlier, after experiencing a passionate, secret but largely physically unexpressed lesbian relationship with an exotic Polish émigré staying at Windy Brow,[49] and suffering a virtual breakdown as a result, Eliza had known she had to get away from home. Naturally clever and diligent, she had started her first novel, set in ancient Egypt. A close friend of her father's persuaded the vicar to allow his twenty-three-year-old daughter to go down to London for a year under his wing, to carry out the necessary research for the novel at the British Museum. Eliza was ecstatic, 'and set my face towards The Promised Land where I was to find work, fame, liberty and happiness'.[50] But she soon realised that the income from novel-writing would never keep her in London, and pondered the alternatives. She then wrote an article on 'Aborigenes', which she sent to the editor of the *Morning Chronicle*.

Surprisingly perhaps, she was called to an interview. She arrived punctual to the moment, 'with beating heart and a very high head',[51] she tells us, to wait half an hour before being greeted by the editor: 'So, you are the little girl who has written that queer book and want(s) to be one of the press-gang are you?' When she replied, 'Yes, I am that woman', she received the response, 'Woman, you call yourself, I call you a whipper-snapper.' She was then further insulted: 'I say though, youngster, you never wrote all that rubbish yourself! Some of your elder brothers must have helped you. You never scratched all those queer classics and mythology into your own numbskull without help! At your age it is impossible.'

Having taken all this with good humour, Eliza finally heard the glorious, if profoundly patronising, words: 'You are a nice kind of little girl, and I think you'll do.'[52] The editor then put her through a tough three-and-a-half-hour test, the results of which he energetically admired, and there she was: a staff member of the *Morning Chronicle*, the first woman journalist to draw a fixed salary in Britain. At the age of twenty-five she was, suddenly, on 20 guineas a month, rather than £30 a year. For the next two years she was not merely self-sufficient and 'supremely happy', she became positively well off, and was 'taken up' by many of the luminaries of mid-Victorian literary London. This feisty, negligently brought-up, entirely self-educated vicar's daughter from Crosthwaite had achieved something truly remarkable. But, true to previous form, Eliza lost her job by fighting back once too often in 1851 – the editor shaking his fist in her face. However, she had faith in her new novel *Realities*, soon to be published, and stayed in London.

Life in the Parish in the 1840s

ELIZA LYNN HAD been returning to the vicarage twice yearly[1] for long harmonious visits. She must have been impressed by the amount of money spent and raised in the 1840s by the local chapel vestries, rebuilding and improving their chapels and, in some cases, their schools. St John's School was rebuilt in 1848, and its master paid from a combination of the quarter-pence, a £5 annual endowment and an annual subscription of £21 from five of the better-off parishioners, so he probably enjoyed a decent salary in local terms. In very different circumstances, Newlands, Borrowdale and Thornthwaite had been the last three chapels of ease in the diocese to move their teaching out of their chapels.[2] That change had started when Borrowdale built a schoolhouse in 1825. Both there and at Wythburn, where the Thirlmere valley had its first recorded school 'attached to the chapel' by around 1833,[3] the curates probably remained schoolmasters, as the teacher's only wage came from the quarter-pence paid by the children.

Newlands did not get its schoolhouse until 1842, the money raised by a subscription organised by the Reverend Monkhouse, the chapel's first wealthy curate, who generously guaranteed a minimum salary of £40 for the schoolmaster to supplement the quarter-pence.[4] And when the new Braithwaite school began its long life in the same year, the £550 costs were paid for in part by an émigré, John Crosthwaite Esq. of Liverpool, although the bulk, as ever, came from James Stanger, who had become one of the largest landholders in 'Underskiddaw' by then.[5] Originally, both benefactors gave £10 annually to the schoolmaster, but, in time, after the school came 'under government inspection', the teacher's salary was aided by a grant from the committee of the council for education.

So, in a major break from the long history of the grammar school, all the chapel schools charged for attendance. And, until Braithwaite got into its stride later, Crosthwaite free grammar school had more pupils than all the chapelry schools combined. During the 1840s, changes there were on the educational side. In the summer of 1844, on the master's resignation, the eighteen trustees – now in their twilight, and including, significantly, the JPs James Stanger and Thomas Spedding, as well as a Banks, a Dowthwaite, a Mawson, et al. – had met at Mrs Dixon's Hare and Hounds to discuss improving their education system, which was now their main concern.[6] Stanger was delegated to write to the governor of the Inspectors for Schools to establish which of the training institutions he thought best to provide 'modern fashionable teaching'. The current number of scholars was, rather surprisingly, given the 1818 published figures, under 150, but a good master would, Stanger thought, attract more, and they would pay that individual £70 per annum, or £80 if they felt it would affect 'the proficiency, happiness and number of pupils'.

Since the income from the endowments was more than £80, there was a discussion about whether it might not be better to employ two teachers, but it was felt 'the funds are manifestly insufficient for the support of two *able* men' – which throws some doubt on the level of teachers available in the chapels of ease – although a decision was taken later to include an assistant teacher. The Monitorial or Madras System was chosen, which, true to its name, appointed pupil teachers, as well as emphasising the importance of punctuality, cleanliness and prayers to begin and end the school day. The trustees were sufficiently confident to print a flyer to be distributed throughout the Parish, stressing the system's efficiency and success.[7] Hours were to be 9.00 a.m. to 12 noon and 1.30 to 4.00 p.m. in the winter and 8.30 a.m. to 12 noon and 2.00 p.m. to 5.00 p.m. in the summer. According to the flyer, 'Any child may be admitted by applying to one of the trustees', and subjects for teaching in the upper school included Latin, Greek and philosophy.

The examiners in 1845, James Stanger, the Reverends John

Monkhouse and Christie as trustees, plus the Reverend Myers, Joshua Stanger, Miles Dover and more, found 'the knowledge and intelligence displayed by the children was highly satisfactory and gratifying'. It was encouraging for general Parish health to see the involvement of Myers, and all were equally pleased with the children the next year, when the examiners included John and Mrs Spedding as well.[8] It should be added that a later government inspection in 1855 thought 'there were great deficiencies in respect of order and method', although how much of that was down to the children taking little notice of strangers is impossible to know.[9] The school was still living off its endowments (which were augmented that year by a £500 legacy from a Miss Ogle, largely funding the purchase of more than twenty acres of land in Newlands)[10] but, since it was then under government inspection, it was possible for it to receive a grant from the government as well. This had its dangers.

Even more work was done on the chapels than the schools. Wythburn, happy with its single belfry and no clock, was the only Church of England building in the Parish to be left untouched in the 1840s; £915 was spent on Thornthwaite-cum-Braithwaite,[11] and the largest sum, £1,000, was spent in Borrowdale, on a parsonage, of which £800 came from Abraham and Joseph Fisher Esqs. Further down the valley, at Grange, and after much opposition from Borrowdale's curate, a Miss Heathcote was eventually allowed to erect a small chapel, using a local builder who had a passion for raising the lintels so they sat upon the windows like quizzical eyebrows. Consecrated in 1861, the chapel was also to be used as a school, and a year later a vicarage was built in Wythburn.

Newlands spent £200 in 1843, raised by subscription, to renovate its chapel, which included a new gallery, as there was 'no convenient place for the administration of Holy Communion'.[12] And St John's in the Vale raised £290 by subscription and a local levy organised by the churchwardens for an 1845 rebuild by John Richardson,[13] a considerable dialect poet and, later a schoolmaster,* who introduced a generous porch and a delightful, indigenous

---

* It is said that a copy of his *Cummerlan Talk* could be found in 'every farmhouse in the country'.

nod to the need for a tower.[14] In the same year, the Bishop of
Carlisle raised £800 from 'two societies' to build a parsonage for
Thornthwaite-cum-Braithwaite, hoping that some of the money
would be left over to invest for future income as well.

The giving for church and school buildings included the new
Parish names but also bore witness to the real involvement of local
statesmen and their families. All of the chapels of ease, except
Borrowdale, had lost their civic role as official townships: Newlands
chapel and Thornthwaite-cum-Braithwaite district church had
become Above Derwent and St John's, Castlerigg and Wythburn
had been amalgamated into one township. Nevertheless, we have
seen the various vestries continuing to look after their chapels, and
the vestry minutes reveal that many statesmen remained deeply
involved in looking after their communities. At Newlands, for
instance, the local families gave their labour for the school building for free, including paying the costs to convey the necessary
materials to the site.[15] The 'few free sittings' provided when the
chapel was renovated were financed by the thirty that were rented
by the likes of the Mawsons, Wrens (who had three), Thwaites,
Harrimans, Fishers etc., plus a few new names.[16]

In 1851 the government had organised its one and only church
census, which indicated, to the astonishment of all, that the dissenting churches commanded the allegiance of nearly half the
population of England and Wales. Wordsworth and Southey
would have been horrified, even though in the Parish, where the
only dissenting chapels of the time were in Keswick, the overall
pattern did not then apply. The Congregational chapel was in a
period of decline, about to be revived; the Primitive Methodists
had yet to build a place of worship; and while the Methodist chapel
had been active, with a full-time minister since 1836, there is no
record of exceptional numbers. And Chancellor Fletcher's diocesan notebooks from 1814–45 at no time express any anxiety
about the growth of Methodism.[17] Nevertheless, Newlands and
Thornthwaite were two of the only four diocesan chapels that still
practised pew-to-pew communion in Bishop Percy's day, a Scottish
custom seen as a naturally dissenting practice.[18]

Another census finding – that the average attendance at church or chapel in Cumberland and Westmorland was between 25 and 33 per cent of the population[19] – might also have given Wordsworth and Southey pause for thought. The papers of the Wythburn vicar record that his chapel had an average attendance of twenty adults, and a maximum of fifty-six between 1849 and 1852; his catchment area at that time numbered 203 souls. So the average attendance at Wythburn appears to be substantially below the lowest county estimate.[20] The attendance at St John's chapel seems higher and is likely to have included more summer visitors; sometime between 1828 and 1846, Bishop Percy's notes record average summer sittings of 130 and winter sittings of 50, before he assigned some of the chapel's territory to the new church of St John the Evangelist in Keswick. It has to be said, however, that diocesan notes often seem over-optimistic about average percentage attendance generally.* St John's, with a catchment area of 296, had just rebuilt its church to seat 230 people. In all the concerted local efforts to improve the chapels, combined with the building of St John the Evangelist in Keswick, were in real danger of 'over-seating' the Parish.

Mining, bobbins and tithes

Given Eliza's attitude to the miners at Caldbeck when she was a child (see pages 408–9), she may not have welcomed a forty-year revival of the Parish mining industry. Starting in 1840, there were determined attempts to mine Helvellyn from the Wythburn side. There had always been one or two mining families living in the Thirlmere valley, whose men walked strenuously to and fro, either over Helvellyn, to the productive mine at Glenridding above Ullswater, or to some mines beneath Blencathra. These miners were as much a part of the local community as the blacksmiths. But from 1840 onwards the valley changed, the new lead-miners

* For example, at Wythburn they record average congregations of forty in the morning and seventeen in the afternoon, yet judge the total population to be about seventy, suggesting two-thirds of the chapel's potential congregation attended church. The correct population figures were 191 in 1841 and 203 in 1851. Armstrong, *Thirlmere*, pp. 14, 33.

originally coming from other Cumbrian mining areas, including Thornthwaite, Keswick and Caldbeck, in search of work.[21] But once the mine, Wheal Henry, opened in the 1830s, they came from further afield as well, their families setting up homes in the valley – clustering around the City,* Fisher Place or Back Lane Cottages.

The new miners kept to their own kind (a miner's daughter almost inevitably marrying a miner's son) despite cheerful banter with the farmers at the Cherry Tree and the Nag's Head and mutual respect between the two groups. Mining remained a tough, and still fairly primitive, job. Shot holes were painstakingly bored to a depth of 2 feet, swabbed with a rag knotted on the end of a stick to remove any water, and the gunpowder poured in – either from a narrow tin measure or a hollow cow's horn – followed by the insertion of a narrow brass rod called a 'pricker'. Using a wooden charging stick, clay was tightly packed around the pricker, which was then removed and replaced with a home-made straw fuse. The miner lit the fuse with his tallow candle, made from sheep fat – and ran.[22]

The 'count-house' for the mine, an office and a smithy, with a stone-built toilet a few yards further south, were built 1,650 feet up Helvellyn, to the south side of what became known as Mine Gill,[23] and packhorses were used to transport equipment to the count-house and bring down what treasure had been found. But by 1857, Wheal Henry had come to a standstill, and new talent was needed.

Sir Henry Vane was considered to have overcharged for his royalties on the land's mineral rights, and in August the new prospectus announced that he had now 'greatly reduced them', to one-sixteenth.[24] It explained that 'Rich ore is now being raised, experienced miners engaged, and first-rate talent employed, which will prove this property to be unsurpassed by any lead-mine in England'. Despite the hyperbole, the mine's manager, Captain John Muse, 'a devout Wesleyan whose dedication and loyalty to mineral mining were as deep and steadfast as his Christian beliefs', was indeed an exceptional miner, and came from Alston. However,

---

* Just north of Wythburn Chapel: a 'few white cottages, enlivened by the green leaves of the cheerful hollin tree, [its name] The City, a corruption undoubtedly from some more homely epithet'. Guide book by William Ford, 1839.

with only modest results to offer his shareholders, he was distinctly economical with the truth in his regular reports and, inevitably, support for the company collapsed again.

Upon its rebirth in 1861, Wheal Henry became known as Wythburn or Helvellyn Mine and, for the first time, the mine was well capitalised. By the 1860s the miners made up a sizeable proportion of the valley population. The old, short sections of wooden trunking outside the mine, the original Elizabethan delivery method for the ventilation mechanisms, were replaced, largely by zinc tubing, and Elizabethan hand-dressing methods were mechanised too.[25] Then the packhorses were phased out by the introduction of a 600-foot tramway, which descended the gill at a gradient of 1 in 3 and worked by gravity, the fully laden mine tub heavy enough to lift an empty one on the circulating miner-operated cable system. Safe, cheap-to-run, gravity-operated inclines were to continue in the slate mines and quarries of the Lake District and Parish until shortly after the Second World War.[26] The mine had temporarily closed again but reopened when Manchester Corporation acquired Thirlmere and its surrounding land in 1879 to build a reservoir. It continued to operate in a reduced capacity but was finally forced to close in 1882.

Many other much smaller mines in the Parish, in Newlands and Borrowdale, mirror the story of the rise and fall at Wythburn,* the miners, in productive times, predominantly off-comers born into a profession that was a way of life. The constant starts and stops of investment, and therefore of employment, explain their sense of fraternity in adversity; they were members of a skilled tribe who knew how to work together, often had to move on and were often to meet up again. But in Newlands, as elsewhere, the younger sons of some old valley names (for instance, two Fishers, a Hardisty and a Hodgson) turn up in the mining accounts as well.[27]

The mine at Force Crag, southwest of Braithwaite, was the last mine[28] in the Lake District to remain working in the twentieth

---

* The story of the greatest Parish mining tragedy, in which a dam burst and the miners were buried in sand and mud as they worked, was handed down in folklore, and probably occurred at Barrow.

century,[29] and you can still see signs of the tramway that used to carry the ore to Braithwaite in the 1940s. It had employed fourteen miners in the 1850s,[30] but by the 1870s it was closed, until Captain Muse took over in 1873. He had left Wheal Henry the year before, after one takeover too many, and moved to Cockermouth with his family. Opening up two upper levels in Grisedale Pike, he started mining barytes – a mineral he had been throwing out at Wythburn – as its price had risen dramatically once it was found to be useful industrially, particularly for glass manufacture.[31]

Two other Parish mines were considerably larger operations. Over Catbells from Force Crag, above Brandelhow Bay, the Keswick Mining Company started work in 1847 on two shafts at Brandley Lead Mine, whose management had gone bankrupt eleven years earlier, having sunk a 40-yard shaft and created a 34-foot-diameter water wheel. 'The liberty' of its workings was 'about six square miles',[32] and in time the company would employ some eighty men, producing 300 tons of lead a year. A steam engine replaced the old wheel to pump out the water, and one shaft was deepened to a remarkable 100 yards by steam power, with the strength of 26 horsepower – the other, driven by water of 12 horse power, still plunged 60 yards. Shut for fourteen years after 1865, the mine then reopened and expanded again until, in 1891, the water became impossible to deal with and it finally closed. In their day, its spoil tips had quite obscured the old shore road, but by then everyone was using Lord William Gordon's new road, which was much better maintained and skirted the workings. The Brandley spoil tips remain a feature of the lake shore to this day.

In the mid-century, Goldscope, in the Newlands valley – the *pièce de résistance* of the Elizabethan mining boom, and as sophisticated as Brandley – was reworked by some fifty men, extending a vein in places 20 feet wide and around 190 fathoms deep, in a westerly direction. About 2,000 tons of lead were mined in the six years after 1853, as well as a little silver and some useful minerals, but after a long and expensive battle between the owners,[33] the mine closed in 1864,[34] not to be breached again for fifty years. And, in time, the brief echo of the Parish's Elizabethan national mining glory would subside again.

By the mid-1830s the Lake District had started on the road to becoming, for a time, the bobbin-producing centre of the world. The two Keswick bobbin mills were the only ones in the north Lakes. The smaller of the two, with between ten and thirty lathes, lay at the edge of the town on the Greta and the 1841 census records nine bobbin-makers and their families at Briery Cottages, none of them indigenous to the Parish. These numbers had more than doubled by the 1851 census, including just three young men from Keswick, as the bobbin business had expanded into the larger Briery Mill further upstream, both mills originally turning only local wood. In due course, Briery Mill would expand to more than fifty lathes and its success was to be prodigious; at its peak, the mill was producing forty million bobbins each year, which, as the information outside the old mill proudly proclaims, would have stretched more than 800 miles if placed end to end.

There were two main buildings, a small two-storey factory building, which still stands, and an open barn supported by pillars. This was the original drying shed, where the good wood (ash, birch, alder, willow and sycamore) was seasoned for about a year. Coppice wood was universally used for the simpler types of bobbin, and extensive stretches of woodland, obviously previously coppiced, remain on Greta-side today. Cut into slices a few inches in diameter, the wood was then formed into smaller cylinders and dried out before being bored and rinsed, i.e., 'the ends were cleared, usually by a boy on a machine with a rotating bit'.[35] Then two small squares of wood were glued together, cross-grained and attached to each end of the shaft, and an adult turned the 'rough' more precisely, sometimes bevelling it, polishing it with beeswax or dyeing it.

Elsewhere, the pattern of employment at mills generally illustrated a shift in industrial working relationships after Shaftesbury's 1833 Factory Act. Originally, family employment had been the norm, reflecting the way families had worked together on the land. This arrangement was popular with both workers and philanthropists, including Charles Dickens, who saw it as a way of preventing families from falling into poverty. The Act 'broke the kinship system to pieces'[36] and the imposition of discipline and work by foremen and managers, as opposed to family members, came to seem intolerable to factory hands and led to waves of protest. However, the 1833 Act did not cover the bobbin industry, where conditions remained tough, although hardly sensationally so by Victorian standards, despite the average working conditions in the Lake District including a thirteen-hour working day; longer than that in the northern industrial towns.

The biggest problem in the bobbin mills was the permanent clouds of dust, little or no ventilation, and thigh-deep piles of wood shavings.[37] The 1842 report from the Royal Commission of Inquiry into Children's Employment (originally set up by Lord Shaftesbury) brings this problem alive. In the words of a seventeen-year-old boy, ten years into his career, 'it is so dusty and stuffs you up so ... alder and ash are very bad, if dry. The dust chokes up your stomach, and you are obliged to spit it out or you couldn't get on. It stops you breathing.'[38] It is unsurprising that a doctor commented that the workers 'are as a class, a very pale, anaemic, strumous [affected by a chronic swelling of the lymph glands] race of men very different in physical powers with agricultural workers in the neighbourhood'. According to a Troutbeck man, 'if a man has several sons ... unless he will bring them the master will very likely refuse to have the man'.[39]

By the 1860s, the mills had become sensitive to patterns in the wider, global economy. In 1860, Dickens's magazine *Household Words* said of the Ambleside mill that 'their purchase of (local) coppices depend mainly on whether the cotton crop in America has been a good or deficient one ... if Manchester is in good spirits, these bobbin makers on the mountains may make up their minds to pay as high for coppice as they ever do, even up to eighteen pounds per acre.'[40] By this date, Scandinavian mills had entered the market, and cotton manufacturers began to use all-metal machines, producing cheap paper bobbins. In 1867, an extension to the Factory Act laid down that children aged from eight to thirteen could work only part-time and must have a minimum of ten hours' schooling per week, which initially affected productivity. Hence, a photograph of the Briery workforce taken just over a hundred years ago shows over eighty workers, of whom only about 10 per cent were children, a very different proportion from earlier days.

The market rose and the market fell, in part because of the introduction of automatic yarn-winding,[41] and about a dozen Lakeland
mills closed between 1867 and 1873. But Briery thrived, and in the
early 1920s a railway halt was built especially for it. Burma teak
and Caribbean boxwood were imported, and the bobbins, as well as
being exported, as before, to the United States and 'busy Belgium',
began to reach as far away as South Africa, Russia and Hong Kong.
In a brief and spectacular burst of national fame, it was Briery
bobbins that were used for the silk in Queen Elizabeth II's coronation dress in 1953 – before the factory finally closed five years later.

*

Eliza Lynn's views on the bobbin mills are not recorded, and it
would have been amusing to have heard her reaction to the long
battle her father fought over the issue of tithes, which had its last
hurrah in 1847 with the forfeiting of a cow, two years after she had
left home.

Tithes had long been the bane of farmers, particularly of
the poorer ones, as the tax fell indiscriminately upon all those
involved in agricultural production, and several parishioners had
brought lawsuits against Lynn for the removal of 'unaccustomed
and unheard of tithes' in 1833.[42] The intention of the 1836 Tithe
Commutation Bill was that each tithe holder would get around two-
thirds of their old gross receipts. That same year, the great and the
good of the Parish, Messrs Pocklington, Stanger, Abraham Fisher
and Joseph Dover, formed a committee to look into the matter
in the Parish context. Having paid for a search of the records at
Lambeth Palace and the Cottonian Library in Oxford, they agreed
two years later to offer £300 a year for the tithes acknowledged to
be due, plus another £100 for other tithes claimed by Lynn, and a
fair sum for rates.[43]

But the vicar, who had enjoyed checking, and then grumbling
about, each farmer's offer at Caldbeck, was never simply going to
accept, and the dispute rumbled on for another ten years (actually a reasonably quick agreement by national standards). It was
concluded that the vicar would receive just under £450, over a

third more than his average living of £312,[44] the 'impropriators' (the inheritors of the monastic lands)[45] just under £300, and that the corn tithes were worth just over £100. The high proportion of tithe money paid to tithe holders other than the vicar was a potent reminder of the importance of the abbeys of Fountains and Furness in the Parish story.

The commissioner in charge of the Parish, J. Job Rawlinson, duly produced the Tithe Award of 1844 – apportioning what was to be paid – but the back-up work proved pretty poor, as nothing tallied: neither the maps of the whole with the maps of the distinct areas, nor the total figure for the commons of a township with the acreage of its named fells. In Borrowdale, even Rawlinson admitted his valuers' claims about three of the fells, including Langstrath, were 'misleading', since 'many of the owners have no other property in the parish'.[46] In which case, of course, they should not have had any claims to the commons. The muddle, as so often, probably went back to the Great Deed, but it caused no trouble until, at the very last minute, Sir John Woodford entered into his new demesne – Lord William Gordon's estate at Waterend – the property having remained largely unoccupied since Gordon's death in 1823.

The Gordons' only child had died in 1831, and three years later Lady Gordon had decided to give their estate to her nephew Major General Sir John Woodford,[47] who had had a long and distinguished army career. Sir John had intended an immediate sale and John Marshall II had again had the idea of purchasing it. However, when Sir John came to see his property for himself in October 1835, he was entranced by it, and by Marshall's early death in 1836 no deal had been agreed. In 1841, having missed out on the post he most wanted, through his own miscalculation, Sir John decided to retire from the army,[48] though he did not come to settle in Derwent Bay until early 1845. This was the exact moment when the final objections to the 1844 Tithe Award were being heard by the commissioners. A man used to rousing the troops, the general immediately set about trying to rouse the 'Gentlemen and Yeomen of Borrowdale', writing a pamphlet stressing that, while they were due to pay the tithes paid by the Abbot of Furness at the time of the Dissolution, they were otherwise exempt.

Their right of exemption, he claimed, had been proved and acknowledged when the assistant commissioner showed that the tithes due to the vicar from Borrowdale were just £51 16s. ¾d. His neighbours had agreed to pay over 50 per cent more, he argued, because they were being terrorised by the threat of a speculative and experimental lawsuit. Woodford then wrote a letter to the whole Parish, saying that he had taken an objection to the 'Court of Queen's Bench' in Westminster. He intended to point out that, while the local commissioners had accepted the case that Monk Hall was exempt from tithes, because of its history, they had denied the equally valid claim for Birkett Wood,[49] which 'you know belongs to the poor of the parish, the indigent and infirm occupants of the alms-houses at Keswick, who have no audible voice'.[50]

Sadly for Sir John, he discovered that he too had no audible voice, as the judge refused to listen to most of his affidavit, saying that he was out of time. The judge was entirely wrong, of course, and had he but listened he would have known it.

In all this, Sir John was behaving much in character. In his forty-one years in the army he had nearly lost his foot at the Battle of Corunna and served on Wellington's staff at Waterloo, but his promotion was often delayed. This was because his humane approach – as a colonel he had banned flogging in his Guards battalion, and he later abolished the standard punishment of 'standing under arms'[51] in 1830 – was distinctly unpopular with the army's senior establishment. And, when Woodford came up with his proposals, he stuck to his guns unwaveringly if he thought he was in the right. King William IV, who strongly disapproved of his reforms, remarked: 'Colonel Woodford should be tried by court martial three times a week, if he had his just deserts.'[52] The king's words may have been spoken on the occasion when Sir John had, entirely on his own initiative, cancelled the Trooping of the Colour ceremony because he thought the rain would be too unpleasant for the troops.[53] He had made tireless efforts to improve the lot of the common soldier and would continue his efforts through correspondence from the shores of Derwentwater.

When the agreed tithes became due, he published his reactions:

'I deny that the rent charge demand by the Vicar is morally, lawfully, or fairly due to him, and I refuse to pay the proportion assessed on my estate; and I look forward to the recovery of the rights of the parish according to justice and the laws.'[54] And this is where the cow comes in. The tithe collector had to seize something from the miscreant who had not paid his tithes, and each year the same cow was duly seized and then resold on the spot to Sir John for the sum demanded. A present of a crown piece to the

Sir John Woodford.

collector accompanied this annual ceremony, until, in due course, the cow died. Sir John consistently said that he and Lynn were very good friends, his difference was with the *vicar* of Crosthwaite.

Yet, whatever he had said about Lynn, the general cannot have made any 'good friends' in the Parish. For, despite a voluminous correspondence with the outside world and a daily correspondence with his even more eminent brother, Field Marshal Sir Alexander Woodford, he refused all private invitations, as he was not going to reciprocate. Until Sir John was a very old man, no visitor was allowed in his house; any business that needed doing was done standing in front of it. He placed a hoarding all around his house to barricade himself from any wandering tourists who might disturb his home too. Animals were welcome: moles disported themselves on Lord William Gordon's immaculate lawns, and rats and mice were caught and carefully carried far away from the house; jays nested in his chimneys.[55] Everything was left to the rule of nature; living in the relatively modest Derwent Bay, Sir John entirely neglected Gordon's ground-breaking home and did not even thin the woods. So, by the end of his life, the innovative, consciously picturesque piece of landscaping along the western shore of Derwentwater had become a wilderness.[56]

The Parish came to feel an affection for their eccentric new general. Showing little concern for his income, he was kind to his tenants and polite to everyone he met as he roamed the mountains and his terrain. He was particularly interested in the welfare of the children. He endowed the Boys Band of Fifers and Drummers with a military cap and enjoyed their annual performance at Silver Hill field,[57] where he welcomed all the Crosthwaite Sunday school children for their summer tea in its cottage, presenting each of them with an especially made berry pasty as they left. In 1863, to celebrate the marriage of the Prince of Wales to Princess Alexandra of Denmark, he presented a Danish flag to be hoisted up the church tower, along with its British counterpart. He also engaged some boys to trail branches of wood up to the top of Swinside for bonfires to mark that and other major public events. (The fuel-carrying boys were paid for their efforts, to impress upon them further the significance of the event he was celebrating.) And Woodford always made sure, when the herbage of the mountain was let, that his right to light bonfires on the Queen's birthday was reserved.

Life in Keswick

Eliza Lynn's new novel, *Realities*, a call for women's political, social and sexual freedom, which had already been expurgated,* received a hostile reception when it was published in 1851, around the time she was dismissed, and Eliza was shattered. She was not to publish another novel for fourteen years and retreated to the Lake District. Crosthwaite must have provided a haven, both nourishing her profound connection with the Lakes and allowing her to keep up with her local friends, who must by then have included Henry Marshall. Henry had joined the family firm in 1828, more concerned with commercial development than process, and in 1837, to family approval, he had married Catherine Spring Rice, daughter of the Whig grandee Thomas Spring Rice, who was then chancellor of the exchequer. Henry was a hard-working man who seems also

* The cuts were approved by George Eliot.

to have had a startling presence. Once he had become mayor of Leeds in 1842, he thought it high time he found a summer estate, duly purchasing the Pocklington house on Derwent Island when Mrs Peachy and Captain Henry put it on the market.[58] He was the second youngest of the Marshall brothers.

Between them, the brothers had major holdings around, and usually at the head of, six of the area's most beautiful lakes, prompting the phrase that 'There was a Marshall on every Lake'. Eliza would have been aware that her neighbours' early misgivings about welcoming the new industrial family to the area had long since changed into considerable admiration for what they had achieved. Henry's new home, in a wonderful position, was also free of any problems with the neighbours, as, in 1850, he bought St Herbert's Island from Lawson.[59]

But the Peachy house would not do. So, Salvin was called in yet again, adding two new wings that gave it an Italianate air, and the Parish was introduced to a style of living to which it was far from accustomed. Fresh water was piped in under the lake, fleets of boats carried necessaries to and fro, and some twenty servants – who, we are told, had to enter the house via an underground passage from the landing stage and lived in the cellars – ensured the comfort of family and guests. The island became a haven for many of John and Jane Marshalls' numerous grandchildren – there were thirty-eight of them by the end of the 1840s.

The year 1842 had also seen the arrival of a new vicar at St John's. The Reverend Frederick Myers was succeeded by his curate, Thomas Battersby, who, like his predecessor, had taken time to find his own theological niche. Deeply impressed by the sincerity and holiness of the Oxford Movement, he had decided to take holy orders after listening to a sermon by Archdeacon Henry Manning. But by the time he learnt there was a curacy in the offing, he had moved to a strongly evangelical position, which, according to Eliza, placed him in 'the most exaggerated section of the Evangelical school'.

Before the end of the year, Battersby had settled Myers's co-educational primary school at Brigham into a new building. Here, supported by fees and voluntary contributions,[60] it began its long and successful march into the future with fifty-eight pupils, to complement the 140-odd in the grammar school. The new vicar also continued Myers's mission to improve the condition of the town. In 1855 he added a lecture hall to the library, where he later housed the 'Mechanics Institute' and the 'Keswick Literary and Scientific Society',[61] one of the oldest lecture societies in the country, which, under a different name, still flourishes today.[62] Four years later, Battersby launched the 'Evangelical Union for the Diocese of Carlisle',[63] the first step in a process that would culminate in the establishing in 1875 of his greatest legacy, the Keswick Convention, an annual gathering of evangelical Christians that today draws 15,000 visitors from all over the world.

By 1851, the Parish population had risen to around 5,250 souls, and the number of summer visitors lay somewhere between 8,000 and 10,000[64] – although Mr Frank of the Queen's Head Hotel calculated a confident 15,000. Tourist and directory observations continued much as before: according to Whellan's directory of 1860, the inhabitants of St John's were still 'a shrewd, sensible, and primitive set of people, remarkably peaceful, honest and upright in their dealings'.[65] The parishioners were fast retreating from their wartime arable expansion; the amount of arable land in the Keswick Vale dropped by a remarkable 88 per cent between the late 1830s and 1875, with a 77 per cent reduction in Borrowdale.

Keswick had far more tourist amenities than its rivals, Crosthwaite's museum still attracted a thousand visitors in a good year[66] and, the year before Eliza retreated from London, a new 'splendid pavilion', the Odd Fellows Hall, had opened in Market Square, large enough to hold 2,000 people and even to host equestrian spectaculars. The Blücher hotel in Portinscale made its entrance, complete with aviary and pleasure gardens, in 1847 and, for quieter moments, Myers's library now held some two thousand books and a reading room with all the local and national newspapers. The town hall now offered theatrical performances and concerts to complement its powerful new draw – Flintoff's remarkable map.

A Yorkshire man, the landscape painter Flintoff had come to Keswick in 1823 to enjoy the hunting, shooting and fishing life, but soon found he wanted more to occupy his time. And, with no Ordnance Survey map to help him, he meticulously created a three-dimensional model of the 1,200 square miles of the Lake District, on a scale of 3 inches to the mile. An extraordinary feat of exploration and measurement, his model won the wholehearted admiration of Adam Sedgwick and the other leading geologists of the day. It had taken Flintoff six years to complete and was considered to be 'one of the finest specimens of geographical modelling in England'.[67]

However, by the time Eliza returned, living conditions in the old Keswick burgage lots were, if anything, more cheek by jowl than ever. In 1848, a year of severe economic depression, 42,000 vagrants had been reported to be passing through Derwent Ward,[68] and the next year's figures were not much better. Southey had been right to say that there was much to improve in Keswick, and men like Peter Crosthwaite and Jonathan Otley had been passionate advocates of clean 'sweet' water. But the town's sanitation problem wasn't really addressed until the year after Eliza's withdrawal from London, 1852, when her father, Joshua Stanger JP and the solicitor Joseph Hall led a group of 141 ratepayers to petition the General Board of Health to apply the provisions of the 1848 Public Health Act to Keswick.

The original local reaction was much like their original reaction to the creation of the turnpike roads – a good deal of grumbling: no one had asked them what they thought, things were fine, sewers had recently been expensively installed, the statistics only looked bad because of the number of old and decrepit people in the town – and anyway, what about the huge amount of money it would cost? More than three times as many signed a counter-petition asking to be left alone, and some signed both petitions.[69] While it is true that there had been some civic improvements – new gas lighting and a small lock-up jail – it is hardly surprising that the original petitioners won the battle.

When the proselytising public health inspector, Robert Rawlinson, came to report the following year, he found that things were just as bad as before. 'The whole place is encompassed by foul middens, open cesspools and stagnant ditches, or by still fouler drains.'[70] Only the detritus and stink of the leather trade had been largely removed. The bulk of the poor had no water rights of their own, and near one place where they went to get water, at Greta Bridge, an outlet was discharging human soil and liquid refuse from the town's new gasworks. 'At The Forge, workmen apart, seventy people had to share one open trough and one privy.'[71] The pump at Hutton's yard was said to supply half of the town, while the drain under the houses there was so foul that, when Miss Hutton's nephew came to visit, 'the effluvium made him vomit'. And so on and so on. Inspector Rawlinson's judgment upon Braithwaite was even worse, maintaining that it contained 'in proportion to its population more dirt, disease and death than any decent town. It is one of the most romantic and filthy villages in England.'[72]

Abraham Wigham and his donkey constituted 'the town's cleaning department' as late as 1870, according to the artist Joseph Brown.

It is difficult not to see a bit of proselytising here, but a statistical report Rawlinson received from Dr Leitch makes pretty grim reading, even though the mortality rate he recorded, twenty-three per thousand, compares reasonably well with Penrith's twenty-six per thousand in 1849.[73] Over time, Rawlinson's recommendations would do a great deal of real good. A proper local board of health was set up to oversee the essential reforms. These included regulation of slaughterhouses and common lodgings – where the appallingly crowded, potentially infectious conditions could be dangerous – and the provision of public baths and wash-houses. Dr Leitch, the Reverend Battersby and John Fisher Crosthwaite set up a Waterworks Company in 1856, which opened up a supply of pure Skiddaw water for the town. Proper law enforcement was made easier the next year when Keswick's police force was established, with one inspector, one sergeant and two constables.[74] And, twenty years later, the national Sanitary Record declared that the death rate in Keswick was 'the lowest yet registered in any part of the United Kingdom'.[75]

When, in 1847, to Wordsworth's horror, 'the railway gateway to the Lakes' opened at Windermere for Bowness, those two towns, along with nearby Ambleside, started to vie for Keswick's tourist crown, and the balance of the Lake District tourist trade began to change. In 1841 Keswick had had a population of nearly two and a half thousand, while the combined population of Bowness and the vestigial Windermere was under fifteen hundred. Within twenty years, the population of both towns had overtaken Keswick's, a position that has never since been reversed.[76] For Eliza, Keswick remained what it was when she first stopped living in the Parish and had been throughout the previous seventy years of the tourist explosion: 'the metropolis' of the Lake Country, 'the centre of the district'. But, as early as 1855, Harriet Martineau's directory, *A Complete Guide to the English Lakes*, listed forty 'Esqs.' in Windermere and Bowness, twenty-seven in Ambleside, fourteen in Keswick and ten in Hawkshead[77] – and the number of boarding houses lined up the same way. So when, in 1864, Eliza wrote, 'Keswick is the largest and most important of the Lake County towns', she was out of date.

New hotels ushered in the future, as the railway directors ensured that enough were built to welcome their genteel travellers,[78] and the large growth in the number of tourists had an inevitable effect on the old innkeepers throughout the Lake District. It is lucky, as has been said,[79] that hoteliers are trained, not born, 'as the Cumbrian was not conceived with a deferential mien and a napkin over his arm'. Gradually, however, the local statesmen who generally set up these hotel businesses gained in experience, and the old complaints about accommodation began to drop off. As their status rose, the hoteliers used their personalities to promote their businesses: the Royal Oak in Keswick became 'Wilson's Royal Oak', and over the Raise it was 'Rigg's Windermere Hotel' or 'Scotts' Old England Hotel'. But since the original innkeepers had usually been farmers as well, most of the grander hotels kept some sort of farming connection, several of them having farm servants and labourers living on the premises.[80]

The Parish felt the loss of Keswick's previously unchallenged position as Tourist Queen strongly, as the town's proportion of the total Parish population dropped, completely against the national trend of a demographic shift to the towns and cities. The 1860 directory even stated (wrongly) that fewer people lived in the town than twenty years earlier. But Keswick remained a draw and, by 1862, was to be grandly described as the greatest surviving coaching centre in the nation. Twenty-two coaches made daily trips from Keswick throughout the summer,[81] and 15,240 visitors had been recorded as taking the trip to Keswick from the array of coaches provided at Windermere station by Riggs of Windermere Hotel.[82]

With the coming of the railways, day trippers began to come to the Lakes for the very first time, Whitsuntide being the favourite holiday for Lancastrians; by the 1860s, some ten thousand 'excursionists' were arriving in the Lake District on summer Saturdays as well, giving Windermere and Bowness a far more mixed clientele than their rivals.[83] For Keswick continued, despite its lamentable sanitation, to attract 'the cathedrals',* even without the lure of living Lake Poets; and 'better-class' visitors from the universities, London, Bristol and abroad became the mainstay of its economy. In time, the Royal Oak, no longer just one of Keswick's two most popular inns, would claim to be 'Patronized by HRH the Prince of Wales, the King of Saxony and other Distinguished Visitors'. Elsewhere, however, middle-class incomers of the same type as settled in Brighton and Bournemouth had descended on the Lake District, making up all those Esqs. who appeared in Harriet Martineau's *Complete Guide*.[84] And, even though a railway arrived in Keswick in 1865, it was not until the 1890s that the town's growth figures would take it back to the top of the tourist table.

* The old parish word for students from university.

Eliza and the Lakes and the
End of the Parish

I N 1852 ELIZA Lynn had taken a job as a correspondent in Paris; the position was considerably worse paid and more precarious than she was used to, but she soon had a considerable professional breakthrough, beginning her long stint writing for Charles Dickens and his magazine *Household Words*. In 1854, however, she had to return to Crosthwaite again, as her father was seriously ill and needed her help. The ever present Dr Leitch mentioned her name to the revolutionary republican and brilliant engraver William James Linton, as an ardent radical, writer and novelist. Linton had just bought Brantwood and its 10-acre estate near Coniston,[1] and, along with his partner Emily, who was delicate but a regular producer of children, invited Eliza both to stay and to contribute to their paper, *The English Republic*. Her first article acclaimed Mary Wollstonecraft's *A Vindication of the Rights of Woman* as 'one of the bravest and boldest things ever published'.[2]

The scene at Brantwood, with its totally unkempt garden, astonished Eliza, as did the children, 'all dressed exactly alike in long blue blouses of that coarse blue flannel with which housemaids scrub floors; and all had precisely the same kinds of hat – the girls distinguished from the boys only by a somewhat broader band of faded ribbon'.[3] This pre-Bohemian attire, which inevitably aroused scorn and abuse from the local children, won her heart, and the Lintons' high-minded poverty, and Emily's long illness, seductively promised tragedy and drama. When their paper folded early in 1855, Eliza poured in her strength, energy, time and money as ballast. 'They had fascinated me by their strangeness, linked to so much goodness and beauty,' she remembered, still then capable of adding, without irony, 'The simplicity with which they accepted all I did for them, as of the natural order of things, had also its charm.'[4]

The force of their need had allowed Eliza to romance herself into 'that frame of mind which made benevolence my greatest solace and my only happiness. I had the desire to sacrifice myself for the well-being of others ... to give myself up as an offering to God, through man.'[5] Underneath, other things were happening to her, for she wrote stories for *Household Words* about young women taking on widowers with small children,[*] including a woman who was entirely repelled by the widower. 'Those restless, burning fingers passing perpetually over her hand irritated her beyond her self-command ... When he held her, her teeth set hard and her nerves strung like cords. She felt sometimes as if she could have killed him when he touched her.'[6] Chilling. Up until the last year of her life, Eliza could not speak of the time of Emily's final illness. Unable to do anything for herself and clinging to Eliza, before she finally died in December 1856, Emily bequeathed her household to her new friend: 'I die quite happy, sure that you will accept your charge and fulfil its obligations.'[7]

The Reverend Lynn had also died at the beginning of the year and had named Eliza his co-executor, with instructions to sell Gad's Hill Place, with which the young Charles Dickens – fascinated by its bell-turret – had fallen in love the same year the Lynns had moved to Crosthwaite. Dickens's father had said to him, 'if ever I grew up to be a clever man, perhaps I might own that house'.[8] And so he did, making his bid anonymously, anxious that the price might be raised once his interest was known and meanly refusing the sum Eliza and her brother asked for some ornamental timber. Referred to arbitration, Eliza was delighted to record that the arbitrator gave them nearly twice the sum Dickens had rejected.[9]

She was to have a third of the proceeds and £1,500, which, were

---

[*] A story written a whole year before Emily's death.

she to marry, would be divided equally between herself and the two married beneficiaries. Landor wrote to her to say he believed she had made a serious mistake in making it clear she would marry Linton. He knew him to be a man of intellect and worth, but, as he finished with scorn, 'I would share my wealth with the woman I loved, but I would not invite her to share my poverty. Fly rather – die rather.'[10] He feared for Eliza, who would lose £1,000 of her £1,500 if she went ahead, and was soon sending her money from his own modest income.

But Landor had failed to grasp the strength of emotion felt by someone who was herself a motherless child, born into a disordered household, for other motherless children left entirely adrift, and Eliza and Linton were married in London on 24 March 1858. The children were rapidly given more conventional clothes, the boys sent to school and a governess hired for the girls, to Linton's amusement. For a short time, the radical succumbed to the charms of order and comfort; the family moved to a good house in London, and Eliza called him 'Manny'.[11] However, far too old to change his spots, Linton soon reverted to absence, disorder and revolutionary politics, while Eliza took on any journalistic job that came her way, including those she would have previously thought beneath her, to keep the family going. Linton's biographer concluded that, despite Linton's admiration for his wife, the marriage remained unconsummated; while Eliza, before the first two months were up, doubted that the whole thing would last.[12]

She was right to be doubtful, of course, and by the time the marriage ended she had lost all her capital.[13] Nevertheless, the marriage had produced two considerable memorials. Linton's youngest daughter remembered no other mother and, as her elder sister wrote, 'owing to our own mother's ill health, we had had but little training till she took us in hand, and it must have been no easy task she undertook'.[14] She added that it was impossible to express strongly enough 'how truly she was a mother to us all … from first to last the "true friend and mother" she always signed herself'.[15] It seems that, in everything Eliza did, she tried to avoid any possibility of repeating the damage of her own childhood. And, even after the marriage was finally over and the children had joined their father – who had moved to America, in part to find work, in 1867 – the two daughters then living with Linton still spoke and wrote of Mrs Linton as a loving mother. The eldest daughter later went to live with Eliza in Hampstead.

In the ten years she spent with them, she gave the Linton girls what they needed, substantially improving their chances in life, a memorial indeed. In later years, Eliza's biographer reports, she often 'marvelled how her belief in goodness and right, unsupported [by then] as it was by religion, supported the onslaughts of this trial. But she never lost her faith in her kind.'[16] She had developed an active humanism, underlined by her natural inclination and her upbringing as a vicar's daughter, to find strength and warmth in a wide variety of people outside the confines of her class.

The second lasting achievement of the Linton marriage was essentially created when Eliza and her husband roamed the Lake District between May and August 1863 to gather material for a memorial to their lives there. *The Lake Country*, their only joint book, was, they wrote, a 'love-book', made to share; just as Alfred Wainwright later wrote of the first volume of his *Pictorial Guides*, 'It is, in very truth, a love-letter'. Perhaps for this reason, I find theirs the most beautifully produced of all the books about the Lake District that I have come upon, the preeminent tribute to William Linton's book-making skills.

Eliza argues that, once people learnt for themselves that the ascent of Blencathra could be made without a fit of apoplexy and the necessity of bloodletting, that Borrowdale had nothing maniacal about it, and that Newlands was rather remote but not in the least degree terrifying, a reaction to the picturesque and the romantic had set in – and only guides containing useful roadside information were asked for. Descriptive books, as opposed to measuring scales, had gone quite out of fashion, but 'It seemed to my husband and myself that a pleasant book could be made by treating the Lake Country with the love and knowledge – artistic and local – belonging of right to natives and old inhabitants.'[17] A faithful description of scenes and places and their history rather than a tour made up of personal adventures. Fifty-five years after their book was published, Canon Rawnsley could still say it was 'not likely to be superseded'.[18]

We have seen Eliza's repeatedly anthologised description of the Honister slate-workers and her beautifully expressed awe and love of the Crosthwaite valley and Derwentwater, but there are other little jewels of Parish history too; often unrecorded elsewhere, some of them close to the limits of living human memory. She tells us, for instance, of the old custom of 'the bearers and mourners in the funerals from under Skiddaw [Applethwaite and Millbeck, etc.] raising the psalm' in the Lairthwaite fields at Crosthwaite, as they approached St Kentigern's. 'This striking custom is still kept up. At a given spot ... the clerk, who heads the funeral procession, gives out the Old Hundredth, and the mournful wail may be heard far and wide thru the valley.'[19] She also tells us of a tall flat-topped stone, called the Justice Stone, in Thirlmere, situated halfway between the City and Armboth, 'where the dalesmen of Wythburn, Legburthwaite, and St John's in the Vale, used to meet to settle public matters, such as the letting of the sheep – runs, repairing roads, etc. An old man now living in Wythburn remembers being taken by his father to the last of these meetings.'[20]

Then, in the book's excellent appendix, 'Provincialism of the Lake District', we learn, apart from a dialect lesson, that clay-daubin was as good as over, whittlegate had lingered on for a Wasdale schoolmas-ter,* sweet butter (with rum and sugar) was still put into the baby's mouth, as its first taste of earthly food, and that Collop Monday was still kept. Now, 'if a girl loses her lover she is rubbed with pea straw (pez-strae) by the young men of the village; and the same thing is done to a youth by the girls if he is jilted by his sweetheart'. On Halloween, the night before All Saints Day or Allhallow Mass, 'the girls try charms such as melting lead, or breaking the white of an egg into a tumbler of water, tying up their garters, peeling apples before the glass, burning nuts and other like efficacious manner of prophesy for the matrimonial future'. The word, porridge, was always plural, as in 'serious grand things for making banging bairns',[21] gooseber-ries had to be 'knopped', rather than topped and tailed, and 'hack pudding', made of suet, sheep's heart, sugar and dried fruits, was now to be eaten on Christmas morning.

* Although it was to stop the next year, upon the schoolmaster's death.

The year the book was published, 1864, Walter Savage Landor died, and, apart from a profound sense of sadness and loss, Eliza received another of the knocks that fate dealt her. Landor's behaviour had made him the centre of unpleasant Bath gossip and, rebutting it with his usual vigour, he had been forced to flee to Italy in 1858 to avoid a libel suit. His family had refused to receive him, and Eliza had fretted that all her new responsibilities did not allow her to go and nurse him or be his companion. But they had corresponded as ever and, upon his death, it emerged that he had left her some 'really' good pictures. But the poet Robert Browning, his executor, wrote to Eliza asking her to forego them, as he maintained Landor's wife and a daughter needed all the money they could get. Eliza, typically, immediately agreed, but received no thanks. And, despite her repeated requests to be told whom they had been sold on to, Browning never wrote her a single word in response.[22]

Landor had been 'fondly over-generous'[23] to a young woman in the Bath scandal, but implicitly to reduce Eliza's eighteen-year relationship with him to a similar level was disgraceful and must have been painful. So, it is good to have *The Lake Country*, such a beautiful and affirmative inheritance from Eliza's time in the Parish, as a memorial to what she had been given – as opposed to all the traumas, family and otherwise, that she had suffered.

Goodbye to the statesman poet and the Parish

Wordsworth would have warmed to Eliza's tale of the bearers and mourners at the funerals of his Applethwaite neighbours still firmly 'raising the psalm' for all to hear in 1864. At Rydal, by the year of his own death in 1850, a hearse vehicle had become the new method of transport, but Wordsworth had asked for the old way for himself. This was less than three years after the poet's 'fixed and irremoveable grief'[24] at the death of his beloved daughter, Dora, had caused his family to fear that his pain could leave him as undone as Southey in his final years.

The poet had rallied again, when, in March 1850, a cold went to his lungs. At the shock of this, Dorothy, long an invalid, seemed to recapture a little of her old strength, becoming 'almost the Miss Wordsworth we knew in past days'.[25] On 23 April, her brother died peacefully, and the Rydal blinds were drawn. Four days later, at the funeral to which only the family and the doctor were invited, Wordsworth's son-in-law records a day 'which will be long remembered in these vales, for almost all their population was in the Church and Churchyard of Grasmere';[26] and Rawnsley was told of a 'great procession headed by Sir Richard Le Fleming'.[27]

Matthew Arnold identified the poet's 'healing power' as central to his genius,[28] asking who else could 'make us feel'. The philosopher John Stuart Mill had earlier read himself out of a two-year depression with Wordsworth's poems. They had been 'a medicine for my mind', expressing 'states of feeling, and of thought coloured by feeling, under the excitement of beauty ... I gradually, but completely, emerged from my habitual depression, and was never again subject to it ... I seemed to draw from a source of inward joy, of sympathetic and imaginative pleasure, which could be shared in all human beings.'[29] A joy that had been laid down in the poet's childhood at home and school, a childhood peopled with stories about, and empathy for, the statesmen he came to so cherish.

Wordsworth (and Southey, in the *Colloquies*) had captured for ever the essence of the life of the Lake District statesman, but his death came thirty years after what he had seen as the end of the dying fall of the old life. And, almost as witness to this, the 1850s would see the Parish, the locus of the Eighteen Men, who had de facto overseen its governance for 450 years, lose its 700-hundred-year-old boundaries, as a new parish for St John's was carved out of it. A fact that Eliza, in her ambiguous position, never publicly commented upon nor reported.

However, when Canon Gipps took over the Parish on Vicar Lynn's death in 1855, the year before this happened, he would have discovered, had he been interested, that the representation of all the old districts of the Parish in its oversight appeared to have been unaffected both by the arrival of St John's and the creation of two district churches. Over the previous seven years, churchwardens had still been drawn from all over the Parish, including Borrowdale, Newlands, Watendlath, Thornthwaite, Braithwaite,

St John's and Wythburn. In 1849, a unanimous vote on a vestry land issue not only reflected all parts of the Parish, but involved fourteen people with old names – Wren, Crosthwaite, Scott, two Bowes, Wilson, Hall, three Dovers, Fisher, Dowthwaite, Hodgson and Howe – plus four I've not spotted in the old records, and so who may or may not have long been established in the Parish: Clark, Hawkrigg, Scrambler and Slack (the son of the man who had berated the pugilistic schoolmaster).[30]

Gipps must have been impressed, and perhaps surprised, by all the church-building that had gone on in the Parish in the 1830s and 1840s. Only two new churches had been built in the whole diocese in the eighty years before 1830, when two more were built in Carlisle, followed by St John's in Keswick.[31] And, as we know, every single Parish chapel, except for Wythburn, had been rebuilt or improved in the 1840s, and St Kentigern's had been entirely refurbished. In 1864 the Church Extension Society was founded,[32] offering financial help, promoting an extraordinary, ever expanding wave of church-building and renovation throughout the country, until close to the end of the century. But in the Parish, although much of the church work had been seigneurial, the chapel work was done by the parishioners, organised by clergy earning between £51 and £63 in 1835. It had been an impressive Parish effort.

It was Canon Gipps's relationship with Bishop Percy, with whom he had worked at Canterbury years earlier, that brought him to Crosthwaite. In 1845, he had become a residentiary canon at Carlisle, with a particularly fine house on the cathedral close.[*] Their friendship was somewhat out of character for the latter, as all agree that Percy was 'dictatorial and distant from his clergy',[33] and few 'were admitted to his society',[34] only meeting their bishop on public occasions. Hugh Percy had been Bishop of Carlisle since 1827 and, disliking the new ecclesiastical commission, which came into existence in the 1830s following the Great Reform Act, had refused to give permission for its legislated change to the boundaries of his

---

[*] It seems his children always stayed at Crosthwaite once the family had moved there. Philips, *Walter Howard Frere, A Memoir*, p. 17.

diocese. The commissioners duly waited until his death to enlarge
the diocese to encompass the whole of Cumbria.

In the reforming decade of the 1830s, the fact that he was a
duke's grandson had not been to the advantage of Hugh Percy;
bricks had been thrown and his effigy burned around the time
of the Reform Bill. And later, in 1842, the Chartist threat had
been taken so seriously that muskets, hidden in oak packing
cases labelled 'hardware', had been brought into Rose Castle
and sentries placed on the Carlisle road; although the worst that
actually happened was some rioting nearby.* Percy had accepted
the unreformed Marshall plan for Keswick's new church and
approved the consequent decision that the other Marshall church,
at Thornthwaite, should be a district church. So, he was, unsurprisingly, behind the seigneurial approach but he didn't appear to
like changing structures. Might a sense of clerical inadequacy at
Crosthwaite have played a part in his apparent lack of concern for
the status of the Parish church? Despite granting Lynn five years'
respite from his parishes, Percy may have been less than enchanted
by him – the only Crosthwaite vicar he had come across.

Southey, whom Percy approved of, hadn't thought much of the
two vicars he had endured either. He had despised Lynn's predecessor Isaac Denton, whom he thought had slept on the magistrates'
bench. And he had told his friend William Wilberforce, 'Our population is in a deplorable state both as to law and to gospel. The
magistrates careless to the last degree; whilst the clergyman of
--- has the comprehensive sin of omission to answer for. The next
generation I trust will see fewer of these marrying and christening
machines.'[35] Southey had actively disliked Lynn, as we have seen,
not for his manners but for his conduct; and in 1825, two years
before Hugh Percy's appointment, he had berated Lynn's father-
in-law, Bishop Goodenough:[36] 'Our bishop is a sleeping one and

---

* However, Percy's strong support for the Carlisle Infirmary and his 'unwearied
perseverance' (*Carlisle Patriot*, 9 February 1856) caused much gratitude, still
expressed in 1950 at the hospital, Percy Ward, see Bouch, *Prelates and People*,
p. 386. Yet his new dean in 1849 noted in his diary 'with much dismay' that the
day after his inauguration, a Sunday and the Feast of Epiphany, there were only
nine or ten communicants. Ibid, p. 383.

this place has been shamefully neglected. No confirmation has been held here within the living memory of man.'

The previous century, one of which the church as a whole had little reason to be proud, had seen some serious clerical care for St Kentigern's and the parishioners. In the nineteenth century, however, as Southey pointed out, except for the odd outburst from – or real care on the part of – a curate, and the pleasure of hearing a vicar with a fine preaching voice, all indeed had seemed to be sleeping. More importantly, major church matters had almost entirely relied on lay support, pre-eminently James Stanger's and the Marshalls', to get anything done. Perhaps the Parish had been losing its heart as the statesmen, who had always been at its centre, were losing their status.

The directories suggest the decision to split the Parish was taken after Blandford's New Parishes Act of May 1856, which amended old Peel legislation to enable 'populous' parishes to be divided for the purposes of church work. Percy's rare friendship with Gipps makes it very unlikely that he would have offered Gipps the Parish in 1855 without also telling him that he intended to split it and create a separate parish for St John's the next year, if that was his intention. Alternatively, since the Bishop refused to brook change to the Carlisle diocese, and was a country cler-gyman at heart, spending his Sunday afternoons on the farm and offering his expert advice on his neighbour's horses, he may have been averse to the idea. If so, the decision to create a new parish would have been made, extremely speedily, by his successor, Bishop Hugh Montagu Villiers, who was consecrated on 13 April 1856, just weeks before the Blandford Act was passed (Percy had died in February).

Villiers was a strong evangelical, well known for his effective preaching to the poor – 'no minister in London was more popular than Villiers'.[37] The new bishop would therefore have provided the perfect climate for Battersby to start his Evangelical Union from St John's.[38] In this scenario, Gipps would have been given little time to adjust; new to the neighbourhood himself, he may have had little sense of the historic centrality of the Parish to the people, or of any need to maintain it.

It is impossible to gauge what feelings surrounded this historic, seven-hundred-year full-stop. While recorded names tell us that the representation of the old districts of the Parish had continued, the churchwarden's minutes had always been extraordinarily discreet. There had been no whisper of the major Parish battle of 1832, when the Eighteen Men called their extraordinary meeting. Fees for destroying five young foxes, five ravens and eight young ravens had been duly paid; a decision had been taken to flag the floor of the north aisle to prevent dry rot and patch the roof; the only hint of any trouble was the record that a large majority had voted down a suggestion from Stanger and Whiteside to move the pulpit and reading desk into the chancel. Nothing at all about the creation of the district churches was noted. And the creation of the new parish was equally absent from the minutes.[39]

The change made extraordinarily little difference to the way the traditional territory of the Parish was reported four years later in Whellan's 1860 directory too. Everything described under the heading of Crosthwaite Parish was as before: eight pages of text describing St Kentigern's and its history, and just twenty-seven lines for St John's. The correct information is included – 'Until 1856 Keswick was comprised in the parish of Crosthwaite but, since the passing of Lord Blandford's act, in that year, that portion of the town situated east and south of the Town Hall, together with an assigned district, had for all ecclesiastical purposes become a separate and distinct parish'[40] – but the acknowledgment just floats, ignored and entirely unexplored, subsumed by the old and understood context. Even today, books and articles about Canon Rawnsley describe a Thirlmere event as 'part of his pastoral duties' and assign him the role of Keswick's vicar.

Whatever the ecclesiastical changes imposed by the state, in 1868, and almost certainly until 1874, the Eighteen Men contin- ued to be confirmed on Ascension Day, taking their sacred oath between morning prayers and the litany the following Sunday. However, just as the new gentry, with their new power as Keswick JPs, had materially affected the status of the statesmen, the arrival of St John's in Keswick had changed the status of St Kentigern's and the Old Crosthwaite Parish. At the same time, following the arrival in the Parish of James Stanger, from the 1810s the gentry had become much more involved with the organisation of the church. Eliza Lynn recalled: 'Munificence had a hard fight with chronic obstructiveness before it got leave to bestow; and every stone that was laid and every ornament that was added was subjected to hostile criticism and opposition.'[41] So, everything interconnects. But whether the first change or the second change to the old Parish was felt most, it is impossible to know.

*

Probably inevitably, in this busy period of church reorganisation and extension, change would continue.[42] St John's in the Vale and Wythburn* both became separate parishes in 1863, with Legburthwaite attached to St John's, in accordance with its history. Newlands became a separate parish in 1868 and Borrowdale at much the same time.

The genesis of these changes, as we know, was the stark disconnection between the numbers of people and the numbers of churches in the new industrial areas. Manchester's population in the 1760s was around 18,000; by 1800 it was 40,000 and in 1830 more than 180,000. By the time Southey's friend Charles Wynn was working on the Commons enquiry into the state of the dioceses and church numbers in 1835, the parish of St Anne's in Manchester had a population of more than 270,000. When Southey had reported to Wynn that the relatively new town of Maryport had 4,000 inhabitants and one church, which seated around 600 at that time, he made his own view clear: 'no thousand inhabitants ought to be without a church and a clergyman', and 'equally, more than a thousand no clergyman, even with the assistance of a curate, can deal with'.[43]

Thirty years later, the lack of churches in the enormous new industrial centres had begun to be dealt with, although many of the new churches lay half empty. The problem had proved to be – rather than raising money for a church – raising sufficient money to house and provide for a clergyman. Had Southey known

---

* Wythburn had held neither marriages nor burials before then.

that 50 per cent of England favoured the dissenting churches, and that only 25–33 per cent of the Cumberland population attended church or chapel, might his maximum figure for the ideal size of a Parish, despite his natural conservatism, have increased? And what, in these new conditions, would he have thought of this plethora of parishes in the old Parish he loved? *Five* new parishes created from the old chapels serving a total population of 1,799 people – that is an average catchment area of just 361; little more than a third of his maximum number.[44] Within thirty years, the Newlands Parish's catchment area would contain only just over a hundred inhabitants.[45]

The principle that 'the cure of souls' requires geographical proximity to a church, which was the principle behind the chapels, had always made sense. But would Southey not have felt that the creation of the new parishes sufficiently diminished the whole concept of a 'parish' as to make it meaningless at some level? If you become a parish, your ideas grow and your sense of the need for bigger churches grows too. And, as we have seen, and perhaps as a compensatory assertion of status after the creation of the district churches, this had already been happening in the Parish, in an expensive operation, *before* Keswick St John's became a separate parish. At the same time, the creation of the new small parishes threw away the possibility of bringing together large numbers of people, spread over a large, sparsely populated area, for significant occasions (at least three of the chapels still used St Kentigern's for marriages during Bishop Percy's tenure). And it was expensive. St Kentigern's, a church with the capacity to seat 900–1,000, which used to play the role of central gathering place, remained, while St John's had continued to expand the size of its building and its seating.

And the money wasn't there, despite the goodwill of parishioners and the great ecclesiastical push of the Victorian era. In the diocese, where the balance between 'literate' and 'graduate' clergy had changed,[46] clergy salaries remained so low in 1864 that only three of the twenty-two literates and ten of the thirty-three graduates ordained between 1856 and 1862 were still working there.[47] The rest had gone, usually down south, for a better living. Something clearly was not right. The state certainly thought so; when an 1866 Act[*] created civil parishes, Borrowdale was the only old chapel of ease whose ecclesiastical parish coincided with its civil parish. All the others fell into two larger civil groups, for reasons the numbers make clear.

It is difficult to see the reasoning behind the new move and why the old Parish church and Parish chapel system would not have been preferable. It may just be that, with the crossover between a new Parish church in Keswick, which had become the serious population centre of the old Parish, and Crosthwaite, it seemed too difficult politically to administer a church and chapel system. Equally, the whole concept of the 'mother churches' in Cumberland had lost force, as more attention was paid to patterns suitable for large centres of population than to those suitable for the rural world.

So, we leave the Parish behind, dramatically shrunk from 90,000 acres to 9,200, then and now consisting of a part of Keswick, Portinscale and Underskiddaw; with St John's, despite its original claim to be supplying only half of the town population, soon to call itself the Keswick Parish Church.[48] Just like that of the statesmen, who had for so many generations provided the backbone to its administration, the status of the Parish was utterly transformed.

* The Poor Law Amendment Act.

The End of the Mountain Republic

OW THE EIGHTEEN Sworn Men were to lose their free grammar school as well as their Parish. It seems improbable that Canon Gipps had come across a select vestry before, certainly one in total charge of a school, and he may have had little idea of its importance to the Parish and the offence he was causing, when, in 1861, he invited the Charity Commission to look at all the Parish charities. Aware of his new bishop's concern about educational provision, and the general Whig belief in change and progress, he probably thought he was making a wise move, but this time the Parish, once it understood the terms, felt sure it would win the fight, as it always had. The Charity Commission ruled that Crosthwaite grammar school should no longer be free, and all girls were to be excluded. Surely not.[1]

The trustees, led by their foreman, Joseph Todd, initially relied on the ancient oath they still made annually at St Kentigern's, when 'they were bound and sworn, to hand the school down to posterity, as they received it'.[2] This was profoundly felt, and was based on good principles, but it was a somewhat weak defence in that the trustees had striven, rightly, for change themselves, to keep up to date. So, they then employed the political acumen they had always shown in battle by dealing with every one of the commissioners' specific criticisms.

An extra classroom was built, a new teacher employed to teach the girls sewing and knitting, lest they should lose their useful feminine qualities, and the playground enlarged, all paid for by a fairly easily raised public subscription of £350. Finally, in a major historic change, the eighteen trustees took up a suggestion from the 1831

Vestries Act and changed the age-old system of annual appointments to a three-year tenure, to deal with the argument that lack of experience damaged school management. So, from then on, only six men of the eighteen were to retire each year, to ensure continuity. Every objection dealt with, the eighteen trustees maintained their control, the school remained free, and girls were as welcome as boys.

The Parish was entirely satisfied with this response, but it is said that Canon Gipps, seen as the prime mover for the attack, lost much of his popularity. The situation can only have got worse three years later, when it turned out that the trustees' triumph had been a classic case of winning the battle, not the war. A new educational code deprived the school of a £60 per annum grant and disallowed salaries for pupil teachers, a crucial adjunct of the Madras teaching system the trustees had chosen in 1844. The great hopes of the Eighteen Men, when they advertised what they had been told was the best modern education system, were in ruins. And yet, throughout the 1850s the average attendance at the school was over 150,[3] indicating a successfully run institution. How could the Parish possibly cope with or understand what was being done to them? The power of the Eighteen Sworn Men had already been severely weakened once 'the strangulation of the parish' had been initiated by the 1834 Poor Law. Did this latest government intervention presage a knockout blow?

The impotent anger of some of the parishioners about the new order of things had rung clear in the 1859 letter praising *habeas corpus* and scorning the behaviour of the vicar – both for allowing the damage to the Derwentwater effigies and mistreating 'the Duchess'. But in fact the government was behind the curve of Prussia (soon to be a unified Germany) in having a national educational policy; they dreaded the inevitable fracas that would erupt between the established Church and the Nonconformists, should they try to create one.[*]

---

[*] Gipps's brother Sir George Gipps, governor of New South Wales (1838–46), had found it impossible to reconcile the competing educational requirements of Anglicans, Catholics and Nonconformists in Australia. His failure to get support for his proposal for a comprehensive, non-denominational system paid for by the government is considered to have contributed to his early death.

So it was not until the era of Gladstone and Disraeli and the 1867 Reform Act, which gave the vote to all male householders and any male tenant paying £10 or more in rent, that self-interested spines stiffened, as the need for Parliament to take an interest in its new electorate seemed clear. So, in 1870, the Elementary Education Act legislated for universal education for children up to thirteen, with grants to church schools theoretically doubled, and 'board schools' – the board elected by local ratepayers – created where the cupboard was bare. On the surface, the act did not look too bad for Crosthwaite grammar school.

It was widely known that Cumbrian literacy, particularly in the rural areas, 'is probably greater than in any county in England, although the amount of education may be but moderate'.[4] And Crosthwaite provided secondary education as well. The Bishop of Carlisle, Harvey Goodwin, wrote in his pastoral letter, 'I apprehend that if this diocese had been an average sample of England, the elementary Education Act would not have been passed.' Much was far from perfect, of course, 'but still so much had been done and there is such goodwill in the diocese to do more, that it would have been quite possible to bring up, in the course of a few years, educational appliances to educational needs'.[5] Thirty years later, Bishop Ware of Barrow-in-Furness was to add, 'as regards to the northwest of England, I doubt whether the changes in modern legislation ... may not have made it more difficult for the poor man's clever son to rise in the world than it was then'.[6]

The Parish had certainly had its share of those, and any argument that the statesmen obstructed education for farming needs seems partial, but, four years later, the suspended Damocles sword fell from on high. The 1874 Endowed Schools Act took Henry Denton's £500 legacy for the school (and perhaps some more from his brother William), along with the rest of the school's endowments (then valued at £4,000), for the general administration fund of the charity commissioners.[7] At a stroke, this undid the long history of the governance of the old Parish. So, it may almost have been a good thing that the Eighteen Men were outlawed too; the many from the old Parish families who had nurtured the endowment for generations could not have borne it.

The high-handedness of the charity commissioners' dealings with the endowed grammar schools had already provoked
angry national headlines.[8] They had been given 'such powers as
it is believed have never before been given by parliament to any
persons, and never must be again ... The Commissioners at once
proceeded to attack the well-managed schools, and gave no attention to the bad ones ... [They] contemplated a general reversion of
trusts, however wholesome and beneficent their purpose, a sweeping disestablishment of the existing governing bodies ... Gratuitous
education was declared to be a cause of demoralisation to the poor',
the commissioners' intention being to apply the sequestered funds
to establish 'cheap schools for the middle classes'.[9]

From now on, the school was to be governed by twelve 'governors', five still nominated by the (open, it is assumed) vestry, two by
the magistrates, with five co-opted, who reported to the commissioners. The Parish, through the Eighteen Men it had elected, had
been solely responsible for running its own education for almost
500 years, the generosity and competence of the parishioners
having provided far better for this purpose initially than the state.
And, as the considerable Opie, Denton and promised Dover
bequests illustrated, there were clear Parish intentions to continue
to expand its funding. Now control of the age-old endowments was
moved to London, fees were charged, and, in time, the girls removed
to the National School as the title of Crosthwaite's 'grammar
school' was lost. The people of the Parish were numbed – until, in
1880, when, despite much protest, the grant for the school remained
just £50 a year and the value of the upper school was completely
written off by the governors – an offence which finally unleashed
their feelings.

There was an orgy of window-smashing, not by the children,
but by the parents. In an impotent desire to stop everything their
ancestors had worked for being stolen by London, and their children disrespected, they smashed eighty-four panes of glass around
Keswick in fourteen months.[10] Eight years later, upon the death of
Arthur Dover's widow, feeling ran equally high about where the
£800 Dover legacy for the grammar school would end up.

In 1859 the endowments had provided £113 p.a., sufficient for a headmaster, Mr Harrison, who taught the higher school (primarily Latin, Greek, algebra and geometry),[11] an assistant teacher and two pupil teachers. It seems farcical, and deeply unfair, that fifteen years later the state would leave the school with just one schoolmaster, the same Mr Harrison, on a severely reduced salary of £50 and reliant on the help of his wife and whatever assistance he could get for £10 a year to make the school tick over. This would have been unfair to him and unfair to any community but would have been particularly felt by the naturally independent-minded, land-and family-hefted members of the Parish, whose forebears had forever administered the school – the type that Canon Gipps had originally offended and the type the tourists had dignified with their particular name of 'statesmen', just as change diminished them.

It is hardly surprising that, as stated by the Keswick expert George Bott, the move 'did little to increase the efficiency and achievements of the school';[12] by 1878, only three boys studied Latin, and the inspector's reports most certainly did not become more positive.

But the long reign of the Eighteen Men was over.

A pure commonwealth?

It can be argued that there are no full-stops in social history, just tipping points and consequences, both planned and unforeseen. But there was a full-stop for Great Crosthwaite Parish, and there was a full-stop for the Eighteen Men, the trustees of Crosthwaite grammar school. And the lives of and perceptions of Parish statesmen were forever changed from the mid-nineteenth century, after JPs took over local governance from the manor courts. Had anything significant been lost? Was Wordsworth right when he famously described the Lake District in his *Guide* as an 'almost visionary mountain republic'?[13]

'Towards the head of these Dales was found a perfect Republic of Shepherds and Agriculturalists, among whom the plough of each man was confined to the maintenance of his own family, or to the occasional accommodation of his neighbour ... The chapel was the only edifice that presided over these dwellings, the supreme head of this pure Commonwealth; the members of which existed ... like an ideal society or an organised community, whose constitution had been imposed and regulated by the mountains which protected it. Neither high-born nobleman, knight, nor esquire was here; but many of these humble sons of the hills had a consciousness that the land, which they walked over and tilled, had for more than five hundred years been possessed by men of their name and blood.'[14]

So much stems from this. For Wordsworth, the Lake District mountains, 'surpassed by none',[15] provided the essential unifying and controlling force that allowed the existence of this hallowed place – 'a termination and last retreat ... divided from the world / As if it were a cave';[16] home to the special statesman community – to whom the mountains lent their strength. And although the mountains towered above 'the little family of men' at the shepherd's fair on Helvellyn, they were also the source of their fraternal solidarity. Rousseau had provided a republican prototype in the owner-occupier cantons of the Swiss mountains where work and pleasure were not distinct; and Wordsworth, finding the same republican balance of civic virtue and social restraint in the Lake District, believed it to be the ideal way to live.

That Wordsworth lived in the only area of the core Lake District that was then home to a 'high-born nobleman' – the Le Flemings of Rydal – but totally ignored this fact, may jar.* However, in the wider Lake District, the Le Flemings's only equivalents had been the Derwentwaters in the Parish, who had lost their home there in the Civil War. The Lowthers or the Fletcher-Vanes might own Lake District land, but they lived (just) outside the area. Wordsworth's portrayal of statesman society in his description of the chapel priest may jar too: he was 'the sole distinguished individual among them; everything else, person and possession, exhibited a perfect equality, a community of shepherds and agriculturalists, proprietors, for the most part, of the lands which they occupied and cultivated'.[17]

As we know, this image of perfect equality of 'person and

---

* They had bought the rectory of Grasmere church after the Reformation, were the patron of the curacy for the chapel in Ambleside, and built Rydal Chapel, beloved of Wordsworth, in 1824.

possession' is, in a literal sense, inaccurate; the wealthier statesman families had enjoyed greater power and influence for some time.

We know too that the landless or disabled poor in the Lake District had become as adversely affected as anywhere else in England after the introduction of the original Elizabethan poor laws. But Wordsworth had always understood that poverty could undo the values he found in his 'pure commonwealth', which is why he fought so hard to prevent it. The statesmen understood this too, hence their fight to maintain their old working practices, designed to ensure that, as was reported as late as 1834 to the Poor Law commissioners for Cumberland and Westmorland, 'scarcely any who can be called able-bodied men are on the poor rates'.[18]

Essentially, Wordsworth had been right with regard to the Parish, and probably to the rest of the core Lake District too, about the frequent longevity of habitation for farm families. The lives of men such as Jonathan Otley and John Dalton illustrate the passionate connection between the statesman and the land from which he came. Otley was only absent from Keswick and his daily climate observations during his annual pilgrimage back to the 14 acres from which he sprang near Loughrigg Tarn, a trip he still managed in his mid-eighties.[19] And Dalton, a man who always exhibited his 'unbending fellside Quakerism'[20] and whose funeral procession in Manchester was over a mile long, almost always returned for a fortnight to visit his home village, Eaglesfield, 'te hev a reet gud crack'.[21]

Wordsworth had also incorporated the old Parish principles of 'good neighbourhood' and 'ancient custom' in an important footnote to his famous passage in the *Guide*: 'One of the most pleasing characteristics of manners in secluded and thinly-peopled districts, is the sense of a degree of human happiness and comfort dependant on the contingency of neighbourhood ... This mutual helpfulness is not confined to out-of-doors work; but is ready upon all occasions.'[22] For the basic tenets of Lake District society had *come* from the hill farmers' way of life; there is a reason that the biblical analogy for care – of people or animals – is shepherding; taking care of your flock was the be-all and end-all of the shepherd's life. A life founded on a literal 'commonwealth', for the wealth of the Lake District shepherd was the commons, on which he could graze his sheep.

'Old Perfection', a prize Herdwick, proudly shown by the Wilsons of
Watendlath and Wasdale Head.

In turn, the effective use of the commons depended on hefted
stock and mutual cooperation between shepherds. Cooperation not
just for strays, to be 'luffyngly and easefully rechased and driven
agayn', in the old fourteenth-century ruling, but to be exercised
throughout the year; for bringing the flocks down from the hills,
'boon clippings' to help get the sheep sheared, and much more.
This ingrained habit of necessary cooperation was part of village
life too, whether for the 'child of the village' or the mentally hand-
icapped. And the indigenous sense of equality, largely caused by
the demands of nature and the mountains, as the hill farmer went
about his everyday life, is exhibited too in the wills of the time,
which demonstrate a strong ethic to provide equally for every son
and every daughter. Similarly, and attractively, a husband farmed
'in the name of his wife', if she had inherited the land.

The Lake District hill farmer's life had always been different
from that of farmers in virtually all the rest of England; subject to
an authority that was uniquely weak, except in times of border war.

From its very beginnings, their ancestors' lives had been exceptionally unsullied by internecine conquest; only cooperation had been necessary to accommodate new waves of immigrants, or, in the case of the Normans, overlords. By 1292, certainly in the Derwentwater lands in the Parish, there were no bondsmen or serfs, yet more than half the population of England remained bound in 1350. Then, for 150 years after the Reformation, most Lake District Parish chapels were left without any clergy, and the natural statesman qualities of resourcefulness and community* made the bankrupt system work with 'whittlegate' and 'harden sack'.

New gentry did not move into the Lake District during the period of huge national change that followed the Reformation; by 1626,† Cumbria was the only area of England that had a significant preponderance of customary tenants including inheritance in their tenancies. This history had created a statesman community that had been welded together in a unique cohesion that, latterly, had given them more power than their landlords. Hence, to repeat W. G. Collingwood's lovely phrase, from then on, and throughout the reign of the Georges, the hill farmers 'were practically their own masters. They were forced to be careful but had no-one to cringe to'.[23] So, fundamentally, Wordsworth's passage from the *Guide* reflects the essential truth of the time he was writing about, pre-1770.

A commonwealth in a mountainous area breeds a hard-working egalitarian way of life, in which you are responsible for your own life and you work within a mutually reinforcing autonomous community that orders behaviour; this results in a morally neutral organisation of society, neither necessarily good nor bad, and likely to be assessed according to your view of human nature. Wordsworth never pretended that everyone in the Lake District possessed his ideal temperament: 'Manners erect, and frank simplicity'.[24] Even in his 'hallowed spot ... I came not dreaming of unruffled life, / Untainted manners'. 'Born among the hills / Bred

---

* And the humility of the readers.
† The formal ratification of the judgment on the Kendal fight to keep inheritance as part of customary tenancy was dated 29 January.

also there',[25] he knew that ribaldry, drunkenness, envy and revenge would play their part, but believed that all was potentially gentled by the redemption of labouring for oneself. In *The Excursion*, the whole of 'The Ruined Cottage' is a portrait of the capacity for 'idleness', caused by continual unemployment, to effect an absolute disintegration of mind and character; the poet forever aware of the relationship between poverty and brutality. He admits in that poem too that the 'thriving churl', of 'Wide, sluggish, blank, and ignorant, and strange'[26] expression, was commonplace.

Coleridge rightly wrote that Wordsworth's ideal pertain not to 'low and rustic life in and for itself' but to 'a particular mode of pastoral life, under forms of property, that permit and beget manners truly republican'.[27] The poet was not lauding a fantasy, he was lauding the conditions in which he believed humanity could best flourish and be true to its better nature; in a place offering 'the perpetual pleasure of the sense' and 'an image for the soul, / A habit of Eternity and God'.[28] Hill farming and shepherding were 'not languid and effeminate, but full of hardship, effort, and danger, and diversified by the fluctuations of hope and fear'.[29] It was frequently a borderline existence, restrained by nature, the mountains and relative poverty, but one in which hardship was made palatable by independence and community. This was the world Michael inhabited; 'Intent on little but substantial needs',[30] but able to call on the 'virtuous habit' of custom and self-reliance to avoid being undone by fear, and any other otherwise ungovernable emotion.

This society was a vital antidote to the prevailing forces in much of the rest of the country, where man's better nature was easily perverted; for, if people had too much time or money, they 'invite the temptations of luxury and idleness' – for Wordsworth, the undoing of a man. In the town and factory, as he had warned in 1800, it was almost impossible to avoid blunting 'the discriminatory powers of the mind, and unfitting it for all voluntary exertion, to reduce it to a state of almost savage torpor [and] a craving for extraordinary incident'.[31] From this the Lake District was protected; protected too from the frequently hypocritical talk of the powerful about truth and justice, and, by its environment, from the destructive effects of divided labour.

Its unique history had required stoicism and independence, as much as cooperation, and Eliza Lynn's observation that, after the gentry's arrival, 'Munificence had a hard fight ... before it got leave to bestow'[32] would have been shared by the many. The sense that longevity of connection earned control was not going to be easily given up. So, the comment in an 1864 issue of *The Saturday Review*, bemoaning the 'superabundant humility' of the southern labourer in contrast to 'the independent bearing of the Cumberland peasant',[33] rings entirely true. Similarly, throughout the Lake District, the lack of really large farming estates ensured that the egalitarian relationship between large farmer and labourers remained; the farmer continued to 'dine with their servants, and on particular occasions plough, or harrow, and do various operations of husbandry themselves'.[34]

Just before the First World War, almost a hundred years after Wordsworth believed his visionary mountain republic to be over, there remained more than five thousand Cumberland proprietor/farmers, the vast majority holding less than a hundred acres of land – a class that had been swept away in most of the rest of England a quarter of a millennium earlier.[35] The Cumbrian statesman had stuck to his last.

*

A 'perfect republic' can only be judged so by its actions, and here I put forward the case that the vast old Crosthwaite Parish offers a pre-eminent example both of Wordsworth's pure commonwealth and his sense that the condition of farming your own land and flock in the Lake District allowed the essential humanity of man to flourish; a humanity expressed in love of family and closeness to the natural world and the needs of those around you.

Essentially, this is because of the history and achievements of its Eighteen Men. The Parish, with its combination of abbey and secular landholding before the Reformation, had created its vestry governance and the Eighteen Men ('from among the most responsible men, gentle and simple') unusually early, the latest possible date being the foundation of the school, since its foundation

– 'donor and date unknown'[36] – necessitated it. And the pre-Tudor date of the school was equally exceptional. Of the five hundred or so Cumberland and Westmorland charities listed in the 1821 Parliamentary returns, there were just three sixteenth-century endowments or gifts for Cumberland schools, all of them made around the time, 1571, when the Eighteen Men were told to modernise their financial practices, to enable their schoolmaster to earn more money.*

So, in the core area for the 'perfect republic', Parish pastoral and agricultural small hill farmers uniquely oversaw the money and land given to found and fund the school, entirely without gentry oversight,† for nearly 500 years, including a lengthy period when there may have been no vicar. In the early days, before the year 1400 – at the time when Sir Thomas de Eskhead probably instituted the school – the Eighteen Men would have had little, or even no, education themselves. Yet rent was taken, land was bought, the school building protected against the weather, schoolmasters hired and overseen, and everything kept going. By 1817, the free grammar school was teaching nearly three times as many children as any other school in Cumberland.

When the 1874 Act removed their control of the school, no other church school in the Lake counties had a vicar who had been legally required to have nothing to do with running his Parish school, underlining the originality of Crosthwaite's governance.[37] It produced some spectacular battles, on occasion between two warring sides in the Parish, but usually the battles – always successfully fought up until the decade before the axe came down in 1874 – were about maintaining the Eighteen Men's absolute control of the school. This principle was probably embedded during the long pre-Reformation

---

* At Great Blencow, Dean and St Bees. Queen Elizabeth, somewhat meagerly, as we have seen, refounded the Penrith Grammar School in 1563, and there was one other date and donor unknown, school recorded, at Hutton in the Forest. In the Lake District, but in Lancashire North of the Sands, Hawkshead, originally owned by Fountains Abbey, founded its grammar school in 1585. Schools in the other main Lake District areas came later – Bowness in 1665, Grasmere's in 1684 and Ambleside in 1721 – all, though, still early rural schools. Parson and White, *History, Directory and Gazetteer*.

† Except on the two or three occasions the Eighteen Men went to court.

period without a vicar, and there is no single recorded instance of any vicar or bishop interfering with any success.

After the select vestry was publicly acknowledged, towards the end of the reign of Elizabeth, as responsible for the temporal well-being of the Parish, the Eighteen Men – hill farmers soon to be joined by the occasional miner – *officially* oversaw every aspect of Crosthwaite Parish life until 1846. They continued to favour necessary domestic use over profitability and, still with no indigenous gentry oversight, fought through the maelstrom of land change and potential poverty after the Reformation, in time probably even buying rights themselves to sell on to the customary landowners. Their power was reflected, perhaps unconsciously, when the 1616 judgment named them as 'jurors', for, combined with the juries for the regular manor courts, the statesmen of the Parish had broadly created their own laws, and looked after their own, since the cusp of the fourteenth/fifteenth century.

The five chapels were still maintained after the Reformation, even though they (and only one other Cumbrian parish) had had to wait for a full 200 years to get even a deacon. And a unique Parish strand continued throughout the seventeenth century, this time the strong early charitable tradition, an embodiment of the ancient custom of helping your neighbour. Bishop Nicolson had reported in 1702 that, largely due to John Bankes, the Parish had more substantial resources for its poor than any other parish in the diocese, which was remarkable enough, given the number of its inhabitants and the absence of living-in gentry, but it was far more than that. Crosthwaite's 1821 charity income produced by pre-eighteenth-century endowments was £424 a year, magnificently higher than all the other Cumberland parishes; just two produced a bit under half that sum, both from single individual gifts.*

In the eighteenth century, the fact that the Reverend Christian and his parishioners remained on good terms, despite his early fight to correct the underpayment of tithes, indicates that basic

---

* The parish of St Bees, producing £200 a year from the gift of Archbishop Grindal and King James to endow its school, and Great Blencow £201, £191 of which came from Thomas Burbank's endowment of the school there.

neighbourliness continued. And, at the end of the century, when new donations had only increased Crosthwaite's 1821 charity income to £454 a year, still no other Cumberland parish came near to receiving half its income, except for Penrith, which did slightly better than half at £235 (largely produced by two large eighteenth-century donations). At times, the system may have led to a self-perpetuating oligarchy (although who would *choose* to be the surveyor of the roads?), but complaints could be made, and there were no doubt other invitations for the full vestry (i.e. all the parishioners) to meet, apart from the big legal fights and the time when the Reverend Whiteside caused sufficient fury to get the Sunday school banned from meeting in the school – the locus of the Parish representatives' absolute freedom.

It is difficult to believe that any Lake District parish had provided better provision for the poor than Crosthwaite. Its poorhouse had been the best house in Keswick until the state took over, and both St Kentigern's and the grammar school had always welcomed the poor. In the mid-nineteenth century the Marshall Parish enclosure, the only large core Lake District enclosure, was a largely stinted, fairly distributed commons, free from the rectangles drawn in the rest of the district.

Combine all this with the population figures that we have seen elsewhere in the year that Crosthwaite's remarkable charities were first properly recorded, 1821: Carlisle's population 14,531; the parish of St Bees, including Whitehaven, 19,969; Workington 7,188; compared to Crosthwaite's 4,087 – a figure that was similar to Wigton, a quarter less than Penrith and a third less than Cockermouth – and the Parish and its parishioners must have felt uniquely punished, almost raped, by London's removal of its authority over the two areas their forefathers had given their money and land for: the poor and the school. The parishioners' pro rata contribution over the more than 450-year reign of the Eighteen Men had been heroic, as was the care the Eighteen Men took of it.

While it is perhaps ironic that the strength of the Parish continued to be witnessed at the beginning of the twentieth century by a legal, rather than a clerical, definition – a nod to the memory of the administration of the Eighteen Men rather than the clergy – briefly remain it did, as we have seen, as a description of a ward. Crosthwaite ... including Applethwaite, Braithwaite, Castlerigg, Keswick, Millbeck, Newlands, Portinscale, St John [sic], Thornthwaite and Wythburn: 90 square miles with a history of which its people should be very proud.

By then, Wordsworth's almost visionary, pre-1770 mountain republic was hardly even a memory, but his description of a pure commonwealth remained; even if, as Norman Nicholson suggests, it describes a state 'which, if never quite fulfilled, has always been aimed for, or at least, hoped for'.[38] The Parish, governed by the Eighteen Men and the progenitor of some exceptional and charitable people, a home to genius, and for ever alive with the beauty and use produced by its farmers and their sheep, surely approaches both the literal description of 'a pure commonwealth' and, given the parishioners' actions, Wordsworth's sense of the worth of its community. Without doubt, it fits his description of a unique English society, and provides a rare example of a way of life that is self-respecting, community-driven, and just.

*

Here endeth the tale, you might think. And it did. But there was to be a glorious afterglow. The top of many of Wordsworth's mountains became permanently free for the people – the people not only of the Lake District but of the world – when a vicar from St Kentigern's, inspired by both the area's history and its beauty, and working with two others, brought the poet's ambition to fruition. Wordsworth had written that he and 'persons of pure taste throughout the whole island ... deem the district a sort of national property, in which every man has a right and interest who has an eye to see and a heart to enjoy'. And in 1895, Canon Rawnsley, working from his study in St Kentigern's vicarage, started the National Trust with Octavia Hill and Robert Hunter. The Trust now owns and preserves – for everyone for ever – a quarter of the most beautiful and productive land of the Lake District.

Afterglow

Crosthwaite's young vicar.

Marrying the Parish

O N 8 JULY 1883, Hardwicke Drummond Rawnsley became vicar of Crosthwaite's new Parish. The tradition was that the new incumbent rang the bell once for each of the years he intended to stay, and the thirty-one-year-old vicar strode, alone, into St Kentigern's. Locking out the accompanying party, he tolled the bell sixty-four times. Not enough ... After a pause came another forty-one strokes. An entirely characteristic display, which showed he was there to stay – which he did, for almost thirty-four years.

Rawnsley's Parish was a different place from the one we left. A passenger railway had arrived in January 1865 and Keswick had again become 'the generally accepted capital of the Lake District',[1] as boarding houses and temperance hotels had been built for the new excursion tourists. In 1880 the guide-writer Henry Jenkinson had learnt that all of the Le Flemings' old Monk Hall estate north of the Greta was to be offered for sale as building plots and having negotiated a bulk price, intended to transform the area into a place of recreation for the people of the town – Fitz Park. Keswick St John's had been enlarged, with a north and south aisle, and an early arts and crafts Crosthwaite Parish Room had been built by Greta Bridge and licensed for worship by the bishop. There was also a new Wesleyan chapel, accommodating 200, and a new, smaller Primitive Methodist chapel.

The Speddings and the Lawsons were still in residence, the Sir Wilfrid Lawson of that era habitually corresponding in rhyme with Rawnsley. But all that was left of John Bankes's grand poorhouse was an annual £300 from his trust, used for various causes, including the support of ten poor people in their homes. Separately, a 'vagrant

ward' had been created in the east of town, with accommodation
for eighteen, and the petty sessions had moved from the Moot Hall
to the new county court buildings on Main Street. Making pencils
had become the staple industry of the town. The great campaign
against Manchester Corporation's plan to turn Thirlmere into a
reservoir* had been lost. However, it represented a milestone in the
history of conservation in England, the government legislating, for
the first time, both an environmental clause, stipulating that 'all
reasonable regard'[2] should be shown to preserve the area's scenic
beauty, and a clause protecting existing rights of access.

Hardwicke Rawnsley was a man of prodigious energy and
enthusiasms, a magpie with 'almost a lust of perpetual motion',[3]
and he was, above all, effective. His sustenance came from beauty
and the natural world, his primary hero was Wordsworth, and one
of his mentors was John Ruskin. He had an over-romanticised sense
of history, common at the time, and the history of St Kentigern's,
from its sixth-century foundation, was certainly romantic and its
backdrop as beautiful as you will find. This was the perfect place
for Rawnsley, and the Bishop of Carlisle, Harvey Goodwin, knew
it: 'In my opinion the post which I can offer you is as near Heaven
as anything in this world can be.'[4]

Rawnsley would already have been known to many of his new
parishioners, as he had first flexed his formidable fighting and
cheerleading skills to protect the Lake District earlier in 1883, the
year he joined them. Discovering that a bill allowing a railway
from Braithwaite to Honister Pass had reached the committee stage
in Parliament, he issued a public warning: 'Let the slate train once
roar along the western side of Derwentwater, let it once cross the
lovely vale of Newlands, and Keswick as a resort of weary men in
search of rest will cease to be.'[5] This was just the start. The new
vicar was an unabashed and tireless networker, and he so energised
the campaign that, just three weeks later, thirteen major newspapers were up in arms.

By 14 April the *Spectator* could write, 'Even the promoters
of the line, who persisted until they reached the Lords, felt the

---

* The water level was raised by 54 feet.

indignation of every educated man in England.'[6] Five days later, the bill was withdrawn. Rawnsley was widely credited for 'slaying the Dragon of Honister' and when a later bill promoting a railway along the shores of Ennerdale reached committee stage, he gave evidence amid a blaze of publicity. Upon the withdrawal of that bill, the press promoted him to 'Defender of the Lakes'.

At the same time, the vicar, with Gordon Somervell and W. H. Hills, was promoting a 'Permanent Lake District Defence Society'. The existing English Lake District Association had an entirely local base, mostly connected to the tourism industry, and, once its membership had been persuaded that promotion was more important than conservation, it hadn't even waved a finger at the proposed bills.[7] Rawnsley's ambitions were simple, but larger and disinterested: 'to protect the Lake District from those injurious encroachments upon its scenery which are from time to time attempted from purely commercial or speculative motives, without regard to its claim as a national recreation ground'.[8] And it was to the Wordsworth Society that he made his first appeal, dedicating his successful battles to the poet 'in the strength of whose spirit the victory was gained'.[9]

The vicar's passion for Wordsworth had already made a unique contribution to our knowledge of the poet in 1880–81, when, demonstrating a considerable natural skill for oral history, he had collected reminiscences from Grasmere's elderly inhabitants, providing a source that has since been used by virtually every Wordsworth biographer. A decade later, after Dove Cottage was acquired, Rawnsley became a founding trustee and first chairman of what became the Wordsworth Trust, and in 1891, Dove Cottage would be opened to the public for the first time. His next immediate task however, was to win the support of Britain's oldest amenity group, the Commons Preservation Society, which would provide much of the legal back-up he needed to launch the Lake District Defence Society (LDDS); its leading lights included the other founders of the National Trust, Octavia Hill and Robert Hunter.

Rawnsley would live his life on the big stage, but in his early years he threw himself wholeheartedly into his role as Crosthwaite's vicar. In the first issue of his new Parish Magazine he wrote, 'I believe strongly that the law of Christ and the love of Christ should embrace and govern the whole round of active practical life', adding that we 'sometimes forget that our love to God involves love and very present duties to neighbours'. Strangely, the month Rawnsley joined Crosthwaite, just as the congregation for the 1883 Keswick Convention was arriving, Canon Battersby, the charismatic evangelical vicar of Keswick St John's, the creator of the Convention, had died.

Rawnsley's admiration for the canon and his achievements comes across clearly in the Parish Magazine as he celebrated 'the unselfish life that has served Keswick for so long' and stressed Battersby's contribution to the pure water and improved sanitation of Keswick. Battersby had perfectly fulfilled the 'very present duties to neighbours' – a task that Rawnsley himself imaginatively embraced. He offered prizes for the best Herdwick sheep at the Keswick agricultural show and, a year later, introduced cookery lessons at the National School for Girls to win back absentees. But, pre-eminently, 1884 was the year in which he and his wife Edith prepared the ground for the Keswick School of Industrial Art.

The couple had married in 1878, when Rawnsley took up his first post as vicar at Wray, near the western shore of Lake Windermere. A year and a half later their son, Noel, was born. During Edith's pregnancy, the couple had introduced woodworking classes, the vicar having been inspired by long talks with Ruskin, living over the fells on the east side of Coniston. Edith was a talented artist who had exhibited at both the Royal Academy and the New Watercolour Society in London[10] before turning her attention to the School of Industrial Art. Initially, the couple intended both to try and rekindle a love of the native carving skills, evident in every old Lake District house, and to fill the long winter evenings with cheerful activity. But before they left Wray, Edith had added metal repoussé skills to her armoury.

More fundamentally, the Rawnsleys hoped 'to counteract the pernicious effects of turning men into machines without possibility of love for their work' and aimed to open their workers' eyes to 'what they used to pass by without notice in flower life and bird life' and 'the beauty of cloud and sunshine upon the fell-side of their native vale'.[11] Rawnsley's godfather and first mentor, Edward Thring, the headmaster of Uppingham, had taught his pupils to observe nature both closely and passionately, as the visible manifestation of God's gift to mankind, and had also taken his young pupil to see Wordsworth's grave and inspired his love of poetry. Thring believed that mere outward success was of little value; the test of a man was honesty and good intent and the ability to endure defeat bravely after efforts boldly sustained. These beliefs were fundamental to both Rawnsleys, and the vicar would spend many hours exploring them with children in the Parish schools.

Keswick, with its winter dip in the number of hours worked and its thriving tourist market for local goods, seemed the perfect place to extend their ambitions. And the couple quickly began talking to their new neighbours. John William Oddie of Lyzzick Hall, a friend of Ruskin who ran Keswick's sketching club, was originally an integral part of the new venture.[12] The official opening of the school took place on 1 November 1884, in the Parish Room. Free woodworking* and repoussé classes were offered for three evenings a week, woodcarving and brass-hammering taking place under the same roof, yet within a month simple, saleable work was produced.[13] The committee bore all the risk and the workers, unless unemployed, waited to receive their share, a quarter of the sale price,[14] until their work was sold. The next year there were more applications for the classes than space and the school had its first local exhibition at the town hall. In 1886 an old stable was rented for a woodcarvers' workshop, apprentices aged fifteen and upwards were accepted, and by 1888 the school was self-supporting, sales raising £288.

Rawnsley could be found at art meetings 'surrounded with shining pots and pans, which he waved before a delighted audience as he expatiated on their merits, their cheapness and their moral influence in raising the tone of their makers'.[15] The number of hands, aged between fifteen and fifty-five, increased to forty-four:

* The teaching costs were subsidised by an afternoon paying class.

boatmen, ostlers, coachmen, shopworkers, shepherds and labourers, and more.[16] They made sconces, ornamental dishes, menu holders and other items, in copper, brass or silver, and wooden furniture. As the 'presiding genius', Edith took responsibility for the repoussé classes and oversaw the quality of all the work, approving, then stamping, each finished product. And displayed above the scene of activities was her husband's invocation:

> *The makers are the poets! Ply your skill!*
> *Beat rhythmic hammers! Work, harmonious will!*
> *Coleridge and Southey watch from yonder hill!!*

Edith knew the skills of each worker and would allocate work accordingly. A finished object would cause a halt as, one by one, all went over to examine it: 'everyone has something to say except the worker, and he just listens and smiles, and goes on with the work in front of him'.[17]

Workers at the Keswick School of Industrial Art *c.*1900. R. Temple holds the jardinière and J. Sparke the flagon.

When the land and money was found for a permanent home for the School of Industrial Art, the school itself was able to provide £300 towards the costs, a sum equalled by donations from the Friends, who included the celebrated artists William Holman Hunt, Walter Crane and George Frederic Watts.[18] Standing on the Crosthwaite side of Greta Bridge, the attractive house with art nouveau overtones (designed by the Lancaster architects Sharpe, Paley and Austin) included both Wordsworthian chimneys and a nod to the old farmhouse spinning galleries. Surrounded by gardens to provide extra inspiration, the building, proudly displaying the handwritten couplet 'The loving eye and skilful hand / Shall work with joy and bless the land', was opened on 4 April 1894. And, although the school would close in the 1980s, the poetic inscription still refreshes passers-by in Keswick today.

*

The Parish and Crosthwaite would become the centre of Rawnsley's life, providing the restorative calm at the centre of his storms. And the church *breathed* its history for him – as well it might, with the seventeenth-century seat-owners' local names, which recur repeatedly over the years, almost all still familiar: Williamson, Stanger, Thwaite, Calvert, Wilkinson, Fisher, Birkett, Jackson, Crosthwaite ... Brownrigg and Lowther. Since Rawnsley had an overdeveloped sense of the heroic, it was irresistible for him to bring the Parish's mistily remembered past of Celtic religion and saints back to life. Southey had left his challenge: 'Not a bell rings on St Kentigern's day ... the saint utterly forgotten.'[19] And Rawnsley took it up. Within eighteen months of his arrival, he had written the first of four annual 'sermon-lectures', and duly inaugurated his first St Kentigern's Day service on 13 January 1885.

Telling gripping stories that honoured the deeds of the good and strong, with a moral to adorn the tale, was one of his essential skills. So when he offered some remarkable specificity about the actions of King Arthur,[20] *we* may think that a passion for local colour could have distorted his pedagogic saunters through the past – but such a suggestion would have been unlikely to disturb their author. For the vicar's passion for historical context frequently lacked much relationship with pedestrian fact.*

However, a huge amount of work must have gone into researching his talks and, for me, Rawnsley redeemed himself when he collected all four lectures, plus one on St Herbert, into a book[21] that included a brief note on St Kentigern's and a list of vicars – in which he had the emotional intelligence to include John Herynge, the vicar at the time of the church's rebuilding, whose name was subsequently removed from the official roll (see page 81). The service when he first revived the story of St Herbert is a typical one.[22] The congregation sang Psalm 60, to echo the monks of Lindisfarne when they received the torchlight news of St Cuthbert's death, then out rang the words 'Once again from out of the darkened centuries sounds the old command that came from Rose Castle in the year 1374 to the then Vicar of this parish'. And Rawnsley let glorious rip as his imagined procession to St Herbert's Island became a very grand scene indeed:[23]

> 'In front of the people walked the players, playing two pipes of silver ... behind these a cross-bearer, bearing a copper cross ... twenty-nine candle-bearers, bearing the brazen or latyne candlesticks that in those days stood on the three altars of Crosthwaite Church; four priests in vestments; after these came the Elder and Vicar of the Parish ... carrying the silver Paxe beneath a hanging canopy; banner bearers marched behind waving painted cloths or banners, whereupon were rudely drawn pictures of St Peter, St Paul and the Holy Trinity; and last walked the people gathered from the neighbouring dales ... with certain monks from Fountains Abbey lately come for a sojourn at the monastery in the Monks Halls meads.'

---

* In the case of the Calverts, Raisley and William, Rawnsley claimed William quite literally, proudly recording that his remains lay in Crosthwaite churchyard between the tombs of Robert Southey and William Jackson. Which they clearly did not, since William Calvert had died, and was buried, in London. Eeles, *The Parish Church*, p. 72.

He had conjured up a stirring account, and impressively every single object mentioned was one of those that, back in 1571, the church had been commanded to destroy or sell – but imagine the transport that would have been needed to ferry this multitude to the island.* Rawnsley's bishop, Harvey Goodwin, shared his sense of the vitality that honouring its history gives to a church, and when consecrating some additional Parish burial ground in 1885, knowledgeably used the foundation of St Kentigern's to prompt a call for crosses to be used again in churchyards – a practice he felt had been unnecessarily abandoned after the Reformation. The Rawnsleys responded to the challenge with brio, Edith's wonderful Celtic crosses becoming a feature of the churchyard.

Canon Saunders, Rawnsley's fellow Carlisle canon, who had been vicar of Thornthwaite-cum-Braithwaite, described him convincingly: 'When he made professional excursions into theology, he was, of course, off his beat. The fruits were sometimes grotesque.' The canon continued that Rawnsley's reading in church was 'quite admirable' – at times, as with the story of the shepherds at Christmas, he would read impressively in dialect – and he 'was a great draw for tourists ... for the charm of his voice and the cultivated presentation of attractive religious and ethical ideas'.[24]

Another description of Rawnsley before he was a fully fledged vicar, acting as 'half parson half policeman' in Bristol – 'an energetic public spirited, dancing, laughter-loving curate'[25] – rings true too. From the moment he arrived in the Parish he started to look for prizes to give or historic occasions to celebrate, and, with his reintroduction of May Queens to Keswick in 1885, more dancing too. As in the case of the School of Industrial Art, behind all this activity was the desire of a dedicated temperance man to divert his parishioners from excessive drinking. The May Queen was chosen by her peers, while the twelve maypole dancers – each dressed by Edith to represent a different flower – had been the most regular attenders at school.[26] The celebrations were unstinted and the enthroned queen, with her crown and sceptre of flowers, would

* On occasion, to underline the story's importance, Rawnsley would give a lecture on St Herbert's Island, on the ancient bishop's appointed day.

give prizes to many. Young Cameron Highlanders piped her cere-monial ride through the streets; there were fiercely fought skipping competitions, wrestling and racing, horse's hurdle-leaping, intri-cate maypole dancing, and then dancing for all.

Rawnsley would lead the queen on her white horse to the mar-ketplace, where her proclamation was delivered. Children were instructed to be kind and good to their families and every animal under the sun, and the boys were 'not to use catapults ... not to rob birds' nests, nor be cruel to nestlings or hunt any living thing, but to learn by heart the notes of the birds, and to know how they fly, and what they say'. All participants 'young and old, residents and visitors, [must] do no damage to shrubs or growing crops ... seats or fences', and they all must keep to footpaths.[27] The queen's proc-lamations were posted all over Keswick and have been described as the first children's country code. Ruskin, when sent a description, was moved to respond: 'My dearest Rawnsley – You have made this day snow-white for me and it began grey, with your letter and the proclamation and the quite lovely poem, the best piece of sacred song I have read this many a day.'[28]

Rawnsley was a knowledgeable and enthusiastic cheerleader for his church choir and the church's first-class bell-ringers, too, reporting on Christmas Eve 1895 'the greatest number of changes that has been rung by Crosthwaite men upon the Crosthwaite bells for over a quarter of a century'. Music was a passion and, later, he organised many a competition, and promoted music fes-tivals in both Cumberland and Westmorland. In 1884 he became a trustee of the Fitz Park Trust, to which he devoted considerable time and energy. Promotion of health and well-being remained a lifelong mission, whether taking active steps to improve sanitation or offering chances for personal education in how to deal with illness and hygiene.

In 1885 the vicar experienced the duplicity of the Manchester Corporation in their dealings over the Thirlmere reservoir. Anxious to preserve the Rock of Names inscribed by the Wordsworth entou-rage, he had got their permission to remove either the rock itself or its face, later finding that the nature of the rock's composition made that impossible. He was then informed that 'as far as Manchester

Corpn. is concerned the Rock of Names need not be interfered with for four years or so ... The Corporation has every desire ... to respect the wishes of those people who nationally have warm feelings as to its protection.'[29] Within a year the rock had been dynamited (to provide material for the dam, Rawnsley tells us), with the chairman of the Corporation Water Works inaccurately claiming that it had broken up while being moved. Hardwick and Edith Rawnsley spent two desperate days in the rubble, searching for every relic of the rock carving they could find, workmen reconstituting it as best they could higher up the fell.[30]

*

In 1884, the year after his arrival, the vicar had joined the governors of Crosthwaite's sadly languishing school. Four years later, most unusually, he lost a battle. We left the grammar school flattened by far too little money to be effective (see pages 561–2) and soon no longer to be a grammar school. The headmaster, Peter Harrison, had been in his job since 1850 (when his salary had been adjusted to allow for the loss of the cock-penny) and had much enjoyed teaching the upper school before the state takeover.

The government-appointed school inspectors, however, had judged that the grammar of 'the higher classes' displayed 'gross ignorance' and when, in 1880, the governors accepted their decision to close the upper school entirely (the headmaster notwithstanding) the window smashing had begun. Four shillings were now to be charged each quarter for special subjects, the girls would be removed to the National School, and the governors were instructed to 'save' half the money allocated to the school and put it into a fund for a new high school. The pupils' reaction is perhaps indicated by the Inspectors that year ordering that 'spitting on the floor should be checked'.[31]

A shaft of light had penetrated the gloom on 9 June 1882, when a letter arrived from Henry and Thomas Hewetson, two of ten Keswick children impoverished by the early death of their father. As an adolescent, Henry had been taken under the wing of a London uncle and found himself excelling in the family cloth-trading business, becoming extremely rich. The Hewetson pair had kept in touch with their old schoolmaster and had long since acquired 25 acres of land, yielding about £143 per annum, with the intention of offering to help the school in due course. Now, it seemed, the time had come, and they had just three conditions. A sum should be put aside to pay Peter Harrison when he retired; the new high school should welcome girls; and the girls should be given an equal right to gain scholarships. All this was in accord with the history of the school; but not being in accord with the educational views of the charity commissioners, they refused to accept the conditions.

They equally maintained their refusal to raise the £50 allowance for what was now called the 'Old School', implying that money should be raised locally. The governors pointed out that £1,500 had recently been raised for the new south aisle of St John's church and £100 for the enlargement of their school; £800 would be needed for an addition to the churchyard, and money was still needed for Fitz Park.[32] But to no avail. And, inevitably, with two parish churches and two lots of schools, money was becoming more difficult to raise.[*] Nevertheless, Rawnsley was lucky to have become a school governor after the Hewetson offer, which might promise a good future for the first time since the Eighteen Sworn Men had been dismissed. During his first year, the two benefactors had acquired more land, offering to transfer it for the new school when appropriate. Meanwhile, despite the 1887 Ordinance Survey map still recording the old school a 'Grammar School (Endowed)' the school remained in the doldrums throughout the 1880s, and in 1888, upon Mrs Jane Dover's death, the long-awaited storm broke about the Dover bequests.

When Arthur Dover bequeathed his £300, a new high school had not even been contemplated, and Mrs Dover, strongly opposed to diverting money from the old school, had left it £500, specifying that the income should be paid to its headmaster.[33] All clear, one would think. Nevertheless, the charity commissioners instructed that just half of Arthur's legacy should go to the

---

[*] Brigham School was doing really well under the Hightons – Edward and Thomas, father and son – the school roll soon approaching 200.

old school, the rest, along with all of his wife's legacy was to go into the building fund. The governors, backed by legal opinion, insisted that all the funds should go to the old school and the resounding silence which followed was only broken when they approached their MP, J. I. Lowther, asking whether a question in the House of Commons would help matters.[34] Four months later, the commissioners modified their position, offering to halve all monies. And there they stuck.

Rawnsley went to London to protest – and thought he had got somewhere. It is likely that Lowther, one of the commissioners, had privately tipped him off that they had the makings of a successful case. Indeed, legal counsel reported that they would be likely to win – but, even if they did, the costs would outweigh the benefits. For once, there was nothing Rawnsley could do.[35]

*

In the year that he became a school governor, and the Parish started its history lessons, Rawnsley was trying both to persuade the LDDS wholeheartedly to back the defence of footpaths and the old rights of way and to induce the government to look into the issue. There had been a growing two-way pressure for the past thirty years or so, a realisation by walkers that enclosure had curtailed access to some of the high fells, and a realisation by landowners who had habitually granted permissive access to their lands that the arrival of the railways – above all, the weekend outings – had considerably increased the numbers expecting access, some of whom were igno-rant of the 'country code'.

Rawnsley's prompt in Keswick was a large house at Fawe Park. It had originated in the late 1850s as a shooting lodge for James Spencer-Bell and stood close to the old corpse road from Newlands, one of the district's ancient rights of way. In the early 1880s Spencer-Bell had tried to block it with a gate, which Sir John Woodford, among others, had persuaded him to remove.[36] In 1885 his widow went further, installing two chained gates, for-tified with brambles and sticks, claiming the pathway interfered with her privacy.

Some believed that, when the LDDS was formally established, the society had been hampered by its upper-middle-class
bias and lack of support from local people, who at times made up
only 10 per cent of the membership. On the other hand, a society
that had attracted Tennyson, Browning, Ruskin and the Duke of
Westminster would not be without influence and, for Rawnsley,
having a national base was the whole point – above all, to capitalise on the publicity he could generate, but also to underline that
the society saw the Lake District as belonging to everyone, regard-
less of education, wealth or domicile, who wanted to preserve its
unique beauty.

The canon had moved on from Wordsworth and Ruskin here,
as, unlike them, he was fighting to save recreational space for the
masses as well as the elite – a genuine resource for all. Fell-walking
had become a particularly classless occupation, and in 1893
Rawnsley would become a trustee of the Co-operative Holiday
Association, a nonconformist working-class organisation introducing rambling to the workers of the Lancashire mill towns and, from
then on, would frequently act as guide on their walks.[37] But, at
this moment, the make-up of the membership of the LDDS did not
prove helpful, causing it to meander around the access issues. So,
in March 1886, Rawnsley called a meeting to revive the Keswick
and District Footpath Preservation Association. Under Rawnsley
as president, the Reverend W. Colville, Keswick's Congregational
minister, and W. Routh Fitzpatrick became vice-presidents; Henry
Irwin Jenkinson was put in the key role of honorary secretary. This
time the membership was almost entirely local, and Rawnsley was
the only person to belong to both societies.[38]

The adoption by the Footpath Association of an anti-trespass
and anti-litter stance, along with its motto 'arbitration not war',
underlined its desire to attract landowners too. But this was not to
be; both the Speddings and the Marshalls had already entered the
fray. Upon William Calvert's death, the Speddings had bought his
estate, which had acquired, after the Brundholme Enclosure Act,
the old commons of Latrigg and its access pathway to Skiddaw
from Spooney Green.[39] Calvert had built another access road from
his house and, in 1885, the Speddings had closed both roads and

planted conifers on the zigzag path to the summit. At the same time, the absentee Reginald Dykes Marshall closed the footpath near Castlehead, the centre of Southey's old tree preservation battles with Greenwich Hospital. Negotiations with the landowners continued for well over a year, Mrs Spencer-Bell rejecting an alternative route away from the house as walkers 'might frighten the horses',[40] and the Speddings rejecting the offer of reducing the claim to only one of the two paths. The principle of permissive, rather than absolute, right of access remained fundamental to all three landowners and needed, they thought, to be tested by law.

On 29 August 1887 the tone of discussions changed when a Keswick Footpath Association meeting chaired by Colville passed a motion to 'make arrangements for asserting the public rights to the paths on Latrigg and Fawe Park Estates'.[41] The next day they went to Fawe Park, where – although Jenkinson and Fitzpatrick were punctiliously polite when Mrs Spencer-Bell attacked them all, declaring the people of Keswick to be 'a lot of hungry sharks'[42] – members of the association removed the obstructions she had erected.

When Colville chaired the next association meeting on 23 September, attended by around 150 members,[43] and stressed the need to respect the rights of others and show moderation, the motion to remove the barricades was carried unanimously, and the date of Saturday, 1 October 1887, was set for a protest at Latrigg. The dispute became a national story. Eliza Lynn Linton described Latrigg as a test case about whether a private owner could 'block out the public from a mountain',[44] and Jenkinson said on the day of the mass trespass, 'If we do not have the right of access to the summit of Latrigg then we have no right to ascend other similar mountains in Britain' – a sentiment endorsed by the *Manchester Guardian*.[45] This view, based on the widely perceived need for a manufacturing nation to enjoy restorative health-giving activities, was everywhere strongly felt and expressed.

To help raise funds, Jenkinson sent a circular letter to those who had supported the fight to stop the Braithwaite Honister railway, asking for the surplus money to be transferred to the Keswick Footpath Association. One of the few who objected was Frank

Marshall, a Harrow schoolmaster, one of Henry's sons, later a considerable benefactor of the National Trust; Marshall believed the association's decision would prove counterproductive and cause 'a much more rigid assertion of their rights by the landowners of the neighbourhood'.[46] The perceived depreciation of the value of an estate was not something to be trifled with. Marshall, a first cousin of Reginald Dykes Marshall, was in an excellent position to know what was going on and also wrote twice asking others to persuade Rawnsley to 'moderate the speeches and conduct of his supporters'.[47]

The trespass itself was a triumph. On 1 October crowds of people got off trains from Whitehaven, Workington, Maryport and Cockermouth, and by the time the threshold was crossed there were about two thousand people, accompanied by reporters. 'Rule Britannia' was taken up by the crowd, Jenkinson attempting to stop the singing in response to the gamekeepers' fear that it might disturb the game, and the top was reached by 4.30 p.m. Having gained its outstanding viewpoint, Jenkinson pointed out to all where he believed that Dykes Marshall had agreed to open up a path through Great Wood and over Walla Crag for the people.* Then, as 'God Save the Queen' rang out over the fells, the protesters retired, having behaved impeccably. The paths were kept to, no one suggested that harm had been done, and the *Cumberland Pacquet*[48] acknowledged that credit should be given both to Jenkinson and the Keswick Footpath Association 'for the tact, forbearance and good temper they have all along shown in asserting what they conceive to be a public right of way over the roads named'.

It was a month before John James Spedding took legal action against eight association members to prevent their renewed trespass,[49] whereupon the hunt for a guarantee fund began in earnest. Rawnsley won support from members of the Commons Preservation Society, who thought it improper that 'gentlemen like Mr Rawnsley should be exposed to so vast a burden and so great

---

* Later in the day, the reformer and ex-Derby MP, Samuel Plimsoll, also referred to the agreement, but nothing was to happen. Jenkinson would tell the *Cumberland Pacquet* on 13 July 1888 that Dykes Marshall 'did not keep faith with us in what he promised to do before'.

a responsibility',[50] and the canon travelled the cities of the country to drum up support.

Mary Stanger, Cuthbert Southey and the former headmaster Peter Harrison were among fourteen elderly parishioners who gave evidence in the case, which opened at Carlisle Assizes on 6 July 1888. All said that they had regularly used the paths – for instance, Harrison had for many years led his father's horses over Calvert Bridge and along his 'Terrace Road'. Mary Stanger said she believed her father had intended to give the path from Spooney Green to the public – in part because it was the old route for the Easter Monday Keswick pace-egging – but that he was prevented from doing so by 'his unfortunate habit of procrastination'.[51] In the event, a compromise was reached, obviating the need for a judgment of principle. The Footpath Association offer of 1886 was accepted; the verdict was entered for the plaintiff on the issue of 'Terrace Road' and for the defendants on the issue of 'the Latrigg road'.

When Jenkinson and the other members of the association returned to Keswick, they were met by a large crowd and a brass band and escorted into town by the band playing Handel's 'See the Conquering Hero Comes'. Celebrations continued all evening. And the costs of the case, close to £1,000, were covered, without recourse to the Footpath Association's reserves. The resulting gentlemen's agreement proved effective and was much praised. Mrs Spencer-Bell held her peace, although she ensured that her household withdrew from St Kentigern's to worship at St John's, and, now that the court case was over, a general agreement appeared to have been reached with Dykes Marshall.

The negotiations were complicated and took two years to complete and they left a nasty taste within the Footpath Preservation Association as their vice-president, Routh Fitzpatrick, resigned, unable to go along with the compromise Rawnsley had accepted. So it must have felt particularly chilling to read in the *English Lakes Visitor and Keswick Guardian*,[52] just three years later, that Dykes Marshall had withdrawn permission for public access in all the land around Friar's Crag, Castlehead Wood and Walla Crag, except on staked-out single-width public footways. Even the footway between Castlehead Wood and Borrowdale Road was to be closed. Southey's ghost would have paled.

Nevertheless, the Latrigg mass trespass remains England's largest successful popular action to retain public access to this day, the Kinder Scout protest in Derbyshire, half a century later, attracting some five hundred people. At the time, however, its national fame had ruffled feathers at the LDDS. In response to a provocative letter from Fitzgerald in 1890, W. H. Hills replied, 'this side of the Raise ... in relation to footpath preservation, I do not hesitate to say that [we have] done ten times the work which your Keswick Society has done'[53] for almost no cost. Hills then alluded to Spedding's reaction to the court decision, erecting barbed-wire fencing on either side of the public path and planting a large number of fir trees at the summit, planned, in due course, to block the fabled view.[54] The landlords were hitting back.

Rawnsley has historically been portrayed as marching to the barricades at the head of the protesters – but, as is now known, he had actually been absent from all the meetings during the five-week battle. No more details are known, but the *Pall Mall Gazette* of 1 October 1887, the very day of the mass protest at Latrigg, announced that Rawnsley had been abroad.[55] Today this has prompted amusement and criticism but contemporary opinion simply expressed gratitude.

The *Cumberland Pacquet*'s editorial the week after the trespass observed that 'The Rev. H. D. Rawnsley, the president, has shown an active interest in all that concerns the welfare of Keswick', and a correspondent in the *Manchester Guardian* wrote, 'It is infinitely to his credit that, with a hope ... of mediating between an impatient public and landowners who were personal friends, he risked all chance of being socially ostracised and took the helm of the movement.'[56] Rawnsley had even, with some naivety, invited John James Spedding to be president of the association. Also, there were many intervals during his working years when he became ill, succumbed to stress, had a breakdown – the terms vary. In 1886 he had had to leave the battle about a possible railway from Windermere to Ambleside entirely to W. H. Hills, as he was *hors de combat*.

Traditionally, Rawnsley's childhood ailments have been seen as the precursor to a general 'weak health' that persisted throughout his life, but his enormous physical and, usually, mental stamina undermines this interpretation. And ignored in descriptions of the frantic whirl of his public life, his marvellous ability to make friends, his rare talent as a raconteur and his sense of fun are both the muddles he got into and, more importantly, the moments of quiet that provided the necessary balance.

Eleanor Simpson, Rawnsley's second wife, who wrote his biography, gives a charming example of her husband's propensity for muddle, describing the canon writing a congratulatory sonnet on a friend's marriage with instructions to the verger to give it to the couple as they left the vestry. But 'the postcard on which it was written bore only the Christian name of the bridegroom and was addressed to the wrong cathedral!'[57] This touched on an enduring problem. Rawnsley had long impressed serious men (who all commented on his entire lack of self-consciousness) such as Benjamin Jowett at Oxford, who warned, 'You must get rid of all excitable ways which will altogether unfit you for any place of responsibility or authority ... and you must be on your guard against it.'[58] Similarly, the art historian Professor Baldwin Brown had written to Rawnsley at Wray, 'As is always the case, what is best in you – your zeal for helpful work – is mixed up with one of your great difficulties, a tendency to be carried away with the immediate present.'[59]

Here are two randomly chosen passages from *Months at the Lakes* that illustrate Rawnsley's extraordinarily clear eye for the particularity and colouring of the changing scene. 'How it comes about I know not, but in February this fading of the bracken, and some change in the bleached grasses, some hint of life returning to our lower valley slopes produces the curious effect of coral pink upon our mountain sides which we see at no other time of year.'[60] And the following month: 'Never are the contrasts of grey and green so sure to bring the purples of the woodland into prominence. Dim purple of oak, dark purple of alder, rich purple of birch and sweet gale, all these are emphasised by the greys of the stems of the oaks and the greens of the mosses in the wood and the background of grey green fellside, while always the silver grey of the naked ash tree branches rise up in mid woodland with such an effect as almost to make one think the wild cherry is just blossoming.'[61]

These passages could only have been written by someone who sees with acute precision yet can equally allow the parts to meld into a whole, by someone who is sustained by what he sees – indeed, by someone who *needs* to be sustained by what he sees. This, in turn, needs solitude, and part of Rawnsley's cherished dream was to preserve 'the possibilities of loneliness that the rural footpaths and mountain walks offer to meditative England'.[62] Wordsworth's lines on St Herbert, which he quoted to his parishioners in his sermon, were, I think, deeply meaningful for him:

> ... *a self-secluded man*
> *After long exercise in social cares*
> *And offices humane, content to adore*
> *The deity with undistracted mind,*
> *and meditate on everlasting things*
> *In utter solitude.*

And the epitaph he wrote in 1912 for his own grave hints at the same impulse:[63]

> *Here rests at last a man whose best*
> *Was done because he could not rest,*
> *His wish to work, his wish to serve*
> *Were things from which he could not swerve,*
> *Till Death came by with gentle hand*
> *And said – 'Sleep now – and understand.'*

Beauty and truth were close companions for Rawnsley. Equally, he had a thirst for knowledge and new experience, and any periods when the whirlwind was such that it occluded both were dangerous for him. Also, as Eleanor observed, Rawnsley's fertile observations and ideas would only crystallise for him once he had written them down and 'caught' them.[64] More need for solitude. People write for many reasons, but it seems Rawnsley *had* to write – another habit Jowett criticised – and an explanation perhaps of the considerable variability of standard in his work. So, in all, I feel there are many reasons why Rawnsley, whether consciously or subconsciously, found himself to be absent from the five weeks of protest in the late summer of 1887.

*

Having shown, I hope, that Rawnsley, in spite of his absences, married his Parish in the years after his arrival, I would like to leave them there together, on the evening of 22 June 1887, the day of celebration for Queen Victoria's golden jubilee – and the day after a debt-free Fitz Park had finally been opened to the people. Rawnsley is standing with more than four hundred people on the top of Skiddaw, milling around a bonfire at a jubilee celebration that he had arranged. The vicar had already warned his Parish that, despite the drama of George III's jubilee, 'We do not intend to wake the echoes of Skiddaw by artillery from Crosthwaite Church tower', adding that the singing of hymns would 'by usage link ourselves on to the celebration of a former Jubilee'.[65]

The thread of history, as always, added cumulative effect for Rawnsley and much was made too of the summit's earlier celebration – with Southey, after the victory at Waterloo. This time, more than seventy years later, under Rawnsley's capable Cumbria-wide organising umbrella, the parishioners were able to see 145 answering celebratory flames – an occasion remembered for generations[*] throughout the area. And, after a lusty rendition of the national anthem, the parishioners seized their vicar and carried him shoulder-high through the cheering crowd.[66]

---

[*] 'Eh, man, but it was a grand sight. A wadn't missed sek a sight for forty pund', said one, quoted in the October Parish Magazine. And, away in Ulverston, seeing this bonfire was one of my grandmother's best early memories.

Marrying the World

I N AN ATTEMPT to impose order on an evolving, ad hoc system creaking at the seams, the Local Government Act of 1888 introduced county councils. Rawnsley found the idea of a wider scope of influence irresistible and stood for election as an Independent Liberal, topping the poll of the four Keswick candidates. However, for part of his Parish, the vicar seems by this time to have lost his magic. The issue, which could have been unifying, was how to honour John Bankes, the great benefactor of the poor – and two main proposals were presented to Rawnsley as chairman of the organising committee. Eliza Lynn Linton wrote in favour of them in *The Times* but, following 'a movement in the town to replace Rawnsley as chairman', the whole committee resigned, and the project failed.[1] For Eliza, the problem was familiar: 'I see the dear vale keeps up its fighting blood ... I wonder they all accept the arithmetic of the schoolmaster ... that some of them do not take off their coats to two and two making five!'[2]

However, some significant animus was abroad and Rawnsley must have been seen as too big for his boots by those with little interest in high-flying nonsense about beauty or worth. And perhaps some were fed up with the restraints of temperance and being told how to behave, quite forgetting their feelings on top of Skiddaw eighteen months earlier. Apparently unperturbed, the vicar continued enthusiastically to support his myriad of potentially improving causes: the KSIA and May Days went from strength to strength, some fine memorials were erected, beekeeping and the making of haver bread were promoted for health and wealth, a TB sanitorium on Blencathra was established and the Smoke Abatement Society supported. In 1897 a purpose-built museum opened in Fitz Park, with his strong support and, over time, he would both open an extension for an Art Gallery and sow the seeds of the importance of its literary collection, bringing many bequests, particularly from Southey's family. The number of the poet laureate's original letters and documents there still surprise people today.

Towards the end of the decade, 'indecent literature' and 'rude' postcards began to exercise and activate the canon and in 1912 he became an honorary chaplain to George V. But Rawnsley steered himself through his maelstrom with one clear intent: that, in the next decade, and for the rest of his life, he would give the education of the Parish children and the evolution and effectiveness of the National Trust his full attention.

From the first moment Rawnsley stepped up to fight to conserve the Lake District he had envisaged something like the National Trust, asking 'When will true public spirit awake, and in the best interests of its age ... protest and claim State protection in a matter that concerns the State only?'[3] and the concept had been fleshed out the following year. A descendant of the diarist and gardener John Evelyn had wished to leave his London house and garden to the nation, and Octavia Hill and Robert Hunter had realised that, unless a land company was formed to protect the public interest in the 'open spaces of the country',[4] there was no effective way of dealing with this. But the concept was opposed by George Shaw-Lefevre, vice-president of the Commons Preservation Society, who feared it might weaken his society's primacy.[5]

So all went quiet on the home front, waiting for a further catalyst. In the United States, however, the idea flourished, after the landscape architect Charles Eliot had visited Hill and Hunter, and then, in 1886, travelled unannounced to the Lake District to meet Rawnsley. On his return to America, Eliot had successfully proposed legislation in Massachusetts to set up a non-profit corporation to hold 'special bits of scenery ... which possess uncommon beauty and more than usual refreshing power', and the Appalachian Mountain Club was born. Two years after the American breakthrough, in May 1893, when several Lake District properties, including important land on the Derwentwater shore that encompassed the Lodore

Falls,[6] came on the market,* Rawnsley too was faced with a specific *need* for a national landholding company. Having gathered advice from Charles Eliot, who had achieved his aim so quickly, he went to London to confer.

The fabled appeal of Derwentwater unlocked Shaw-Lefevre's original disapproval of the principle; Hunter started work on a draft constitution, and Hill and Rawnsley set out to get broad support for an inaugural gathering at Grosvenor House on 16 July 1894. The Duke of Westminster, the Lords Dufferin, Rosebery, Ripon and Carlisle, the Master of Trinity College, Cambridge, and the President of Magdalen College, Oxford,[7] were among the great and good in attendance. Rawnsley raised cheers when he said they were establishing 'a great National Gallery of national pictures' and 'but for such action many a lovely bit of England would be irretrievably ruined'.[8] Octavia Hill said 'the trust, like St Francis of old, would be strong in poverty and, like him, would ask for gifts'. The support of the Society for the Protection of Ancient Buildings and the National Gallery was offered, and the National Trust for Places of Historic Interest or Natural Beauty was launched, constituted as a legal company on 12 January 1895.

A council of fifty members, half elected and the other half nominated by relevant societies (the British Museum, the Royal Academy and others) oversaw the Trust, while an executive committee, with Hunter as chairman and Rawnsley as honorary secretary, did the day-to-day work. In 1899 Rawnsley undertook a tour of the United States, to generate interest and to raise funds; his lectures on the literary associations of the English Lakes proved extremely popular, with the result that the Anglo-American link became a firm plank in the Trust's financial support.

There were many small acquisitions during the Trust's first decade, each indicating new routes forward, whether for education, or saving a historic site, or in memory of someone, as upon Ruskin's death in 1900. A mentor of both Hill and Rawnsley, Ruskin had

---

* Also Grasmere Island, which was originally seen as less significant. See Waterson, *The National Trust,* pp. 33–36. Its profile has risen in the twenty-first century since the National Trust bought Allan Bank.

promoted ideas that, following Wordsworth, had contributed to the Trust's formation. And Rawnsley's erection of a fine monolith of Borrowdale slate on Friar's Crag, with Ruskin's portrait in bronze relief, immortalises the seer's words about how the view had awakened his eye and his soul. But these remained tentative steps and the membership of the Trust had only risen from its original 110 in January 1895 to 260.[9]

The situation changed dramatically in 1902, when the 100-acre Brandelhow estate, the centre of Lord William Gordon's old demesne, was *offered* to Rawnsley, as long as the Trust could raise £6,500.[10] Both Rawnsley and Hill were born for such a challenge. The fundraising leaflet went out to all 'lovers of Ruskin', and Rawnsley organised appeals to factory workers in Manchester, Liverpool, Leeds and Birmingham, from whom several touching responses were received. A thousand pounds more than needed was raised in five months.

The Brandelhow opening ceremony on 16 October proved to be a classic Lake District moment: two hours before the ceremony was due to start, the great marquee 'went up to the sky like a balloon and came down a wreckage of snapped masts and poles'.[11] After frantic efforts to clear up, Octavia Hill recalls her amusement when 'the little red dais was out under the free sky' surrounded by 'happy and orderly' locals as well as the grander guests. Rawnsley threw his long speech in his light voice to the wind and presented a written copy to the Trust's president, Princess Louise, in a special silver casket created by the Keswick School of Industrial Art. To the enthusiastic rendering of the national anthem by the band of the Border Regiment, the princess, having earlier been steered to the school for some judicious purchases,[12] duly declared the land open to all. The locked gates and notices of prosecution for trespass had been replaced by stiles, latched gates and Rawnsley's stone-built fireplaces on the shore, for boiling kettles. *The Times* called for a similar salvation for the rest of the nation's 'more beautiful places of resort'.[13]

In the year that Rawnsley was campaigning to get Brandelhow to offer itself to the Trust, Beatrix Potter was staying with her family at Lingholm, the new mansion neighbouring Fawe Park, for the sixth summer.* In September, as she began her work on *The Tale of Squirrel Nutkin*, she sketched the view of St Herbert's Island, soon reimagining it as Owl Island for Squirrel Nutkin's boating adventure[14] (see colour images). Most Potter biographies suggest that, had she not known Rawnsley, she might never have got her children's books published, but that is debatable. The two had first met at Wray Castle, which the Potter parents had rented, in 1882, the year before the Rawnsleys came to Crosthwaite, when Rawnsley had just turned thirty and Beatrix was a shy sixteen.

Rupert Potter, Beatrix's father, the first life member of the National Trust, became an intimate friend of Hardwicke Rawnsley, and there are good reasons why his daughter and Rawnsley would connect too. At school, Rawnsley would 'stuff birds and small deer' in his study 'and in hot weather, when the skinning and disembowelling processes that precede preservation were necessarily interrupted by the inconvenient demands school

An 1885 photograph of Rupert, Helen and Beatrix Potter, with Rawnsley and his only child, Noel, who remained attached to Beatrix.

* The Potters' final summer on the Derwentwater shore was 1903.

work makes upon time, his study became an object of marked interest to the rest of the school, but at a safe distance'.[15] As a child, Beatrix kept a menagerie on her nursery floor and, to improve her drawings, would skin rabbits there, boil their bones and reassemble the skeletons.[16]

Rawnsley was the first published writer Beatrix had met; he would have been bound to respect her anatomical investigations, to critique her sketches and, later, her animals' tales, and to want to see her work published. In 1900, he encouraged her to take the initiative, and *The Tale of Peter Rabbit and Mr McGregor's Garden* (set in the garden of Fawe Park) was born.[17] Six publishers were chosen, and six publishers said no. So, again with Rawnsley's backing, Beatrix had her story privately printed and the canon, who had enjoyed success with his *Rhymes for the Young*, rewrote the story in rhyme, hoping that might help.* It certainly reminded the publishers Frederick Warne how much they had liked the illustrations and, with Beatrix agreeing to colour them and shorten her text, a deal was struck – for *The Tale of Peter Rabbit*.

Warne sent the offer to Rawnsley, who passed it on. Beatrix's reply was firm: 'I do not know if it is necessary to consult Canon Rawnsley, I should think not.'[18] She knew exactly what she wanted. Astonishingly, the first edition of 6,000 sold out before publication on 2 October 1902, and by the following Christmas there were 50,000 copies in print.[19] In less than a decade, the old Parish had become not only the spur to get the National Trust off the ground and the occasion for its first major successful fundraising, but also the inspiration for some of the most successful children's books in the world.

In 1906 Rawnsley had an even greater Lake District success when 1,600 people raised the necessary £12,800 to purchase Gowbarrow fell and park at Ullswater, which included the majestic Aira Force.† At the official opening, Lord Ullswater (a Lowther and

---

* One of the reasons given for the manuscript's rejection 'this time' was 'because the publisher wants poetry'. Letter from Potter to Marjory Moore, quoted in Rawnsley, R., 'A Nation's Heritage'.
† The Crosthwaite Parish Magazine had made an appeal right back in September 1904 and the canon had been on his travels to promote the scheme.

the Speaker of the House of Commons) congratulated all 'who had fallen victims to Canon Rawnsley and Miss Hill' and commented, 'We have all heard of the mountain in labour that brought forth a mouse, this time the mice have been in labour and brought forth a mountain.'[20] The Trust's crucial first pillar[21] was cemented; it had shown that, with the right people, sufficient money could be raised for important properties despite the small size of the Trust itself.

There was, however, a major problem. Ten years after it had been launched, the membership stood at just 450,[22] a *third* less than the membership of the Lake District Defence Society some five or so years after it had started.[23] Given the status and influence of the Trust's governing body, this seems extraordinary. Yet the following year, as we know, Rawnsley, Hill and the Lake District would raise more than £12,000. The acquisitions at Brandelhow and Ullswater remain seminal in histories of the Trust, frequently the only two mentioned between 1895 and 1914.[24] So a real argument can be made that the Lake District, and Rawnsley's lifetime of promoting it, was crucial to the very existence of the Trust in the pre-war years. He had cheerfully, and self-deprecatorily, written, 'I came and preached until I bust, the sacred name of the National Trust', but without him the Trust could have withered on the vine – which is indeed what might have happened had he taken the post of Bishop of Madagascar offered by the Archbishop of Canterbury in 1897, two years after the Trust was born.

The decision seems to have been a very hard one – in light of the strongly felt need to respect the Christian concept of being 'sent', however unsuitable the place might have been for someone of Rawnsley's constitution. Almost all the vicar's friends advised him not to take the job, but I suspect that Octavia Hill's letter, brilliantly underlining the particularity of his contribution to the National Trust, will have clinched the matter. She acknowledged the worth of the missionary job and the possibility of duty, but doubted 'whether sudden change of life and work where there has been no special connection between the old and the new, often is a duty'. Crucially, she continued, 'What work you have in England! It seems to me almost unique. I am sure the National Trust owes, and must owe, much of its special character to your influence. If it is to gather in the givers, if it is to seize upon the importance and opportunities for good, if it is to retain some element of poetry and of hope, it seems to me it must depend on you ... All that I feel sure of is that you fill for us a unique place, and that if we must lose you it will be a great loss.'[25]

*

The 1890s were a good decade for Rawnsley's other major interest, the education of the children in his Parish. After some unsatisfactory replacements following Peter Harrison's retirement (see page 586), in 1891 the old school finally got the right headmaster. Henry Swinburn was young and quite unscarred by bureaucratic battles. He would stay for thirty-five years, introducing subjects such as woodwork, local history and nature study, and, with Rawnsley's help and to his considerable pride, established what may have been the first school garden, complete with beehives and a barometer. Swinburn maintained the long tradition of stern discipline and it wasn't long before the school was again claiming the best attainments in the county.[26]

In 1894 Keswick became an urban district, expanding its boundary north from the Greta to the railway line and, for the very first time, incorporating Crosthwaite. So when Henry Hewetson died a year later and left a legacy of £33,000 to the new school, unlocking its future, its grounds would be under the same administration as Crosthwaite.[27] The charity commissioners agreed that Rawnsley and the other governors could now raise the necessary money.* The school was to hold 'not less than 80 day scholars and 24 boarders' aged between seven and seventeen years. It was to cost 'not more than £6,000 for the building' and to lie on the dedicated Hewetson land just southeast of Greta Hall. Tuition fees were to be set at between £6 and £12 per annum, the boarding fee at £50, the headmaster's salary at £120, and there were to be some scholarships.†

* Hewetson also bequeathed £200 per annum to augment the much improved rents from his earlier gift.
† It took almost two years for the Endowed School's Branch of the Charity Commissioners to publish these requirements.

True to the school's ancient history, and to both the Hewetsons' and Rawnsley's original wishes, it would be co-educational – making it the first co-educational boarding school in the country. For the rest of his life, Rawnsley 'never lost the opportunity of inspiring' all connected with the school that 'they were embarked on a great venture, watched by a wider world than that that lay hemmed in between Skiddaw and Scafell'.[28]

With the energy of a long pent-up burst of steam, all was ready for the official opening in September 1898 – which proved to be another Lake District moment. In headmaster Grant's words, 'Lakes Derwentwater and Bassenthwaite had chosen the occasion to unite their waters in our schoolroom, so that we were soon taking refuge in the neighbouring Parish Room!'[29] Apparently unperturbed, the Bishop of Hereford* launched forth, dismissing the suitability of just an 'intermediate or technical college' for Keswick and promoting the idea of a liberal education, including Latin and Greek, and the study of the literature of the children's 'own native district'. He also gave the headmaster a coded warning: 'He knew Cumberland people did not give themselves away, they were cautious people and he was one. They would give the Master a welcome and their affection when they had summer'd and wintered him.'[30]

Cecil Grant, a twenty-eight-year-old clergyman married to a young headmistress, had been chosen from 116 applicants. He wished his students to learn 'there was but one object in life – the betterment of your fellow men',[31] a belief that would have strongly appealed to Rawnsley. The local take-up was originally just forty-one, with twenty boarders, and at the beginning of the first term the headmaster, unable to judge academic prowess,† had to sort pupils into forms by their relative heights.[32] The following summer, the Rawnsleys presented a fine silver cup to the two (one male, one female) *victores ludorum* at the school's first sport day,

---

* John Percival, the headmaster of Clifton, which sponsored Rawnsley's tough mission work in Bristol. Some accounts suggest that Percival fired him; if so, he must have had a serious change of heart as he was Rawnsley's chief supporter, among the bishops, in the new school's early years.

† Grant had established that just one pupil (who had come with him from his previous post) had ever been taught Latin or French.

and an extra £2,000 from the beneficent Hewetson family was responsible for several new classrooms. The school seemed to be generating strong Keswick support on the field too. Having learnt the rudiments of rugby that autumn, its team was beaten 66-nil in their first match against Carlisle grammar school and the well-known referee reported his conversation with a spectator: "'Eh! But the local lads put up a grand show." "You mean the Carlisle team?" "Naay! I mean nobbut t' Keswick lads. First team I ever saw play, beaten from t' staart yet playing better after every try scored gainst 'em.'"[33]

In 1901, Greta Hall came on to the market and Rawnsley joined with Robert Slack (the grandson of the man who attacked 'Peppery Bill') to buy the property and let it to the school* for a separate girls' boarding house.[34] Then, in 1902, a new Education Act moved the responsibility for education to county councils, and created county grammar schools along with county education authorities to fund the new schools jointly with the Board of Education. Keswick School resumed the status of its predecessor and, in return for providing scholarships for 25 per cent of each new intake, received a grant from the two bodies that would cover around 20 per cent of its running costs.[35]

Grant and his wife had never been to the North before their arrival in Keswick and, despite the Bishop of Hereford's public warning, it had indeed taken them a year or so to value 'the true, loyal, staunch Cumbrian character'.[36] Grant had argued for the need for religious education in all state schools, to no avail, and from then on had chafed under the 'shackles' of the two new grant-givers and 'the constantly increasing interference from the County Council'.[37] At the same time, Rawnsley had become chairman of the committee dealing with secondary school and higher education, and appointed Courtenay Hodgson to the post of Cumberland Director of Education. Hodgson considered Rawnsley not only 'the real founder of Keswick High School'[38] but would also write that

---

* The vicar did not mention his own involvement in *The Church Monthly* when he announced that the headmaster had 'obtained a lease [of Greta Hall] for a term of years'.

his 'fresh enthusiasm and courage'[39] had played a crucial part in the eventual creation of six other Cumberland secondary schools.

This makes the attack in 1904 from Rawnsley's co-committee member of the Carlisle School Association, Reginald Dykes Marshall, particularly surprising. Dykes Marshall proposed, in the *Carlisle Patriot*, that the £100 grant to Keswick School be removed, as 'the management of the School had been notoriously bad for some time' and its form of education was, 'contrary to the wishes of the Hewetsons, not of that commercial character which was suitable for the sons of tradesmen'.[40] This was a – presumably conscious – misreading of the two brothers, whose stated aim was 'the blessings and benefits of a really high class education, the want of which has too often hindered the due development and care of many a noble nature there in my time and before it'.[41] Rawnsley responded with 'An Open Letter on the Constitution and Work of Keswick High School' and reprinted in full the four inspectors' reports from October 1900 onwards, which were uniformly excellent,[42] and the furore subsided.* So when, just a year later, Rawnsley lost his seat on the county council to, of all people, Reginald Dykes Marshall, that must have hurt – a lot. Even Eleanor Rawnsley describes it as 'a keen disappointment',[43] although she does not name the victor in the contest.

The canon, therefore, may not have been at his most robust at the end of June 1906, when Cecil Grant announced that he would be leaving at the end of the year to start a public school in Hertfordshire. The loss was brutal: he would take *forty* boarders with him and seven (almost all) of the teaching staff.[44] Nevertheless, Rawnsley behaved with great generosity towards him. Showering Grant with praise at his final speech day, he soon became chairman of the public school's governors.

The loss of the headmaster of a new school that had been entirely identified with him was a severe body blow for everyone connected with it. Grant had excelled at getting the school off the

---

* In July 1900 the first of the copper shields commemorating Keswick School's Oxford entrants was placed in the School Room, awarded to Edmund Curtis for an exhibition at Keble, and in 1904 Norman Hastings won the Hastings Scholarship. Allen, *Keswick School*, pp. 25–32.

ground, and has been nationally recognised as a pioneer of co-education, but the achievements and longevity of his successor, Charles Hudson, a mountain walker, show him to have been personally more suited to the position of headmaster of Keswick School. At first, the finances and emotional equilibrium of the school stood on a knife-edge. Five new teachers were installed,[45] with just eighty pupils on the roll[46] and virtually all the boarders gone. The editor of the school magazine described the dismal atmosphere: 'in the classrooms, empty desks meet the eye, reminding us of last term's occupants; on the football field, fewer merry sportsmen and a more subdued noise of voices' and – he must have been one of the few remaining boarders – 'in the house a desolate loneliness!' But he finished with the spirit the Grants had come to admire: 'Yet in our fourscore left there is much life, a strong vitality; which augurs well that what has been shall be again.'[47]

Rawnsley recovered from his double blow and by 1908 was showing a relish for his freedom from the officialdom of councils and boards. There was a general feeling that the individual secondary schools needed more heft to combat the bureaucracy of the Board of Education and 'the supineness of the local authorities',[48] and in January 1908 he was appointed honorary secretary of a new Secondary School Association, remaining in post until his death. While it would take a long time to restore the school's numbers, by the time Charles Hudson left the institution in 1922 it was in good heart and had 200 pupils.[49]

Canon Rawnsley had steered the Parish through the wilderness created by the state's abolition of the school's governance by the Eighteen Men and arrived in the right place. Old Crosthwaite School, still based in the small building by St Kentigern's (where it had been since the historical record began), remained in business until the 1960s, and today's formidable Keswick School proudly traces its origins back to its foundation. The canon could be rightly proud of his stewardship.

*

In the week before Christmas 1899, a large new reredos was installed

at St Kentigern's. Soon after his arrival, Rawnsley had started thinking about introducing more interest into George Gilbert Scott's empty
interior at St Kentigern's, and his first, small step had provoked the
traditional uproar, but the judgment of the agreed arbitrator went
against the rebels and the plan was endorsed by fifty-seven votes
to ten. A great deal of restoration went on in the church over the
years and, for me, Rawnsley's creation of the reredos, in collaboration with Charles Ferguson, is one of the church's highlights.
A pamphlet was placed on every seat on Christmas Day,* proudly
praising the quality of the materials used and the workers, including
'the leading firm of mosaic makers in England',[50] who incorporated
all the traditional symbols of St Kentigern into the design of the
floor. The mosaics, along with the three large bronze panels,[51] one
designed by Edith Rawnsley, are what stand out today. The panels
too are a remarkably fine piece of work and, joyously for the Parish,
they, along with the text, were worked entirely by students of the
Keswick School of Industrial Arts.

Eliza Lynn Linton had died in July 1898, and the following
Sunday the congregation of St Kentigern's sang a memorial hymn
to her. The turbulence of her life had increased when, the year
after her husband's departure for America, she made a vehement
stand against female suffrage in *The Girl of the Period*. Her views
were shared by Octavia Hill, who regarded politics as 'man's business', and while it is striking to find two of the most influential late
Victorian women, manifestly in charge of their own lives, taking
such a position, various explanations are possible for Eliza's state of
mind, including her reason for not returning to her old home. The
year before her death, she wrote to Rawnsley, 'My heart clings to
Keswick ... nothing but the climate prevented me from going back
to live and die at the foot of the dear old mountains which seemed
ours, exclusively ours.'[52] And indeed, she died after a bout of bron-
chial pneumonia. But it seems she may have found some peace,
telling the writer H. Rider Haggard that a wonderful change had
taken place in her mind.[53] At her request, her ashes were interred
next to her father's grave in the old Crosthwaite churchyard.

---

* The pamphlet was republished in the January 1990 Parish Magazine.

In 1899, a 'Herdwick Sheep Association, for improving and bringing into greater prominence in the country, our beloved breed of little mountain sheep'[54] was inaugurated,* with Rawnsley as its first president. The October Parish Magazine tells us that Stanley-Dodgson and Noel Rawnsley (aged nineteen or twenty) are to be in charge and 'many farmers have already sent in their names as anxious to join the association'. However, they did not seek to establish a flock book, and, ever independent, in 1916 the Herdwick shepherds would establish their own 'Herdwick Sheep Breeders Association' of which Stanley-Dodgson was to be president.[55] Many years later, in March 1943, in what was a revolutionary appointment for a woman at the time, Beatrix Potter was appointed that association's first female president-elect.†

Her life had started on its new journey to becoming a Herdwick sheep farmer (a move Rawnsley encouraged) in 1905 – a destination that would become solidified by her marriage to her local solicitor, William Heelis, whose brother had been a curate of Rawnsley's. Beatrix would live until 1943, and Hunter Davies's discovery that very few of the old shepherds and farmers who remembered seeing Mrs Heelis at shows and auctions knew where her money came from – presuming it must be her husband's – speaks volumes.[56] Beatrix Potter and Mrs Heelis had had two very different, and separate, lives, and Rawnsley had spanned them both. She had no doubt that the National Trust was Rawnsley's work,‡ for, as late as 1933, when she had become extremely knowledgeable about the Trust, she would write, 'I am glad that my parents and I were able to help in the great work that has sprung about miraculously from the small beginnings initiated by Canon Rawnsley.'[57]

Two years later, she added 'The Canon's original aim for complete preservation by acquisition of as much property as possible was the right one for the Lake District',[58] and, once Rawnsley

---

* Salving was now well on its way out, replaced by sheep dipping, which became mandatory in 1905.
† She was to die before her inauguration took place.
‡ Rawnsley did indeed produce the spark that lit the touch paper for the Trust, but it was only the complementary activities of the *three* founders that allowed the Trust to come into being.

died, and with her husband's wholehearted support, Mrs Heelis decided to take on this task herself. Rawnsley's work had inspired her. He had facilitated her first career as a writer and encouraged her second, as a sheep farmer; the two shared views and passions about conservation and the animal world and had equally, usually effective, authoritarian tendencies. That this relationship would lead, in 1945, after William's death, to the National Trust's most significant gift in the Lake District – 4,000 acres of land, vast flocks of Herdwicks, and many farms and cottages – would surely have surpassed even the canon's capacity for optimism. Beatrix Potter had proved to be an exceptional woman and her foundational gift to the Lake District one of the two remarkable afterglows of Rawnsley's life and achievements.

*

Rawnsley had long been the rural dean of Keswick, despite his remuneration, at the turn of the century, being £260 compared to the vicar of St John's £431[59] and in 1903 he had been made an honorary canon of Carlisle Cathedral. He became a residentiary canon at the end of the decade and a description by his second wife, Eleanor, of the ritual followed on his return to Crosthwaite for New Year after a Carlisle Christmas beautifully captures the remaining centrality of the Parish for him, his sense of theatre, of the past, of the centrality of religion to occasion, and his love of the bells – which still usher in the new year for the valley:

> 'The vicarage was always reopened by the last day of the year, when, according to long established custom, the bell ringers and their wives and all present and former curates who could come, a party of about twenty four, met together for a social evening. At half past eleven "Auld lang syne" was sung and then came an adjournment to the belfry. The bells were rung up and a short touch was given upon them. Then at five minutes to twelve the funeral bell was tolled for the dying year.
>
> 'There was silence until midnight. The bells clashed out and, after firing several volleys, they rang a change and ush-

ered in the New Year. It was a Rembrandt-like scene, as in the silence just before midnight Hardwicke would read some short poem which, just because it was the expression of his thoughts at the time, caught the attention of all and lifted up their hearts. Then at the first moment of the New Year, as the ringers with their hands on the ropes waited to pull the bells off, all reverently listened as Hardwicke prayed to "God our heavenly Father to be with us in goings-out and our comings-in from this time forth for evermore." The memory of that little service far outlived the year.'[60]

In the tough years from 1907, after Grant had swept away much of the school, St Kentigern's may have provided real comfort for its vicar. It will have been a proud couple on 8 August 1909 who attended the service of dedication for Austin and Hayley's new baptistry in Crosthwaite church, created to commemorate Rawnsley's twenty-five years' service in his Parish. The font was moved to its present position and mounted on grey/green Lake District Elterwater slate above a purple red breccia base inlaid with Carrara marble. Its new cover was 'an exact reproduction' from a remaining physical fragment and a seventeenth-century drawing;[61] its new ewer, designed and made by the Keswick Society of Industrial Art – a nod to Edith.

The fact that 1907 had seen the National Trust erect its second foundational pillar must have supplied its own balm. The National Trust Act had reached the statute book[62] that year and had incorporated Robert Hunter's declaration that the Trust's land and buildings could not 'be compulsorily acquired by Government departments, local authorities or any other agency without special parliamentary procedure' – that is, its property was to be held inalienably. Hunter would augment this success when he persuaded the Chancellor of the Exchequer, Lloyd George, in his budgets of 1909 and 1910, to authorise the value of gifts of land or buildings to the Trust to count as cash when assessing death duties.[63] The structure of the organisation was in place – an achievement that, as Rawnsley observed, 'served to partly lift the veil from the future and disclose the enormous amount of work within the scope of the National Trust'.[64]

In the Parish, a national subscription was raised in 1908 to begin the process of buying Rowland Stephenson's old land around Manesty. Like the land that became Fitz Park, this had been surveyed for building plots, and by 1916 the Trust had acquired almost 100 acres (and 9 acres of the bed of the lake), just one house having been built on the Derwentwater shore there.[65] Then in 1910, Borrowdale's Grange Fell, including Pocklington's Bowder Stone, came on the market. The whole fell has been described as being 'of great beauty, typical of Lakeland at its best'[66] and Rawnsley secured a five-year option to buy. A successful appeal allowed the purchase of the more than 300 acres, and by now it was clear that the nation, especially the educated elite, recognised both the exceptional beauty of the Lake District and its fragility, and that the area had become 'a forcing house for new ideas about the proper relationship between man, property, morality and environment'.[67]

The next decade brought great changes to the Trust following the deaths of Octavia Hill in 1912 and Robert Hunter in 1913. Rawnsley was now the last man standing from a remarkably harmonious threesome. When one of the founders wrote to another, the letter would often be annotated and passed on to the third and, despite expressions of considerable irritation with other people, 'there seems never to have been a disagreement with each other or the slightest hint that they were not completely united in a common purpose'.[68] The remaining seven years of Rawnsley's life, in the opinion of the National Trust historian Merlin Waterson, were 'indispensable to the success of the Trust'.[69] For the canon had established a firm base that would light up his own achievements with an afterglow – just as his part in founding the National Trust and overseeing education in Keswick had rekindled an afterglow of the old Parish.

*

At five o'clock in the morning of 29 or 30 June 1914, Canon Rawnsley attended a church service in Innsbruck, held in remembrance of the murdered Archduke Ferdinand of Austria and his wife. By seven o'clock, he was making his way back to Schwaz, where he was researching the story of the miners who had come over to Keswick in Elizabethan times, and he returned safely to England before the declaration of war on 28 July.[70] In mid-August his son, Noel, was called to the front, proudly watched by his parents and much of Keswick as he marched off amid a cohort of local young men. In September, the canon was exhorting the other young men of Cumberland to join up.[71] By then, Edith had become badly crippled, apparently by rheumatoid arthritis, her condition brought starkly alive in Beatrix Potter's letter to Rawnsley after Edith's death: 'You can imagine what a shock it was to see her last summer [1915 or 1916] – it seemed to me that was the real – the cruellest death – death in life.'[72] The couple had begun to consider retirement but, once war was declared, the canon felt it his duty to stay with his Parish for the duration.

The following winter, Hardwicke and Edith were on their three-month sojourn in Carlisle when Hardwicke was struck down with virulent influenza and Edith, who attended two services on Christmas Day, became, quite suddenly, acutely ill. She would die on 31 December, her husband unable to attend the funeral on 3 January. Edith's steady capacity to ground him and help him with his work, illuminated by her strong reactions to beauty, had enabled both Rawnsley's achievements and his happiness. The service she chose for her funeral paints its own portrait of this remarkable woman.

Edith had never believed that a funeral should add sorrow; the bells were not to be muffled, nor were stones or heavy clods of earth to be dropped on to the coffin. Eight friends, holding white ribbons, bore the coffin to the grave, which was entirely lined with silver fur and sprays of yew, the planks at the side covered with moss and white heather, with white poinsettia bordering the grave's edge. After the service had finished, the mourners filled the empty space in the ground with the tributes they had been given, sprays of yew, holly, rosemary, lavender, Christmas roses or jasmine. As they did so, a joyous peal from the eight bells rang out.[73]

Rawnsley wrote in the February 1917 Parish Magazine, 'I have not the strength to go on doing parish work, and the public work that has come to me to do, without my wife's help.' Immensely touched by his parishioners' tributes both to Edith and himself, he preached his last service at St Kentigern's on the first Sunday after

Easter, and left a poetic message in the April magazine:[74]

> *I shall come back again*
> *Silent through storm or rain*
> *Sunshine or cloud, for these I shall not care.*
> *I shall come back to rest*
> *In your God's acre blest,*
> *Of all church-yards pre-eminently fair.*

In mid-May he moved to Allan Bank in Grasmere, the first house that the Wordsworths had rented after Dove Cottage. His nearest neighbours were the Simpson family, long-term friends of both the Rawnsleys. A gate was opened between the two houses to allow easy access, as Eleanor, the author of the Grasmere dialect plays, who had helped Edith considerably when she became crippled, continued to offer her secretarial services to the canon. In June 1918 she and Hardwicke married, and this too was clearly a happy marriage. On Armistice Day, 11 November, the couple were in Carlisle and a young chorister tells us:

> '[We] were playing football in the school yard when the bustling figure of Canon Rawnsley hurriedly arrived to ask where our master was. We explained that he had not yet appeared to begin school at 11.00 am, so presumably he was still in the Cathedral. "Come with me," said the Canon. "The war is over, so we must go up the tower and sing the National Anthem at 11 o'clock."' Which they, and Eleanor, duly did, 'to the accompaniment of all the hooters and sirens in the City celebrating the end of the war'.[75]

Rawnsley had continued with most of his interests, including bonfires, spending his honeymoon touring National Trust properties in Wales and the west of England and duly dictating to his new wife. And his last battle was about a road rather than a railway. A solicitor and businessman, John Musgrave of Wasdale Hall, had wanted the west coast to share in the tourist trade billowing out from Keswick. Arguing for a road over Sty Head into Borrowdale, he had bought both Thorneythwaite and the old Fisher Seathwaite Farm in 1885,[76] so he would own most of the land over which the road might travel.[77] Reginald Dykes Marshall became chairman of the Sty Head Road Promoters, buying more Borrowdale land himself, and in 1898 advertised the welcome change that would provide 'villas and farms', turning the area into 'a smiling valley instead of a desert, as it is at present'.[78] One proposal was to build a vast sanitorium at the top of the pass to compete with the sun-and-air cures of Switzerland, Italy and Norway. Rawnsley remarked that, with a rainfall of 156 inches and 'cloud banks for days, nay weeks together, above it', there would indeed be 'no place in Britain better for a water cure'.[79]

The battle was a long one and Rawnsley's apt invective was given full rein. Reginald's grandfather, John Marshall, had had two sides, and Reginald's actions seem a distant echo of his father's, executing the millocrat's parsimony in his dealings with the Derwentwater tenants in Keswick, the facet of John Marshall exposed by Southey. The ambitions of Wordsworth's Marshall, the munificent landscape-conserver of the Lake District, had been taken on by Reginald's Uncle Henry and his family. They carried on Jonathan Otley's measurements of the height of the lake, became considerable conservers of the area themselves and were important supporters of the National Trust. But neither side of the family was to affect the Sty Head road battle, as whether it was Rawnsley or the First World War that finally put paid to it is unclear. Both Musgrave and Marshall had died just before the war, with no direct male heirs, and their trustees took no action, sensibly waiting until the war was over before putting their estates on the market.

In 1920, Rawnsley's final book, *A Nation's Heritage*, was published – a record of his and Eleanor's honeymoon trip to the National Trust properties in the west, complete with an application form to join the society printed on a perforated page at the back of the book.[80] Fittingly, it was dedicated to the First Duke of Westminster, Octavia Hill and Sir Robert Hunter, without whom ... It was the canon's time and, aged sixty-nine, after two heart attacks, he had died at home at Allan Bank. While it is possible that, without his work, the National Trust would not have been able to survive, for those who love the Lake District it is quite clear how much they are in his debt. In the view of the writer Hunter Davies, 'No one has achieved more for the Lake District in the last 200 years'.[81]

At the time, it took a town in a county with their own pastoral landscape to say: 'It was given to Canon Rawnsley ... to worthily hold aloft the Sacred Lamp that had been borne by Wordsworth, by Southey ... and the giants of a past era. Look where we will, we can see no one to fill his place. For the time being at all events the succession to a great tradition must be regarded as broken.'[82] But it was *The Times* who, I think, best caught the man:

> 'His enthusiasm was only equalled by his resource and kindness, his influence was all for the good, and by virtue of an excellent heart and pen which rather looks up to the hills than thinks it rules the mountains, gained more and better results than many more gifted and powerful but selfish characters. It is no exaggeration to say – and it is much to say of anyone – that England would have been a much duller and less healthy and happy country if he had not lived and worked.'[83]

Friars Crag and the opening of Scarf Close Bay, which still today bear witness to

So would the Parish.

The National Trust searched for some time for exactly the right place to choose for their memorial to the canon. Then, in 1922, the Marshalls' Castlerigg Manor estate was put on the market and the 1922 Law of Property Act presaged the end of customary tenancy: each remaining customary tenant could extinguish any dues (usually in exchange for paying a small sum to the lord of the manor).* Quickly, the Trust bought Friar's Crag and some surrounding land – it seemed the perfect choice. The lordship, and the rest of the manor, was bought by Herbert Wilson Walker, who came from a prosperous and philanthropic Whitehaven family. Two years earlier he had bought the Wasdale estate, closer to his home territory, and in the old Marshall land he soon reverted to

---

* The following 1925 Law of Property Act executed the 1922 Act's intentions. Only the mineral rights failed to transfer – a situation that, even today, generates revenue, as new road-makers can be asked to make some recompense for their loss. Before the end of the 1930s no customary tenants remained in Cumberland, but their Commoners rights remain robustly to this day.

Canon Rawnsley's inspired acquisition of Lake District land for the National Trust.

using 'Derwentwater' estate rather than 'Castlerigg' in his correspondence.[84] He would enable Rawnsley's last hurrah.

As the service of commemoration dawned, Rawnsley joined his
mentor, Ruskin, at Friar's Crag. The land of Lord's Island and 8
acres of Scarf Close Bay, next to the iconic point, was also bought
in his honour and, on the walk along the Derwentwater shore,
from Keswick to Friar's Crag, the subscribers 'who wish that his
name shall not be forgotten' engraved their memorial for a man
'who greatly loving the fair things of nature and of art set all his
love to the service of God and man'.

Due to the National Trust, it would not be long before the
people of the Parish could walk as far along the eastern shore of
Derwentwater as, since 1902 and Rawnsley's Brandelhow acquisition, the Trust had already enabled them to do on the west.

Epiphany

T HE CARNAGE OF the First World War had inspired Rawnsley's greatest initiative since the National Trust's foundation: honouring the dead in a way that would liberate them from the association with mud and trench and encompass them within the country's ideal of freedom for all. Why not, he said, combine their memorials with freeing the tops of the mountains for the people – a joint celebration in places that would continue to uplift man's spirit for ever.

He made his own contribution in 1917, buying a small Borrowdale knoll for the Trust, prematurely naming it Peace How, and dedicating it to the memory of the Keswick fallen. In 1920 the 3rd Lord Leconfield, the proprietor of the old Percy land, magnificently lifted the bar by taking up Rawnsley's suggestion to him of donating the summit of Scafell Pike, 40 acres of the highest peak in England, to the Trust, in honour of the men of the Lake District who had given their lives in the war.[1] A hundredweight slab of Borrowdale stone inscribed 'this summit of Scafell was given to the Nation, subject to any Commoners rights' was carried up from the valley and built into the cairn on the summit.[2] The gift to the Trust of some 1,300 acres of Scafell, in part through the generosity of Wordsworth's grandson Gordon, followed in 1925.[3]

Described as 'the World's Greatest War Memorial',[4] the donation that would lift the Trust's fading national profile was 3,000 acres of mountain tops, by far the largest acreage received by the organisation before the 1940s. The Fell & Rock Climbing Club had determined to 'buy a fell' in memory of their fallen colleagues.[5] Their idea, to buy all of the Great Gable and Great End fells over 1,500 feet, won the support of their owner Herbert Walker, also the new lord of the old Derwentwater manor, who generously agreed to accept £400[6] for the 3,000 acres,[*] which were duly handed over to the National Trust in 1923.[7]

On 8 June 1924, the day on which twelve mountain summits[†] were dedicated to the memory of those who had loved them – and were now to be free for all mankind – the Parish lay at the heart of the celebrations.

Geoffrey Winthrop Young, the leading mountaineer of his time, was due to speak.[8] Along with his lifelong friend G. M. Trevelyan, who would soon have land in the old Parish and become one of the great re-energisers of the Trust, Young had served with the first British Red Cross ambulance unit in Italy, and had had his left leg amputated. Using a slender steel leg, with a specially adapted gripping plate at its end, he had resumed climbing. But 8 June was a wet and windy day, and he had needed assistance to reach the top of Great Gable, where some five hundred people were waiting.

Coming from a place that resonates with Wordsworth, with Rawnsley and with the ethic of the old Parish, Young delivered his tribute with a 'trumpet voice' so that 'climbers who had only reached the top of Green Gable, across Windy Gap, said afterwards that they heard every word'. This is what he said:

> 'Upon this mountain summit we are met today to dedicate
> this space of hills to freedom. Upon the rock are set the
> names of men – our brothers, and our comrades upon these
> cliffs – who held, with us, that there is no freedom of the
> soil where the spirit of man is in bondage; and who sur-
> rendered their part in the fellowship of hill, and wind, and
> sunshine, that the freedom of this land, the freedom of our
> spirit, should endure.'

---

* In 1944 the National Trust established that c.1800 acres of the gift were actually part of the unenclosed commons of Borrowdale.
† Kirk Fell, Great Gable, Green Gable, Brandreth, Grey Knotts, Base Brown, Lingmell, Broad Crag, Great End, Seathwaite Fell, Allen Crags and Glaramara.

The president of the club pulled aside a Union Jack which flew in the
Battle of Jutland from the brass monument; 'Oh God our help in ages
past' and the National Anthem were sung by all – who became silent as
the last post rang out over the mountain fells of the Parish.

Appendix 1

Additional information to support Wordsworth's view about the timing of the loss of statesman holdings (see Chapter 14).

C. E. Searle's analysis

In his thesis '"The odd corner of England": A study of a rural social formation in transition, Cumbria *c*.1700–*c*.1914', C. E. Searle distinguishes between what he describes as the 'Lake Margins' (using the land-tax returns for Grasmere and Windermere for his analysis) and the 'Lake Dome', the central highlands (using the land-tax returns from Crosthwaite, Eskdale and Wasdale and Loweswater) and his work has been referred to liberally in late twentieth-century academic papers about the Lake District and/or customary tenancy. In his 1800 and 1830 tables[1] showing the percentages of land held by various groups, he uses the term 'peasantry' in preference to his earlier usage of 'customary tenants' and 'peasant proprietors' to denote the same or a similar group, and the change is confusing for our argument, as it is impossible to ascertain the precise relationship between the peasantry and the customary tenants of his previous survey.

There are, I believe, three basic reasons for the change. Firstly, Searle broadly works within a Marxist concept of society, so the changed vocabulary is second nature to him. He is aware, of course, of Marx's view that, 'by about 1750 the yeoman had disappeared, and in the closing decades of the eighteenth century the last traces of communal ownership of land followed in their train', but he scrupulously details the particularities of this 'odd corner of England'.

Secondly, Searle continues his investigation beyond the end of the nineteenth century, when the majority of commentators had ceased to use customary tenancy as part of their analysis, choosing instead the size of a holding as the classifying factor; so he could not have used his earlier terminology for much longer anyway. Thirdly, the numbers of enfranchised customary tenants had grown rapidly from the beginning of the nineteenth century, introducing a third category to the customary tenant/small freeholder arena. However, in regard to the Parish, with its historical lack of small freeholders, Searle's 'customary tenants' and 'peasantry' must have constituted broadly the same group, so I have taken this to be the case.

Two contemporary reports of the period underline the conclusions I have taken from Searle's work more generally. Pringle's 1794 survey of Westmorland observed the daily disappearance of the statesman class and claimed that the conditions of the previous forty years 'has compelled many a Statesman to sell his property and reduced him to working as a labourer...';[2] while a 1770 article by a south Cumberland contributor to *The Gentleman's Magazine*[3] had suggested the same fate for the smaller statesmen but concluded that they had to 'remove to towns, to gain a livelihood by handicrafts and commerce'. Evidence of a decline was clearly visible a generation or two before 1794. Also, since Searle's analysis that the numbers of customary tenures in the Lake Dome area remained broadly the same between 1800 and 1829, Nicolson and Burn's 1777 observation that 'the practice of accumulating farms hath not here made any considerable progress'[4] underlines the importance of Wordsworth's emphasis on the years 1770–1800.

There is support too from the work of others who have diligently collated local and national records to describe the historical make-up of their chosen areas. What stood out most dramatically in the Leath Ward was Uttley's breakdown of the non-resident landowner class, including the old customary tenants who let their land and the customary tenants who farmed some of their holdings but let others. In the eleven years after 1818 their numbers had dropped by 29 per cent, compared to a mere 7 per cent drop amongst the indigenous statesmen working their land.[5] We have seen the major holdings of old customary absentee landlords in Derwentwater and Castlerigg in the Parish and, it seems possible, indeed likely, that Searle did not include the landholdings of those who had left the area entirely amongst his 'peasantry', so Uttley's work would suggest that his figures would change post-1818 had he done so.

However, Arthur Duxbury's work on Ravenstonedale in Westmorland,[6] another pastoral Parish, also deals with non-resident holders of customary land and offers not even a hint of a fall in the comparative numbers for non-residents between 1818 and 1829. So, since the work has not been done for the Parish, in fact, no possible conclusions can be drawn. There is however a traceable timing difference between the Parish and the Ravenstonedale experience of non-residency. In 1790 their yeomen were split virtually equally between owner-occupiers and those who also let or rented land, which Duxbury believed to be a new phenomenon there[7] but, in the Parish, where some 'non-resident' landholders with large holdings had left the area altogether (not an experience recorded at Ravenstonedale), non-residency has more time-depth. More significantly for my argument, the years between 1778 and 1803 strongly stand out in Duxbury's picture as those with the highest rate of loss of indigenous customary tenants during the general arc between 1778 and 1826.[8]

The Leath Ward was a much more varied area, including Penrith, and Uttley's excellent analysis shares the exceptional (and I think proven) drop in statesman numbers between 1780 and 1829,[9] but, as previously stated, it strongly emphasises the years after 1815 without offering any real statistical evidence to back that up.[10] Jonathan Healey's work on Grasmere, and, to a lesser extent, Great Langdale[11] demonstrates that, as in the Parish, the smallest tenements had held their own from the 1770s to 1830, although times had been tough in the years around the turn of the century and many became poorer, as they were joined by some who would be mildly better off by 1809.[12] He also demonstrates that both the number and size of large estates had risen substantially between 1717 and 1771 as some Grasmere statesmen began to buy more than one major farm – one buying four.[13] This process had reversed by 1789, some estates breaking up, but reversed again from 1808 so that, by 1830, the position had largely reverted to that established in 1773.[14]

Although the span of years from which he can gather hard evidence, 1665–1789,[15] is fairly short, Healey's description of Grasmere, not surprisingly, broadly illustrates the Parish position of a strong core of long-held land, usually by the better-off, underpinning an otherwise more fluctuating land market. And, as in Whyte's work in Watermillock shows no evidence of a sharp decline in numbers between 1815 and the 1840s.[16] Finally, if my estimate, based on Uttley's work, of the minimum percentage of customary tenants (30 per cent) in the Parish in 1913 (see Chapter 22) is correct, there would have been a 28 per cent decline in the numbers of Parish customary tenants between 1829 and 1914 (or 3.3 per cent a decade). However, this figure is likely to have been weighted more towards the twenty years before 1850 than the sixty-four years after it, as there is both evidence and general agreement that there was relatively little change in the number of grazier farmers after 1851 throughout Cumberland and Westmorland.[17]

The old consensus that 'the demise' broadly started after 1815 derives largely from Blamire and the directories from 1829 onwards, which were used as the basis for charting the chronology of decline, an approach now proven to be statistically unreliable (see pages 599–600). However, it is almost equally relevant that much of both contemporary and twentieth- and twenty-first-century comment about the 'demise' relates to Cumberland or Cumbria as a whole, and that the experience of lowland farming was distinctly different from that of the Lake District hill farmers in the period we have been examining. Also, what twentieth-century work was done on the Lake District tended to have a strong south Lakeland bias.[18] So, if we want greater certainty in the debate about the fate of the Lake District hill-farmers, yet more work still needs to be done.

Additional Parish detail

Early clusters of similar names in particular parts of the Parish highlight the traditional tendency for family members to live near each other in one area, and around the turn of the twentieth century much play was made of old 'clans' and intermarriage in the upland areas of Cumbria.[19]

Medieval records are usually blank from the fourteenth century, with its wars and plagues, until the late fifteenth century, but Setmabanning, one of the oldest farms in the Parish, breaks the general silence. A 1446 charter tells us that Walter Fitz Walter of Threlkeld had 'by this present Charter ... confirmed to Sir Adam de Crosthwaite, All that land of Mosshouse, in Setmabanwick which formerly belonged to my father Roger...'.[20] This was the first reference to the Mosses and Crosthwaites in the Parish. And there, in the 1623 indenture, Percivall Crosthwaite of Setmabanning is 'enfranchised', while the Mosses remained at Moss Dyke until 1692.[21]

The Derwentwater manor, outside Keswick, had a large expanse of demesne land, used as parkland or farmed on lease, so, combining that with the scant reference to tenant ownership in the fifteenth century (and a relative scarcity in the sixteenth), one would expect that, statistically, any provable customary tenure of more than 150 years in the manor would be rare – so the figures on page 338 are particularly notable.

The twentieth-century assertion that the smaller holdings had disappeared by the early nineteenth century is evidentially problematic. Three cottages in the Derwentwater manor with small amounts of land were consistently left out of the records until the census of 1841 which, following the Population Act of 1840, was the first centralised census in the UK.* So, before 1841, any assertion about the universal loss of smallholdings must have been largely intuited, without the evidence of abandoned buildings.

The danger of the New Historicists

Analysis of Wordsworth's poem 'Michael' lies at the heart of a late twentieth-century school of literary criticism known as New Historicism; the critics' charge being that Wordsworth betrayed or distorted history. However, the two texts I have studied, David

---

* They would subsequently take place each decade.

Simpson's *Wordsworth's Historical Imagination* and *Roger Sale's English Literature in History 1780–1830*, misinterpret the nature of customary tenancy, which necessarily distorts their conclusions about the poem's historical subtext. Michael's story had originally been told to Wordsworth by Ann Tyson, probably around 1780 after the wool price had dropped, and it is almost universally agreed that its crisis was set earlier, within the 1720–50 period, when half the statesmen's estates consisted of credits.

Sale largely depended upon Bailey and Culley, whose judgment that 'customary tenure is allowed, on all hands, to be a great grievance'[22] ignored almost all of the long and dogged fight we have witnessed, the people the commissioners had been describing, and most of the people whose lives we have been following; they were addressing themselves simply to their utilitarian fellow improvers. Furthermore, John Housman judged that 'oppression is little known' among the hill-farming customary tenants, and Pringle,[23] the Westmorland commissioner, referred to by both Simpson and Sale, reported of the statesman that 'The consciousness of their independence renders them impatient with oppression or insult ... but they are gentle and obliging when treated by their superiors with kindness and respect'.[*]

Simpson and Sale believed that Wordsworth had simply got it wrong, Simpson maintaining that the statesmen did not live 'upon their own little properties', as that was true only of freeholders. Customary tenants might live 'as if they were freeholders', but in fact their existence was 'determined by the condescension or indolence of the landowners'. Yet Michael farmed in Grasmere, where rents for the larger 'customary acre' had cost the equivalent of two days' earnings, or a bit less, for a skilled mason or carpenter as far back as 1524; and, as had long been pointed out, even 'when we add fines to rents the total amounts which could be raised from each tenant were of risible proportions'.[24] Grasmere's fine had been two years' customary rent for the death of the lord, and three for

---

[*] Simpson even quotes this passage, but it seems to have prompted neither him nor Sale to any recognition of the possibility that the customary tenant had an inviolable connection to his land, leaving their misunderstanding of the actual historical conditions of the cast of 'Michael' (and 'The Brothers') intact.

the tenant since their 'enfranchisement' in 1619 – distinctly cheap.[25] And there was nothing the landlord could do to change that, unless the tenant committed a criminal act.

Michael's story was set on the other side of Dunmail Raise from the Parish, where, as we know, freeholders (apart from the two large landowners and Lawson, all living outside the Parish) were an almost non-existent class until enfranchisement, a noun virtually absent from the work of both authors. The Derwentwater manor had offered semi-enfranchisement in 1623 and fixed the fines on the death of the lord and tenant at four times the ancient rent, a pittance by the nineteenth century. A hundred years later, fines were, de facto, fixed in the old Percy manor at a maximum of two years' current rent (the same rate as for the far smaller number of Derwentwater 'arbitrary' tenants) and it had seemed advantageous for the landlord to offer enfranchisement from 1759.

However, Sale claims that Michael raises 'the issue of land tenure ... very much the grievance of grievances as far as the Lakeland farmers were concerned', and that the poem 'must be seen as pro-paganda for the local gentry and aristocracy', whom 'historical evidence' shows – and this is 'more of a probability than a possi-bility' – were 'Michael's real enemies'.[26] What does this mean? In fact, Michael is a crystal-clear portrait of the danger of mortgage debt, which the shepherd had not only inherited but failed to take on board, as he risked more when he agreed, as a relatively young man, to be 'bound in surety for his Brother's Son'. An extension too far of the rules of 'domestic affection', the problem was a relatively new one in Michael's youth, and lessons had not been learnt.

It seems that both authors see Wordsworth's later, more estab-lishment position, including his somewhat utopian warmth of feeling for the large landowner, as present in 1800, when 'Michael' and 'The Brothers' were written. Yet that was just seven years after the poet's excoriation of the aristocracy in his letter to the Bishop of Llandaff and eight years before his work on Cintra, in which he wrote 'the voice of the people is the voice of God.'[27] Sale rein-forced this belief by maintaining that Wordsworth became entitled to vote because 'Lowther had bought him a freehold'[28] – which would have been a useful point, had it been accurate. But, as we know, the poet gained that right years earlier, after Beaumont gave him his land in Applethwaite in the Parish. So, it may have been the New Historicists' view of history itself that obscured their capacity to comprehend the historical truth of the position of the customary tenant.

Appendix 2

I AM PARTICULARLY GRATEFUL to Richard Hoyle, the eminent scholar of rural history, for the invaluable prompts towards finding more detail on the history of Crosthwaite Parish in his 1987 paper on tenant right. In that paper he makes the primary case that customary tenancy or tenant right emerged far later than was previously thought, and his view is universally respected. While I fully acknowledge the importance of Hoyle's argument, I feel I should register here, in the form of a brief appendix, my demurral from some parts of it with regard to my particular focus. I make no claims to have any detailed scholarly knowledge outside the Old Crosthwaite Parish, but I think the evidence from this locality does cast some doubt on his conclusion. Of course, the lack of available sources, which Hoyle fully and frequently acknowledges, inevitably makes every argument on the subject incapable of incontrovertible proof.

Hoyle considers 'border service' to fall under general common law and defines taking a fine upon the death of the lord as the fundamental principle of tenant right. He states that surviving sixteenth-century Cumbrian manorial court rolls suggest this was largely an innovation of the 1560s (in the Parish some Derwentwater fines were taken in the 1530s) except for the earlier actions of the Percy manors (also in the Parish) and one other estate. He also, though, comments that a God's penny marks the making of a new contract but 'often passed unremarked in descriptions of custom', so I would query how we can know whether there had or had not been contracts that marked the death of the lord earlier still, albeit with this virtually symbolic exchange of money.

Hoyle points to a few manors with those conditions in the second half of the sixteenth century, including the dubious Borrowdale agreement, but does not appear to consider whether these transactions were a crucial part of the customary agreement long before they could be manipulated into fines in sixteenth-century conditions. Yet how could the fining have arisen without some earlier customary basis of agreement between lord and tenant? Hoyle himself suggests 'at some prehistoric time, [there were] tenants held by the payment of a God's penny on their entry and a God's penny on the death of the lord', so is it not plausible to make the connection? And, the most important question of all, for me, is this: if tenant right, with Hoyle's determining condition, arose only in the sixteenth century, how could it suddenly become so strong that in that same century, as he says, 'a lord had only a small chance … of breaking tenant right by illegal means'. I do not think that wands wave that quickly.

Essential to understanding customary tenancy, I think, is determining the chronology (never universal in a manorial custom system) of the form of agreement with the lord, the power to sell tenant right by deed and hereditary rights. These are timing questions which available sources may never allow us to answer fully. Hoyle's answer to the last question is the sixteenth century – prompted, I think, by his unequivocal view that customary tenancy evolved from a system of life leases. His only direct evidence for this comes from some court rolls. However, he says elsewhere that 'often tenant right holders had leases or warrants from their lords' (a practice that was consistent in the two large Parish manors) and so negotiated directly, keeping their own copy of any written agreement made, while copyholders *de jure* surrendered their agreement to the court. This distinction, I think, puts some strain on the value of his court-roll evidence.

Despite this, it allows Hoyle to say about copyhold, which emerged during the fourteenth century, 'some copy-hold might have no greater antiquity than all of tenant right'. While that remark is, of course, fully justified if we accept his determining characteristic, it leaves wide open the whole question of what customary tenancy was before the sixteenth century. Equally, it ignores the particular strength of hereditary tenant right/customary tenancy, which held its position in Cumberland better than hereditary copyhold land elsewhere, much of which had been converted to leasehold as well as to freehold – a conversion which both forms of tenancy experienced liberally. This was largely because when the rights, including inheritance rights, of customary tenancy began to be referrable to the central courts of equity and common law from the mid sixteenth century to the early seventeenth century, copyholds of inheritance remained forever under the sole purview of the manor courts (see Oxford *Dictionary of Law*), a clear indication of the government's view of the relative significance of the two forms of tenancy.

Undoubtedly, I would argue, some of the early tenant relationships in the Parish reflect arrangements made before the Normans arrived. For instance, the various cornage relationships, such as the one between the Derwentwaters and the monarch, or the Norman acceptance that tenants could continue to exercise their common rights, principally grazing and turbary, after the barons had asserted their control of the vast no-man's-land of Lake District upland waste. Perhaps that has some relationship to the evolution of customary tenancy? Unknowable. But my sense is that, for Hoyle, even asking the question is impossible, so that, quite apart from a very late timing of hereditary customary tenancy, some fundamental issues are left hanging. I am left feeling that there is an absence of explanation here, which an earlier dating of customary tenancy might help to rectify.

Acknowledgements

Writers of books covering a long time span inevitably, I think, access much of their raw material through the diligent work of those before them and Lake District research has a long and fine tradition. The archives of the CWAAS are, of course, quite invaluable and, more recently, Stephen Mathew's publishing for Bookcase has led to a flowering of more local history for the region. It would be impossible to list every writer whose work has unravelled a vital strand in the book but three local history books, difficult to access outside the area but part of a national resource of raw material not often enough complimented, are foundational: Susan Grant's *The Story of the Newlands Valley*, Geoff Darrell's *Rediscovering Our Past* (a history of the houses within the old Derwentwater manor, written in collaboration with the householders of the area), and George Bott's *Keswick* (a book which has been consistently in print since 1994). For more essential insight into the area, I also owe particular thanks to Angus Winchester for all his meticulous work and to the theses of C. E. Searle and Derek Denman; equally my book would not have been conceived without the work of all who have debated the role of the customary tenant and the 'demise of the statesman' from Collingwood and Rawnsley onwards.

On the literary side I have been particularly lucky to have had the new resource of all Robert Southey's Letters from 1791–1821 available to me, free of access, from Romantic Collections and am most grateful for the extraordinary scholarship of Lynda Pratt, Tim Fulford and Ian Packer. I am also most grateful for the collegiality of the late Bill Speck in discussing Robert Southey, and the relatively recent perceptions of Lucy Newlyn in *William and Dorothy Wordsworth: All in Each Other* and Jonathan Bate in *Romantic Ecology*. Above all, I owe a major debt to the generations of work and scholarship concerning Wordsworth and his poetry and was particularly lucky to come across Jonathan Wordsworth's 1985 edition of The Pedlar, Tintern Abbey, and The Two-Part Prelude early on, which, for me, sparked a new line of thought. My knowledge about Canon Rawnsley was especially enhanced by material in Rosalind Rawnsley's essays, hosted by hdrawns-ley.com, and Merlin Waterson's The National Trust: The First Hundred Years. Behind everything lie many great classics, such as Keith Thomas's Religion and the Decline of Magic and Diarmaid MacCulloch's A History of Christianity.

Every historian of the Lake District of the last forty-five years owes their thanks to both Michael Moon and to the former Cumberland County Library for their reprints of the classic directories and here the Covid Year makes its entrance. Stephen White at Carlisle Library has helped me all through the long years and the closure of libraries has been a difficulty, as has the closure of some picture sources. However, Jeff Cowton, the curator of the Wordsworth Trust, was wonderfully helpful, photographing pictures himself for us which were essential for the book; so eventually we have suffered only one significant loss to The Year. You do not meet your publishers in The Year either, which, for an ex-publisher, inevitably feels peculiar. However, I would like to express my real gratitude to Anthony and Nic Cheetham for publishing the book. The Head of Zeus design and production standards are, I think, exemplary, and they have made a beautiful book, for which so many thanks. I am also particularly grateful to Matilda Singer, my editor's editorial assistant, who only arrived in January and has been isolated by Covid but has done a wonderful job of work and in whose hands I felt safe. Thank you.

I have been awed by my editor Richard Milbank's capacity to lay his hands, almost instantly, on obscure facts and quotations and he asked many productive questions which much improved the manuscript. But I also profoundly owe my friend Geoffrey Strachan for his great generosity in giving me his editorial thoughts before I offered the manuscript, Tom de Wesselow for gracefully and kindly giving it a last-minute polish (and offering an excellent editorial suggestion) and Henrietta Heald for putting the effects of an editorial evolution onto the text and skilfully steering me through a writer's block. Since then, my family have been heroic, coping with a luddite made distinctly irritable through the effects of a rare ignorance of how to use a computer. My husband, Anthony, has been wonderfully diligent and helpful tracing lost footnotes and my step-daughter, Lucy, has, with great patience, saved both the publishers and myself (and her father) by ferrying the manuscript corrections and endnotes onto the correct text without damage. I felt safe in her hands too. Thank you and thank you to the many friends who have also supported me along the way – so much.

Bibliography

Archive sources are cited in Endnotes.

Articles are cited from volumes in three series from the Transactions of the Cumberland and Westmorland Antiquarian and Archaeological Society: 1st Series (*CW1*) 1870–1900; 2nd Series (*CW2*) 1901–2000; 3rd Series (*CW3*) 2001–

Allan, Sue (2017), 'Merrie England, May Day and More: Morris Dances in Cumbria in the Early Twentieth Century', London: English Folkdance and Song Society/Historical Dance Society.

Allen, Howard (2018), *Keswick School, The English Lake District, 1898–1998*: Keswick School.

Andrews, Malcolm (1989), *The Search for the Picturesque: Landscape Aesthetics and Tourism in Britain, 1760–1800*, Aldershot: Scholar Press.

Anon. (1943), 'A Fragment of Forgotten History. Monk Hall, Crosthwaite (Keswick)', *CW2*, 43, pp. 200–6.

Appleby, Andrew B. (1978), *Famine in Tudor and Stuart England*, Liverpool: Liverpool University Press.

Armitt, M.L. (1912), *The Church of Grasmere*, Kendal: Titus Wilson.

Armstrong, Margaret (1989), *Thirlmere, Across the Bridges to Chapel 1849–1852*, Keswick: Peel Wyke Publications.

Armstrong, Margaret (2002), *Linen and Liturgy*, Keswick: Peel Wyke Publications.

Bailey, John and Culley, George (1794), *General View of the Agriculture of the County of Cumberland*, London: C. MacRae.

Bampton People (2003), *Ploughing in Latin: A History of Bampton*, Carlisle: Bookcase.

Barker, Juliet (2001), *Wordsworth: A Life*, London: Penguin.

Barker, Juliet (ed) (2003), *Wordsworth: A Life in Letters*, London: Penguin.

Barraclough, Eleanor R. (2016), *Beyond the Northlands: Viking Voyages and the Old Norse Sagas*, Oxford: Oxford University Press.

Bate, J. and Engell, J. (eds) (1992), *The Collected Works of Samuel Taylor Coleridge: Biographia Literaria*, Vol 2, Princeton: Princeton University Press.

Bate, Jonathan (1991), *Romantic Ecology*, London: Routledge.

Bate, Jonathan (2020), *Radical Wordsworth*, London: William Collins.

Battrick, Elizabeth (1987), *Guardian of the Lakes: A History of the National Trust in the Lake District from 1946*, Kendal: Westmorland Gazette.

Beale, Robert and Kirkman, Richard (2015), *Lakeland Waterways: A history of travel along the English Lakes*, Isle of Man: Lily Publications Ltd.

Beckett, J.V. (1982), 'The Decline of the Small Landowner in Eighteenth- and Nineteenth-Century England: Some Regional Considerations', *Agricultural History Review*, 30 (2), pp. 97–111.

Beckett, J.V. (1984), 'The Peasant in England: A Case of Terminological Confusion', *Agricultural History Review*, 32 (2), pp. 113–23.

Berry, G. and Beard, G. (1980), *The Lake District, a Century of Conservation*, Edinburgh: J. Bartholomew.

Bicknell, Peter (ed) (1984), *The Illustrated Wordsworth's Guide to the Lakes*, Exeter: Webb & Bower (Publishers).

Birley, Eric (1954), 'The sources of Clarke's Survey of the Lakes', CW2, 54, pp. 273–5.

Bishop of Barrow-in-Furness (1904), 'On the Readers in the Chapelries of the Lake District' CW2, 5, pp. 89–105.

Bott, George (1994), *Keswick: The Story of a Lake District Town*, Cumbria: Cumbria County Library.

Bott, George (2009), *A Cumbrian Anthology* selected by George Bott, Carlisle: Bookcase.

Bouch, C. M. L. (1948), *Prelates and People of the Lake Counties*, Kendal: Titus Wilson.

Bouch, C. M. L. (1951), 'Local Government in Appleby in the 17th and 18th centuries', CW2, 51, pp. 147–69.

Bouch, C. M. L. and Jones, G. P. (1961), *The Lake Counties 1500–1830: A Social and Economic History*, Manchester: Manchester University Press.

Bradley, Ian (1997), *Abide with Me: The World of Victorian Hymns*, London: SCM Press Ltd.

Bradshaw, Penny (ed) (2014), Ann Radcliffe's *Observations during a Tour to the Lakes of Lancashire, Westmoreland and Cumberland*, Carlisle: Bookcase.

Bragg, Melvyn (1990), *Land of the Lakes*, London: Hodder and Stoughton.

Broadway, Ian (2007), *The Journal of a short tour to the Lakes in 1822 by John May*, Carlisle: Bookcase.

Broatch, M. (1934), *Keswick and Derwentwater*, Penrith: Printed by The Herald Printing Company.

Brodie, Ian O. (2012), *Thirlmere and the emergence of the landscape protection movement*, Carlisle: Bookcase.

Brown, Geoff (2009), *Herdwick Sheep and the English Lake District (A Cumbria Guide)*, Wigtonshire: Hayloft Publishing.

Bruce, Ian (2001), *The Loving Eye and Skilful Hand*, Carlisle, Bookcase.

Brunskill, R. W. (2002), *Traditional Buildings of Cumbria*, Republished 2010 by Yale University Press in association with Peter Crawley.

Bulmer's *History, Topography and Directory of Cumberland 1901*, Preston: T. Snape and Co.

Burke, Edmund (1757), *A Philosophical Enquiry into the Origin of Our Ideas of the Sublime and Beautiful*.

Butland, Cameron (2015), *Grasmere Church*, Printed by Kay Jay Ltd.

Butler, Marilyn (1981), *Romantics, Rebels & Reactionaries: English Literature and its Background 1760–1830*, Oxford: Oxford University Press.

Byatt, A. S. (1997), *Unruly Times: Wordsworth and Coleridge in Their Time*, London: Vintage.

Campbell, Mildred (1960), *The English Yeoman*, London: Merlin Press.

Carlisle, Nicholas (1818), *A Concise Description of the Endowed Grammar Schools in England and Wales Volume 1*, London: Baldwin, Cradock and Joy.

Carruthers, F. J. (1979), *People called Cumbri*, London: Robert Hale.

Carter, C. Sydney (1948), *The English Church in the Eighteenth Century*, London: Church Book Room Press Ltd.

Chadwick, Owen (1966), *The Victorian Church*, Part 1, London: Oxford University Press.

Chadwick, Owen (1970), *The Victorian Church*, Part 2, London: A & C Black Ltd.

Chaplin-Brice, Graham H., Cordon, Peter and Pattinson, Joanne (2000), *The Parish of St. Johns, Castlerigg and Wythburn Millennium Book*, Keswick: Graham H. Chaplin-Brice.

Church Warden Accounts of Crosthwaite Parish Church from 1699, transcribed by Tom Wilson. Bound copy from Hugh Walpole's Library.

Clarke, J. (1787), *A survey of the lakes of Cumberland, Westmorland and Lancashire*, London: J. Clarke.

Collingwood, W. G. (1902), *The Lake Counties*, revised by William Rollinson (1988), London: J. M. Dent and Sons Ltd.

Collingwood, W. G. (1904), 'The Home of the Derwentwater Family', *CW2*, 4, pp. 257–87.

Collingwood, W. G. (1912), *Elizabethan Keswick: Extracts from the Original Account Books, 1564–1577, of the German Miners, in the Archives of Augsburg*, Cumberland and Westmorland Archaeological and Antiquarian Society Tractarian Series VIII, Kendal: Titus Wilson.

Collingwood, W. G. (1921), 'Thirteenth Century Keswick', *CW2*, 1, pp. 159–173.

Colman, Clark Stuart (2001), 'The Paralysis of the Cumberland and Westmorland Army in the First Civil War *c.*1642–45', *CW3*, 1, pp. 123–38.

Hargrave, F. (1792) *Collectanea Juridica*, London.

Corner, Martin (ed) (1994), *The Works of Samuel Taylor Coleridge*, Ware: Wordsworth Editions.

Cousins, John (2009), *Friends of the Lake District: the early years*, Lancaster: Centre for North-West Regional Studies at the University of Lancaster.

Cowell, Ben (2013), *Sir Robert Hunter*, Stroud: Pitkin Publishing.

Crosthwaite, J. Fisher (1874), The Last of the Derwentwaters: A Paper Read to the Keswick Literary Society, and Appendix, Cockermouth and Keswick: Printed by R. Bailey.

Crosthwaite, J. Fisher (1881), *Brief Memoir of Major-General Sir John George Woodford*, U.S.: Kessinger Legacy Reprints.

Crosthwaite, J. Fisher (1883), 'The Colony of German Miners at Keswick', *CW1*, 6, pp. 344–54.

Crosthwaite, J. Fisher (1886), 'The Traditions of Crosthwaite Church Belfry, Keswick', *CW1*, 8, pp. 48–54.

Cumbria Archive Service. Carlisle and Whitehaven. cumbria.gov.uk/archive.

Cumbrian Manorial Records, Lancaster University (on the net).

Cunliffe, Barry (2013), *Britain Begins*, Oxford: Oxford University Press.

Curtis, Jared (ed) (2007), *The Fenwick Notes of William Wordsworth*, Humanities-Ebooks: Tirril.

Curwen, John F. (ed) (1926), *Records relating to the Barony of Kendale*, Vol 3: Cumberland and Westmorland, Antiquarian and Archaeological Society, Record Series, 6.

Darrall, Geoffrey (2006), *Wythburn Church and the Valley of Thirlmere*, Keswick: Piper Publications.

Darrall, Geoffrey (2009), *The Story of St John's-in-the-Vale*, Keswick: Piper Publications.

Darrall, Geoffrey (ed) (2012), *Rediscovering our Past: A history of the Houses of St John's in the Vale, Castlerigg and Wythburn*, Keswick: Piper Publications.

Davies, Hunter (1988), *Beatrix Potter's Lakeland*, London: Frederick Warne.

De Quincey, Thomas (1907), *Reminiscences of the English Lakes Poets*, Everyman's Library, London: J. M. Dent & Sons.

Denman, Derek (2011), 'Materialising Cultural Value in the English Lakes, 1735–1845: A Study of the Responses of New Landowners to Representations of Place and People', Lancaster University Ph.D. thesis, https://eprints.lancs.ac.uk/id/eprint/61596/1/DenmanThesisEprint.pdf.

Denman, Derek (2012), 'The published topographical work of John Housman from 1793 to 1800, and its Relevance to Cumbrian Identities', *CW3*, xii, pp. 217–30.

Denman, Derek, Thornthwaite and the start of local forestry in the nineteenth century, https://derwentfells.com/pdfs/journal/Journal50.pdf.

Denyer, Susan (1991), *Traditional Buildings & Life in the Lake District*, London: Gollancz/National Trust.

Dickinson, William (1876), *Cumbriana, Or, Fragments of Cumbrian Life*, London: Whittaker and Co.

Dilley, Robert S. (1967), 'The Cumberland court leet and use of the common lands', *CW2*, 67, pp. 125–51.

Dilley, Robert S. (1997), 'Rogues, Raskells and Turkie Faced Jades: Malediction in the Cumbrian Manorial Courts', *CW2*, 97, pp. 143–51.

Dodds, H. M. and R. (1915), *The Pilgrimage of Grace, 1536–1537 and the Exeter Conspiracy*, 1538, Cambridge: Cambridge University Press.

Donald M. B. (1955), *Elizabethan Copper*, London: Pergamon Press.

Drabble, Margaret (2009), *A Writer's Britain*, London: Thames and Hudson.

Drake, Robert (2008), *A Solitary Trade: The Art and Craft of Dry Stone Walling*, Carlisle: Bookcase.

Duggett, Tom (2013), 'Southey's *Colloquies* and Romantic History', Xi'an Jiaotong-Liverpool University.

Duxbury, A. H. (1994), 'The decline of the Cumbrian yeoman – Ravenstonedale: a case study', *CW2*, 94, pp. 201–13.

Edwards, B. J. N. (2004), 'The damaged carvings on the font, St Kentigern's Church, Gt. Crosthwaite', *CW3*, 4, pp. 257–64.

Eeles, Francis C. (1974), *The Parish Church of St. Kentigern Crosthwaite*, Kendal: Titus Wilson.

Ellis, Roy (2008), 'The Keswick Trespasses: Working Class Protest or Gentleman's Agreement?' Unpublished Dissertation.

Ellis, Roy, William Calvert, Unpublished M.A.

Ellwood, T. (1899), 'The Mountain Sheep: their origin and marking', *CW1*, 15, pp. 1–8.

Elsas, Madeleine (1945), 'Deeds of the Parish of Crosthwaite [1571–1636]', *CW2*, 45, pp. 39–48.

Fairbairn, Charlotte, *The Story of Lowther*, Penrith: Jarrold Publishing and Lowther Castle.

Fairlie, Simon (2009), 'A Short History of Enclosure in Britain', *The Land*, 7.

Farrer, William and Travis Clay, Charles (eds) (1947), *Early Yorkshire Charters, Volume 7: The Honour of Skipton*, Cambridge: Cambridge University Press.

Fell, Clare (1972), *Early Settlement in the Lake Counties*, Yorkshire: Dalesman Books.

Ferguson, Richard S. (1890), *A History of Cumberland*, London: Elliot Stock.

Fleming, Daniel (1983), *The Memoirs of Sir Daniel Fleming*, London: Forgotten Books.

Frain, Seán (2010), *Hunting in the Lake District*, Ludlow: Merlin Unwin Books.

Franks, A. W. (1883) 'Crosthwaite Church, Keswick', *CW1*, 6, pp. 413–16.

Fulford, Tim (2011), 'Virtual Topography: Poets, Painters, Publishers and the Reproduction of the Landscape in the Early Nineteenth Century': Nottingham Trent University. www.erudit.org/en/journals/ron.

Fulford, Tim (2013), *The Late Poetry of the Lake Poets*, Cambridge: Cambridge University Press.

Gibson, William Sydney, *Dilston Hall: Or Memoirs of James Radcliffe, Earl of

Derwentwater, A Martyr in the Rebellion of 1715 (1850), available on the net.

Gill, Stephen (ed) (1984), *William Wordsworth, The Major Works*, London: Oxford University Press.

Gilpin, William (1792), *Observations relative chiefly to Picturesque Beauty*, London: Printed for R. Blamire.

Graham, T. H. B. (1926), 'Cumberland', *CW2*, 26, pp. 274–84.

Grainger, Francis (1903), 'The Sixteen Men of Holme Cultram', *CW2*, 3, pp. 172–213.

Grant, Susan (2006), *The Story of the Newlands Valley*, Carlisle: Bookcase.

Greenhow, Ray (2017), *The Derwentwater Disaster: 12th August, 1898*, Carlisle: Bookcase.

Griffin, Carl J. (2014), *Protest, Politics and Work in Rural England, 1700–1850*, London: Macmillan.

Hague, William (2007), *William Wilberforce*, London: HarperCollins.

Hall, Ian (2017), *Thorneythwaite Farm Borrowdale: The 1,000 year story of a Lakeland farm and its valley*, Keswick: Orchard House Books.

Hall, Ian (2019), *Derwentwater: In the Lap of the Gods*, Keswick: Orchard House Books.

Hankinson, Alan (1993), *Coleridge Walks the Fells*, London: Fontana HarperCollins.

Hardie, C., 'The Lakes Through a Glass Darkly', Cumbria Historic Landscape Characterisation Programme. www.aenvironment.co.uk/index.php/online-library/

Harrison, S. M. (1981), *The Pilgrimage of Grace in the Lake Counties 1536–7*, Studies in History 27 pviii: Royal Historical Society.

Hattersley, Roy (2017), *The Catholics*, London: Chatto & Windus.

Hay, Daisy (2010), *Young Romantics*, London: Bloomsbury.

Hazlitt, William *The Spirit of the Age*, Robert Woof (ed) (2007), Grasmere: The Wordsworth Trust.

Healey, Jonathan (2007), 'Agrarian Social Structure in the central Lake District, c.1574–1830: The fall of the "Mountain Republic"?', *Northern History*, 44(2), pp. 73–91.

Hewitt, Rachel (2017), *A Revolution of Feeling: The Decade that Forged the Modern Mind*, London: Granta Publications.

Hindle, Paul (2001), 'The first large scale county maps of Cumberland and Westmorland in the 1770s', *CW3*, 1, pp. 139–54.

History of Parliament Online: historyofparliamentonline.org.

Hodgson, T. H. (1903), 'Extracts from Acts of the Privy Council relating to Cumberland and Westmorland, 1558 to 1568, being the first ten years of the reign of Elizabeth', *CW2*, 3, pp. 126–49.

Housman, John (1800), *A Topographical Description of Cumberland, Westmoreland, Lancashire, and a Part of the West Riding of Yorkshire*, London: British Library, Historical Print Editions.

Housman, John (1800), *A descriptive tour, and guide to the lakes, caves, mountains,... in Cumberland, Westmoreland, Lancashire...*, Carlisle: Jollie.

Hoyle, R. W. (1984), 'Lords, Tenants, and Tenant Right in the Sixteenth Century: Four Studies', *Northern History*, 20(1), pp. 38–63.

Hoyle, Richard W. (1987), 'An ancient and laudable custom: The definition and development of tenant right in north-western England in the sixteenth century', *Past and Present*, 116, pp. 24–55.

Hughes Edward, 'North Country Life in the Eighteenth Century', Inaugural lecture to Durham, 1940.

Humphries, Andrew (1996), *Seeds of Change: 100 Years contribution to Rural Economy, Society and the Environment*, Newton Rigg College.

Hutchings, Richard J. (1977), *The Wordsworth Poetical Guide to the Lakes*. Isle of Wight: Hunnyhill Publications.

Hutchinson, William (1797), *The History of the County of Cumberland*, Volume I, Wakefield: E. P. Publishing Ltd. in collaboration with Cumberland County Library, Reprint 1974.

Hutchinson, William (1797), *The History of the County of Cumberland*, Volume II, Wakefield: E. P. Publishing Ltd. in collaboration with Cumberland County Library, Reprint 1974.

Hutton, Ronald (1996), *The Stations of the Sun*, Oxford: Oxford University Press.

Jackson, Violet (*c.*1955), 'Lakeland Parsonage,' private paper.

Jackson, William (1880), 'An Historical and Descriptive Account of Cockermouth Castle', *CW1*, 4, pp. 109–38.

Jackson, W. (1881), 'The Curwens of Workington Hall, and Kindred Families', *CW1*, 5, pp. 181–232.

Jackson, W (1883), 'A Sketch of the History of Egremont Castle', *CW1*, 6, pp. 150–62.

Johnson, Susan (1981), 'Borrowdale, its land tenure and the Records of the Lawson Manor', *CW2*, 81, pp. 63–72.

Jones, G. P. (1958), 'Some population problems relating to Cumberland and Westmorland in the 18th century', *CW2*, 58, pp. 123–39.

Jones, G. P. (1962), 'The Decline of the Yeomanry in the Lake Counties', *CW2*, 62, pp. 198–223.

Kaye, J. W. (1957), 'The Millbeck Woollen Industry', *CW2*, 57, pp. 158–73.

Kaye, J. W. (1966), 'Governor's House, Keswick', *CW2*, 66, pp. 339–46.

Keswick Historical Society, Friends of Keswick Museum & Art Gallery (2006), *Keswick Characters*, Volume One, Carlisle: Bookcase.

Keswick Historical Society, Friends of Keswick Museum & Art Gallery (2007), *Keswick Characters*, Volume Two, Carlisle: Bookcase.

Keswick History Group and Friends of Keswick Museum and Art Gallery (2012), *Keswick Characters*, Volume Three, Carlisle: Bookcase.

Kirby, D. P. (1962), 'Strathclyde and Cumbria: a survey of historical development to 1092', *CW2*, 62, pp. 77–94.

Knight, William (ed.) (1897), *Journals of Dorothy Wordsworth,* Vol. 1, London: MacMillan and Co.

Koot, Gerard M., 'The Standard of Living debate during Britain's industrial revolution', warwick.ac.uk.

Layard, George Somes (1901), *Mrs Lynn Linton: Her Life, Letters and Opinions,* London: Methuen.

Lees, Thomas (1883), 'S. Kentigern and his Dedications in Cumberland' and 'S. Herbert of Derwentwater', *CW1,* 6, pp. 328–43.

Lefebure, Molly (1964), *The English Lake District,* London: Batsford.

Lefebure, Molly (1970), *Cumberland Heritage,* London: Gollancz.

Lefebure, Molly (1977), *Cumbrian Discovery,* London: Gollancz.

Lefebure, Molly (1986), *The Bondage of Love: A Life of Mrs Samuel Taylor Coleridge,* London: Gollancz.

Lindop, Grevel (2005), *A Literary Guide to the Lake District,* Wilmslow: Sigma Leisure.

Linton, E. Lynn (1864), *The Lake Country,* London: Smith Elder and Co.

Linton, E. Lynn (1885), *The Autobiography of Christopher Kirkland,* Reprinted in three volumes by U.S.: Kessinger Publishing Reprints.

Lowther, Tom (1977), The Parish of Borrowdale with Grange. Pamphlet.

Lucas, John (1990), *England and Englishness,* London: Chatto & Windus.

Macaulay, Thomas Babington, Lord, 'Review of Sir Thomas More; or, Colloquies on the Progress and Prospects of Society, by Robert Southey', *Edinburgh Review,* January 1830, www.econlib.org/library/Essays/macS1.html.

MacCulloch, Diarmaid (2009), *A History of Christianity,* London: Penguin Books Ltd.

MacCulloch, Diarmaid (2018), *Thomas Cromwell: A Life,* London: Penguin Books Ltd.

MacFarlane, Alan (1984), 'The myth of the peasantry; family and economy in a northern parish' from Richard M Smith (ed), *Land, Kinship and Life-cycle:* Cambridge: Cambridge University Press.

Mahoney, John L. (2003), *William Wordsworth of Rydal: Religious Experience and Religious Practice,* Rydal: Rydal Church Trust.

Manders, H. (1853), *The History of the Church of Crosthwaite, Cumberland,* London: Printed by John Bowyer Nichols and Sons.

Mannix and Whellan (1847), *History, Gazetteer and Directory of Cumberland,* printed for the authors by W. B. Johnson, Beverley.

Marshall, J. D. (1971), *Old Lakeland: Some Cumbrian Social History,* Newton Abbot: David & Charles.

Marshall, J. D. (1972), '"Statesmen" in Cumbria: the vicissitudes of an expression', *CW2,* 72, pp. 248–73.

Marshall, J. D. (1973) 'The domestic economy of the Lakeland yeoman, 1660–1749', *CW2,* 73, pp. 190–219.

Marshall, J. D. (1980) 'Agrarian wealth and social structure in pre-industrial

Cumbria', *The Economic History Review*, 2nd series, 33 (4), pp. 503–21.

Marshall, J. D. and Walton, John K. (1981), *The Lake Counties from 1830 to the mid-twentieth century*, Manchester: Manchester University Press.

Mason, Nicholas, Stimpson, Shannon and Westover, Paul (2020), *Introduction to Romantic Circle's Edition of Wordsworth's Guide*.

Mathias, Peter (1983), *The First Industrial Nation: The Economic History of Britain 1700–1914*, London: Routledge.

Matthews, Stephen (2014), *The Gentleman who Surveyed Cumberland*, Carlisle: Bookcase.

McCormick, Terry (2018), *Lake District Fell Farming: Historical and Literary Perspectives, 1750–2017*, Carlisle: Bookcase.

McCulloch, J. R. (1837), *A Descriptive and Statistical Account of The British Empire*, London: Longman, Brown, Green and Longmans.

McIntosh, Marjorie Kenniestone (2011), *Poor Relief in England 1350 – 1600*, Cambridge: Cambridge University Press.

McFadzean, Alen (1987), *Wythburn Mine and the Lead Miners of Helvellyn*, Ulverston: Red Earth Publications.

Mee, Arthur (1994), *The Lake Counties*, London: Bracken Books.

Meem, Deborah T. (ed) (2002), *The Rebel of the Family: Eliza Lynn Linton*, Canada: Broadview Press.

Moorhouse, Geoffrey (2008), *The Last Office: 1539 and the Dissolution of a Monastery*, London: Weidenfeld and Nicolson.

Moorman, M. (1968), *William Wordsworth: A Biography – The Early Years 1770–1803*, Oxford: Oxford University Press.

Morris, Harrison & *Co's Directory & Gazetteer of Cumberland, 1861*, Nottingham; Facsimile edition Whitehaven: Michael Moon.

Morris, J. E. (1903), 'Cumberland and Westmorland Military Levies in the time of Edward I. and Edward II', *CW2*, 3, pp. 307–27.

Mounsey, George Gill (ed) (1846), *Authentic account of the occupation of Carlisle in 1745 by Prince Charles Edward Stuart*, London: Longmans.

Muchin, J. R. (1977), 'The Great Rebuilding: A Reassessment', *Past and Present*, Vol. 77, pp. 33–56.

Magna Britannia, Vol. 4, Cumberland (1816), London.

Murphy, Graham (2002), *Founders of the National Trust*, National Trust Enterprises Limited.

Murray, John R. (2011), *A Tour of the English Lakes with Thomas Grey & Joseph Farington*, London: Frances Lincoln Limited.

National Archives: nationalarchives.gov.uk.

Newby, Howard (ed) (1995), *The National Trust: The Next Hundred Years*, The National Trust.

Newlyn, Lucy (2013), *William & Dorothy Wordsworth: All in Each Other*, Oxford: Oxford University Press.

Nicolson, Adam (2011), *When God spoke English: The Making of the King James Bible*, London: Harper Press, Harper Collins Publishers.

Nicolson and Burn (1777), *The History and Antiquities of the Counties of Westmorland and Cumberland*, London: W, Strahan and T, Cadell.

Nichols, J (ed.) (1840), *Fuller: The History of the Worthies of England* (1811), London: Thomas Tegg.

Nicholson, J. Holme (1891), 'The Parish Registers of Orton, Westmorland', *CW1*, 11, pp. 250–65.

Nicholson, Norman (1949), *Cumberland and Westmorland*, London: Robert Hale.

Nicholson, Norman (1995), *The Lakers: The Adventures of the First Tourists*, London: Cicerone Press.

Nicholson, Norman (1963), *Portrait of the Lakes*, London: Robert Hale.

Nicholson, Norman (1969), *Greater Lakeland*, London: Robert Hale.

Nickalls, John L. (ed) (1975), *Journal of George Fox*, London: Religious Society of Friends.

Owen, W. J. B and Worthington Smyser, Jane (ed) (1974), *The Prose Works of William Wordsworth, Volume 1*, Oxford: Clarendon Press.

Oxford Dictionary of National Biography online: www.oxforddnb.com.

Parson, William and White, William (1829), *A History, Directory and Gazetteer of Cumberland and Westmorland with Furness and Cartmel*, Whitehaven: Michael Moon republished 1984.

Pearsall, W.H. (ed) (1969), *Lake District: National Park Guide No. 6*, London: Her Majesty's Stationery Office.

Pearson, William (1863), *Letters, Papers and Journals*, 2005 facsimile, Kirkby Stephen: Hayloft Publishing.

Pennant, Thomas (1772), *A Tour in Scotland and Voyage to the Hebrides*, Chester: John Monk (1774).

Percy, Thomas (ed) (1765), *Reliques of Ancient English Poetry*, London: J. Dodsley.

Phillips, C. S. (1947), *Walter Howard Frere, Bishop of Truro*, London: Faber and Faber.

Platt, Jane (ed) (2015), *The Diocese of Carlisle, 1814–1855: Chancellor Walter Fletcher's 'Diocesan Book', with additional material from Bishop Percy's parish notebooks*, The Surtees Society, Vol. 219.

Powley, Miss (1876), 'Past and Present among the Northern fells, No.2', *CW1*, 2, pp. 354–74.

Pratt, Lynda, Fulford, Tim and Packer, Ian (eds) (2014), *The Collected Letters of Robert Southey 1791–1821*, Romantic Circles romantic-circles.org.

Pringle, Andrew (1794), *General View of the Agriculture of the County of Westmorland*, Edinburgh: Chapman and Company.

Rawnsley, Eleanor (1923), *Canon Rawnsley: An Account of his life*, Glasgow: MacLehose, Jackson and Co.

Rawnsley, Hardwicke Drummond: (1883), 'The Proposed Permanent Lake District Defence Society', Paper read before The Wordsworth Society: Cumberland Association for the Advancement of Literature and Science

Transactions, Part 8.

(1887), 'Our Industrial Art Experiment at Keswick', *Murray's Magazine* 2, pp. 756–68.

(1888), *Five Addresses on the Lives and Work of St Kentigern and St Herbert. Delivered in St Kentigern's Church, Crosthwaite*, Carlisle: Chas Thurnam and Sons; London: George Bell and Sons.

(1899), *Life and Nature at the English Lakes*, Glasgow: James MacLehose and Sons.

(1900), *Memories of the Tennysons*, Glasgow: James MacLehose and Sons.

(1901), *Literary Associations of the English Lakes Vol.1.: Cumberland, Keswick and Southey's Country*, Reproduced by Lightning Source UK Ltd 2010.

(1901), *Ruskin and the English Lakes*, Reproduced by Cambridge University Press 2011.

(1903), *Lake Country Sketches*, Glasgow: James MacLehose and Sons.

(1906), *Months at the Lakes*, Glasgow: James MacLehose and Sons.

(1910), 'The Light of the World', Sermon in memory of Holman Hunt.

(1916), *Past and Present at the English Lakes*, Glasgow: James MacLehose and Sons.

Rawnsley, Rosalind (2016), 'A Nation's Heritage: Beatrix Potter and Hardwicke Drummond Rawnsley', Lecture given at Allan Bank, Grasmere. hdrawnsley.com.

Rawnsley, Rosalind (2017), 'No Man is an Island', Lecture given at Allan Bank, Grasmere, hdrawnsley.com.

Rawnsley website, hdrawnsley.com.

Rebanks, James (2015), *The Shepherd's Life: A Tale of the Lake District*, London: Allen Lane.

Redmayne, W. B. (1948), *Cumberland Scrapbook*, Carlisle: Chas. Thurnam and Sons.

Registers of Crosthwaite Church, Vol. I 1562–1600, Vol II 1600–1670, Vol. III 1670–1812.

Reid, Rachel R. (1921), *The King's Council in the North*, London: Longman.

Reid, Robert (2017), *The Peterloo Massacre*, London: Random House.

'Report of the commissioners into English Charities for the Education of the Poor' (1821), Parliamentary Papers Online.

Rice, H. A. L. (1967), *Lake Country Portraits*, London: The Harvill Press.

Richardson, John (1871), *'Cummerland Talk'; Being Short Tales and Rhymes in the Dialect of that County: together with a Few Miscellaneous Pieces in Verse*, Leopold Classic Library printed by Amazon. Originally published in London: John Russell Smith.

Roberts, Alice (2015), *The Celts*, London: Quercus.

Roberts, Ros (2015), *The Keswick Painting*, Carlisle: Bookcase.

Roberts, William (ed) (2001), *Thomas Gray's Journal of his Visit to the Lake District in October 1769*, Liverpool: Liverpool University Press.

Robertson, Eric (1911), *Wordsworthshire*, London: Chatto & Windus.

Robinson, Thomas (1709), *An Essay Towards a Natural History of Cumberland and Westmorland* in 2 parts: London.

Roebuck, Peter (2015), *Cattle Droving through Cumbria 1600–1900*, Carlisle: Bookcase.

Rollinson, William (1974), *Life and Tradition in the Lake District*, London: J. M. Dent.

Rollinson, William (1978), *A History of Cumberland & Westmorland*, Chichester: Phillimore.

Rollinson, William (1978), *Lakeland Walls*, Yorkshire: Dalesman Books.

Rollinson, William (1997), *The Cumbrian Dictionary of Dialect, Tradition and Folklore*, Otley: Smith Settle.

Ruskin, John (1885–9), *Praeterita*, published in one volume in 1949, London: Rupert Hart-Davis.

Ruskin, John (ed. James S. Dearden 1969), *Iteriad or Three Weeks Among the Lakes*, Newcastle upon Tyne: Frank Graham.

Ruskin, John (2004), *On Art and Life*, London: Penguin.

Sales, Roger (1983), *English Literature in History 1780–1830*, New York: St. Martin's Press.

Searle, C. E. (1983), '"The odd corner of England": A study of a rural social formation in transition: Cumbria *c*.1700–*c*.1914'. Unpublished PhD thesis, University of Essex.

Searle, C. E. (1986), 'Custom, class conflict and agrarian capitalism: the Cumbrian customary economy in the eighteenth century', *Past and Present*, 110, pp. 106–33.

Searle, C. E. (1993), 'Customary tenants and the enclosure of the Cumbrian commons', *Northern History*, 29(1), pp. 126–53.

Sedgefield, W. J. (1915), *The Place-Names of Cumberland and Westmorland*, Manchester: Manchester University Press.

Seward, Anthony (ed) (2016), William Hutchinson's *An Excursion to the Lakes in Westmoreland and Cumberland 1773 and A Tour through Cumberland in 1774*, Carlisle: Bookcase.

Sharpe, Richard (2006), *Norman Rule in Cumbria 1092–1136*, Cumberland and Westmorland Archaeological and Antiquarian Society Tractarian Series XXI, Kendal: Printed by Titus Wilson & Son.

Shepherd, Margaret E. (2011), *Across the Oceans: Emigration from Cumberland and Westmorland before 1914*, Carlisle: Bookcase.

Simpson, David (1987), *Wordsworth's Historical Imagination: The Poetry of Displacement*, London: Methuen & Co. Ltd.

Sisman, Adam (2006), *The Friendship: Wordsworth and Coleridge*, London: HarperCollins.

Smith, Richard. M. (1985), *Land, Kinship and Life-cycle*, Cambridge: Cambridge University Press.

Smith, Thomas Fletcher (2007), *Jonathan Otley, Man of Lakeland*, Carlisle: Bookcase.

Smith, Thomas Fletcher (2014), *John Dalton: A Cumbrian Philosopher*, Carlisle: Bookcase.

Smith, Thomas Fletcher (2017), *Pencil People: The Story of a Lakeland Industry*, Carlisle: Bookcase.

Somervell, D. C. (1950), *A Short History of our Religion: from Moses to the Present Day*, London: G. Bell and Sons, Ltd.

Songs of the Fell Packs (1971), Produced by the Hunt Show Committee of the Melbreak Hunt. Cleator Moor: Bethwaites.

Southey, Robert (1850), *The Poetical Works in One Volume*, London: Longman, Brown, Green and Longmans.

Southey, Robert and Coleridge, S. T. (1812 with additions), *Omniana,* London: Centaur Press Ltd., 1969.

Southey, Robert, *Sir Thomas More, or, Colloquies on the Progress and Prospects of Society*, available www.gutenberg.org ebooks

Speck, W. A., 'Robert Southey, Lord Macaulay and the Standard of Living Controversy', *History* Vol. 86(284), pp. 467–77.

Speck, W. A. (2006), *Robert Southey: Entire Man of Letters*, Newhaven and London: Yale University Press.

Storey, Mark (1977), *Robert Southey, A Life*, New York: Oxford University Press.

Storey, R. L. (1962), 'The Chantries of Cumberland and Westmorland, Part II', *CW2*, 62, pp. 145–70.

Stretton, E. H. A. (1994), *Dacre Castle*, Penrith: Dalemain Estates.

Stevenson, John (1992), *Popular Disturbances in England 1700–1832*, London: Longman.

Sutherland, Douglas (1965), *The Yellow Earl*, London: Cassell & Company Ltd.

Sutton, Shelagh (1961), *The Story of Borrowdale*, Keswick: Borrowdale Women's Institute.

Tate, W. E. (1943), 'A Handlist of Enclosure Acts and Awards', *Proceedings of the Society of Antiquaries of Newcastle upon Tyne*, 4th Series, X, No. 3., pp. 175–87.

Tate, W. E. (1983), *The Parish Chest*, Chichester: Phillimore.

Taylor, Michael W. (1893), 'Some Manorial Halls in the Vale of Derwent', *CW1*, 12, pp. 147–66.

Thomas, Keith (1971), *Religion and the Decline of Magic*, Harmondsworth: Penguin.

Thompson, B. L. (1946), *The Lake District and the National Trust*, Kendal: Titus Wilson and Sons.

Thompson, B. L. (1954), 'The Windermere "Four and Twenty"', *CW2*, 54, pp. 151–64.

Thompson, E. P. (1991), *Customs in Common*, London: Merlin Press.

Thompson, E. P. (1997), *The Romantics*, Woodbridge: Merlin Press.

Thompson, I. (2010), *The English Lakes: A History*, London: Bloomsbury Publishing.

Thompson, W. N. (1904), 'The Derwentwaters and Radcliffes', *CW2*, 4, pp. 288–324.

Thurley, Simon (2013), *The Building of England*, London: William Collins, HarperCollins.

Trevelyan, G. M. (1904), *England Under the Stuarts*, London: Methuen.

Trevelyan, G. M. (1944), *English Social History*, London: Book Club Associates edition (1973).

Tullie, Isaac (1840), *A Narrative of the Siege of Carlisle in 1644 and 1645*, 1988 reproduction by Michael J. Moon.

Turner, Hugh (1990), *Fletcher Christian: Some facts, Some fallacies*, Cockermouth: The Printing House.

Tyler, Ian (1995), *Seathwaite Wad and the Mines of the Borrowdale Valley*, Carlisle: Blue Rock Publications.

Tyson, Blake (2001), The Estate and Household Accounts of Sir Daniel Fleming of Rydal Hall, Westmorland from 1688 – 1701, Record Series, Vol. XIII, *CWS*.

Uglow, Jenny (2014), *In These Times*, London: Faber & Faber.

Uttley, David (2007), 'The Decline of the Cumbrian Yeoman: Fact or Fiction?' *CW3*, 7, pp. 121–34.

Uttley, David (2008), 'The Decline of the Cumbrian "Yeomen" Revisited', *CW3*, 8, pp. 127–46.

van Thal, Herbert (1979), *Eliza Lynn Linton*, London: George Allen and Unwin.

The Victoria County History of Cumberland, Two volumes, I (1901) and II (1905).

Walpole, Hugh (1930), *Rogue Herries*, London: Macmillan. And ensuing series.

Walton, John K. (1986), 'The strange decline of the Lakeland yeoman: some thoughts on sources, methods and definitions', *CW2*, 86, pp. 221–34.

Waterson, Merlin (1994), *The National Trust: The First Hundred Years*, The National Trust.

Watson, George (1899), 'Keswick', *CW1*, 16, pp. 146–51.

Watts, S. J. (1971), 'Tenant-Right in Early Seventeenth-Century Northumberland', *Northern History*, Vol. 6(1), pp. 64–87.

Weir, Alison (1989), *Britain's Royal Families: The Complete Genealogy*, London: The Bodley Head.

West, Thomas (1778), *A Guide to the Lakes of Cumberland, Westmorland and Lancashire*, reprinted 2008, Cumbria: Unipress Cumbria.

Weston, David W. V. (2013), *Rose Castle and the Bishops of Carlisle: 1133–2012*, Kendal: CW Extra Series, No. XL.

Whalley, Joyce Irene and Bartlett, Wynne (2010), *Beatrix Potter's Derwentwater*, Ammanford: Sigma Press.

Whellan, William (1860), *History and Topography of the Counties of Cumberland and Westmorland*, Pontefract: Published by W. Whellan and Co., London: Whittaker & Co.

Whyte, I. D. (2009), 'The Customary Tenants of Watermillock c.1760–c.1840: Continuity and Change in a Lake District Township', CW3, 9, pp. 161–74.

Wilcox, Timothy, Introduction and Notes 2017, *Francis Towne's Lake District Sketchbook*, a facsimile reconstruction, Lewes: The Winterbourne Press.

Wilkinson, Rev. Joseph, (1821), *Select Views in Cumberland, Westmoreland and Lancashire*, London: Rodwell and Martin.

Wilkinson, Thomas (1812), *Thoughts on inclosing Yanwath Moor and Round Table*, Penrith: J. Browne.

Williams, Raymond *The Country and the City*, OUP New York,

Wilson, Frances (2008), *The Ballad of Dorothy Wordsworth*, London: Faber and Faber.

Wilson, Tom (1949), *The history & chronicles of Crosthwaite Old School: the story of a struggle by 'The eighteen sworn men' for better education in the ancient parish of Crosthwaite*, Keswick: G. W. McKane & Son Ltd.

Wilson, Tom (1955), The History and Romance of Crosthwaite Church Bells, Keswick. Manuscript.

Wilson, Tom (1939, revised J. M. Kaye 1970), *History of Crosthwaite Parish Church*, Keswick: Printed by G. W. McKane & Son Ltd.

Winchester, Angus J. L. (1987), *Landscape and Society in Medieval Cumbria*, Edinburgh: John Donald Publishers Ltd.

Winchester, Angus J. L. (1988), 'Wordsworth's "Pure Commonwealth"? Yeoman dynasties in the English Lake District c.1450–1750', *Armitt Library Journal*, 1, pp. 86–113.

Winchester, Angus J. L. (1990), *Discovering Parish Boundaries*, Princes Risborough: Shire Publications.

Winchester, Angus J. L. (2000), *The Harvest of the Hills: Rural Life in Northern England and the Scottish Borders, 1400–1700*, Edinburgh: Edinburgh University Press.

Winchester, A. (ed) (2003), *Thomas Denton: A Perambulation of Cumberland 1687–8*, The Surtees Society. Vol. 207.

Winchester, Angus J. L. (2005), 'Regional Identity in the Lake Counties: Land Tenure and the Cumbrian Landscape', University of Leeds, *Northern History* 42(1), pp. 29–48.

Winchester, Angus J. L., with Crosby, Alan G. (2006), *The North West*: England's Landscape Vol 8, London: Collins.

Winchester, Angus J. L. (2006), 'Village byelaws and the management of a contested common resource: bracken (Pteridium aquilinum) in highland Britain, 1500–1800', Paper read at IASCP Europe Regional Meeting, Italy. Available on the net.

Winstanley, Michael, 'The Poor Law in Cumbria', Cumbria County History Trust.

Winter, H. E. (1997), *History of Cumberland Villages*, illustrated edition, Regentlane Ltd.

Wohlgemut, Esther, 'Southey, Macaulay and the Idea of a Picturesque History',

University of Prince Edward Island. www.erudit.org/en/journals/ron.

Woof, Pamela (2013), *Dorothy Wordsworth: Wonders of the Everyday*, Grasmere: Wordsworth Trust.

Wordsworth, Dorothy (ed. William Knight 1897), *Journals of Dorothy Wordsworth, Vol. 1*, London: Macmillan.

Wordsworth, Dorothy (ed. Ernest de Selincourt 1941), *Journals of Dorothy Wordsworth*, 2 vols, London: Macmillan.

Wordsworth, Dorothy (1987), *Dorothy Wordsworth's Illustrated Lakeland Journals*, London: William Collins.

Wordsworth, Jonathan (ed) (1985), *William Wordsworth: The Pedlar, Tintern Abbey, The Two-Part Prelude*, Cambridge: Cambridge University Press.

Wordsworth, William and Coleridge, Samuel Taylor (1798), *Lyrical Ballads, with a Few Other Poems*, London: Humphrey Milford.

Wordsworth, William (1793), 'A Letter to the Bishop of Landaff'.

Wordsworth, William (1814), *The Excursion*, G. B.: Printed by Amazon.co.uk.

Wordsworth, William (1819), 'The Waggoner' from *The Complete Poetical Works*, 1888, London: Macmillan and Co., Bartleby.com, 1999. www. bartleby.com/145/.

Wordsworth, William, *1835 Guide to the Lakes*, edited de Selincourt, Ernest, with a preface by Stephen Gill (2004), London: Frances Lincoln.

Wordsworth, William (1892), *The Poetical Works of Wordsworth with memoir, explanatory notes etc*, London: Frederick Warne & Co.

Wordsworth, William, *William Wordsworth 1770–1970*, ed. Nesta Clutterbuck (1970), Grasmere: Trustees of Dove Cottage.

Wordsworth, William (2011), *The Major Works*, Oxford: Oxford University Press.

Worthen, John (2014), *The Life of William Wordsworth*, Chichester: John Wiley & Sons Ltd.

Young, Arthur (1771), *A Six Months Tour through the North of England*, London: W. Strahan.

Yu-san Yu (2007), 'Revolutionary or Apostate?: Wordsworth's Cintra Tract', *EuroAmerica* 27(3), Institute of European and American Studies, Academia Sinica.

Exhibition Catalogues

Bainbridge, Simon and Cowton, Jeff (eds) (2015), *Wordsworth, War & Waterloo*, Grasmere: The Wordsworth Trust.

Bicknell and Woof (1983), *The Lake District Discovered 1810–1850*, Grasmere: The Wordsworth Trust.

Catalogue (2005), *The Spooner Collection of British Watercolours*, Kendal: printed by Titus Wilson.

Hebron, S., Shields, C. and Wilcox, T. (2006), *The Solitude of Mountains*,

Constable and the Lake District, Grasmere: Wordsworth Trust.

Hebron, Stephen (2008), *In the Line of Beauty: Early Views of the Lake District by Amateur Artists*, Grasmere: The Wordsworth Trust.

Murdoch, John (1984), *The Discovery of the Lake District: A Northern Arcadia and Its Uses*, London: The Victoria and Albert Museum.

Thomason, David and Woof, Robert, Commentary and Notes (1986), *Derwentwater: The Vale of Elysium*, Grasmere: The Trustees of Dove Cottage.

Woof, Robert (ed) (1985), *Thomas De Quincey: An English Opium Eater 1785–1859*, Grasmere: Trustees of Dove Cottage.

Woof, Robert (2005), *Treasures of the Wordsworth Trust*, Grasmere: Wordsworth Trust.

Endnotes

Introduction

1. Wordsworth, William, *1835 Guide to the Lakes*, edited de Selincourt, Ernest (2004), Section 2, p. 75.
2. In his anonymous introduction to Wilkinson, Joseph (1821), *Select Views in Cumberland, Westmoreland, and Lancashire*.
3. It is often said that Thirlmere is a recent name but in fact it predates Leathes Water; Leathe's 1557 purchase included the fishing of Thyrlemyre. For another early name, see Brodie, Ian O. (2012), *Thirlmere and the emergence of the landscape protection movement*, p. 15.
4. Wordsworth, William, *1835 Guide to the Lakes*, ft on p. 98.
5. Collingwood, W. G. (1902), *The Lake Counties*, revised by William Rollinson (1988), p. 109.
6. Winchester, Angus J. L. (1987), *Landscape and Society in Medieval Cumbria*, p. 97.
7. See Chapter 3.
8. See Chapters 2 and 4.
9. Collingwood, *The Lake Counties*, p. 142.
10. Wordsworth, William, *1835 Guide to the Lakes*, Section 2, p. 54.
11. Wordsworth's Letter to Charles Fox, 1801, quoted in Barker, Juliet (2003), *Wordsworth: A Life in Letters*, p. 64.
12. Letter to Fox, 1801.
13. Linton, E. Lynn (1864), *The Lake Country*, p. 61.
14. From the National Trust notice at St Margaret's Church at Wray.
15. UNESCO citation.

Chapter 1

1. Carruthers, F. J. (1979), *People called Cumbri*, p. 142.
2. Conran, T. (trans) (1986), *Welsh Verse*, 2nd edition. Bridgend, p. 117.
3. Lees, Thomas (1883), 'S. Kentigern and his Dedications in Cumberland' and 'S. Herbert of Derwentwater' *CW1*, 6, pp. 339, 340.
4. Ibid.
5. Ibid.
6. Cambridge University Press (1911), *The Cambridge Medieval History*, Vol. 1, p. 384.
7. Cunliffe, Barry (2013), *Britain Begins*, p. 447. These are the words of Alcuin, an English scholar working at the Frankish court of Charlemagne, in a

letter to King Aethelred of Northumbria.

8. Rollinson, William (1978), *A History of Cumberland & Westmorland*, p. 33.

9. Bragg, Melvyn (1990), *Land of the Lakes*, pp. 64–6.

10. After a renascent push into Northumbria and the capture of Viking York.

11. Weir, Alison (1989), *Britain's Royal Families: The Complete Genealogy*, p. 179.

12. Ibid, pp. 168–96.

13. Wordsworth, William (1819), 'The Waggoner' from *The Complete Poetical Works, 1888*.

14. There never was a King of Cumberland. It is on record that Owen, styled King of Cumbria (the only time that title is recorded), was present at a tripartite meeting with the 'Kings' of England and Scotland in 926–7. But the Welsh, Scots and English all hold different views about his identity, a split that makes any certain identification of Dunmail impossible. That a usually particularly reliable English source says that 'the kingdom of Cumbria or Strathclyde came to an end with Dunmail in 945' – Bouch, C. M. L. and Jones, G. P. (1961), *The Lake Counties 1500–1830: A Social and Economic History*, p. 7. – and the average Scottish source ignores the fell battle at Dunmail Raise entirely (although the *Annales Cambriae* records that Strathclyde was wasted the same year – Graham, T. H. B. 'Cumberland', *CW2*, 26

p. 277) underlines the obscurity of the period.

15. *Magna Britannia*, Vol. 4, Cumberland (1816), p. 56.

16. www.english-lakes.com/dunmail_raise.html.

17. As described by the *Anglo-Saxon Chronicle*.

18. Jackson, W. (1883), 'A Sketch of the History of Egremont Castle', *CW1*, 6, p. 151.

19. Jackson, W. (1881), 'The Curwens of Workington Hall, and Kindred Families' *CW1*, 5, pp. 181–3.

20. History of Parliament Online www.historyofparliamentonline.org/; biographies of Sir John Derwentwater and Sir Nicholas Radcliffe.

21. Collingwood, W. G. (1921), 'Thirteenth Century Keswick', *CW2*, 1, p. 167.

22. Farrer, William and Clay, Charles Travis (eds.) (1947), *Early Yorkshire Charters, Volume 7: The Honour of Skipton*, p. 11.

23. In compensation for his abolition of the traditional Scottish system of tribal land tenure.

24. Dates confirmed by Farrer and Clay, *Early Yorkshire Charters, Vol. 7*, pp. 10–11.

25. Jackson, 'A Sketch of the History of Egremont Castle', p. 153.

26. One source – Manders, H. (1853), *The History of the Church of Crosthwaite, Cumberland*, p. 13 – suggests that William the Noble took part in the 'Revolt of the Earls' at Perth in 1160, which aimed to make him King of Scotland.

27. Farrer and Clay, *Early Yorkshire Charters, Vol. 7*, p. 10.
28. Ibid, p. 13.
29. Wordsworth, William, *The Force of Prayer*, line 2
30. Ibid, p. 51.
31. Collingwood, *The Lake Counties*, p. 101.
32. Winchester, Angus J. L. (1990), *Discovering Parish Boundaries*, p. 11.
33. *c.*1181, quoted in Eeles, Francis C. (1974), *The Parish Church of St Kentigern Crosthwaite*, p. 8.
34. Ibid, pp. 1, 2, 9.
35. Today demonstrated by some stones, now by the Radcliffe memorials.
36. See From William I to Henry II, Encyclopaedia of British Coins of the British Isles, Colonies, and Commonwealth.
37. Collingwood, 'Thirteenth Century Keswick', p. 172.
38. Winchester, *Landscape and Society*, p. 97.
39. Southey, Robert, *Sir Thomas More, or, Colloquies on the Progress and Prospects of Society*, Colloquy X.
40. Percy, Thomas, Bishop (ed) (1765), *Reliques of Ancient English Poetry*.
41. Wordsworth, William, *The White Doe of Rylstone*, Lines 141–150.

Chapter 2

1. Farrer and Clay, *Early Yorkshire Charters, Vol. 7*, pp. 16–17.
2. Ibid, p. 17.
3. Ibid, p. 18.
4. Jackson, William (1880), 'An Historical and Descriptive Account of Cockermouth Castle', *CW1*, 4, p. 113.
5. Farrer and Clay, *Early Yorkshire Charters, Vol. 7*, p. 18.
6. Collingwood, 'Thirteenth Century Keswick', p. 162.
7. Crosthwaite, J. Fisher (1881), *Brief Memoir of Major-General Sir John George Woodford*, p. 49.
8. Wilson, Tom (1949) *The history & chronicles of Crosthwaite Old School*, p. 15, CRO, Enfranchisements, Lawson, 1805 description of the bounds of Borrowdale. Quoted Johnson, Susan (1981) *Borrowdale, its land tenure and the Records of the Lawson Manor, CW2*, 81, pp. 66–67; Clarke, J, (1787) *A survey of the lakes of Cumberland, Westmorland and Lancashire*, p. 99, Thompson, B.L. (1946), *The Lake District and the National Trust*, pp. 185–186; and a book of old Lake District Parish Boundaries produced for the Carlisle Library.
9. Winchester, Angus. J. L. (2000), *The Harvest of the Hills: Rural Life in Northern England and the Scottish Borders, 1400–1700*, p. 97.
10. Winchester, *Landscape and Society*, p. 40.
11. Parson. William and White, William (1829) *A History, Directory and Gazetteer of Cumberland and Westmorland with Furness and Cartmel* (Crosthwaite and Keswick).

12. Bragg, Melvyn (1990), *Land of the Lakes*, p. 21.

13. Brodie, *Thirlmere and the emergence of the landscape protection movement*, p. 30.

14. Winchester, *The Harvest of the Hills*, p. 27.

15. Farrer and Clay, *Early Yorkshire Charters, Vol. 7*, p. 19.

16. Aelred, Abbot of Rievaulx 1147–67.

17. Bouch and Jones, *A Social and Economic History*, p. 132.

18. Bouch, C. M. L. (1948), *Prelates and People of the Lake Counties*, p. 27.

19. Winchester, *Landscape and Society*, p. 104.

20. Winchester, *The Harvest of the Hills*, p. 63.

21. More than twenty farm buildings recorded in the Derwentfells before 1300 had fewer than 5 customary acres of core arable land: the top holding being only 10. Winchester, *Landscape and Society*, p. 64.

22. Document from King John's reign. VCH1, p. 425 referred to by Bouch and Jones in *A Social and Economic History*, pp. 7–14.

23. See Winchester, A. (ed.) (2003), *Thomas Denton: A Perambulation of Cumberland 1687–8*.

24. See Appendix 2.

25. Farrer and Clay, *Early Yorkshire Charters, Vol. 7*, p. 19.

26. Dilley, Robert S. (1967), 'The Cumberland court leet and use of the common lands', CW2, 67, pp. 125–51.

27. All quotations from Inq. Postmortem, 31Ed.1., n.15, quoted in Thompson, W. N. (1904), 'The Derwentwaters and Radcliffes', CW2, 4, pp. 291–3.

28. Bott, George (1994), *Keswick: The Story of a Lake District Town*, p. 12.

29. Appleby, Andrew B. (1978), *Famine in Tudor and Stuart England*, p. 69. ASK Map 7–9.

30. Denman, Derek (2011), 'Materialising Cultural Value in the English Lakes, 1735–1845: A Study of Responses of New Landowners to Representations of Place and People', Lancaster University PhD thesis, p. 83.

31. Winchester, *The Harvest of the Hills*, p. 126.

32. Winchester, Angus J. L., (2005), "Regional Identity in the Lake Counties: Land Tenure and the Cumbrian Landscape", University of Leeds, *Northern History* 4 (1), p. 37.

33. Winchester, *Landscape and Society*, p. 62.

34. Winchester, *Landscape and Society*, p. 68.

35. Bouch, *Prelates and People of the Lake Counties*, p. 35.

36. Ibid, p. 32.

37. Bouch and Jones, *A Social and Economic History*, p. 5.

38. Ibid, p. 11.

39. Bouch, *Prelates and People of the Lake Counties*, pp. 20–22.

40. It seems that the narrow sides of the Derwentwater valley, before it opened up into Borrowdale, may have made it a rare exception, as no remaining evidence can be found, the early farming in the valley concentrating on the far wider open land around

Keswick. Hardie, C., 'The Lakes Through a Glass Darkly', Cumbria Historic Landscape Characterisation Programme, ch. 16, p. 263.

41. Winchester, *The Harvest of the Hills,* p. 87.
42. Ibid, p. 57.
43. *c.*1270 at Keskadale.
44. At Fawe.
45. Winchester, *The Harvest of the Hills*, pp. 292–6.
46. Winchester, *Landscape and Society*, p. 42.
47. Collingwood, 'Thirteenth Century Keswick', p. 168.
48. Bouch, *Prelates and People*, p. 34.
49. Robert de Curtenay.
50. Winchester, *Landscape and Society*, p. 111.
51. Collingwood, 'Thirteenth Century Keswick', p. 161.
52. Ibid.
53. Ibid.
54. Ibid.
55. In 1291.
56. Manders, *The History of the Church of Crosthwaite*, p. 103.
57. Three wealthy Cumbrian parishes stand out; the richness of the first two, Greystoke at £120 and Kendal at £123, demonstrated by the remarkably similar valuation of the Carlisle bishopric, at £126 7s. The third richest parish, Brigham, valued at £80, was centred on an old and lovely small church thought to have originated, like St Kentigern's, in the sixth century. Its parish enveloped Cockermouth and its castle, which was only a chapelry, underlining the central importance of Celtic history to Cumberland parishes. Bouch, *Prelates and People*, pp. 60–61.
58. Manders, *The History of the Church of Crosthwaite*, p. 103.
59. Ibid.
60. In 1315 and 1316.
61. From 1319 to 1321.
62. Winchester, *Landscape and Society*, p. 45.
63. Morris, J. E. (1903), 'Cumberland and Westmorland Military Levies in the time of Edward I. and Edward II', CW2, 3, p. 308.
64. By 1319.
65. Manders, *The History of the Church of Crosthwaite*, pp. 95–6.
66. The *Nonarum Inquisitiones.*
67. Bott, *Keswick: The Story of a Lake District Town*, p. 13.
68. This was younger than the usual official age for a clergyman.
69. Bouch, *Prelates and People*, p. 90.
70. Ibid.
71. Ibid, p. 98.

Chapter 3

1. Eeles, *The Parish Church*, p. 45.
2. Hall, Ian (2019), *Derwentwater in the Lap of the Gods*, p. 19.
3. Rawnsley, Hardwicke Drummond (1888), *Five Addresses on the Lives and Work of St Kentigern and St Herbert. Delivered in St Kentigern's Church, Crosthwaite*, p. 47.
4. Rawnsley, Eleanor (1923), *Canon Rawnsley: An Account of His Life*, p. 55.

5. Manders, *The History of the Church of Crosthwaite*, pp. 133–4.

6. Cumberland, Westmorland, Northumberland and Durham. Edwards, B. J. N, (2004), 'The damaged carvings on the font, St Kentigern's Church, Gt. Crossthwaite', *CW3*, 4, pp. 257–264.

7. Jackson, 'An Historical and Descriptive Account of Cockermouth Castle', *CW1*, 4, p. 124.

8. Grant, Susan. *The Story of the Newlands Valley*, p. 14–5.

9. Cumbrian Manorial Records, Lancaster University, pp. 1–6.

10. Webb, Sidney and Beatrice (1906), *English Local Government, the Parish and the County*. p. 175.

11. Thompson, B.L. (1954), *The Windermere Four and Twenty*. *CW2* 54. p. 151

12. Uttley, David (2008), 'The decline of the Cumbrian "Yeoman" Revisited', *CW3*. 8, p. 130. A description of Winchester, Angus J. L. (1988) 'Wordsworth's "Pure Commonwealth"? Yeoman dynasties in the English Lake District *c.*1450–1750', *Armitt Library Journal*, 1, pp. 86–113.

13. Hoyle, R. W. (1984), 'Lords, Tenants and Tenant Right in the Sixteenth Century: Four Studies'. *Northern History*, 20(1), p. 39.

14. 19 June 1625. The Kings Bench ruled that the Border service was *not* a necessary part of tenant right and customary tenancy in Cumbria was saved.

15. A schoolmaster is mentioned there at least twice before 1371.

16. Carlisle, Nicholas (1818), *A Concise Description of the Endowed Grammar Schools in England and Wales, Volume 1*, pp. 191–2.

17. Manders, *The History of the Church of Crosthwaite*, p. 3.

18. Ibid, p. 28.

19. Wilson, *The history & chronicles of Crosthwaite Old School*, p. 16.

20. Winchester, *Landscape and Society*, p. 48.

21. Such as a flock of 50–80 sheep summering in the Derwentfells between 1473 and 1503, having travelled from land near Wokington. Winchester, *The Harvest of the Hills*, p. 96.

22. Ibid, pp. 114–15.

23. Ibid, p. 115.

24. See Ibid, pp. 103–4, for paragraph.

25. Nicholson, Norman (1963), *Portrait of the Lakes*, p. 113.

26. Bouch and Jones, *Social and Economic History*, p. 347 and Nicholson, *Portrait of the Lakes*, p. 117.

27. Winchester, *Landscape and Society*, p. 107.

28. Ibid.

29. Wordsworth, William, *1835 Guide to the Lakes*, p. 45.

30. For £10 6s. 8d. per annum.

31. Bouch, *Prelates and People,* p.33.

32. The Portinscale fishery would be abandoned by 1547.

33. Winchester, *Landscape and Society*, p. 63.

34. Winchester, *The Harvest of the Hills*, pp. 90–9.

35. Bouch, *Prelates and People*, p. 158.

36. Rawnsley, Hardwicke Drummond (1916), *Past and Present at the English Lakes*, p. 216 – his remark about Wythburn chapel there sounds inclusive.

37. Platt, Jane (ed.) (2015), *The Diocese of Carlisle, 1814–1855: Chancellor Walter Fletcher's 'Diocesan Book', with additional material from Bishop Percy's parish notebook*, p. 111.

38. Bouch, *Prelates and People*, Appendix XIII, pp. 374–5.

39. Darrall, Geoffrey (2006), *Wythburn Church and the Valley of Thirlmere*, ch. 5.

40. See Hutton, Ronald (1996), *The Stations of the Sun*, ch. 22.

41. Lefebure, Molly (1970), *Cumberland Heritage*, p. 222.

42. Rawnsley, Hardwicke Drummond, (1903), *Lake Country Sketches*, pp. 147–9.

43. Rollinson, William (1974), *Life and Tradition in the Lake District*, p. 70.

44. Ferreiro, Alberto (ed.) (1998), *The Devil, Heresy and Witchcraft in the Middle Ages: Essays in Honor of Jeffrey B. Russell* on Google Books.

45. Linton, *The Lake Country*, p. 305.

46. Lefebure, *Cumberland Heritage*, pp. 218–19.

47. Rollinson, *Life and Tradition*, p. 68.

48. Lefebure, Molly (1977), *Cumbrian Discovery*, p. 83.

49. Lefebure, *Cumberland Heritage*, p. 81.

50. Ibid.

51. Manders, *The History of the Church of Crosthwaite*, pp. 35–7.

52. For more information on this paragraph, see Thomas, Keith (1971), *Religion and the Decline of Magic*, pp. 521–40.

53. Rollinson, *Life and Tradition*, p. 69.

54. Lefebure, *Cumbrian Discovery*, p. 83.

55. Ibid, pp. 82–3.

56. Housman, John (1800), *A Topographical Description of Cumberland, Westmoreland, Lancashire, and a Part of the West Riding of Yorkshire*, p. 75.

57. Rollinson, *Life and Tradition*, p. 67.

58. Housman, *A Topographical Description*, p. 77.

59. Rollinson, *Life and Tradition*, p. 52.

60. Coulton, G. E. (1921), *Medieval Studies*, 14 (2nd edition), pp. 24–5, quoted in Thomas, *Religion and the Decline of Magic*, p. 36.

Chapter 4

1. The musters for Allerdale Below Derwent 1580 specify Keswick, Naddle, Legburthwaite, Castlerigg, and Wythburn from the Parish, and Tallentire outside it.

2. History of Parliament Online, Biography of Sir John Derwentwater.

3. Ibid, Biography of Sir Nicholas Radcliffe.

4. The couple still held the Vill of Threlkeld. Ibid.

5. See Thompson, 'The Derwentwaters and Radcliffes', CW2, 4, p. 304. and Crosthwaite, J. Fisher (1874), 'The Last of the Derwentwaters: A paper read to the Keswick Literary Society', and Appendix, pp. 8–9.

6. In both 1523 and 1524.

7. Eeles, The Parish Church, p. 3.

8. Manders, The History of the Church of Crosthwaite, p. 71.

9. Ibid, p. 100.

10. Southey, Colloquies, Colloquy X, Vol. 2, pp. 1, 2.

11. Eeles, The Parish Church, p. 12.

12. Feet of Fines, Cumbl., Easter, 6ed.V1, 1552., described in Thompson, 'The Derwentwaters and Radcliffes', CW2, 4, p. 309.

13. All quotations, unless mentioned, from Ibid, pp. 308–9.

14. Watson, George (1899), 'Keswick', CW1, Vol. 16, p. 148.

15. Bouch, Prelates and People, p. 178.

16. I have used the local spelling of both names rather than the Leighton and Lee used by Diarmaid MacCulloch in his masterly biography of Cromwell (2018), Thomas Cromwell: A Life.

17. Letters and papers, foreign and domestic, of the reign of Henry VIII, 1X, p. 955. quoted in Moorhouse, Geoffrey (2008), The Last Office: 1539 and the Dissolution of a Monastery, p. 121.

18. Ibid, p. 124.

19. MacCulloch, Thomas Cromwell, p. 305.

20. Letters and papers, foreign and domestic, of the reign of Henry VIII, 1X, p. 955. quoted by Moorhouse The Last Office, p. 121.

21. MacCulloch, Thomas Cromwell, pp. 118–19.

22. Moorhouse, The Last Office, p. 125.

23. Kendal largely because of the loss of Windermere and Grasmere. Kirkoswald, in the Eden Valley, some 9 miles from Penrith, was the third. Bouch and Jones considered Crosthwaite to be the highest of the 130 'taxable benefices' in their region – see Bouch and Jones, A Social and Economic History, p. 60.

24. See Bouch, Prelates and People, Appendix XIII, pp. 473–6.

25. Ibid, Appendix XIII, pp. 473–6.

26. MacCulloch. Thomas Cromwell. p.374.

27. Hoyle, Richard W. (1987), 'An ancient and laudable custom: the definition and development of tenant right in north-western England in the sixteenth century', Past and Present, 116, p. 26.

28. Ibid, p. 28.

29. Bouch, Prelates and People, p. 186.

30. For instance, this right was recorded in the Percy Parish lands in the survey, albeit at that time requiring that it be recorded by the steward in open court. Quoted in Bouch and Jones, A Social and Economic History, p. 67. from a Percy

survey at Cockermouth Castle.

31. PRO C1 878.67. Quoted in Harrison, S. M. (1981), *The Pilgrimage of Grace in the Lake Counties 1536–7*, Studies in History 27 p.viii: Royal Historical Society, p. 52.

32. PRO C1/923/8.

33. Hoyle, 'An ancient and laudable custom', p. 31.

34. MacCulloch, *Thomas Cromwell*, pp. 378–9.

35. Ibid, pp. 381–4.

36. Ibid, p. 387.

37. See Appendix 2.

38. PRO C1/727/12 and PRO C1/923/8.

39. MacCulloch, *Thomas Cromwell*, p. 378–9.

40. Ibid, pp. 399–400.

41. Bouch, *Prelates and People*, p. 186.

42. Moorhouse, *The Last Office*, p. 154.

43. Ibid, pp. 154–5.

44. MacCulloch, *Thomas Cromwell*, p. 464.

45. Ibid, p. 421.

46. Moorhouse, *The Last Office*, pp. 180, 181.

47. MacCulloch, *Thomas Cromwell*, p. 529.

48. Moorhouse, *The Last Office*, p. 218.

49. Manders, *The History of the Church of Crosthwaite*, pp. 108–112.

50. Bouch, *Prelates and People*, p. 194.

51. Ibid, p. 198.

52. Ibid, p. 200.

53. Reid, Rachel R. (1921) *The King's Council in the North*, p. 195.

54. Quoted in Bouch, *Prelates and People*, p. 204.

55. Manders, *The History of the Church of Crosthwaite*, p. 106.

56. Ferguson, Richard S. (1890), *A History of Cumberland*, pp. 249–50.

57. Bouch, *Prelates and People*, p. 205.

58. Lord Hudson quoted Ibid.

59. Reid, *The King's Council in the North*, p. 194.

60. Divided into eighteen tenements.

61. The 'other lands' included 'Wanthwaite', presumably the small valley of that name in St John's in the Vale, where some land provided income for the school. Nicolson and Burn (1777), *The History and Antiquities of the Counties of Westmorland and Cumberland*, p. 92.

62. E Sandford, quoted Taylor, Michael W. (1893), 'Some Manorial Halls in the Vale of Derwent', *CW1*, 12, p. 152.

63. Taylor, 'Some Manorial Halls in the Vale of Derwent', pp. 148–52.

64. Manders, *The History of the Church of Crosthwaite*, p. 100.

65. For £732.

66. E.g. PRO C2/ELIZ/D3/41.

67. This appears not have been fully understood by the commissioners of the Crosthwaite Ruling, when they recommended the purchase of what they called 'some free and good Manors of Lordshipps'. That would be surprising given the amount of upland Parish land, all still technically subject to Forest Law.

So, it may be that most of the commissioners' land had never been subject to it.

68. Winchester, 'Wordsworth's "Pure Commonwealth"?', pp. 90–1.

69. Hattersley, Roy (2017), *The Catholics*, p. 123.

70. Ibid, p. 133.

71. Trevelyan, G. M. (1904), *England Under the Stuarts*, p. 61.

72. Bishop of Barrow-in-Furness (1904), 'On the Readers in the Chapelries of the Lake District', CW2, 5, p. 89.

73. Bouch, *Prelates and People*, p. 205.

74. Ibid, p. 239.

75. Ibid, p. 238.

76. Bulmer's *History, Topography & Directory of Cumberland 1901*, p. 485.

77. Dodds H. M. and R. (1915), *The Pilgrimage of Grace, 1536–37 and the Exeter Conspiracy, 1538*, ii, p. 227.

Chapter 5

1. Elsas, Madeleine (1945), 'Deeds of the Parish of Crosthwaite [1571–1636]', CW2, 45, p. 40.

2. Eeles, *The Parish Church*, p. 58.

3. Quotations in this paragraph Ibid, pp. 59–60.

4. Quotations in this paragraph Ibid, p. 61, unless otherwise stated.

5. Ibid, p. 61.

6. Elsas, 'Deeds of the Parish', p.40.

7. Bouch and Jones, *A Social and Economic History*, p. 152.

8. All quotations in this paragraph from Elsas, 'Deeds of the Parish',

p. 42, unless otherwise stated.

9. There are many sources that quote from the Crosthwaite Ruling, primarily the ones I have used, and occasional discrepancies arise. For instance, the 2d. fine is occasionally reported as a mixture of 1d. and 2d. fines. Here I have taken the majority view, which includes the 1821 Parliamentary Report. I have been unable to find the originals last reported, by Elsas, 'Deeds of the Parish', pp. 39–48, as belonging to the Governors of Keswick School, whose staff have been most helpful.

10. 'Report of the Commissioners into English Charities for the Education of the Poor' (1821), Parliamentary Papers Online, p. 72.

11. For paragraph, see Elsas, 'Deeds of the Parish', p. 40.

12. 'Report of the Commissioners', p. 72.

13. Lefebure, *Cumberland Heritage*, p. 55.

14. Wilson, *The history & chronicles of Crosthwaite Old School*, p.15.

15. Rollinson, *Life and Tradition*, p. 89.

16. Winchester, *The Harvest of the Hills*, p. 105.

17. Lefebure, *Cumberland Heritage*, p. 108.

18. Wordsworth, William, *1835 Guide to the Lakes*, p. 69.

19. Lefebure, *Cumberland Heritage*, p. 102.

20. Winchester, *The Harvest of the Hills*, pp. 64–5.

21. Searle, C. E. (1993), 'Customary tenants and the enclosure of the

Cumbrian commons', *Northern History*, 29 (1), p. 131.

22. Winchester, *The Harvest of the Hills*, p. 71.

23. Ibid, p. 73.

24. Steads document dated 1606 quoted in Darrall, *Wythburn Church*.

25. Winchester, *The Harvest of the Hills*, p. 84.

26. A 1606 Steads document copied by Darrall, *Wythburn Church*, pp. 160–163.

27. All the following quoted by Lefebure, *Cumberland Heritage*, pp. 103–9.

28. Ibid, p. 108.

29. Donald, M. B. (1955), *Elizabethan Copper: The History of the Company of Mines Royal*, p. 7; Keswick Historical Society, Friends of Keswick Museum & Art Gallery (2006), *Keswick Characters* Vol. 2, p. 17.

30. Robinson, Thomas (1709), *An essay Towards a Natural History of Cumberland and Westmorland*, two parts.

31. Donald, *Elizabethan Copper*, p. 110.

32. Calendar of State Papers Domestic: Edward VI, Mary and Elizabeth, 1547–80, p. 279, quoted in Hall, *Derwentwater in the Lap of the Gods*, p. 39.

33. Both quotations Donald, *Elizabethan Copper*, p. 152.

34. Donald, *Elizabethan Copper*, pp. 153–4, 156–7.

35. Bott, *Keswick: The Story of a Lake District Town*, p. 17.

36. Donald, *Elizabethan Copper*, p. 151.

37. Rawnsley, *Past and Present at the English Lakes*, p. 68.

38. Grant, Susan (2006), *The Story of the Newlands Valley*, p. 32.

39. Bott, *Keswick: The Story of a Lake District Town*, p. 19.

40. Collingwood, W. G. (1912), *Elizabethan Keswick: Extracts from the Original Account Books, 1564–1577, of the German Miners, in the Archives of Augsburg*, p. 35.

41. Hardie, The Lakes Through a Glass Darkly, p. 273.

42. Donald, *Elizabethan Copper*, p. 157.

43. Bouch and Jones, *A Social and Economic History*, pp. 121–2.

44. Ibid, p. 121.

45. Rollinson, *A History of Cumberland & Westmorland*, p. 62.

46. Robinson quoted Grant, *The Story of the Newlands Valley*, p. 27.

47. Rollinson, *A History of Cumberland & Westmorland*, p. 55.

48. Lefebure, Molly (1964), *The English Lake District*, p. 173.

49. Winchester, *Thomas Denton*, p. 137.

50. Grant, *The Story of the Newlands Valley*, pp. 26–27.

51. The appalling plague toll that occurred around the turn of the century, along with the subsequent demise of the mining industry, brought the Parish's population back to close to its pre-German numbers by 1688. This was a mysteriously low figure as the average increase of population in the Carlisle

diocese was some 45 per cent between these two dates. Bouch and Jones, *A Social and Economic History,* p. 82.

52. From the Old Norse words *thveit* and *sef.*

53. Tyler, Ian (1995), *Seathwaite Wad and The Mines of The Borrowdale Valley,* p. 69.

54. Ibid, p. 70.

55. Ibid, pp. 72, 212.

56. Lefebure, *Cumberland Heritage,* p. 91.

57. Lefebure, *Cumbrian Discovery,* p. 190.

58. Tyler, *Seathwaite Wad,* p. 75.

59. Bouch and Jones, *A Social and Economic History,* p. 73.

60. Grant, *The Story of the Newlands Valley,* pp. 37–8.

61. Grant, *The Story of the Newlands Valley,* p. 31.

62. Bouch and Jones, *A Social and Economic History,* pp. 68–9.

63. Winchester, 'Wordsworth's "Pure Commonwealth"?', p. 93.

64. Ibid, p. 94.

65. Winchester, *Landscape and Society,* p. 63.

66. Grant, *The Story of the Newlands Valley,* p. 32.

67. Winchester, *The Harvest of the Hills,* p. 16.

68. Winchester, *Landscape and Society,* pp. 66, 96.

69. Winchester, 'Wordsworth's "Pure Commonwealth"?', endnote 37.

70. Winchester, *The Harvest of the Hills,* pp. 18–19.

71. Winchester, 'Wordsworth's "Pure Commonwealth"?', pp. 96–7.

72. Winchester, *The Harvest of the Hills,* p. 18.

73. PRO C 2/Eliz/DE/41.

74. Marshall, J. D. Agrarian Wealth and Social Structure in Pre-Industrial Cumbria. *Economic History Review* 33 (1980) pp. 517–19.

75. McIntosh, Marjorie Keniston (2011) *Poor Relief in England 1350–1600,* p. 131.

76. Leonard, E. M, (2013), *The Early History of English Poor Relief,* Cambridge University Press, p. 81.

77. Hodgson, T. H. (1903), 'Extracts from Acts of the Privy Council relating to Cumberland and Westmorland, 1558 to 1568, being the first ten years of the reign of Elizabeth', CW2, 3, Art VIII, p. 147.

78. Leonard, E. N. *The Early History of the Poor Relief.* p. 87.

79. Lambarde, William (1951), *Eirenarcha, in Tudor Constitutional Documents, A.D. 1485–1603, with an Historical Commentary,* ed. J. R. Tanner, p. 459.

80. Sometime before 1634.

81. Grant, *The Story of the Newlands Valley,* p. 42.

82. Ibid.

83. Winchester, *The Harvest of the Hills,* p. 39.

84. Rollinson, *Life and Tradition,* p. 74.

85. Ibid.

86. Thomas, Keith. *Religion and the Decline of Magic,* p. 295.

Chapter 6

1. Searle, C. E. (1983), 'The odd

corner of England': a study of a rural social formation in transition: Cumbria *c*.1700–*c*.1914. Unpublished PhD thesis, University of Essex, p. 26.

2. Lefebure, *Cumbrian Discovery*, p. 126.

3. Lefebure, *Cumberland Heritage*, p. 49.

4. Quoted in Bouch, *Prelates and People*, p. 270.

5. PRO C2/ELIZ/D3/41.

6. Both quotes in Bouch and Jones, *A Social and Economic History*, p. 75.

7. Quoted in Bouch, *Prelates and People*, p. 249.

8. Bouch and Jones, *A Social and Economic History*, p. 76.

9. Bouch, *Prelates and People*, pp. 244–5.

10. Ibid.

11. A Chillingham.

12. Thompson, 'The Derwentwaters and Radcliffes', p. 315.

13. All quotations from the decree, unless stated, Elsas, 'Deeds of the Parish, pp. 45–7.

14. A point made by George Bott.

15. 'Report of the Commissioners', p. 72.

16. The two entrepreneurs, James Whitemore and Jonas Verdon, are consistently so described but, mysteriously, Tyler, a local mining expert, also records a Jonas Verdon as one of the 'freeholders' who bought 'lands affecting the wadd mines' in the Great Deed. Tyler, *Seathwaite Wad*, p. 73.

17. Johnson, 'Borrowdale, its land tenure', p. 63.

18. Tyler, Seathwaite Wad. p. 73.

19. CRO/D Law/1 168/4, Cumbria Archive Centre.

20. Fleming, Daniel (1983), *The Memoirs of Sir Daniel Fleming*, p. 60.

21. Manders, *The History of the Church of Crosthwaite*, p. 97.

22. Daniel, like his father, dropped the 'Le' in his surname, but the family restored it in the eighteenth century.

23. See 1911 February lecture to the Literary and Scientific Society, Joseph Broatch, reprinted 17 December 1976.

24. Manders, *The History of the Church of Crosthwaite*, p. 100.

25. Fleming, *The Memoirs of Sir Daniel Fleming*, p. 60.

26. Ibid, p. 70.

27. Clarke, *A survey of the lakes*, p. 100.

28. As his father had done briefly. Fleming, *The Memoirs of Sir Daniel Fleming*, p. 70.

29. History of Parliament Online.

30. Nicolson and Burn, *The History and Antiquities*, p. 92.

31. Ibid.

32. See 1911 February lecture to the Literary and Scientific Society, Joseph Broatch, reprinted 17 December 1976.

33. Winchester, *The Harvest of the Hills*, p. 125. Quoting John Norden, writing in 1618.

34. Ibid, p. 124.

35. Grant, *The Story of the Newlands Valley*, p. 47.

36. Hoyle, 'An ancient and laudable custom', p. 38.

37. Quoted in Bouch, *Prelates and People*, p. 251.

38. Thompson, 'The Derwentwaters

and Radcliffes', p. 317.

39. All quotes from 1623 Indenture from a copy of the deed in Keswick Museum.

40. Oddly, Alston Moor, purchased by Edward in 1629, was another virtual enfranchisement, a 1,000-year lease having been granted in 1611.

41. Bouch and Jones, *A Social and Economic History*, p. 76.

42. Quoted from a July 1621 play in Kendal. McCormick, Terry (2018), *Lake District Fell Farming: Historical and Literary Perspectives, 1750–2017*, p. 16.

43. Bouch, *Prelates and People*, p. 251.

44. McCormick, *Lake District Fell Farming*, p. 16.

45. This subject is discussed fully in Watts, S. J., (1971), 'Tenant-Right in Early Seventeenth-Century Northumberland', *Northern History*, Vol. 6 (1), pp. 64–87.

46. Manders, *The History of the Church of Crosthwaite*, pp. 131–132.

47. Redmayne, W. B. (1948), *Cumberland Scrap Book*, p. 16.

48. Rawnsley, *Past and Present at the English Lakes*, p. 83.

49. Bott, *Keswick: The Story of a Lake District Town*, p. 20.

50. Nichols, J. (ed.) (1840), *Fuller: The History of the Worthies of England* (1811), p. 344.

51. Oxford Dictionary of National Biography online, www.oxforddnb.com.

52. Winchester, *Thomas Denton*, p. 470.

53. D/BKL Family and estate papers at Dorset History Centre, quoted in Kingston Lacy (National Trust Guidebooks) by Anthony Mitchel.

54. See Tyler, *Seathwaite Wad*, pp. 74–5, 82, for this and the following paragraph.

55. Ibid, p. 75.

56. Ibid, p. 73.

57. Robert Jopson, William Braithwaite, John Birkett and John Fisher.

58. Tyler, *Seathwaite Wad*, p. 75.

59. Oxford Dictionary of National Biography online, Bankes.

60. By then, Isaac Singleton.

61. Oxford Dictionary of National Biography online, Bankes.

62. MacCulloch, Diarmaid (2009), *A History of Christianity*, p. 638.

63. Ibid.

64. Oxford Dictionary of National Biography online.

65. Tullie, Isaac (1840), *A Narrative of the Siege of Carlisle in 1644 and 1645*, p. 39.

66. Johnson, 'Borrowdale, its land tenure', p. 64.

67. Lefebure, *Cumbrian Discovery*, p. 112.

68. Ibid.

69. Bouch, *Prelates and People*, p. 262.

70. In the 1641 marriage articles of his daughter Elizabeth, after he had ascended to the baronetcy. Gibson, William Sydney (1850), *Dilston Hall: or Memoirs of James Radcliffe, Earl of Derwentwater, A Martyr in the Rebellion of 1715 (1850)*, p. 17.

71. Thompson, 'The Derwentwaters and Radcliffes', p. 317.

72. Crosthwaite, 'The Last of the

Derwentwaters', pp. 15–16.

73. Johnson, 'Borrowdale, its land tenure', p. 64.

74. Collingwood, W. G. (1904), 'The Home of the Derwentwater Family', CW2, 4, pp. 257, 271.

75. Johnson, 'Borrowdale its land tenure', pp. 64, 70.

76. As stated by Nicolson and Burn, The History and Antiquities, Vol. 2, p. 69.

77. Quoted in Bott, Keswick: The Story of a Lake District Town, p. 21.

78. Collingwood, 'The Home of the Derwentwater Family', p. 275.

79. Bott, Keswick: The Story of a Lake District Town, p. 20.

80. Clarke, A survey of the lakes, p. 85.

81. Bouch, Prelates and People, p. 266.

82. See Grant, The Story of the Newlands Valley, p. 51.

83. Bott, Keswick: The Story of a Lake District Town, p. 131.

84. Grant, The Story of the Newlands Valley, p. 51.

85. Manders, The History of the Church of Crosthwaite, p. 128.

86. The Works of the Reverend and Learned John Gregoire, 3rd Edition (1684), London M. Clark, p. 122.

87. Nickalls, John L. (ed. 1975), Journal of George Fox, p. xxxix.

88. Ibid, p. 148.

89. Ibid, p. 151.

90. Ibid, p. 153.

91. Ibid, p. xxv.

92. Ibid, p. 160.

93. Ibid, p. 162.

94. Ibid, p. 163.

95. Ibid, p. 164.

96. Ibid, p. 170.

97. Grant, The Story of the Newlands Valley, p. 52.

98. Fleming, The Memoirs of Sir Daniel Fleming, p. 77.

99. Thompson, 'The Derwentwaters and Radcliffes', pp. 318–20.

100. Ibid, p. 320.

101. MacCulloch, A History of Christianity, p. 653.

102. Nickalls, Journal of George Fox, pp. 469–70.

103. Curwen, John F. (1926), Records relating to the Barony of Kendale, Vol. 3, Cumberland and Westmorland Antiquarian and Archaeological Society, Record Series, 6.

104. Nickalls, Journal of George Fox, p. 454.

105. Ibid, p. 455.

106. Original Quaker Records 1660–66 Cumberland. Other Quaker families in the Parish included the Graves, the Bewleys, the Heads and the Birketts. The Quaker Crosthwaite Trustees for Tickell's will, p. 78. PPEC.

107. Bott, Keswick: The Story of a Lake District Town, p. 130.

Chapter 7

1. Bouch and Jones, A Social and Economic History, p. 142.

2. Parliamenary Papers Online, Public Act 14, Charles II c.22 1662.

3. Bott, Keswick: The Story, p. 29.

4. Tyler, Seathwaite Wad, p. 90.

5. Ibid, p. 86.

6. Ibid.

7. Robinson quoted in Lefebure, *Cumberland Heritage*, p. 84.

8. Bouch and Jones, *A Social and Economic History*, p. 97.

9. Searle, C. E. (1986), 'Custom, class conflict and agrarian capitalism: the Cumbrian customary economy in the eighteenth century', *Past and Present*, 110, p. 122.

10. Hargrave, F. (1792), *Collectanea Juridica*, p. 345.

11. Bailey, John and Culley, George (1794), *General View of the Agriculture of the County of Cumberland*, p. 184.

12. Searle, 'Custom, class conflict and agrarian capitalism', p. 112.

13. Grant, *The Story of the Newlands Valley*, p. 66.

14. Dilley, 'The Cumberland court leet', p. 143.

15. See Winchester, *The Harvest of the Hills*, for more on the topic.

16. Winchester, *Landscape and Society*, p. 140.

17. Lefebure, *Cumberland Heritage*, p. 41.

18. Ibid.

19. For more on this subject, see Ibid, pp. 28–44.

20. Winchester, *Thomas Denton*, p. 138.

21. For more on this, see Winchester, *The Harvest of the Hills*, pp. 133–8.

22. Bouch, *Prelates and People*, p. 242.

23. Robert Herrick, 'The Fairies', lines 5 and 6.

24. The Bishop of Carlisle's Court 'Visitation and Correction court books' from 1663, all quotations in Bouch, *Prelates and People*, pp. 235–8.

25. Details in Manders, *The History of the Church of Crosthwaite*, pp. 116–18, unless otherwise attributed.

26. 'Report of the Commissioners, p. 82.

27. Bulmer's 1901 Directory. St John's in the Vale, Castlerigg and Wuthburn, *Charities*.

28. 'Report of the Commissioners', p. 78.

29. Bott, *Keswick: The Story of a Lake District Town*, p. 141.

30. Probably a reference to the schoolmaster's loyalty to the Stuarts rather than the Le Flemings.

31. Fleming, *The Memoirs of Sir Daniel Fleming*, p. 73.

32. Sandford, quoted in Taylor, 'Some Manorial Halls in the Vale of Derwent', p. 153.

33. From a George Brown.

34. All quotations from 'Report of the Commissioners', pp. 74–5.

35. All paragraph detail: Ibid.

36. Clarke, *A survey of the lakes*, p. 101.

37. Ibid.

38. Manders, *The History of the Church of Crosthwaite*, p. 116.

39. Crosthwaite, 'The Last of the Derwentwaters', p. 13.

40. See Marshall, J. D. (1980), 'Agrarian wealth and social structure in pre-industrial Cumbria', *Economic History Review*, 2nd series, 33 (4), pp. 503–21.

41. 46 per cent of the sample.

42. Marshall, 'Agrarian wealth', p. 510.

43. Marshall, J.D. (1973), 'The

domestic economy of the Lakeland yeoman, 1660–1749', *CW2*, 73, p. 215.

44. Denton considered that Parish corn and hay tithes were worth a third of the value of the sheep and wool tithing them. Quoted in Hardie, C., 'The Lakes Through a Glass Darkly', p. 292.

45. Quoted in Winchester, *The Harvest of the Hills*, p. 21.

46. For this and the last paragraph, see Searle, 'Customary tenants and the enclosure of the Cumbrian commons', pp. 134–5.

47. After the 1745 rebellion customary tenants may also have been helped by the Duke of Cumberland calling for lower Cumberland rates after tenants both gave his marching soldiers food and carried their arms as they ate. Clarke, *A survey of the lakes*, p. 119.

48. Beckett, J. V. (1982), 'The Decline of the Small Landowner in Eighteenth- and Nineteenth-Century England: Some Regional Considerations', *Agricultural History Review*, 30 (2), p. 102.

49. 1686 Michalmas [sic] Petitions. Q/11/1/14/11 and Q/11/1/5/12.

50. Marshall, J. D. (1971), *Old Lakeland: Some Cumbrian Social History*, p. 37.

51. Muchin, J. R., (1977), 'The Great Rebuilding: a Reassessment', *Past and Present*, Vol. 77, p. 48.

52. Wordsworth to Lady Beaumont, 10 May 1810.

53. Manders, *The History of the Church of Crosthwaite*, p. 128.

54. Sandford (*c.*1675) quoted in Taylor, 'Some Manorial Halls in the Vale of Derwent', p. 148.

55. Nicolson and Burn, *The History and Antiquities*, p. 80.

56. Bridge House and Fornside in St John's in the Vale and Brigholme and Castlerigg.

57. Winchester, 'Wordsworth's "Pure Commonwealth"?', pp. 95–6.

58. The Registers of Crosthwaite. Vol. 111.

59. The names of the farms in the deed are hard to place, High Row probably referring to some, usually unnamed, cottages at Dale Bottom (or possibly Stone Cottage and Piper House) and Beck House, probably being Brown Beck Farm.

60. See Winchester, 'Regional Identity in the Lake Counties', pp. 34–9.

61. The Registers of Crosthwaite. Vol. 111.

62. Eeles, *The Parish Church*, pp. 62–4.

63. Bouch, *Prelates and People*, p. 295.

64. Article I of the Treaty of Union.

65. Ireland, however, keen to join, remained legally subordinate to Great Britain until 1784.

66. Crosthwaite, 'The Last of the Derwentwaters', pp. 17–18.

67. Ibid, pp. 20–1, including the poem.

68. Bouch, *Prelates and People*, p. 304.

69. Mounsey, George Gill (ed.) (1846), *Authentic account of the occupation of Carlisle in 1745 by Prince Charles Edward Stuart*.

70. Crosthwaite, 'The Last of the

Derwentwaters', pp. 22–3.

71. Ibid, p. 27.

72. As reported by Lady Nithsdale, who rode from Scotland. Ibid, p. 26.

73. Ibid, p. 27.

74. Ibid.

75. Ibid, p. 37.

76. Ibid, pp. 32–5.

77. Ibid, p. 38.

78. Ibid, pp. 32–5.

79. 17 July 1715, quoted in Gibson, *Dilston Hall: or Memoirs of James Radcliffe*, p. 17.

80. Lefebure, *Cumbrian Discovery*, p. 192.

81. Ibid, p. 221.

82. Collingwood, 'The Home of the Derwentwater Family', p. 272.

83. Ibid, pp. 273–5.

84. Crosthwaite, 'The Last of the Derwentwaters', Appendix p. vi.

85. Ibid, Appendix p. iv.

86. Ibid, p. 38.

87. An amusing comment from Denman, Derek, 'Thornthwaite and the start of local forestry in the nineteenth century', http://derwentfells.com/pdfs/journal/Journal50.pdf.

88. Ibid.

Chapter 8

1. Searle, 'Custom, class conflict and agrarian capitalism', p. 122.

2. Ibid.

3. Searle, '"The odd corner of England"', p. 102.

4. Ibid, p. 123.

5. TNA/ADM 79/1 1738 Derwent Estate Rent Roll.

6. TNA/ADM/79/6 Spelt out in rental for 1788, 1788/9 Derwentwater Estate Rent Roll 1788–1805.

7. Collingwood, 'The Home of the Derwentwater Family', p. 285.

8. Marshall, 'Agrarian wealth', p. 509.

9. Marshall, 'The domestic economy', p. 213.

10. Marshall, 'Agrarian wealth', p. 514.

11. Searle, '"The odd corner"', p. 255.

12. Ibid, p. 256.

13. Marshall, 'Agrarian wealth', p. 509.

14. Ibid, p. 519.

15. Butler, J. (1740), *The Analogy of Religion*.

16. Dilley, 'The Cumberland court leet', p. 132.

17. Butler, J. (1740), *The Analogy of Religion*.

18. Rawnsley, *Past and Present at the English Lakes*, p. 79.

19. Platt, *The Diocese of Carlisle, 1814–1855*, p. xxi.

20. Manders, *The History of the Church of Crosthwaite*, p. 124.

21. Lefebure, *Cumbrian Discovery*, p. 198.

22. Grant, *The Story of the Newlands Valley*, p. 76.

23. Waugh, 'A Survey of the Diocese of Carlisle' *c.*1749. Quoted in Eeles, *The Parish Church*, p. 65.

24. The following quotations from the case all from Grant, *The Story of the Newlands Valley*, pp. 73–4.

25. Eeles, *The Parish Church*, p. 65.

26. Ibid.

27. Ibid.

28. See Jackson, Violet, (*c.*1955),

'Lakeland Parsonage', Private paper, pp. 3, 5.

29. Ibid.

30. 'Report of the Commissioners, p. 73.

31. Eeles, *The Parish Church*, p. 65.

32. Bishop of Barrow-in-Furness, 'On the Readers in the Chapelries of the Lake District', p. 100.

33. Ibid, p. 95.

34. Ibid.

35. Manders, *The History of the Church of Crosthwaite*, pp. 118–19.

36. 'Report of the Commissioners', p. 82.

37. Darrall, Geoffrey (2009), *The Story of St John's-in-the-Vale*, p. 21.

38. Platt, *The Diocese of Carlisle, 1814–1855*, p. 112.

39. Southey, *Colloquies*, Colloquy 2, p. 60.

40. Newlands received three augmentations of £200 from 1748, and John Fisher was ordained deacon in 1749. Wythburn received its £200 in 1745, after the chapel was rebuilt. By 1751 their local lay reader, John Mallison, had become deacon. In 1772 two more augmentations (one from the Dowager Countess Gower, a Clifford, and an exceptionally generous benefactor to many chapels in the Lake District) must have improved the paltry £3 17s. living of 1739. Thornthwaite's living that year was almost as low as Newlands, at £2 16s. 8d., a sliver over half of the sum received at the beginning of the century and was augmented in 1747. The next year, Thomas Addison 'literate' was ordained deacon, and received £4 19s. 8d. a year, a salary helped by another Bounty of £200 a year later. The Borrowdale living was £3 5s. throughout the century, until the first £200 was received in 1743, and the local reader again ordained deacon a year later. In 1752, when John Harrison, 'literate', a better educated deacon, was appointed, a second batch was received, and a further augmentation was given by the Dowager Countess Gower ten years later. Sources: The Directories; Grant, *The Story of the Newlands Valley*, p. 100; Eeles, *The Parish Church*, p. 67; Lowther, Tom (1977), The Parish of Borrowdale with Grange.

41. Thompson, 'The Derwentwaters and Radcliffes', Appendix. p. iv.

42. Lefebure, *Cumberland Heritage*, pp. 184–5.

43. Ibid, p. 185.

44. Fairlie, Simon (2009), 'A Short History of Enclosure in Britain', *The Land*, 7, p. 7.

45. Crosthwaite, 'The Last of the Derwentwaters', p. 39.

46. TMA/ADM/79/1. The three most valuable holdings, in diminishing order, were Stable Hill and Lord's Island, held by Edward Waterson, Grave and John Wilson, Castlehead Farm held by John Younghusband, and Goosewell held by John Crosthwaite. However, in the 1723 roll, Edward Stephenson is reported as paying more than

half the total sum of the receipts from the demesne land, £30, and more than any individual in 1738. in Unfortunately, the source does not indicate what this was paid for. Collingwood, 'The Home of the Derwentwater Family', p. 284.

47. Denman, 'Materialising Cultural Value', p. 83. plus following unless stated.

48. Ibid, pp. 91–4.

49. Ibid, p. 136.

50. Peter Crosthwaite letter to the head of the Derwentwaters in 1800 quoted in Crosthwaite, 'The Last of the Derwentwaters', which also describes the height. Appendix p iii.

51. Hardie, 'The Lakes Through a Glass Darkly', p. 269.

52. See Matthews, Stephen (2014), *The Gentleman who Surveyed Cumberland*, p. 320.

53. Denman, 'Materialising Cultural Value', pp. 109–10.

54. Ibid, pp. 98–103.

55. Ibid, p. 109.

56. Roberts, William (ed.) (2001), *Thomas Gray's Journal of his Visit to the Lake District in October 1769*, p. 59.

57. Housman, John (1800), *A descriptive tour, and guide to the lakes, caves, mountains,....*', p. 267.

58. Crosthwaite, 'The Last of the Derwentwaters', Appendix p. ii.

59. Crosthwaite, 'The Last of the Derwentwaters', Appendix p. vi.

60. Bouch, *Prelates and People*, p. 352.

61. West, Thomas (1778), *A Guide to the Lakes of Cumberland, Westmorland and Lancashire*, p. 45.

62. Bouch, *Prelates and People*, p. 352.

63. Crosthwaite, 'The Last of the Derwentwaters', Appendix pp. viii–ix.

64. Ibid, quoting Clarke, *A survey of the lakes*.

65. Published in *The Gentleman's Magazine* May 1750, p. 200. See Matthews, *The Gentleman*, p. 311.

66. *The Gentleman's Magazine*, October 1754, George Smith.

67. Gilpin, William (1792), *Observations, Relative Chiefly to Picturesque Beauty*, pp. 35–6.

68. *The Gentleman's Magazine* 1751, pp. 389–90, from a 1749 letter probably from one of George Smith's party. Matthews, *The Gentleman*, p. 310.

69. *The Gentleman's Magazine*, May 1750, p. 200.

70. Ibid.

71. *The Gentleman's Magazine*, October 1754, George Smith.

72. *The Gentleman's Magazine*, 1751, pp. 389–90.

73. *The Gentleman's Magazine*, October 1754, George Smith.

74. Matthews, *The Gentleman*, p. 12.

75. He tells of his welcome by John Shepherd, who had bought a quarter of the lease, broadly covering the Seatoller commons and the higher wadd hole thirteen years earlier.

76. Hutchinson, William, (1797), *The History of the County of Cumberland*, Volume II, p. 214.

77. Lefebure, *Cumberland Heritage*,

p. 85.

78. *The Gentleman's Magazine* February 1751, George Smith.

79. Ibid.

80. Tyler, *Seathwaite Wad*, pp. 92–5.

81. Thomason, David and Woof, Robert, Commentary and Notes (1986), *Derwentwater: The Vale of Elysium*, (The Trustees of Dove Cottage), p. 29.

82. Tyler, *Seathwaite Wad*, p. 96.

83. Ibid, p. 90.

84. Thomason and Woof, *Derwentwater*, p. 30.

85. Matthews, *The Gentleman,* p. 328.

86. Tyler, *Seathwaite Wad*, pp. 118, 213.

87. Ibid, p. 108.

88. Ibid, p. 122.

89. Ibid, p. 116.

90. Ibid, p. 119.

91. Linton, *The Lake Country,* pp. 196–7.

92. See Lowther, 'The Parish of Borrowdale with Grange'.

93. Matthews, *The Gentleman*, p. 306.

Chapter 9

1. Searle, 'Custom, class conflict and agrarian capitalism', p. 125.

2. Griffin, Carl J. (2014), *Protest, Politics and Work in Rural England, 1700–1850*, p. 7.

3. Grant, *The Story of the Newlands Valley*, p. 17.

4. Hutchinson, William (1797), *The History of the County of Cumberland*, Volume I, p. 182.

5. Grant, *The Story of the Newlands Valley*, p. 81.

including the quotations in the following paragraph.

6. Denman, 'Thornthwaite and the start of local forestry', p. 9.

7. After a never-ending battle between the Hospital and some Fishers of Jenkin's Hill.

8. Denman, 'Thornthwaite and the start of local forestry', pp. 10, 15.

9. £1,537. Searle, 'Custom, class conflict and agrarian capitalism', p. 126.

10. Ibid, p. 131.

11. Ibid, p. 110.

12. Ibid, p. 108.

13. See Lowther, 'The Parish of Borrowdale with Grange'.

14. In *The Gentleman's Magazine* XXXVI (1766), see Bouch and Jones, *A Social and Economic History*, p. 219.

15. The names of the months are not as clearly defined in the original, but much used in quotations.

16. *The Gentleman's Magazine* XXXVI (1766), see Bouch and Jones, *A Social and Economic History,* p. 229.

17. Nicholson, Norman (1955), *The Lakers: The Adventures of the First Tourists*, p. 46.

18. Parson and White, *A History, Directory and Gazetteer*, p. 69.

19. As printed by Hutchinson, *The History of the County of Cumberland*, Volume II, p. 180.

20. Ibid.

21. Bouch and Jones, *A Social and Economic History,* p. 241, using the figures from Young, Arthur, (1771), *A Six Months Tour through the North of England*.

22. Lefebure, *Cumberland Heritage,* p. 109.

23. Two paragraphs from Young observations in 1768, published on pp. 179–81, Hutchinson, *The History of the County of Cumberland*, Volume II, p. 180. They exclude the Dickinson verse.

24. Bouch and Jones, *A Social and Economic History,* p. 222.

25. Searle, 'Customary tenants and the enclosure of the Cumbrian commons', p. 136.

26. Dilley, 'The Cumberland court leet', p. 144.

27. Ibid, p. 146.

28. Winchester, Angus J. L., *Harvest of the Hills*, p. 133.

29. Ibid.

30. Ibid, p. 3.

31. Grant, *The Story of the Newlands Valley*, p. 73.

32. Ibid, pp. 69–71.

33. The new families included Radcliffes, Harrimans and two branches of the Wren family from St John's in the Vale.

34. Grant, *The Story of the Newlands Valley*, pp. 79–80.

35. CRO/NT/12. George Scott at High Snab and Littledale, who paid £199, John Cowper also at High Snab, who paid £144 to enfranchise his two tenements totalling some 60 acres.

36. Grant, *The Story of the Newlands Valley*, pp. 84–5.

37. Denman, 'Materialising Cultural Value', p. 170.

38. Lefebure, *Cumberland Heritage,* p. 114.

39. Denman, 'Materialising Cultural Value', pp. 170–1.

40. Ibid, p. 169.

41. From Dean, and so unlikely to be one of the Parish Stangers.

42. Denman, 'Materialising Cultural Value', pp. 171, 174.

43. Ibid, p. 174.

44. Grant, *The Story of the Newlands Valley*, p. 71.

45. Ibid, p. 86.

46. Ibid.

47. In major part due to absence of the old destructive plagues.

48. Four years after the start date of his first enfranchisement.

49. In the Parish land north-north-east of the Greta the process had started even earlier and was completed by 1795. Thorthwaite started to enfranchise the same year as Newlands, all their tenants enfranchised by 1814. And by 1831 any burgage holder in Keswick or customary tenant in the old Derwentwater lands to the east of the lake, not already holding property in 'freehold', were enfranchised too.

50. Parson and White, *History, Directory and Gazetteer,* p. 327.

51. In the town, there was a toll gate at Brigham at the east end of the town, several, apparently move-able, toll gates on the Ambleside road and one at Crosthwaite, just over the Greta on High Hill. Bott, *Keswick: The Story of a Lake District Town*, p. 30.

52. 12 August 1745. www.geocities.ws/gizmo_42/threlk.html.

53. Examined by Lefebure, *Cumberland Heritage*, Ch. 2, from which the quotations of the next three paragraphs all come.

54. For instance, in 1694, when the

inhabitants of Underskiddaw had made a vital repair to a bridge over the Derwent, they counter-sued 'Crosthwaite Parish above and below Derwent' at the Cumberland Quarter Sessions for its previous 'non-repair'. The judgment was that all parties should present their case to two JPs whose adjudication would finalise the matter. Four years later, when J. Birkett refused to be constable, 'unlesse he take his oath to execute the office … before a Justice of the Peace … within ten days next' was to be severely punished. Dilley, 'The Cumberland court leet', p. 132.

55. 'Report of the Commissioners, p. 75. This may have been connected to the introduction of three churchwardens at the beginning of the century.

56. Ibid.

57. Keswick Museum, 1997-3-21.

58. Drabble, Margaret (2009), A Writer's Britain, p. 37.

59. Wilson, The history & chronicles of Crosthwaite Old School, p. 23.

60. Platt, The Diocese of Carlisle, 1814–1855, p. 119.

61. Eeles, The Parish Church, p. 66.

62. Carlisle, A Concise Description of the Endowed Grammar Schools, p. 168.

63. Wilson, The history & chronicles of Crosthwaite Old School, p. 35.

64. Bott, Keswick: The Story of a Lake District Town, p. 141.

65. Wilson, The history & chronicles of Crosthwaite Old School, pp. 20–3.

66. See Kaye, J.W. (1966) 'Governor's House, Keswick', CW2, 66, pp. 339–46, from which the following material comes.

67. On Lake Road.

68. George Smith quoted in Matthews, The Gentleman, p. 211.

69. Bouch and Jones, A Social and Economic History, p. 260.

70. Dalton quoted in Matthews, The Gentleman, p. 322.

71. Bouch, Prelates and People, p. 341.

72. Bampton People (2003), Ploughing in Latin: A History of Bampton, p. 55.

73. Turner, Hugh (1990), Fletcher Christian: Some facts, Some fallacies, p. 8.

74. Lefebure, Cumberland Heritage, p. 51.

Chapter 10

1. Nicholson, The Lakers, p. 67.

2. Roberts, Thomas Gray's Journal, p. 87.

3. Andrews, Malcolm (1989), The Search for the Picturesque: Landscape Aesthetics and Tourism in Britain, 1760–1800, p. 158.

4. Roberts, Thomas Gray's Journal, p. 39.

5. Ibid, p. 59.

6. Ibid, p. 87.

7. Wordsworth, William, 1835 Guide to the Lakes, p. 35.

8. Roberts, Thomas Gray's Journal, p. 46.

9. Matthews, The Gentleman,

pp. 307, 308.

10. Roberts, *Thomas Gray's Journal*, p. 47.
11. Ibid.
12. Housman, *A Topographical Description*, p. 273.
13. Burke, Edmund (1757), *A Philosophical Enquiry into the Origin of Our Ideas of the Sublime and Beautiful.*
14. Some of which had been published in 1767.
15. Quoted in Andrews, *The Search for the Picturesque*, p. 179.
16. Ibid, p. 177.
17. Roberts, *Thomas Gray's Journal*, p. 15.
18. Ibid, p. 18.
19. Ibid, p. 45.
20. West, *A Guide to the Lakes*, p. 51.
21. Nicholson, *The Lakers*, p. 29.
22. West, *A Guide to the Lakes*, p. 57.
23. Sykes, William Brownrigg, *Keswick Characters* Vol. 3, pp. 36, 39.
24. Clarke (1786), *A Descriptive Tour of the Lakes of Cumberland and Westmorland*, p. 65.
25. Andrews, *The Search for the Picturesque*, p. 191.
26. To £3 7s. 6d.
27. The ringers were paid £3 3s. a year, rising with expertise and inflation to £9 by 1812. Wilson, Tom (1955), 'The History and Romance of Crosthwaite Church Bells', p. 16.
28. Darrall, Geoffrey (ed.) (2012), *Rediscovering our Past, A history of the Houses of St John's in the Vale, Castlerigg and Wythburn*, p. 134.
29. Quoted in Manders, *The History of the Church of Crosthwaite*, p. 39.
30. Thompson, I. (2010), *The English Lakes: A History*, p. 64.
31. Wilson, *The history & chronicles of Crosthwaite Old School*, p. 23.
32. Thompson, *The English Lakes*, p. 71.
33. Ibid, p. 76.
34. Thomason and Woof, *Derwentwater*, Section 80.
35. Ibid, Section 95.
36. Thompson, *The English Lakes*, p. 73.
37. Hutchinson, William, (1797), *The History of the County of Cumberland*, Vol. 2, p. 154.
38. Nicholson, *The Lakers*, p. 193.
39. P. Break, quoted in Thompson, *The English Lakes*, p. 72.
40. Embleton is just outside the Parish at the west end of the Derwentfells.
41. Denman, 'Materialising Cultural Value', p. 168.
42. From Miles Ponsonby of Haile. D NT 6 Cumbria Record Office.
43. Andrews, *The Search for the Picturesque*, p. 182.
44. Thomason and Woof, *Derwentwater*, pp. 60, 61.
45. 1784, 1789 and 1793.
46. Denman, 'Materialising Cultural Value', p. 63.
47. Quotations here and in the next two paras from *The Cumberland Pacquet*, September 1782, quoted in Housman, *A descriptive tour*, pp. 233–4.
48. Thomason and Woof, *Derwentwater*, Sections 80 and

83.

49. Clarke, *A survey of the lakes*, p. 65.
50. Thomason and Woof, *Derwentwater*, Section 60.
51. Coleridge Journal quoted in Lindop, *A Literary Guide to the Lake District*, p. 149.
52. Thompson, *The English Lakes*, pp. 67, 68.
53. October 1787.
54. Thomason and Woof, *Derwentwater*. Text for Exhibit No. 63.
55. Quoted from Elizabeth Diggle's Journal, 1788 in Andrews, *The Search for the Picturesque*, p. 183. Pocklington was helped by the Ladymans, the Keswick builders, who had also built the house.
56. Nicholson, *The Lakers*, p. 95.
57. See 1809 map.
58. Thomason and Woof, *Derwentwater*, Section 95.
59. Quoted in Nicholson, *The Lakers*, p. 81.
60. Parson and White, *A History, Directory and Gazetteer*, p. 74.
61. CRO/NT/19.
62. CRO/NT/19.
63. Denman, 'Materialising Cultural Value', p. 153.
64. Ibid.
65. Ibid.
66. Reducing the wood's value to a mere £16 for 27 oak trees, a few alders and a little coaling wood.
67. For £450 and an annual rent of 14s. 10d.
68. 5,052 numbered trees, some 22,734 feet valued at 8d. a foot. Denman, 'Materialising Cultural Value', p. 153.

69. Ibid.
70. Ibid, pp. 180–3.
71. Hall, *Derwentwater in the Lap of the Gods*, p. 120.
72. Denman, 'Materialising Cultural Value', p. 184.
73. Ibid.
74. CRO/D Sen 14/16/11. Pocklington sold the house when he left the island.
75. Housman, *A Topographical Description*, p. 274.
76. Denman, 'Materialising Cultural Value', p. 192.
77. Crosthwaite, *Brief Memoir of Major-General Sir John George Woodford*, pp. 41, 42.
78. Sutton, Shelagh (1961), *The Story of Borrowdale*, p. 14.
79. Denman, 'Materialising Cultural Value', p. 193.
80. Ibid, pp. 194–6.
81. Henry Skrine quoted in Denman, 'Materialising Cultural Value', p. 195.
82. Quoted in Hall, *Derwentwater: in the lap of the gods*, p. 116.
83. At Swinsdale and Hause End.
84. Except, of course, from Pocklington.
85. Denman, 'Materialising Cultural Value', chart on p. 182.
86. Quoted from Elizabeth Diggle's Journal, 1788 in Andrews, *The Search for the Picturesque*, p. 183.
87. Nicholson, *The Lakers*, p. 34.
88. Quoted in Byatt, A. S. (1997), *Unruly Times: Wordsworth and Coleridge in Their Time*, p. 255.
89. Quoted in Nicholson, *The Lakers*, p. 48.
90. Andrews, *The Search for the Picturesque*, p. 63, p. 171

follows.

91. Observations on several parts of England, particularly the mountains and lakes of Cumberland and Westmoreland.
92. Quoted in Nicholson, *The Lakers*, p. 35.
93. Ibid, p. 41.

Chapter 11

1. Nicholson, *The Lakers*, p. 86.
2. Ibid, p. 96.
3. Mr Grant in *The British Tourists*, William Mavor (1798–1800), quoted in Nicholson, *The Lakers*, p. 96.
4. Nicholson, *The Lakers*, pp. 96–7.
5. Bradshaw, Penny (ed. 2014), Ann Radcliffe's *Observations during a Tour to the Lakes of Lancashire, Westmoreland and Cumberland*, pp. 148–149.
6. Nicolson and Burn, *The History and Antiquities*, p. 92.
7. PRO/ C78/73/3. The full attribution of the 1592 document gives a good insight into the preoccupations of those times, the case being started by several tenants of 'the manor of Crosthwaite (late of Fountains Abbey), Applethwaite and Ormathwaite, Cumberland, ancient towns near the border of Scotland'.
8. Nicolson and Burn, *The History and Antiquities*, p. 92.
9. PRO/ C78/73/3. 14 June 1592.
10. Nicolson and Burn, *The History and Antiquities*, p. 87.
11. This sale included some adjoining land outside the Parish from Caldeck fells on the west side of Skiddaw.
12. Nicolson left some important historic documents and books to the Dean and Chapter, which remain in their care today.
13. Nicolson and Burn, *The History and Antiquities*, Vol. 1, pp. viii–ix.
14. Hutchinson was a Yorkshire solicitor and a Fellow of the Society of Antiquities.
15. Seward, Anthony (ed.) (2016), William Hutchinson's *An Excursion to the Lakes in Westmoreland and Cumberland 1773 and A Tour through Cumberland in 1774*, pp. xxviii and xxix.
16. Hutchinson, *The History of the County of Cumberland*, Volume II, pp. 562–3.
17. Young, Arthur (1771). *A Six Month Tour through the North of England*, p. 411.
18. Clarke, *A survey of the lakes*, p. 100.
19. Nicholson, *The Lakers*, p. 32.
20. Rice, H. A. L. (1967), *Lake Country Portraits*, p. 62.
21. Lindop, Grevel (2005), *A Literary Guide to the Lake District*, p. 25.
22. Rice, *Lake Country Portraits*, pp. 63–4.
23. Ibid, p. 72.
24. Wordsworth, William (1805), *The Prelude IX*, lines 219–221.
25. Ibid, lines 219–221.
26. Ibid, lines 521–526.
27. Ibid, lines 629–693.
28. Ibid, line 289.
29. Wordsworth, William, *The

Prelude X, lines 701–702.

30. Worthen, John (2014), *The Life of William Wordsworth*, p. 81.

31. Owen, W. J. B. and Worthington Smyser, Jane (eds.) (1974), *The Prose Works of William Wordsworth*, Vol. 1, p. 35.

32. Wordsworth, William, *The Prelude X*, lines 234–238.

33. Owen and Worthington Smyser, *The Prose Works*, Vol. 1, p. 29.

34. Ibid, p. 32.

35. Ibid, p. 35.

36. Ibid, p. 35.

37. Ibid, p. 48.

38. Ibid, pp. 39–40.

39. Ibid, p. 40.

40. Ibid, p. 46.

41. Ibid, p. 49.

42. Wordsworth, William, *The Prelude XI*, line 759.

43. Wordsworth, William, *The Prelude X*, lines 311–312.

44. Wordsworth, William (1793), 'A Letter to the Bishop of Llandaff', pp. 33, 38.

45. Wordsworth, William, *The Prelude XI*, lines 252–253.

46. Ibid, lines 59–60.

47. Ibid, line 193.

48. Wordsworth, William, *Tintern Abbey*, lines.70–72.

49. Wordsworth, William, *The Prelude X*, lines 374–380.

50. Barker, Juliet (2001), *Wordsworth: A Life*, p. 24.

51. Quoted in Newlyn, Lucy (2013), *William & Dorothy Wordsworth: All in Each Other*, p. 4.

52. Worthen, *The Life*, p. 99.

53. Quoted in Barker, *Wordsworth: A Life*, p. 86.

54. Worthen, *The Life*, p. 102.

55. All from DW to Jane Pollard, 24 April 1794. See Barker, *Wordsworth: A Life in Letters*, p. 26.

56. Newlyn, *William & Dorothy*, who points this out.

57. Quoted in Barker, *Wordsworth: A Life*, p. 97.

58. Wordsworth, William, *The Prelude X*, lines 910–911 and 919–921.

59. 'Septimi Gades', 11, 10–12, quoted in Newlyn, *William & Dorothy*, p. 32.

60. Newlyn, *William & Dorothy*, p. 37.

61. Wordsworth, William, *The Prelude X*, lines 466–467.

62. Ibid, lines 577–580, 584–585.

63. Ibid, lines 411–412.

64. Quoted in Barker, *Wordsworth: A Life*, p. 102.

65. Thomason and Woof, *Derwentwater*, p. 1.

66. Quoted in Barker, *Wordsworth: A Life*, p. 102.

67. Letter to Matthews in London November 1795, quoted Ibid, p. 104.

68. Wordsworth, William, *The Prelude XI*.

69. Letter to Jane Pollard, 2 September 1795, see Barker, *Wordsworth: A Life in Letters*, pp. 32–4.

70. Quoted in Barker, *Wordsworth: A Life*, p. 105. Earlier letter to Jane Pollard.

71. Worthen, *The Life*, p. 116.

72. Wordsworth, William, *The Prelude X*, lines 889–901.

73. The Seditious Meetings Act and the Treason Act of 1795 aimed to limit the size of political

gatherings to fewer than fifty people and to make it more difficult to license premises for lectures and debates.

74. Quoted in Barker, *Wordsworth: A Life*, p. 121.

75. *The Letters of Wordsworth and Dorothy Wordsworth; The Early Years*, p. 161. Quoted in Newlyn, *William & Dorothy*, p. 40.

76. Their expenses in 1787–8 were £110.

77. Worthen, *The Life*, p. 109.

78. For more detail see Ibid, pp. 108–9.

79. Published in 1807. To the memory of Raisley Calvert.

Chapter 12

1. Wilberforce to Ralph Creke, 8 January 1803, quoted in Hewitt, Rachel (2017), *A Revolution of Feeling: The Decade that Forged the Modern Mind*, p. 142.

2. A theme fully explored by Hewitt.

3. Bouch, *Prelates and People*, p. 375.

4. Hutchinson, *The History of the County of Cumberland*, Volume II, pp. 154, 156.

5. Rollinson, *Life and Tradition*, p. 49.

6. Chadwick, Owen (1970), *The Victorian Church*, Part 2, pp. 8–9.

7. Mathias, Peter (1983), *The First Industrial Nation: An Economic History of Britain 1700–1914*, p. 59.

8. Ibid, p. 16.

9. Quoted in Simpson, David (1987), *Wordsworth's Historical Imagination: The Poetry of Displacement*, p. 90.

10. Hutchinson, *The History of the County of Cumberland*, Volume I, p. 501.

11. Ibid, Volume II, p. 161.

12. Ibid, Volume II, pp. 163, 169.

13. Housman's notes, Ibid, Volume II, p. 181.

14. Housman's notes, Ibid.

15. Bailey and Culley, *General View of the Agriculture*, p. 19.

16. Bailey and Culley (1794), *A General View of the Agriculture of the County of Cumberland*, p. 19.

17. Housman's notes in Hutchinson, *The History of the County of Cumberland*, Volume II, p. 182.

18. Arthur Young's notes in Hutchinson, *The History of the County of Cumberland*, p. 182.

19. Ibid, Volume I, p. 501.

20. Whellan, William (1860), *History and Topography of the Counties of Cumberland and Westmorland*, p. 60.

21. Bailey and Culley, *General View of the Agriculture*, pp. 16, 17, 19.

22. Hutchinson, *The History of the County of Cumberland*, Volume II, pp. 180–1.

23. 'The Two Drovers', *Chronicles of the Canongate*, Vol. I (1827), quoted in Marshall, *Old Lakeland*, pp. 77–8.

24. Ibid, map on p. 82.

25. Housman, *A Topographical Description*, p. 79.

26. Bouch and Jones, *A Social and Economic History*, p. 243.

27. Ibid, p. 244.

28. Seward, William Hutchinson's

An Excursion, p. 140.

29. All Hutchinson, *The History of the County of Cumberland*, Volume II, p. 181.

30. Bailey and Culley, *General View of the Agriculture*, p. 37.

31. Ibid, p. 12.

32. Ibid, p. 49.

33. Ibid, pp. 31 and 47.

34. Ibid, p. 36.

35. Ibid, p. 38.

36. Ibid, p. 37.

37. Clarke, *A survey of the lakes*, p. 75.

38. Rollinson, *Life and Tradition*, p. 99

39. Pringle, Andrew (1794), *General View of the Agriculture of the County of Westmorland*, p. 41.

40. Bailey and Culley, *General View of the Agriculture*, p. 31.

41. Housman, *A Topographical Description*, p. 64.

42. Ibid.

43. Tate, W. E. (1983), *The Parish Chest*, p. 21.

44. Hughes, Edward, 'North Country Life in the Eighteenth Century', Inaugural lecture to Durham, 1940, p. 119.

45. Bailey and Culley, *General View of the Agriculture*, p. 23.

46. Hughes, 'North Country Life in the Eighteenth Century', p. 121.

47. Young, Arthur, *Annals of Agriculture and other useful arts*, Vol. xxi, pp. 445–56.

48. Housman, *A Topographical Description*, p. 68.

49. Re-brought to modern attention by Denman, Derek (2012), 'The Published Topographical Work of John Housman, from 1793 to 1800, and its Relevance to Cumbrian Identities', CW3, xii, p. 219.

50. Eden, Vol. I vii–viii, quoted Ibid, p. 221.

51. Housman quoted in Winchester, 'Wordsworth's "Pure Commonwealth"?', p. 89.

52. Housman, *A Topographical Description*, pp. 64, 70.

53. Quoted in Bouch and Jones, *A Social and Economic History*, p. 245.

54. Housman, *A Topographical Description*, p. 64.

55. Hutchinson, *The History of the County of Cumberland*, Volume II, p. 180.

56. Ibid, Volume I, p. 39.

57. Ibid, p. 33.

58. Housman, *A descriptive tour*, p. 154.

59. Pringle, *General View of the Agriculture*, p. 41.

60. Bailey and Culley, *General View of the Agriculture*, p. 46.

61. Ibid, pp. 45–7.

62. Housman, *A Topographical Description*, p. 65.

63. Bailey and Culley, quoted in Marshall, J. D. (1972), '"Statesmen" in Cumbria: the vicissitudes of an expression', CW2, 72, p. 259.

64. Winchester, *Regional Identity in the Lake Counties*, p. 42.

65. Bouch and Jones, *A Social and Economic History*, p. 218.

66. Housman, *A Topographical Description*, p. 266.

67. Ibid, p. 268.

68. Seward, William Hutchinson's *An Excursion*, p. 49.

69. Hutchinson, *The History of the County of Cumberland*, Volume

II, p. 153.

70. Housman, *A Topographical Description*, p. 266.

71. Bott, *Keswick: The Story of a Lake District Town*, p. 36.

72. Hutchinson, *The History of the County of Cumberland*, Volume II, p. 153.

73. Wilson, *The history & chronicles of Crosthwaite Old School*, p. 27.

74. Ibid, p. 25.

75. Ibid.

76. From Lyzzick Hall.

77. Wilson, *The history & chronicles of Crosthwaite Old School*, p.25.

78. Ibid.

79. Housman, *A Topographical Description*, p. 72.

Chapter 13

1. On receiving an account that his only sister's death was inevitable, an early Coleridge sonnet, written in 1794.

2. To the Rev. George Coleridge, lines 18–20.

3. Wordsworth, William, *Tintern Abbey*, lines 117–120.

4. Barker, *Wordsworth: A Life*, pp. 138, 139.

5. In a letter of May 1796 to the radical journalist John Thelwall. Quoted in Worthen, *The Life*, p. 138.

6. Ibid, quoted p. 146.

7. Curtis, Jared (ed.) (2007), *The Fenwick Notes of William Wordsworth*, p. 112.

8. Wordsworth, William, 'The Old Cumberland Beggar', lines 94–97.

9. Ibid, lines 188, 189.

10. Wordsworth, William, 'The Pedlar', lines 26–28.

11. Ibid, line 109.

12. Ibid, lines 122–123.

13. Wordsworth, Jonathan, ed. (1985), *William Wordsworth: The Pedlar, Tintern Abbey, The Two-Part Prelude*, Intro, p. 4.

14. Wordsworth, William, 'The Pedlar', lines 99–106.

15. Ibid, lines 278–290.

16. Ibid, lines 251–253.

17. Barker, *Wordsworth: A Life*, p. 142.

18. Wordsworth, William, *Tintern Abbey*, lines 76, 77.

19. Newlyn, *William & Dorothy*, phrase following, p. 64.

20. Wordsworth, William, *Tintern Abbey*, line 92.

21. Ibid, lines 94–97, 101–103, 108–112.

22. I am grateful to Lucy Newlyn, who brought this unconscious realisation to the front of my mind on p. 65 of *William & Dorothy*.

23. Wordsworth, William, *Tintern Abbey*, lines 34–36.

24. Letter to Southey, July 1797.

25. Both quoted in Barker, *Wordsworth: A Life*, p. 149.

26. Wordsworth, J., *William Wordsworth*, p. 7.

27. The 1799 *Two-Part Prelude* was first published in 1973 and given full attention by Jonathan Wordsworth in his 1985 edition.

28. Newlyn, *William & Dorothy*, phrase, p. 85.

29. A phrase from the 1805 version of *The Prelude*.

30. Wordsworth, William, 1799,

Two-Part Prelude 1, lines 292–294, and *Two-Part Prelude 2*, lines 364–367.

31. Wordsworth, William, *Two-Part Prelude 2*, lines 446–451 and 459–460.

32. Ibid, lines 63–68.

33. Ibid, line 72.

34. Quoted in Bate, Jonathan (2020), *Radical Wordsworth*, p. 214.

35. Sisman, Adam (2006), *The Friendship, Wordsworth and Coleridge*, p. 181.

36. Ibid, p. 298.

37. Ibid, p. 301.

38. Ibid, p. 302.

39. Ibid, p. 302

40. Rawnsley, Hardwicke Drummond (1910), 'The Light of the World, Sermon in memory of Holman Hunt', p. 17.

41. Ibid, p. 19.

42. Ibid, p. 24.

43. Ibid, p. 94.

44. Quoted in Campbell, Peter, *Coleridge's Note-taking*, *London Review of Books* Vol. 31, No 4, 26 February 2009.

45. See Newlyn, *William & Dorothy*, pp. 115, 116.

46. Lefebure, Molly (1986), *The Bondage of Love, a Life of Mrs Samuel Taylor Coleridge*, p. 113.

47. Ibid, p. 91.

48. Ibid, p. 93.

49. Ibid, p. 127.

50. Ibid, p. 127.

51. Uglow, Jenny (2014), *In These Times: Living in Britain through Napoleon's Wars, 1793–1815*, pp. 330–1. HB AFM 9/14/4 Sophia Thrale 'Tour through Derbyshire to the Lakes'. Hoare's Bank Archives.

52. Hewitt, *A Revolution of Feeling*, p. 174.

53. Ibid, pp. 171, 172.

54. Lefebure, *The Bondage of Love*, p. 134.

55. Hall, *Derwentwater in the Lap of the Gods*, p. 62.

56. Southey to Wade Brown, 31 December 1818.

57. Lefebure, *The Bondage of Love*, p. 130.

58. Sisman, *The Friendship*, p. 321.

59. Ibid, p. 92.

60. Ibid, pp. 145–6.

61. Ibid, p. 31.

62. Ibid, p. 344.

63. Coleridge 'Dejection Ode' Stanza 16.

64. *Letters of Samuel Taylor Coleridge*, 1895, Heinemann, London Vol 1, p. 796.

65. Wordsworth, William, *Resolution and Independence*, lines 71–7.

66. Ibid, lines 145–146.

67. *Letters of Samuel Taylor Coleridge*, 1895, Vol. 1, Chapter 6.

68. Letter to Sara Hutchinson, quoted in Hankinson, Alan (1993), *Coleridge Walks the Fells*, p. 49.

69. Letter to Sara Hutchinson, quoted Ibid, p. 18.

70. Sisman, *The Friendship*, pp. 344–6.

71. Lefebure, *The Bondage of Love*, p. 154.

72. Ibid, p. 155.

73. Letter to Sara Hutchinson, quoted Ibid, p. 186.

74. Letter to Sara Hutchinson, quoted Ibid, pp. 135–7.

75. Lindop, *A Literary Guide*, p. 217.
76. Hankinson, *Coleridge Walks the Fells*, p. 142.
77. Corner, Martin (ed.) (1994), *The Works of Samuel Taylor Coleridge*, p. vii.
78. Ibid, p. vii.
79. Coleridge, Samuel Taylor, 'Dejection, An Ode', lines 21–24, 84–86.
80. Lefebure, *Cumberland Heritage*, p. 135.
81. In a letter to Francis Wrangham, December 1800.
82. Sisman, *The Friendship*, p. 326.
83. Ibid, p. 355.

Chapter 14

1. Barker, *Wordsworth: A Life*, p. 191.
2. Preface to the *Lyrical Ballads*.
3. Quoted in Byatt, *Unruly Times*, p. 111.
4. All quotations in the next four paras Barker, *Wordsworth: A Life in Letters*, p. 64–66.
5. Wordsworth, William. Footnote on p. 113 of 'The Brothers'.
6. Wordsworth, William, 'The Brothers', lines 175–180.
7. Ibid, lines 181–182.
8. Wordsworth, William, 'Michael', lines 84–87.
9. Ibid, lines 113–115.
10. Rawnsley's phonetic transcription in 'The True Story of "D'Ye Ken John Peel?"', *Baileys* magazine, March 1897, p. 10.
11. Ibid.
12. Wordsworth, William, 'The Brothers', lines 160–163.
13. Based on Robert Bateman building Ing chapel on the Kendal–Ambleside road at his birthplace, complete with a startling marble floor.
14. Wordsworth, William, 'The Brothers', lines 274–275.
15. Ibid, lines 272–273.
16. Ibid, lines 205–207.
17. Ibid, lines 296–298.
18. Ibid, lines 337–340.
19. Ibid, lines 353–356.
20. Ibid, lines 149–152.
21. Ibid, line 422.
22. Barker, *Wordsworth: A Life*, p. 90.
23. Ibid, p. 194.
24. Curtis, *The Fenwick Notes*, p. 56.
25. Wordsworth, William, 'Michael', lines 21–23.
26. Wordsworth, William, *The Prelude Book VIII: Retrospect*, importantly titled *Love of Nature Leading to Love of Mankind*, lines 392–395.
27. Wordsworth, William, 'Michael', lines 30–33.
28. Ibid, lines 122–124.
29. Ibid, lines 19–21.
30. Ibid, lines 43–45.
31. Ibid, lines 56–58.
32. Ibid, lines 62–79.
33. Ibid, lines 96–97.
34. Ibid, lines 208–213.
35. Ibid, lines 231–232.
36. Ibid, line 251.
37. Ibid, line 254.
38. Ibid, lines 255–257.
39. Ibid, lines 302–313.
40. Ibid, lines 373–374.
41. Ibid, line 418.
42. Ibid, lines 420–422.
43. Ibid, lines 457–459.

44. To Thomas Poole, 9 April 1801.
45. Wordsworth, William, 'Michael', lines 469–475.
46. See Newlyn, *William & Dorothy*, p. 137.
47. Barker, *Wordsworth: A Life in Letters*, p. 65.
48. Gill, Stephen (ed.) (1984), *William Wordsworth, The Major Works*, xviii Intro.
49. Letter to Charles Fox, 14 January 1800.
50. Wordsworth, William, *The Prelude Book XIII*, lines 255–259.
51. Wordsworth, William, *The Prelude Book XIII*, line 272.
52. Walton, John K. (1986), 'The strange decline of the Lakeland yeoman: some thoughts on source, methods and definitions', CW2, 86, p. 228.
53. Bouch, *Prelates and People*, p. 375.
54. Knight, William (ed.) (1897), *Journals of Dorothy Wordsworth*, Vol. 1, p. 33.
55. Beckett, 'The Decline of the Small Landowner', p. 106.
56. McCormick, *Lake District Fell Farming*, p. 114.
57. Beckett, J.V. (1984) 'The Peasant in England: A Case of Terminological Confusion', *Agricultural History Review*, Vol. 32, No. 2, p. 121; MacFarlane, Alan (1984), 'The myth of the peasantry; family and economy in a northern parish' from Richard M Smith (ed.), *Land, Kinship and Life-cycle*, pp. 333–349. MacFarlane's exploration of the issue at Kirkby Lonsdale, 'seems very much uncharacteristic of the region', Healey, Jonathan (2007), 'Agrarian Social Structure in the Central Lake District, c.1574–1830: The fall of the "Mountain Republic"?' *Northern History*, XLIV, p. 91.
58. For instance, Walton, 'The strange decline', p. 225; Marshall, *Old Lakeland*, p. 37.
59. There were also two Wilkinsons, Allisons, Howes, Mosses and Buntings, and one Wharton, Rabye, Williamson, Wood, Birkhead, Fisher, Jackson, Walker, Fletcher, Wallas, Taylor, Radcliffe, Ritson and Richardson, many of whom were also still in the manor.
60. Darrall, *Rediscovering our Past*, pp. 141–2.
61. Ibid, p. 10.
62. Ibid, p. 101.
63. Ibid.
64. Ibid, p. 100.
65. Recorded as farming 14 acres in 1851, they seem to have been significant landowners as at one stage as they owned twenty-one grasses on Helvellyn, seven and a half at Armboth and five others elsewhere, which would have been a lot of hefted sheep for Manchester to reallocate.
66. Winchester, 'Wordsworth's "Pure Commonwealth"?', p. 95.
67. Ibid.
68. The Crosthwaites at Setmabanning, in the Wanthwaite township, lived there before 1446, Ibid, p. 180, and after the 1623 'enfranchisement' and the Harrimans at Shundraw, in the Burns

township from, at the latest, 1696 to 1868, Ibid, p. 43.

69. It is possible, but not provable that the Buntings may have stayed at Moor Farm from 1569 until the early 1800s.

70. Thomas Wilson lived at Hollin Root, also at Burns, before 1689 and his family, passing by his sister's marriage to Thomas Crosthwaite, until 1857, Darrall, *Rediscovering our Past*, p. 30. In Wanthwaite Valley the Wrens stayed at Birkett from before the 1623 Indenture until at least 1787 (Ibid, p. 166), and the Gasgarth family at Hilltop, from at least 1600–87 (Ibid, pp. 172–3), and the Williamsons built the fine Lowthwaite farm there in the 1700s, staying there until at least 1856 (Ibid, pp. 177–8). The Hodgsons were linked with Brotto at Legburthwaite for 'at least 150 years' (Ibid, p. 95).

71. The Mosses at Mosse Dyke in Burns township from sometime before 1575 to 1692 (Ibid, p. 3), and the Wilkinsons at Shoulthwaite in Naddle (Ibid, p. 163), who were there for more than a hundred years before their forced sale to Manchester.

72. Winchester, 'Wordsworth's "Pure Commonwealth"?', p. 103.

73. A mansion indeed, Fieldside would have another period of rebuilding, creating extra cottages for its estate. Darrall, *Rediscovering our Past*, p. 170.

74. Rawnsley, Hardwicke Drummond (1901), *Literary Associations of the English Lakes, Vol. 1.: Cumberland, Keswick, and Southey's Country*, p. 113.

75. Beckett, 'The Decline of the Small Landowner', pp. 100–2 concludes that Dickinson's 1852 essay establishes that it was no longer economically viable to farm with less than 40 acres by that date.

76. Marshall, J. D. and Walton, John K. (1981), *The Lake Counties from 1830 to the mid-twentieth century*, p. 61.

77. Armstrong, Margaret (1989), *Thirlmere, Across the Bridges to Chapel 1849–1852*, p. 33. Excepting, as usual, the Leathes manorial holding of, then, 150 acres farmed by Daniel Thwaite.

78. Winchester, 'Wordsworth's "Pure Commonwealth"?', p. 108.

79. Shepherd, Margaret E. (2011), *Across the Oceans: Emigration from Cumberland and Westmorland before 1914*, p. 16.

80. Ibid.

81. A. B. Humphries, 'Agrarian Change in East Cumberland, 1750–1900', Unpublished thesis, p. 318, quoted Uttley, 'Decline, Revisited', p. 134.

82. Housman, *A Topographical Description*, p. 58.

83. Wordsworth maintained, taking his history mainly from Furness and Thomas West, that tenements combined 'often in the proportion of four to one' after the union and the Restoration, during the 'Great Rebuilding'. Wordsworth, William, *1835 Guide to the Lakes*, p. 68.

84. Winchester, 'Wordsworth's "Pure

Commonwealth"?', p. 103.

85. Searle, '"The odd corner of England"', p. 275, between £1 and £5; see also Table 5.5, p. 209.

86. Risen from £76 in 1750–5 to £154 in 1770–5, despite wool prices dropping until the beginning of the war.

87. Wordsworth, William, *Guide to the Lakes*, p. 74.

88. Bailey and Culley, *General View of the Agriculture*, p. 11.

89. Searle, 'Custom, class conflict and agrarian capitalism', p. 110.

90. Searle, 'The Odd Corner of England', Table 5.1 and Table 7.11, p. 387.

91. Uttley, David (2007) 'The Decline of the Cumbrian Yeoman: Fact or Fiction?' *CW3*, 7.

92. Uttley, 'The Decline', p. 130; Uttley, 'The Decline, Revisited', p.141.

93. Uttley, 'The Decline', p. 128.

94. Uttley, 'The Decline, Revisited', pp. 135, 130–1.

95. In 'Decline, Revisited', Uttley somewhat modifies this position: 'most of this [decline] after 1817' (p. 139), and the decline occurred 'mainly in the post-war years' (p. 142).

96. Simpson, *Wordsworth's Historical Imagination*, pp. 93–4.

97. Ibid, p. 142.

Chapter 15

1. Barker, *Wordsworth: A Life*, p. 215.

2. 'Wordsworth and the Peasantry' in Rawnsley, *Lake Country Sketches*, p. 53.

3. Sisman, *The Friendship*, p. 360.

4. On 15 October.

5. Barker, *Wordsworth: A Life*, p. 225.

6. Ibid.

7. Newlyn, *William & Dorothy*, p. 209.

8. The quotation relating to this incident from Rawnsley, *Literary Associations of the English Lakes Vol. 1*, pp. 86–94.

9. Clonfer, David Ross Leitch, *Keswick Characters Vol. III*, p. 54.

10. Robert Southey to Charles Watkin Williams Wynn, 9 January 1802.

11. Speck, W. A. (2006), *Robert Southey: Entire Man of Letters*, p. 91.

12. Ibid, p. 98.

13. Ibid, p. 91.

14. Curry, Kenneth (ed.) (1965), *New letters of Robert Southey*, Vol. I, p. 108. Note, quoted Ibid, p. 65.

15. Sisman, *The Friendship*, p. 42.

16. Hewitt, *A Revolution of Feeling*, pp. 173–5.

17. Speck, *Robert Southey: Entire Man of Letters*, p. 43.

18. Ibid, pp. 176, 183.

19. Ibid, pp. 200–3.

20. Ibid, p. 272.

21. Sisman, *The Friendship*, p. 103.

22. Speck, *Robert Southey: Entire man of Letters*, p. 273.

23. Ibid, p. 276.

24. Hewitt, *A Revolution of Feeling*, p. 410.

25. Rawnsley, *Literary Associations of the English lakes, Vol. 1*, p. 60.

26. Ibid.
27. Speck, *Robert Southey: Entire Man of Letters*, p. 104.
28. In Hazlitt, William (2007, Robert Woof ed.) *The Spirit of the Age*.
29. To Thomas Southey, 29 October 1803.
30. Rawnsley, *Literary Associations of the English Lakes, Vol. 1*, p. 66.
31. Ruskin, John (1969 edition), 'Hero Worship' in *Iteriad, or Three Weeks Among the Lakes*.
32. Lindop, *A Literary Guide*, pp. 43, 44.
33. Rawnsley, *Literary Associations*, p. 68.
34. Quoted in Lindop, *A Literary Guide*, p. 250.
35. Ibid, p. 140.
36. Watson, 'Keswick', p. 147.
37. Ibid.
38. Manders, *The History of the Church of Crosthwaite*, p. 28.
39. Ibid, p. 30.
40. Ibid, pp. 28, 29.
41. CRO DB p. 191. Abstract of the title of Forge Mill for all the following information unless otherwise stated.
42. Sisman, *The Friendship*, p. 375.
43. To Charles Danvers, 15 January 1804.
44. Speck, *Robert Southey: Entire Man of Letters*, p. 101.
45. Rawnsley, *Literary Associations of the English Lakes, Vol. 1*, p. 46.
46. Letter to Mary Barker, 11 May 1805.
47. Lefebure, *The Bondage of Love*, p. 22.
48. Letter to Mary Barker, 8 August 1813.
49. Lefebure, *The Bondage of Love*, p. 168.
50. Speck, *Robert Southey: Entire Man of Letters*, p. 110.
51. Quoted in their 'Intro to Letters. Untitled review', *Imperial Review*, 5 (1805), pp. 465–73; reprinted in Madden, Lionel (ed.) (1972), *Robert Southey: The Critical Heritage*, pp. 104–5.
52. To William Taylor, 9 March 1805.
53. Uglow, *In These Times*, p. 350.
54. Storey, Mark (1977), *Robert Southey: A Life*, p. 167.
55. Elegiac Stanzas II, 5, 14, 15.
56. Gill, *Wordsworth's Major Works*, p. 714.
57. Lefebure, *The Bondage of Love*, pp. 169–70.
58. Letter to Wynn, quoted Storey, *Robert Southey*, p. 182.
59. Sisman, *The Friendship*, p. 379.
60. Ibid, p. 381.
61. Ibid.
62. Lefebure, *The Bondage of Love*, p. 172.
63. Ibid, p. 382.
64. Bate, *Radical Wordsworth*, p. 303.
65. Rawnsley, *Literary Associations of the English Lakes, Vol. 1*, p. 42.
66. Lefebure, *The Bondage of Love*, p. 175.
67. Sisman, *The Friendship*, p. 388.
68. Lefebure, *The Bondage of Love*, p. 175.
69. Southey quotations in this para in Sisman, *The Friendship*, pp. 388–9.
70. Lefebure, *The Bondage of Love*, p. 176.

71. Coleridge to William Wordsworth.

72. Letter to Wynn, 18 March, quoted in Speck, *Robert Southey: Entire Man of Letters*, p. 148.

73. Letter to Thomas Southey, 25 February 1807.

74. Hazlitt, *The Spirit of the Age*, p. 119.

75. Speck, *Robert Southey: Entire Man of Letters*, pxvi.

76. Speck, W. A., 'Robert Southey, Lord Macaulay and the Standard of Living Controversy', *History*, Vol 86 (284) p. 475.

77. 27 September 1807.

78. Robert Southey to Walter Savage Landor, 26 March 1810.

79. This post continues in Scotland but ceased in England in the first half of the nineteenth century.

80. Barker, *Wordsworth: A Life*, p. 349.

81. Speck, *Robert Southey: Entire Man of Letters*, pxvi.

82. Rawnsley, *Literary Associations of the English Lakes, Vol. 1*, p. 74.

83. *Edinburgh Review*, 1 October 1802 – Jan. 1803, article VIII.

84. Quotations in Sisman, *The Friendship*, pp. 366–7.

85. Southey, Letter to John May, 11 March 1803.

86. To the Revd George Coleridge.

87. Speck, *Robert Southey: Entire Man of Letters*, p. 7.

88. Ibid, p. 34.

89. Raisley Calvert for Wordsworth, Greville Wynn, a school friend for Southey and Thomas Wedgwood for Coleridge.

90. Speck, *Robert Southey: Entire Man of Letters*, p. 123.

91. Letter to Caroline Bowles, 13 January 1824.

92. Storey, *Robert Southey*, p. 198.

93. Barker, *Wordsworth: A Life*, p. 263.

94. Prelude 1805 X, pp. 723–7.

95. Storey, *Robert Southey*, p. 213.

96. Speck, *Robert Southey: Entire Man of Letters*, p. 25.

97. Ibid, p. 30.

98. Letter to Charles Wynn, 12 January 1804.

99. See Newlyn, *William & Dorothy*, p. 217.

100. Ibid, p. 219.

101. Description of his proposed *Book of the Church* to John Murray, 13 December 1811, quoted in Speck, *Robert Southey: Entire Man of Letters*, p. 148.

Chapter 16

1. Rawnsley, Hardwicke Drummond (1906), *Months at the Lakes*, p. 135.

2. To Bedford, 1 June 1811.

3. Grant, *The Story of the Newlands Valley*, p. 62.

4. Lefebure, *Cumberland Heritage*, p. 245.

5. Ibid, pp. 236–7.

6. Ibid, p. 246.

7. Ibid, p. 241.

8. Woodcock-Graves, quoted in Frain, Seán (2010), *Hunting in the Lake District*, p. 81. See pp. 72–90 for more on this period of Lake District hunting. Also see Lefebure, *Cumberland Heritage*, pp. 234–56.

9. 9 February 1808.

10. Letter to Humphrey Senhouse, 19 November 1808.

11. Southey, *Colloquies,* Colloquey 12, Part 2.

12. Letter to Grovesnor Bedford, 9 July 1809.

13. Quoted in Speck, *Robert Southey: Entire Man of Letters*, p. 134.

14. Letter to Grovesnor Bedford, 12 August 1809.

15. Letter to T.W. Smith, 13 November 1809.

16. Storey, *Robert Southey*, p. 171.

17. Derwent Hill brochure, available in the house.

18. From William Rowbotton, a hand-loom weaver working near Oldham, 30 November 1806. Quoted in Uglow, *In These Times*, p. 444.

19. Ibid, pp. 545–8 for the rest of the paragraph.

20. *Edinburgh Annual Register* for 1809 (published in 1811), p. 122.

21. Letter to John Spedding, 27 March 1811.

22. *The Gentleman's Magazine*, 109 (March 1811).

23. Letter to Elizabeth Hitchener, 2 January 1812.

24. Speck, *Robert Southey: Entire Man of Letters*, p. 146.

25. Ibid, p. 147.

26. Ibid.

27. Uglow, *In These Times*, p. 545.

28. Ibid, p. 547.

29. Letter to William Peachy, 22 January 1813.

30. Letter to James Burney, February 1812.

31. Letter to John Rickman, 2 November 1812.

32. Letter to John Rickman, 17 March 1818.

33. 1801–1854, National Portrait Gallery. A new tenor bell was added to St Kentigern's in 1882 dedicated to the two 'brothers and benefactors of this Parish'. Wilson, 'The History and Romance of Crosthwaite Church Bells', p. 34.

34. Lefebure, *The Bondage of Love*, p. 210.

35. Letter to Grovesnor Bedford, 4 November 1814.

36. Letter to Charles Danvers, 9 December 1813.

37. Letter on 13 November 1811.

38. Quoted in Storey, *Robert Southey: An Entire Man of Letters*, p. 224.

39. Letter to Mary Barker, 8 October 1813.

40. Letter to Edith Southey, 25 September 1813.

41. Letter to Mary Barker, 8 October 1813.

42. Rawnsley, *Literary Associations of The English lakes, Vol. 1,* p. 109.

43. Letter to Grosvenor Charles Bedford, 26 December 1813, and Pratt, Lynda, Fulford, Tim and Packer, Ian (eds.) (2014), *The Collected Letters of Robert Southey 1791–1815*, p. 5. Introduction to Part 4 of Southey's *Letters.*

44. *Quarterly Review*, 1812, p. 347.

45. Barker, *Wordsworth: A Life in Letters*, p. 297.

46. Ibid, p. 317.

47. Ibid, p. 315.

48. Ibid, p. 320.

49. Medwyn, Journal of the Conversations of Lord Byron, p. 135, quoted Bate, *Radical Wordsworth*, end note, p. 554.

50. Bate, Jonathan (1991), *Romantic Ecology*, p. 41. from which I have learnt a lot of the material here and passim about Wordsworth and ecology.

51. November 1814 edition.

52. Byron (1809).

53. Bate, *Radical Wordsworth*, p. 386.

54. 'Ode to Duty', written 1805, published 1807.

55. A phrase from Hazlitt's review.

56. Wordsworth, William, *The Excursion*, Book 4, lines 10–16.

57. Worthen, *The Life*, pp.376–7.

58. Quoted in Barker, *Wordsworth: A Life*, p. 328.

59. Wordsworth, William, *The Excursion*. Book 5, p. 161.

60. Sermon at Pimperne, 21 April 1844.

61. See Bate, *Radical Wordsworth*, pp. 177–485 for an expansion of this point, which includes an interesting Parish story.

62. Wordsworth, William, *Guide to the Lakes*, p. 70.

63. Wordsworth, William, *The Excursion*, line 372.

64. Ibid, line 280.

65. Wordsworth, William, *The Excursion*, VIII, lines 154–157.

66. Bate, *Romantic Ecology*, p. 59.

67. Letter to James Hogg, 24 December 1814.

Chapter 17

1. Barker, *Wordsworth: A Life*, p. 324.

2. Marshall, *Old Lakeland*, p. 136.

3. Review of Pratt, Lynda, Packer, Ian and Bolton, Carol (2012), *Robert Southey, Later Political Works, 1811–1838* by Stuart Andrews, Review19, www.nbl-19.org.

4. See Fulford, Tim (2013), *The Late Poetry of the Lake Poets*, pp. 8–10.

5. Ibid, to which I owe the perceptions of this paragraph.

6. Denman, 'Materialising Cultural Value', p. 123.

7. Letter to Wade Brown, 5 November 1812.

8. To be joined by the enclosure of another 76 acres, the Ladstocks common field, in 1843.

9. From whom the Hospital received just over £10 a year in rent from these customary tenants and an average of £30 from fines when the tenancies changed hands.

10. For £21.

11. Denman, 'Thornthwaite and the start of local forestry'.

12. Platt, *The Diocese of Carlisle, 1814–1855*, p. 107.

13. Searle, '"The odd corner of England"', p. 291.

14. All Tate, W. E. (1943) 'A Handlist of Enclosure Acts and Awards', *Proceedings of the Society of Antiquaries of Newcastle upon Tyne*, 4th Series, X, No.3., p. 183.

15. Rollinson, *Life and Tradition*, p. 139.

16. Ibid.

17. Ibid.

18. Searle, 'Customary tenants and

the enclosure of the Cumbrian commons', p. 150.

19. Ibid.

20. Bouch and Jones, *A Social and Economic History*, p. 239.

21. Quoted Ibid, ft, p. 238.

22. Letter to Wade Brown, 22 June 1815.

23. Bott, *Keswick: The Story of a Lake District Town*, p. 75.

24. All quotations of the event, unless specified, come from Southey's letter (2649) to his brother Henry, 23 August 1815.

25. Rawnsley, *Literary Associations of the English Lakes, Vol. 1*, p. 168.

26. Quoted Ibid, p. 172.

27. Butler, Marilyn (1981), *Romantics, Rebels and Reactionaries: English Literature and its Background 1760–1830*, p. 138.

28. Letter to John Rickman, 13 March 1815.

29. Barker, *Wordsworth: A Life*, p. 337.

30. Denman, 'Materialising Cultural Value', p. 118.

31. In Watson's Park.

32. Winchester, *Thomas Denton*, p. 118.

33. Letter to Grovesnor Bedford, 17 April 1816.

34. Letter to John Estlin, 17 March 1815.

35. Quoted in Storey, *Robert Southey*, p. 246.

36. Letter to Wynn, 7 December 1816.

37. To Catherine Cookson, April, quoted in Storey, *Robert Southey*, p. 262.

38. Bradshaw, Ann Radcliffe's *Observations*, p. 69.

39. Southey, Robert, *The Poet's Pilgrimage to Waterloo*, Part II, lines 139–144.

40. Fulford, *The Late Poetry*, p. 41.

41. Southey, *The Poet's Pilgrimage to Waterloo*, Part 1, Verse V.

42. Letter to William Peachy, 6 December 1816.

43. Butler, *Romantics*, p. 138.

44. Hazlitt was the exception.

45. Both quotations in Ibid, p. 141.

46. Quoted in Bate, *Radical Wordsworth*, p. 381.

47. Ibid.

48. Published in *Alastor; or, The Spirit of Solitude, and Other Poems*, 1816, London.

49. Bate, *Radical Wordsworth*, pp. 417–18.

50. *A Letter to a Friend of Robert Burns*, quoted Ibid, p. 397.

51. Ibid, p. 225.

52. Ibid, p. 397.

53. Quoted in Speck, *Robert Southey: Entire Man of Letters*, p. 170.

54. Ibid, p. 171.

55. Review of *Robert Southey, Later Political Works* by Stuart Andrews, Review19 www.nbl-19.org.

56. 9 April 1817.

57. Quoted in Speck, *Robert Southey: Entire Man of Letters*, in ft on p. 280.

58. Letter to Wynn, quoted in Storey, *Robert Southey*, p. 239.

59. Robert Southey to William Smith, 17 March 1817.

60. Letter to The Earl of Liverpool, 9 March 1817.

61. Preface to *Joan of Arc*, 1837

Collected Edition of Poems.
62. *Quarterly Review* in 1815.
63. Letter to Humphrey Senhouse, 1 April 1817 and fts.
64. Letter to Henry Herbert Southey, Easter Sunday (6 April) 1817.
65. Letter to Charles Watkin Williams Wynn, Easter Sunday (6 April) 1817.
66. Letter to Walter Landor, 14 June 1817.
67. Letter to Henry Koster, 26 August 1817.
68. Battrick, Elizabeth (1987), *Guardian of the Lakes: A History of the National Trust in the Lake District from 1946*, p. 82.
69. Letter to Wade Browne, 4 November 1817. There is more detail on this story in the letters (and their footnotes) numbers 2960, 2961, 2964, 2994, 2970, 3037 and 3390 in Pratt, Fulford and Packer, *The Collected Letters*.
70. Letter to Bedford, 15 June 1817.
71. Letter to Sharon Turner, 7 August 1820.
72. 'The Poor', *The Quarterly Review*, 15 (April 1816), 219, quoted Lynda Pratt, Robert Southey and His Age: Ageing, Old Age and the Days of Old, p.11 https://www.euppublishing.com/loi/rom
73. Letter to Wade Browne, 31 December 1818, demonstrates Southey's approval.
74. Manders, *The History of the Church of Crosthwaite*, p. 29.
75. Platt, *The Diocese of Carlisle, 1814–1855*, p. 109.
76. Carlisle, *A Concise Description

of the Endowed Grammar Schools*, p. 180.
77. Ibid.
78. Ibid, p. 163.
79. Letter to Henry, 8 April 1818.
80. Letter to Bedford, 27 February 1819.
81. Letter to Henry, 16 June 1819.
82. Just north of Littletown.
83. Letter to Wade Brown, an ex-neighbour, 31 December 1818.
84. Letter to Henry, 16 June 1819.
85. Letter to Grovesnor Bedford, 5 May 1819.
86. Grant, *The Story of the Newlands Valley*, p. 115.
87. Ibid.
88. Thomas Oldfield, *Representative History of Great Britain*, 1816.
89. Reid, Robert (2017), *The Peterloo Massacre*, p. 28.
90. Letter to Peachy, 15 October 1819.
91. Pratt, Fulford, Packer, *The Collected Letters*, Introduction, Vol. 6, p. 10.
92. Bate, *Radical Wordsworth*, p. 406.
93. See Ibid.
94. Quoted in Ibid, p. 412.
95. Speck, *Robert Southey: Entire Man of Letters*, p. 186.
96. Ibid.
97. Rawnsley, *Literary Associations of the English Lakes, Vol. 1*, pp. 69–73.
98. Ibid.
99. Ibid.
100. Ibid.
101. Speck, *Robert Southey: Entire Man of Letters*, p. 91.

Chapter 18

1. Linton, E. Lynn (1885), *The Autobiography of Christopher Kirkland*, Vol. I, p. 11.
2. All Ibid, Vol. I, p. 5.
3. Ibid, Vol. I, p. 7.
4. Ibid, Vol. I, p. 8.
5. Ibid.
6. Bush to John Marshall, 14 April 1836, CRO PR 167/7/1
7. Linton, *The Autobiography of Christopher Kirkland*, Vol. I, p. 13.
8. Denman, 'Materialising Cultural Value', pp. 131–4.
9. Ibid, p. 150.
10. Ibid, p. 139.
11. Ibid, pp. 134–5.
12. Ibid, p. 137.
13. 'Report of the Commissioners, p. 73.
14. Carlisle, *A Concise Description of the Endowed Grammar Schools*, p. 182.
15. In 1805.
16. Lefebure, *Cumberland Heritage*, p. 126.
17. Winchester, Angus J. L., with Crosby, Alan G. (2006), *The North West*, England's Landscape Vol. 8, p. 178.
18. Letter of 2 May in Keswick Museum.
19. Also, the home of the Richardson's blacksmith, white-smith, scythe and edge business.
20. Smith, Thomas Fletcher (2007), *Jonathan Otley, Man of Lakeland*, p. 25.
21. By the name of Plasett.
22. Platt, *The Diocese of Carlisle, 1814–1855*, pp. xlviii–xlix.
23. Letter to Wade Brown, 1 August 1821.
24. Letter to Wade Brown, 1 August 1821.
25. Linton, *The Autobiography of Christopher Kirkland*, Vol. I, p. 17.
26. Meem, Deborah T. (ed. 2002), *The Rebel of the Family: Eliza Lynn Linton*, p. 442.
27. *My Literary Life*, p. 36. Quoted in Meem, *The Rebel*, p. 442.
28. Linton, *The Autobiography of Christopher Kirkland*, Vol. I, p. 16.
29. Ibid, Vol. I, p. 14.
30. Ibid, Vol. I, p. 18.
31. Ibid, Vol. I, p. 34.
32. Ibid, Vol. I, pp. 15–16.
33. Ibid, Vol. I, p. 49.
34. Ibid, Vol. I, p. 62.
35. Ibid, Vol. I, p. 10.
36. Ibid, Vol. I, p. 50.
37. Ibid, Vol. I, p. 49.
38. Ibid, Vol. I, pp. 77–88.
39. To Mrs Septimus Hodson, 1 March 1837.
40. Smith, Thomas Fletcher (2014), *John Dalton: A Cumbrian Philosopher*, p. 77.
41. Ibid, p. 23.
42. Ibid, p. 117.
43. Ibid, p. 10.
44. Ibid, pp. 110–13.
45. Ibid, p. 42.
46. Ibid, p. 43.
47. Ibid, pp. 44–5.
48. Ibid, p. 92.
49. Both Ibid, p. 77.
50. Ibid, p. 94.
51. Ibid, pp. 37, 109.
52. Ibid, p. 110.
53. Quoted in Storey, *Robert Southey*, p. 297.
54. Letter to William Wordsworth,

11 April 1822.

55. Bott, *Keswick: The Story of a Lake District Town*, p. 75.

56. Speck, *Robert Southey: Entire Man of Letters*, p. 201.

57. Letter to Herbert Southey, 8 July 1826.

58. Ibid, pp. 201–2.

59. Southey, Cuthbert (ed.) (1899), *The Life and Correspondence of Robert Southey*, Vol. 5, p. 252.

60. Bouch and Jones, *A Social and Economic History*, p. 317.

61. Bott, *Keswick: The Story of a Lake District Town*, p. 83.

62. Parson and White, *History, Directory and Gazetteer*, p. 326.

63. Ibid.

64. Ibid, p. 325.

65. Lefebure, *The Bondage of Love*, p. 242.

66. Ibid, p. 243.

67. Ibid.

68. Ibid.

69. Speck, *Robert Southey: Entire Man of Letters*, p. 319.

70. Letter from Mary Wordsworth to Edward Quillinan, 26 July 1828. See Barker, *Wordsworth: A Life in Letters*.

71. Thomas Colley Grattan, 25 June 1828. Quoted Ibid, p. 189.

72. Lefebure, *The Bondage of Love*, p. 246.

Chapter 19

1. Chadwick, Owen (1966), *The Victorian Church*, Part 1, p. 47.

2. Ibid, Part 1, p. 51.

3. Hewitt, *A Revolution of Feeling*, p. 26.

4. Chadwick, *The Victorian Church*, Part 1, p. 21.

5. Letter to Uncle Herbert, 16 November 1817, quoted in Speck, 'Robert Southey, Lord Macauley'.

6. Storey, *Robert Southey*, p. 167

7. Southey, *Colloquies*, Colloquy 2, p. 27.

8. Ibid, Colloquy 1, p. 18.

9. Ibid, Colloquy 2, p. 38.

10. Letter to Henry, 17 August 1809.

11. Tom Duggett, from whom the thought in the footnote on this page comes.

12. Letter to John Rickman, January 1820.

13. Williams, Raymond, *The Country and the City*, pp. 44, 45.

14. The word Southey used for the first time on 25 June 1823 in a letter to Joseph Cottle.

15. Westall also provided the illustrations for Southey's *History of the Peninsular War*, published in three volumes between 1823 and 1832.

16. Speck, 'Robert Southey, Lord Macauley', p. 475.

17. Letter to Wordsworth, May 1817.

18. Letter to Henry Koster, 26 August 1817.

19. Letter to Henry Koster, late February 1818.

20. Letter to Bedford, 31 January 1818.

21. Fulford, Tim (2011), 'Virtual Topography: Poets, Painters, Publishers and the Reproduction of the Landscape in the Early Nineteenth Century', Nottingham Trent University,

www.erudit.org/en/journals/ron para. 23.

22. Ibid.

23. Ibid, para. 5.

24. Ibid, para. 6.

25. *Views of the Lakes, etc. In Cumberland And Westmorland. Engraved from Drawings Made By Joseph Farington, RA*. Individual plates had been published since 1874.

26. Fulford, 'Virtual Topography', pp. 8–9.

27. Ibid, para. 6.

28. Southey, *Colloquies*, Colloquy 10, p. 59.

29. Bicknell and Woof (1983), *The Lake District Discovered 1810–1850*, p. 7.

30. Thomason and Woof, *Derwentwater,* Section 95.

31. Letter to Henry Koster, Late February 1818.

32. Fulford, *The Late Poetry*, p. 43.

33. Sara Hutchinson to John Monkhouse, 15 October 1820, quoted Ibid.

34. Fulford, *The Late Poetry*, p. 45.

35. Letter to William Westall, 8 December 1820.

36. Fulford, *The Late Poetry*, p. 45.

37. Southey, *Colloquies*, Colloquy 6, p. 122.

38. Ibid, Colloquy 4, p. 62.

39. Ibid, Colloquy 4, p. 73.

40. Ibid, Colloquy 4, p. 94.

41. Ibid, Colloquy Intro, p. 18.

42. Ibid, Colloquy 4, p. 88.

43. Ibid, Colloquy 4, p. 79.

44. Ibid.

45. Ibid, Colloquy 4, p. 82.

46. Ibid, Colloquy 5, p. 99.

47. Ibid, Colloquy 5, p. 96.

48. Ibid, Colloquy 4, p. 81.

49. Ibid, Colloquy 5, p. 98.

50. Burke, Edmund (1790), *Reflections on the Revolution in France*, London: J. Dodsley.

51. Edmund Burke quoted Fulford, *The Late Poetry*, Ch.1, Ft. 32.

52. Ibid, p. 39, who highlights this point.

53. Proem IV.

54. This thought was prompted by Fulford, *The Late Poetry*, which I only read after I had embarked upon the publishing process.

55. Southey, *Colloquies*, Colloquy 6, p. 119.

56. Ibid, Colloquy 12, p. 102.

57. A thought prompted by Storey, *Robert Southey,* pp. 317–18.

58. Southey, *Colloquies*, Colloquy 15, p. 324.

59. Quoted in Storey, *Robert Southey*, p. 303.

60. A solution Southey liked, which was originally prompted by the actions of his friend Thomas Clarkson, the anti-slavery campaigner. Ibid, p. 298.

61. Southey, *Colloquies*, Colloquy 15, p. 326.

62. Quoted in Duggett, Tom (2013), 'Southey's "*Colloquies*" and Romantic History', p. 88.

63. Wohlgemut, Esther, 'Southey, Macaulay and the Idea of a Picturesque History', University of Prince Edward Island. www.erudit.org/en/journals/ron .

64. *Edinburgh Review*, January 1830 (Vol. 50, pp. 528–65).

65. Jane Millgate, Ch. 2 of *Macaulay*, quoted by Wohlgemut in 'Southey'.

66. As Lowther wrote to the Secretary of State for the

colonies the previous year. See ft. 97, Speck, *Robert Southey: Entire Man of Letters*, p. 284.

67. Macaulay, Thomas Babington, Lord, 'Review of "Sir Thomas More; or, Colloquies on the Progress and Prospects of Society, by Robert Southey', *Edinburgh Review*, January 1830, para. 19.
68. Duggett, 'Southey's "*Colloquies*"', p. 90.
69. Macaulay, 'Review of Sir Thomas More;...', para. 20.
70. Southey, *Colloquies*, Colloquy 2, p. 22.
71. Ibid, Colloquy 4, p 83.
72. Macaulay, 'Review of Sir Thomas More;...', para. 10.
73. Southey, *Colloquies*, Colloquy 7, p. 173.
74. Ibid, p. 174.
75. Ibid, pp. 173 and 174.
76. Macaulay, 'Review of Sir Thomas More;...', para. 23.
77. Duggett, 'Southey's "Colloquies"', p. 87.
78. See *The Excursion*.
79. Wordsworth, William, *1835 Guide to the Lakes*, p. 52.
80. Macaulay, 'Review of Sir Thomas More;...', para. 23.
81. From Wordsworth and Dorothy to Lady Beaumont, 10 May 1810.
82. Wordsworth, William, *1835 Guide to the Lakes*, p. 70.
83. Macaulay, 'Review of Sir Thomas More;...', para. 20.
84. Parson and White, *History, Directory and Gazetteer*, pp. 32–6.
85. See Kaye, J. W. (1957), 'The Millbeck Woollen Industry',

CW2, 57.
86. Speck, 'Robert Southey, Lord Macaulay', p. 475.
87. Macaulay, 'Review of Sir Thomas More;...', para 21.
88. Koot, Gerard. M. 'The Standard of Living debate during Britain's industrial revolution', p. 7.
89. Hewitt, *A Revolution of Feeling*, p. 383.
90. John Daniel Banks.
91. Southey (1817), 'On the Rise and Progress of Popular Disaffection', *Quarterly Review*, 16, pp. 511–52.
92. Southey, *Colloquies*, Colloquy 11, p. 242.
93. Speck, *Robert Southey: Entire Man of Letters,* p. 151.
94. Cutmore, Jonathan B. (ed.) (1991), 'The "Quarterly Review" under Gifford: Some new attributions', *Victorian Periodicals Review*, 24(3), pp. 137–42.
95. Speck, 'Robert Southey, Lord Macaulay', p. 472.
96. Macaulay, 'Review of Sir Thomas More;...', para 21.
97. *Quarterly Review* xvi, 1812, p. 320. Southey's article on the poor.
98. Duggett, Southey's "*Colloquies*"', p. 1/87.
99. Quoted Storey, *Robert Southey,* p. 270.
100. Quoted Ibid, p. 327.
101. Speck, 'Robert Southey, Lord Macaulay', p. 477.

Chapter 20

1. Vol. 4, Cumberland.

2. Devout religious involvement was strong in Cambridge too.

3. Chadwick, *The Victorian Church*, Part 1, p. 174.

4. Then the Oxford Regius Professor of Hebrew.

5. Chadwick, *The Victorian Church*, Part 1, p. 179.

6. Ibid. p. 194.

7. Ibid, p. 174.

8. Ibid, p. 230.

9. Ibid.

10. Ibid, p. 174.

11. Manders, *The History of the Church of Crosthwaite*, p. 29.

12. Keswick museum.

13. Wilson, *The history & chronicles of Crosthwaite Old School*, p. 32.

14. Ibid, p. 33.

15. Chadwick, *The Victorian Church*, Part 1, pp. 34, 36–8.

16. Letter to Wynn, 29 March 1832.

17. Letter to Henry Southey, 15 October 1831.

18. Speck, *Robert Southey: Entire Man of Letters*, p. 218.

19. Letter to Mrs Septimus Hodson, 24 October 1832.

20. Wilson, *The history & chronicles of Crosthwaite Old School*, p. 31.

21. A poster in the Keswick Museum.

22. Letter to Wade Brown, 18 December 1832.

23. Linton, *The Autobiography of Christopher Kirkland*, Vol. 1, p. 33.

24. Bott, *Keswick: The Story of a Lake District Town*, p. 187.

25. Parson and White, *History, Directory and Gazetteer*, p. 327.

26. Mannix and Whellan (1847), *History, Gazetteer and Directory of Cumberland*.

27. Oxford Dictionary of National Biography online: www.oxforddnb.com.

28. Rimmer. W. G. (1960), *Marshalls of Leeds Flax-Spinners 1788–1886*, quoted in Denman, 'Materialising Cultural Value in the English Lakes, 1735–1845', Lancaster University Ph.D. thesis, p. 213.

29. Denman, 'Materialising Cultural Value in the English Lakes, 1735–1845', Lancaster University Ph.D. thesis, p. 217.

30. Ibid, p. 237.

31. Ibid, p. 229.

32. Ibid, p. 238.

33. Ibid, p. 149.

34. The Spanish had entered the market and the price of lead dropped from a stable £25 6s. a ton in 1825 to £19 in 1826, reaching its floor of £13 10s. in 1832. Ibid, p. 130.

35. Letter to Wade Brown, June 1819.

36. Denman, 'Materialising Cultural Value in the English Lakes, 1735–1845', Lancaster University Ph.D. thesis, p. 14.

37. 341 acres.

38. Wordsworth to John Marshall, late February 1832. Quoted in Denman, 'Materialising Cultural Value', p. 264.

39. Ibid, p. 265.

40. Ibid.

41. 12 December 1832.

42. Linton, *The Autobiography of Christopher Kirkland*, Vol. 1, p. 12.

43. Lefebure, *Cumberland Heritage*,

pp. 94–6.

44. *The Illustrated Magazine of Art*, 1854.

45. This and the following quotes from Lefebure, *Cumberland Heritage*, pp. 94–6.

46. Whellan, *History and Topography*, p. 342.

47. Wordsworth, William and Wilkinson, Rev. Joseph (1821), *Select Views in Cumberland, Westmorland and Lancashire*.

48. Letter to Catherine Clarkson, 18 November 1809. Quoted in Barker, *Wordsworth: A Life in Letters*, p. 100.

49. Following sales figures from Mason, Nicholas, Stimpson, Shannon and Westover, Paul, (202), *Introduction to Romantic Circle's Edition of Wordsworth's Guide*.

50. This and subsequent quote from Smith, *Jonathan Otley, Man of Lakeland*, p. 51.

51. He had printed 600 copies of the first edition, 1,000 of the second, 1,200 of the third, and another 2,200 by 1835: Ibid, pp. 51–2.

52. Letter to Adam Sedgwick, March 1842. All letters quoted in this para from Mason, Stimpson and Westover, *Introduction*.

53. Letter to John Hudson, April 1842.

54. 11 May 1842.

55. See figure 13 in Mason, Stimpson and Westover, *Introduction*.

56. Smith, *Jonathan Otley, Man of Lakeland*, pp. 99–100.

57. Ibid, p. 77.

58. Ibid, p. 98.

59. Ibid, p. 52.

60. Ibid, p. 101.

61. Quoted in Rawnsley, *Literary Associations of The English Lakes, Vol. 1*, pp. 132–3.

62. Smith, *Jonathan Otley, Man of Lakeland*, p. 117.

63. Ibid, p. 124.

64. Oldroyd, David, Lecture at 30th International Geological Congress, Beijing 1996, p. 203. Having given generous credit to Otley.

65. Part of a eulogy to him by the eminent geologist Clifford Ward.

66. A point made in Winchester and Crosby, *The North West*, p. 200.

67. Wordsworth, William, *1835 Guide to the Lakes*, p. 58.

68. Ibid, p. 45.

69. Ibid, p. 58.

70. Ibid, p. 46.

71. Ibid, p. 44.

72. Ibid, p. 79.

73. Ibid, p. 80.

74. Ibid, p. 78.

75. Ibid.

76. Ibid, p. 86.

77. Ibid, p. 82.

78. Ibid, p. 86.

79. Ibid, p. 90.

80. Bate, *Radical Wordsworth*, p. 124.

81. Wordsworth, William, *1835 Guide to the Lakes*, p. 54.

82. As pointed out by Thompson, *The English Lakes*, pp. 154 and 160 and whose chapter 9 is useful on the subject.

83. Letter to Jacob Fletcher, 17 January 1825.

Chapter 21

1. Dale Bottom itself and two others.
2. Out of some land around Dale Bottom.
3. From Borrowdale, and Portinscale, within the Parish and Bassenthwaite and Greystoke outside it.
4. https://www.cumbria.gov.uk/archives/Online.
5. Tate, *The Parish Chest*, p. 23.
6. 'Report of the Commissioners, p. 76.
7. Clarke, *A survey of the lakes*, p. 101.
8. 'Report of the Commissioners', p. 76. Eliza Lynn Linton also mentions 'a row of quaint old fashioned almshouses', also referred to by Sir John Woodford provided by the Bankes's endowment, which had been replaced by a bank by 1864.
9. http://www.workhouses.org.uk/
10. Winstanley, Michael, 'The Poor Law in Cumbria', Cumbria County History Trust p. 4.
11. Bouch and Jones, *A Social and Economic History*, p. 304.
12. Storey, *Robert Southey*, p. 326.
13. Whellan, *History and Topography*, p. 336.
14. Lefebure, *The Bondage of Love*, p. 254.
15. Storey, *Robert Southey*, p. 334.
16. Letter to HS, 111834, Keswick Museum.
17. Quoted at The Poetry Foundation: www.poetryfoundation.org/poets/robert-southey.
18. Speck, *Robert Southey: Entire Man of Letters*, p. 224.
19. Linton, *The Autobiography of Christopher Kirkland*, Vol. 1, p. 33 for paragraph.
20. Letter to Henry Southey, 2 October 1834, Keswick Museum.
21. CRO PR 167/7/1 provides all the following information and quotations, unless otherwise referenced, until the end of this section. Its contents were still held at the Vicarage of St John's when described by Canon Watson. I was led to them by Hall, *Derwentwater in the Lap of the Gods*, ft p. 72.
22. See Armstrong, Margaret (2002), *Linen and Liturgy*, p. 6.
23. See the appendix XX for more detail on the two plans and the negotiations.
24. See letter to Wynn, February 1835, when Wynn was on a Government Commission on the subject.
25. Lefebure, *Cumbrian Discovery*, p. 215.
26. Weston, David W. V. (2013), *Rose Castle and the Bishops of Carlisle: 1133–2012*, p. 93.
27. A minimum of 300,000 cubic feet.
28. Denman, 'Materialising Cultural Value', p. 236.
29. *The Economy of Social Life*.
30. Denman, 'Materialising Cultural Value', pp. 277–83.
31. Ibid.
32. *Cumberland Pacquet*, 16 July.
33. *Cumberland Pacquet*, 23 July.
34. Bott, *Keswick: The Story of a lake District Town*, p. 58.
35. See Dilley, 'The Cumberland court leet, pp. 138–9.

36. As Sir William Blackstone famously wrote of the English legal system.

37. Since the seventeenth century the court baron had become for free tenants and the customary, or leet court, for everyone else. By 1897 the annual Derwentwater manor court was simply described as a Court Baron.

38. Mannix and Whellan, *History, Gazetteer and Directory of Cumberland* for the rest of the paragraph.

39. The court for Allerdale above Derwent had been naturally much less locally influenced and the seventeen JPs there then included John Christian Curwen, a Spedding, two Lowthers and, again, Humphrey Senhouse.

40. Winchester, *Regional Identity in the Lake Counties*, p. 32.

41. Thomas Wilkinson (1812), *Thoughts on inclosing Yanwath Moor and Round Table*.

Chapter 22

1. Devised by Joseph Walker, acknowledging the help of Robert Mounsey and William Jackson of Martindale (Marshall's neighbours).

2. Wythburn, Legberthwaite [sic], St Johns, Wanthwaite and Burns, Borrowdale and Newlands.

3. Powley (1875), 'Past and Present in the Northern Fells', *CW1*, 75, p. 358.

4. Also Braithwaite in the old Percy manor.

5. Darrall, *The Story of St John's-in-the-Vale*, p. 24.

6. Powley, Miss (1876), 'Past and Present among the Northern fells, No 2', *CW1*, 2, pp. 369–70.

7. Jones, G.P. (1962), 'The Decline of the Yeomanry in the Lake Counties', *CW2*, 62, p. 220.

8. Beckett, 'The Decline of the Small Landowner'. Almost all agreed with this assessment, from Bailey and Culley, to the acerbic critic writing in *The Gentleman's Magazine* in 1766.

9. Quoted in Marshall and Walton, *The Lake Counties*, p. 5.

10. Quoted in Beckett, 'The Decline of the Small Landowner', p. 109.

11. Darrall, *Rediscovering our Past*, p. 7.06.01.

12. Ibid, p. 144.

13. Marshall and Walton, *The Lake Counties*, Appendix 4, p. 249.

14. Rawnsley, *Lake Country Sketches*, p. 32.

15. Wordsworth,William (1935) Appendix to Poems 1835... Of Legislation to The Poor.

16. Quoted in Daunton, M. J., *The Historian*, 22 September 1994.

17. Beckett, 'The Peasant in England', pp. 120–1.

18. Ibid, p. 121.

19. Marshall and Walton, *The Lake Counties*, p. 6.

20. Uttley, 'The Decline Revisited', p. 141.

21. Quoted in Marshall and Walton, *The Lake Counties*, p. 5.

22. Beckett, 'The Peasant in England', p. 122.

23. Good discussion in Walton, 'The strange decline', pp. 228–31.

24. Uttley, 'The Decline, Revisited',

pp. 140–2.

25. Ibid, p. 142.

26. Walton, The Strange Decline, pp. 229–30.

27. Parson and White, History, Directory and Gazetteer. See Uttley, 'The Decline', pp. 123–31 for reasons it was the first 'proper' directory.

28. Enumerated in Bouch and Jones, A Social and Economic History, p. 334.

29. This does not accord with much comment, e.g. 'The word yeoman being "accepted by the community" for anyone holding an estate of inheritance, either freehold or customary tenure.' Beckett, 'The Decline of the Small Landowner', p. 100.

30. At Shoulthwaite in the Naddle Valley.

31. Marshall and Walton, The Lake Counties, p. 249.

32. Ibid, p. 61.

33. Ibid, p. 249.

34. Uttley, 'The Decline', p. 130, and Uttley, 'The Decline, Revisited', p. 141.

35. Uttley, 'The Decline, Revisited', p. 137.

36. Searle, '"The odd corner of England"', p. 338.

37. Ibid, pp. 425–6.

38. Carlisle Journal, 3 March 1893, quoted Ibid, p. 436.

39. Ibid, p. 188.

40. Ibid.

41. Rawnsley, Months at the Lakes, p. 104.

42. Bouch and Jones, A Social and Economic History, pp. 225–6.

43. Bouch, Prelates and People, pp. 410–11.

44. CRO/ DB/191.

45. Dilley, 'The Cumberland court leet', p. 150.

46. Crosthwaite, Brief Memoir of Major-General Sir John George Woodford, p. 50.

47. J. R. McCulloch, the 1837 Statistical Account of the British Empire. Quoted in Bouch and Jones, A Social and Economic History, p. 236.

48. This had apparently been suspected more generally in England some time ago by Campbell, Mildred in The English Yeoman, (1960), who wondered whether the general demise of the 'yeoman class' in rural communities may not have been more 'psychological' than numerical after the triumph of 'landlordism'. See Uttley, 'The Decline, Revisited', p. 139.

49. Searle, '"The odd corner"', p. 314.

50. Marshall and Walton, The Lake Counties, p. 62.

51. Ibid, Appendix, p. 4.

Chapter 23

1. Keswick Museum, 24 March 1835 to Bertha Southey.

2. Letter to John Horseman, 21 December 1835.

3. Conversation with Derek Denman.

4. CRO PR 167/7/1.

5. Letter to Mrs Septimus Hodson, 1 March 1837.

6. Letter to General Peachy, 6 May 1836.

7. Manders, The History of the

Church of Crosthwaite, p. 51.

8. Quoted in Speck, *Robert Southey: Entire Man of Letters*, p. 238.

9. Kewick Museum, 26 November 1837.

10. Bodleian, 28 December 1837 to HS.

11. Speck, *Robert Southey: Entire Man of Letters*, p. 241.

12. Ibid, p. 244.

13. The correspondence of Robert Southey with Caroline Bowles, ed. Edward Dowden, Dublin 1881.

14. Both quotes from Speck, *Robert Southey: Entire Man of Letters*, p. 245.

15. From Thomas Story Spedding's diary, quoted in Armstrong, *Linen and Liturgy*, in the foreword.

16. Linton, *The Autobiography of Christopher Kirkland*, Vol. 1, pp. 42–3. And, in time, St John's held a monthly communion, while St Kentigern's held the service five times a year.

17. Storey, *Robert Southey*, pp. 342–3.

18. Ibid, p. 343.

19. Ibid, p. 250.

20. Speck, *Robert Southey: Entire Man of Letters*, p. 240.

21. Barker, *Wordsworth: A Life*, pp. 470–2.

22. Linton, *The Autobiography of Christopher Kirkland*, Vol. 1, p. 11.

23. Storey, *Robert Southey*, p. 203.

24. Ibid, p. 254.

25. Rawnsley, *Literary Associations of the English Lakes, Vol. 1*, p. 65.

26. Speck, *Robert Southey: Entire Man of Letters*, p. 254.

27. To Mrs Hughes, 9 March 1843, Storey, *Robert Southey*, p. 211.

28. Manders, *The History of the Church of Crosthwaite*, p. 46.

29. Eeles, *The Parish Church*, p. 74.

30. Ibid, pp. 45–6.

31. Manders, *The History of the Church of Crosthwaite*, p. 128.

32. Ibid, p. 47.

33. Lefebure, *Cumbrian Discovery*, pp. 193–7.

34. Eeles, *The Parish Church*, p. 73.

35. Barker, *Wordsworth: A Life*, pp. 48–78.

36. Quoted in Rawnsley, *Literary Associations of the English Lakes, Vol. 1*, p. 83.

37. Journal of George Tickner, Harvard University 8 May 1838: quoted in Barker, *Wordsworth: A Life in Letters*, p. 246.

38. Barker, *Wordsworth: A Life*, p. 484.

39. Letter to Isabella Fenwick, 17 July 1844. Those words could have been written as easily by an evangelical as by a High Churchman, and some in the movement over-claimed him as a partisan; when Faber became a Roman Catholic in 1845, Wordsworth certainly felt betrayed.

40. Letter to Isabella Fenwick, 13 May 1845.

41. Barker, *Wordsworth: A Life*, p. 489.

42. To Professor Henry Reid, 5 July 1844.

43. Rawnsley, *Literary Associations of the English Lakes, Vol. 1*, p. 82.

44. Barker, *Wordsworth: A Life*, p. 484.
45. Storey, *Robert Southey*, p. 344.
46. Linton, *The Autobiography of Christopher Kirkland*, Vol. 1, pp. 98–9.
47. Layard, George Soames (1901), *Mrs Lynn Linton: Her Life, Letters and Opinions*, p. 73.
48. Linton, *The Autobiography of Christopher Kirkland*, Vol. 1, p. 98.
49. Ibid, p. 73.
50. Ibid, p. 87.
51. Ibid, pp. 92–3.
52. Layard, *Mrs Lynn Linton*, pp. 56–7.

Chapter 24

1. Dowden, quoted by the scholars.
2. Platt, *The Diocese of Carlisle, 1814–1855*, p. xii.
3. *Victoria County History of Cumberland*, Vol. 2.
4. Until his death in 1861.
5. Mannix and Whellan, *History, Gazetteer and Directory of Cumberland*.
6. This and following from papers in the Keswick Museum.
7. Details from the flyer, which is reproduced in Wilson, *The history & chronicles of Crosthwaite Old School*, pp. 33–4.
8. Keswick Museum papers.
9. Quoted in Bott, *Keswick: The Story of a Lake District Town*, p. 142.
10. Whellan, *History and Topography*.
11. Bouch, *Prelates and People*, p. 402.
12. Grant, *The Story of the Newlands Valley*, p. 109.
13. Brian Wilkinson on John Richardson, *Keswick Characters*, Vol. 1 for an excellent account of the man and his work.
14. A note in the church today claims a total expenditure of £98, which seems unlikely.
15. Grant, *The Story of the Newlands Valley*, p. 131. They had earlier paid John Marshall £10 a year plus free board and lodging during his brief tenure as teacher.
16. Ibid, pp. 9–10.
17. Platt, *The Diocese of Carlisle, 1814–1855*, p. xlii.
18. Ibid, p. xxxv.
19. Armstrong, *Thirlmere*, p. 33.
20. Ibid, passim.
21. McFadzean, Alen (1987), *Wythburn Mine and the Lead Miners of Helvellyn*, p. 4.
22. Ibid, pp. 6–7.
23. Ibid, p. 6.
24. Ibid, p. 11.
25. Ibid, p. 18.
26. Ibid, p. 19.
27. Grant, *The Story of the Newlands Valley*, p. 119.
28. Until the Honister slate mine reopened in 1997.
29. Industrial History of Cumbria, www.cumbria-industries.org.uk.
30. Whellan, *History and Topography*, p. 351.
31. McFadzean, *Wythburn Mine*, pp. 35–6.
32. Ibid, p. 35.
33. Bott, *Keswick: The Story of a Lake District Town*, p. 27.
34. Grant, *The Story of the*

Newlands Valley, p. 122.

35. A description of how bobbins made Marshall, *Old Lakeland*, p. 147. See pp. 142–53 for more information on Lakeland bobbin mills generally.

36. Mathias, *The First Industrial Nation*, p. 182.

37. Marshall, *Old Lakeland*, p. 151.

38. Children's Employment Commission 1865, pp. 250–1. Quoted in Ibid, p. 148.

39. Children's Employment Commission 1865, pp. 250–1. Quoted Ibid, p. 151.

40. Children's Employment Commission 1865, pp. 250–1. Quoted Ibid, p. 144.

41. Winchester, *The North West*, p. 122.

42. Lowther, The Parish of Borrowdale with Grange, p. 68.

43. Crosthwaite, *Brief Memoir of Major-General Sir John George Woodford*, p. 49.

44. Manders, *The History of the Church of Crosthwaite*, p. 99.

45. Whellan, *History and Topography*, p. 334.

46. Lowther, The Parish of Borrowdale with Grange, p. 68.

47. Crosthwaite, *Brief Memoir of Major-General Sir John George Woodford*, p. 41.

48. Ibid, p. 46.

49. Birkett Wood was part of the land John Bankes had left for the use of the Parish poor.

50. Crosthwaite, *Brief Memoir of Major-General Sir John George Woodford*, p. 51.

51. Ibid, p. 36.

52. Ibid, p. 37.

53. Ibid, Appendix pp. xviii and x.

54. Ibid, p. 51.

55. Bott, *Keswick: The Story of a Lake District Town*, p. 62.

56. Crosthwaite, *Brief Memoir of Major-General Sir John George Woodford*, pp. 59–60.

57. Ibid, p. 58.

58. CRO/D NT/6. Marshall paid £3,440.

59. Ibid. Marshall paid £300 at auction for the island.

60. Although there was a small endowment of £8.

61. Armstrong, *Linen and Liturgy*, p. 20.

62. Bott, *Keswick: The Story of a Lake District Town*, p. 113.

63. Ibid, p. 133.

64. Ibid, p. 91.

65. Ibid, p. 91.

66. Marshall and Walton, *The Lake Counties*, p. 25.

67. Bulmer's *History, Topography and Directory*, p. 402.

68. Marshall, *Old Lakeland*, p. 126.

69. For paragraph, see Bott, *Keswick: The Story of a Lake District Town*, pp. 85–6.

70. Quoted in Bouch and Jones, *A Social and Economic History*, p. 92.

71. Bott, *Keswick: The Story of a Lake District Town*, p. 87.

72. Marshall and Walton, *The Lake Counties*, p. 93.

73. Ibid, p. 92.

74. Bulmer's *History, Topography and Directory*, p. 403.

75. Bott, *Keswick: The Story of a Lake District Town*, p. 88.

76. Marshall and Walton, *The Lake Counties*, p. 25.

77. Bouch, *Prelates and People*, p. 413.

78. Marshall, *Old Lakeland*, p. 169.
79. Ibid, p. 168.
80. Ibid, p. 177.
81. Marshall and Walton, *The Lake Counties*, p. 188.
82. Marshall, *Old Lakeland*, p. 174.
83. Marshall and Walton, *The Lake Counties*, p. 184.
84. Bouch and Jones, *A Social and Economic History*, p. 411.

Chapter 25

1. van Thal, Herbert (1979), *Eliza Lynn Linton*, p. 59.
2. Ibid, p. 46.
3. Linton, *The Autobiography of Christopher Kirkland*, Vol. 3, p. 7.
4. Ibid, Vol. 3, p. 11.
5. Ibid, Vol. 3, p. 12.
6. Meem, *The Rebel*, p. 432.
7. Linton, *The Autobiography of Christopher Kirkland*, Vol. 3, p. 11.
8. Quoted in John Walsh's *Sunday Times*, 30 July 2017 review of *House of Fiction* by Phyllis Richardson.
9. van Thal, *Eliza Lynn Linton*, pp. 15–16.
10. Ibid, p. 62.
11. Ibid, p. 64.
12. Linton, *The Autobiography of Christopher Kirkland*, Vol. 3, p. 13.
13. Ibid, Vol 3, p. 22.
14. Layard, *Mrs Lynn Linton*, pp. 104–5.
15. Ibid.
16. Ibid, p. 66.
17. Linton, *The Lake Country*, pp. ix–x.
18. Eeles, *The Parish Church*, p. 76.
19. Linton, *The Lake Country*, pp. 83–4.
20. Ibid, p. 45.
21. Ibid, p. 34.
22. Layard, *Mrs Lynn Linton*, pp. 72–3.
23. www.poetryfoundation.org/poets/walter-savage-landor.
24. Barker, *Wordsworth: A Life in Letters,* p. 300.
25. Ibid, p. 522.
26. Edward Quinnilan to Sara Coleridge, 28 April 1850.
27. Rawnsley, *Past and Present at the English Lakes*, p. 276.
28. Newlyn, *William & Dorothy*, p. 311.
29. Ibid, p. 312.
30. 'Church Warden Accounts of Crosthwaite Parish Church from 1699', transcribed by Tom Wilson.
31. Bouch, *Prelates and People*, Appendix xi.
32. Ibid, p. 437.
33. Ellen Goodwin quoted Ibid, p. 387.
34. *Carlisle Patriot* obituary, 9 February 1856.
35. To Henry Crabb Robinson, 17 June 1838.
36. A letter to Wynn quoted in Bott, *Keswick: The Story of a lake District Town*, p. 126.
37. *Dictionary Of National Biography*: Bishop Hugh Montague Villiers.
38. Bouch, *Prelates and People*, p. 421.
39. 'Church Warden Accounts of Crosthwaite Parish Church from 1699'.
40. Whellan, *History and*

Topography, p. 343.

41. Linton, *The Autobiography of Christopher Kirkland*, Vol. 1, p. 33.

42. Much as it did in Hawkshead, a parish we have previously compared to Crosthwaite's.

43. Letter to Wynn, 8 February 1835.

44. Taking the figures of the 1851 census.

45. Bulmer's *History, Topography and Directory*, p. 311.

46. Platt, *The Diocese of Carlisle, 1814–1855*, xxvi.

47. Bouch, *Prelates and People*, p. 423.

48. 1830s document at Keswick Museum.

Chapter 26

1. See Wilson, *The history & chronicles of Crosthwaite Old School*, pp. 36–7.

2. Ibid, p. 36.

3. Whellan, *History and Topography*, p. 336.

4. Marshall and Walton, *The Lake Counties*, p. 142.

5. Bouch, *Prelates and People*, pp. 408–9.

6. Ibid.

7. Wilson, *The history & chronicles of Crosthwaite Old School*, p. 39 and Bott, *Keswick: The Story of a Lake District Town*, agree.

8. See 'The endowed schools commission: shall it be continued?' Anonymous, 1873, W. H. Allen & Co. London.

9. Ibid.

10. Wilson, *The history & chronicles of Crosthwaite Old School*, p. 40.

11. Ibid, p. 36.

12. Bott, *Keswick: The Story of a Lake District Town*, p. 142.

13. Wordsworth, William, *1835 Guide to the Lakes*, p. 75.

14. Ibid, p. 74.

15. Ibid, p. 45.

16. Wordsworth, William, *Home at Grasmere*, lines 166, 823, 824.

17. Wordsworth, William, *1835 Guide to the Lakes*, p. 69.

18. Captain Pringle's Report to the Poor Law Commissioners 1834, quoted in Searle, '"The odd corner of England"', p. 364.

19. Smith, *Jonathan Otley, Man of Lakeland*, p. 117.

20. Lonsdale, Henry, *The Worthies of Cumberland*, John Dalton 1874, quoted in Smith, *John Dalton*, p. 30.

21. Ibid, p. 141.

22. Wordsworth, William, *1835 Guide to the Lakes*, p. 74.

23. Collingwood, *The Lake Counties*, p. 142.

24. Wordsworth, William, *The Prelude 9*, line 220.

25. Wordsworth, William, *Home at Grasmere*, lines 348–349.

26. Wordsworth, William, *The Excursion 8*, lines 404 and 410.

27. Bate, J. and Engell, J. (eds), *The Collected Works of Samuel Taylor Coleridge: Biographia Literaria*, Vol. 2.

28. Wordsworth, William, *Home at Grasmere*, lines 214–215.

29. Quoted Simpson, *Wordsworth's Historical Imagination*, p. 71.

30. Wordsworth, William, *The*

Prelude 8, line 209.

31. Preface to *Lyrical Ballads*, 1800, Gill, *William Wordsworth, The Major Works*, p. 599.

32. Linton, *The Autobiography of Christopher Kirkland*, Vol. 1, p. 33.

33. Quoted in Marshall, *Old Lakeland*, p. 154.

34. William Blamire, MP, giving evidence to the Agricultural Committee of the House of Commons in 1833.

35. Searle, 'The odd corner of England', p. 314.

36. As listed in the 1821 Parliamentary returns.

37. Bouch, *Prelates and People*, p. 408.

38. Nicholson, *The Lakers*, p. 9.

Chapter 27

1. Bulmer's *History, Topography and Directory*, p. 397.

2. Manchester Corporation Waterworks Act: 1879, Clause 13.

3. Canon Saunders, a friend, quoted in Bouch, *Prelates and People*, pp. 454–5.

4. Rawnsley, E., *Canon Rawnsley*, p. 55.

5. Murphy, Graham (2002), *Founders of the National Trust*, p. 84. Rawnsley's letter to *The Standard*.

6. Rawnsley, Hardwicke Drummond (1883), 'The Proposed Permanent Lake District Defence Society', Paper read before The Wordsworth Society: Cumberland Association for the Advancement of Literature and Science Transactions, Part 8, p. 71.

7. Berry, G. and Beard, G. (1980), *The Lake District: A Century of Conservation*, p. 73.

8. Rawnsley, 'The Proposed Permanent Lake District Defence Society", Part 8, p. 71.

9. Ibid, p. 69.

10. Rosalind Rawnsley on Edith Rawnsley, *Keswick Characters*, Vol. 2, pp. 126–7.

11. Rawnsley, Hardwicke Drummond (1901), *Ruskin and the English Lakes*, p. 128.

12. Ruskin had particularly high praise for the work of Lucy Gipps, one of Canon Gipp's daughters. And Oddie, by 1890, was exhibiting metalwork separately from the KSIA, apparently having started his own Lyzwick [sic] Hall Art School. Dearden, James (1998) John Ruskin, J.W. Oddie and the Keswick Sketching Club, *CWS* 2, *98*, pp. 287–296.

13. Rawnsley, Hardwicke Drummond (1887), 'Our Industrial Art Experiment at Keswick', *Murray's Magazine*, 2, p. 759.

14. Bruce, Ian (2001), *The Loving Eye and Skilful Hand*, p. 18.

15. Professor Baldwin Brown, quoted by Rawnsley, E., *Canon Rawnsley*, p. 67.

16. Rawnsley, 'Our Industrial Art Experiment', p. 760.

17. Ibid, p. 763.

18. Bruce, *The Loving Eye*, p. 35.

19. Southey, *Colloquies*, Colloquy X.

20. Rawnsley, *Five Addresses*, p. 16.

21. Ibid.

22. Following material Ibid, pp.42–9.

23. Ibid, p. 46.

24. Bouch, *Prelates and People*, pp. 454–5.

25. Rawnsley, E, *Canon Rawnsley*, pp. 32, 34.

26. Rawnsley, Hardwicke Drummond (1902), *Life and Nature at the English Lakes*, p. 66.

27. Ibid, pp. 57–8.

28. Rawnsley, E., *Canon Rawnsley*, p. 70.

29. CCC CRO Carlisle 24/16/1 Quoted in Brodie, *Thirlmere and the emergence of the landscape protection movement*, p. 136.

30. Ibid, pp. 133–56.

31. Wilson, *The history & chronicles of Crosthwaite Old School*, p. 37.

32. Ibid, p. 49.

33. Following para, see Bott, *Keswick: The Story of a Lake District Town*, p. 143 and Wilson, *The history & chronicles of Crosthwaite Old School*, pp. 46–8 – who disagree with each other over whether the £500 and £300 bequests were owned by husband or wife. While Wilson is a far more muddled thinker, I have taken his figure as he supplies more detail.

34. Wilson, *The history & chronicles of Crosthwaite Old School*, p. 38.

35. Ibid, p. 39.

36. Ellis, Roy (2008), 'The Keswick Trespasses: Working Class Protest or Gentleman's Agreement?', unpublished dissertation, p. 30

37. Murphy, *Founders*, p. 109.

38. hdrawnsley.com. Keswick Footpath Disputes.

39. Calvert purchased some of this land *after* the Enclosure Act.

40. Ellis, 'The Keswick Trespasses', p. 31.

41. Ibid, p. 36.

42. Ibid, p. 37.

43. Ibid, p. 38.

44. *The English Lakes Visitor and Keswick Guardian*, 1 October 1887.

45. *Manchester Guardian*, 7 October 1887.

46. Ellis, 'The Keswick Trespasses', pp. 48–9.

47. CRO/DSO24/7/3 Quoted Ibid, p. 49.

48. 6 October 1887.

49. hdrawnsley.com. Keswick Footpath Disputes.

50. Ellis, 'The Keswick Trespasses', p. 49.

51. *Cumberland Pacquet*, 12 July, quoted Ibid.

52. March 1893.

53. Ellis, 'The Keswick Trespasses', p. 64.

54. hdrawnsley.com. Keswick Footpath Disputes.

55. Ibid.

56. *Manchester Guardian* article copied in *The English Lakes Visitor and Keswick Guardian*, 10 October 1887.

57. Rawnsley, E., *Canon Rawnsley*, p. 89.

58. Ibid, pp. 24–5.

59. Ibid, p. 67.

60. Rawnsley, *Months at the Lakes*, p. 21.

61. Ibid, p.35.

710 MOUNTAIN REPUBLIC

62. Rawnsley, E, *Canon Rawnsley*, p. 73.
63. Ibid, p. 264.
64. Ibid, pp. 87–8.
65. June 1887 Parish Magazine.
66. Rawnsley, E., *Canon Rawnsley*, p. 75.

Chapter 28

1. Brian Wilkinson on John Bankes, *Keswick Characters*, Vol. 1, ch. 1, pp. 15–16. The Bankes project stalled until 1894, when a bronze cast of Bankes, set on a plinth of Aberdeen granite, was placed in Fitz Park – and not all the Fitz Park trustees had been in favour of that either.
2. Quoted in Elizabeth Kissack, 'Eliza Lynn Linton', Ibid, Vol. 2, p. 96.
3. 2 February 1803 letter to the *Standard,* quoted in Murphy, *Founders*, p. 84.
4. Waterson, Merlin (1994), *The National Trust: The First Hundred Years*, p. 29.
5. Ibid p. 32.
6. The old Stephenson estate.
7. *Spectator*, 7 July 1894.
8. Waterson, *The National Trust*, p. 37, for both HRD and Octavia quotes.
9. Ibid, p. 60.
10. Murphy, *Founders*, p. 109.
11. Para Rawnsley, E., *Canon Rawnsley*, p. 112. Unless stated.
12. *The Times*, 17 October.
13. *The Times*, 16 October.
14. Waterson, *The National Trust*, p. 46.
15. Rawnsley, E., *Canon Rawnsley*,

p. 12. Quoting a contemporary of her husband, Professor Baldwin Brown.
16. Davies, Hunter (1988), *Beatrix Potter's Lakeland*, p. 17.
17. Ibid, p. 30.
18. Letter 18 December 1901, quoted in Rawnsley, Rosalind (2016), 'A Nation's Heritage: Beatrix Potter and Hardwicke Drummond Rawnsley', A lecture given at Allan Bank, Grasmere, hdrawnsley.com.
19. Davies, *Beatrix Potter's Lakeland*, pp. 35, 49.
20. Rawnsley, E., *Canon Rawnsley*, pp. 112–13.
21. Down south there had been an equal success the same year, orchestrated by Hunter, as another 750 acres were acquired, the greater part of it *given*, around Hindhead Common and the Devil's Punch Bowl.
22. Waterson, *The National Trust*, p. 60.
23. Marshall and Walton, *The Lake Counties*, p. 214.
24. e.g. David Cannadine in Newby, Howard (ed) (1995), *The National Trust: The Next Hundred Years*, p. 12.
25. Quoted in Rawnsley, E., *Canon Rawnsley*, pp. 137–8.
26. Wilson, *The history & chronicles of Crosthwaite Old School*, p. 51.
27. The VCH Project, Keswick. The new urban district also incorporated the extra-parochial Briery Cottages, home to many of the bobbin makers.
28. Cecil Grant quoted by Rawnsley, E., *Canon Rawnsley*, p. 168.

29. Allen, Howard (2018), *Keswick School, The English Lake District 1898–1998*, p. 18.
30. Ibid.
31. Ibid.
32. Ibid, p. 19.
33. Ibid, pp. 26–27.
34. Bott, *Keswick: The Story of a Lake District Town*, p. 147.
35. Allen, *Keswick School*, p. 42.
36. Ibid, p. 25.
37. Ibid, pp. 34–5.
38. Rawnsley, E., *Canon Rawnsley*, p. 159.
39. Ibid, pp. 160–1.
40. Allen, *Keswick School*, p. 23.
41. Bott, *Keswick: The Story of a Lake District Town*, p. 143.
42. Ibid, p. 147.
43. Rawnsley, E, *Canon Rawnsley*, p. 33.
44. Allen, *Keswick School*, p. 43.
45. Ibid, p. 39.
46. Ibid, p. 41.
47. Ibid, p. 37.
48. Quoting Cecil Grant, Rawnsley, E., *Canon Rawnsley*, p. 165.
49. Allen, *Keswick School*, p. 37.
50. Messrs Burke and Son.
51. Cartoons drawn by Mr Margetson.
52. Quoted in Elizabeth Kissack, 'Eliza Lynn Linton', *Keswick Characters*, Vol. 2, p. 98.
53. Quoted in Elizabeth Kissack, Ibid, Vol. 2, p. 99.
54. October 1899 Parish Magazine.
55. Brown, Geoff (2009), *Herdwick Sheep and the English Lake District (A Cumbria Guide)*, pp. 23–27.
56. Davies, *Beatrix Potter's Lakeland*, p. 124.
57. Rawnsley, R., 'A Nation's Heritage', hdrawnsley.com.
58. Ibid.
59. *1897 Kelly's Directory of Cumberland*.
60. Rawnsley, E., *Canon Rawnsley*, pp. 213–14.
61. The Dedication of the Baptistry in St Kentigern's Church, Crosthwaite, 8 August 1909, Canon Rawnsley.
62. The 1907 National Trust Act.
63. Cowell, Ben (2013), *Sir Robert Hunter*, p. 22.
64. Battrick, *Guardian of the Lakes*, vii.
65. Thompson, *The Lake District and the National Trust*, pp. 44, 210.
66. Ibid, p. 97.
67. Marshall and Walton, *The Lake Counties*, p. 219.
68. Waterson, *The National Trust*, pp. 56–7.
69. Ibid, p. 57.
70. Rawnsley, *Past and Present at the English Lakes*, pp. 90–1, 101.
71. Rawnsley website, hdrawnsley.com.
72. Rosalind Rawnsley on Edith Rawnsley, *Keswick Characters*, Vol. 2, p. 129.
73. Rosalind Rawnsley on Edith Rawnsley, from a contemporary handwritten account, Ibid, Vol. 2, pp. 126–7.
74. Rawnsley, E., *Canon Rawnsley*, pp. 245–6.
75. Stanley Ritchie. Quoted by Rosalind Rawnsley in her lecture 'Figures in a Landscape at Crosthwaite Old Vicarage', March 2008.

76. Battrick, *Guardian of the Lake*, p. 80.
77. Hall, *Derwentwater: In the Lap of the Gods*, pp. 106–7.
78. *Carlisle Journal*, 29 July 1898, letter from Canon H. D. Rawnsley.
79. Ibid.
80. Rawnsley website, hdrawnsley.com. Rosalind Rawnsley 'No Man is an Island', lecture given at Allan Bank, Grasmere, September 2017.
81. Davies, *Beatrix Potter's Lakeland*, p. 26.
82. *Derby Daily Telegraph*, 29 May 1920.
83. *The Times*, 29 May 1920.
84. Hall, *Derwentwater in the Lap of the Gods*, p. 108.

Epiphany

1. Thompson, *The Lake District and the National Trust*, p. 182.
2. Ibid.
3. Ibid, p. 183.
4. Waterson, *The National Trust*, p. 70.
5. Ibid, p. 68.
6. Ibid, p. 69.
7. In 1944, the same year as the Heelis/Potter bequest, the Trust established that c.1,800 acres of the land gifted to it was actually part of the unenclosed commons of Borrowdale, and so, to all intents and purposes, already accessible. From the Great Deed to the tithe computations, there had always been different views about Borrowdale land, but this legal discovery would have made General Woodford (see page 534–6) even more incensed that the courts had not listened to him. See Thompson, The Lake District and the National Trust, pp. 185–6.
8. For following, see Ibid, pp. 69–70.

Appendix 1

1. Searle, '"The odd corner of England"', Table 5.1, p. 188 and Table 7.11, p. 387.
2. Pringle, *General View of the Agriculture*, p. 40.
3. Bouch and Jones, *A Social and Economic History*, p. 128.
4. Nicolson and Burn, *The History and Antiquities*, p. 9.
5. Uttley, 'The Decline' *CW3*, 7, Table 3, p. 128.
6. Duxbury, A. H. (1994), 'The decline of the Cumbrian yeoman – Ravenstonedale: a case study', *CW2*, 94, pp. 201–13.
7. Ibid, p. 206.
8. Ibid, Table 4, p. 207.
9. Uttley, 'The Decline' p. 127.
10. Ibid, pp. 121–34.
11. Healey, 'Agrarian Social Structure in the Central Lake District'.
12. Ibid, Tables 9 and 1.
13. Ibid, Table 3.
14. Ibid, Table 9.
15. Ibid, Table 10.
16. Whyte, I. D. (2009), 'The Customary Tenants of Watermillock *c.*1760–*c.*1840: Continuity and Change in a Lake District Township', *CW3*, 9, p. 171.
17. Nevertheless, it is worth

remembering some 1859 Parliamentary papers in which Richard Abbott Esq maintained that the numbers of 'statesmen' at Torpenhow had reduced from forty-five to two or three in the previous thirty years, all remaining in the village but becoming labourers.

18. Particularly the excellent work of J. D. Marshall.

19. MacFarlane, 'The myth of the peasantry;', p. 335.

20. Darrall, *Rediscovering our Past*, p. 180.

21. Ibid, p. 35.

22. Bailey and Culley, *General View of the Agriculture*, p. 46.

23. Pringle, *General View of the Agriculture*, p. 18.

24. Searle, 'Custom, class conflict and agrarian capitalism', p. 118.

25. Ibid, pp. 106–33. And Jones,

'The Decline of the Yeomanry in the Lake Counties', p. 205.

26. See Winchester, 'Wordsworth's "Pure Commonwealth"?', pp. 87–8 for the opposite argument.

27. Cintra Tract, lines 971–972, quoted in Yu-san Yu (2007), 'Revolutionary or Apostate?: Wordsworth's Cintra Tract', *EuroAmerica*, Vol. 27 (3).

28. Sales, Roger (1983), *English Literature in History 1780–1830*, p. 53.

Image credits

Integrated Images

p. ii, Old Shepherd postcard (Courtesy of the author).

p. 11, *Crosthwaite Church and Skiddaw*, William Westall (© The Trustees of the British Museum).

p. 21, *Dunmail Raise*, Joseph Wilkinson (Originally published electronically on the University of Colorado's Romantic Circles website).

p. 36, Derwentwater and Bassenthwaite Lake, from Thomas Rose, *Westmorland, Cumberland, Durham and Northumberland* (1832).

p. 38, Derwentwater and the village of Grange, from Thomas Rose, *Westmorland, Cumberland, Durham and Northumberland* (1832).

p. 58, The Vale of St John, George Pickering, from Thomas Rose, *Westmorland, Cumberland, Durham and Northumberland* (1832).

p. 92, Thirlmere Bridge, Crag, Thomas Allom, from Thomas Rose, *Westmorland, Cumberland, Durham and Northumberland* (1832).

p. 104, Lug Marks, *The Shepherd's Guide*, from Angus Winchester, *The Harvests of the Hills*.

p. 110, Sorting the Ore, from *Keswick Characters Vol 11*, Elizabeth Battrick and Daniel Hechstetter.

p. 125, Honister Crag, Thomas Allom, from Thomas Rose, *Westmorland, Cumberland, Durham and Northumberland* (1832).

p. 155, Scafell Pikes, Thomas Allom, from Thomas Rose, *Westmorland, Cumberland, Durham and Northumberland* (1832).

p. 156, Fisher postcard of Styhead Pass (Courtesy of the author).

p. 157, *Stockley Bridge*, William Green (© Jean Norgate and courtesy of The Armitt Library).

p. 168, Cottages at Braithwaite, Joseph Wilkinson (Originally published electronically on the University of Colorado's Romantic Circles website).

p. 173, James, Earl of Derwentwater (Chronicle/Alamy Stock Photo).

p. 196, Legburthwaite Mill, Joseph Wilkinson (Originally published electronically on the University of Colorado's Romantic Circles website).

p. 198, Map of the Black Lead Mines in Cumberland, George Smith (© Cumbria County History Trust).

p. 214, *A Turnpike near Keswick*, John Thornton, (© Bridgeman Images).

p. 225, Coleridge, George Dance (© The Wordsworth Trust, Grasmere); Wordsworth, Henry Edridge (Digital Image Library/Alamy Stock Photo);

Southey, Henry Edridge (Granger Historical Picture Archive/Alamy Stock Photo).

p. 238, *Pocklington's Island*, J.Merigot, John 'Warwick' Smith (© National Trust / Robert Thrift).

p. 240, Derwentwater and Lodore, from Thomas Rose, *Westmorland, Cumberland, Durham and Northumberland* (1832).

p. 242, Barrow Fall, from Thomas Rose, *Westmorland, Cumberland, Durham and Northumberland* (1832).

p. 268, Drawing of William Calvert, Mary Calvert (© The Wordsworth Trust, Grasmere).

p. 282, Grisedale, Thomas Allom, from Thomas Rose, *Westmorland, Cumberland, Durham and Northumberland* (1832).

p. 295, Amos Green Dove Cottage (© The Wordsworth Trust, Grasmere).

p. 304, Castle Crag, from Thomas Rose, *Westmorland, Cumberland, Durham and Northumberland* (1832).

p. 332, View in St John's Vale, Joseph Wilkinson (Originally published electronically on the University of Colorado's Romantic Circles website).

p. 341, Ennerdale from How Hall, from Thomas Rose, *Westmorland, Cumberland, Durham and Northumberland* (1832).

p. 345, Derwentwater from Applethwaite, Henry Gastineau, from Thomas Rose, *Westmorland, Cumberland, Durham and Northumberland* (1832).

p. 359, Thirlmere from Raven Crag, from Thomas Rose, *Westmorland, Cumberland, Durham and Northumberland* (1832).

p. 387, Hog Hole, from William Rollinson, *Life and Tradition in the Lake District*.

p. 391, Derwentwater from Castle Head, from Thomas Rose, *Westmorland, Cumberland, Durham and Northumberland* (1832).

p. 402, Crosthwaite Free School, Tom Wilson, from *The History and Chronicles of Crosthwaite Old School*.

p. 414, *Skiddaw from Applethwaite*, from Thomas Rose, *Westmorland, Cumberland, Durham and Northumberland* (1832).

p. 431, William Westall, by William Daniell (Glasshouse Images/Alamy Stock Photo).

p. 433, *Sketch of Sir George Beaumont and Joseph Farington painting a waterfall*, Thomas Hearne (© The Wordsworth Trust, Grasmere).

p. 435, *Derwentwater, Bassenthwaite-Water and Skiddaw from Walla Crag*, William Westall (© The Trustees of the British Museum).

p. 451, *Fields, River and Greta Hall*, William Westall (© The Wordsworth Trust, Grasmere).

p. 478, Lodore Cataract, from Thomas Rose, *Westmorland, Cumberland, Durham and Northumberland*(1832).

p. 488, Keswick from Greta Bridge, from Thomas Rose, *Westmorland, Cumberland, Durham and Northumberland* (1832).

p. 511, Lithograph of the Church of St John, (© Cumbria Image Bank).

p. 521, Elizabeth Lynn Linton, Samuel Lawrence (Wikimedia Commons).

p. 536, Major-General Sir John Woodford (© Look and Learn).

p. 541, *Keswick Main Street*, Joseph Brown (© Keswick Museum and Art Gallery).

p. 565, Prize Herdwick postcard (Courtesy of the author).

p. 573, Young Hardwicke Rawnsley (© Rosalind Rawnsley, The Rawnsley Archive).

p. 580, Men at the Keswick School of Industrial Art (© Pricewalker Antiques).

p. 600, Rupert, Helen and Beatrix Potter with Hardwick and Noel (© Rosalind Rawnsley, The Rawnsley Archive).

p. 616, *Keswick Lake from Friars Crag, Evening*, William Westall (© The Wordsworth Trust, Grasmere).

p. 621, Great Gable Monument postcard (Courtesy of the author).

Plate Images

1. Sir John Bankes M.P. (© National Portrait Gallery, London).

2. Upper Wadmine, Borrowdale, Joseph Wilkinson (© The Wordsworth Trust, Grasmere).

3. Crest of The Mines Royal Company, from *Elizabethan Copper* by M.B. Donald.

4. *Rosthwaite in Borrowdale*, Thomas Allom (© Ash Rare Prints).

5. *Lancaster Sands*, Joseph Mallord William Turner (© The Trustees of the British Museum).

6. *Regatta at Keswick in Cumberland*, Robert Smirke (© Bridgeman Images).

7. Crosthwaite Church, Lucy Gipps,

photographed by Val Corbett (© Keswick Museum and Art Gallery).

8. *Skiddaw and Derwentwater*, Joseph Farington (© Yale Center for British Art, Paul Mellon Collection).

9. *Windy Brow*, Joseph Wilkinson (© The Wordsworth Trust, Grasmere).

10. *Doctor Syntax Sketching the Lake*, Thomas Rowlandson (© The Wordsworth Trust, Grasmere).

11. *Wanderer above the Sea of Fog*, Caspar David Friedrich (classicpaintings/Alamy Stock Photo).

12. *William Wordsworth*, Benjamin Robert Haydon (Painters/Alamy Stock Photo).

13. *Robert Southey*, Thomas Lawrence (© Bridgeman Images).

14. Jonathan Otley, unknown artist (© Keswick Museum and Art Gallery).

15. Sarah Coleridge, engraved after a miniature by Matilda Betham (Hulton Archive/Stringer).

16. Crosthwaite Vicarage, Lucy Gipps, photographed by Val Corbett (© Keswick Museum and Art Gallery).

17. *Keswick Lake from the East Side*, William Westall (© The Wordsworth Trust, Grasmere).

18. *Skiddaw*, William Westall (© The Wordsworth Trust, Grasmere).

19. John Marshall, John Russell (© University of Leeds Art Collection).

20. Jane Marshall, John Russell (© University of Leeds Art Collection).

21. *Woollen Mills at Millbeck*, Sir Joseph Flintoff (© National Trust).

22. *South Window of the Study of*

Index

Italic type indicates a reference to a text illustration.